GAZETTEER of Irish Stained Glass

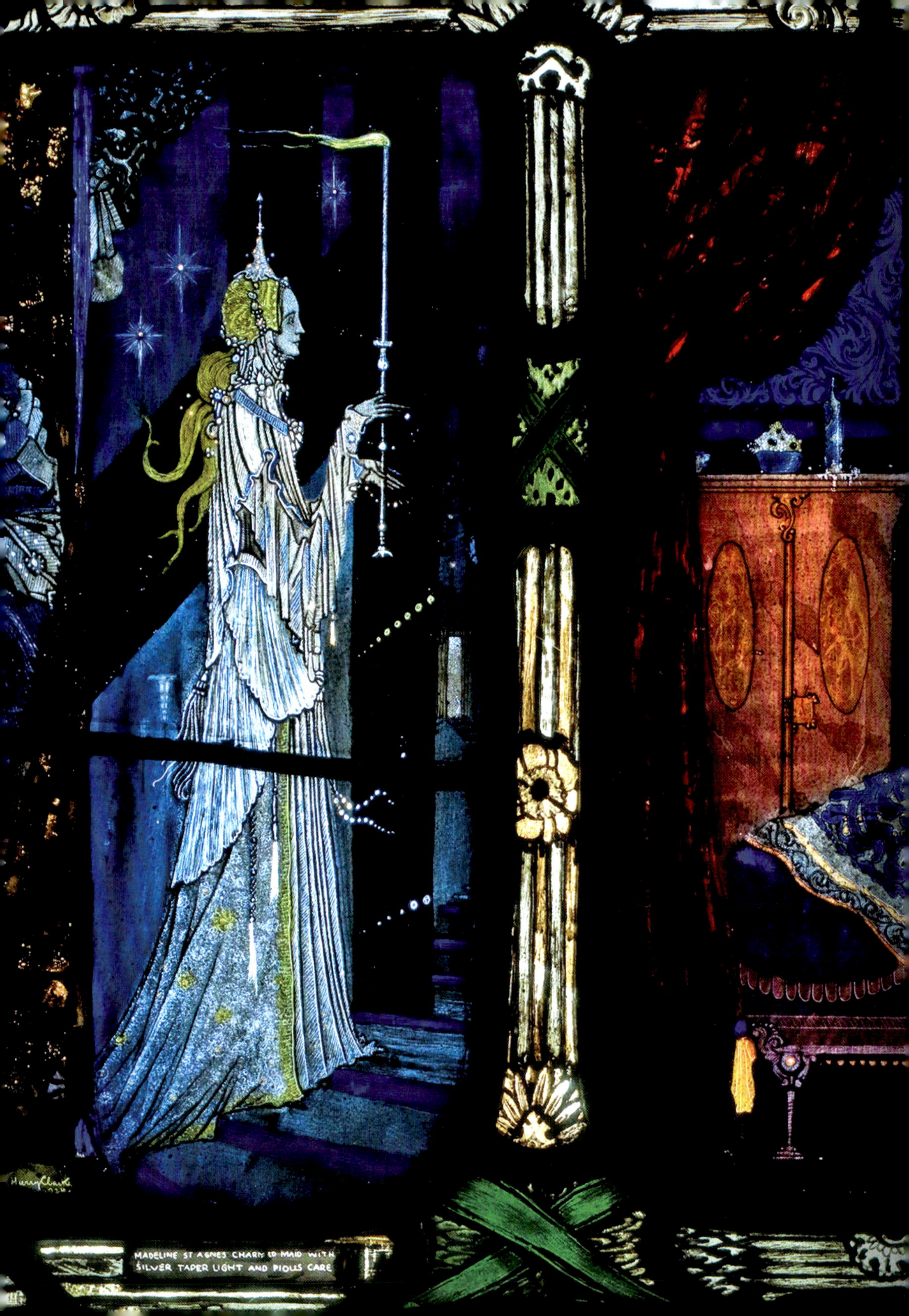
Harry Clarke
MADELINE ST AGNES CHARMED MAID WITH
SILVER TAPER LIGHT AND PIOUS CARE

GAZETTEER of Irish Stained Glass

THE WORKS OF HARRY CLARKE,
THE ARTISTS OF AN TÚR GLOINE (THE TOWER OF GLASS)
AND ARTISTS OF SUCCEEDING GENERATIONS
TO THE PRESENT DAY

REVISED NEW EDITION

NICOLA GORDON BOWE, DAVID CARON
& MICHAEL WYNNE

EDITOR: DAVID CARON

CONTRIBUTORS: PAUL DONNELLY, WILLIAM EARLEY,
BART FELLE, FINOLA FINLAY, BRIAN McAVERA,
JOSEPH McBRINN, REILTÍN MURPHY, RUTH SHEEHY

PRINCIPAL PHOTOGRAPHY: JOZEF VRTIEL

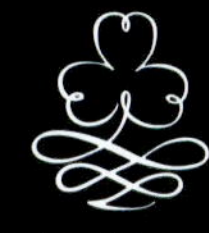

IRISH ACADEMIC PRESS

First published in 1988 by Irish Academic Press
10 George's Street
Newbridge
Co. Kildare
Ireland
www.iap.ie

978 1 78855 175 5 (Paperback)
978 1 78855 132 8 (PDF)

Revised Edition published in hardback in 2021
This paperback edition published in 2024

A CIP catalogue record for this book is available from the British Library.

Cover design and book design: edit+ www.stuartcoughlan.com
Typeset in Garamond Premier Pro

Title page: Harry Clarke, *Eve of St Agnes* (1924), detail of the panels depicting Madeline, St Agnes's maid (panel 9), and St Agnes sleeping (panel 10), Dublin City Gallery The Hugh Lane, Parnell Square, Dublin. Collection and image © Hugh Lane Gallery, Dublin (Reg. No. 1442)

Front cover: left to right: Wilhelmina Geddes, detail of '*The Leaves of the Tree Were for the Healing of the Nations*' (1920), Church of Ireland (St John's), Malone Road, Belfast, County Antrim; Michael Healy, detail of *St Victor* (1930) Church of Ireland (St Catherine's and St James's), Donore Avenue, Dublin; Harry Clarke, detail of *St Gobnait* (1916), Honan Chapel (St Finbarr's), University College Cork, Western Road, Cork, reproduced courtesy of the Honan Trust; Evie Hone, detail of *The Cock and Pot, Vulgo The Betrayal* (1945), National Gallery of Ireland, Merrion Square, Dublin. Collection NGI. © The Artist's Estate. Photograph © National Gallery of Ireland

Back cover: Richard King, *The Paschal Lamb* (1966–7), Dominican Convent, Wicklow Town

Irish Academic Press is a member of Publishing Ireland.

Contents

In memory of
Nicola Gordon Bowe and Michael Wynne

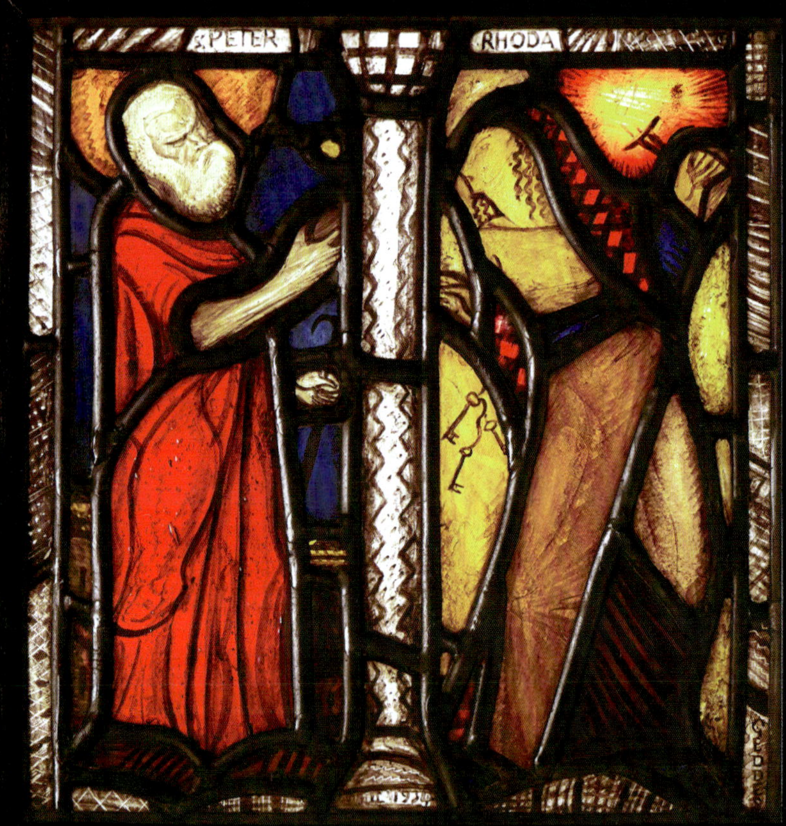

Wilhelmina Geddes, *Rhoda Opens the Door to St Peter* (1934),
National Museums NI Collection: Ulster Museum (BELUM.U2132)

Sponsors

For over a century, since 1916, the Jesuits in Ireland have commissioned stained glass from leading Irish artists working in the medium: Margaret Becker, Frances Biggs, Harry Clarke and the Harry Clarke Studios, Evie Hone, Michael Healy, Richard King, Patrick Pollen, Patrick Pye, Charles Simmonds and George W. Walsh. Windows and panels by these artists can be found in a dozen locations throughout the island, mainly Jesuit institutions, and in some instances gifted by the Jesuit Order to local churches and convent chapels.

The author would like to gratefully acknowledge financial sponsorship for this new edition of the *Gazetteer of Irish Stained Glass* from the following:

Belvedere College S.J.

Clongowes Wood College S.J.

Gonzaga College S.J.

The Irish Jesuit Province

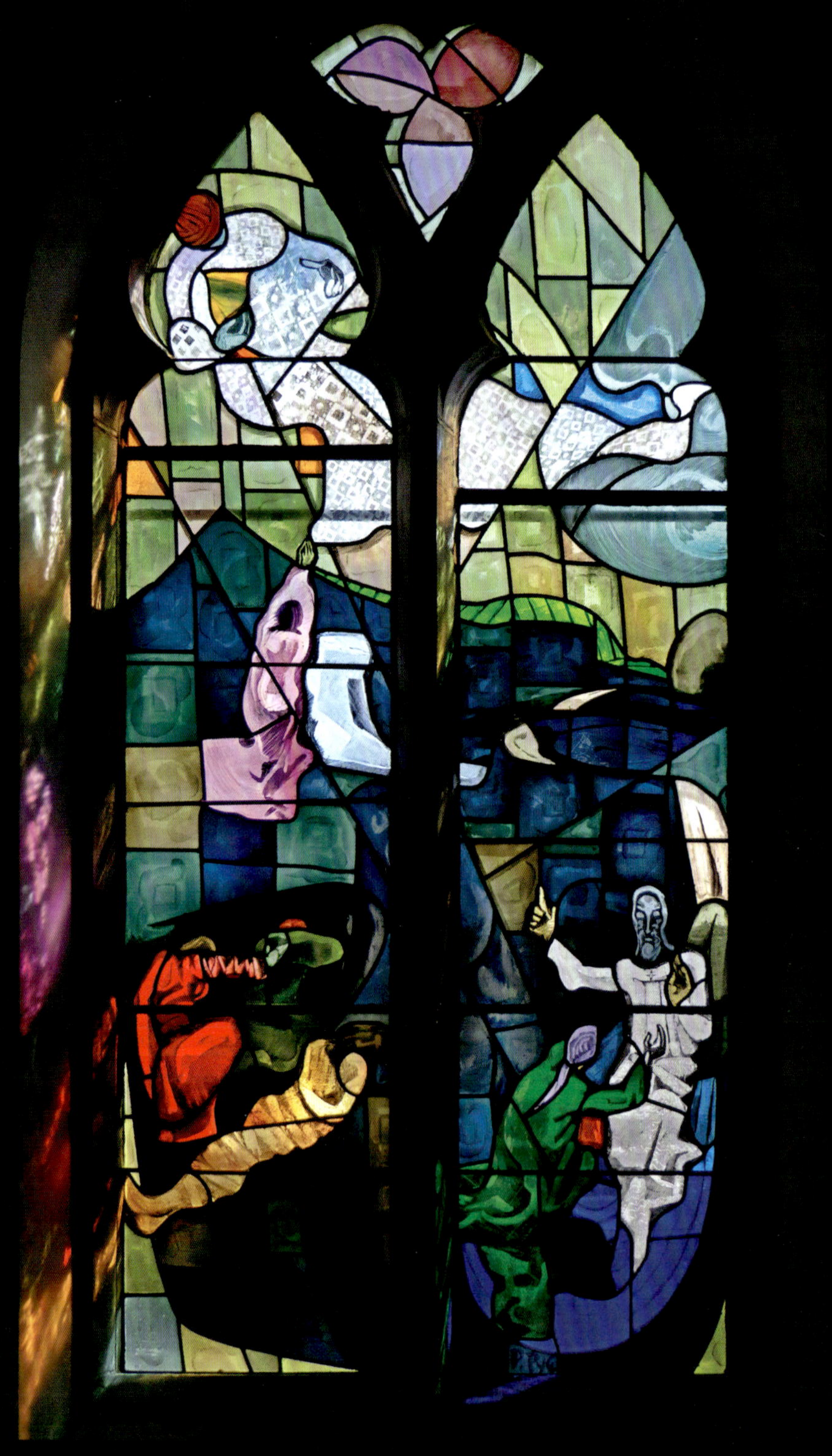

Acknowledgements

As with the first edition, this work has been a collaborative project. I would like to particularly thank the eight contributors who generously provided their specialist knowledge of specific artists, compiled exhaustive lists of the artists' windows and panels, and wrote the biographical notes on them: Paul Donnelly, William Earley, Bart Felle, Finola Finlay, Brian McAvera, Joseph McBrinn, Reiltín Murphy and Ruth Sheehy. Additionally, they contributed to this *Gazetteer* in many other ways: advising on the parameters of the new edition, informing me of less well-known artists and alerting me to windows they uncovered in their research, and providing feedback on what I had written.

I want to record my sincere gratitude to Jozef Vrtiel – whose idea it was to produce a new edition of the *Gazetteer* – for taking the vast majority of the photographs. Without his photographic expertise, his knowledge of Irish stained glass and discerning eye, and his eager willingness to travel all over the island (even to offshore islands) to record windows by these artists, this new edition may not have happened at all, and certainly would not be as comprehensively illustrated as it is.

I would also like to record my gratitude to the following: Michael Earley, PhD candidate at NCAD, for generously sharing his expert knowledge of Earley & Company; Róisín de Buitléar for her overview and insights into contemporary Irish stained glass; Colm O'Brien (currently compiling *Dublin Suburbs and County* in the *Pevsner Architectural Guides: Buildings of Ireland* series), who kindly shared his considerable knowledge and research.

The contributors and I would like to record our specific thanks to the many artists, their descendants and the studios where they worked who provided us with key information, specifically: Margaret Becker; Conor Biggs; Fiona Biggs; Lua Breen; Phyllis Burke; Mary Clarke; Maud Cotter; Debbie Dawson; Anthony Devitt; David

Left: Patrick Pye, *Christ Praying in Gethsemane, the Entombment, and the Resurrection* (*c.*1986), Catholic Church (Our Lady of Lourdes), Creagh, near Ballinasloe, County Galway

Esler; Katharine Lamb; Peadar Lamb; Mary Mackey; Patrick Muldowney; Cristín Ní Éanaigh; Bríd Pollen; Naoise Pye; Ken Ryan; James Scanlon; Killian Schurmann; Bonnie Shawcross; Neil Shawcross; Alan Tomlin; George W. Walsh; Manus Walsh; Peter Young.

We would like to express our gratitude to Donna Romano, Librarian, National College of Art and Design, and to Jennifer Fitzgibbon, Administrator of the National Irish Visual Arts Library, and the dedicated staff in the archive for their support and ongoing policy to expand their collection of stained glass-related material.

Many individuals assisted us in a myriad of ways, from site visits in far-flung locations to checking records: Edwin Alkin; Dr Jasmine Allen, Stained Glass Museum, Ely; Ken Anderson; Patti Benane; Helena Bergin, Fingal County Council; Michael Bevan; Dr Eileen Black; Stephen Bonnlander; Paddy Bowe; David Britton; Dr Richard Butler; Damien Byrne, Jesuits Archives; Dick Byrne; Martin Byrne; Susan Byron; Fr Eamon Cahill; Stephen Callaghan; Jo Cannon; Fr Aodháin Canon; Fr Gerard Cassidy; Tom Cassidy, Limerick Architectural Conservation Officer; Maeve Clancy; Aidan Clarke; Harold Clarke; Fr Colm Clinton; Dr Paul Colton, Bishop of Cork; Gillian Cooke; Peter Cormack; Elizabeth Coyle; Martin Crampin; Christy Cunniffe; Nigel Curtin and Marian Thérèse Keyes, DLR Lexicon Library; Patricia Curtin-Kelly; Mary Cuthbert; Marcel Daloze; Mairéad Delaney, Abbey Theatre; Ciaran Diamond; Catherine Doherty; William Doherty; Evelyn Donnellan; Deborah Douglas, HERoNI; Anne Marie Duffy; Barbara Dunne; Mavis Dunton; Fiachra Etchingham, Gonzaga College; Robert Flatley; Dr John Fitzgerald; Lisa Flanagan; Colin Flinn; Sarah Foster; Alan Furlong; Vincent Galligan; Rev. Mark Gardner; Emma Gilleece; Julian Girdham, St Columba's College; Olivia and Roger Goodwillie; the late Lindy Guinness; Fr John Harris, OP, Newbridge College; Robert Harris; Rev. Patrick Harvey; Colin Hatrick; Fr Tom Hayes; Enda Headd; John M. Hearne; Eamon Hedderman; Claire Hegarty; Gillian Hennessy; Rev. Canon Tom Hever; Patrick Hickey; Anne Hodge, NGI; Geraldine Hone; Dr Susan Hood, Church of Ireland RCB Library; Amy Hourie, Administrator, Girls Friendly Society; staff of the Irish Architectural Archive; Fr Piaras Jackson, SJ, Manresa, Dollymount; Iris Noyek Jacob; Fern Jolley, RCB; Peter Jones; Roisín Keag; Fr Bob Kelly, Terenure College; Sr Gerty Kelly; Monsignor Liam Kelly; Dr Barry Kennerk, Temple Street Children's Hospital; Jimmy Laffey; Ken Langan; Laura Larkin, Athy Public Library; Pascal Letellier, Arts Council of Ireland; Anna Liesching, Ulster Museum; Canon Stuart Lloyd; Clare Lymer, NIVAL; Brendan Lyons; Niall McAuley; Fr Joseph McCann; Dr Darina McCarthy, Galway Diocesan Archive; Fr Bernard McCay-Morrissey; Damon McCaul, Gonzaga College; Fr Brendan McGuinness; Gerard McInerney; Niamh MacNally, NGI; Mary Macken, Lagan College, Belfast; Brendan Maher, NGI; Angela Mehegan; Eugene Mehegan; Ellen

Moiselle, Holy Child School, Killiney; Louise Morgan, NGI; Bridget Mulcahy, Irish Arts Review; Grace Mulqueen; Fr Declan Murray, SJ, Milltown Park; Fr Tom Murray; Brendan Nash; V Rev. Eamonn O'Connor; Jim O'Crowley; Raymond O'Donnell, Galway Cathedral; Monsignor James O'Donnell; Fr Silvester O'Flynn; Anne and Jack O'Keefe; Emer O'Neill; Bernard O'Reilly, Limerick Civic Trust; Fr Henry O'Shea, Glenstal Abbey; Isabelle Peyrat, NCAD; Patricia Plunkett; Carole Pollard; Monsignor Francis Puddister; the family of Patrick Pye; Audrey Rebbeck; Karen Reihill; Robin Roddie; Frank Rogers; Kevin Rooney; Vera Ryan; staff of the Royal College of Surgeons in Ireland; Jack Searle; Fr Michael Sheil, SJ; Fr Paul Shelley; the Sisters of Charity, Temple Street; Doug Smith; Leslie Smith, BSMGP; Paul Gerard Smith; Nora Timlin, Terenure Synagogue; Ewoud van den Bourg; Janet Walsh; Fr Padraig Walsh; Stephen Walsh; Eibhear Walshe; Dave Webster; Frank Whelan; Rev. David White; Len Wilson.

Finally, we would like to warmly thank the many individuals in addition to those listed above who kindly allowed us to examine and record their stained glass windows.

Sincere thanks to the team at Irish Academic Press who made this new edition of the *Gazetteer* a reality: Conor Graham, Patrick O'Donoghue, Wendy Logue and Maeve Convery; to copy editor Dermott Barrett; and to the book's designer, Stuart Coughlan.

About the Author

David Caron was born in Dublin and studied Visual Communication at the National College of Art and Design, to which department he returned in due course as lecturer and was subsequently appointed Head of Department. He was one of the three original compilers of the first edition of the *Gazetteer of Irish Stained Glass* in 1988. David's PhD research at Trinity College Dublin focused on the stained glass artist Michael Healy and the artists of An Túr Gloine studio. He has written articles on various aspects of Irish stained glass over the years, most often for the *Irish Arts Review*.

Abbreviations and Notes on Text

ATG	An Túr Gloine
CC	Catholic Church
C of E	Church of England (Anglican)
C of I	Church of Ireland (Anglican)
C of S	Church of Scotland (Presbyterian)
HERoNI	Historic Environment Record of Northern Ireland
NGI	National Gallery of Ireland
NIVAL	National Irish Visual Arts Library
NLI	National Library of Ireland
RHA	Royal Hibernian Academy
TCD	Trinity College Dublin
UM	Ulster Museum

Note: Where the name of a work is followed by an asterisk, this means that the work has been attributed to the artist by one or more of the compilers.

All windows are single lights unless otherwise stated.

Harry Clarke windows

Where no abbreviation appears after the name of the work, this means that Harry Clarke was entirely responsible for its design and execution.

Where (A) appears, Clarke was actively involved in part of the window's execution, the rest being executed under his supervision in his studio.

Where (B) appears after the name of the work, it was initially conceived and designed by him but executed by his studio under his close supervision.

There is no work listed under Harry Clarke which was carried out by the studios rather than by him.

Photographic Credits

I am enormously grateful to all those owners and custodians of Ireland's stained glass heritage who allowed their windows and panels to be photographed. The vast majority of photographs in this edition are by Jozef Vrtiel, and both he and I have always been facilitated and made welcome whenever we asked to photograph stained glass throughout the island of Ireland. Unless otherwise noted, photographs are by Jozef. I would also like to thank Finola Finlay and Anthony Hobbs for kindly taking photographs specifically for the *Gazetteer*. My gratitude also to Fr James Bradley; Martin Crampin; Jake Kelly; Joseph McBrinn; Kevin McQuinn; Roland Paschhoff; Frank Whelan.

I would like to express my gratitude to the following galleries and institutions for kindly providing photographs of works from their collections: Dublin City Gallery The Hugh Lane; National Gallery of Ireland, Dublin; National Irish Visual Arts Library, Dublin; Sisters of St Joseph, CentreWest Region South Australia; The Stained Glass Museum, Ely Cathedral; The Wolfsonian-Florida International University, Miami; Ulster Museum, Belfast.

Additionally I would like to thank the estates of the artists who kindly provided copyright permission: the children of Frances Biggs for her estate; Mary Clarke for the estate of Terry Clarke; Geraldine Hone and the estate of Evie Hone; Elizabeth Kerr and family for the estate of Wilhelmina Geddes; William Cooper for the estate of George Campbell; Anne Marie Doherty for the estate of Richard King; Helen Callan for the estate of Helen Moloney; the children of Patrick Pollen for his estate; the family of Patrick Pye for his estate. To the estates of other deceased artists whom I have not been able to trace, I would be happy to acknowledge them in any subsequent edition of this *Gazetteer*. I would also like to express my gratitude to all the living artists who kindly gave permission to have photographs of their work reproduced.

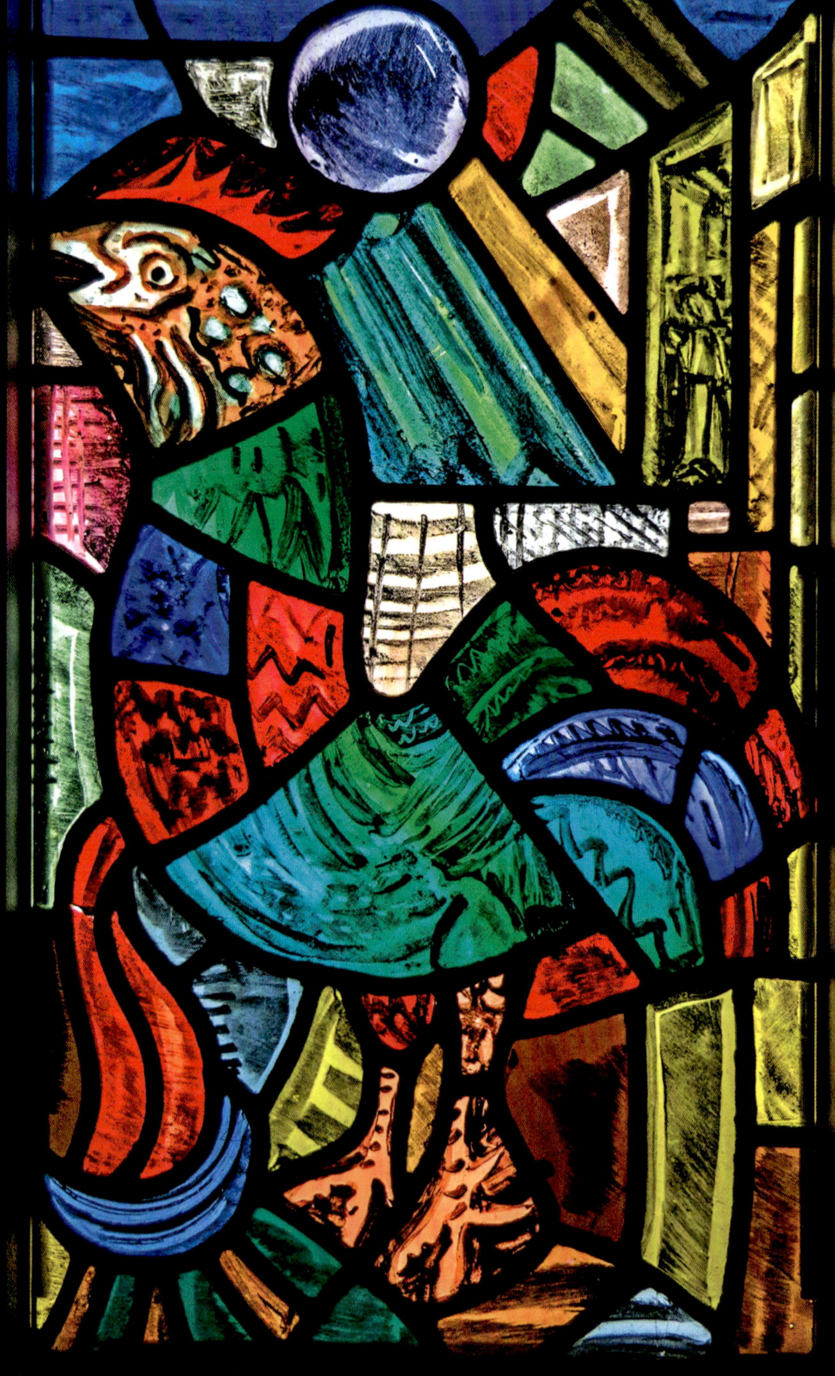

Preface

David Caron

The original 1988 edition of this *Gazetteer* was the brainchild of the late Nicola Gordon Bowe, who also wrote the introduction and biographical notes on the artists,[1] and she, the late Michael Wynne and I compiled the 800 or so entries. We set out to document all stained glass works known to us, excluding those in private collections, by Harry Clarke[2] and the nine artists of An Túr Gloine (Sarah Purser, Alfred Ernest Child, Michael Healy, Catherine O'Brien, Ethel Rhind, Beatrice Elvery, Wilhelmina Geddes, Hubert McGoldrick and Evie Hone). The time frame of the study was essentially determined by the founding of An Túr Gloine in 1903 and the deaths of both Hone and Geddes in 1955, though the last surviving An Túr Gloine artist, Catherine O'Brien, continued to produce windows into the early 1960s. The original *Gazetteer* also included a number of works made in opus sectile mosaic, which was a side speciality at An Túr Gloine, and we have retained them in this new edition.[3]

The twin ambitions of this new edition of the *Gazetteer of Irish Stained Glass* were: firstly, to update the original information; and secondly, to include windows by significant artists who were contemporaries of Clarke and those of An Túr Gloine, and in particular to highlight work by those distinguished artists who followed, bringing it up to the present day. By casting a wider net than the original *Gazetteer*, one has to acknowledge an unavoidable element of subjectivity in the selection and to counter this I have greatly valued the advice of the key contributors and others in the field: historians, researchers and practitioners. Artistic merit, individual voice and excellence

Left: Evie Hone, *The Cock and Pot, Vulgo The Betrayal* (1945), National Gallery of Ireland, Merrion Square, Dublin. Collection NGI. © The Artist's Estate. Photograph © National Gallery of Ireland

in the craft have been key criteria, though as Nicola Gordon Bowe made clear in the original introduction, 'By no means all the windows listed in this *Gazetteer* can be regarded as masterpieces.' The total number of entries in this edition has increased to well over 2,500.

The *Gazetteer* includes work by those who are generally recognised (and self-identified) as Irish artists, though not all were necessarily Irish-born, such as Patrick Pye and Patrick Pollen. All the stained glass listed was made on the island with a few exceptions, such as the windows made by Clarke and Geddes in London and those made by Pollen after he moved to North Carolina. We have included the windows made by Kathleen Quigly while in Ireland, but not the large number, over 100, made after she emigrated to South Africa in the mid-1930s. We have not included work by international artists made for Irish churches, but we have included some windows by the Scottish artist John Blyth, created by him during the eight years he worked at Clokey and Company, Belfast.[4]

Recent investigations have discovered nine new verifiable windows by the artists of An Túr Gloine, including in locations as far away as New York[5] and India,[6] and we have been able to include eleven missing or previously unrecorded small panels by Evie Hone.[7] Through additional research, we have been able to state with certainty which specific artist from this studio was responsible for nearly seventy windows that in the first edition we had only been able to attribute to various artists based on stylistic grounds.

We have included a few new additions by Harry Clarke,[8] though in respect of Clarke we have taken a particularly cautious approach. As scholars and enthusiasts of Clarke know, he had a cohort of highly skilled fellow artists trained to execute windows in his distinctive style. Additionally, in his final years he was seriously ill, spending protracted periods convalescing abroad, and there was increasing pressure on others in the studio to create 'a Harry Clarke' in order to meet the demand of eager patrons. Without clear documentary evidence determining his precise involvement, one is navigating a minefield of supposition and conjecture.

Nicola Gordon Bowe, in the concluding paragraph of her introduction to the original edition wrote: 'It is hoped that this study will encourage an appreciation and interest in a little documented area to which Irish artists contributed so much earlier this century.' This has undoubtedly come to pass and though the considerable loss of both Nicola and Michael's knowledge and scholarship has made this task more challenging, I have been greatly assisted by a dedicated team of highly knowledgeable researchers and compilers. The specific contribution of these compilers can be found in the acknowledgements and biographical notes on the key artists. Due to their diligence and expertise we are in a position to include complete lists of work – or, in some cases, as near complete as it has been possible to ascertain – by many 'new' artists, including Richard King, Patrick Pye, Patrick Pollen, Helen Moloney, Johnny Murphy, Róisín Dowd Murphy, Phyllis Burke, George W. Walsh and Lua Breen, together with accompanying biographical notes. This has possibly been the most rewarding aspect of compiling this new edition of the *Gazetteer*, as it has provided an opportunity to highlight the significant artists who followed on after Clarke and those of An Túr Gloine whose work has been largely eclipsed or, in many instances, totally forgotten.

In keeping with the approach of the original *Gazetteer*, we have generally constrained ourselves to include only those artists who designed and made their own windows (with the assistance of glaziers, etc.) and we did not set out to survey all work by the larger, more commercial firms, where many hands may have been involved in the production process and the role of attribution can become very fraught, if not impossible. Additionally it would have been a vast undertaking. So, with regret, the many hundreds of windows produced by the Harry Clarke Studios, Earley Studios and Abbey Stained Glass Studios, among others, will not be listed here, but we are delighted to note that doctoral-level research into Clarkes and Earleys is underway and will in time shed more light and clarity. We have, however, included a selection of the finest windows created at these and other studios where the attribution of artist/designer is unambiguous.[9]

It is with sadness that we acknowledge the undeniable trend which has emerged in recent years, that of the high number of places built for religious worship which have shut their doors for a final time. Convent chapels in particular, of which there were hundreds throughout the island, have been quietly closing with increasing regularity; sometimes the stained glass windows have been relocated, sometimes put into long-term storage, sometimes buildings have found a new function, sometimes purchased by developers and left to languish, and sometimes simply abandoned to a very uncertain future. We note that one of Geddes's finest windows, her *Psalm 100*, for the former Egremont United Reformed Church, Wallasey, was severely damaged in 2017 when vandals smashed through it in order to enter the church;[10] a clear indicator of what can and does happen to stained glass left in abandoned buildings.

A major challenge now and in the coming years will be to see how religious buildings can be appropriately and sensitively repurposed, perhaps ideally for community use. It is generally acknowledged that in most instances relocating a stained glass window should be a last resort as it was made for a specific window opening, taking into account the building's architecture, the viewing height and its orientation.

One factor which may be contributing to the lack of value placed on windows created by artists is the fact that often the religious custodians themselves and/or the local communities have no record or knowledge of who the artists are, nor an awareness of the merit of the pieces. It is hoped that this new edition of the *Gazetteer* may go some way towards highlighting forgotten windows, some now requiring attention due to age and neglect.[11] This *Gazetteer* never set out to be an inventory of *all* stained glass in Ireland, though this would be a wonderful legacy for future generations were it to happen. We would like to salute the magisterial research undertaken by Dr David Lawrence over a twenty-six-year period on behalf of the Church of Ireland for their website, which documents the majority of stained glass in their churches throughout the island.[12]

It is worth noting that when the original *Gazetteer* was published, the only stained glass-related archive in Ireland was in the National Gallery, preliminary designs and order books, etc., from An Túr Gloine, which had been generously gifted by Patrick Pollen and catalogued by Michael Wynne. Since then the National Irish Visual Arts Library has acquired original material by among others: Lua Breen, Phyllis Burke, Earley & Company, Helen Moloney, Murphy-Devitt Studios, Patrick Pollen and Patrick Pye, as well as Evie Hone's papers; Trinity College Dublin acquired and digitised the hugely significant Clarke's Stained Glass Studios Collection; the National Library acquired the Harry Clarke Papers; the Crawford Art Gallery, Cork, acquired the Watson Archive; and the Northern Ireland Environment Agency acquired the Clokey Stained Glass Collection. As with the original *Gazetteer*, where there is a preliminary design or cartoon in a public collection for a window/panel we have noted it in the entry.

From time to time I and the other compilers have encountered works of merit, but due to lack of signatures, plaques or easily accessible records, we have been unable to identify the artist or studio and have therefore not listed these 'anonymous' windows. As with the first edition of the *Gazetteer*, one hopes that this publication may act as a spur for fresh research, whether by professional art historians, students, or individuals living in local communities, which will shed further light on Ireland's rich and precious holding of stained glass.

Notes

1 While we have retained Nicola's introduction and her biographical notes on Clarke and Geddes, in the light of additional research we have written new biographical notes for the other An Túr Gloine (ATG) artists.

2 See N. Gordon Bowe, *The Life and Work of Harry Clarke* (Dublin: Irish Academic Press, 1989) and reprinted as *Harry Clarke: The Life and Work* (Dublin: The History Press, 2012). Also numerous articles and exhibition catalogues on Clarke written by N. Gordon Bowe from 1979 onwards.

3 This type of mosaic is similar to stained glass in structure with large pieces cut to specific shapes – rather than tiny square tesserae – though it is composed entirely of glazed opaque tile with painted details. It was considered suitable for works which were traditionally wall-mounted, such as Stations of the Cross, and liable to degrade in the damp Irish climate. Some artists, particularly those who had trained at Clarke's studio, such as Richard King, George Stephen Walsh and William Dowling, also worked in a variant of opus sectile mosaic using 'opal glass' and we have included examples by them in this edition of the *Gazetteer*.

4 Another exception is Marthe Donas (1885–1967), a Belgian refugee who worked at An Túr Gloine for some of 1915 and up to the 1916 Rising. In unpublished reminiscences, written in her eighties, she recalled making three large windows at the studio, but it has only been possible to identify one with certainty, *The Deposition* for the Catholic Church, Ballinderreen, County Galway. She went on to become a leading abstract and cubist artist, residing mainly in France. (I am indebted to Marcel Daloze, curator of the Musée Marthe Donas, for this information). A further exception are the windows in County Carlow Military Museum (formerly St Dympna's Catholic Church) by August Weckbecker (1888–1939), a German artist who lived in Ireland in the mid-1920s. It is likely that the windows, though designed by him while in Ireland, were actually fabricated in Germany.

5 Beatrice Elvery's *Christ Blessing Children* (1912) in the Episcopalian Church, Pelham, NY.

6 Ethel Rhind's *Woman with the Anointment, Good Shepherd, Parable of the Ten Virgins* (1912–13) for Columba's Hospital Chapel, Hazaribagh.

7 Two in Terenure College Chapel, Dublin; two in County Kilkenny, in the Catholic churches at Bennetsbridge and Clara (which were donated by descendants of the artist); one each in the Mortuary Chapel, Tallaght Hospital, Dublin; St Maelruain's C of I, Tallaght, Dublin; St Columba's College, Rathfarnham; Little Company of Mary, Churchtown, Dublin; Catholic Church, Dulverton, Somerset; Catholic Church, Wootton Wawen, Warwickshire; and Boston College.

8 *Sacred Heart and St Francis*, Holy Trinity Church, Fr Mathew Quay, Cork. This window was discovered by Patricia Curtin-Kelly and verified by Nicola Gordon Bowe; a 'lost' decorative window which had formerly been in Rathfarnham Castle and was transferred to the Sisters of Charity Convent, Temple Street, Dublin, in the 1980s.

9 In the listing section of the *Gazetteer*, after some entries we have indicated, in parentheses, at which studio the window was made. We have done this mainly in two instances: (1) in the case of windows made in the Clarke Studios which might initially appear to be the work of Harry Clarke himself but are by artists such as Terry Clarke, William Dowling and Richard King; (2) in the case of windows made at Abbey Stained Glass Studios, which employed several significant artists including George Campbell, Willie Earley and George W. Walsh.

10 I am indebted to Joseph McBrinn for bringing this to my attention.

11 The Heritage Council has produced an excellent booklet, *The Care of Stained Glass* (2004), written on their behalf by Dr David Lawrence and available to download in PDF form from the Council's website.

12 See www.gloine.ie.

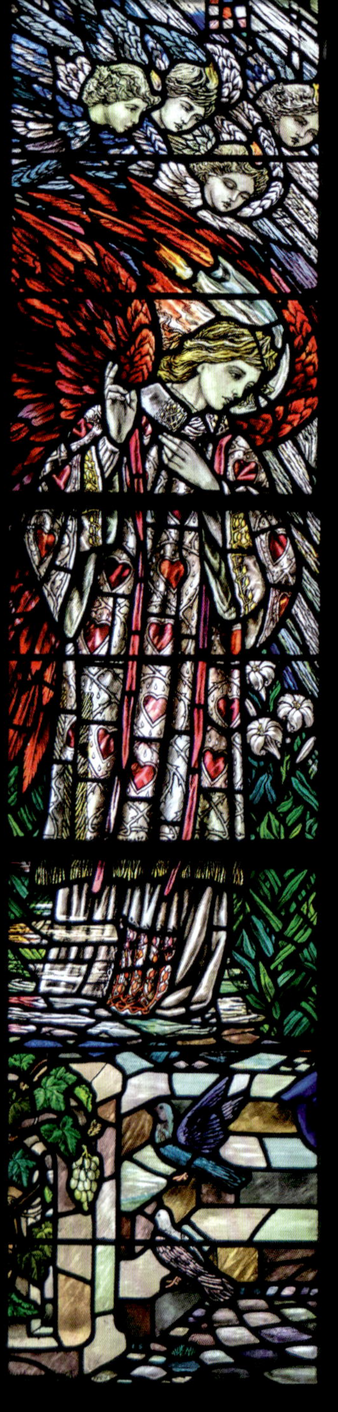
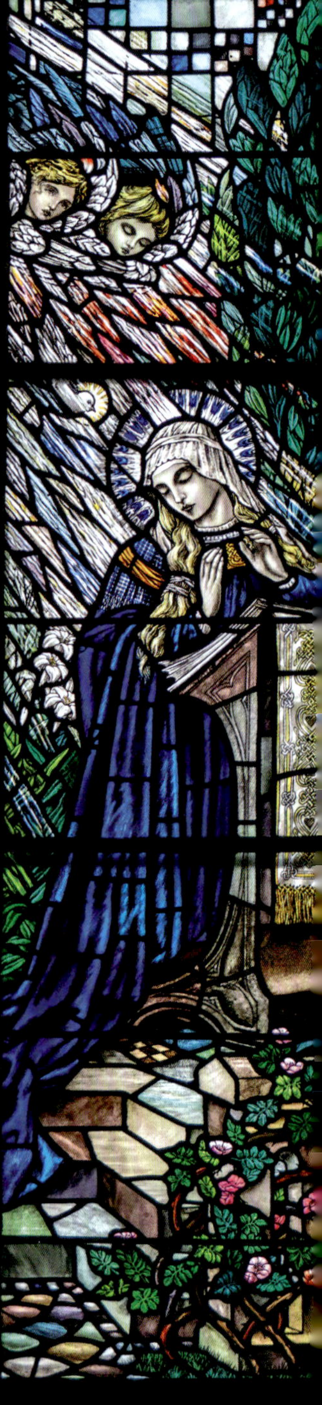

Introduction

Early Twentieth-century Irish Stained Glass in Context

Nicola Gordon Bowe

Fortunately, George Moore's despairing words at the beginning of the twentieth century – 'All modern stained glass is so utterly bad and so beastly ugly, that it is simply throwing away money trying to improve it – in fact, the sooner it dies the better'[1] – were not to be entirely prophetic. The problem in Ireland was clearly identified by George (Æ) Russell: 'We have bad stained glass ... in our churches because there is no authority in matters of taste to indicate what is poor and what is truly beautiful.'[2]

Between 1903 and as late as 1955, a small group of Irish artists established an unqualified reputation for their work all over the world, encouraged and supported by a handful of enlightened patrons. John Piper, in his seminal appraisal of the art of stained glass, traces the story of modern art in relation to glass 'through strange, devious channels' as it 'pressed on strongly against the tide of the browns and mauves and plentiful dirty whites, and the demoralised Gothic, of establishment Edwardian windows' and began to 'infiltrate in odd places. ... It was through the sympathetic influences of Harry Clarke, Wilhelmina Geddes and Evie Hone that positive constructive relations were again established between stained glass and painting. Ireland had a strong influence at this time.'[3]

The combination of an inspired painter expressing his or her art through the difficult, demanding and deceptively beguiling techniques of stained glass is very rare. By no means all the windows listed in this *Gazetteer* can be regarded as masterpieces. However, the best of Clarke, Geddes, Healy and Hone are second to none and worth

Left: A.E. Child, detail of *The Annunciation* (1903; based on original designs by Christopher Whall, painted by A.E. Child, Michael Healy and Catherine O'Brien), Catholic Cathedral, Loughrea, County Galway

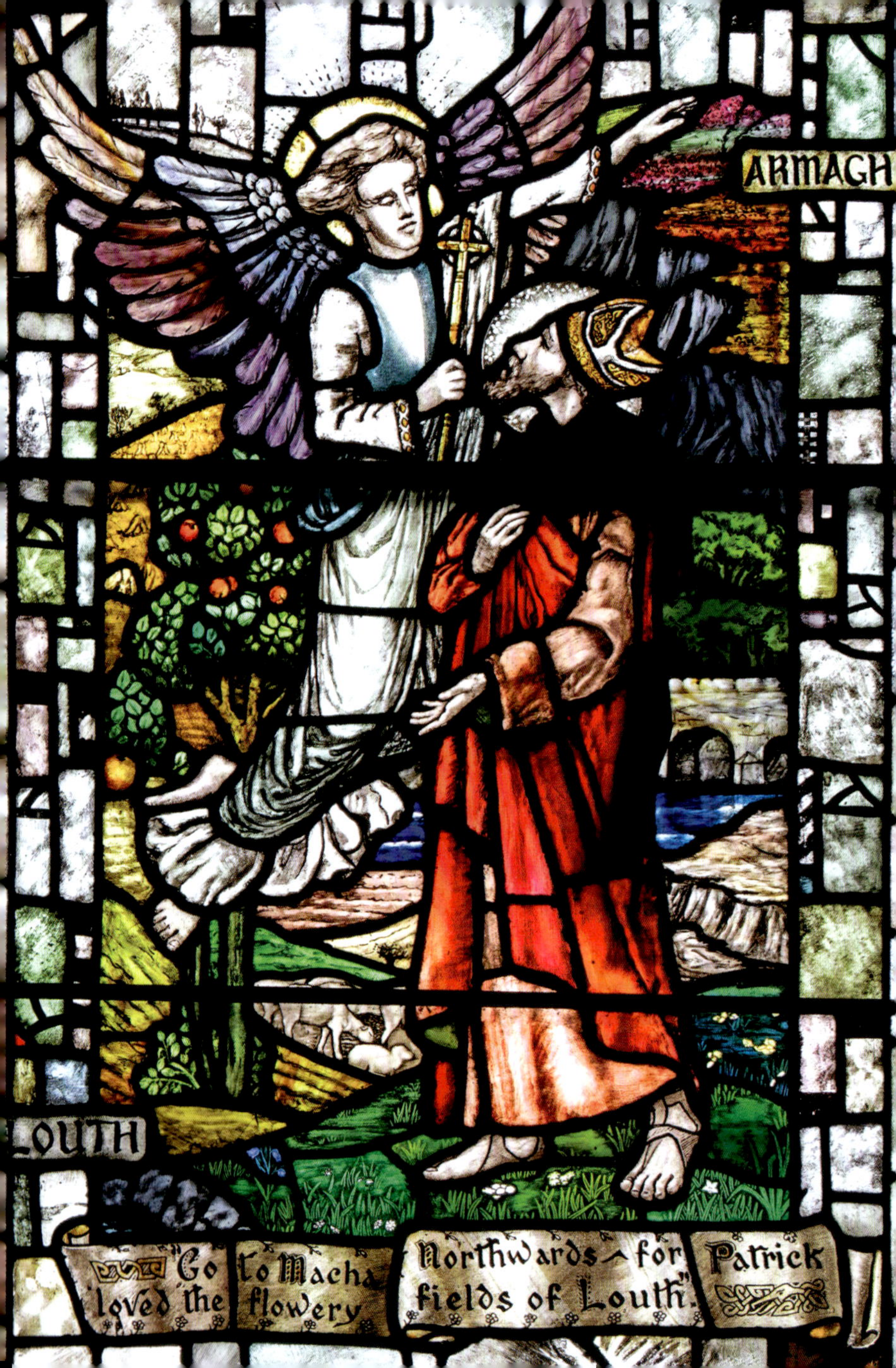
ARMAGH
LOUTH
"Go to Macha Northwards – for Patrick
loved the flowery fields of Louth."

any journey, while the collective work of An Túr Gloine co-operative set high standards and marks a unique chapter in Ireland's cultural history.

George Moore was not alone in decrying the 'sham, imitative, defective work of the commercial exploiter'[4] which prevailed in Ireland at the turn of the century. George Bernard Shaw described the ubiquitous imitation chromo-lithographs of medieval panelled saints 'in garish crudity'[5] as comparable with dirty linoleum. The most vehement and constructive critic in Ireland was Edward Martyn,[6] a key figure in the Irish cultural revival, who wrote in his preface to Robert Elliott's scathing *Art and Ireland* (1906) that the blame for 'the miserable decadence of church art' lay with the ill-educated clergy, trade architects, 'the crude paw of the tradesman' and an undiscerning public. They seemed not to be able to distinguish between the work of an artist and the trade salesman 'with an oily tongue and an ever-ready kiln' as they readily squandered money they could ill afford on the comparatively large number of new churches being erected since Catholic Emancipation. Although the general decoration of these was not, Messrs Elliott and Martyn felt, much worse than the modern churches of any other country, they considered stained glass to be the most degraded art in Ireland.

Because the lowest tender for a window was usually sought, regardless of quality or aptness, commissions frequently went to the large commercial firms in France, England, Scotland and Germany (like Mayer's of Munich, Hardman's of Birmingham and Heaton, Butler and Bayne), who offered competitive prices, conveyor-belt designs and no consideration of the site, light or circumstances involved. All too often windows from the lower end of the market reveal peeling enamels, cheap, thinly coloured glass, indiscriminate use of lead, silver stain, antimony and stay bars, and generally turgid subject matter. The few native firms still in business at the turn of the century had to struggle against the odds, all too often producing competitive commercial work to survive. From 'Munichized Dublin', Martyn took up the banner in his role as a Celtic revivalist and nationalist cultural reformer: 'If we are determined to have bad work, it is better to have it bad Irish than bad foreign.'[7] It was with this aim that he turned to Christopher Whall (1849–1924), the acknowledged father of the English Arts and Crafts stained glass revival, for advice in trying to establish a native school. It is here interesting to summarise briefly the history of stained glass in Ireland.

Although written evidence shows that there were windows glazed, sometimes with stained glass, long before the eighteenth century in Ireland,[8] so far none of the medieval glass which has been excavated, or the few pieces still *in situ*, have been proved to be of indigenous production; several examples have been shown to be of

Left: Sarah Purser, detail of *Scenes from the Lives of St Colmcille, St Patrick and St Brigid* (painted by Catherine O'Brien) (1908–9), Catholic Church (St Brigid's), Kilcurry, County Louth

foreign manufacture. The dating and provenance of other random fragments are as yet necessarily speculative. The small heraldic, narrative or genre panels, so popular in seventeenth-century England after the Reformation and the destruction of the Lorraine glasshouses, were also imported into Ireland after the departure of Cromwell. His troops' desecration of notable windows, such as the reputedly magnificent East window in St Canice's Cathedral, Kilkenny, is legendary. In the eighteenth century, three of the leading painters in England were Irish-born or Dublin-trained – Thomas Jervais (d.1799), who worked for distinguished patrons in Ireland and England, Richard Hand (d.1816), who worked in Ireland for at least fifteen years before settling in England, and James Pearson (1739/40–*c.*1838). Most windows during this period were based on cartoons or paintings by well-known contemporary painters like Sir Joshua Reynolds or Old Masters, interpreted in enamel colours on rectangles of glass inserted into a lead or cast-iron grille. Thus they ignored the basic tenets of stained glass – that is, a two-dimensional, fundamentally architectural art form which employs a complex relationship of pieces of translucent coloured glass whose surfaces, in turn, are variously manipulated by paint, stain, and acid and resist, and orchestrated by the disciplining rhythm of lead calmes within glazing bars.

At the beginning of the nineteenth century, the tradition of transparencies painted onto glass continued for festive occasions as well as for windows. In the first half of the century, George M'Allister (1786–1812) provides a link between the two centuries, and ladies like Louisa Beaufort, Anna Maria Dawson and Louisa, Marchioness of Waterford, designed creditable windows. Michael O'Connor (1801–1867), a native of Dublin who had a stained glass studio here after training with Willement in London, was well known in England, where he worked in Bristol and then, in 1845, established a thriving business in London.

The Gothic Revival in England and the ensuing interest it generated in the lost secrets of the chemical properties of medieval stained glass encouraged a more sensitive architectural approach. Martin Harrison has written that 'It was Pugin who, as a leading figure in establishing a basis of archaeological accuracy for the Gothic Revival in architecture, laid the foundations for the successful revival of the medieval principles of stained glass design.'[9] Pugin collaborated with O'Connor on the design for a series of windows in Leeds and, although 'in direct contact with five of the leading stained glass firms working in the Gothic style in the early Victorian period ... the firm whose direction he controlled most completely, John Hardman and Co., was the one which by 1850 set the standard at which all the rest aimed.'[10] On Pugin's death, John Hardman Powell became the firm's chief designer. There is a strong link with Ireland here. Thomas Earley, born of Irish parents in Birmingham, had worked for Pugin in England, France and Belgium before setting up a stained glass manufacturer's practice under the name of Messrs John Hardman and Co. in Dublin in 1864 with Henry Powell, who had conducted Hardman's stained glass department for some years.

The chemical analyses of medieval glass instigated by barrister Charles Winston (1814–1865), author of *An Inquiry into the Difference of Style Observable in Ancient Glass Paintings especially in England; with Hints on Glass Painting* (1847), at the Royal College of Chemistry led to James Powell and Sons successfully reproducing glass which revealed many of the qualities of colour and texture lost for so long, and enabled them to re-establish the technology of medieval pot metal glass at their Whitefriars Glass Works in London. Although they became very important manufacturers of glass, Powells only succeeded in appointing a permanent designer in 1857, the painter Edward Burne-Jones, who left four years later to join William Morris, and then Henry Holiday.[11]

Burne-Jones, Morris and Holiday were to be vital in developing stained glass from High Victorian Gothic to the Aesthetic Style of the 1870s. The latter also worked very briefly with W.G. Saunders, whose firm made windows and worked closely with William Burges, the architect of St Fin Barre's Cathedral, Cork. Burges, who was a close friend of Winston and a wide circle of Pre-Raphaelites with shared ideals, was responsible, with W.G. Saunders, H.W. Lonsdale and Fred Weekes, for the 'fine and extensive' scheme of windows in 'rich and hotly coloured stained glass'[12] (*c.*1875–81) in St Fin Barre's.

Unfortunately, glass of such quality had little influence on the many small studios (over fifty) which proliferated in Ireland during the nineteenth century. Michael Wynne has remarked on the ubiquitous eclecticism 'clearly discernible from 1830 onwards. The absence of pronounced styles, developments and patterns of treatment ... make it very difficult to give reasonable attributions without substantiating documentation.'[13] Not until 'the sources of Irish nineteenth-century architecture are more thoroughly sifted and indexed' can the threads of any stylistic evolution be evaluated. F.S. Barff's spirited Celtic Revival clerestory windows (1863) in St Patrick's Cathedral, Dublin, deviate from an increasingly eclectic sameness.

Such was the Victorian demand for stained glass that competent, respected firms in Ireland like Messrs J. and D. Casey and Messrs Earley and Powell (formerly Hardman's) of Dublin and, before the end of the century, Watson and Co. of Youghal, Joshua Clarke of Dublin and Campbell Brothers and Ward and Partners of Belfast were faced with stiff competition from commercial firms abroad, who did not have the extra handicap of having to import all the raw materials of their craft.

On the crest of the new wave of Irish nationalist and Revivalist fervour, Edward Martyn, probably at W.B. Yeats's suggestion, decided to seek out the most influential contemporary stained glass artist and try to persuade him to come over to Ireland to work and train a new breed of young Irish men and women in this demoralised but increasingly ubiquitous art. Christopher Whall, a Catholic convert, had been trained as a painter before designing his first window in 1880. While working for Saunders and for Hardman and Powell, he became increasingly frustrated by the division of labour practised by such large firms, whose commercial competitiveness found little time for the traditional technical precepts advocated earlier by Winston and company, or for the William Morris-inspired philosophy that a man should be responsible for every stage in the production of an art work.[14] A growing number of artists and craftsmen and women, raised on Morris and Ruskin, wanted to consider a window's architectural setting, to sketch out, design and cartoon each window, select, paint and fire the glass and participate in its leading and eventual fixing. 'A more or less strictly interpreted adherence to this ideal, together with Pre-Raphaelite-inspired figure design and a fondness for plant-form backgrounds derived from Ruskin and Morris are the chief elements which may be said to typify Arts and Crafts stained glass.'[15]

During the 1880s, in true Arts and Crafts spirit, Whall taught himself every facet of stained glass, received his first commissions, exhibited at the first Arts and Crafts Society exhibition, joined the Art Workers' Guild, contributed to the Century Guild's journal and became a friend of the Guild's pioneering stained glass artist, Selwyn Image.[16] In 1896 he began teaching stained glass at the Central School of Arts and Crafts in London. By then, he had become 'a passionate admirer of medieval stained glass and, like Winston, he understood that its beauty lay not so much in its formal stylistic characteristics as in the way in which, through superb craftsmanship, light and colour were made almost in an abstract way the instruments of artistic expression'.[17] In 1898, at Walter Crane's invitation, he joined the staff of the Royal College of Art, where his teaching colleagues were the leading artists and craftsmen of the day. The architects he collaborated with (like E.S. Prior, Lethaby, Sedding and Henry Wilson) were the most progressive and shared a common belief in a thorough 'knowledge of materials as a basis for style'.[18] Just as Winston's rediscovery of 'antique' pot metal glass had stimulated an earlier generation of stained glass designers, so in 1889, just as Whall's independent career was beginning, the invention by E.S. Prior of the deliberately lumpy 'early English' or Norman slab glass provided Whall, and the new school of artist/craftsmen and women he fathered, with a fundamental ingredient of their designs.

By 1901, when Martyn approached him, Whall was designing and executing windows with a devoted following of pupils and associates from the workshops of Lowndes and Drury's, soon to move premises to the purpose-built Glass House in Fulham.[19] Four years later, his philosophy and teaching would be published in Lethaby's Artistic Crafts series of technical handbooks, as *Stained Glass Work*, a seminal and enormously influential reference book for several succeeding generations of aspiring stained glass students. Whall came over to Ireland, visited Martyn's parish church at Labane, near

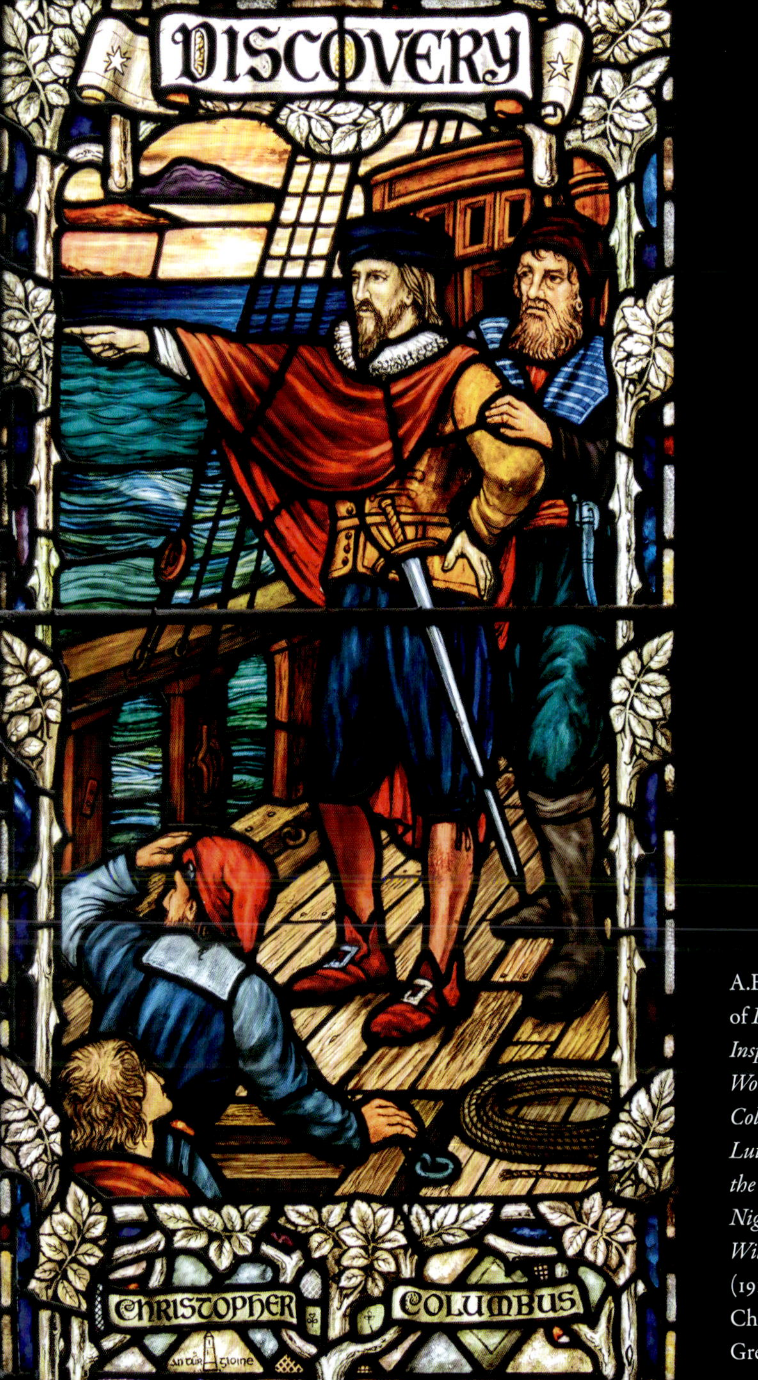

A.E. Child, detail of *Discovery, Truth, Inspiration, Love, Work, with Christopher Columbus, Martin Luther, Christ in the Temple, Florence Nightingale, and William Caxton* (1917–18), Unitarian Church, St Stephen's Green, Dublin

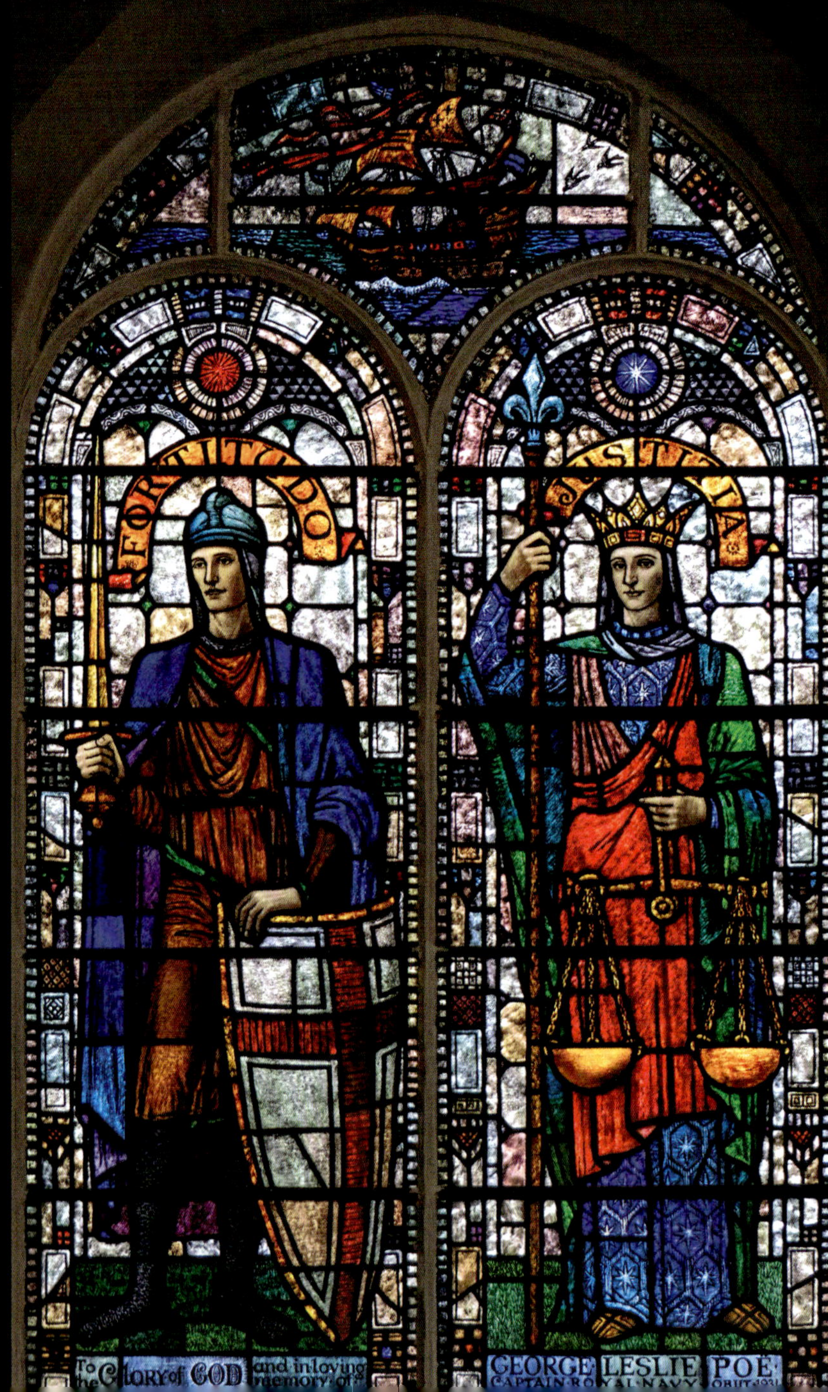
FORTITUDO
JUSTITIA
To the Glory of God and in loving memory of
GEORGE LESLIE POE
CAPTAIN ROYAL NAVY

Ardrahan in County Galway and arranged that his old friend and colleague Selwyn Image (1849–1930) should provide two single-light windows for it, *St Robert* and *St Anna*; he himself subsequently designed a fine *St Elizabeth* window[20] for the church. But he was not free to stay and set up stained glass classes at the Dublin Metropolitan School of Art, newly removed from London control and placed under the auspices of the Department of Agriculture and Technical Instruction since April 1900. Not only was Martyn able to arrange provision for such classes in Dublin through his old friend, the Department's sympathetic Secretary T.P. Gill, but even more important was a commitment from his County Galway neighbour, the Bishop of Clonfert and his enlightened administrator, in April 1901 that the new cathedral they had been building at Loughrea since 1897 should have stained glass executed in Ireland by Irish craftsmen, even if the designs had to come from abroad.[21]

Enthusiastic and supportive as Whall was, he could not abandon his own work in England and therefore, in July 1901, sent over his 'chief assistant' and 'favourite pupil',[22] Alfred Ernest Child, to take up an appointment in September as Instructor in Stained Glass at the Dublin Metropolitan School of Art. Meanwhile, Martyn had found committed active and financial support from Sarah Purser the painter,[23] in their decision to establish a co-operative stained glass workshop, somewhat along the lines of the Lowndes and Drury workshops in Chelsea. Here, under Miss Purser's direction and Alfred Child's management and instruction, the best of the newly trained students could begin to take commissions.

The first of January 1903 marked the inaugural tea party of An Túr Gloine (The Tower of Glass) on the site of two former tennis courts behind 24 Upper Pembroke Street – 'not at all the shimmering edifice the name suggests. But it provided what was necessary: a big, light studio, a small office, a workshop with benches for the glaziers, a gas fired furnace.'[24] Twenty-five years later Sarah Purser wrote of the venture which was to absorb so much of her interest and energy until her death forty years later: 'The shop was quite new and oh, so cold! We gathered round the kiln and drank champagne out of tea cups – it didn't taste very well and we betook ourselves to the tea pot.'[25] As well as Child, Whall also sent over Mr Drury's half-brother, Charlie Williams, as glazier; he was joined by the colourful Dubliner, Tommy Kinsella, as second glazier.

Sarah Purser was determined the workshop should adhere to true Arts and Crafts philosophy: 'Each window is the work of one artist who makes the sketch and cartoon and selects and paints every morsel of glass him or herself.'[26] This was reiterated in their twenty-fifth anniversary booklet: 'Now *we* hold each window should be in all its artistic

Left: Catherine O'Brien, *Fortitude and Justice, with Job and St John the Baptist* (1935), Church of Ireland (St Pappin's), Santry, Dublin

parts the work of one individual artist, the glass chosen and painted by the same mind and hand that made the design and drew the cartoon, in fact a bit of stained glass should be a work of free art as much as any painting or picture.'[27] They were to be devoted to enhancing the nature of the glass and the strength of their designs by the use of leading and to try and combine the former Celtic glories of metal work, illumination, jewellery and sculpture. The studio began with a bank loan; then, out of investments by Purser and Child, was able to pay for overheads, materials and the services of the craftsmen; the artists were given a fee for a design and paid according to the hours spent on a particular commission (in principle), with a bonus at the end of a successful year. In 1925 it was formally made into a co-operative society and registered as An Túr Gloine Stained Glass Works Ltd.

The workshop's first commission in 1903, a two-light *Annunciation* window for Loughrea, was painted by Child but directly adapted from a design by Whall.[28] Miss Purser's first recruit was Michael Healy, who painted an angel in the window as part of his apprenticeship and made his own first window for the cathedral the following year. Indeed, Loughrea Cathedral in its various phases of decoration represents successive stages of Healy's development as an artist in stained glass,[29] from his sensitive, exquisitely painted and stippled early academic style, to the dramatic use of aciding, almost neon in effect, in a rich Byzantine glowing tapestry of colour and line, through to the expressionist, powerfully linear *Last Judgement* (1937–40). His early involvement with the Dominican Order and Florentine and Umbrian Renaissance art was succeeded by a total devotion to the craft he quickly learnt from Child. Although Miss Purser held him in as much respect as she would later Wilhelmina Geddes, she despaired at the slow, painstaking care he took over each piece of glass. Sarah Purser herself only ever painted one public window, for the porch in Loughrea, although she advised on points of design.[30] Her main role was as a tireless defender and promoter of the 'shop', relentlessly pursuing commissions for her artists, ensuring the work was fairly and fittingly distributed, never for her own financial gain but to ensure quality at all cost.

From the Dublin School of Art, Catherine O'Brien joined in 1903, Beatrice Elvery followed in 1904 but only stayed until 1912; Ethel Rhind in 1906; Wilhelmina Geddes, trained initially in Belfast, came in 1912 and left ten years later; Hubert McGoldrick from Earley's in 1920. In 1925, Child, Rhind, O'Brien, Healy, Geddes and McGoldrick all joined Miss Purser, her nephew John Geoghegan and the writer and artist George Russell (Æ), as shareholders in the co-operative. That year Geddes went to work in London, from a studio in the Glass House. The painter, Evie Hone, became a member

Right: Michael Healy, *Last Judgement* (1936–40), Catholic Cathedral, Loughrea, County Galway

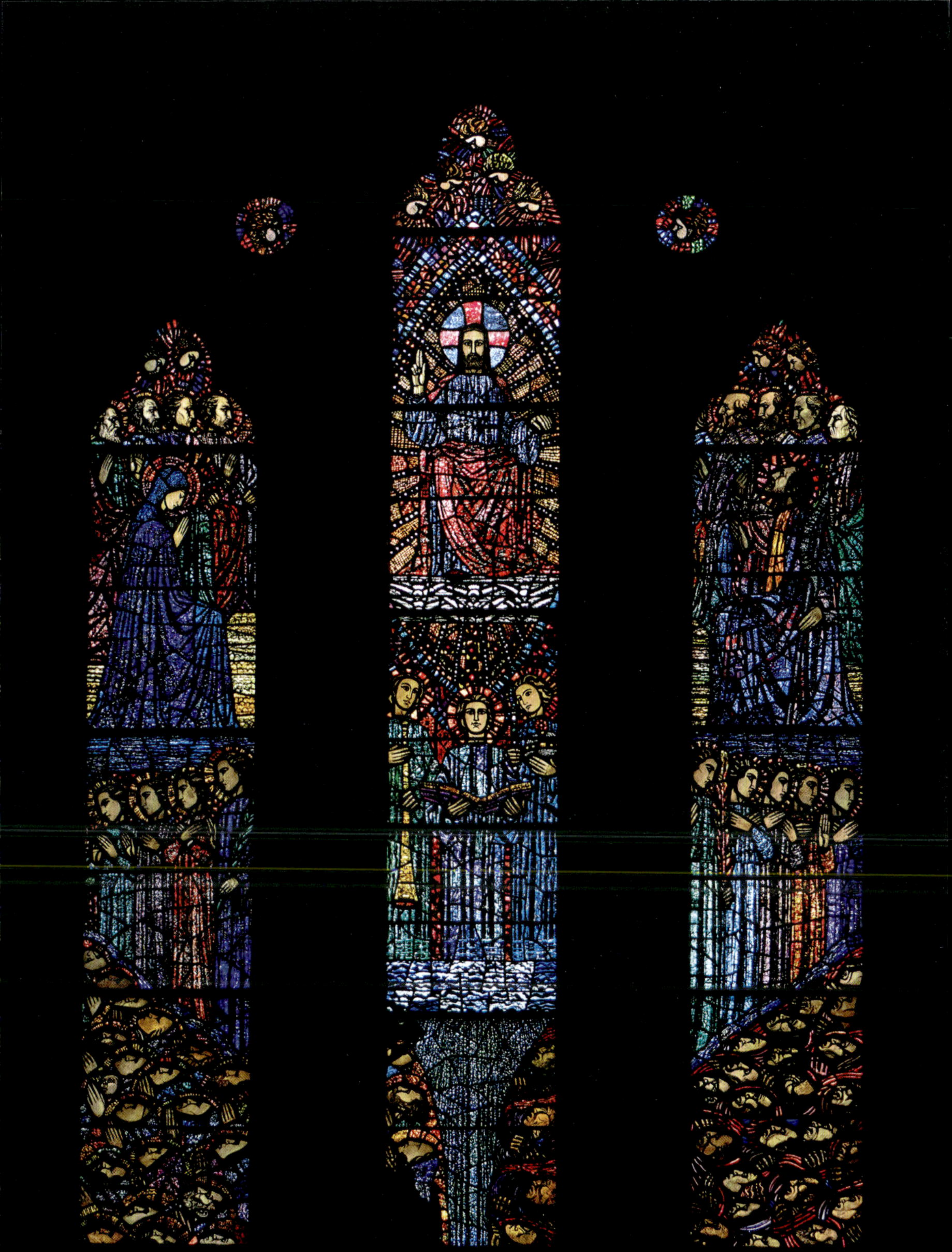

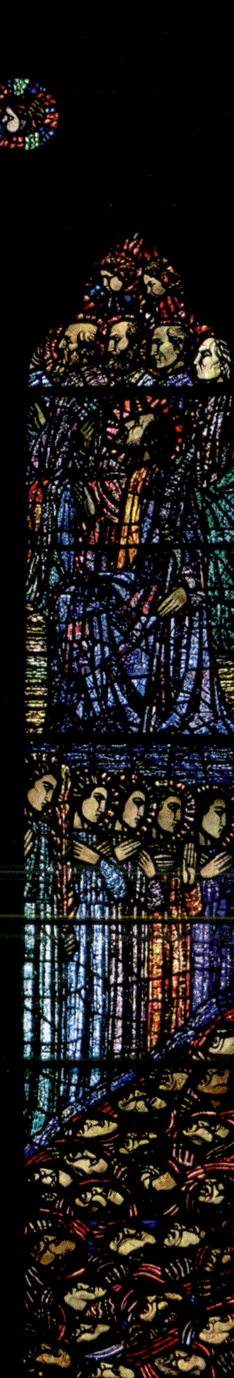

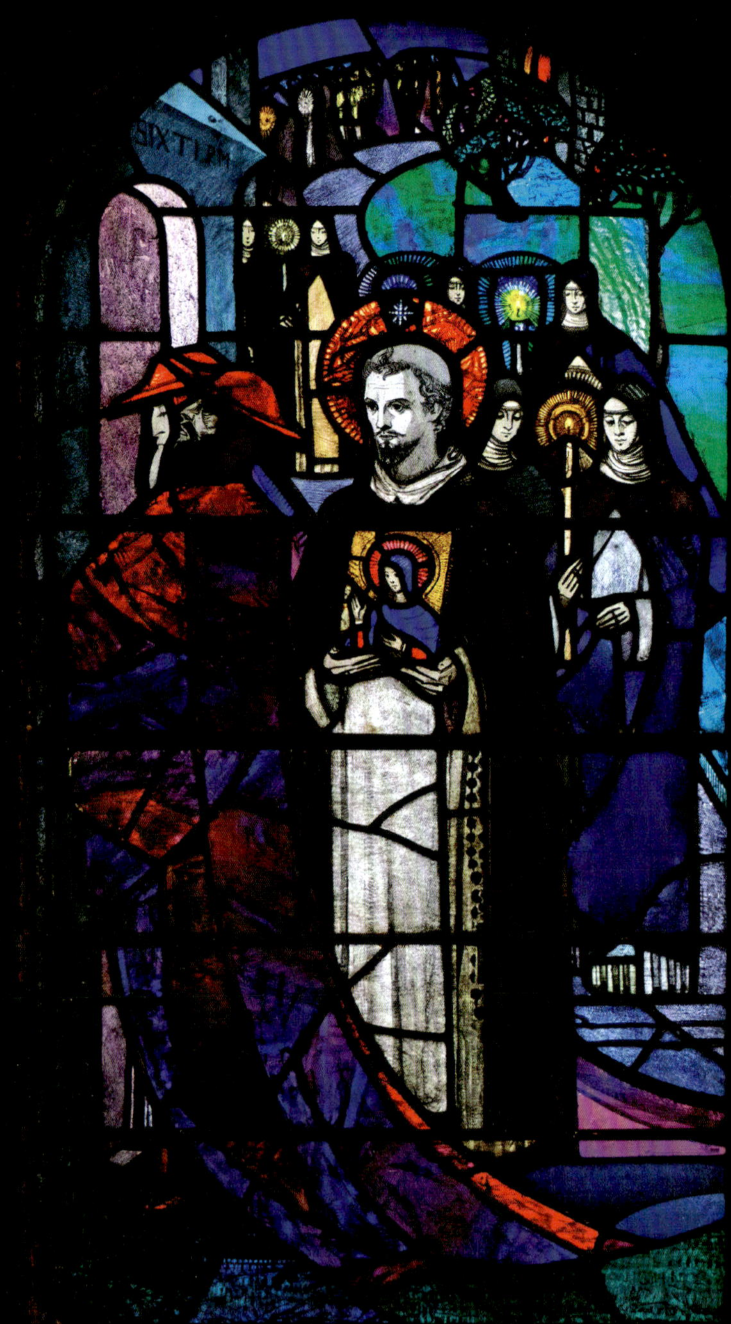

Hubert McGoldrick, *St Dominic Carrying the Icon of the Madonna of San Sisto and leading Nuns Across the Tiber to their New Hone, the Dominican Convent of San Sisto* (1939), Catholic Church (St Mary's), Claddagh, Galway City

of the co-operative in 1935 until its dissolution in January 1944, five years before Child's death, O'Brien's appointment as Secretary and Manager and Miss Purser's resignation (aged 91) of her studio involvement. The year 1943 saw the death of Sarah Purser and only Hone, O'Brien and McGoldrick actively producing glass. The following year the co-operative was dissolved and Catherine O'Brien took over the studio and its contents; unfortunately much of the latter were destroyed in a fire in 1958.[31] Evie Hone rearranged her painting studio in Rathfarnham, County Dublin for glass painting and glazing.

Child trained a steady number of students and apprentices over the years at the Dublin Art School. Kathleen Fox (1880–1963), like Elvery a gifted all-round craftsworker, who soon devoted herself to painting, designed and executed a window, *St Tobias*, in the Whall manner in Child's classes in 1909.[32] Others who were particularly good included Hugh Barden (who had been one of Child's first students, from 1902–7, and is recorded much later as working in the 1950s in Pembroke Street) and Kathleen Quigly.[33]

Harry Clarke had been brought up at 33 North Frederick Street in Dublin which housed the (mainly church) decorating business his father had established in 1886. In 1905, by the time he had enrolled, aged 16, for Child's night classes at the Dublin Metropolitan School of Art in stained glass, he had absorbed a certain amount about the 'shop' from his father's stained glass craftsman, Pope from Nottingham,[34] then William Nagle, a skilled painter, and Arthur A. Orr, a freelance designer and craftsman in Middlesex, who worked mainly for A.J. Dix but often sent designs over to Joshua Clarke to have made up in glass. The first piece of glass Clarke painted in 1906 was a copy of one of Orr's designs. This was to enable him to spend two months at the South Kensington Art School, where he may well have been instructed in stained glass by Whall, and a disastrously short apprenticeship in a trade house in Nottingham. He was soon back in Dublin studying with Child at night, working as an apprentice in his father's studios by day.

In 1910 Joshua Clarke took on William MacBride, trained at Heaton, Butler and Bayne's, to replace his son who had been awarded the newly created scholarship in stained glass at the art school.[35] The panels he proceeded to make established an early reputation in Britain, winning him the coveted Gold Medal for three successive years in the annual Board of Education National Competition,[36] a continuing scholarship and, in 1914, a travelling award to study medieval stained glass in France and England. Whall was one of the judges who selected panels by Clarke and Geddes (as well as Anning Bell, Karl Parsons and Douglas Strachan) for the Exposition des Arts Décoratifs de Grande-Bretagne et d'Irlande in Paris that year. He returned to Ireland in 1915 when he received his first commission from another enlightened patron, Sir John O'Connell, for the Honan Hostel Chapel, Cork. As Loughrea had done for An Túr Gloine, this major opportunity (eleven windows) justifiably established his reputation and the jealously watchful eye of Sarah Purser.[37] She and Joshua Clarke were already arch rivals in Dublin, so young Clarke's success only compounded the animosity between the two studios.

Until his father's death in 1921, Clarke designed from a studio he adapted in the garden of the house in Blackrock, County Dublin, which he shared with his painter wife, Margaret; he also rented studio facilities in Frederick Street. He was assisted by Austin Molloy, another ex-student of Child, sometime silver medallist in the National Competition, who continued to assist him until the mid-1920s. Then he acquired and converted two large Georgian houses over the road, at 6 and 7 North Frederick Street. Nagle worked at the Studios until his death in 1923. MacBride had gone his own way in 1918, after prestigious commissions for war memorial windows in St Patrick's Cathedral, Dublin and St John's, Malone Road in Belfast; the following year he joined Albert Power, the sculptor, in the formation of the Craftworkers' Guild in Harcourt Street, Dublin.[38] Kathleen Quigly (1888–1981) worked with Clarke, notably on his *Eve of St Agnes* window, from October 1921 to January 1924, and A.A. Orr discovered Philip Deegan from Worthing, who worked skilfully but closely in Clarke's style from September 1921 onwards. In May 1923, Leo Cartwright, who would subsequently leave in August 1926 to work with Charles Connick in Boston, joined the Studios. Millicent Girling, who had studied graphic illustration with Clarke at the School of Art, came from January 1924 until July 1926. Michael Dunne was the invaluable chief glazier. In no time there was a large studio successfully producing Clarke-style windows to his designs or under his supervision. Until incipient tuberculosis began to crush his health, Clarke had hopes of setting up a London studio with, first, the book illustrator John Austen and secondly, more realistically, his old friend Karl Parsons (1884–1934), a leading exponent of the Whall school, whom he had first met through Orr and Joseph Nuttgens before the First World War. Clarke shared Parsons' studio at Lowndes and Drury's Glass House in 1926 and again in 1927, when their assistant was Leonard Potter, who came over to Dublin in 1928 to help with the running of the Studios.[39]

Shortly before his death in January 1931, the decorating side of the Clarke Studios was liquidated and the stained glass department became the Harry Clarke Stained Glass Studios Ltd, with an artist, Charles Simmonds, recommended by Parsons and Will Rothenstein as manager. The Studios were finally closed in 1973, shortly before Earley's.[40]

Curran wrote of Harry Clarke that his 'windows shine with an incomparable jewelled splendour. An artist of great virtuosity he created a world of his own, through which passed strange figures, insubstantial and disquieting, figures whose frailty bear with difficulty the almost insupportable burden of their glittering ornament.'[41]

Right: Harry Clarke, *Eve of St Agnes* (1924), Dublin City Gallery The Hugh Lane, Parnell Square, Dublin. Collection and image © Hugh Lane Gallery, Dublin (Reg. No. 1442)

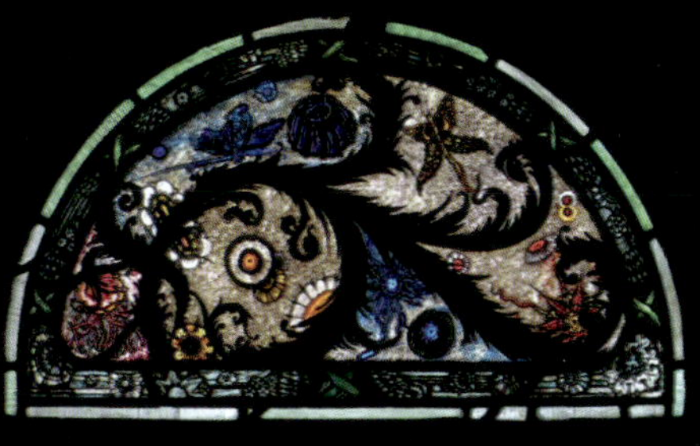
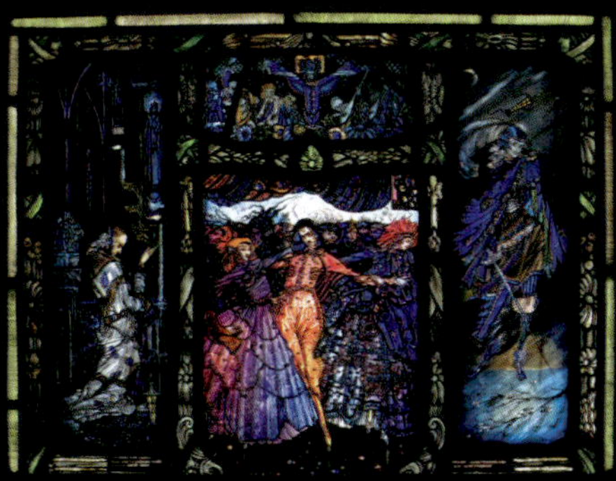
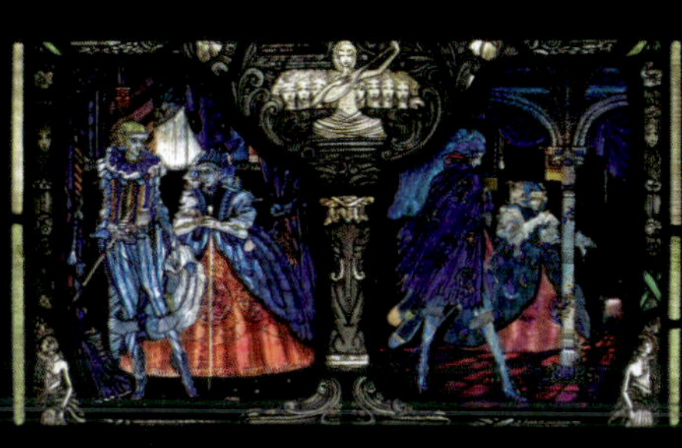
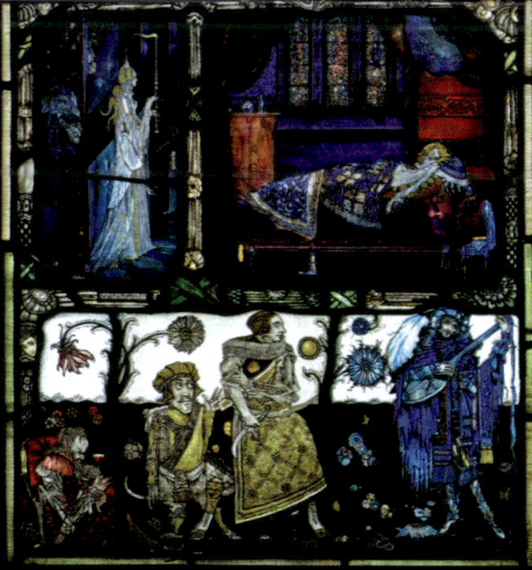
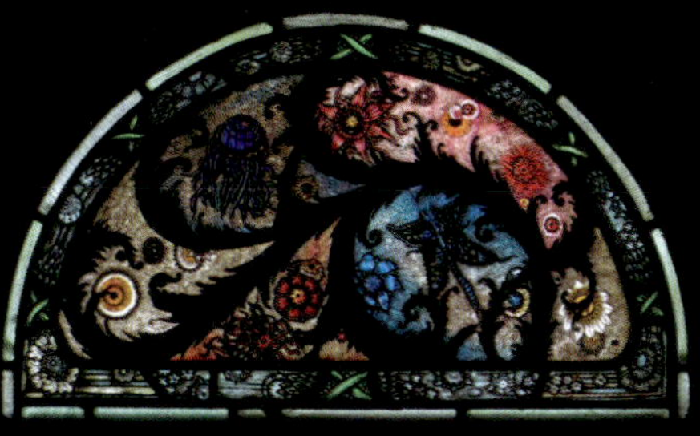
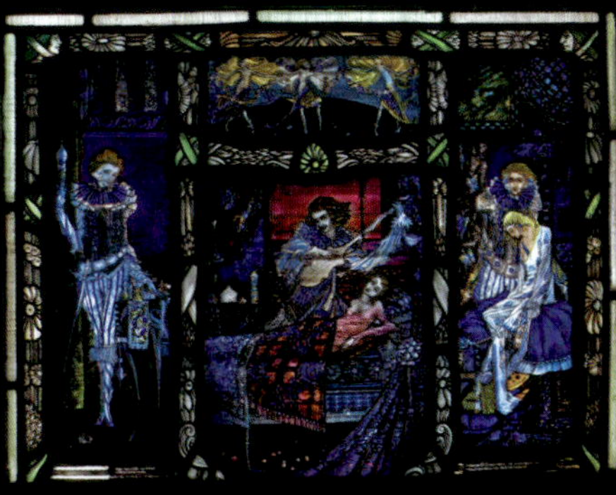
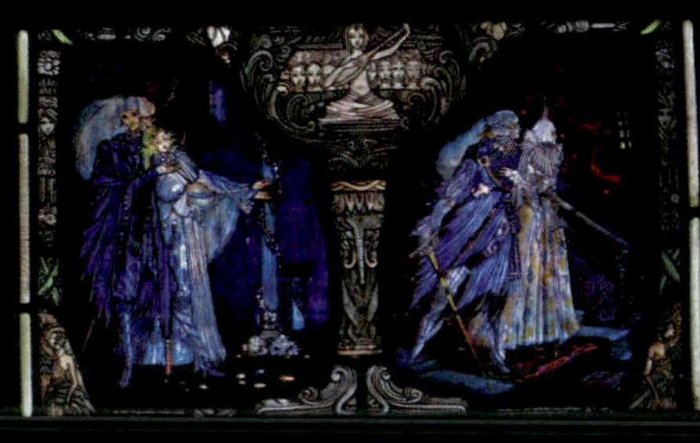
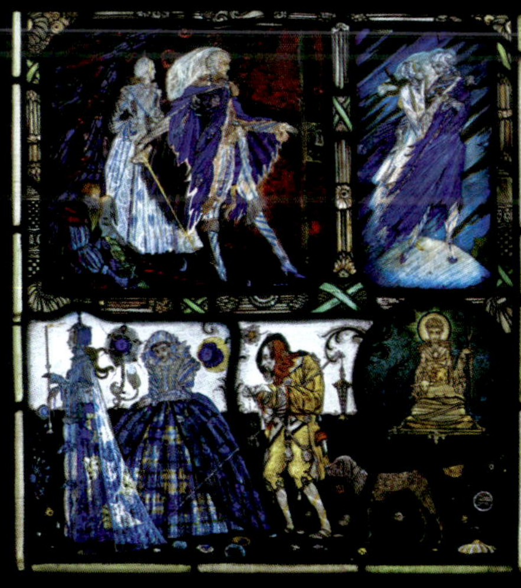

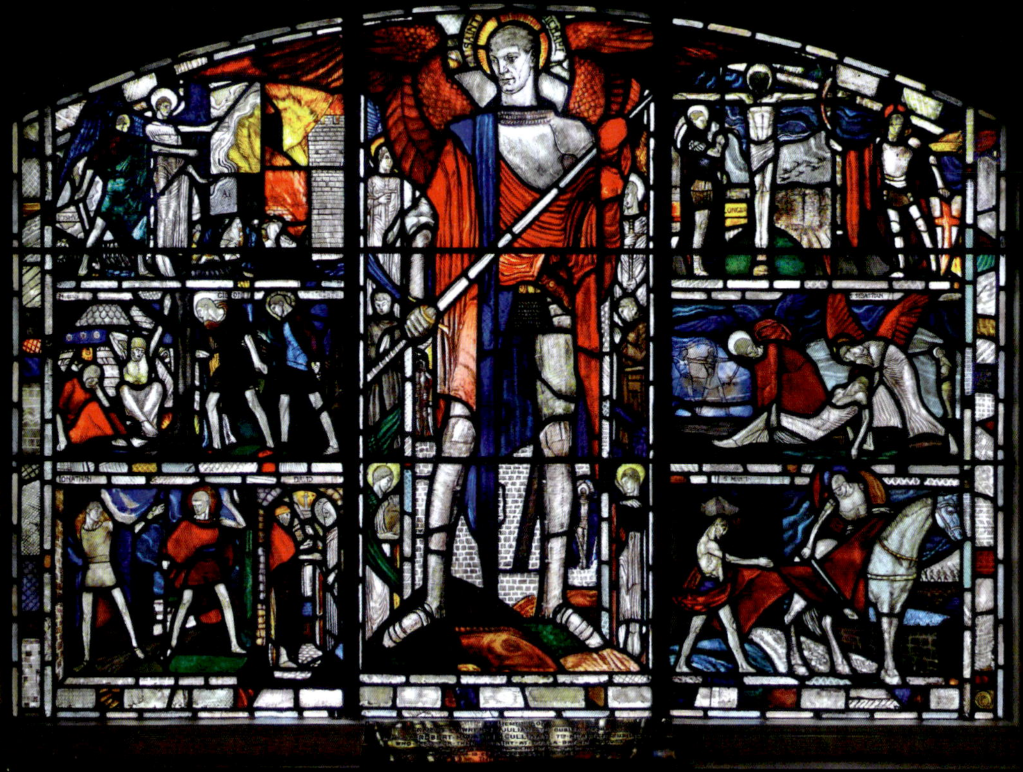

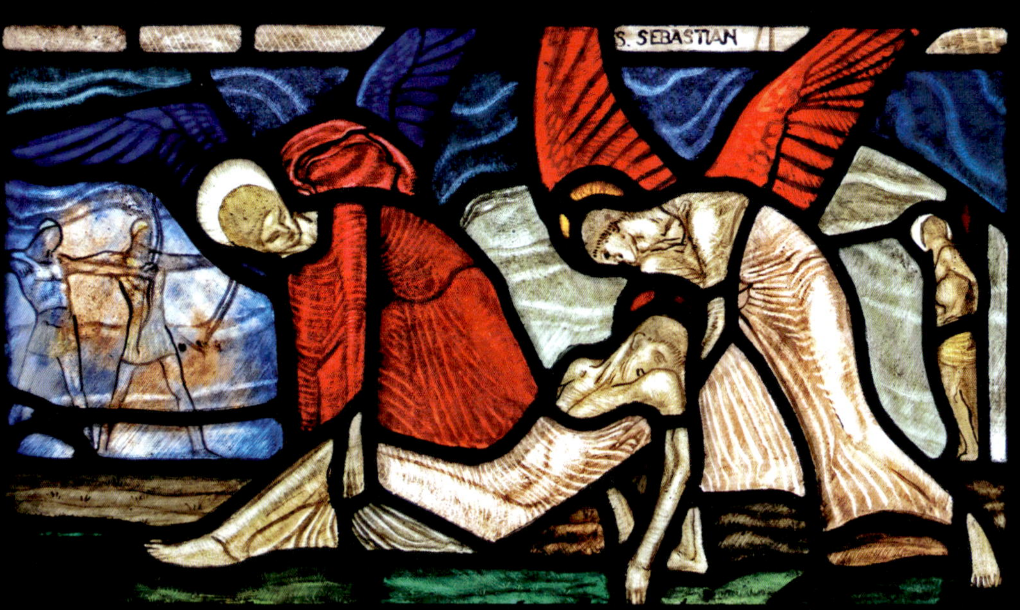
S. SEBASTIAN

Like Clarke, Wilhelmina Geddes also rented studio space at the Glass House in London when she moved there in 1925, having left An Túr Gloine in 1922. Geddes started working in glass after talking to Sarah Purser, who had been so struck by her illustrative work when it was exhibited in Dublin in 1910 that, even though the young student had never worked in glass,[42] she invited her to join the studio the following spring. Geddes returned to the Belfast Art School, which she had been attending since she was 16, and in 1911 made her first panel, *Sir Walter Raleigh*, whose cartoon won her a bronze medal in the National Competition. She then came down to the Dublin School of Art, enrolled in Orpen's life and painting classes, and took lodgings. The ensuing three small illustrative panels depicting *St Colman MacDuagh* she made for Sarah Purser to give to Edward Martyn demonstrate how well her powerful graphic skills were suited to stained glass. In 1912, she joined An Túr Gloine. Her impressive first full-scale window made that year, for the Church of Ireland at Inishmacsaint, County Fermanagh, reveals Child's Whall-inspired teaching as well as a number of idiosyncratic features which she would develop in successive windows; indeed, much more so than in her next *Innocence Walking in the Fields of Paradise* window in nearby Monea Church of Ireland. This may well be because, although responsible for the design, she only executed sections of the window. Her other two windows designed in 1913, for Townsend Street Presbyterian Church in Belfast and St Ann's, Dawson Street in Dublin, are more consistent in execution and treatment. Through family contacts she brought a number of welcome Northern commissions to the Tower of Glass and, although dogged by poor health which necessitated frequent retreats to Belfast, she was very close to Sarah Purser, whose judgement and encouragement she greatly valued. In 1914, she and Catherine O'Brien accompanied Miss Purser on the first of a number of trips to look at thirteenth-century stained glass in France.

By the time she left An Túr Gloine, she had produced seventeen windows of unprecedentedly powerful original design and treatment, the Duke of Connaught's Ottawa *War Memorial* (1919) and the controversial Wallsend *Crucifixion* (1922) being the most famous. Due to recurring ill health, she left Michael Healy to execute in glass her designs for Bardsea and (with Rhind) Curraun. Her first window made at the Glass House, for Laleham in Middlesex, develops her unique power to achieve a deep spiritually moving effect with a raw physical intensity through arresting compositional devices and consummate technical skill. Even more than Clarke and Healy, she set herself almost impossibly high standards, taking infinite pains with each piece of glass,

Left: Wilhelmina Geddes, full window and detail of *Archangels Raphael and Michael, and Jacob's Angel with Joshua, Gideon's Vision, David and Jonathan, St Longinus, St Sebastian and St George* (1918), Church of Ireland (St Ann's), Dawson Street, Dublin

and consequently often completing work at great financial loss to herself. In between lengthening bouts of illness, she worked from Studio B at the Glass House until the early 1950s, making windows for both sides of the Irish Sea and exhibiting widely. Always a loner, her inimitable style was revered by her stained glass colleagues and discerning critics and patrons who sought out her work. Pevsner, when describing her *Crucifixion* window at Wallsend,[43] ascribed it to the much better known Evie Hone, to whom Geddes had taught the rudiments of glass in London in 1933.

Evie Hone had been painting and exhibiting regularly when she became interested in expressing her art through glass in the early 1930s. Her religious aspirations, involvement with pure colour and the principles of abstraction, added to a love of the work of Giotto, Fra Angelico and Rouault, culminated in her designing three exploratory panels, two abstract and one an *Annunciation*, in 1933. Her lifelong friend, the painter Mainie Jellett, with whom she had returned year after year to France seeking to come to grips with abstraction and a return to the two-dimensional surface, 'suggested she should ask Sarah Purser to let her carry them out at An Túr Gloine. Miss Purser was entirely discouraging and told her if she wanted to learn the craft to join Mr Child's class in the School of Art. She went there but found her own opinion of her proposed master no higher than his opinion of her designs.'[44] Back in London she was put in touch with Bernard Rackham at the Victoria and Albert Museum, who advised her to go to Geddes at the Glass House.[45] There she was kindly and appreciatively received by a kindred artist, taught the rudiments of stained glass and helped to effectively translate her designs onto glass. Hone showed these panels to Roland Holst (well known as a stained glass artist, teacher and Director of the Amsterdam Rijksakademie), who encouraged her to persist in her newfound medium.

On her return to Dublin the three panels were acquired by the Rector of Taney Church, County Dublin, for composition into a window, and she was given her first commission, for Ardcarne Church, Boyle, County Roscommon. Even with these commissions, Sarah Purser remained adamantly disinclined to offer her facilities. When Hone eventually became a member in 1935, she had already completed the Ardcarne commission and, with Michael Healy's help, adapted her three panels into an *Annunciation* window. Healy and Tommy Kinsella taught her the tricks of the trade. Healy's death in 1941 ended plans they had made to set up a workshop together; Kinsella glazed all her windows until his death in 1953. When An Túr Gloine was dissolved in 1944 (to her relief by then) she was free to rearrange her own studio at Marlay, Rathfarnham, across the yard from the Dower House in which she lived

Right: Evie Hone, *The Sacred Heart and Jesuit Saints* (1945), Manresa House, Dollymount, Dublin (formerly in Tullabeg, County Offaly)

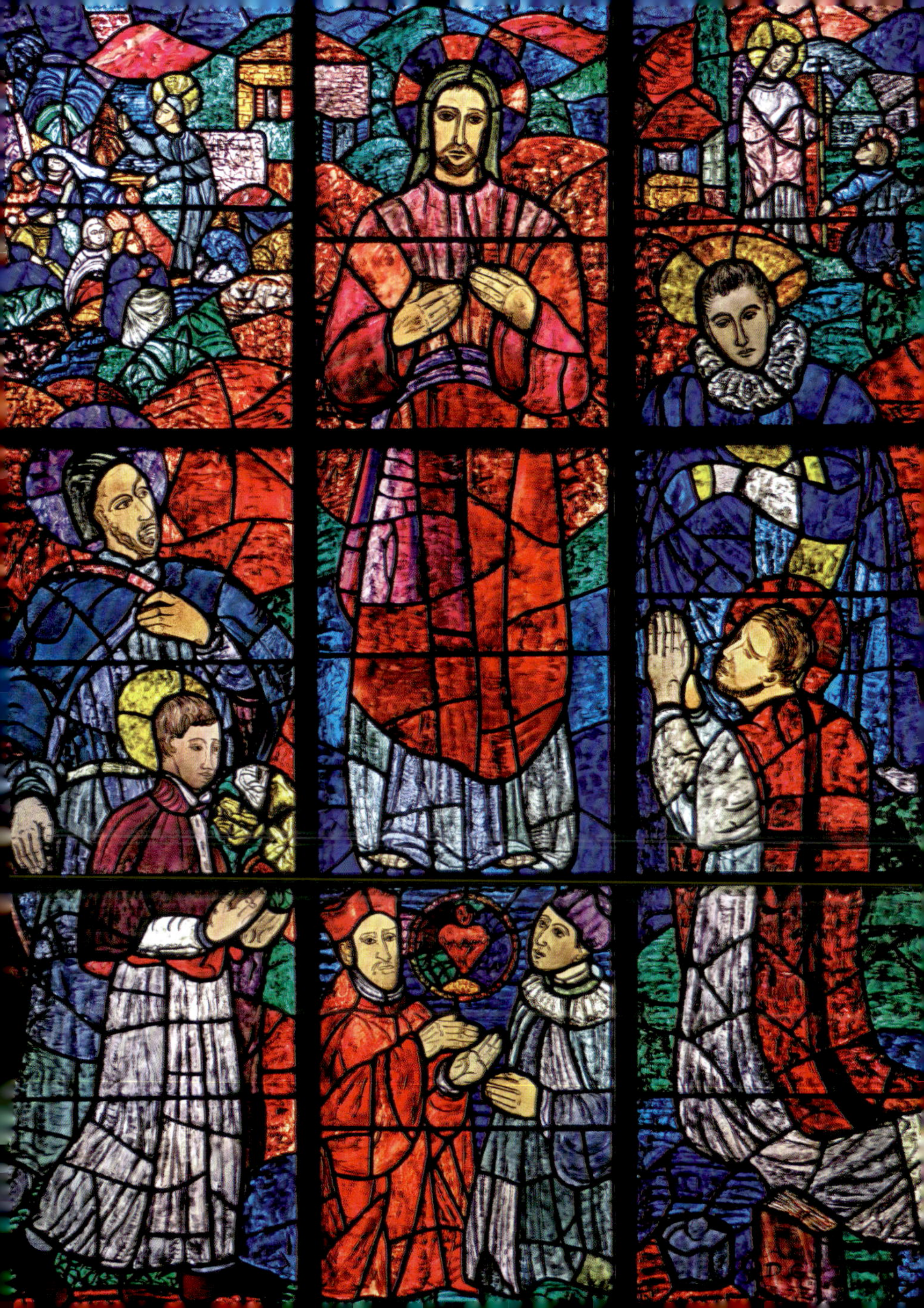

below the Dublin mountains. Although she had already been acclaimed for a dozen or so windows, including her large abstract composition *My Four Green Fields*, made for the New York World's Fair of 1939, she now proceeded to make the windows she herself judged her best – the series at Tullabeg, County Offaly and Kingscourt, County Cavan, whose loosely painted, deeply coloured glass pulsates in solemn, even anguished intensity. Any early influence of Geddes and Healy has been assimilated; her maturity as a painter and profound religious sentiment were now expressed through her concern with the painted surface of the glass, the value of colour and the rhythm of line. Her study and understanding of early Irish medieval stone carving had a profound effect on her treatment of both the figure and composition. Although she too studied and admired French and English early medieval glass (as well as modern French and Dutch glass), unlike Healy and Clarke she rarely used acid on flashed glass nor, unlike them and Geddes, plated her glass. Her five symbolic windows in Hatch Street, Dublin (1947) reveal a particularly successful abstract treatment. Her monumental nine-light *Crucifixion and Last Supper* window (1949–51), for Eton College Chapel, given to her on the strength of her Tullabeg and Kingscourt windows, had an enormous impact on a wide circle of her contemporary artists both in stained glass and other media.

John Piper wrote in 1957 that 'Léger's glass at Audincourt seems to me to be the modern masterpiece in the medium, and after these windows I would put Evie Hone's Eton east window, if only for its glassy-ness'.[46] Patrick Reyntiens has written of the Eton window's 'dramatic breakthrough ... the herald of a new period of co-operation between the eye of the painter and the eye of an artist in stained glass'.[47] Martin Harrison has said, 'Compared to her glass, always direct, simple and primitive, the work of her contemporaries looks distinctly anaemic',[48] but he, like Piper and an increasing number of contemporary critics, feels her reputation should not eclipse that of the more reclusive Geddes, who died five months after her, similarly dogged by ill health, in August 1955.

The legacy of Clarke, Geddes and Hone and, to a lesser extent, Healy, An Túr Gloine and the Clarke Studios is undeniable not only in Ireland and the British Isles but also in America, where Charles Connick was the first to realise the importance of their work,[49] Canada, New Zealand[50] and Australia. In the following gazetteer, drawn principally from An Túr Gloine's work journals in the National Gallery of Ireland Archives and the Harry Clarke Stained Glass Studios' manuscripts in Trinity College Dublin, as well as the observations and investigations of Michael Wynne, David Caron and myself variously over the past twenty or so years, the windows are attributed to the individual artist where possible. It is hoped that this study will encourage an appreciation and interest in a little documented area to which Irish artists contributed so much earlier this century.

Notes

1 In his evidence before the Royal Commission of Art in Ireland, quoted in *The Irish Builder*, 29 December 1906.

2 *The Irish Statesman*, 14 November 1925, pp. 310–12, reprinted as 'Light in Dark Places', *The Living Torch*, ed. Monk Gibbon (New York: Macmillan, 1937), p. 195.

3 J. Piper, *Stained Glass: Art or Anti Art?* (London; Studio Vista, 1968), pp. 37–8.

4 R. Elliott, *Art and Ireland* (Dublin: Sealy, Bryers & Walker, 1902), p. 201.

5 Ibid.

6 Edward Martyn (1859–1923), a native of County Galway, was a playwright, co-founder of the Irish Literary (later Abbey) Theatre, founder of the Palestrina Choir and impassioned supporter of the Irish language, sacred music and church art. He bequeathed a Corot, a Monet and two Degas pastels to the National Gallery of Ireland. The establishment of a stained glass school in Ireland was one of the few idealistic ventures he had championed by which he was not ultimately disillusioned.

7 Quoted in Denis Gwynn, *Edward Martyn and the Irish Revival* (London: Jonathan Cape, 1930), pp. 229–36.

8 See Michael Wynne, 'Stained Glass in Ireland, principally Irish Stained Glass, 1760–1963', unpublished doctoral thesis, University of Dublin 1975, chapter on Irish stained glass in the eighteenth century.

9 M. Harrison, *Victorian Stained Glass* (London: Barrie & Jenkins, 1980), chapter 1, 'The Revival of the True Principles of Glass Painting 1837–1951', p. 15.

10 Ibid., pp. 18–19.

11 H. Holiday's book, *Stained Glass as an Art*, published in 1896, was keenly recommended by Robert Elliott (*Art and Ireland*, p. 208) 'to all the priests of Ireland, as one of the few books on art worth reading . . . This man, Holiday, *did* know what he was writing about.'

12 See Harrison, *Victorian*, Chapter 4, 'Stained Glass of the Aesthetic Period', p. 55.

13 M. Wynne, 'Stained Glass in Ireland', p. 151, chapter on Irish stained glass in the nineteenth century; see also his article 'Irish Stained and Painted Glass in the eighteenth century', *Crown in Glory*, ed. Peter Moore (Norwich: Jarrold & Sons, 1982).

14 See A.C. Sewter, *The Stained Glass of William Morris and his Circle*, 2 vols (London 1974–5); Harrison, *Victorian*; P. Cormack, *Christopher Whall 1849–1924; Arts and Stained Glass Worker*, catalogue of an exhibition at The William Morris Gallery (London; William Morris Gallery, 1980); also Whall's own *Stained Glass Work: A Text Book for Students and Workers in Glass* (London: Isaac Pitman & Sons, 1920).

15 Harrison, *Victorian*, Chapter 5, The Arts and Crafts Movement – a return to fundamentals, p. 63.

16 It was Image, through Whall, who would design the first Arts and Crafts windows for Edward Martyn's parish church at Ardrahan, County Galway. Harrison writes (*Victorian,* p. 64) that Image was 'the first of the Arts and Crafts stained glass men to put his ideas into practice, having shown designs for stained glass at the 1878 International Exhibition in Paris. The highly individual mature style at which he had arrived by about 1890 was chiefly characterised by its distinctive lead patterns. This entailed breaking up the overall design for a window into regular geometric shapes, the restless rhythms giving an almost Expressionist effect.' For Image, see also *Studio*, vol. 14, no. 63, 1898, pp. 2–10.

17 P. Cormack, *Introduction to Christopher Whall, 1849–1924: Arts and Crafts Stained Glass Worker:* Catalogue of the Exhibition (London: William Morris Gallery, 1979)

18 Ibid.

19 Whall moved into a studio and workshops specially converted for stained glass production in Ravenscourt Park in 1907. One of Whall's closest friends and pupils, Louis Davis (1861–1941), would later design the fine *St Columba* Law war memorial window in St Patrick's Cathedral, Dublin.

20 Peter Cormack does not think that the Image windows look as though they were made at Powell's of Whitefriars, as was most of the glass from 1890; he suggests it might have been made by Whall at Lowndes and Drury – or, of course, by Child in Dublin, although there is no record

of this. The *St Elizabeth* by Whall, Cormack states, is a reworking of a figure first used at St Saviour's, Folkestone (1901) and All Saints, Brockhampton (1902) and may have been executed by Child in Dublin, since it could date from as late as 1912. Image's windows are marked by the contrast between an intensely leaded dark single saintly figure set against a clear delicately silver-stained background.

21 See D. Caron, 'An Túr Gloine Stained Glass Windows and Mosaic Stations of the Cross in St Brendan's Cathedral, Loughrea, County Galway', undergraduate degree thesis, National College of Art and Design, 1982.

22 C.P. Curran refers to Whall's 'chief assistant' in 'Michael Healy: Stained Glass Worker 1873–1941', *Studies*, vol. 36, March 1942, p. 70; T.P. Gill as a 'favourite pupil' in his speech transcribed in An Túr Gloine's twenty-fifth anniversary celebratory booklet (Dublin: Sign of the Three Candles, 1928), p. 5.

23 Sarah Purser, RHA (1848–1943), from an academic Dublin family, was trained as a painter in Dublin, Paris and Italy and first exhibited at the RHA in 1878. Her success as a portrait painter (not to mention on the stock exchange) enabled her to become a vital force in promoting Dublin's artistic and cultural activities over her long life. She was responsible for drawing Sir Hugh Lane's attention to contemporary Irish art (with an important exhibition of the work of Nathaniel Hone and John Butler Yeats) and his subsequent interest in Irish artistic affairs. In 1924 she founded the Friends of the National Collections of Ireland, partly to encourage good contemporary continental art to reach Ireland, and in 1930 secured Charlemont House as a permanent city gallery. The monthly salons she held at Mespil House from 1911 onwards are still legendary.

24 E. Coxhead, *Daughters of Erin* (London: Secker and Warburg, 1962), p. 140. The image of a glass tower was, apparently, taken from Celtic mythology.

25 Sarah Purser's reply to T.P. Gill transcribed in An Túr Gloine's twenty-fifth anniversary booklet, p. 13.

26 Quoted in *Athenaeum*, 30 July 1919, from An Túr Gloine's anniversary booklet, p. 24.

27 Sarah Purser's reply to T.P. Gill, An Túr Gloine's anniversary booklet, p. 9.

28 I am grateful to Peter Cormack for drawing attention to this. The main design for *The Annunciation* is closely adapted from Whall's windows in All Saints Church, Dogmersfield, Hampshire (1898). Similarly, substantial sections of Child's *Agony in the Garden* window of 1903 are adapted from Whall's design for the same subject in Canterbury Cathedral (1902). The third window in the Loughrea apse of 1903 by Child, *The Resurrection*, is closely related to Whall's version in Canterbury Cathedral (1902) and a window in St Ethelbert's Church, Herringswell, Suffolk (1902). The designs of the windows are reproduced, recorded and analysed in D. Caron's 'An Túr Gloine' where the question is discussed as to why Child should choose to follow Whall's designs so closely when each window in An Túr Gloine was supposed to be the unique and integral production of an individual artist.

29 See Caron, 'An Túr Gloine'.

30 Sarah Purser only ever painted one public window, *St Brendan*, for the porch at Loughrea Cathedral, although she advised on points of design constantly – e.g. her collaboration with Beatrice Elvery (*The Passion*, 1908) and Child (*The Nativity*, 1912) at Loughrea – and made several very small panels for friends and family, depicting subjects such as *St Colmcille* and a beloved toy elephant (see Hilary Pyle, *Irish Art 1900–1950*, catalogue of the ROSC Exhibition, Cork 1975, no. 223 and Nicola Gordon Bowe, *The Dublin Arts and Crafts Movement 1885–1930*, Edinburgh Festival exhibition catalogue, Edinburgh, 1985 no. 122). It is important to record this as it has long been a popular misconception that Sarah Purser was responsible for a number of windows since the Studios were commonly known as 'Miss Purser's Studios'. She herself described her Loughrea window as 'My only output … something in the nature of a curiosity' (in her address in the twenty-fifth anniversary booklet, p. 11), and did not have it entered in the workshop journal.

31 From 1952 until her death in 1963, Miss O'Brien rented space to Patrick Pollen who had come to Ireland to learn about stained glass from Evie Hone on the strength of seeing her Eton window.

32 The window, which was measured by Hardman's of Birmingham in 1907 for St Joseph's Catholic Church, Glasthule,

County Dublin was erected there in 1910 after being exhibited in South Kensington. Kathleen Fox also drew the only portrait of Child which has so far come to light.

33 Kathleen Quigly (1888–1981) was never a member of the co-operative although she did produce a window in the Church of Ireland, Dunmore East, County Waterford and another for the chapel of the Sacred Heart Convent, Newton, Massachusetts with them. She also executed some of the Singapore windows and assisted on others, as she also did with Harry Clarke between 1921 and 1924. In 1919 she had collaborated with him on a lantern incorporating zodiac stained and painted panels, which they exhibited jointly in 1921. In 1925 she established the Columbian Studio in Westmoreland Street in Dublin, where she continued to work with her sister in a variety of media until they emigrated to South Africa in 1934.

34 Probably from Pope and Parr's in Nottingham. He stayed from 1892 to 1904. See Nicola Gordon Bowe, 'The Life and Work of Harry Clarke 1889–1931', unpublished doctoral thesis, University of Dublin, 1982, vol. 1, Chapter 1, pp. 6ff.

35 Ernest Lakeman had been awarded the first scholarship in 1909, but, after initial promise, he left the school and later worked with Henry Wynd Young in America; windows by him can be seen in Denver Cathedral, Colorado.

36 Selwyn Image was among the judges.

37 For a full description, analysis and discussion of these windows, in the context of Clarke's work and the wider contexts of the stained glass revival, the Celtic Revival and European Symbolism, see my 'Life and Work', vol. 1, Chapter 3, pp. 125–97; also my catalogue *Harry Clarke* (Dublin: Trinity College, 1979) nos 149, 150 and Addendum; and 'A Host of Shining Saints', *Country Life*, 12 July 1979, pp. 114–17.

38 MacBride collaborated with Clarke on a three-light window in the Catholic Church of the Sacred Heart, Donnybrook, Dublin in 1924, when he made the central light to Clarke's two outer light designs. He could achieve a rich sumptuous quality using Whall-inspired devices and Clarke-influenced symbolic detail. His production of windows became increasingly spasmodic after he formed the Craftworkers' Guild, where he took increasingly to metalwork.

39 The only collaboration between Clarke and Parsons was the *St Cecilia and a Listening Angel* window in St Michael and All Saints Church, Waterford, Hertfordshire. Parsons designed one window in Ireland, a three-light *Last Judgement* east window in the Church of Ireland, Saintfield, County Down (1928).

40 For a full discussion of Clarke's work in relation to the studios he established, see my unpublished thesis, 'Life and Work', vol. 2, pp. 813ff., Dublin 1982; also *Harry Clarke*, the catalogue I complied for the major exhibition in Trinity College (Dublin: 1979), pp. 45–7.

41 C.P. Curran, 'Michael Healy', pp. 73–4.

42 It had already been suggested to her there that she take up stained glass as admirably suited to her work but she had not done so.

43 N. Pevsner, *The Buildings of England: Northumberland* (Harmondsworth: Penguin Books, 1957), pp. 59 and 309.

44 C.P. Curran, 'Evie Hone: Stained Glass Worker 1894–1955', *Studies*, Summer 1955, pp. 129–42.

45 Rackham had written in praise of Geddes's windows for Rosemary Street in Belfast a few years earlier in 'Stained Glass Windows by Miss W.M. Geddes', *Studio*, vol. 98, 1929, pp. 682–3.

46 J. Piper, 'Abstraction to Creation' in *A Tribute to Evie Hone and Mainie Jellett*, ed. Stella Frost (Dublin: 1957), p. 44.

47 P. Reyntiens, *The Technique of Stained Glass* (London: B.T. Batsford, 1967).

48 Harrison, *Victorian*, p. 73.

49 See his classic account, Charles J. Connick, *Adventures in Light and Colour* (New York and London: 1937) and, more specifically, his enthusiastic discovery of the Tower of Glass in 'Modern Glass – A Review', *International Studio*, vol. 130, no. 329, October 1924, pp. 40–52.

50 Fiona Ciaran, Director of New Zealand Stained Glass Research, is currently examining the contribution of Irish stained glass of this period to the broader New Zealand context.

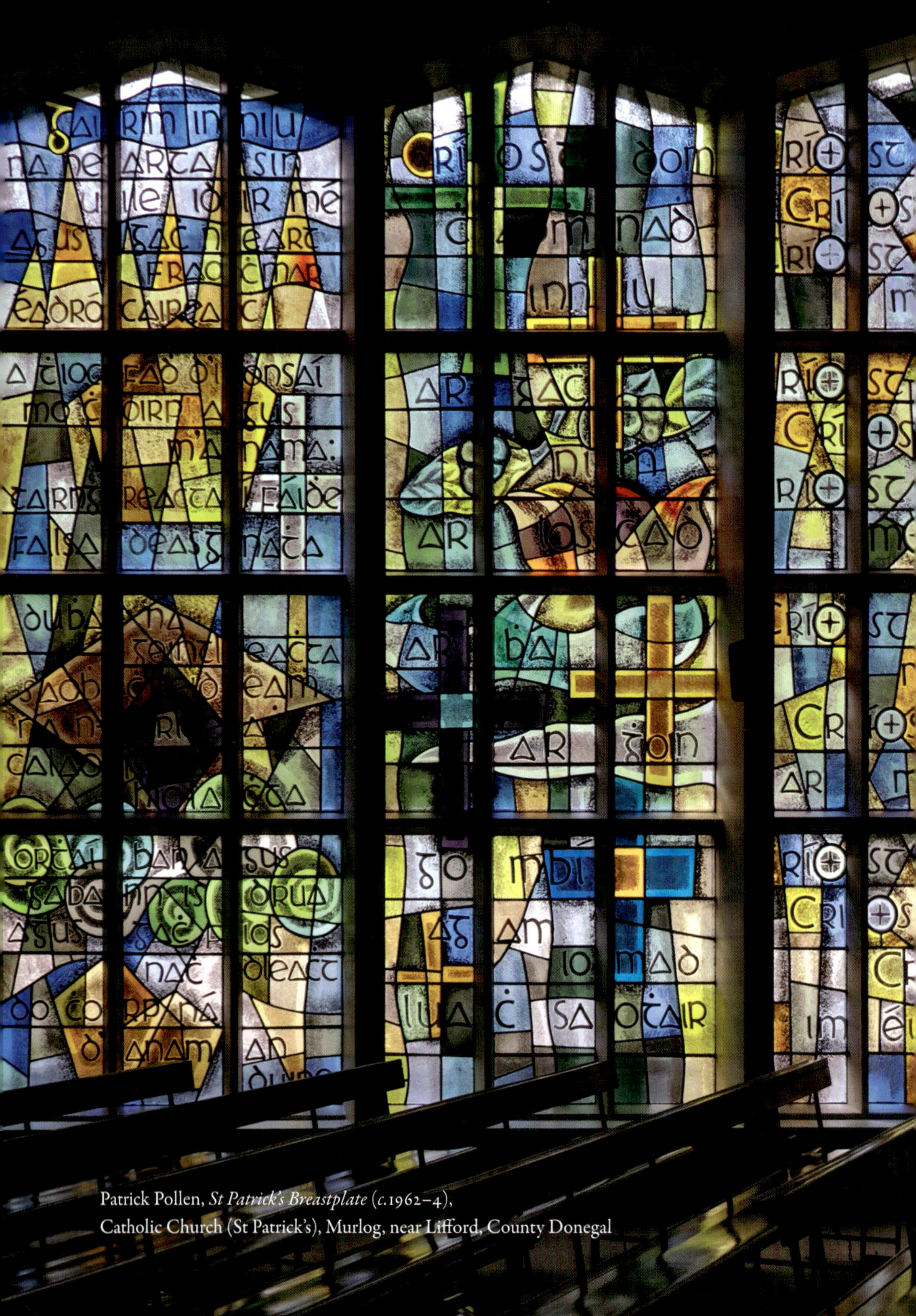

Patrick Pollen, *St Patrick's Breastplate* (*c.*1962–4),
Catholic Church (St Patrick's), Murlog, near Lifford, County Donegal

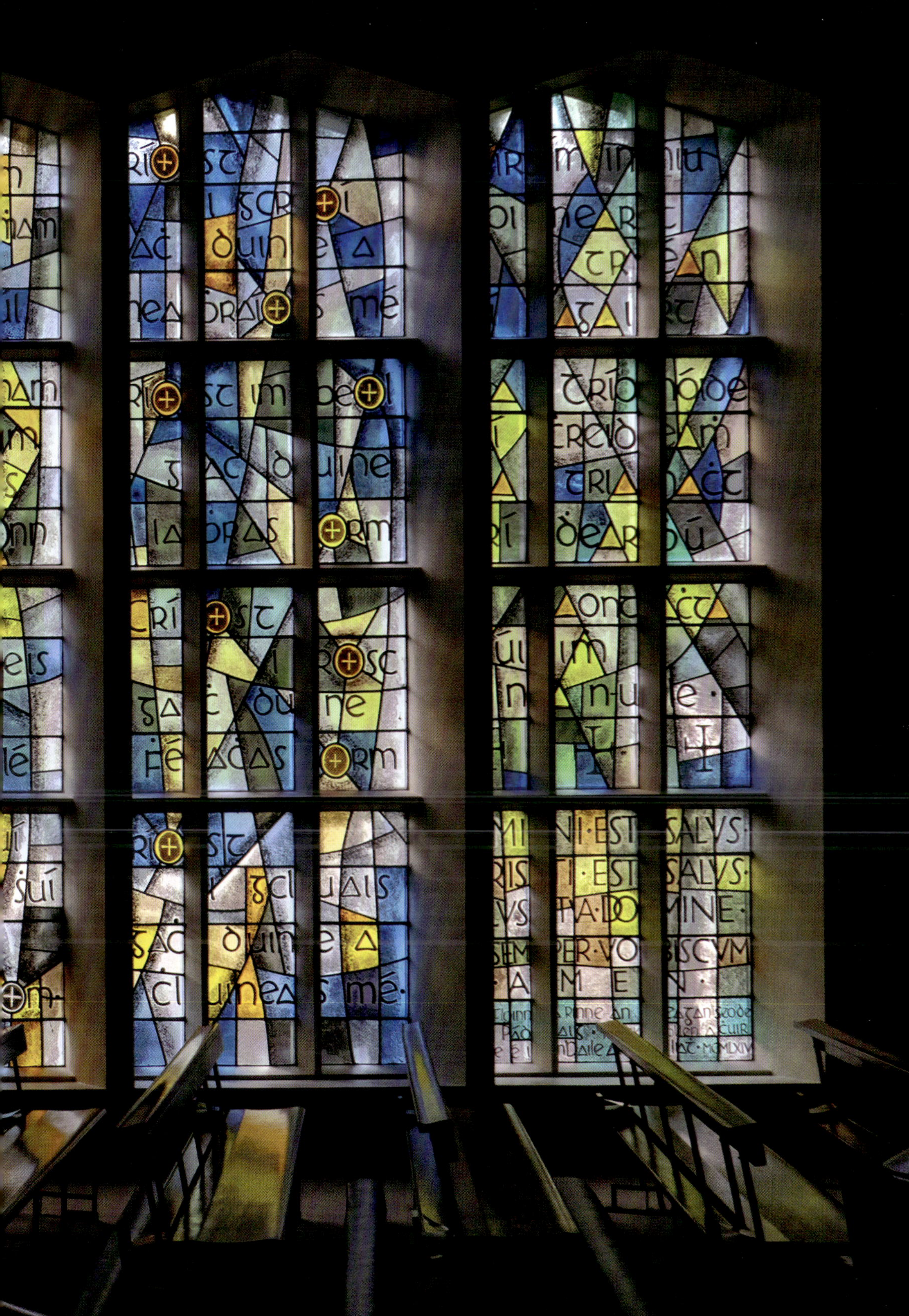

Overview of Irish Stained Glass, mid-Twentieth Century to the Present Day

David Caron

The original edition of the *Gazetteer*, including Nicola Gordon Bowe's comprehensive and erudite introductory essay, had an informal concluding point of 1955 with the death of the two greats, Wilhelmina Geddes[1] and Evie Hone.[2] However, before focusing on the period post-mid-fifties, it is worthwhile briefly stepping back to the previous decade.

During the early 1940s several talented artists emerged from Harry Clarke Studios to pursue independent careers, including two contemporaries, Richard King and George Stephen Walsh.[3] King (b.1907) was the older by four years, and following Harry Clarke's death in 1931, he became principal designer and later also manager of the studios from 1935, departing in 1940. King's artistic development shows that his best work belongs to two periods: 1930–40 while he was still designing within the parameters of the Harry Clarke 'house style' and even more so in the period from 1960–73 when his stained glass windows show his engagement with modernism. Over time he gradually became less insular and more open to influences from Britain, Europe and modernism in general, which produced a lot of stylistic change, experimentation and eclecticism in his work, ultimately finding his authentic voice as a religious artist with a style and expression which became unique to him. From the 1950s onwards King's work became increasingly appreciated overseas in Britain, the USA and particularly Australia.[4]

George Stephen Walsh (b.1911, and not to be confused with his son George W. Walsh whose work is also listed in this publication) left Clarke's studio at approximately the same time as King, *c.*1941, but it appears that it was a highly productive six-year stint in the USA in the late 1950s and early 1960s which had a transformative effect on his artistic development. Employed by a studio in Wisconsin he had the opportunity to work on ambitious stained glass schemes, which were often painted by his son, usually for new-build churches.[5] These schemes were decidedly modern and dynamic, demonstrating what an effective designer he was in choreographing light, colour, line and movement to dramatic effect. Throughout his career G.S. Walsh's work was mostly figurative, sometimes narrative, but when the occasion called he could design a wall of essentially abstract glass incorporating symbols in a distinctly modernist style.[6]

Other artists to leave Clarke's studio during the 1940s were Stanley Tomlin (b.1916), who went on to found Irish Stained Glass,[7] while artists choosing to remain included William J. Dowling (b.1907), who became manager of the studio in 1940. It should be noted that the Harry Clarke Studios continued until 1973, over four decades after Clarke died. During the first decade or so the standard remained consistently high, but over time, for various reasons, the quality declined. Regularly windows are erroneously attributed to Harry Clarke which were made decades after his death and do his reputation no credit. As the studio had the policy of signing windows – if they were signed at all – 'Harry Clarke Stained Glass Ltd' (or variant) it is often difficult to establish accurate authorship.[8] As noted in the Preface, we have largely steered clear of Clarke's studio (and the other large studios too for this reason), but there are instances where verifiable information exists to confirm who was responsible including William Dowling's dazzling, highly jewelled series of *The Fifteen Mysteries of the Rosary* (1938–9) for the Dominican Convent, Wicklow Town, and his remarkable nine-panel guide on 'how to be a good Catholic in 1950s rural Ireland' for Drimoleague Catholic Church, County Cork;[9] also Terry Clarke's (nephew of Harry) sumptuous five-light *Coronation of the Virgin* (1942–3) for Mount Melleray Abbey, County Waterford, and Charles (Cecil) Simmonds's windows for Belvedere College, Dublin (*c.*1934). Likewise, Earley and Company – which finally closed in 1975, two years after Clarke's studio – had a policy of not permitting artists to sign windows. However, recent research has shown that arguably the most talented member of the family, William (Bill) E. Earley, was the designer of lavish and highly populated extravaganzas, such as those for Ringsend and Blackrock Catholic Churches, Dublin.[10]

The other main company of note which was operating in Dublin during those decades was the Dublin Glass and Paint Company, more commonly known as the Abbey Stained Glass Studios, which was managed by Frank Ryan.[11] Other smaller Dublin companies included A.W. Lyons,[12] Myles Kearney & Sons,[13] and The State Glass Company/John Hogan & Company,[14] and the contributions of some of the key artists associated with these studios are highlighted further on in this essay.

As noted above, the original *Gazetteer* essentially concluded with the death of Hone and Geddes, but the mid-1950s was also a period of renewal and emerging talents. With respect to fostering the craft, classes had by then long ceased in the Dublin School of

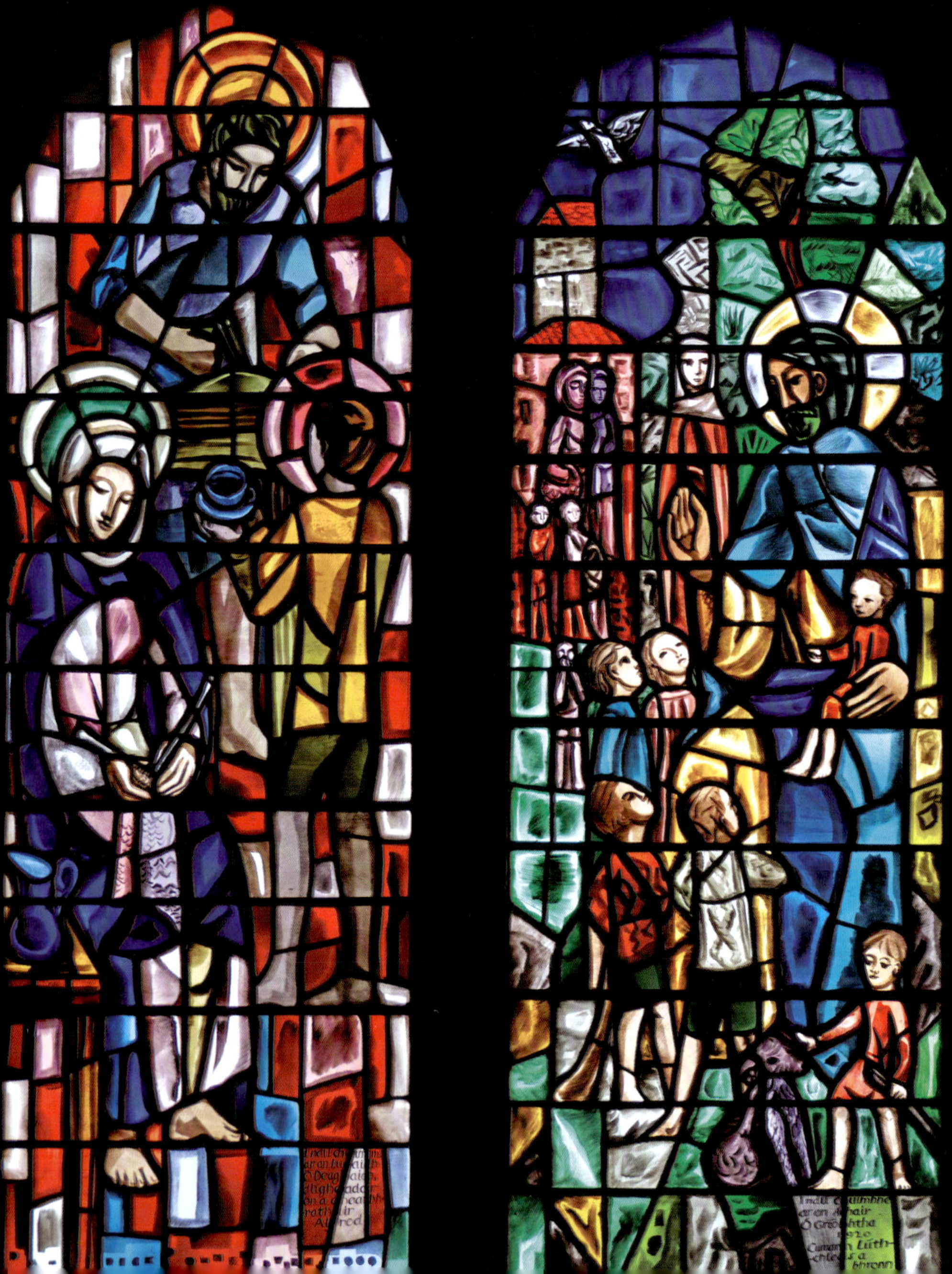

ar an
Alfred

ar an
1920
Lúth-

Art until the arrival of the energetic Johnny Murphy on the scene in 1954. Trained at Clarke Studios – though Harry Clarke himself had died by the time he arrived there – he reintroduced stained glass classes. These were popular, not only with young students straight from school, but also with more mature artists who wanted to learn the craft, such as Patrick Pye, Helen Moloney and Phyllis Burke. Additionally, a talented artist from London, Patrick Pollen, had moved to Ireland to study, initially under his heroine Evie Hone, and he rented half the An Túr Gloine studio at 24 Upper Pembroke Street from the elderly Catherine O'Brien, buying it outright after her death and thereby maintaining a continuum begun in 1903. Through Pollen's generosity, artist friends who had no facilities of their own could avail of a skilled glazier and the use of a kiln.

Significant changes were afoot by mid-century: the Protestant Churches, especially the Church of Ireland in the Republic, had ceased to be major patrons of stained glass, brought about by a mixture of reduced congregations with diminishing wealth, and the reality that many churches had their full complement of stained glass windows. The desire to fund memorial windows for family members who had died on service in the two World Wars had long since passed. The Catholic Church by comparison was on the ascent, exemplified by a gradual nationwide church-building programme brought about by shifting demographics and expanding cities and towns, coupled with increased wealth relative to the austerity of the post-war years and driven by a strong collective sense of religious fervour. In many instances, in contrast to trends in patronage during previous decades, stained glass was then recognised as an integral component of the architect's vision, and often that of the local parish priest and bishop; this changed ambitions from commissioning an occasional window to the desire for an entire scheme of windows with thematic and visual coherence which could transform a new church.

Harking back to the medieval tradition, the Catholic clergy remained acutely aware of the instructional potential of stained glass. The tendency to commemorate local, often obscure, saints began to wane somewhat – and along with it Celtic Revivalist decorative elements – but that certainly did not vanish, and within the Catholic Church the potential to channel specific devotion, such as to the Virgin Mary, the Rosary or the Stations of the Cross, was regularly at the forefront of consideration. It should be noted that many of the artists working in stained glass were themselves deeply religious: in earlier decades Healy and Hone had both considered religious vocations, and many later artists including Richard King, Patrick Pollen and Patrick Pye were profoundly spiritual individuals.

Left: Patrick Pollen, *The Holy Family* (1969) and *Jesus Blessing Children* (1969), Catholic Cathedral, Galway City

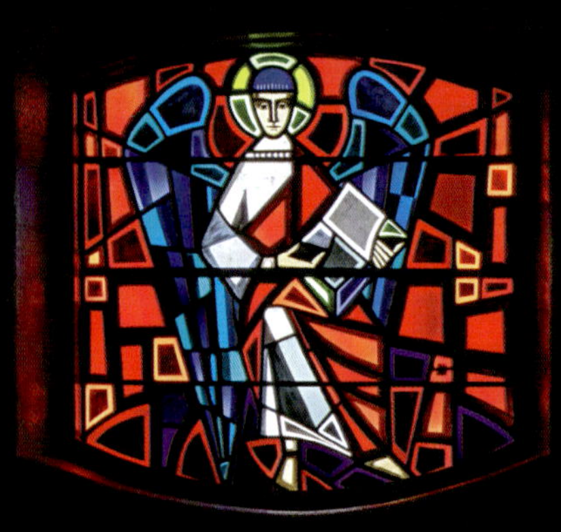
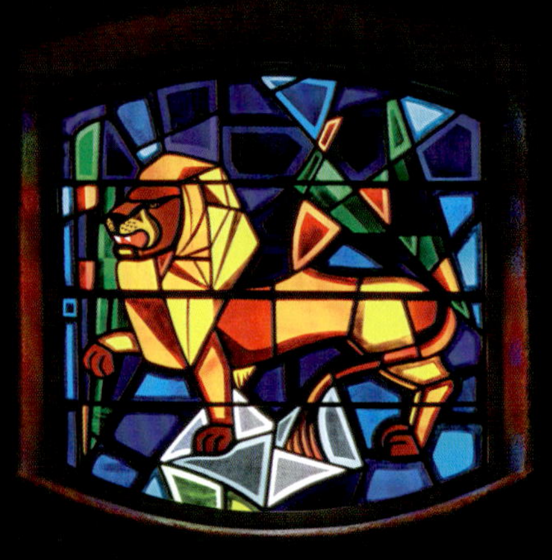
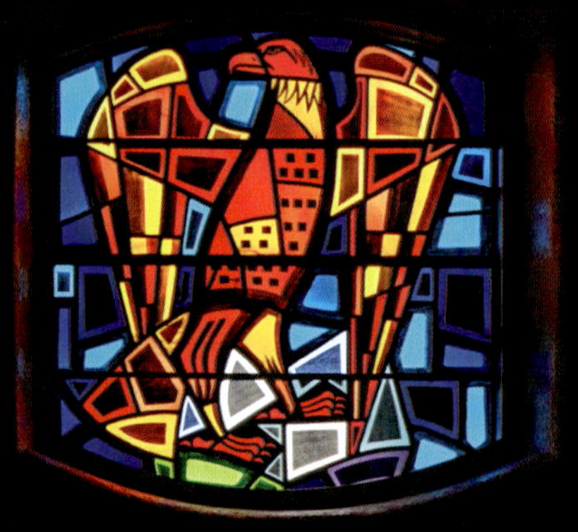
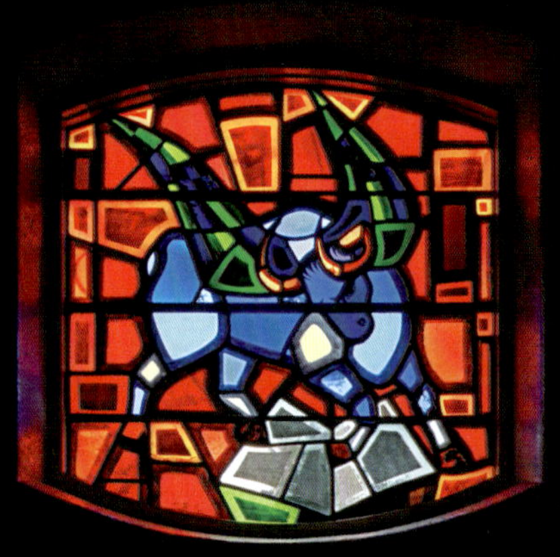
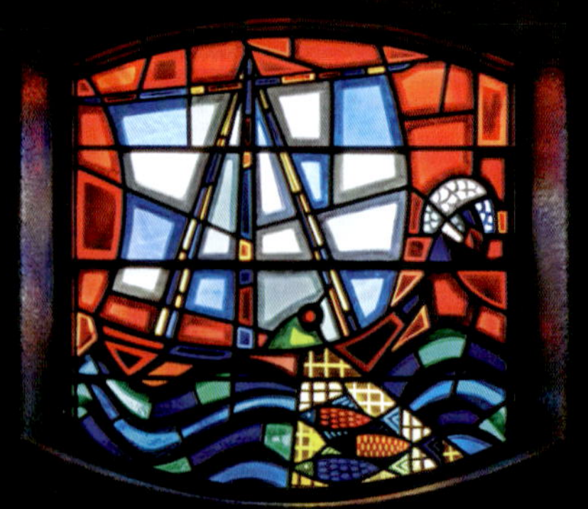
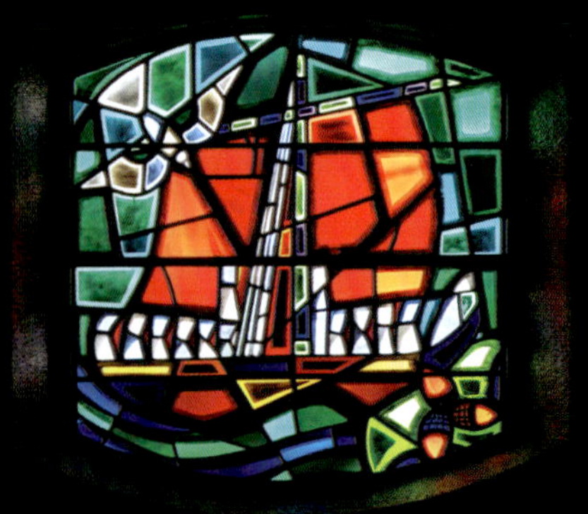

The quality of church architecture during the 1950s and the decades which followed varied considerably. Although the impetus had begun before Vatican II (1962–5), that seismic event had an accelerating effect on the building of new churches, with many designed in a more consciously contemporary idiom, as well as the internal reordering of existing ones.[15] Arguably the most distinguished church architect of his day was Liam McCormick, who designed imaginative, understated and modestly scaled structures in harmony with their surroundings, often rural, with a concentration of exceptional churches in County Donegal. McCormick regularly commissioned stained glass: windows by Patrick Pollen, Patrick Pye, Phyllis Burke, George Campbell, Margaret Becker, Imogen Stuart and Ruth Brandt can be found in his buildings, and, as pointed out by Carole Pollard, 'His close relationship with the artists was central to his design methodology: they were very much part of his design team and many became close friends.'[16] Undoubtedly his preferred stained glass collaborator was Helen Moloney, whose brave combinations of intense colour and punchy design usually incorporating a repertoire of favourite symbols acted as an effective foil for McCormick's muted and restrained interiors, as in the Catholic Churches at Desertegney (1964), Burt (1967), Creeslough (1971), and the Presbyterian Church at Donoughmore (1977), all in County Donegal.[17]

Andrew Devane of Robinson, Keefe & Devane, who had studied under Frank Lloyd Wright, utilised stained glass in an innovative manner from at least the mid 1950s. In his lauded dormitory for Mary Immaculate College, Limerick (1955) he incorporated stained glass windows in colourful, abstract, organic forms which go from the first floor upwards to the top floor like one continuous window,[18] though the artist or studio who created the windows for him remains to be discovered. A similar stylistic treatment featured in the stained glass laylight (subsequently destroyed) of the Robinson, Keefe & Devane-designed mortuary chapel (1955) for the Catholic Church, Naas, County Kildare. Devane's church at Dublin Airport, Our Lady Queen of Heaven, has a series of square Stations of the Cross (1964) by Sheila Corcoran.[19] These expressionistic images verge on abstraction and utilise a palette of intense, vivid colours, where the layers of glass were fused rather than leaded. A radical departure from the norm of their day, they were not appreciated by Dublin's conservative and controlling Archbishop McQuaid.[20]

Another mid-1960s modernist church with significant stained glass is the former Dominican Church, Athy,[21] which has recently been successfully repurposed as a public library. With a hyperbolic paraboloid concrete shell roof it has a dramatic

Left:

Helen Moloney, *St Matthew; St Mark; St John; St Luke; The Church as Fishers of Men; St Columba's Missionary Endeavours* (1964), Catholic Church (Star of the Sea), Desertegney, County Donegal

Abbey during the 1960s. Unlike at the Clarke and Earley studios, each was encouraged to design in his own style. Ryan, who had studied at NCA himself, was a skilled salesman and every two years would travel to the United States, securing enough work from clergy to keep the studio busy for a two-year period until the next trip.[30]

Patrick Pollen and Patrick Pye were both English-born, the former a devout Catholic, the latter a Catholic convert, whose families became close friends, with both men establishing their own stained glass studios south of Dublin City: Pollen in Dundrum and Pye in Piperstown, Bohernabreena. Pollen always remained more traditional, the influence of his mentor Evie Hone often discernible, and without major stylistic developments in a long and productive career devoted exclusively to religious stained glass. His subjects are usually easy to identify and 'read' whether depicting individual saints or narrative scenes, and during his career he undertook two particularly extensive commissions, thirty-three windows for Johannesburg Cathedral (1957–9) during which period An Túr Gloine burned down due to a kiln fire, such was the pressure on production, and secondly for Galway Cathedral which contains twenty-six of his windows (*c.*1965–70). Patrick Pye was an altogether more maverick character who also produced a much larger body of work as a painter and printmaker, and for which he is better known.[31] Despite a smaller stained glass output (and sometimes the windows themselves are relatively small), he is arguably the more intriguing artist, with a very personal, idiosyncratic, even poetic vision where the artist's commentary is often required in order to accurately interpret the imagery.

Like Pollen and Pye, there were other artists who worked independently during this period, such as Phyllis Burke, Margaret Becker[32] and Frances Biggs,[33] and though they had their own individual art or design studios, they did not have their own facilities to fire glass and usually employed freelance glaziers on a job-to-job basis.

Phyllis Burke's career began with an order for stained glass Stations of the Cross for a church in rural Nigeria in 1958, in that instance commissioned by an Irish architect, though indicative of a trend whereby Irish individuals, usually in religious life – priests, brothers and nuns – working in the 'Missions' placed orders for stained glass from Irish artists. Burke had a long and consistent career, often producing distinctly modernist windows in the 1960s and softer, more painterly ones later on.

Margaret Becker's first windows, all abstract, were for Inverin Catholic Church, County Galway, designed by D.J. Kennedy in 1963; it was the first church designed specifically to meet the new liturgy requirements of Vatican II. Becker interwove a career in stained glass, usually figurative, with that as a printmaker, founding the successful Leinster Printmaking Studio in Clane, County Kildare.

Frances Biggs's first window was for the Catholic Church at Cashel. Signed prominently by both Biggs and Rivers, it was designed by her close friend Elizabeth

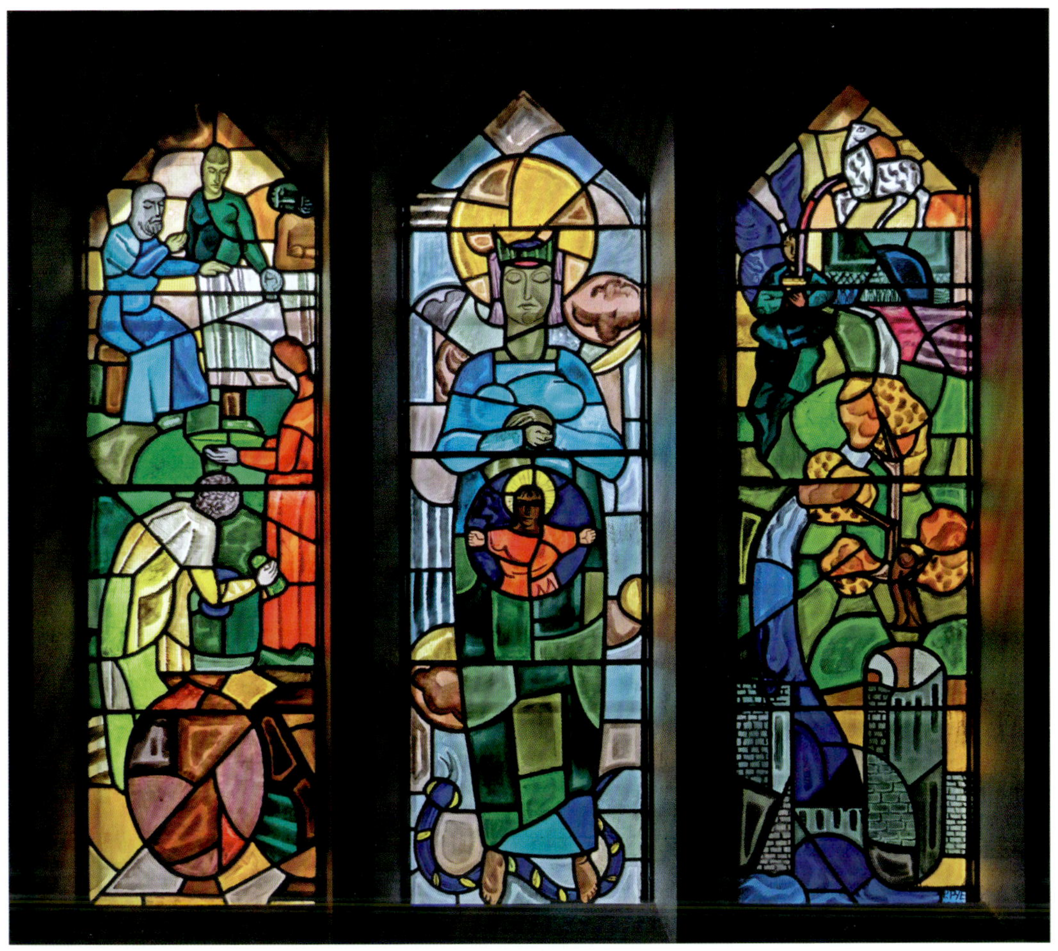

Patrick Pye, *Wedding Feast at Cana; Virgin of the Apocalypse; Lamb of God and the New Jerusalem* (1963–4), (executed by Margaret Becker and painted by Patrick Pye), Glenstal Abbey Church, Murroe, County Limerick

Rivers (who for nine years had worked alongside Evie Hone enlarging her small-scale sketch designs up to full-scale cartoons). However, when Rivers died suddenly from a stroke, it was Biggs who made the window. Biggs produced her first solo window, an essentially abstract design, for the Andrew Devane designed chapel at Gonzaga College, Dublin, in *c.*1969 and approximately a decade later created figurative windows for the remainder of the chapel. Probably her most successful windows are a series of eight single lights for the chapel at Terenure College, Dublin, depicting Carmelite saints, which use intensely coloured glass and eschew any painted detail.

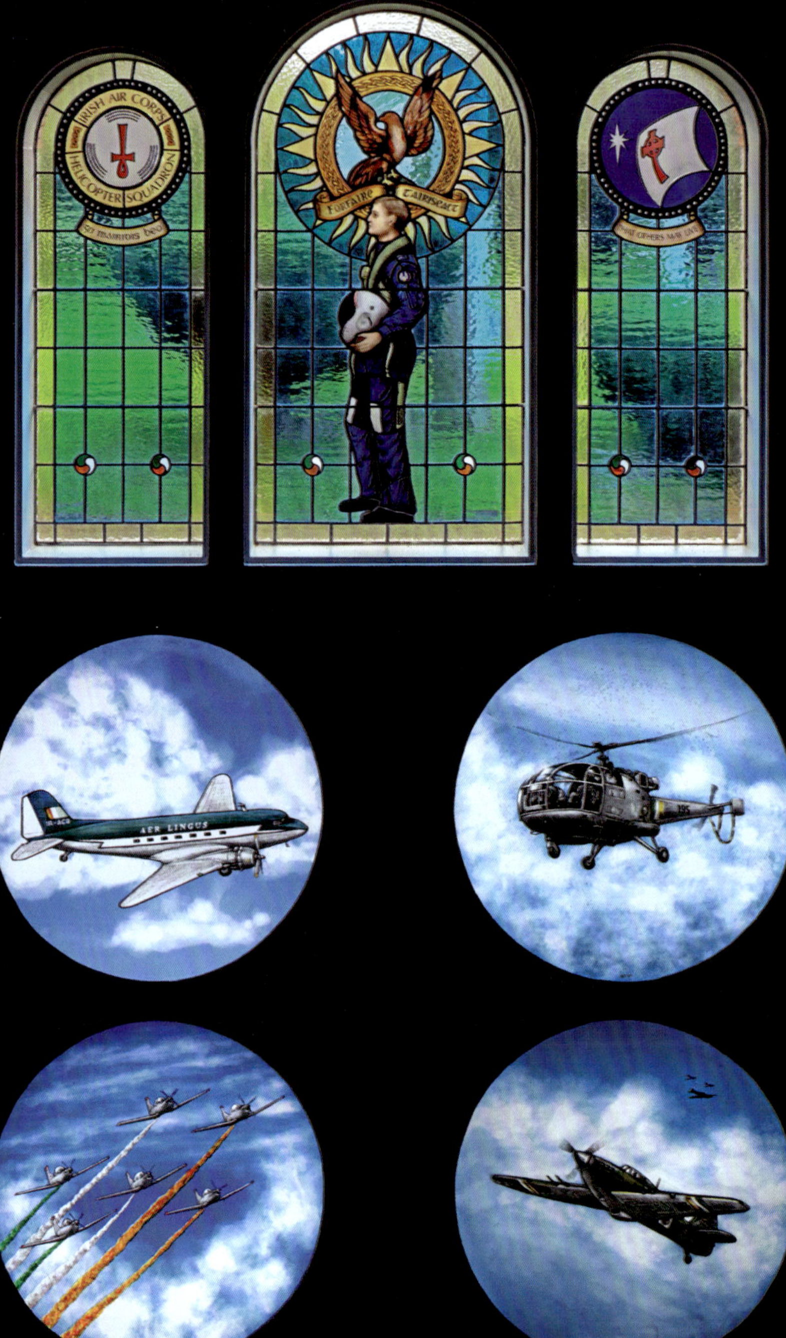
IRISH AIR CORPS
HELICOPTER SQUADRON
AER LINGUS

One distinguishing feature of the 1960s was the number of established artists who created stained glass windows for churches. Though making only a very small number of works, these included the sculptors Imogen Stuart (one window), Benedict Tutty (one window), Gerda Frömel (three known windows), and printmaker John Kelly (abstract schemes for two churches). It is unclear what the motivations may have been, but with classes in the craft then available again and a very visible church-building programme underway it may be that some saw it as potentially a stable part-time income stream.

In addition to Richard King and George Stephen Walsh, there were several other artists who had also received their stained glass training at Harry Clarke Studios and were comfortable moving across different media: Tony Inglis, who had produced both religious and secular panels in Dublin, ultimately pursued a career as a lauded art director in the United Kingdom film industry. Christopher Campbell, another former Clarke employee, who was an accomplished if conventional painter, went on to design a few strikingly modern windows in the 1960s, such as those for Our Lady of Mercy, Artane and the Catholic Church at Tirrane, County Mayo.

A talented graduate of the Dublin Metropolitan School of Art worth noting is Joseph Tierney, who was also a skilled calligrapher; he emigrated to the United States in his mid-30s and as his independent stained glass career really only took off at this point his work is beyond the remit of this *Gazetteer*.[34]

During the second half of the twentieth century and into this century there were several skilled artists who happily worked in a traditional idiom, such as Willie Earley and Kevin Kelly. Earley, a member of the distinguished stained glass dynasty, produced a large body of work, often utilising a colour palette which had a classic Earley and Company appearance. He could also turn his hand to portraiture in stained glass and produced a remarkable set of full-length portraits of 'modern' popes for the Franciscan Church on Merchant's Quay, Dublin. Kevin Kelly arrived at Abbey Stained Glass Studio, Dublin as a 14-year-old in 1941 and worked his way up to become the studio's senior artist. An accomplished restorer of historic stained glass windows, he also produced many original windows, including several sensitive depictions of the Nativity, such as the one for Inchigeela in West Cork, and two interpretations of the subject now displayed in illuminated cabinets in St James's Catholic Church, James Street, Dublin. Both Earley and Kelly died in 2019.

A contemporary artist who also works in a traditional mode is Alan Tomlin (of Irish Stained Glass, founded by his father Stanley). He has developed singular expertise

Left: Alan Tomlin, *Memorial to Air Corps Crew of Rescue 111* (2000); *Commemorative medallions set in leaded lights featuring various models of vintage aircraft, crests and logos* (from 1997 and ongoing), Garrison Church, Casement Aerodrome, Baldonnel, Dublin

painting stained glass in an almost photorealistic style; the best example is an extensive ongoing commission of commemorative medallions for the Garrison Church at Casement Aerodrome, Baldonnel, Dublin. In addition to designing original stained glass windows and many decorative leaded schemes for commercial and domestic clients, he has been responsible for painstakingly restoring to the highest standard much vulnerable decorative Georgian and Victorian stained glass and leaded lights (fanlights, landing windows, etc.) throughout Ireland.

Two artists who seemed to particularly excel when presented with the challenge of filling contemporary churches with complete schemes of stained glass were Johnny Murphy (of Murphy-Devitt Studios),[35] and George W. Walsh[36] (an ability his father had previously acquired during his period in the United States). Both Murphy and Walsh had highly developed design sensibilities, and were at ease drawing the human form and depicting figurative and narrative work, but both could just as easily work abstractly or utilise symbols within largely abstract schemes. They could orchestrate colour, light and movement within a given space, respecting the content or thematic approach agreed with clergyman and architect. Murphy, the older of the two, had a particular ability to rhythmically integrate abstract and figurative passages. In singling out Murphy, one cannot leave out Róisín Dowd Murphy, his regular creative collaborator whose more painterly and lyrical style often enhanced Murphy's schemes. George W. Walsh excelled in incorporating narrative detail, often pertaining to local history, and yet never losing sight of the bigger picture. Walsh continues to work in stained glass though now mainly undertaking smaller commissions, including 3D pieces utilising fused glass.

While the majority of Irish stained glass artists of the twentieth century, and particularly the ones who went on to achieve international reputations, were trained and based in Dublin, there was significant stained glass activity elsewhere on the island. In Cork the long-established company of Watson's of Youghal produced a steady stream of well-crafted, if conventional glass (though regularly with complex Celtic-style ornamentation), mainly for churches in the southern half of the island.[37] In 1980 the artist Maud Cotter established the stained glass department in Crawford College of Art, Cork,[38] run by Debbie Dawson, which is now thriving. Work by them and other highly regarded Cork-based artists of the same generation, such as James Scanlon, Peadar Lamb and Mary Mackey, are listed in this *Gazetteer*.

In Belfast the craft was taught by Scottish-born Edward Murray Marr at Belfast College of Art from 1933 to 1971. Marr himself had been a student of Douglas Strachan, Scotland's most distinguished stained glass artist and teacher, and much of his master's aesthetic was transmitted to Marr. Sadly, unlike Strachan, Marr's own creative output was relatively modest, though his windows in St Columb's Cathedral, Derry (1947), Rosnowlagh Church of Ireland in County Donegal (*c.*1951) and St Anne's Cathedral,

Belfast (*c.*1969) show he was an exceptional talent as well as an important instructor.[39] One of Marr's most promising students was Patricia (Paddy) Robinson, who created an impressive and lively four-light window in 1964 at the age of 19 for Kilbroney Church of Ireland, County Down. The next year she emigrated to Australia, establishing a successful and enduring stained glass practice in New South Wales.[40]

The most significant Belfast studio was Clokey and Company Stained Glass Studios, which had been established in 1904 and continued until *c.*1973. In general terms, from the 1950s onwards, the company favoured a fairly standard 'house style' with a restrained, somewhat cool colour palette, utilising plenty of clear glass, with a strong emphasis on crisp, finely drawn features rather than a more tonal and painterly approach. Clokey artists of note included Olive Henry,[41] who worked at the studio for over half a century, the singular female figure working professionally in the craft in Belfast compared with many prominent female artists working out of Dublin. Other Clokey artists included George Stephen Walsh, John (Jack) Calderwood (1927–98), Daniel Braniff (1911–99) and John Blyth (1915–99), all of whom left to develop successful independent careers in the craft, and while Walsh's work can be seen in various parts of Ireland and the United States, most work by Calderwood and Braniff is in Northern Ireland, the latter's output mainly for churches in Counties Antrim and Down. Blyth returned to his native Scotland where many examples of his artistry can be seen.[42]

During the 'Troubles' in Northern Ireland several windows of merit were sadly destroyed (for instance, windows by both A.E. Child and Catherine O'Brien in Whitehouse Presbyterian Church, County Antrim, and Helen Moloney's large sanctuary window in St MacNissi's Catholic Church, Randalstown, County Antrim), with other windows seriously damaged. In several instances decisions were made to build completely new churches rather than renovate an empty shell, and these new churches often employed comprehensive schemes of stained glass. One artist who secured several large commissions was Dublin-born Lua Breen, a former NCAD colleague of Johnny Murphy, who had relocated to Donegal in 1990 and was comfortable working in both abstract and figurative modes.

Caldermac Studios was a small Belfast stained glass company founded *c.*1958 by Jack Calderwood, with William Hogan and later, David Esler, as principal artists.[43] Subsequently Esler left to join forces with his wife and he designed many windows for both religious and secular venues throughout Northern Ireland and beyond. Perhaps his two finest windows are a beguiling, highly detailed five-light with extensive tracery (2009) for the Church of Ireland, Comber, County Down, and the three-light *Archbishop Simms Memorial Window* (2003) for Armagh Church of Ireland Cathedral. Also noteworthy are a number of windows designed *c.*1964–98 by the distinguished Belfast-based painter Neil Shawcross for several religious venues and for the Ulster Museum.

By the end of the twentieth century church patronage of stained glass artists had diminished to a trickle – with the exception of Northern Ireland, as explained above – though one noteworthy commission to mark the millennium was Patrick Muldowney's spirited series of eight 'Jubilee' windows (including a vignette of Dublin's Millennium Bridge) for the church of St John Vianney, Artane, Dublin, which skilfully integrate detailed narrative images with abstract passages. In some instances when religious communities began to downsize they incorporated an oratory or chapel in their newly built accommodation, and among artists to benefit from such commissions was Mary Mackey, who created a pair of windows (2005) for the Chapel of the Ursuline Convent, Blackrock, Cork, in which gentle organic shapes surround clear glass, framing the views, and creating a tranquil, calming effect. Again reflecting demographic changes, the large number of new-build nursing homes throughout the island often incorporated a prayer room complete with stained glass. These smaller scale works allowed artists to focus more specifically on detail and texture, and the intimate relationship between viewer and art piece, with the subject matter selected sometimes of a spiritual rather than overtly religious nature.[44]

New-build hospitals, or extensions to existing ones, often incorporated stained glass in their chapels, prayer rooms, oratories and chapels of rest (mortuary chapels).[45] James Scanlon, an artist who, since the mid 1980s has created deeply spiritual and evocative windows for churches and cathedrals (those at Galway and Longford specifically), also created two sonorous abstract windows for the new chapel at Tallaght Hospital, Dublin. Of his practice Scanlon has said, 'Glass, for me, is for things that tear the heart out of me – I would put them into glass. And they would mean a lot to me. When you look at it, it brings a calmness over you. I try to put that calmness into the glass. When it's finished and the calmness comes out of it over me, then it's finished.'[46]

An innovative policy, the Per Cent for Art Scheme, initially devised by the OPW in 1978, was revised and significantly expanded in 1997 to allow public bodies engaged in construction projects in the Republic of Ireland to apply for extra funding which is ringfenced for art projects associated with the construction. Several talented stained glass artists were successful, often repeatedly so, in gaining commissions. Consequently schools, hospitals, libraries, even swimming pools[47] have been enhanced with bespoke stained glass commissions. Peter Young, who trained as an illustrator, has created vibrant playful windows for several primary schools, involving the pupils in the creative process.[48] He has also created windows for religious settings: notably a pair of evocative, hauntingly beautiful windows inspired by Dylan Thomas's poem *Fern Hill* for the chapel in the grounds of Borris House, County Carlow. In 2013–14 he created a series of fifteen small, harmonious windows – some figurative, some abstract and everything in between – for a circular prayer chapel adjoining St Sylvester's Church, Malahide,

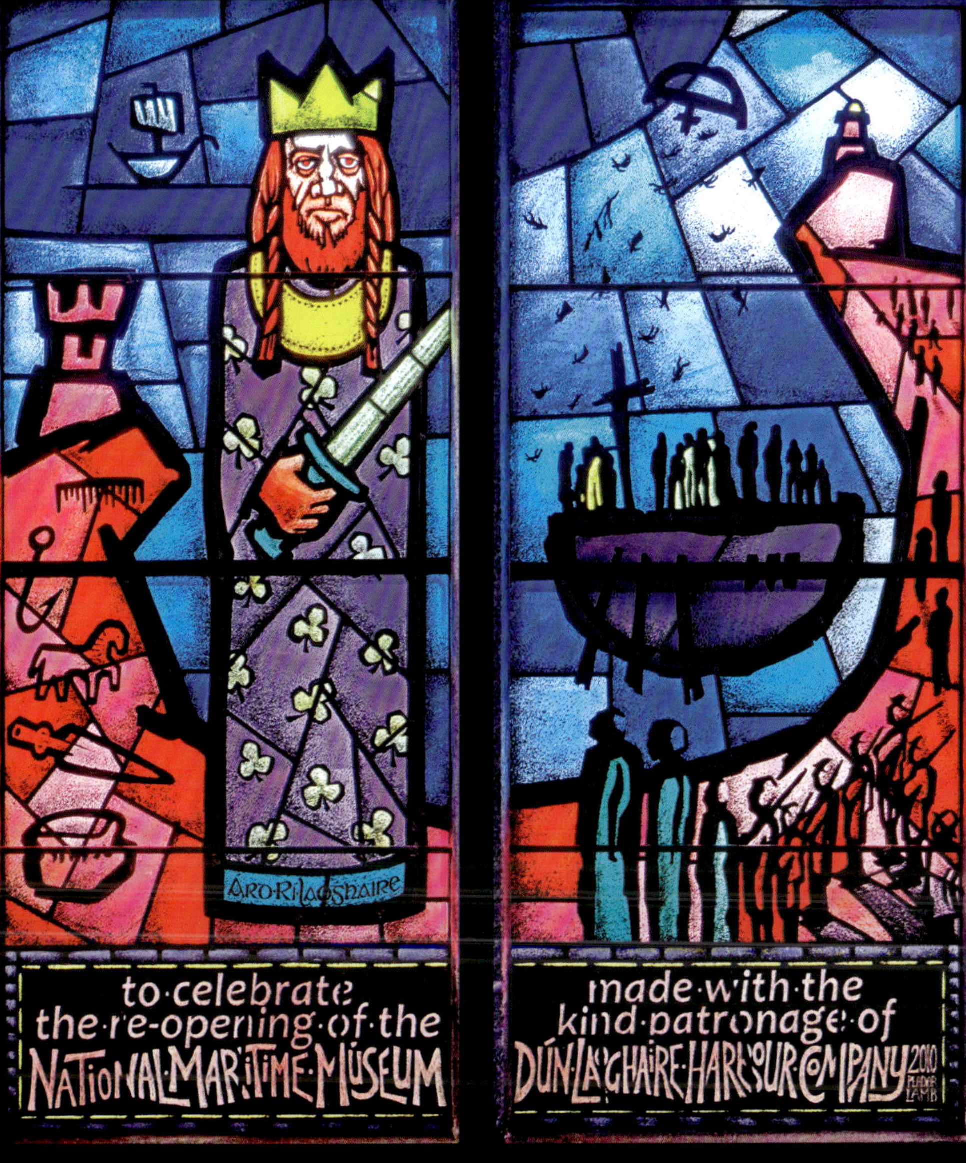

Peadar Lamb, *Dún Laoghaire Diptych* (2010–11), National Maritime Museum (former Mariners' Church), Dún Laoghaire, County Dublin

County Dublin, of which he wrote: 'Horizontally, and closest to the heavens, they represent the New Testament, our religious beliefs and the miracle of the cycle of life in the four seasons. The lower images, originating in the Old Testament, represent the magnificence of the Creation and how we came to be. Thus, in viewing the windows vertically, we will be reminded of and inspired by the transition from this life to heaven.'[49]

Peadar Lamb is an artist who has developed a distinctive personal style and specialises in both large-scale architectural pieces and small-scale light boxes, working to commission and for exhibition. Examples of his work include a series of five panels for the lobby of the Irish Repertory Theatre, New York, inspired by the story of emigration and Irish literature,[50] a quartet of animal panels for Dublin Zoo, windows for the National Maritime Museum drawing on Dún Laoghaire's history, and more recently a large panel commemorating the 1916 Easter Rising for Carlow County Museum. Regularly utilising crisp, confident calligraphic lines, whether in paint or lead, his works can be both bold and direct as well as atmospheric and enigmatic.

Katharine Lamb, an artist with a keen interest in portraiture, has created large multi-portrait panels for Grogan's Pub, South William Street, Dublin (featuring the regular patrons) and for Lucan Public Library, County Dublin (celebrating a local community).

Many of these contemporary artists have also been commissioned by private individuals to create custom pieces for homes and sometimes even free-standing panels for gardens, all going to show that given imagination on the part of clients, stained glass as a medium can be utilised in unexpected ways and can enhance a wide array of venues.

Notes

1 See N. Gordon Bowe, *Wilhelmina Geddes: Life and Work* (Dublin: Four Courts Press, 2015).

2 Dr Joseph McBrinn, University of Ulster, is currently writing the life and work of Evie Hone (a project begun by the late Nicola Gordon Bowe).

3 Both will always be principally recognised as artists in the medium of stained glass, though they were also comfortable working across a range of diverse media.

4 See Ruth Sheehy's meticulously researched and insightful monograph, *The Life and Work of Richard King: Religion, Nationalism and Modernism* (Oxford: Peter Lang, 2020).

5 I am indebted to George W. Walsh for information on his father's career. Regrettably, due to the fact that a significant number of his windows were done for various companies (Clarke, Powells, Clokeys, Pickels) and many while in the United States, it has not been possible to compile an accurate list of all G.S. Walsh's windows at this point.

6 G.S. Walsh designed a striking six-panel 'wall of glass' (date unknown) for the Killarney branch of the Bank of Ireland which has thankfully survived several 'make-overs'.

7 Irish Stained Glass Ltd was established *c.*1957 in Herbert Lane, Dublin, by Stanley Tomlin who had trained at Harry Clarke Studios. It was subsequently based at Hanover Quay, then Fitzwilliam Quay, Ringsend, Dublin and latterly in Sandyford.

8 See Sheehy, *The Life and Work of Richard King*, pp. 36–40; and P. Donnelly, 'Legacy and Identity: Harry Clarke, William Dowling and the Harry Clarke Studios', in Griffith, A., Helmers, M., and Kennedy, R. (eds), *Harry Clarke and Artistic Visions of the New Irish State* (Dublin: Irish Academic Press, 2018), pp. 312–14. I am greatly indebted to Paul Donnelly and Ruth Sheehy for alerting me to various fine Harry Clarke Studios windows, for their painstaking research of the *Clarke's Stained Glass Studios Collection*, TCD, and site visits to confirm the individual artists responsible. I would also specifically like to thank Paul for identifying some excellent windows by Dowling and Terry Clarke in the nearby Catholic Churches at Knockainey and Patrickswell, County Limerick, and to Tom Cassidy for drawing my attention to them in the first instance.

9 R.J. Butler, 'All Saints, Drimoleague and Catholic visual culture under Bishop Cornelius Lucey in Cork, 1952–59', *Journal of the Cork Historical and Archaeological Society*, 120 (2015), pp. 79–97. Also R.J. Butler, 'All Saints, Drimoleague: clarifications and new discoveries', *Journal of the Cork Historical and Archaeological Society*, 121 (2016), pp. 141–3.

10 I am indebted to Michael Earley for information about Earley & Company.

11 Dublin Glass and Paint Company was founded in the mid 1920s by Tom Ryan and was based in Middle Abbey Street, Dublin. When his nephew Frank Ryan (1918–1988) joined as a junior director in the early 1940s, he established Abbey Stained Glass Studios under the umbrella of the larger company, which produced stained glass windows from 1944 onwards. In 1987 Frank's son Ken took over the business and moved it to Kilmainham where it is still based, now mainly specialising in restoration. I am indebted to Ken Ryan for this information.

12 A.W. Lyons was established in 1935 and Stanley Tomlin started the stained glass department *c.*1942. Based at 20 Westland Row, Dublin, it was later bought out by Abbey Stained Glass Studios.

13 Myles Kearney & Sons (founded 1950s, closed 1991). Based at 23 Oakley Road, Ranelagh, its principal artist was James Cox and we have included a small number of his windows in the *Gazetteer* including one of his finest, that of *St Mark and St Ann*, for St Ann's Church of Ireland, Dawson Street, Dublin.

14 The State Glass Company was based in Pembroke Lane and Lower Camden Street, Dublin. John Hogan, who also ran and owned a studio under his own name in the late 1950s and 1960s at 54 and 56 Pembroke Lane, ran the State Glass Company from 1962 until the 1970s at 24 Lower Camden Street, Dublin. For further information see Sheehy *The Life and Work of Richard King*, pp. 215–6.

15 For an analysis of Catholic Church building trends during this period see R. Hurley, *Irish Church Architecture in the Era of Vatican II* (Dublin: Dominican Publications, 2001).

16 C. Pollard, *Liam McCormick: Seven Donegal Churches, vol. VIII – architect + artists* (Kinsale: Gandon Editions, 2011), p. 29.

17 B. Felle, 'Radiant Legacy', *Irish Arts Review*, vol. 37, no. 1, Spring 2020, pp. 120–5.

18 Thanks to Emma Gilleece for information relating to these windows.

19 Little is known of Sheila Corcoran. She was a student at the National College of Art 1960–3 and one of the exhibitors in an exhibition of stained glass by NCA students in Brown Thomas's Little Theatre, June 1963. The only other windows she is known to have created (in 1968, with assistance from Willie Earley) are for the Catholic Church, Ballymun, Dublin.

20 E. Rowley, 'Andrew Devane's Dublin Churches: Catholic Architecture in Ireland in an Age of Tentative Radicalization, 1960–75', in L. Godson and K. James-Chakraborty (eds), *Modern Religious Architecture in Germany, Ireland and Beyond – Influence, Process and Afterlife since 1945* (London: Bloomsbury, 2019), pp. 77–8.

21 O'Connor & Aylward, Pembroke Street, Dublin and John Thompson Architects, Limerick are both credited for the church.

22 George Campbell (1917–79) designed windows at Abbey Stained Glass Studios, Dublin, throughout the 1960s, often painted by his friend George W. Walsh. Campbell's

work varies in style and technique, his earliest windows in Tierneevan, County Galway and Desertegney, County Donegal being either figurative or heraldic, though much of his subsequent work was entirely abstract, sometimes using only unpainted glass as in the (former) Dominican Church, Athy, and other times vigorously and densely painted as in the Dominican Priory, Tallaght, Dublin.

23 Interview with George W. Walsh, 1 February 2020.

24 D. Caron, 'Four Horsemen', *Irish Arts Review*, vol. 36 , no. 2, Summer 2019, pp. 116–21.

25 I am indebted to Ellen Moiselle of the Holy Child School Killiney for drawing my attention to the school's archival material.

26 There are important examples of *dalle de verre* in Ireland by one of the acknowledged masters of the technique, Gabriel Loire (1904–96) of the Loire Studio, Chartres, including in St Patrick's College Chapel, Drumcondra, Dublin (*c.*1965) and in St Augustine's Catholic Church, Cork City (*c.*1972).

27 Dublin-born Patrick Heney worked at Harry Clarke Studios from the early 1930s until 1940. The following year Frank Ryan sought his advice about establishing a stained glass company which would become Abbey Stained Glass Studios. Heney designed Abbey's first stained glass window in 1944 (for the Catholic Church at Bonniconlon, County Mayo) and remained with the studio until the early 1960s, while also maintaining a career as an art teacher. In later years he concentrated on painting, exhibiting regularly. I am indebted to Cristín Ní Éanaigh for information about her father's career.

28 Willie Earley, of the famous stained glass family, spent four years at Dublin's School of Art, gaining his ANCA at 21 in 1941. He then worked part-time at Earley and Company for a few years assisting his uncle William (Bill). Soon he was working for Frank Ryan at Abbey Stained Glass Studios and as a glass painter for Richard King. Earley was full-time in Abbey by the mid 1950s. In 1982 he struck out on his own and formed Earley Studios in a studio in Churchtown, Dublin, previously owned by Patrick Pollen. He was joined there by his daughter Jane, and brothers Jacky and Leo. Information courtesy of Michael Earley, February 2020.

29 K. Reihill, *George Campbell and the Belfast Boys* (Dublin: Adams Auctioneers, 2015), pp. 108–10.

30 I am indebted to Ken Ryan for information about Abbey Stained Glass Studios.

31 See B. McAvera, *Patrick Pye, Life and Work, a Counter-Cultural Story* (Dublin: Four Courts Press, 2013).

32 Margaret Becker was born in Dublin in 1937, graduated from the NCA in 1960 and then went to Rome to study painting. On her return she worked with Patrick Pollen at An Túr Gloine and then joined Patrick Pye at his studio in Herbert Street. After a sojourn in Scotland, Becker returned to Ireland in 1972 to work at the Graphic Studio, Dublin.

33 Frances Biggs was born into a musical family in Salthill, Galway in 1929 and was a violinist in the RTÉ Symphony Orchestra for four decades. Married to the stone sculptor and typographer/letterer Michael Biggs, who most likely encouraged her artistic talent, she attended evening classes at NCA from 1956–62. In addition to stained glass she regularly painted colourful abstract compositions, usually in gouache, and in later years designed tapestries for Monaghan Cathedral.

34 Joseph Tierney (1889–1965) emigrated to the United States in 1924 where he established his own studio, the Church Crafts Centre, New York City. His work can be found throughout New York (Cardinal Spellman favoured him), in Washington DC, Pennsylvania and Massachusetts, and in California: American Martyrs Church, Manhattan Beach; St Timothy's, Los Angeles; St John's Seminary, Camarillo.

35 For more information on Murphy-Devitt Studios, see Finola Finlay, https://roaringwaterjournal.com/stained-glass/; this blog also has other insightful articles on Irish stained glass.

36 See F. Finlay, 'Sacred lights and secular ground', *Irish Arts Review*, vol. 36, no. 1, Spring 2019, pp. 112–17.

37 V. Ryan, 'Divine Light: A century of stained-glass', *Irish Arts Review*, Spring 2015, vol. 32 (2), pp. 272–5.

38 J. McBrinn, '"A mouthful of zephyrs": the Studio Glass Movement in Ireland 1973–2003', in J.M. Hearne (ed.), *Glassmaking in Ireland: From the Medieval to the Contemporary* (Dublin: Irish Academic Press, 2010), pp. 242–3; and N. Gordon Bowe, 'Glazing images', introduction

to *The Light Fantastic: Irish Stained Glass* (Kilkenny: Crafts Council of Ireland, 2007), pp. 6–7.

39 J. McBrinn, 'Edward Marr, 1905–1973', *Perspective: Journal of the Royal Society of Ulster Architects*, vol. 17, 2008, pp. 66–8.

40 As essentially her stained glass career began after she emigrated, we are only listing the one window made by her in Ireland.

41 Olive Henry (1902–1989) joined Clokey's in Autumn 1919 and remained until Easter 1972. Eileen Black, writing in W. Ryan-Smolin, E. Mayes and J. Rogers (eds), *Irish Woman Artists From the Eighteenth Century to the Present Day*, (Dublin: National Gallery of Ireland and Douglas Hyde Gallery, 1987), p. 167, noted that 'most of Olive Henry's time at Clokey's was spent designing windows, although on a few occasions, she had the chance to produce the cartoons and paint herself. However, despite the fact this opportunity only seldom arose (she relished this fuller creative involvement), she enjoyed the work …' I am indebted to Eileen Black for additional information on Olive Henry's career based on her interview with the artist in 1979 and an unpublished essay she wrote on her. HERoNI holds approximately 1,200 Clokey stained glass designs (currently being catalogued), many of which have been attributed to Henry. Aside from her stained glass career Henry was also a talented painter, exhibiting regularly.

42 Edinburgh native John Blyth moved to Clokey and Company, Belfast *c.*1958 to run the studio for Harold Clokey as well as design and make windows. He remained at Clokey's until 1966 and might have stayed longer had his old friend and mentor William Wilson not asked him to return to Scotland to assist him with a major overseas commission. For further information on Blyth's career, see J. Searle, 'John Blyth F.M.G.P., Stained Glass Artist, 1915–1999', *Journal of Stained Glass (British Society of Master Glass Painters)*, vol. XXIII, pp. 95–8. I am indebted to Jack Searle for providing me with a list of Blyth's works in stained glass and additional biographical information.

43 Caldermac Studios was founded by Jack Calderwood (1927–98) in *c.*1958. Initially Calderwood designed the windows himself though soon William (Bill) Hogan became the main artist. Hogan was from Dublin and had worked in stained glass in the United States. David Esler (b.1951) joined as an apprentice in 1968. The company was based at Springfield Road until a bomb destroyed the premises and then the company relocated to Lisburn. Both Hogan and Esler remained with the company for approximately twenty-five years. As the company began to increasingly concentrate on glazing, Bill retired and David opted for redundancy. The company name changed to Sologlass Calderwoods, and later became Calderwood Glass, at which point Bill rejoined. Information kindly supplied by David Esler.

44 Noteworthy is George W. Walsh's fine series of windows (1996), featuring both religious subjects and some non-religious ones titled *Local Interest*, *Reflections on Life* and *Healing Hands* for the chapel at St Camillus Nursing Home Centre, Killucan, County Westmeath.

45 Examples include: Lua Breen's three-light (1986) for the oratory, Mater Private Hospital, Dublin, and Mary Mackay's two-light (1996) for the same hospital's former mortuary chapel (not currently in use), and Phyllis Burke's single-light for the chapel, Beaumont Hospital, Dublin.

46 S. O'Toole, 'The Mastery of Darkness' interview with James Scanlon, *Tracings*, vol. 1, Spring 2000. See also J. McBrinn, '"A mouthful of zephyrs"', p. 243.

47 Mary Mackay created thirty-two panels of acid-etched glass bonded to clear float glass (1998) for Mallow Swimming Pool, County Cork.

48 *Legends* (2008), Scoil Mhuire, Coolcotts, County Wexford; *Big Cheese* (2009), Lourdes Parish Schools, Lower Gloucester Place, Dublin; *Aesop's Fables* (2014), Scoil Bhríde, Naas, County Kildare.

49 Peter Young, 'Second Stage Design Proposal', a document prepared by the artist in January 2014.

50 Hanley, J., 'Drama Through the Window', *Irish Arts Review*, vol. 27, no. 1, Spring 2010, pp. 112–13.

List of Artists

('BN' indicates that there is a biographical note on the artist)

Antrim, Angela (1911–1984)
Barden, Hugh (b.1887)
Becker, Margaret (b.1937)
Biggs, Frances (1929–2006)
Blyth, John (1915–1999)
Brandt, Ruth (1936–1989)
Braniff, Daniel (1911–1999)
Braun, Sebastian (1881–1980)
Breen, Lua (b.1942) BN
Burke, Phyllis (b.1930) BN
Campbell, Christopher (1908–1972)
Campbell, George (1917–1979)
Carrick, Desmond (1928–2012)
Child, Alfred Ernest (A.E.) (1875–1939) BN
Clarke, Harry (1889–1931) BN
Clarke, Margaret (1884–1961)
Clarke, Terry (1917–1968)
Connon, Evan (b.1977)
Corcoran, Sheila (b.*c.*1942)
Corcoran, Terry (b.1947)
Cotter, Maud (b.1954)
Courtney, Dorothy (b.1875)
Cox, James (b.1940)
Dawson, Debbie (b.1965)
Deegan, Philip (b.1896)
Deeny, Gillian (b.1936)
Donas, Marthe (1885–1967)
Dowd Murphy, Róisín (1923–2006)
BN: see Murphy-Devitt Studios
Dowling, William (1907–1980) BN
Dunne, Michael (1921–2005)
Earley, Gerard (1905–2002)
Earley, James (b.1981)
Earley, Leo (1925–2001)
Earley, William E. (Bill) (1872–1956)
Earley, Willie (1930–2019)
Elvery, Beatrice (1883–1970) BN
Esler, David (b.1951)
Ferran, Brian (b. 1940)
FitzGibbon, Ann (b.1949)
Fox, Kathleen (1880–1963)
Frömel, Gerda (1931–1975)

Geddes, Wilhelmina (1887–1955) BN
Guinness, Lindy (1941–2020)
Harriss Crampton, Celia (b.*c.*1942)
Healy, Michael (1873–1941) BN
Heney, Patrick/Pádraig Ó hÉanaigh (1913–2007)
Henry, Olive (1902–1989)
Hensey, Maree (b.1962)
Hone, Evie (1894–1955) BN
Inglis, Tony (1911–1997)
Kelly, John (1932–2006)
Kelly, Kevin (1926–2019)
King, David (1948–2003)
King, Richard (1907–1974) BN
King, Richard Enda (1943–1995)
Lamb, Peadar (b.1966)
Lamb, Katharine (b.1968)
Lyons, Derry/Diarmuid O'Liathain (d.2015)
MacBride, William (1880–1962)
Mac Cana, Carin (b.1957)
Mackey, Mary (b.1960)
Marr, Edward (1905–1973)
McGoldrick, Hubert (1897–1967) BN
Mehegan, Cormac (1924–2015)
Molloy, Austin (1886–1961)
Moloney, Helen (1926–2011) BN
Mooney, Douglas (b.1971)
Muldowney, Patrick (b.1955)
Murphy, Johnny (1921–2006)
BN: see Murphy-Devitt Studios
Murphy, Reiltín (b.1955)
Nevin, Stanislaus (1910–1969)
O'Brien, Catherine (Kitty) (1881–1963) BN
Plunkett, Patricia (b.1966)
Pollen, Patrick (1928–2010) BN
Purser, Sarah (1848–1943) BN
Pye, Patrick (1929–2018) BN
Quigly, Kathleen (1888–1981)
Rhind, Ethel (1877–1952) BN
Rivers, Elizabeth (1903–1964)
Robinson, Patricia (b.1945)
Scanlon, James (b.1952)
Shawcross, Neil (b.1940)
Simmonds, Charles (Cecil) (b.1904)
Stuart, Imogen (b.1927)
Timlin, Michael (b.1958)
Tomlin, Alan (b.1945)
Tomlin, Fergus (b.1949)
Tomlin, Stanley (1916–1976)
Tutty, Benedict (1924–1996)
Walsh, George Stephen (1911–1988) BN
Walsh, George W. (b.1939) BN
Walsh, Manus (b.1940)
Weckbecker, August (1888–1939)
Young, Peter (b.1962)

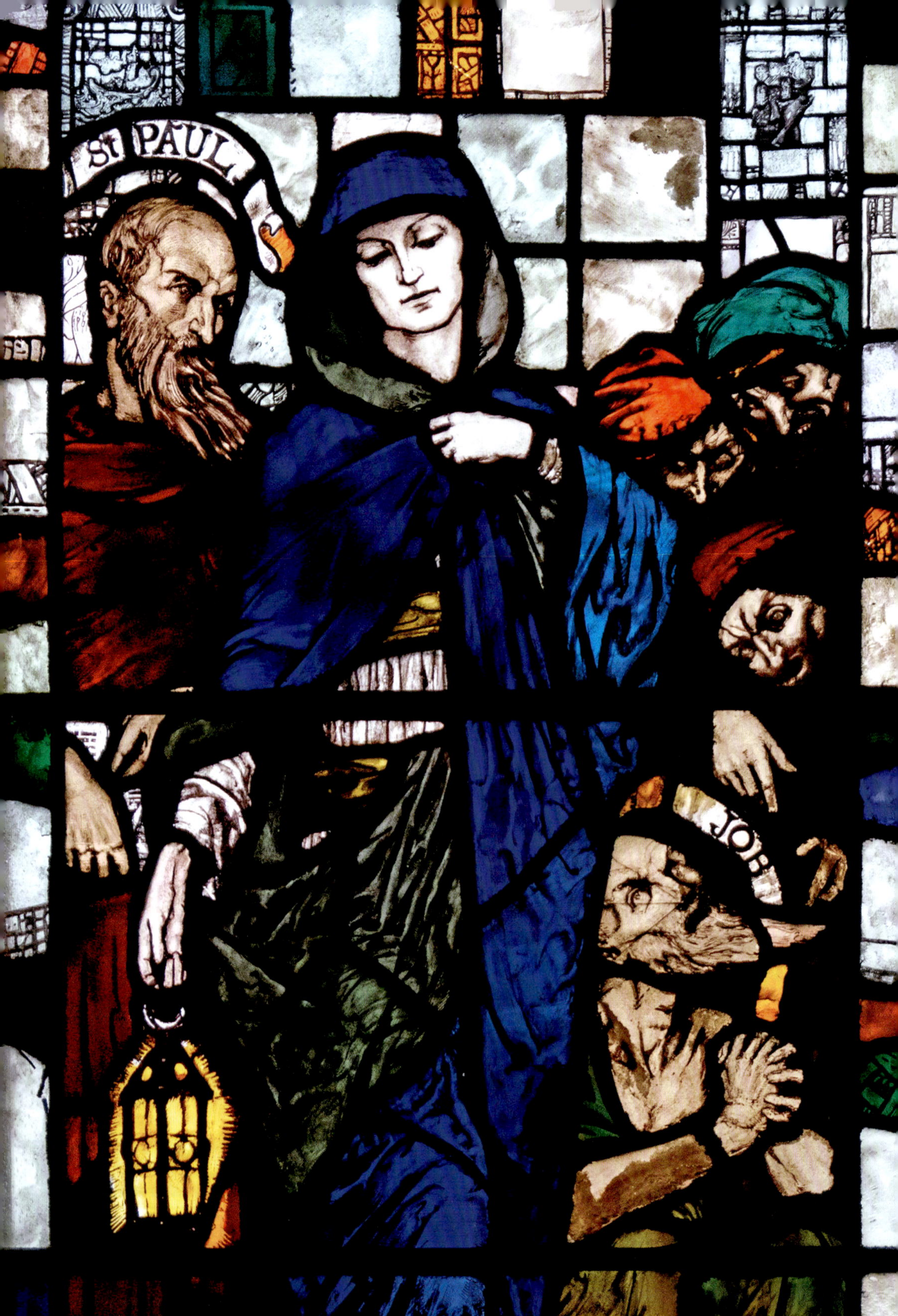
St PAUL

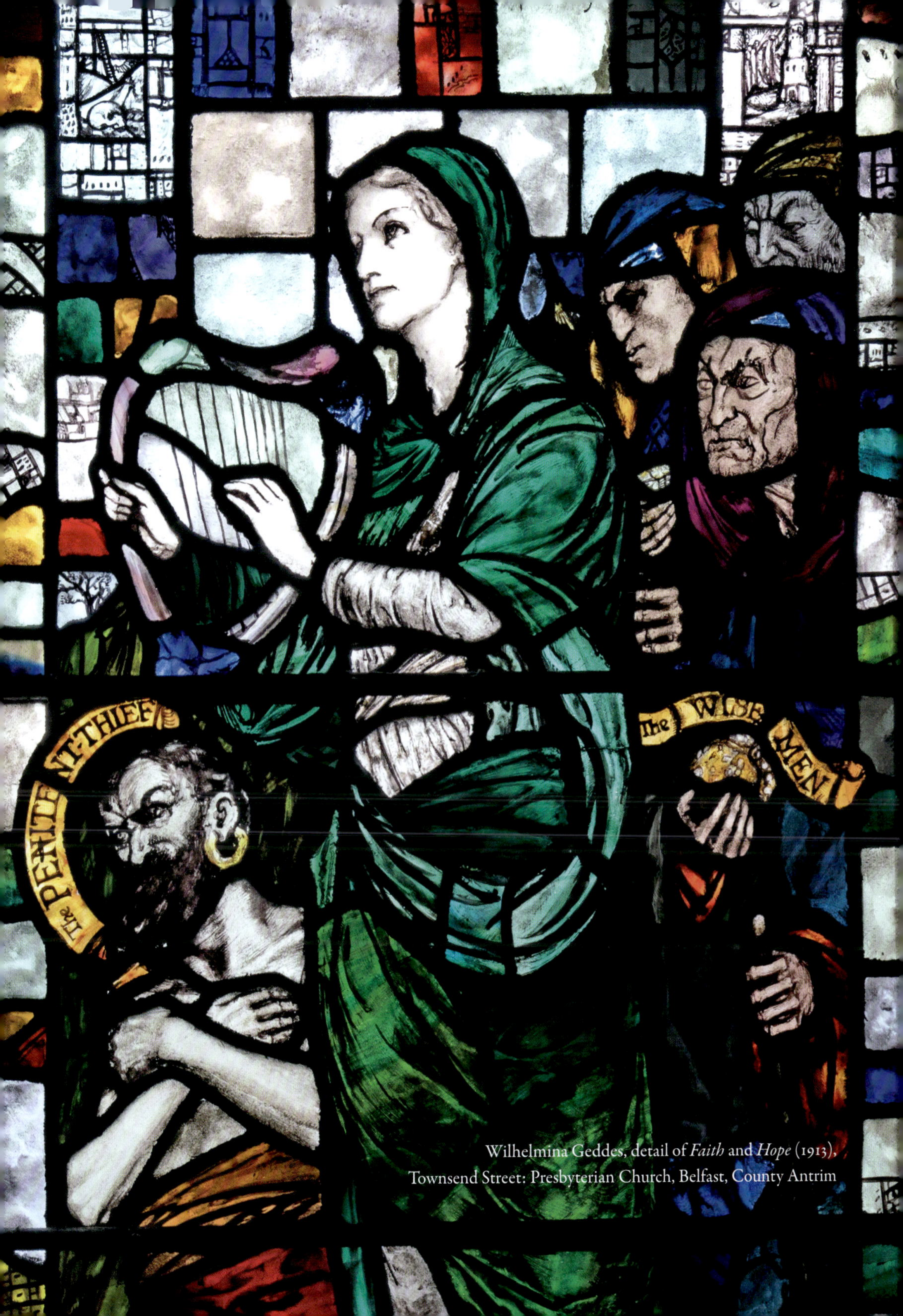

Wilhelmina Geddes, detail of *Faith* and *Hope* (1913),
Townsend Street: Presbyterian Church, Belfast, County Antrim

The Gazetteer of Irish Stained Glass

COUNTY ANTRIM

Ballycastle: Corrymeela Worship Centre
SHAWCROSS, Neil
The Incarnation c.1979

Ballymena: First Presbyterian Church
O'BRIEN, Catherine
Prudence 1920
Valour 1920
Faith 1920
Justice 1920
Benevolence 1920

Ballymena: Gracehill Moravian Church
RHIND, Ethel
John Wycliffe, Jan Huss and Jan Amos Comenius c.1916
Count Zinzendorf, Bishop Peter Boehler and John Cennick c.1916
(Both windows feature three medallions, each with portraits of prominent Moravian figures. Formerly in the Moravian Church, Dublin from where removed in 1959.)

Ballymoney: First Presbyterian Church
McGOLDRICK, Hubert
The Burning Bush, and Heraldry (war memorial) 1920 (3 lights) (sketch design, NGI)

Belfast, Antrim Road: St Clement's Retreat House Chapel (demolished)
MOLONEY, Helen
Some windows salvaged and apparently in storage (unconfirmed)

Belfast, Antrim Road: St Malachy's College Chapel
DOWLING, William
Blessed Oliver Plunkett 1935–6
KING, Richard
The Joyful Mysteries 1935 (five 2 lights)
The Sorrowful Mysteries 1935–6 (five 2 lights)
The Glorious Mysteries 1936–7 (five 2 lights)
St Paul 1935
St Thomas Aquinas 1935
Christ the King 1935
St Joseph 1935–6
St Malachy 1935–6
The Seven Sacraments 1937 (rose)
(All above created at Harry Clarke Studios; sketch designs, TCD)

Belfast, Bloomfield Road: C of I (St Donard's)
BRANIFF, Daniel
Ascension c.1970 (3 lights)
Phoebe and St Paul 1973 (2 lights)
St Peter and St Andrew c.1973 (2 lights)
St Donard and St Patrick 1974 (2 lights)

Belfast, Cavehill Road: Former CC (Church of the Resurrection)
PYE, Patrick
Resurrection 1979 (destroyed by vandals)
Baptism of Christ 1979 (destroyed by vandals)
Three abstract clerestory windows 1979 (condition unknown) (cutline plans for all windows, NIVAL)

Belfast, Donegall Road: C of I (St Simon's)
BLYTH, John
Ascension, with St Simon and St Patrick c.1965 (3 lights)
(Created at Clokey and Company, Belfast.)

Belfast, Donegall Road: Methodist Church
SHAWCROSS, Neil
Stained glass scheme with Angels (either side of entrance doors); *John Wellesley Preaching* (above entrance); *decorative with leaves motif* (side windows) c. early 1970s

Belfast, Donegall Street: C of I Cathedral (St Anne's)
POLLEN, Patrick
Memorial to Soldiers of Irish Regiments Killed in the First and Second World Wars 1979–80 (sketch design, NIVAL)
MARR, Edward
Symbols of Christianity c.1969 (apse, clerestory)
Holy Spirit c.1969 (apse, clerestory)
Holy Communion c.1969 (apse, clerestory)

Belfast, Donegall Square: City Hall
BRANIFF, Daniel
Sir Crawford McCullagh Memorial Window 1951
Lady Margaret McCullagh Memorial Window 1951
(Belfast City Hall has an ongoing policy of commissioning stained glass windows for the building.)

Belfast, Falls Road: Dominican Convent
CLARKE, Harry
Rose Window (A) 1927 (in former chapel, now closed)
HONE, Evie
Our Lady of Mercy Protecting the Dominican Order 1948 (relocated to the convent's new chapel) (cartoon, Hunt Museum, Limerick)

Belfast, Falls Road: St Mary's University College
KING, Richard
Our Lady of Fatima 1937 (2 lights)
Untitled window of two Angels with Chalice and Host 1937 (laylight)
(Both created at Harry Clarke Studios.)

Belfast, Fisherwick Place: Presbyterian Assembly Hall (Church House)
GEDDES, Wilhelmina
The Prodigal Son, the Wise Virgins, the Talents, and the Good Samaritan 1916 (4 lights) (sketch design, NGI)
'Go ye therefore and preach the Gospel to all nations' 1929
'The Delectable Mountains' from Bunyan's The Pilgrim's Progress 1929
(The two last mentioned were rescued from the Presbyterian Church in Rosemary Street after the bombing of 1942 and are rehoused in the Assembly Hall at Church House but were severely damaged in 1972. They are now displayed in light boxes on a landing.)

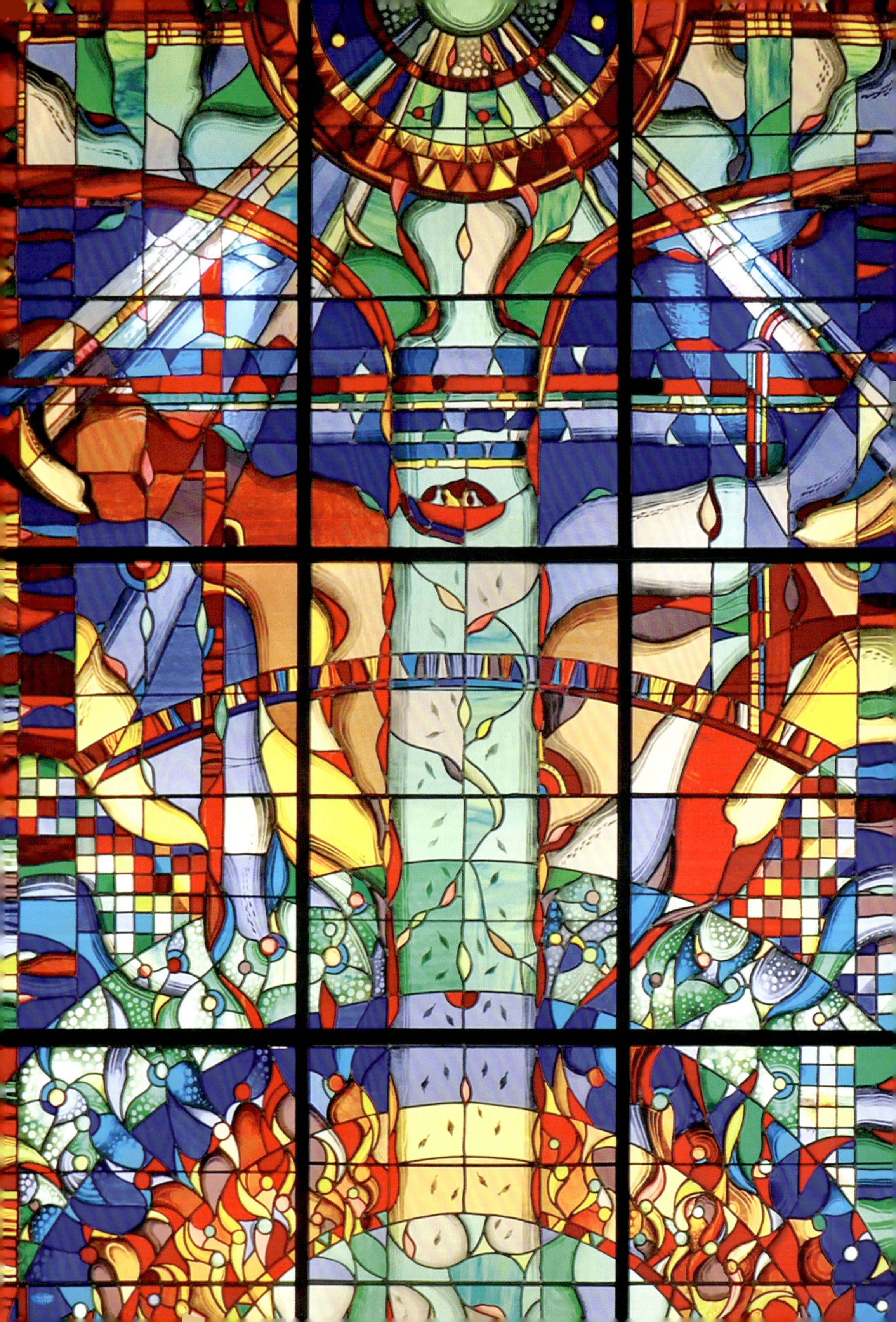

Belfast, Fortwilliam Park: Dominican College Chapel
BRANIFF, Daniel
*Stained glass scheme c.*1964

Belfast, Glen Road, Andersonstown: Christian Brothers' Residence Chapel (adjoining All Saints College)
POLLEN, Patrick
*Twelve abstract windows c.*1961

Belfast, Glengall Street: Grosvenor House (Gallagher Chapel, Belfast Central Mission)
PYE, Patrick
Agony in the Garden 1969 (formerly in the Methodist Church, Donegall Square, Belfast)

Belfast, Holywood Road, Dundela: C of I (St Mark's)
HEALY, Michael
St Luke, St James and St Mark 1932 (3 lights) (sketch design, NGI)

Belfast, Kingsway, Finaghy: Rathmore Grammar School Chapel
WALSH, George Stephen
*Our Lady of the Rosary, with Apparition at Lourdes, Apparition at Fatima c.*1949 (3 lights)
Sacred Heart, Crucifixion, Immaculate Heart of Mary * *c.*1949 (3 lights)
(Created at Clokey and Company, Belfast. It is almost certain that both windows were originally made for the Convent of the Sacred Heart of Mary, Lisburn and transferred (with some modification) *c.*1960s. The chapel has three additional decorative windows with Cross motifs made by Clokey's.)

Left:
George W. Walsh, detail of *Tabernacle screen* (2007), Catholic Church (Holy Family), Newington Avenue, Belfast, County Antrim. Photograph © Finola Finlay

Belfast, Lisburn Road: Agapé Centre (Methodist Community Centre)
ESLER, David
*Five windows on the themes of Peace, Hope, Love, Healing and Justice c.*2011

Belfast, Lisburn Road: Belfast City Hospital, MacMillan Centre
ESLER, David
The Door (inspired by Miroslav Holub's poem) 2010 (free-standing panel)
A Kite for Aibhín (inspired by Seamus Heaney's poem) *c.*2012 (Quiet Room)

Belfast, Lisburn Road: C of I (St Nicholas's)
BRANIFF, Daniel
Christ as Light of the World 1968
*David Playing the Harp to Saul c.*1969
*St Mary at the Crucifixion c.*1970
St Paul 1977

Belfast, Malone Road: CC (St Brigid's), Derryvolgie Avenue
BREEN, Lua
Principal stained glass windows, including Sanctuary window, based on Hallel Psalms 1994
Symbols of the Eucharist 1994
St Malachy 1994
St Oliver Plunkett 1996
St Columba 1994
St Brigid 1994
Martyrdom of Blessed Conor O'Devanney 1994 (2 light)
Abstract with Boat 1994
Abstract with Anchor 1994
Baptism of Christ 1996
Madonna and Child 1996
(sketch designs for all windows, NIVAL)

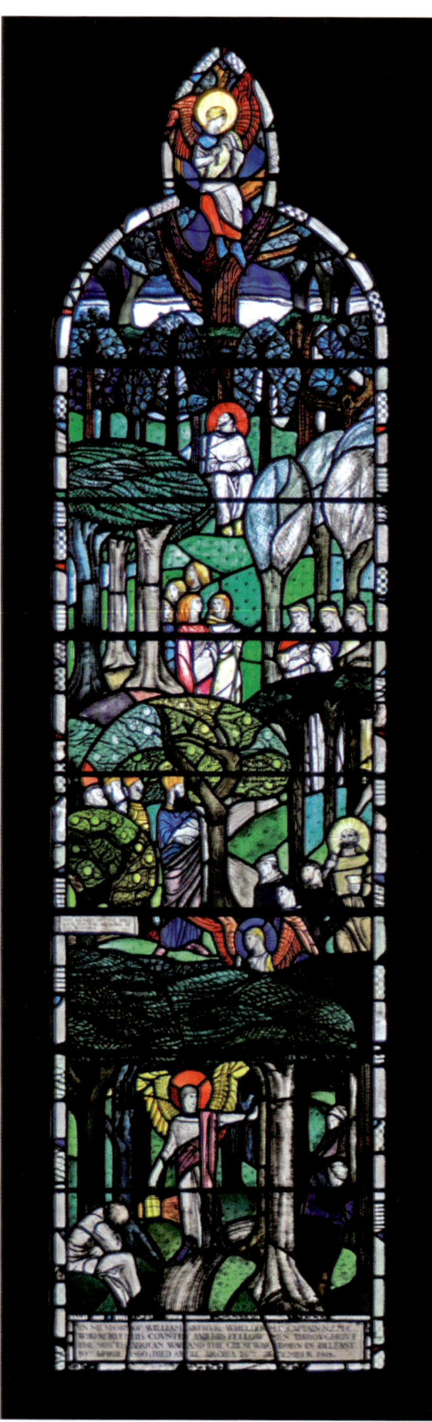

Belfast, Malone Road: C of I (St John's)
GEDDES, Wilhelmina
'The Leaves of the Tree Were for the Healing of the Nations' 1920 (sketch design, NGI)
HONE, Evie
St Columba 1948
Symbols 1947–8 (rose)
St Brigid 1948 (in the porch) (cartoon, Temple Street Convent, Dublin)
MACBRIDE, William
Valour (Seaver war memorial) 1918
Royal Irish Rifles (Capper war memorial) *c.*1918 (2 lights)
Faithful Warrior (Ferguson war memorial) *c.*1918
David (James Ireland war memorial) *c.*1919
O'BRIEN, Catherine
St Patrick 1939

Belfast, Malone Road: Fisherwick Presbyterian Church, Chlorine Gardens
HENRY, Olive and WALSH, George Stephen (initial design by Olive Henry)
*Christ as a Young Man with Nail and Mallet, Christ as an Adult Holding a Crown, Christ Healing a Bedridden Man, Seven Men Representing Different Trades and Occupations c.*1955–6 (6 lights)

Belfast, Manse Road: Lagan College (Faith Space)
WALSH, George W.
Act Justly 2013
Love Mercy 2013
Walk Humbly Together 2013

Left: Wilhelmina Geddes, *'The Leaves of the Tree Were for the Healing of the Nations'* (1920), Church of Ireland (St John's), Malone Road, Belfast, County Antrim

Right: George Stephen Walsh, *Christ as a Young Man with Nail and Mallet, Christ as an Adult Holding a Crown, Eight Men Representing Different Trades and Occupations, Masonic Symbols* (*c.* 1956), Fisherwick Presbyterian Church, Malone Road (Chlorine Gardens), Belfast, County Antrim

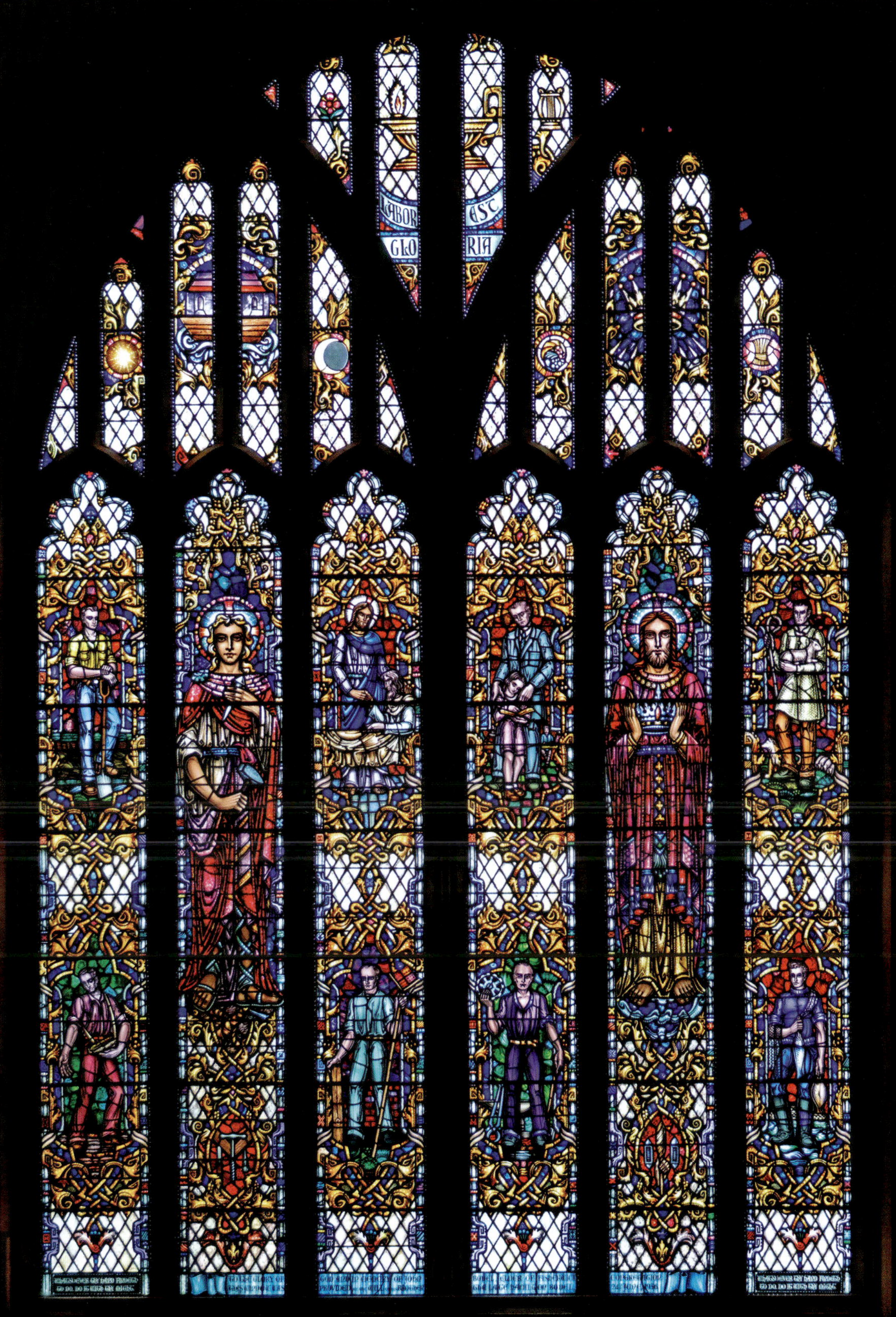
LABOR
EST
GLO
RIA

Belfast, Millfield: C of I (St Stephen's)
BRANIFF, Daniel
*St Luke c.*1965
Mission of St Columba to Ireland (porch) 1966
St Patrick (porch) 1966
*Nativity c.*1966
*Baptism of Christ c.*1966
*Christ as Good Shepherd c.*1966
*Crucifixion c.*1966
*Risen Christ Appearing to Mary Magdalen c.*1966
*Ascension c.*1966
Wedding Feast at Cana 1967
Christ as Bread of Life 1967
Christ Healing at the pool of Bethesda 1967
Miraculous Feeding 1967
Christ Healing the Blind Man 1967
Raising Lazarus 1967
Christ Walking on Water 1967
Moses and the Burning Bush, Samuel Anointing David 1971 (2 lights)
St Peter's Address at Pentecost, Conversion of St Paul 1971 (2 lights)

Belfast, Newington Avenue: CC (Holy Family)
WALSH, George W.
Stained glass scheme, including screen and Tabernacle 2007
Stations of the Cross 2007 (ceramic tile, executed by Laura O'Hagan)

Belfast, Rosemary Street: Presbyterian Church
GEDDES, Wilhelmina
Christ Blessing Little Children 1929 (destroyed by war, 1941)
Moses 1929 (destroyed by war, 1941)

Belfast, Rosetta Road, Knockbreda: St Andrew's Presbyterian Church
SHAWCROSS, Neil
Abstract, with two Intertwined Trees Representing the Presbyterian and Methodist Churches 1971

Belfast, St Peter's Square: Catholic Cathedral (St Peter's)
DOWD MURPHY, Róisín and MURPHY, Johnny
Resurrection 2005 (4 lights) (photograph of cartoons, NIVAL)

Belfast, Stewartstown Road: St Joseph's Training College, Trench House (demolished)
POLLEN, Patrick
All decorative glazing, including twelve painted symbols 1961
(Building closed in 1996 and demolished; unclear if windows were salvaged or destroyed.)

Belfast, Stormont Estate: Stormont Castle
ESLER, David
Man, Fish, and Bird (inspired by John Hewitt's poem) *c.*2009 (3 lights, landing of main staircase)

Belfast, Stranmillis Road: C of I (St Bartholomew's)
HENRY, Olive
St Paul Baptising, St Paul at Ephesus * *c.*1966 (2 lights) (sketch design, HERONI)
(Created at Clokey and Company, Belfast.)
SHAWCROSS, Neil
Christian symbols 1998 (2 lights)

Belfast, Stranmillis Road: Ulster Museum
GEDDES, Wilhelmina
The Fate of the Children of Lir: An Irish legend 1930 (8 panels, one window; in storage)
Rhoda Opens the Door to St Peter 1934 (panel; in storage)
HONE, Evie
The Angel Gabriel 1953 (panel; in storage)
POLLEN, Patrick
Dark Flowers 1966 (panel; in storage) (sketch design and cartoon, UM)
SHAWCROSS, Neil
Ulster countryside theme 1968 (8 lights)
Marine theme 1968 (11 lights)

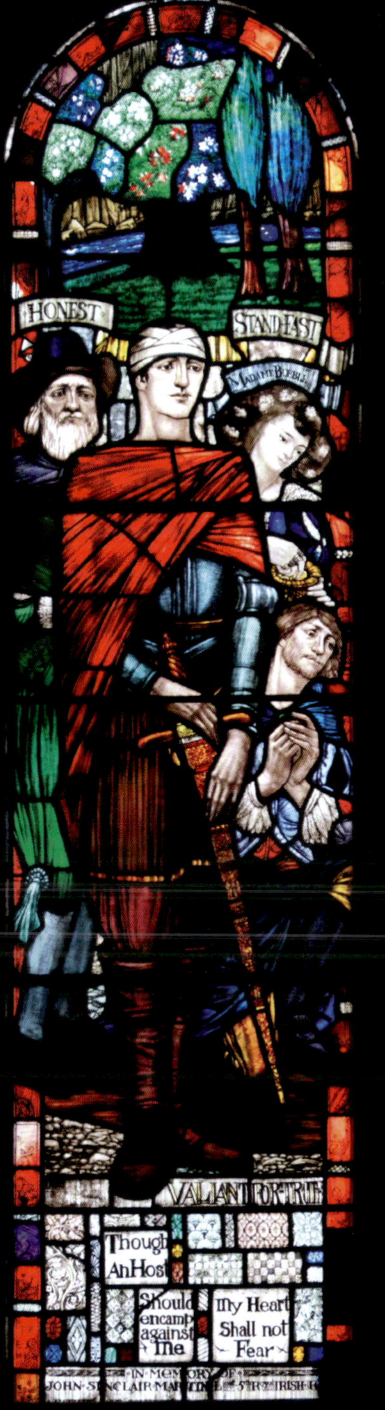

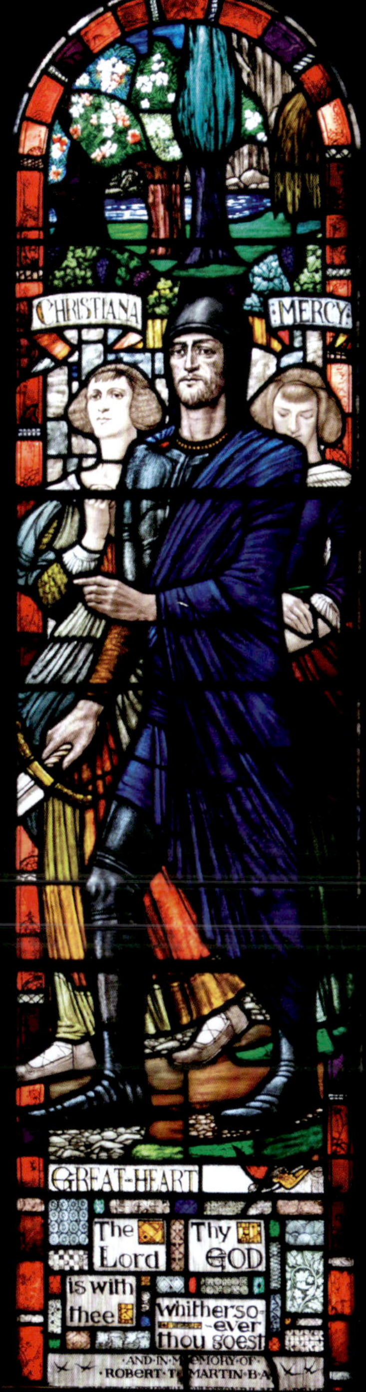

Ethel Rhind,
detail of
Pilgrim's Progress
(1921–2),
Presbyterian Church,
Townsend Street,
Belfast, County Antrim

Belfast, Sydenham: C of I (St Brendan's), Larkfield Road
SHAWCROSS, Neil
*Ten abstract windows with butterfly motifs c.*1966

Belfast, Townsend Street: Presbyterian Church
GEDDES, Wilhelmina
Faith, Hope and Charity 1913 (2 lights) (sketch design, NGI)
RHIND, Ethel
Parables 1913 (2 lights)
Pilgrim's Progress 1921–2 (2 lights)
WALSH, George Stephen
*Knight in Armour ('Valour'), and the Good Shepherd c.*1952 (2 lights)

Belfast, Upper Newtownards Road: C of I (St Patrick's, Ballymacarrett Parish)
HENRY, Olive
*Ascension with Last Supper c.*1954–7 (5 lights; executed, in part at least, by George S. Walsh) (sketch design, UM)
(Created at Clokey and Company, Belfast.)

Belfast, Woodvale Road, Shankill: C of I (St Matthew's)
BRANIFF, Daniel
*Crucifixion c.*1966

Billy, near Bushmills: C of I
HENRY, Olive
*St Columba c.*1969
*St Francis, with St Damian, Christ Walking on the Water c.*1969
(Created at Clokey and Company, Belfast.)
HEALY, Michael
The Risen Christ 1924–5 (sketch design, NGI)
Virgin and Child 1929 (sketch design, NGI)
Ecce Homo 1934–5 (sketch design, NGI)

Carnlough: CC (St John the Evangelist)
BREEN, Lua
Stained glass scheme inspired by the Gospel of St John 1997 (sketch designs, NIVAL)

Carrickfergus: C of I (St Nicholas's)
ELVERY, Beatrice
The Good Samaritan, the Good Shepherd and the Prodigal Son 1911–12 (3 lights)
O'BRIEN, Catherine
St Andrew 1929
RHIND, Ethel
St Columba, St Patrick and St Aidan 1912 (3 lights)
St John 1929

Craigs, Cullybackey: C of I
O'BRIEN, Catherine
Love: Angel of Charity 1947

Cushendall: CC (St Mary's)
MURPHY, Johnny
Baptism of Christ 1958 (2 lights) (sketch design and cartoons, NIVAL)
The Apparition at Lourdes 1958 (2 lights)

Cushendall: C of I (Layde Parish Church)
ELVERY, Beatrice
Christ and Knight 1918 (executed by Ethel Rhind)

Right: Daniel Braniff, *St Columba, St Patrick, St Brendan* (1974), Church of Ireland (Church of the Holy Name), Greenisland, County Antrim

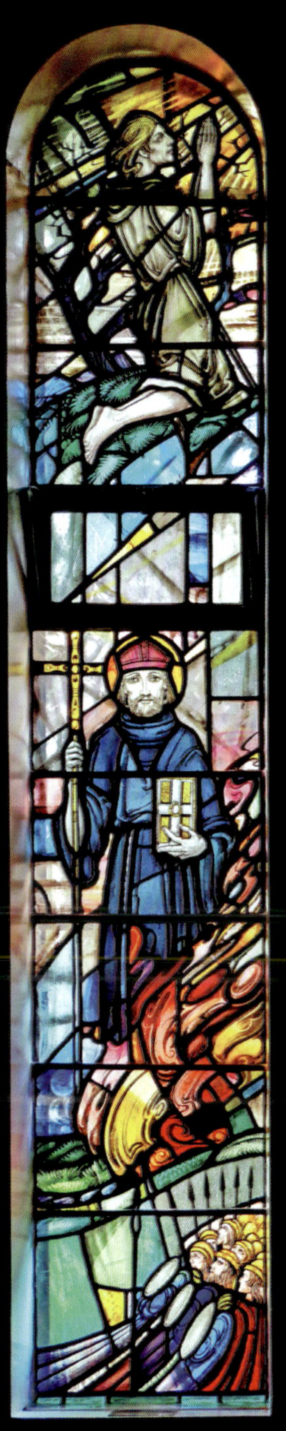
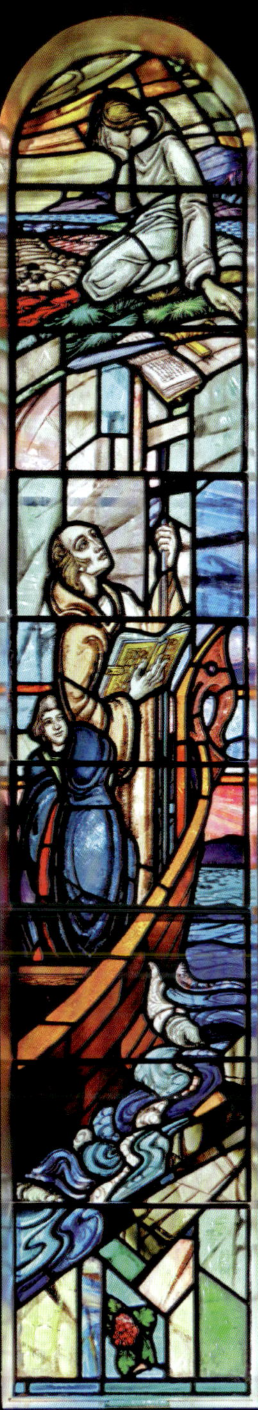
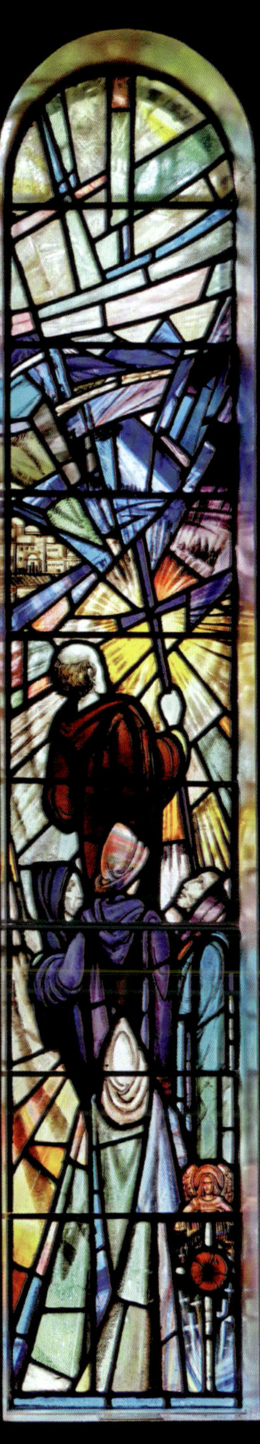

Dunloy: CC (St Joseph's)
BREEN, Lua
Crucifixion 1998
Deposition 1998
Pietà 1998
Entombment 1998
Noli Me Tangere 1998
Road to Emmaus 1998
Incredulity of Thomas 1998
Salvator Mundi 1998
(sketch designs for all windows, NIVAL)

Finvoy: C of I
O'BRIEN, Catherine
Joy 1945
Justice 1946

Glenariffe: CC (St Patrick and St Brigid's)
HEALY, Michael
The Calling of St Peter 1917 (sketch design, NGI)
St Brigid 1917
St Patrick 1917

Glenarm: CC (Church of the Immaculate Conception)
ANTRIM, Angela
Nativity 1961

Glengormley: CC (St Bernard's)
DOWD MURPHY, Róisín and MURPHY, Johnny
Holy Spirit 2003
Stations of the Cross 2003 (cartoons, NIVAL)

Greenisland: C of I (Church of the Holy Name)
BRANIFF, Daniel
Christ Appears to Mary Magdalene, Crucifixion, Last Supper, Christ Arrested 1970 (3 lights)
*Ascension c.*1970
Transfiguration, Temptation, Christ Preaching, Miraculous Feeding, Sermon on the Mount, Christ Healing the Centurion's Servant 1971 (3 lights)
Conversion of St Paul, St Peter Preaching, St Peter Healing the Lame Man at Pentecost 1973 (3 lights)
Three panels (reconfigured, in replacement entrance doors) 1973
St Columba, St Patrick, St Brendan 1974 (3 lights)

Inver, Larne: C of I (St Cedma's)
GEDDES, Wilhelmina
St Patrick and St Columba 1923 (2 lights)
Christ with Martha and Mary 1927 (2 lights)

Lambeg: CC (St Colman's)
SHAWCROSS, Neil
Christ is Risen 1991
A Son is Born to Us 1991

Lisburn: C of I (Christ Church)
O'BRIEN, Catherine
David and Jonathan, Ruth and Naomi, with Infant Christ (in tracery) 1939 (2 lights)

Lisburn: Lagan Valley Island Centre (relocated from Lisburn and Castlereagh City Council HQ)
ESLER, David
La Mon Hotel Bombing Memorial Window 2000
Castlereagh Memorial Window 2000

Magherahoney: CC (St MacNissi's)
MOLONEY, Helen
Symbols of Christian Baptism: a Serpent Denoting Original Sin, Water, a Cross and the Holy Spirit 1967–8 (baptistry) (sketch designs, NIVAL)

Randalstown: CC (*former* St MacNissi's, no longer extant)
MOLONEY, Helen
Blessed Trinity, Fall and Redemption 1972
(Large sanctuary window, destroyed in arson attack, 1979.)

Right: Wilhelmina Geddes, *Christ with Martha and Mary* (1927), Church of Ireland (St Cedma's), Inver, Larne, County Antrim

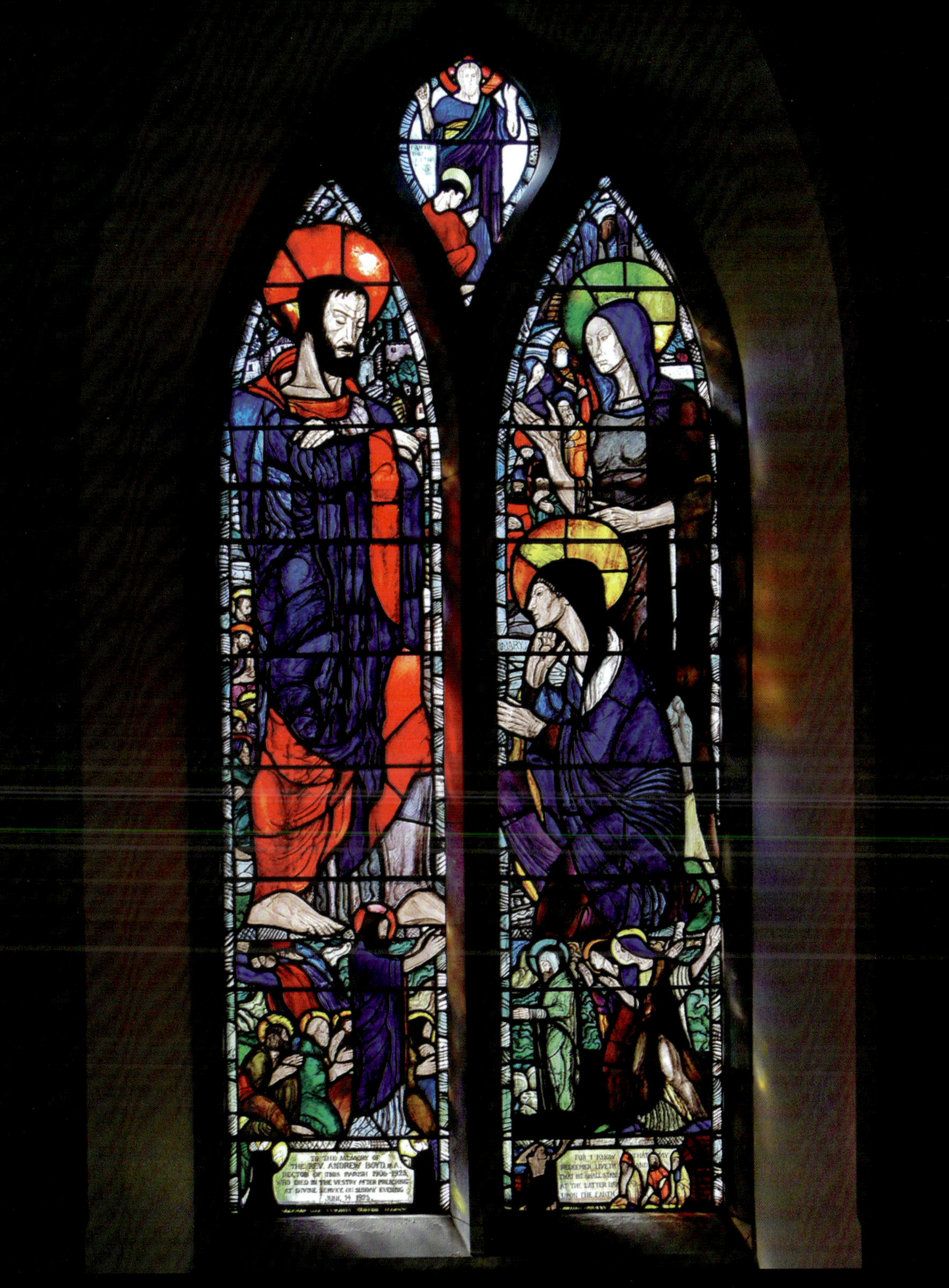
MARY
TO THE MEMORY OF
THE REV. ANDREW BOYD M.A.
RECTOR OF THIS PARISH 1906-1925
WHO DIED IN THE VESTRY AFTER PREACHING
AT DIVINE SERVICE ON SUNDAY EVENING
JUNE 14 1925
FOR I KNOW
REDEEMER LIVETH
AT THE LATTER
UPON THE EARTH

Below: Lua Breen, *One of a scheme of windows based on the period between the Resurrection and the Ascension* (1999), sketch design for the Catholic Church (*new* St MacNissi), Randalstown, County Antrim. Collection National Irish Visual Arts Library (NIVAL), NCAD, Dublin.

Randalstown: CC (*new* St MacNissi's)
BREEN, Lua
Stained glass scheme based on the period between the Resurrection and Ascension 1999 (sketch design, NIVAL)

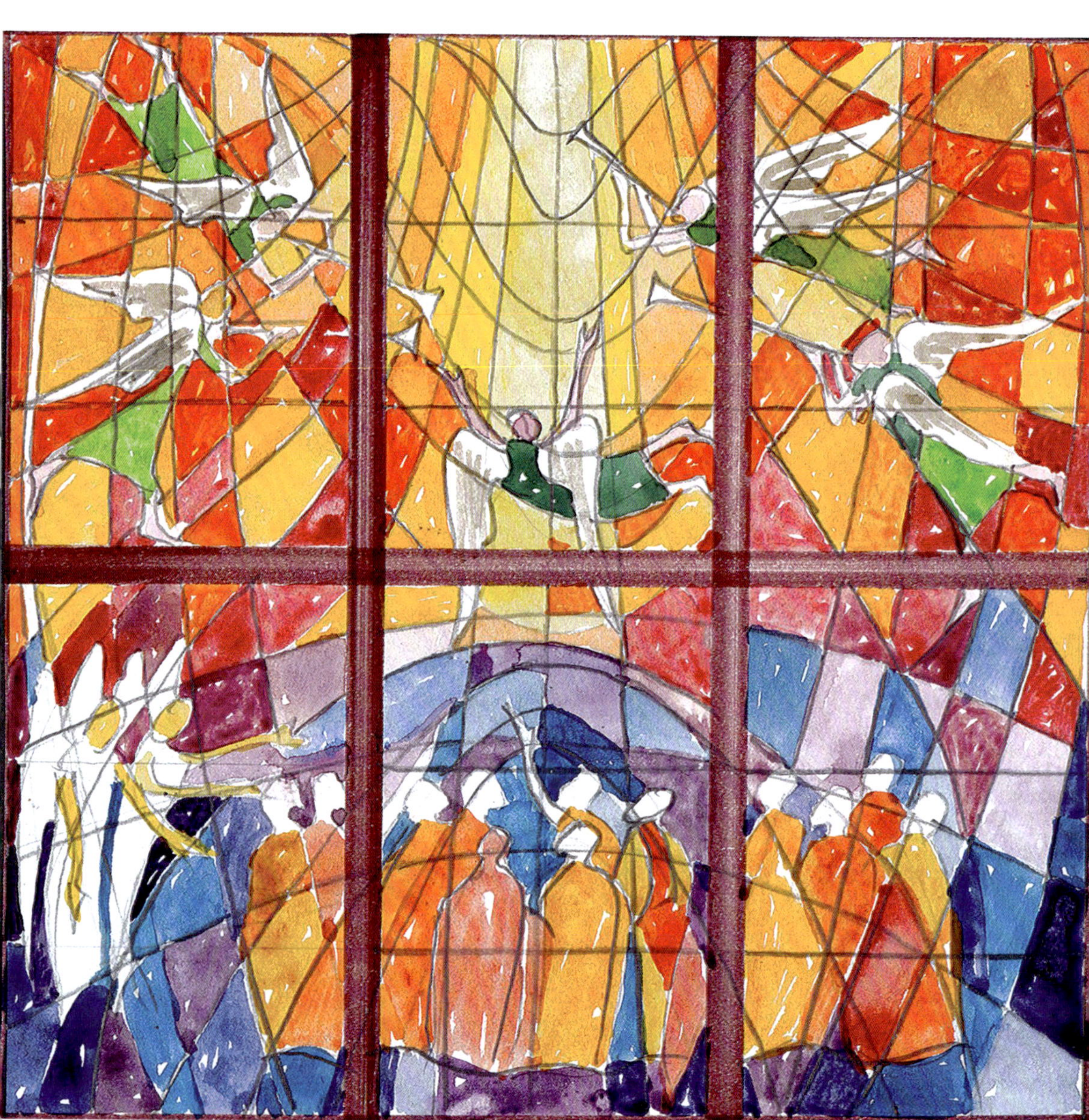

Randalstown: C of I (St Brigid's), Drummaul
CHILD, A.E.
The Risen Christ, Valour, Peace, Pelican, the Nativity, the Agony in the Garden 1923 (3 lights)

Toomebridge: CC (St Oliver Plunkett's)
MOLONEY, Helen
Lamb of God, Eucharist, the Holy Spirit, and Serpent 1976 (*dalle de verre* window, destroyed in reordering of the church, early twenty-first century)

Whitehouse: C of I (St John's)
MacBRIDE, William
St Michael * *c.*1920
Crown of Life *c.*1920

Whitehouse: Presbyterian Church
CHILD, A.E.
Faith 1914–5 (destroyed in arson attack, 2002)
O'BRIEN, Catherine
The Miraculous Draft of Fishes 1943 (destroyed in arson attack, 2002)

COUNTY ARMAGH

Armagh City: C of I Cathedral (St Patrick's)
ESLER, David
Ferdomnach the Scribe with Saints Patrick, Brendan, Columba and Brigid 2003 (3 lights)

Armagh City: C of I (St Mark's)
RHIND, Ethel
St Cecilia and the Good Samaritan 1920 (2 lights)
Beloved Physician and Virtuous Woman 1926 (2 lights)
ESLER, David
Sermon on the Mount 2004 (2 lights)
Archangel Michael 2005 (2 lights)
Christ's Healing Ministry 2008 (2 lights)

Cladymore, near Markethill: CC (St Michael's), Cladymore Road
PYE, Patrick
Coronation of the Virgin 1998
St Michael 1998

Grange (Sallinsgrange): C of I (St Aidan's)
ELVERY, Beatrice
Pentecost, the Four Evangelists, and the Parables of the Lost Sheep, the Sower, the Good Samaritan and the Good Shepherd 1910 (4 lights)

Lurgan: CC (St Paul's), Francis Street
MURPHY, Johnny and DOWD MURPHY, Róisín
Stations of the Cross *c.*1965–6 (14 horizontal panels) (cartoons, NIVAL)

Mullavilly, near Portadown: CC (Immaculate Conception)
BREEN, Lua
Annunciation 1998
Mary Mediatrix 1998
Immaculate Conception 1998
Assumption 1998
Crucifixion 1998 (rose)
Madonna and Child 1998 (2 lights)
Mary, Mother of the Church 1998 (2 lights)
(sketch designs for all windows, NIVAL)

Portadown: C of I (St Columba's), Loughgall Road
SHAWCROSS, Neil
'I Will Make You Fishers of Men' 1970 (7 lights, Iona Chapel)
Six single lights relating to St Columba as Missionary 1970

COUNTY CARLOW

Ardattin (Ardoyne): C of I (Holy Trinity)
O'BRIEN, Catherine
The Ascension 1937 (sketch design, NGI)

Borris: C of I chapel in the demesne of Borris House
YOUNG, Peter
Martin Wills Memorial: (I) 1995 (2 lights)
Martin Wills Memorial: (II) 1995 (2 lights)

Carlow Town, Athy Road: County Carlow Military Museum, (former Catholic Chapel, St Dympna's Hospital)
WECKBECKER, August
God the Father Supporting Christ Crucified, Surrounded by Saints and Angels 1926
Nave windows depicting Irish Saints and Stations of the Cross * *c.*1926

Carlow Town, Athy Road: St Dympna's Hospital, Staff Wellness Centre (former C of I Chapel)
RHIND, Ethel
The Crucifixion, with the Blessed Virgin Mary and St John 1927
The Nativity, with the Annunciation to the Shepherds 1936
The Resurrection, with the Three Marys at the Tomb of Christ 1936
St Stephen 1938
St John the Baptist in the Wilderness 1938

Carlow Town, Church Street: C of I (St Mary's)
O'BRIEN, Catherine
Angels of Prayer and Praise 1930 (2 lights)
Faith and Charity 1934 (2 lights)

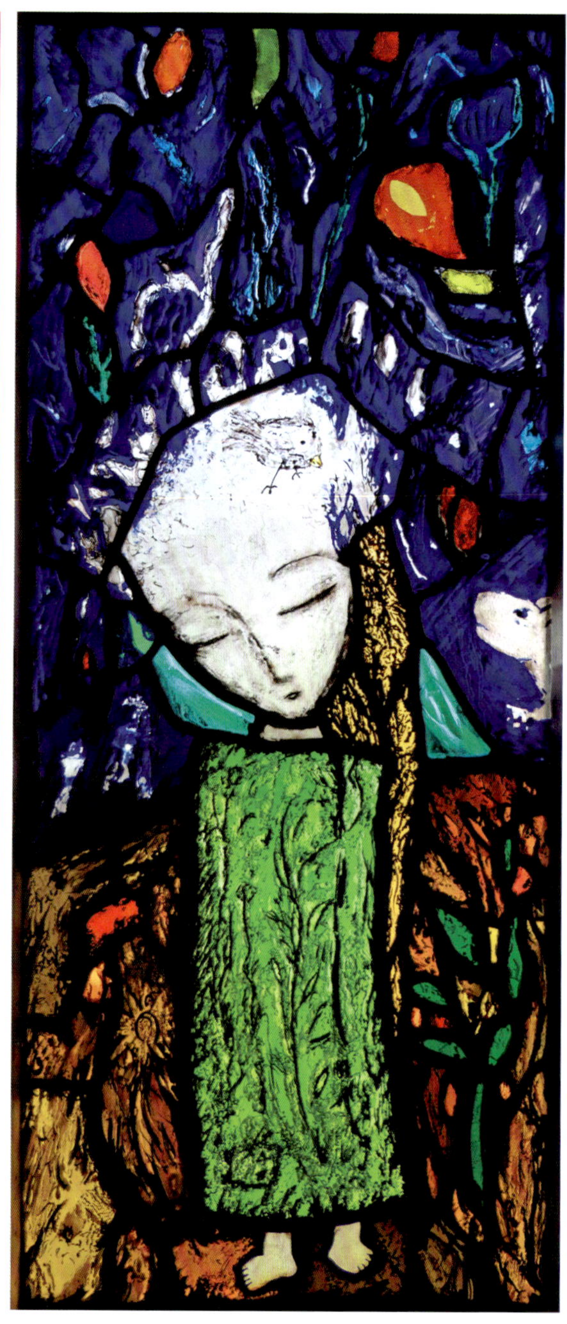

Right:
Peter Young, detail of *Martin Willis Memorial: II* (1995), Church of Ireland chapel in the demesne of Borris House, Borris, County Carlow

Carlow Town, College Street: County Museum
O'BRIEN, Catherine
County Carlow Coat of Arms date unknown (panel; in storage)
LAMB, Peadar
1916 commemorative window 2016

Carlow Town, College Street: St Patrick's College (P.J. Brophy Library)
KING, Richard
Irish or European Saint with Tonsure and Crozier c. early to mid-1930s (Companion window to *St Francis Xavier* in chapel of Belvedere College, Dublin.) (Created at Harry Clarke Studios.)

Killeshin: C of I
O'BRIEN, Catherine
The Sower 1946 (3 lights)

Lorum, near Bagenalstown: C of I
CHILD, A.E.
Knight in Armour * 1933
O'BRIEN, Catherine
The Good Shepherd 1947–8 (sketch design, NGI)

Below from left:
Helen Moloney, *The Serpent* (1974), Catholic Church (St Joseph's), Tinryland, County Carlow

Catherine O'Brien, *Angels of Prayer and Praise* (1930), Church of Ireland (St Mary's), Carlow Town

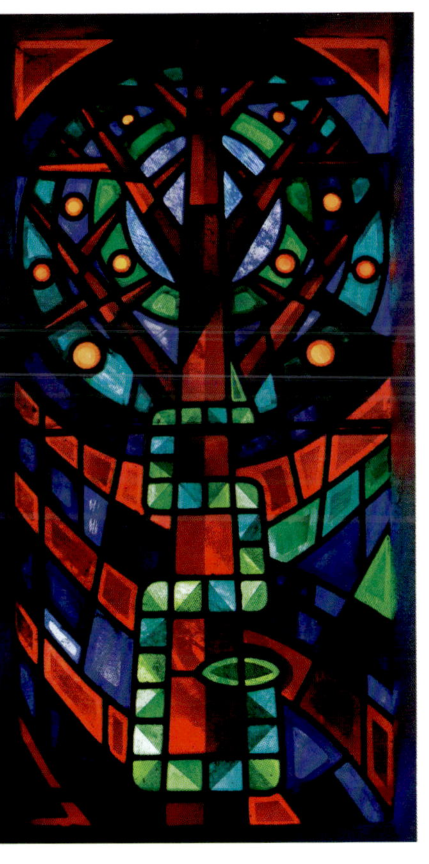

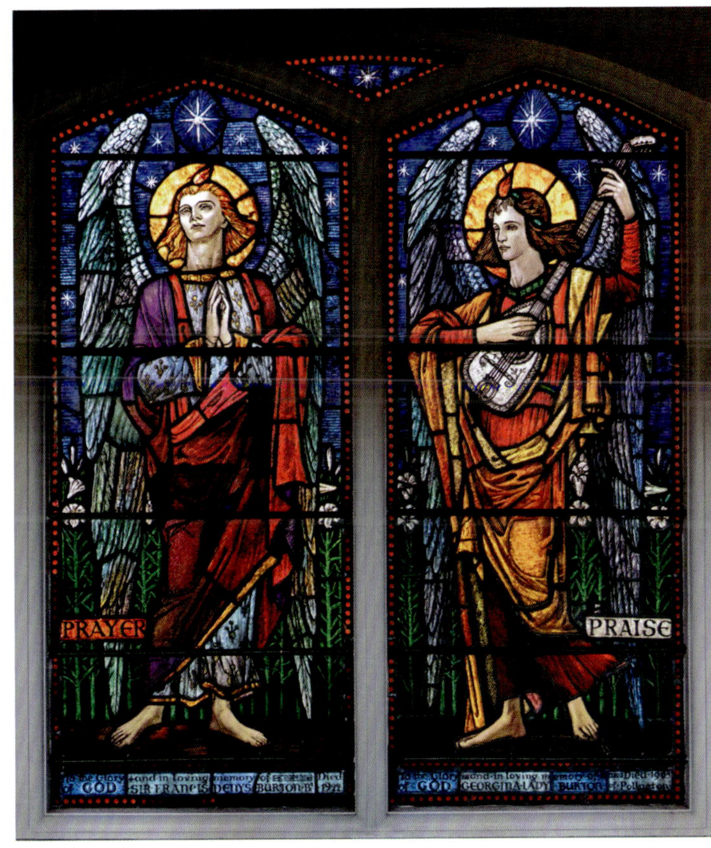

Mayo, Kilabban: C of I
CHILD, A.E.
The Crucifixion, with the Blessed Virgin and St John
1914
O'BRIEN, Catherine
'Blessed are the Pure in Heart' 1925 (sketch design, NGI)

Old Leighlin: C of I Cathedral (St Laserian's)
O'BRIEN, Catherine
Christ, with Saints Moling, Brigid, Fiacre, Canice, Patrick, John, Paul and Laserian 1934 (4 lights with extensive tracery) (sketch design, NGI)

Staplestown: C of I
CHILD, A.E.
St Hubert 1938–9 (adapted from a design by Lionel Edwards)

Tinryland: CC (St Joseph's)
CHILD, A.E.
The Baptism of Christ 1936 (2 lights)
MOLONEY, Helen
The Lamb and Tree of Jesse 1974 (sketch design, NIVAL)
Serpent 1974 (sketch design, NIVAL)

Tullow: CC (Most Holy Rosary)
MURPHY, Johnny
Resurrection, Risen Christ Among His Followers, Descent of the Holy Spirit, Assumption, Our Lady Crowned c.1962 (porch)
(A second window in the porch, for which there in a sketch design in NIVAL, was destroyed; recent replacement loosely based on original.)
WALSH, George W.
Bishop Delany, Brigidine Sisters, Patrician Brothers 2010 (3 lights)
John Paul II, Mysteries of Light (3 lights)
St Brigid's Cross and Sunburst 2006 (lower panel in link door to day chapel)

COUNTY CAVAN

Ballintemple: C of I (St Patrick's)
O'BRIEN, Catherine
Decorative window with symbols c.1957

Ballyconnell: CC (Our Lady of Lourdes)
MOLONEY, Helen
Tree of Jesse, Chalice, Sun, Symbols of the Crucifixion, the Fall, Baptism, Keys of the Kingdom, and other symbols 1967 (18 *dalle de verre* panels in choir gallery)
Symbols Relating to the Life of Christ: Loaves and Fishes, Dove, Lamb, Wine Jars, Symbols of Baptism 1967 (5 *dalle de verre*, entrance) (plan of windows, preparatory drawings and sketches, NIVAL)

Ballyhaise: CC (St Mary's)
WALSH, George W.
Last Supper 1989
St Michael 1989
St Joseph 1989
Crucifixion 1989
Eucharist 1989 (3 lights)
Assumption Flanked by Angels 1989 (3 lights)
Risen Christ Flanked by Angels 1989 (3 lights)
Two abstract single lights 1989

Ballyjamesduff: Pangur Glass Craft, Drumroragh
MULDOWNEY, Patrick
The Art of Glass 1997

Ballynarry: CC (Immaculate Virgin Mary)
WALSH, George W.
St Thérèse of Lisieux 2009
Etched glass, abstract windows 2009

Right: Beatrice Elvery, *St Killian, Immaculate Conception, St Davnet* (1912), Catholic Church (Immaculate Conception), Cross, County Cavan

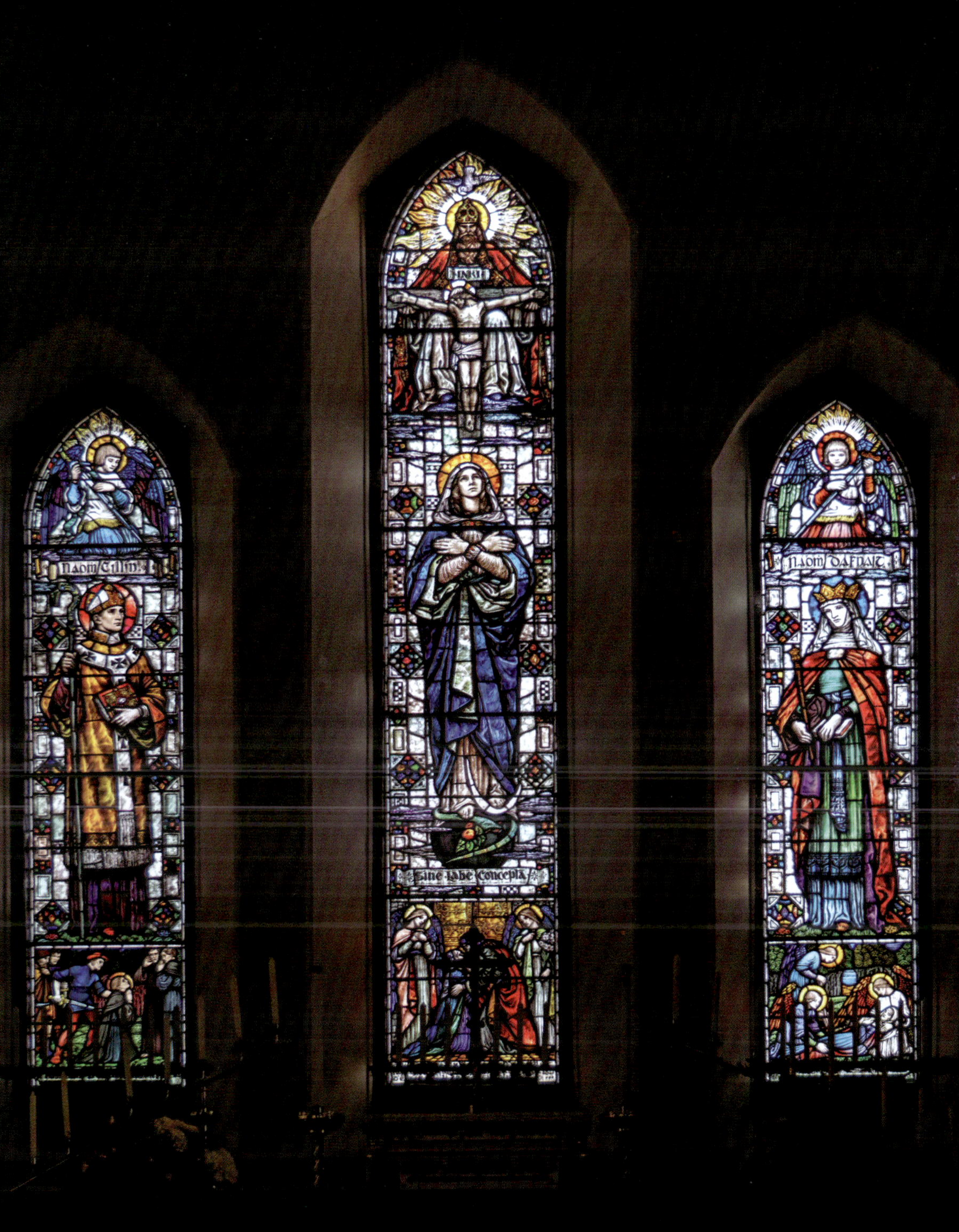
INRI
Sine labe Concepta
Naom Dafnait

Cavan Town, Farnham Street: Catholic Cathedral (St Patrick and St Felim's)
CLARKE, Terry
Risen Christ * 1941–2 (in former mortuary chapel)
DOWLING, William
The Sacred Heart Appearing to St Margaret Mary 1933
Archangel Michael Slaying the Dragon with Attendant Angels 1934
KING, Richard
St Charles Borromeo Giving the Eucharist to St Aloysius Gonzaga * 1933
(The above windows by or attributed to Dowling and King, along with five others dating from 1919–34, created at Joshua Clarke or Harry Clarke Studios, were transferred from the former Sacred Heart Convent, Leeson Street, Dublin, and installed in 1993–4. Artists of other windows yet to be identified.)
EARLEY, William (Bill) E.
Heads of the Apostles set in decorative backgrounds 1942 (twelve single lights in apse)
Lamb of God Surrounded by Angels 1942 (circular, above gallery)

Cross, near Virginia: CC (Immaculate Conception, Parish of Mullagh)
ELVERY, Beatrice
St Killian, Immaculate Conception, St Davnet 1912 (3 lights)

Kilmore: C of I Cathedral (St Fethlimidh's)
BLYTH, John
*Ascension c.*1970 (3 lights)
*St Columba, Christ as Fisher of Men, St Brigid c.*1972 (3 lights)
Both these windows were made by John Blyth for Clokey and Company, Belfast, although he formally ceased working for the company in 1966. Possibly made or part-made at his Scottish studio.
O'BRIEN, Catherine
Joy, Courage, Love 1943–4 (3 lights)
Good Shepherd 1957
Christ Blessing Little Children 1961

Kingscourt: CC (Immaculate Conception)
BECKER, Margaret
St Brigid 1988
St Ernan 1988
St Anne with the Infant Mary 1988
HONE, Evie
*The Annunciation c.*1947–8 (2 lights)
*The Ascension c.*1947–8 (2 lights) (cartoons, NGI)
*The Crucifixion c.*1947–8 (2 lights) (sketch design, Clongowes Wood College; sketch design, Irish American Cultural Institute's O'Malley Art Collection, University of Limerick; cartoons, NGI)
The Apparition of Fatima 1948–9 (3 lights and tracery, in Lady Chapel)
POLLEN, Patrick
Eucharist (abstract) 1968 (3 lights with tracery)

Muff: CC (Our Lady of Mount Carmel)
EARLEY, Willie
Assumption of Our Lady * 1974

Mullagh: CC (St Kilian's)
KELLY, John with DUNNE, Michael
Abstract stained glass scheme 1960s

Redhills: C of I (St Columba's)
O'BRIEN, Catherine
The Sower 1953–4 (3 lights) (sketch design, NGI)

Right:
Evie Hone, *The Apparition of Fatima* (1948–9), Catholic Church (Immaculate Conception), Kingscourt, County Cavan

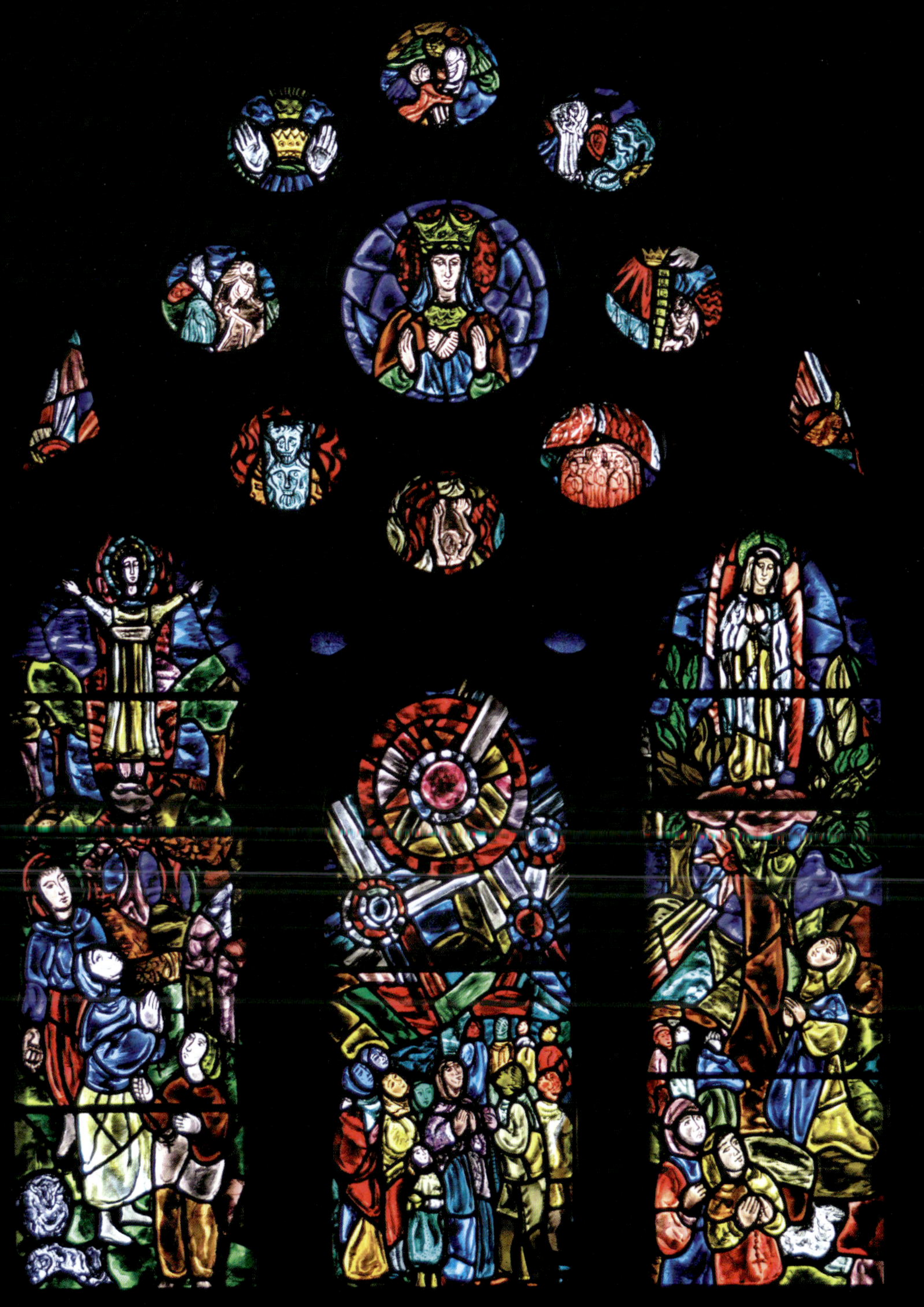

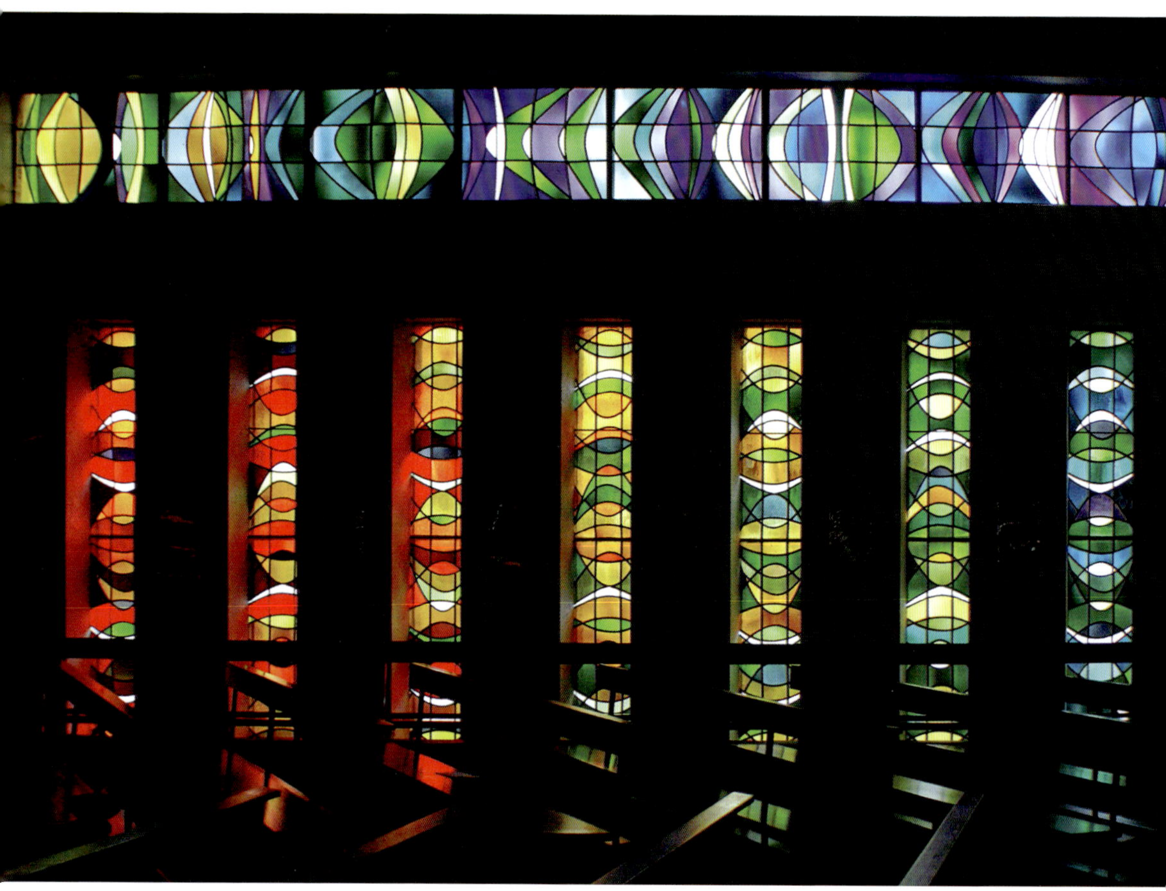

COUNTY CLARE

Ballyvaughan: CC (St John the Baptist's)
WALSH, Manus
Michael Green Memorial 2003
Laudato Si' 2016 (3 lights)

Clarecastle: CC (St Peter and St Paul's)
HEALY, Michael
Veronica's Veil, Christ Meets His Mother, and Ecce Homo 1926–7 (quality compromised by well-meaning 'improvements') (sketch design, NGI)

Above:
Johnny Murphy, *Stained glass scheme: abstract single lights and continual stained glass band,*
Catholic Church (Our Lady Assumed into Heaven)
Doonbeg, County Clare 1976

Corofin: CC (St Brigid's)
BURKE, Phyllis
*St Brigid c.*1997 (cartoons, NIVAL)

Doonbeg: CC (Our Lady Assumed into Heaven)
MURPHY, Johnny
Stained glass scheme: abstract single lights and continual stained glass band at clerestory level 1976 (sketch design, NIVAL)

Ennis, Bindon Street: C of I (St Columba's)
O'BRIEN, Catherine
Reredos 1938–47 (opus sectile mosaic; 22 panels) (sketch design, NGI)
Martha 1957–8 (porch) (sketch design, NGI)
Mary 1957–8 (porch) (sketch design, NGI)

Ennis, Gort Road: Chapel, Our Lady's Psychiatric Hospital (closed 2002, now derelict, state of window unknown)
BURKE, Phyllis
The Annunciation 1962 (circular) (cartoons, NIVAL)

Ennis: Franciscan Friary Church
DOWLING, William
Sacred Heart with Symbols of Christ's Passion 1953 (rose) (preliminary designs, TCD)
(Created at Harry Clarke Studios.)
MURPHY, Johnny
Abstract and symbolic windows including Holy Spirit motif 1967

Kildysart: CC (St Michael's)
DOWLING, William
Crucifixion 1953 (3 lights)
(Created at Harry Clarke Studios.)

Kilkee: CC (Immaculate Conception and St Senan's)
DOWD MURPHY, Róisín and MURPHY, Johnny
Crucifixion, Scenes from the Life of Christ, symbols, and text of the Creed 1963 (14 lights)
'Woman why weepest thou' 1963
'This is my beloved son' 1963
St Patrick 1963 (2 lights)
St Senan 1963 (2 lights)
St Ita 1963 (2 lights)
St Brigid 1963 (2 lights)
St Dympna 1963 (2 lights)
Christ the King 1963 (6 lights)
Star of the Sea 1963 (6 lights)
Abstracts lights throughout the church
(Celia Harriss Crampton of Murphy-Devitt Studios worked on these windows) (cartoons, NIVAL)
Note: *St Flannan* window removed and installed in Lisdeen CC, County Clare.

Killaloe: CC (St Flannan's)
CLARKE, Harry
The Presentation of Our Lord, with the Annunciation and Flight into Egypt (B) 1927

Kilrush: CC (St Senan's)
EARLEY, Willie
Holy Spirit, Annunciation, Nativity, Presentation in the Temple, Jesus Teaching the Elders, Lamb of God date unknown (rose)

Kilshanny: CC (St Augustine's)
WALSH, George W.
Risen Christ and celebration of vocations 1996 (3 lights)

Knockerra: CC (St Senan's)
MURPHY, Johnny (and unidentified NCA student/graduate, supervised by Johnny Murphy)
St Senan and St Imy 1961 (2 lights) (sketch designs, NIVAL)
Baptism of Christ 1961 (3 lights)
Resurrection 1961 (3 lights)
Abstract lights with symbols 1961

Labasheeda: CC (St Ciarán's)
MURPHY, Johnny
Windows with screen-printed pattern 1976 (sketch design, NIVAL)
(Ann FitzGibbon assisted on these windows in Murphy-Devitt Studios.)

Lahinch: CC (Immaculate Conception)
WALSH, George W.
Annunciation, Nativity, Presentation in the Temple 1995 (3 lights)
Our Lady 1995 (circular)

Lisdeen, near Kilkee: CC (St Flannan's)
MURPHY, Johnny
St Flannan 1963 (3 lights) (altered in 2011 when transferred from Kilkee CC, and now signed P.G. Leyden 2011)

Lissycasey: CC (Our Lady of the Wayside)
MURPHY, Johnny and TIMLIN, Michael
Wall of Glass Depicting Everyday Life 1979 (cartoons, NIVAL)
Abstract lead-lights 1979

Monmore: CC (Little Senan's)
DOWD MURPHY, Róisín and MURPHY, Johnny
St Canara 1960
St Imy 1960
St Brigid 1960
St Flannan 1960
St Senan 1960
St Lua 1960
Old Man with Children (inspired by Patrick Pearse's story *Iosagán*) 1960 (3 lights)
Abstract lights 1960
Twelve Apostles c.1960 (cartoons, NIVAL)

Newmarket-on-Fergus: Carrigoran House (care centre)
MURPHY, Johnny
Abstract wall 1974 (*dalle de verre*)

Newmarket-on-Fergus: CC (Our Lady of the Rosary)
MURPHY, Johnny
Scheme of abstract lights 1971
(Paul Britton assisted on these windows in Murphy-Devitt Studios.)

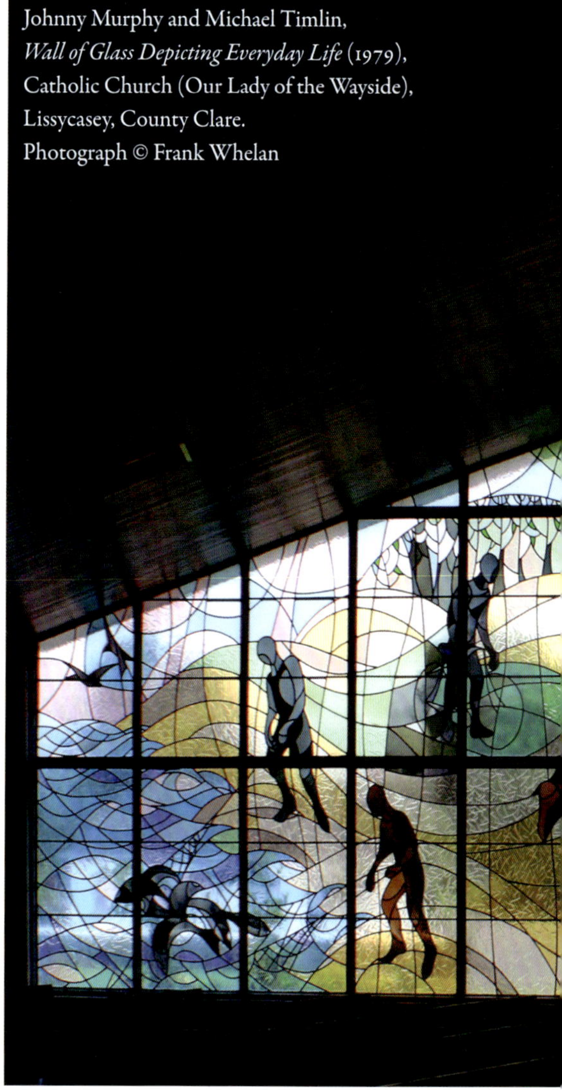
Johnny Murphy and Michael Timlin, *Wall of Glass Depicting Everyday Life* (1979), Catholic Church (Our Lady of the Wayside), Lissycasey, County Clare. Photograph © Frank Whelan

New Quay: CC (St Patrick's)
WALSH, George W.
Our Lady of the Fertile Rock c.1992 (rose)

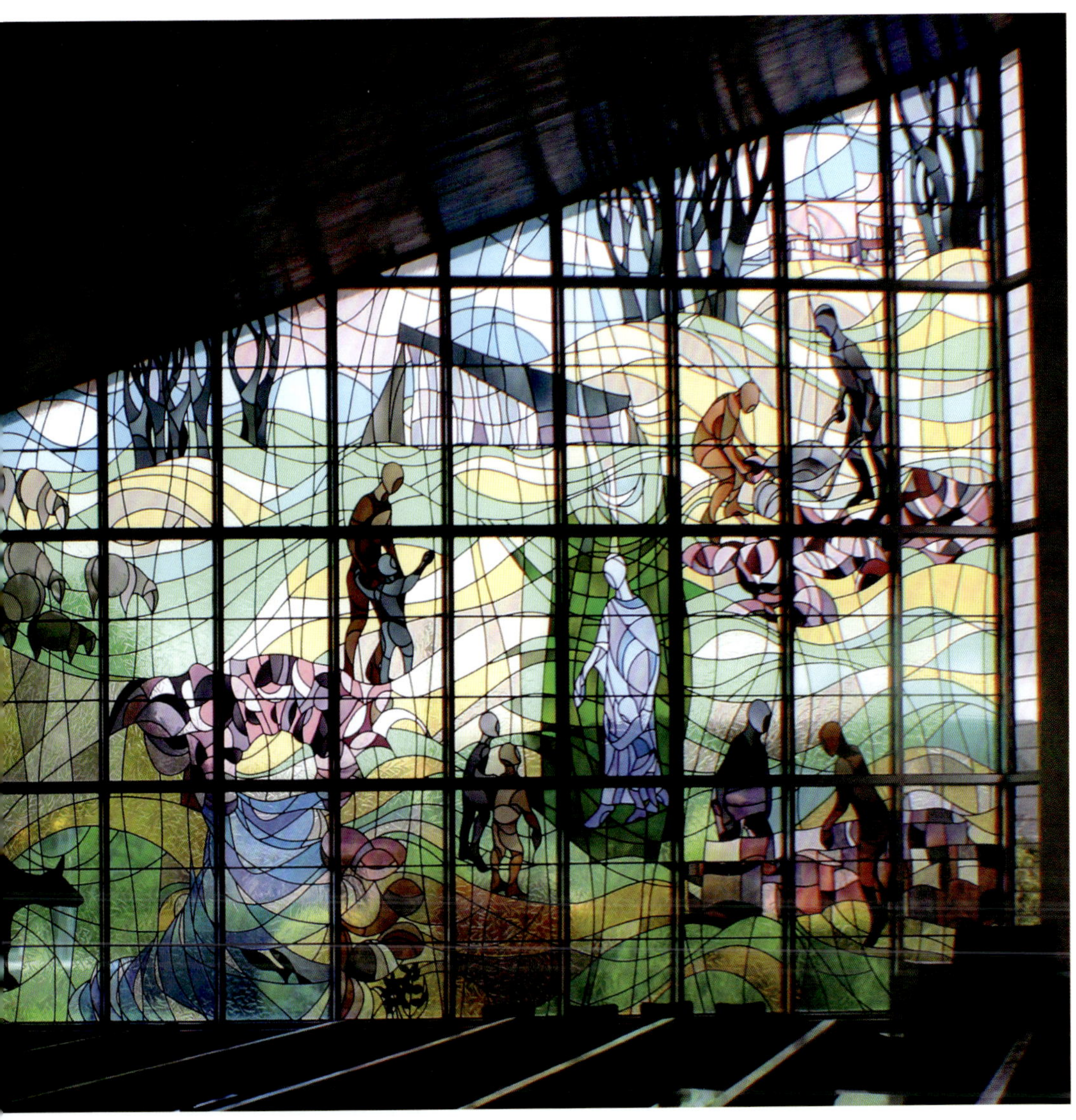

Scariff: CC (Church of the Sacred Heart)
KING, Richard
St Donatus and St Caimin 1930–1 (2 lights)
St Colman MacDuagh and St Flannan 1930–1 (2 lights)
St Brigid and St Clare 1931–2 (2 lights)
St Anthony of Padua and St Augustine 1931–2 (2 lights)
(All above created at Harry Clarke Studios.)

Tuamgraney: C of I (St Cronan's)
CHILD, A.E.
The Risen Christ with Two Angels 1906 (3 lights)
(moved from Sixmilebridge C of I in 1990)

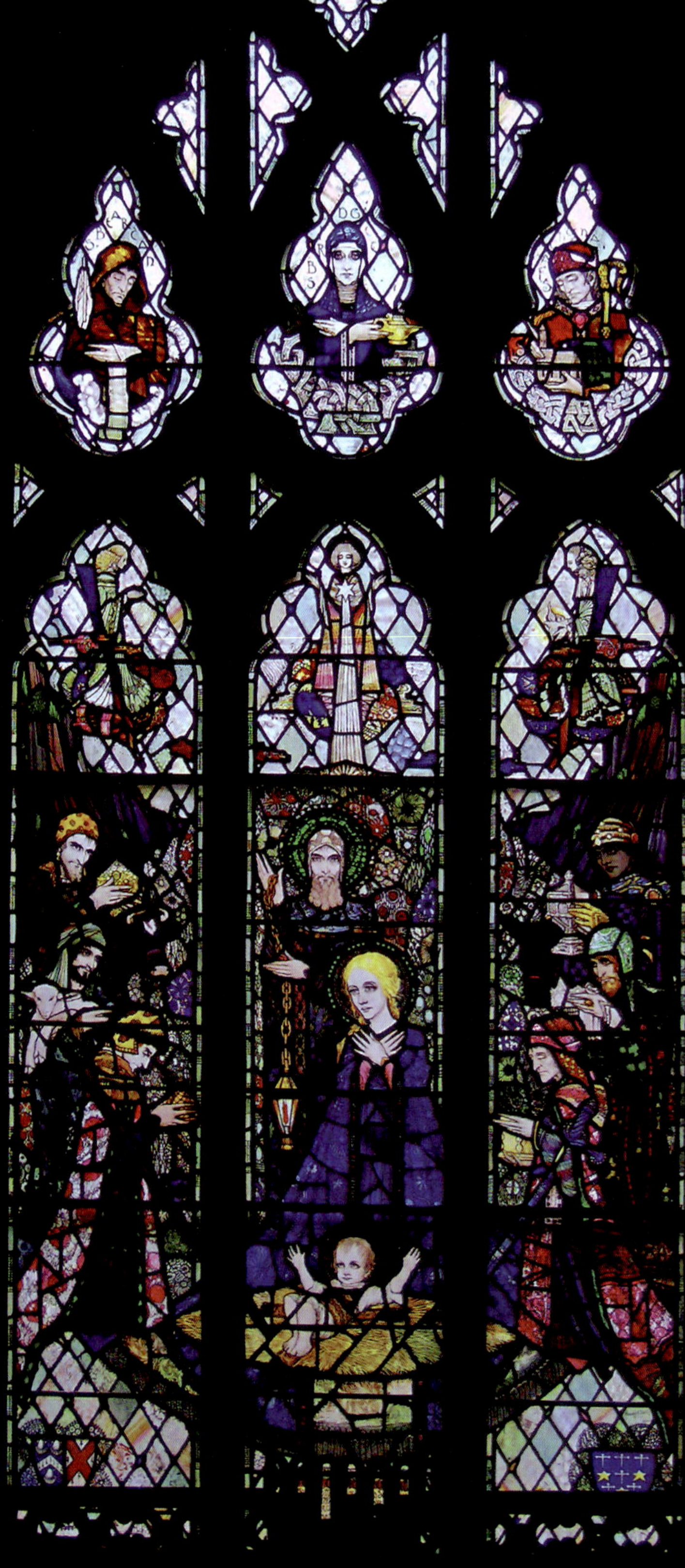

COUNTY CORK

Ballineen (Ballymoney): C of I (St Paul's; church closed in 1991, currently derelict)
O'BRIEN, Catherine
Pilgrim's Progress 1930 (centre light) (sketch design, NGI)
Pilgrim's Progress 1936 (2 side lights) (sketch designs, NGI)

Ballyhooly, near Castletownroche: CC (Nativity of the Blessed Virgin Mary)
MURPHY, Johnny
Scheme of abstract lights 1969 (sketch design, NIVAL)

Bandon: CC (Immaculate Conception)
DOWLING, William
Nativity Surrounded by the Magi and Shepherds * 1948 (5 lights with tracery; drawing, TCD)

Boherbue: CC (Immaculate Conception)
WALSH, George Stephen
Baptism of Christ 1969
Stations of the Cross and cross behind altar 1969 (painted antique glass, laminated on marine ply mounted on marble)

Caheragh: CC (Holy Family)
DOWD MURPHY, Róisín and MURPHY, Johnny
Blessed Thaddeus 1963 (2 lights)
St Fachtna 1963 (2 lights)
St Kieran 1963 (2 lights)
St Finbar 1963 (2 lights)
Church symbols, twin round windows, twin abstracts, dome window, porch windows etc. 1963 (Celia Harriss Crampton of Murphy-Devitt Studios worked on these windows) (sketch designs and cartoons, NIVAL)

Carrigaline: CC (Our Lady and St John)
MEHEGAN, Cormac
Crucifixion with Annunciation and St John date unknown (3 lights)

Carrigaline: C of I (St Mary's)
McGOLDRICK, Hubert
St George (war memorial) *c.*1923

Castletownbere: CC (Sacred Heart)
CHILD, A.E.
St John the Evangelist, The Risen Christ, St John the Baptist, with St John on Patmos, the Deposition, and the Baptism of Christ 1908–10 (3 lights)
O'BRIEN, Catherine
The Adoration of the Lamb of God 1910 (rose)
RHIND, Ethel
The Annunciation 1910 (2 lights)
The Sacred Heart 1910 (2 lights)

Castletownroche: C of I
McGOLDRICK, Hubert
Christ with Crown of Life, Angels and Soldiers 1920–1 (3 lights) (sketch design, NGI)

Castletownshend: C of I (St Barrahane's)
CLARKE, Harry
The Nativity with the Adoration of the Kings and the Shepherds with St Brigid, St Bearcan and St Fachtna (tracery lights) 1918 (3 lights)
St Louis IX, King of France, and St Martin of Tours 1921 (2 lights)
St Luke Attended by St Cecilia, St Barrahane and St Fidelio (A) 1926

Left:
Harry Clarke, *The Nativity with the Adoration of the Kings and the Shepherds with St Brigid, St Bearcan and St Fachtna* (1918), Church of Ireland (St Barrahane's), Castletownshend, County Cork

Clogagh: CC (St Moluada's)
WALSH, George Stephen
Crucifixion date unknown

Cloyne: C of I Cathedral (St Colman's)
PYE, Patrick
Scenes from the Life of St Colman 1962 (2 lights)

Cork City, Ballyphehane: CC (Church of the Assumption), Pearse Road
MEHEGAN, Cormac
Our Lady with Dove c.1956 (5 lights)

Cork City, Blackpool: CC (St Brendan's), Glen Avenue, The Glen
WALSH, George W.
St Brendan the Navigator 1973 (triangular)
Nautical-inspired abstract side windows 1973

Cork City, Blackrock: CC (St Joseph's SMA), Blackrock Road
MEHEGAN, Cormac
St Joseph, Madonna and Child, St Theresa 1950 (3 lights)

Cork City, Blackrock: CC (St Michael's), Blackrock Road
DOWD MURPHY, Róisín and MURPHY, Johnny
'I Will Send Down on Earth a Shower of Roses' c.1960
'Do You at Least Endeavour to Console Me' c.1960 (cartoons, NIVAL)
Twenty windows featuring church symbols 1964 (3 lights)
Holy Spirit 1964 (5 lights, in baptistry)
(Celia Harriss Crampton of Murphy-Devitt Studios worked on the 1964 windows.)

Cork City, Blackrock: Ursuline Convent Chapel, Convent Road
MACKEY, Mary
East window 2005
West window 2005

Cork City, Blackrock: Ursuline Convent Secondary School, Convent Road
MACKEY, Mary
Untitled 2002 (5 lights)

Cork City, Carrigrohane Road: Cork County Council Library
DAWSON, Debbie
Three Colours Blue 2000 (light box)

Cork City, College Road: Poor Clares Monastery Oratory
MULDOWNEY, Patrick
St Clare 2004
St Francis of Assisi 2004

Cork City, Douglas: C of I (St Luke's), Churchyard Lane
O'BRIEN, Catherine
The Good Shepherd 1949 (sketch designs, NGI)

Cork City, Emmet Place: Crawford Municipal Art Gallery
CLARKE, Harry
The Consecration of St Mel by St Patrick 1910 (panel)
The Godhead Enthroned 1911 (panel)
The Meeting of St Brendan with the Unhappy Judas 1913 (panel)
HONE, Evie
St Hubert c.1947 (roundel; in storage)
MACKEY, Mary
Glimpse of Sudden and Brief Freedom 2000 (panel, in storage)
Strange Navigations 2001 (panel, in storage)
SCANLON, James
Lonradh 1993 (on staircase landing)

Cork City, Emmet Place: Luigi Malone's Restaurant
DAWSON, Debbie
Untitled (inspired by Clarice Cliff) 2003 (pyramid-shaped roof lights and door panels for ladies and gents toilets)

Cork City, Grenville Place: Mercy University Hospital
MEHEGAN, Cormac
Archangel Michael date unknown (3 lights, mortuary chapel)

Cork City, Fr Mathew Quay: CC (Holy Trinity)
CLARKE, Harry
Sacred Heart and St Francis (B) 1918–19 (2 lights)
MURPHY, Johnny
Abstract lights 1968

Cork City, Frankfield: CC (Church of the Incarnation), Grange Road
WALSH, George W.
Annunciation and Nativity 1974
Crucifixion and Deposition 1974

Cork City, Frankfield: C of I (Holy Trinity)
SCANLON, James
Abstract window, theme of red 1990
Abstract window, theme of blue 1990
Abstract window, theme of green 1990

Cork City, Grattan Street: Share Housing
SCANLON, James
Five abstract windows 1989–90

Cork City, Liberty Street: CC (St Francis's)
CLARKE, Terry
*St Elizabeth of Hungary c.*1949–51
*St Bernardine of Sienna c.*1949–51
*St Joseph * c.*1949–51
*Ecce Cor * c.*1949–51
DOWLING, William
*St Louis c.*1949–51
*St Francis c.*1949–51
*St Paschal Baylon c.*1949–51
*Blessed Virgin * c.*1949–51
*Abstract c.*1949–51 (7 lights with extensive tracery)
(All above created at Harry Clarke Studios.)
Decorative glazed door panels by the Dublin Glass and Paint Company.

Cork City, Lower Glanmire Road: CC (St Patrick's)
McGOLDRICK, Hubert
The Baptism of Christ 1924
RHIND, Ethel
The Risen Christ and Two Angels 1908 (opus sectile mosaic)

Cork City, Mayfield: CC (Our Lady Crowned), North Ring Road
DOWD MURPHY, Róisín and MURPHY, Johnny
Scheme of Life of Christ, dome and abstracts 1962 (sketch design and cartoons, NIVAL)

Below: Róisín Dowd Murphy and Johnny Murphy, *Risen Christ* (1962), Catholic Church (Our Lady Crowned), Mayfield, Cork. Photograph © Finola Finlay

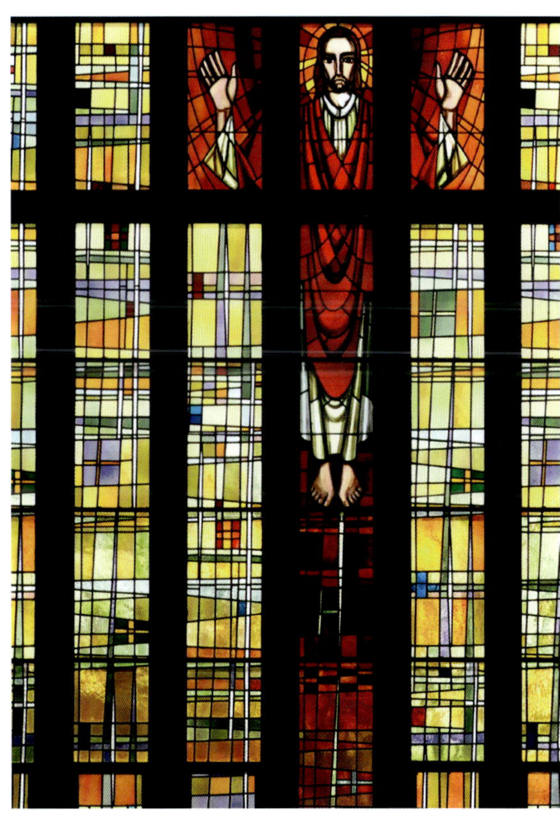

Cork City, Mayfield: CC (St Joseph's), Old Youghal Road
HEALY, Michael
Christ with St Thomas 1915 (2 lights)
Christ with Martha and Mary 1916 (2 lights) (sketch design, NGI)

Cork City, Military Hill: Collins Barracks Chapel
HONE, Evie
Christ in Glory with the Archangel Michael and St Patrick 1938–9 (3 lights)
*Blessed Virgin Mary with a Soldier Kneeling in Thanksgiving c.*1947
*The Sacred Heart and the Miracle of the Bread at Gougane Barra c.*1947

Cork City, Montenotte: St Dominic's Retreat Centre, Ennismore
WALSH, George W.
Abstract stained glass screen 2001
Tabernacle 2001

Cork City, Rochestown: St Francis College (Capuchins), Monastery Road
DOWD MURPHY, Róisín and MURPHY, Johnny
Scenes from the Life of St Francis 1961–2 (chapel)
Canticle of the Creatures 1961–2 (clerestory level, chapel) (sketch design and cartoons, NIVAL)
HEALY, Michael
Saints Kevin, Columba, Enda and Finbarr 1906 (4 lights, over entrance door)

Cork City, Roman Street: Catholic Cathedral (St Mary and St Anne's, also known as the North Cathedral)
DOWLING, William
Crucifixion 1967 (5 lights)
Holy Spirit 1967
Abstract chancel windows 1967
(All above created at Harry Clarke Studios.)
SCANLON, James
Two abstract windows 1995 (Blessed Sacrament Chapel)

Cork City, Summerhill: Tigh Filí Cultural Centre (formerly St Luke's C of I)
CHILD, A.E.
The Resurrection 1912 (sketch design, NGI)
O'BRIEN, Catherine
St Luke 1950
The Light of the World 1950

Cork City, Shandon: C of I (St Anne's), Church Street
McGOLDRICK, Hubert
St Luke 1937 (oval)

Cork City, Tobin Street: Triskel Arts Centre
COTTER, Maud
Route Impeller 1985 (originally sited on second floor, Triskel Arts Centre)

Cork City, Turners Cross: CC (Christ the King), Evergreen Road
McGOLDRICK, Hubert
The Crucifixion, with the Blessed Virgin Mary and St John 1935–6 (opus sectile mosaic)
The abstract windows were designed *c.*1931 by Annette Cremin Byrne, the Chicago-based artist and wife of Barry Byrne, the church's architect. Most likely fabricated in Ireland.

Cork City, Western Road: Honan Chapel (St Finbarr's), University College Cork
CLARKE, Harry
St Patrick, St Brigid and St Columcille 1915 (3 lights)
St Finbarr 1916
St Ita 1916
St Albert 1916
St Gobnait 1916
St Brendan 1916 (Michael Healy prepared a sketch design for this window, NGI)
St Declan 1916
St Joseph 1917
Our Lady of Sorrows 1917

CHILD, A.E.
Our Lord Risen and Triumphant 1916
St Ailbe 1916
St Colman 1916
St Fachtna 1916
O'BRIEN, Catherine
St Flannan 1916 (sketch design, NGI)
St Mainchin 1916
Scenes from the Life of St John 1916
RHIND, Ethel
St Carthage 1916

Cork City, Wilton: Cork University Hospital
DAWSON, Debbie
Water: The Cycle of a River 2001 (Oncology Department. This work in located in three areas: eight panels in entrance doors; eight panels in corridor; wall of glass in waiting area.)
WALSH, George W.
Risen Christ 1972 (Hospital Chapel)
Healing the Sick 1972 (Hospital Chapel)

Crosshaven: Presentation Convent chapel (convent closed, 2015)
DOWD MURPHY, Róisín and MURPHY, Johnny
St Finbarr 1974
Seven windows with church symbols 1974

Darrara: CC (Sacred Heart)
WALSH, George W.
*Archangel Michael c.*1990
*Holy Family c.*1990
*Marian Apparition c.*1990 (rose)

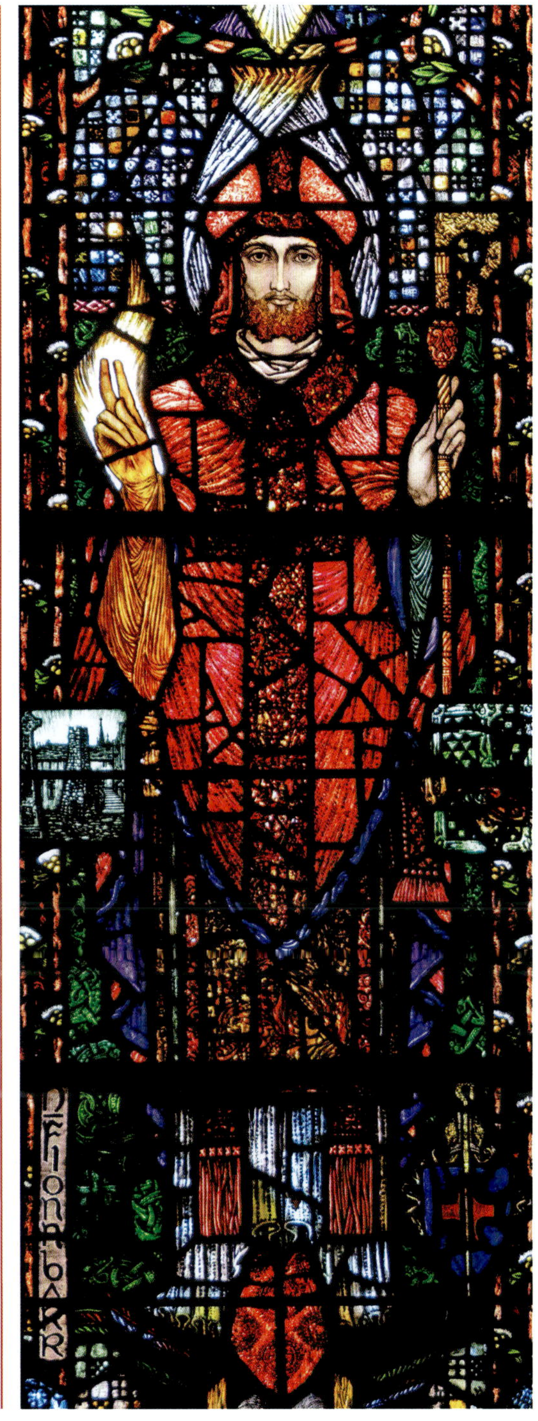

Right:
Harry Clarke, detail of *St Finbarr* (1916), Honan Chapel, University College Cork, Cork City. Reproduced courtesy of the Honan Trust

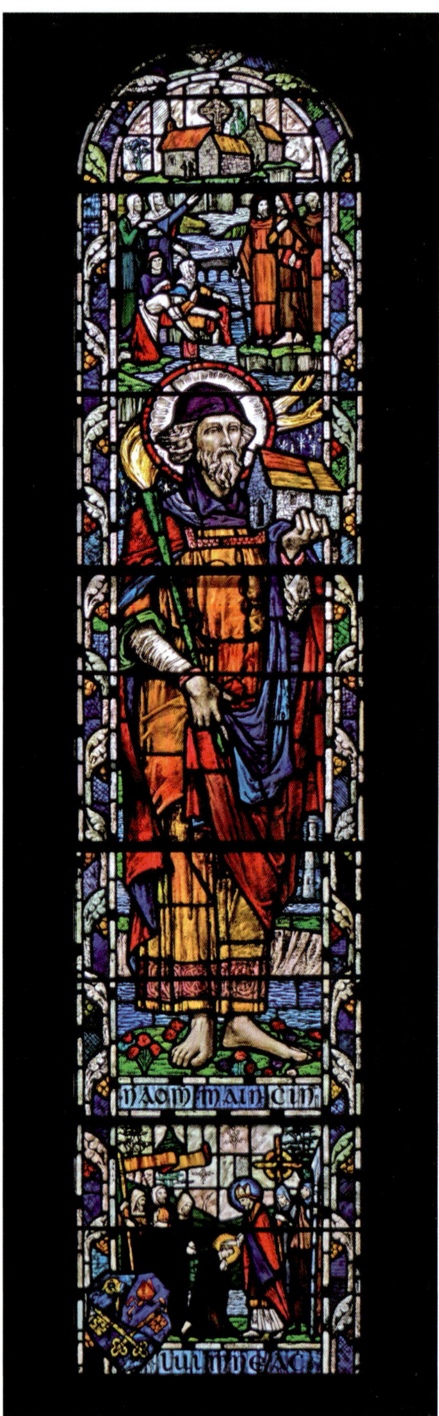

Desertserges, near Enniskeane: C of I (now closed)
O'BRIEN, Catherine
David 1946 (sketch design, NGI)
Good Shepherd 1946 (sketch design, NGI)
St John 1946 (sketch design, NGI)
Our Lord Blessing Little Children c.1955
St Cecilia (sketch design, NGI) 1961

Drimoleague: CC (All Saints)
DOWLING, William
Life Journey of an Irish Catholic: Baptism, Family Prayers, First Communion, Choosing a Way of Life, Mass, Work and Play, Holy Viaticum and Soul Rising to Heaven 1956–62 (wall of glass, comprising eighteen panels, nine figurative and nine abstract) (preliminary drawings, TCD)
(Created at Harry Clarke Studios.)

Dromore: CC (St Joseph's)
EARLEY, Willie
Blessed Virgin, Annunciation, Nativity, with Angels c.1955 (lunette)

Eyeries: CC (St Kentigern's)
WALSH, George W.
History of Ireland, Arrival of Christianity, Life of Christ, Local Life, the Elements 1996 (2 lights)
Fishing, St Brendan 1996 (2 lights)
Farming, Husbandry 1996 (2 lights)
St Finbarr, Emigration 1996 (2 lights)
Evolution, Formation of the Earth 1996 (2 lights)
Prehistory, Megaliths 1996 (2 lights)
Arrival of Christianity 1996 (2 lights)
Resurrection 1996 (2 lights)
Baptism, Eucharist 1996 (2 lights)
Annunciation, Nativity 1996 (2 lights)
Go in Peace 1996 (2 lights)

Left: Catherine O'Brien, *St Mainchin* (1916), Honan Chapel, University College Cork, Cork City. Reproduced courtesy of the Honan Trust

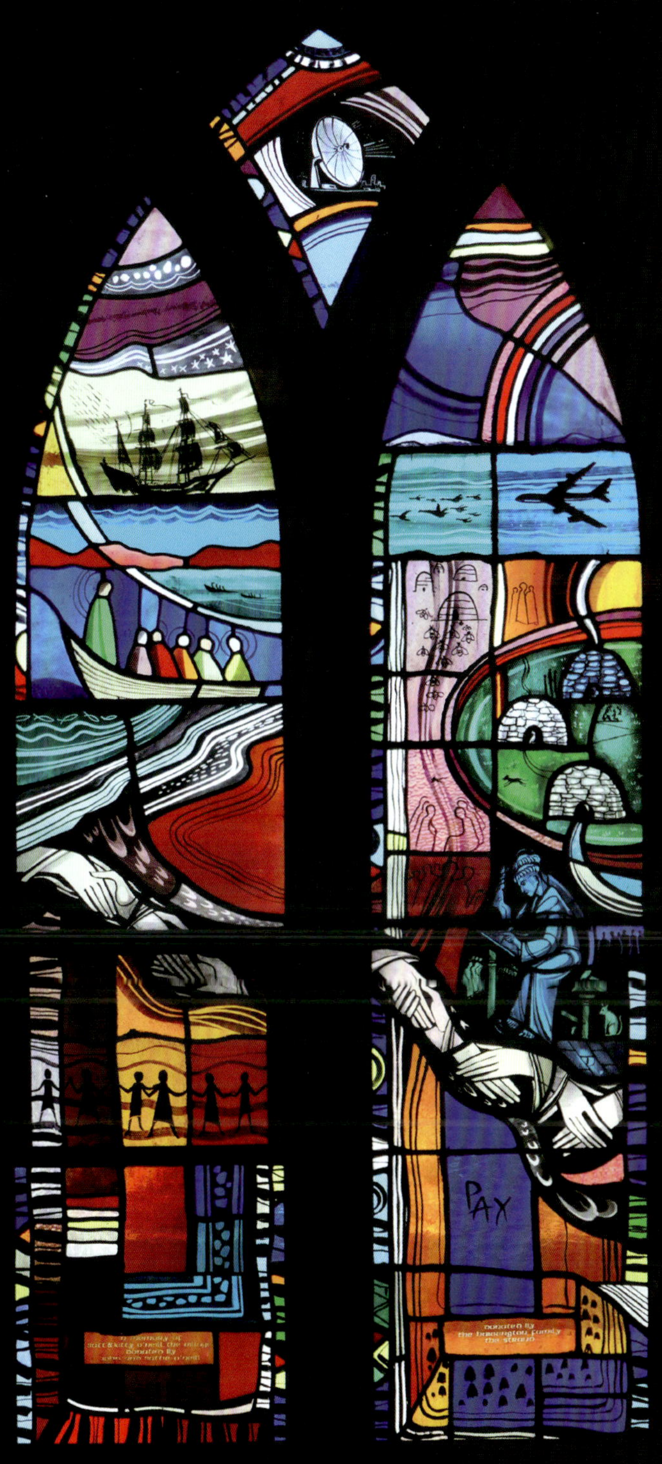

George W. Walsh, *St Finbarr, Emigration* (1996), Catholic Church (St Kentigern's), Eyeries, County Cork. Photograph © Finola Finlay

Glenville (Ardnageehy): C of I (St Mary's)
O'BRIEN, Catherine
St John and the Blessed Virgin Mary, with Cherubs 1926 (2 lights)

Inchigeela: CC (St Finbarr and the Holy Angels)
KELLY, Kevin
Resurrection 2001
Assumption of Our Lady 2002
St Oliver Plunkett 2002
Resurrection 2005 (light box)
Nativity 2005 (light box)
(All above created at Abbey Stained Glass Studios.)

Inniscarra: C of I (St Senan's)
O'BRIEN, Catherine
Angel of Prayer 1918
Angel of Praise 1918

Innishannon: C of I (Christ Church)
CHILD, A.E.
Crown of Life (war memorial) 1919 (2 lights)

Kilbrittain: CC (St Patrick's)
TOMLIN, Stanley
Crucifixion 1951 (in cruciform shape)
Madonna and Child 1951
St Joseph 1951

Kilcoe: CC (Most Holy Rosary)
CHILD, A.E.
Virgin and Child with the Three Magi 1905 (rose) (painted by Catherine O'Brien)
St Patrick, St Brigid, the Crucifixion 1905 (2 lights) (painted by Catherine O'Brien)
CLARKE, Terry
Virgin and Child, Surrounded by Scenes from the Life of Mary 1943 (rose)

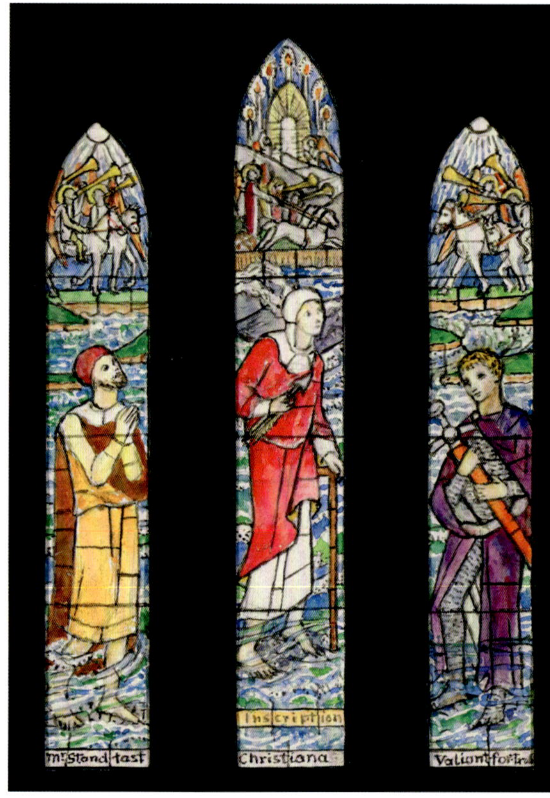

Above: Catherine O'Brien, *Pilgrim's Progress*, Church of Ireland (St Multose's), Kinsale, Co Cork. Collection NGI. Photograph © NGI

Kinsale: C of I (St Multose's)
O'BRIEN, Catherine
The Miraculous Draft of Fishes 1928 (3 lights)
Crossing the Bar 1933 (5 lights)
Pilgrim's Progress: Old Honesty, Christiana, Valiant for Truth 1962 (3 lights) (sketch designs, NGI)

Lowertown: CC (Seven Sacraments)
MURPHY, Johnny
Holy Spirit 1967 (*dalle de verre*) (sketch designs, NIVAL)

Macroom: CC (St Colman's)
MAC CANA, Carin
St Colman mid 1990s (porch)
KING, Richard
*Untitled stained glass panel of Virgin and Child as King and Queen of Heaven c.*1963 (porch)

Mallow: CC (Church of the Resurrection)
DOWD MURPHY, Róisín
Our Lady 1989 (3 light)
MURPHY, Johnny
Crucifixion 1967 (3 light)
Resurrection 1967 (3 light)
MURPHY, Johnny and CORCORAN, Terry
Scenes from New Testament (ten 3 lights) and abstract lights 1967 (sketch designs and cartoons, NIVAL)

Mallow: C of I (St James's)
O'BRIEN, Catherine
The Crucifixion 1950
St Augustine 1950

Mallow: Mallow Swimming Pool
MACKEY, Mary
Untitled 1998 (thirty-two panels fixed inside double glazed units)

Midleton: CC (Most Holy Rosary)
MULDOWNEY, Patrick
Nano Nagle 1996
Edmund Rice 1996
Catherine McAuley 1996

Millstreet: CC (St Patrick's)
DOWLING, William
Adoration of the Magi 1939 (sketch design, TCD)
(Created at Harry Clarke Studios.)

Mitchelstown: CC (Our Lady Conceived Without Sin)
BURKE, Phyllis
*Angels I c.*1995 (cartoons, NIVAL)
*Angels II c.*1995 (cartoons, NIVAL)

Rath: CC (Sacred Heart)
DOWD MURPHY, Róisín and MURPHY, Johnny
Assumption of Our Lady 1963
'I Confess to Almighty God' 1963
St Fachtna 1963
St Teresa 1963
St Francis 1963
St Joseph 1963
St Kieran 1963
St Peter 1963
'Woman, Why Art Thou Weeping' 1963
'This is My Beloved Son' 1963
Holy Spirit 1963
Abstract lights 1963

Reananerree (Reidh na nDoiri), near Ballyvourney: CC
LYONS, Derry (Diarmuid O'Liathain)
Madonna and Child 1951

Rosscarbery: Convent of Mercy (currently closed)
WALSH, George W.
Stations of the Cross early 1970s (seven windows)

Schull: CC (St Mary's)
BURKE, Phyllis
*Scoil Mhuire c.*1988
*Abstract with Boat c.*1988 (in porch)

Skibbereen: Heritage Centre
MAC CANA, Carin
Marine Life in Lough Hyne date unknown (entrance hall)

Timoleague: CC (Nativity of the Blessed Virgin)
DOWLING, William and KING, Richard (under the supervision of CLARKE, Harry)
Holy Family, Flight into Egypt, Coronation of the Virgin, the Assumption, Our Lord Meets His Mother on the Way Calvary, Miracle at Cana, Death of St Joseph 1930–1 (3 lights) (pencil design, TCD)

COUNTY DERRY/LONDONDERRY

Ballinderry: C of I (St John's)
HEALY, Michael
Joshua and the Captain of the Hosts of the Lord, with illustrations of 2 Kings 13:16 and Psalm 34:4 1921 (2 lights) (sketch design, NGI)

Below: Michael Healy, *Joshua and the Captain of the Hosts of the Lord, with illustrations of 2 Kings 13:16 and Psalm 34:4* (1921), Church of Ireland (St John's), Ballinderry. County Derry. Collection NGI. Photograph © NGI

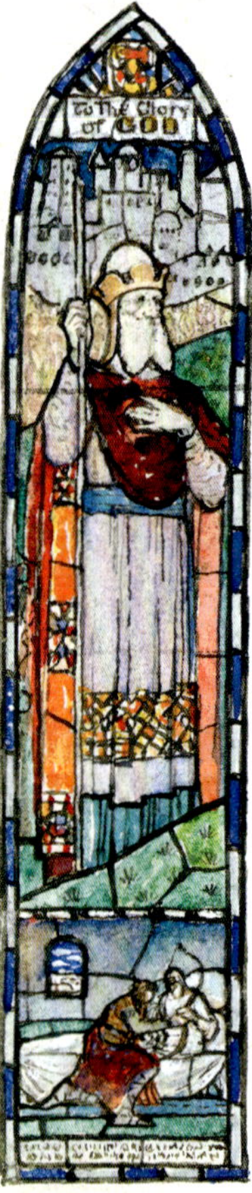

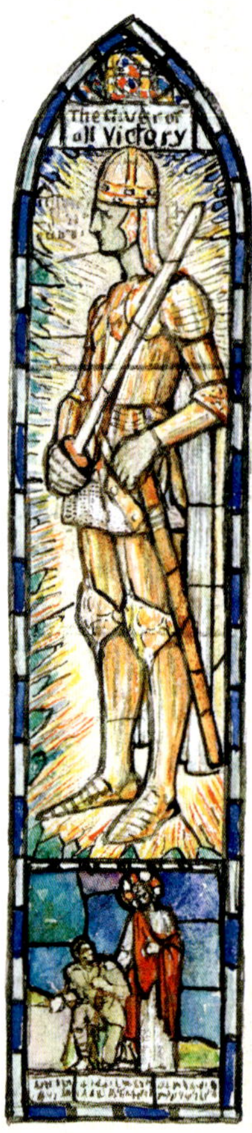

Banagher, near Derrychrier: C of I (St Moresius's)
PURSER, Sarah
'Blessed Are the Pure in Heart' 1904 (painted by Catherine O'Brien)

Castlerock: C of I (Christ Church)
HEALY, Michael
St Patrick and St Columba 1918
'Suffer Little Children to Come unto Me' 1932 (sketch design, NGI)

Coleraine: Causeway Hospital Chapel
DOWD MURPHY, Róisín
'Homage to Grandparents' 2001 (pair of lights)

Culmore: C of I (Holy Trinity)
O'BRIEN, Catherine
St Peter and St Andrew 1948 (2 lights) (sketch design, NGI)

Derry City, Bishop Street: Nazareth House (demolished 2019; plans to salvage the stained glass and incorporate in new apartment building to be built on site in 2021)
POLLEN, Patrick
Christian symbols 1962
Originally a four-light window, it was removed when the chapel was demolished in 2019 and the four lights were reduced in size and installed as individual windows in the replacement building.

Derry City, Buncrana Road: St Columb's College Oratory
MOLONEY, Helen
Christ, with Crucifixion Scene in Background 1979
St Peter, Symbolised by the Key he is Holding and the References to Fishing 1979
St Columb, with Red Globe Indicative of Iona 1979
St Columb, and Monks Voyaging to Iona and Scribe in

lower right corner Symbolising Education 1979 (sketch designs, NIVAL)

Derry City, Culmore Road: C of I (St Peter's)
HENRY, Olive
Agnus Dei * *c.*1966 (3 lights)
(Created at Clokey and Company, Belfast.)

Derry City, London Street: C of I Cathedral (St Columb's)
MARR, Edward
The Ideal Wife and Mother 1947 (3 lights)

Glendermott, Altnagelvin: C of I
BRANIFF, Daniel
*Angel and Women at the Tomb c.*1968 (2 lights)

Macosquin: C of I (St Mary's)
ELVERY, Beatrice
Moses and the Gifts of the Tabernacle, St Peter Raising Dorcas 1907 (2 lights)

Maghera: St Patrick's College Chapel, Coleraine Road
FERRAN, Brian
Three St Patrick-themed windows 1989

Tamnaherin: CC (St Mary's)
KELLY, John
Abstract scheme 1966 (two 6 lights, and two tall 12-panelled windows)
(Created at Abbey Stained Glass Studios.)

COUNTY DONEGAL

Ardara: CC (Holy Family)
HONE, Evie
Christ Among the Doctors, David, Moses and the Symbols of the Evangelists 1953 (rose) (sketch design, NGI; cartoons, TCD)

Ballyshannon: Finner Camp (home of 28th Infantry Battalion, Irish Army), Chapel
WALSH, George W.
How We Remember 2010
Baptism 2010
Communion 2010
Nativity 2010
Resurrection 2010
Stations of the Cross 2010

Buncrana: C of I (Christ Church)
O'BRIEN, Catherine
The Pilgrimage of Life, with St Brigid and St Columba 1951 (2 lights)

Burt: CC (St Aengus's)
MOLONEY, Helen
Continuous band of abstract stained glass representing darkness into light 1967

Carndonagh: C of I
CHILD, A.E.
The Resurrection 1905 (2 lights)

Convoy: CC (St Mary's)
WALSH, George W.
All windows, abstract 1972

Convoy: C of I (St Ninian's)
PYE, Patrick
Three Marys at the Tomb 1967–8 (3 lights)

Creeslough: Ards Friary
DOWD MURPHY, Róisín and MURPHY, Johnny
St Francis 1966 (5 lights)
Our Lady 1966 (6 lights)
Church symbols, abstracts, porch windows 1966 (sketch designs, NIVAL)

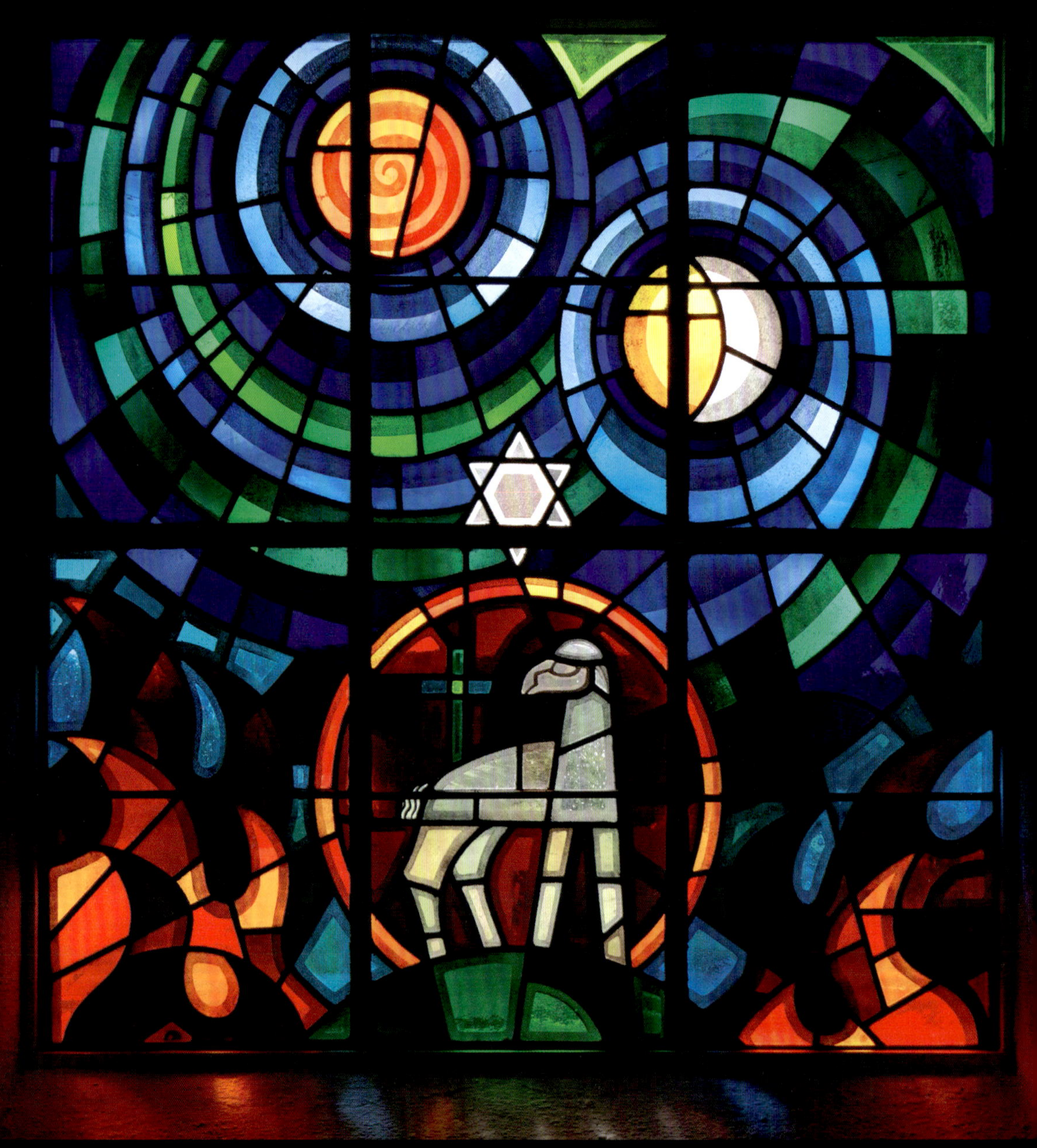

Helen Moloney, *Christ as the Light of the World Symbolised by the Lamb, within a Nimbus Incorporating a Latin Cross Symbolising the Crucifixion* (1977), Presbyterian Church, Donoughmore, near Lifford, County Donegal

Creeslough: CC (St Michael's)
MOLONEY, Helen
The Serpent 1971
Loaves and Fishes 1971
The Dove 1971
The Dice 1971
The Lamb 1971
The Host 1971
(sketch designs, NIVAL)

Culdaff: C of I (St Buadán's)
O'BRIEN, Catherine
War memorial 1947 (opus sectile mosaic)

Derrybeg: CC (St Mary's)
WALSH, George W.
All windows, abstract with religious symbols 1972

Desertegney, near Buncrana: CC (Star of the Sea)
BECKER, Margaret
Virgin Mary 1964
St Patrick 1964
St Brigid 1964
St Columcille 1964
CAMPBELL, George
Baptism of Christ 1964
Armorial Window: Pope Paul's Arms 1964
Armorial Window: Bishop Neil Farren's Arms 1964
MOLONEY, Helen
Man, Symbol of St Matthew 1964
Lion, Symbol of St Mark 1964
Ox, Symbol of St Luke 1964
Eagle, Symbol of St John 1964
St Columba's Missionary Endeavours 1964
The Church as Fishers of Men 1964
Instruments of Christ's Passion 1964
St Brendan 1964
(sketch designs and scaled cartoons for Helen Moloney's windows, NIVAL)

Donegal Town: CC (St Patrick's, also known as the Church of the Four Masters)
KING, Richard
St Patrick 1933 (circular)
The Sacred Heart 1933
Our Lady of Lourdes 1933
(All created at Harry Clarke Studios.)

Donoughmore, Liscooley, near Lifford: Presbyterian Church
MOLONEY, Helen
Light of God's Creation, Concentric Circles Symbolising Darkness Out of Light (repaired) 1977
Light of God's Presence Depicted by a Burning Bush 1977
Light of God's Guidance Depicted by a Pillar of Fire 1977
Light of God's Covenant Depicted by a Seven-Branched Candlestick 1977
Light of God's Word Symbolised by a Star within a Range of Concentric Circles 1977
Christ as the Light of the World Symbolised by the Lamb, within a Nimbus Incorporating a Latin Cross Symbolising the Crucifixion 1977
(sketch designs, NIVAL)

Dungloe: CC (St Crona's)
WALSH, George W.
All stained glass (abstract) 1981

Fahan, Buncrana: C of I
HONE, Evie
St Elizabeth of Hungary 1948–9 (2 lights)

Frosses: CC (St Mary's)
WALSH, George Stephen
The Sacred Heart 1950s
The Blessed Virgin 1950s
Subject not recorded 1950s

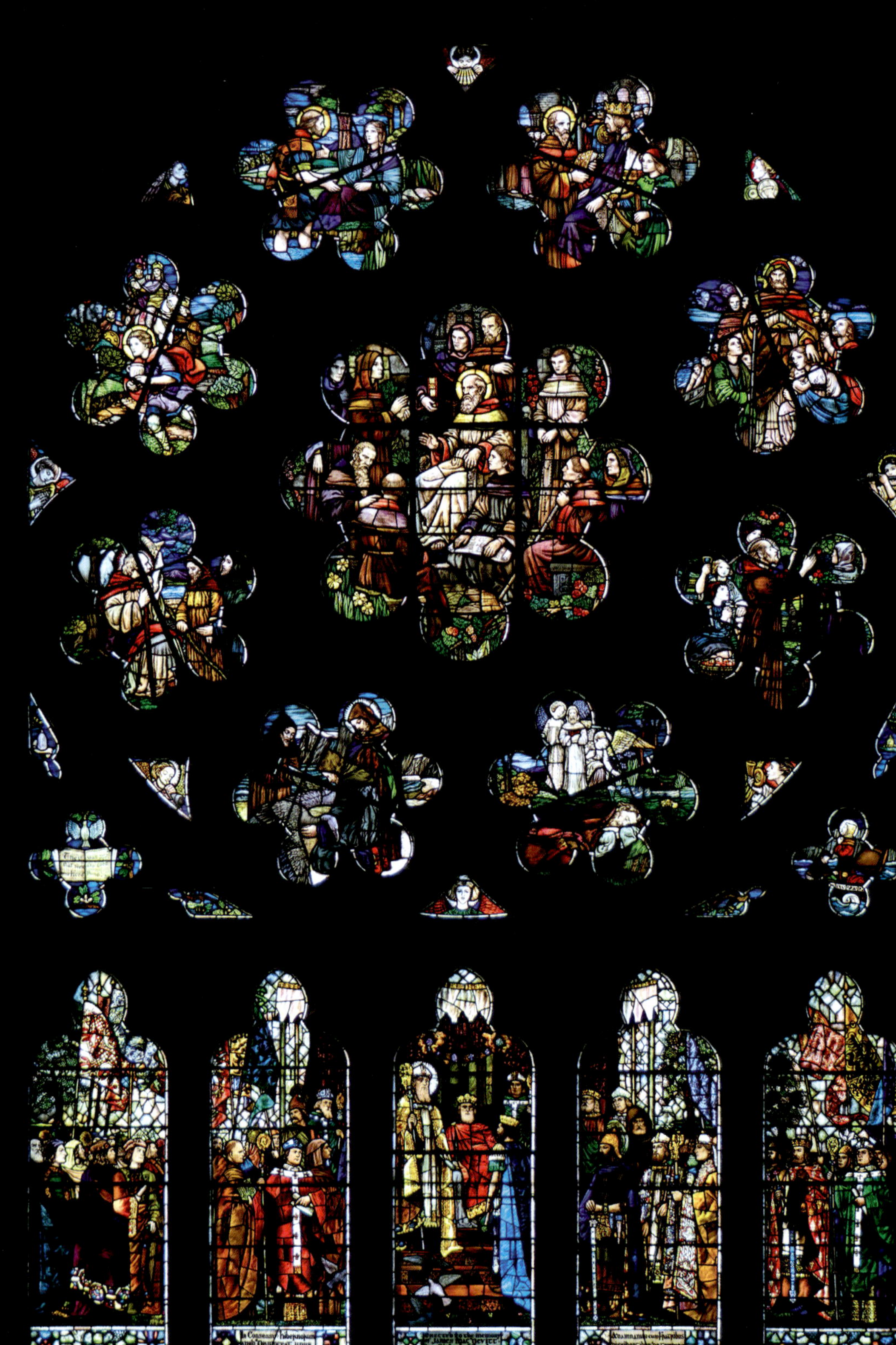

Left:
Beatrice Elvery, assisted by Ethel Rhind, *Scenes from the Lives of St Colmcille and St Eunan* (rose, 1910), with Michael Healy's *Convention of Drum Ceat* (1910) Catholic Cathedral, Letterkenny, County Donegal

Below, from left:
Phyllis Burke, *St Brigid* (1961);
Patrick Pye, *St Eunan* (1961),
Catholic Church (St Peter's), Milford, County Donegal

Killymard: CC (St Mary's)
WALSH, George W.
All stained glass, including Stations of the Cross 1986
Crucifix in opal glass, Tabernacle 1986

Laghey: C of I
BRANIFF, Daniel
*Parable of the Good Samaritan c.*1971

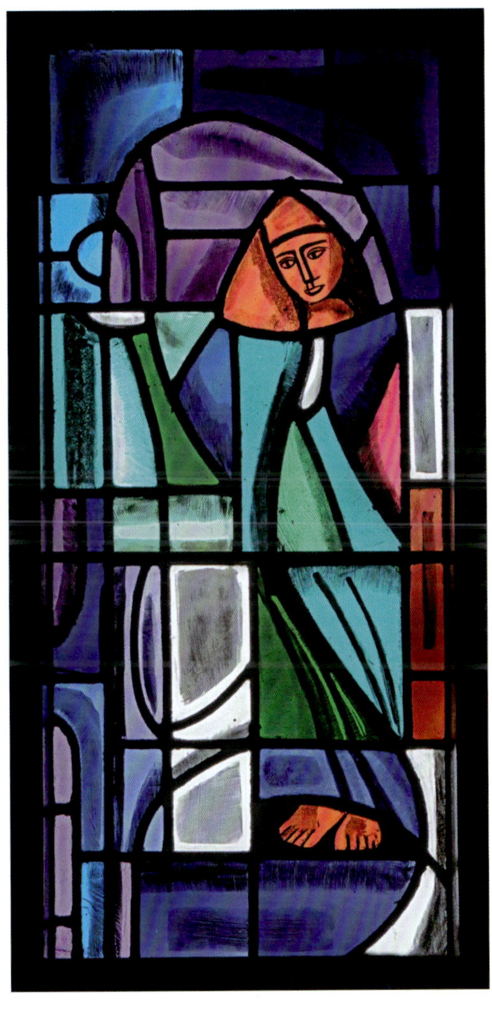

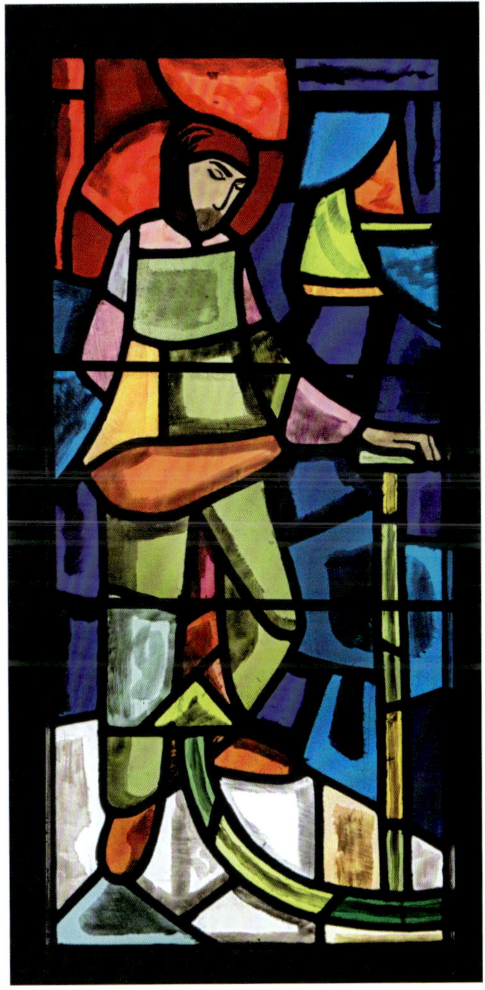

Letterkenny: Catholic Cathedral (St Eunan's)
CLARKE, Harry
Ten decorative clerestory windows (B) 1929 (each 2 lights)
CHILD, A.E.
St Finian of Moville and St Mobhi 1911 (2 lights)
ELVERY, Beatrice
Scenes from the Lives of St Colmcille and St Eunan 1910 (rose; assisted by Ethel Rhind)
St Columbanus and St Gall 1911 (2 lights)
HEALY, Michael
The Convention of Drum Ceat 1910 (5 lights) (sketch design, NGI)
St Conall and Dallán Forgail 1911 (2 lights) (sketch design, NGI)
St Ann 1911
St Hugh 1911
St Helena and Constantine 1914 (2 lights) (sketch design, NGI)
O'BRIEN, Catherine
St Cruitnecan and St Colmcille with St Baithen * 1911 (2 lights)
RHIND, Ethel
St Charles Borromeo 1912 (2 lights)

Milford: CC (St Peter's)
BURKE, Phyllis
St Brigid (cartoon, NIVAL) 1961
St Attracta (cartoon, NIVAL) 1961
St Colman (cartoon, NIVAL) 1961
POLLEN, Patrick
St Columcille 1961
St Adamnan 1961
St Comgall 1961
Abstract glazing throughout the church 1961
PYE, Patrick
St Eunan 1961
St Patrick 1961
St Brendan 1961
STUART, Imogen
St Garvan 1961

Moville: Presbyterian Church
POLLEN, Patrick
The Good Shepherd 1957 (installed in a light box, formerly in the Masonic Girls School, Ballsbridge, Dublin, now the Clayton Hotel) (sketch design, NIVAL)

Murlog, near Lifford: CC (St Patrick's)
POLLEN, Patrick
St Patrick's Breastplate, two 'walls of glass', and all other glazing c.1962–4

Pettigo, Lough Derg: Basilica of St Patrick's Purgatory
BREEN, Lua
Moses and the Burning Bush 2003 (in Room of Contemplation) (sketch design, NIVAL)
CLARKE, Harry
Fourteen single lights incorporating Stations of the Cross (indicated in parentheses below) in vesica-shaped panels held by each figure:
St Peter (Jesus is Condemned to Death) (B) 1929
St Paul (Jesus is Made to Bear His Cross) (B) 1929
St Andrew (Jesus Falls the First Time) (B) 1929
St James Major (Jesus Meets His Afflicted Mother) (B) 1929
St John the Evangelist (Simon the Cyrenaean Assists Jesus to Carry His Cross) (B) 1929
St Philip the Wayfarer (Veronica Wipes the Face of Jesus) (B) 1929
St Bartholomew (Jesus Falls the Second Time) (B) 1929
St Thomas (Jesus Consoles the Women of Jerusalem) (B) 1929
St Matthew (Jesus Falls the Third Time) (B) 1929
St James Minor (Jesus is Stripped of His Garments) (B) 1929
St Thaddeus (Jesus is Nailed to the Cross) (B) 1929
St Simon (Jesus Dies on the Cross) (B) 1929
St Matthias (Jesus is Taken Down from the Cross) (B) 1929
Our Lady (Jesus is Laid in the Tomb) (B) 1929

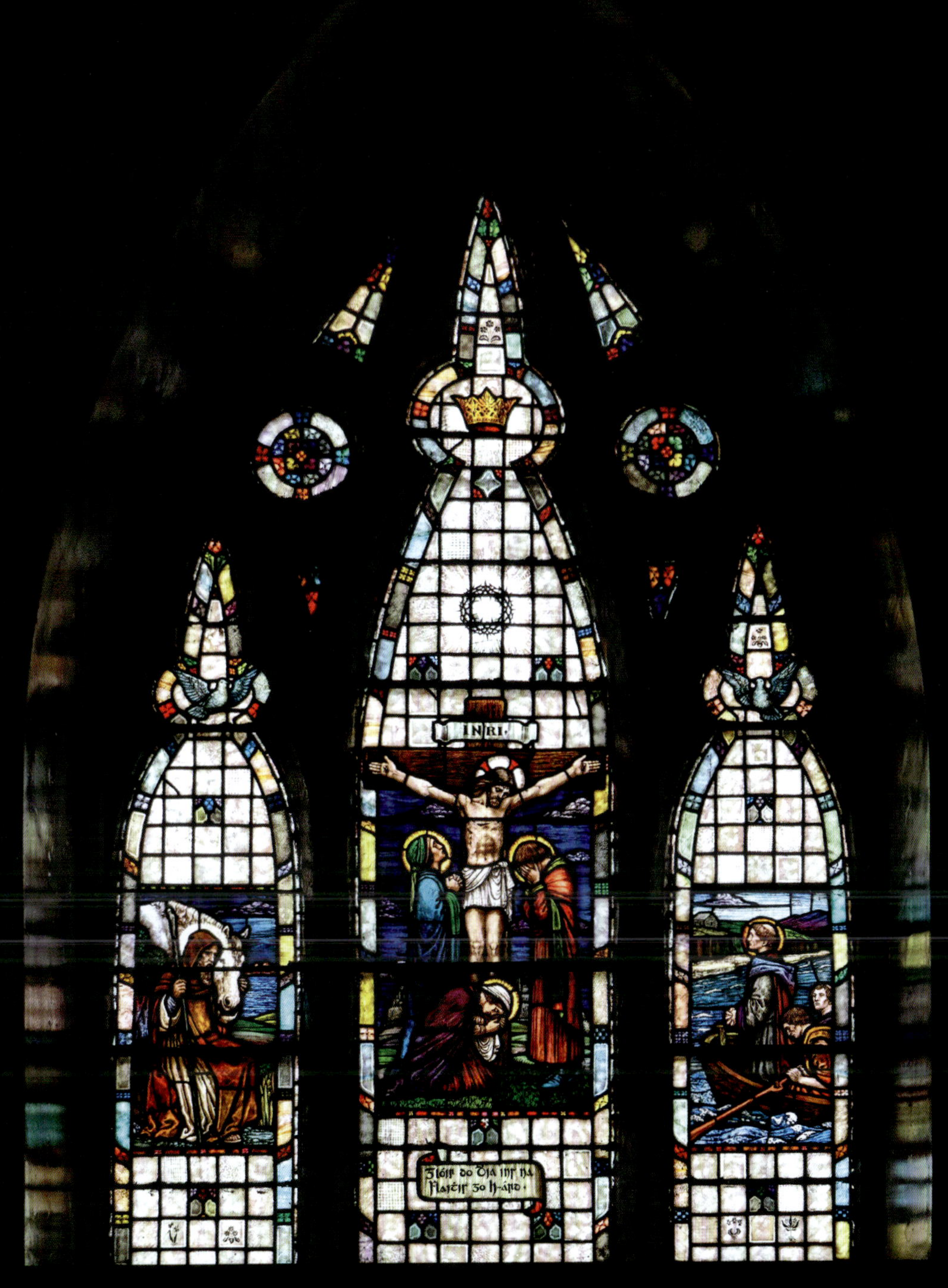

Beatrice Elvery, *St Columba with the White Horse that Foretold his Death, the Crucifixion, St Columba Arriving at Tory Island* (1910), Catholic Church (St Colmcille's), Tory Island, County Donegal

Ramelton: C of I (St Paul's)
POLLEN, Patrick
Benedicte 1975 (3 lights) (sketch designs, NIVAL)

Raphoe: C of I Cathedral (St Eunan's)
CHILD, A.E.
St Mark 1906
St Matthew 1906
St John 1906
St Luke 1906
PURSER, Sarah
St Eunan 1906 (painted by Ethel Rhind)

Rathmullan: CC (St Joseph's)
DOWLING, William
Christ the King 1940
(Created at Harry Clarke Studios.)

Rossnowlagh: C of I (St John's)
MARR, Edward
Resurrection 1951 (3 lights)

Rossnowlagh: CC (Franciscan Friary)
DUNNE, Michael
St Francis Receiving the Stigmata 1962 (porch of repository)
Canticle of the Sun, and St Francis with the Infant Jesus 1962 (porch of repository)
(Also several windows by Harry Clarke Studios in the apse.)

Taughboyne: C of I (St Baithin's)
O'BRIEN, Catherine
The Twenty-third Psalm 1949 (3 lights)

Tory Island: CC (St Colmcille's)
ELVERY, Beatrice
St Columba with the White Horse that Foretold his Death, The Crucifixion, St Columba Arriving at Tory Island 1910 (3 lights) (sketch design, NGI)
POLLEN, Patrick
St Columba 1967 (sketch design, NIVAL)
Christ Calming the Sea of Galilee 1967 (sketch design, NIVAL)
Both of Pollen's windows were commissioned by the artist Derek Hill to thank the islanders for their generosity and kindness.

COUNTY DOWN

Ardglass: C of I (St Nicholas's)
BRANIFF, Daniel
Christ Blessing Children 1971

Ballywalter: C of I (Holy Trinity)
O'BRIEN, Catherine
Downpatrick Cathedral 1960

Banbridge: C of I (Holy Trinity)
MacBRIDE, William
Faith, Hope and Charity * 1920 (3 lights)
Wedding Feast at Cana * 1920 (3 lights)

Bangor: C of I (St Comgall's)
CHILD, A.E.
The Knight 1915
ELVERY, Beatrice
The Sower 1915 (design/cartoon by Beatrice Elvery though executed by another An Túr Gloine artist, most likely Marthe Donas under A.E. Child's supervision)

Bangor, Clandeboye Estate: C of I Chapel (wedding venue)
GUINNESS, Lindy
Annunciation, Madonna and Child, Adoration of the Magi 2018 (3 lights)
Presentation in the Temple, Baptism of Christ 2018 (2 lights)
(Both fabricated by Colin Suckling.)

Carryduff: CC (Immaculate Heart of Mary)
BREEN, Lua
Immaculate Conception 2002
Annunciation 2002
Mary, Mother of the Church 2002
Nativity 2002
Epiphany 2002
Presentation in the Temple 2002
Flight into Egypt 2002
Holy Family at Nazareth 2002
Finding in the Temple 2002
Wedding Feast of Cana 2002
Crucifixion 2002
Resurrection 2002
Pentecost 2002
Assumption 2002
(sketch designs for all in NIVAL)

Comber: C of I (St Mary's)
ESLER, David
Cistercian Monk surrounded by Local References, Symbols of the Evangelists in the Tracery 2008–9 (5 lights)

Gilford, Castle Hill: CC (St John the Evangelist's)
CLARKE, Harry
St Catherine of Siena (A) 1922
Our Lady of Lourdes (B) *c.*1929

Groomsport: C of I
O'BRIEN, Catherine
Christ Blessing Little Children 1951 (sketch design, NGI)

Holywood: CC (St Colmcille's)
BREEN, Lua
Complete stained glass scheme based on the Seven Sacraments (sketch design, NIVAL) 1995
Peacock and Butterflies 1995 (side chapel)

Holywood: Sullivan Upper School, Belfast Road
HENRY, Olive
Untitled cityscape 1964 (sketch design, HERONI)
(Created at Clokey and Company, Belfast.)

Maghera: CC (St Mary's)
MOLONEY, Helen
Windows on the theme of the Eucharist 1974 (7 lights; removed and currently untraced)

Magheralin: C of I (Holy and Undivided Trinity)
CHILD, A.E
St Comgall and St Finian 1908–9 (2 lights)
ELVERY, Beatrice
St Gall and St Columbanus 1908–9 (2 lights)
HEALY, Michael
St Patrick and St Columba 1908–9 (2 lights)
RHIND, Ethel
The Institution of the Eucharist, with Judas, St John, Blessed Virgin Mary, the Miraculous Draft of Fishes 1915 (3 lights)
The Lord Triumphant 1923 (opus sectile mosaic; 3 panels)

Newcastle: C of I (St John's)
CHILD, A.E.
Faith, Love, Work 1916 (3 lights)

Newry: C of I (St Mary's)
BRANIFF, Daniel
Nativity, Blessed Virgin Mary 1968 (2 lights)
Scribe and Shipwreck(?) 1968 (2 lights)

Newry: C of I (St Patrick's)
BRANIFF, Daniel
Nativity 1969
*Ascension c.*1969

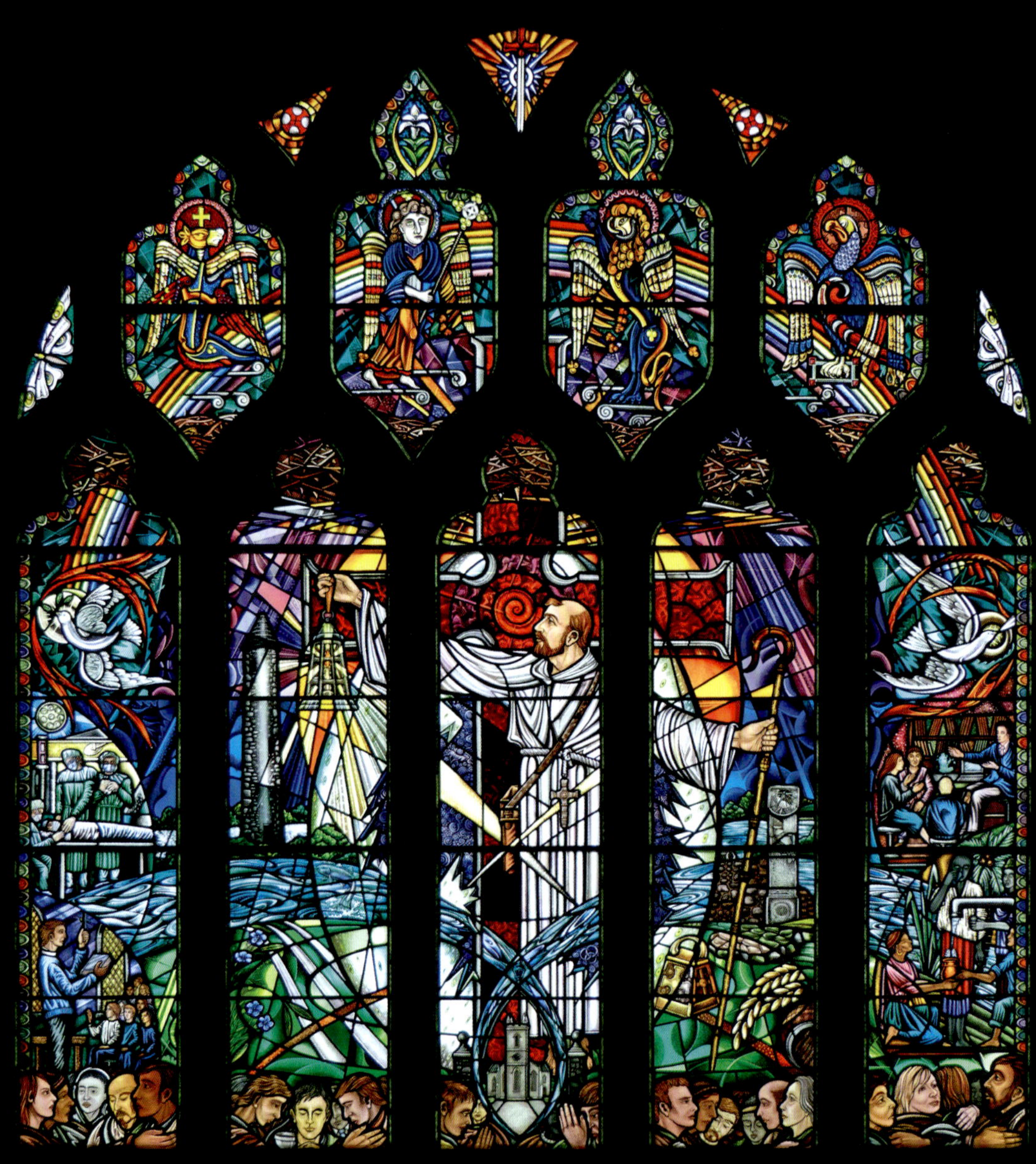

David Esler, *Cistercian Monk surrounded by Local References; Symbols of the Evangelists in the Tracery* (2008–9), Church of Ireland (St Mary's), Comber, County Down

Newry: St Clare's Convent (Sisters of St Clare, formerly a Carmelite convent), Glenvale Road
KING, Richard Enda
Untitled scheme of abstract windows inspired by the poetry of St John of the Cross, based on the theme of God's Love of the Human Soul and the Soul's Journey to God (1979–80)
(Fabricated by J.A. Devitt and Associates, Dublin.)

Newry: St Colman's College Chapel
DOWLING, William
St Aloysius Gonzaga 1938–9 (opus sectile mosaic in opal glass)
KING, Richard
Irish Saints 1937–9
Apostles Window 1937–8
St Michael 1937–8
St Joseph 1937–8
Our Lady of Sorrows 1937–8
The Sacred Heart 1937–8
Presentation of the Child Jesus 1937–8 (2 lights)
Untitled window depicting Scenes from the Old and New Testaments 1937–8 (wheel window)
Stations of the Cross 1937–8 (opus sectile mosaic in opal glass)
St Therese (The Little Flower) 1937–8 (opus sectile mosaic in opal glass)
(All above created at Harry Clarke Studios; sketch designs, TCD)

Old Court: de Ros family chapel, C of I (private property, wedding venue)
CHILD, A.E.
Heraldic Window 1908 (5 lights)
ELVERY, Beatrice
The Supper at Emmaus 1908 (3 lights)
RHIND, Ethel
St Peter, St Patrick, St Columba, St Andrew 1908 (4 lights)

Rostrevor (Kilbroney): C of I (St Bronach's)
ROBINSON, Patricia
Tree of Life and St Elizabeth of Hungary 1964–5 (4 lights)

Saul: C of I (St Patrick's)
O'BRIEN, Catherine
St Patrick 1933

Warrenpoint: CC (St Peter's)
HEALY, Michael
The Annunciation, Christ the King, The Ascension 1929 (3 lights)

Below: Michael Healy, detail of *The Annunciation* (1929), Catholic Church, Warrenpoint, County Down

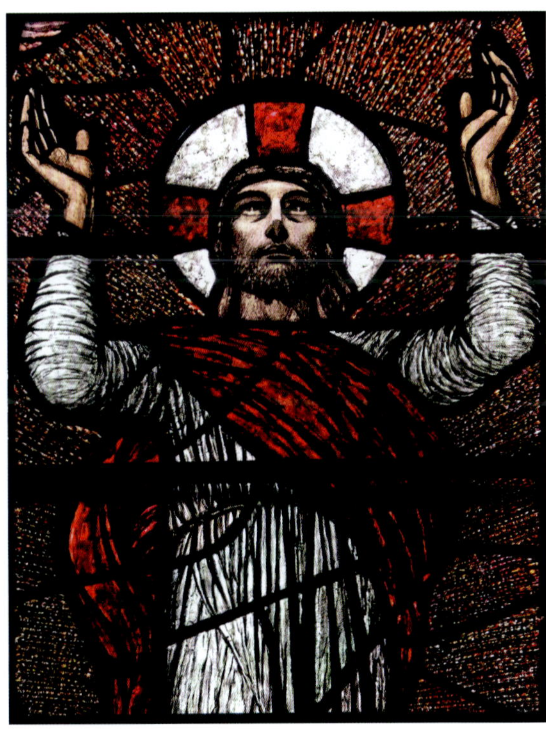

DUBLIN CITY CENTRE

Dublin City, Aughrim Street: CC (Holy Family)
McGOLDRICK, Hubert
The Crucifixion, with the Blessed Virgin Mary and St John 1939 (3 lights)
The Resurrection 1939 (3 lights)
(Both in original mortuary chapel, right of sanctuary.)

Dublin City, Aungier Street: CC (Whitefriar Street Church)
DUNNE, Michael
*St Nuno Alvares c.*1962–71
EARLEY, Leo
Our Lady of Mount Carmel and the Christ Child Enthroned early 1950s (behind altar)
EARLEY, Willie
Our Lady of Perpetual Succour * date unknown
Madonna and Child with St Therese * date unknown
KELLY, Kevin
Risen Christ 1995
(Created at Abbey Stained Glass Studios.)

Dublin City, Bachelors Walk: CC (Blessed Sacrament Chapel)
WALSH, George W.
All stained glass, mostly abstract with symbols 1995
Stations of the Cross 1995 (sandblasted on glass)

Dublin City, Benburb Street: National Museum of Ireland, Collins Barracks
CLARKE, Harry
Judas 1913 (panel, two-thirds of a lancet window)
A Meeting 1918 (panel) (on loan)
DAWSON, Debbie
Falling Slowly 2008 (triptych of panels in light boxes)
MACKEY, Mary
If I … 2007 (diptych in light box)
YOUNG, Peter
Indi 1995/2006 (panel in light box)

Dublin City, Blackhall Place: Incorporated Law Society
HEALY, Michael
Heraldic Window 1930 (elements reconfigured and window relocated within the building)
HONE, Evie
The Risen Christ 1936 (cartoon, Incorporated Law Society)

Dublin City, Camden Street: Keavan's Port
EARLEY, Gerard
*Decorative c.*1940s (circular) (painted by his nephew Jacky Earley)
The building was occupied by Earley Studios for many decades up to its closure in 1975. A replica stained glass fanlight by Joe Sheridan was installed in 2020.
MULDOWNEY, Patrick
St Kevin and the Blackbird 2020 (light box, in bar)

Dublin City, Castle Street: Dublin Castle, Bedford Hall, Bedford Tower
COTTER, Maud
That Sound Meets Sense Straight as Lemons Meet Fish 1988 (preparatory drawing in adjacent room)

Dublin City, Cathal Brugha Street: C of I (St Thomas's) (currently used by Indian Orthodox Community)
O'BRIEN, Catherine
The Way 1931
The Light 1931
The Truth 1931

Dublin City, Christchurch Place: C of I Cathedral (Christ Church)
POLLEN, Patrick
St Luke (memorial window to Catherine O'Brien) 1964
RIVERS, Elizabeth
Head of Christ date unknown (panel mounted in light box)

Dublin City, Church Street: C of I (St Michan's)
O'BRIEN, Catherine
Our Lord Quelling the Tempest 1909

Dublin City, Clarendon Street: CC (St Teresa's Church)
BURKE, Phyllis
St Joseph 1990 (cartoon, NLI)
St Elias 1991 (cartoon, NLI)
St Teresa of Avila 1992 (cartoon, NLI)
St John of the Cross 1993 (cartoon, NLI)
St Thérèse of Lisieux 1994 (cartoon, NLI)
St Patrick 1996 (cartoon, NLI)
St Brigid 1997 (cartoon, NLI)
Prodigal Son with quatrefoil above depicting *Veronica's Veil* 1988 (left porch) (cartoon, NLI)
The Woman at the Well with quatrefoil above depicting *Veronica's Veil* 1988 (right porch) (cartoon, NLI)
Psalm 41/42 (Deer Drinking from Fountain) I c.2005–7 (2 lights) (cartoon, NLI)
Psalm 41/42 (Deer Drinking from Fountain) II c.2005–7 (2 lights) (cartoon, NLI)
St Teresa Benedicta of the Cross (Edith Stein) 2006
EARLEY, William (Bill) E.
Betrothal of Mary and Joseph with circle above depicting *Three Angels* 1936
Elijah, Our Lady of Mount Carmel Presenting the Scapular to St Simon Stock, St John of the Cross 1936 (3 lights)
Ecstasy of St Teresa with circle above depicting *Three Angels* 1936
WALSH, George W.
Resurrection 1970s (3 lights)
Stations of the Cross (with Willie Earley, painted antique glass on polished granite)

Dublin City, Dawson Street: C of I (St Ann's)
COX, James
St Mark and St Ann 1979
GEDDES, Wilhelmina
Charity 1913
St Christopher and Scenes from the Life of Christ 1916 (with Ethel Rhind)
Archangels Raphael and Michael, and Jacob's Angel with Joshua, Gideon's Vision, David and Jonathan, St Longinus, St Sebastian and St George 1918
RHIND, Ethel
*'He Hath Delivered My Soul in Peace from the Battle that Was Against Me'** c.1916

Dublin City, Donore Avenue: C of I (St Catherine's and St James's)
HEALY, Michael
Hope 1915
St Catherine 1923 (sketch design, NGI)
St Victor 1930 (sketch design, NGI)
O'BRIEN, Catherine
St Columba 1952 (sketch design, NGI)
RHIND, Ethel
Charity 1928 (opus sectile mosaic; formerly in St Peter's C of I, Aungier Street, Dublin)

Dublin City, Dublin Castle: Chapel of the Holy Trinity (formerly Chapel Royal)
CHILD, A.E.
Armorials of Viscount French and Viscount FitzAlan, the Marquess of Aberdeen and Viscount Wimborne 1922 (2 lights)

Dublin City, Eccles Street: Mater Private Hospital
BREEN, Lua
Abstract 1987 (3 lights, in oratory, ground floor)
MACKEY, Mary
Untitled 1996 (2 lights, in former mortuary chapel, basement)

Dublin City, Eccles Street: Mater Public Hospital
LAMB, Peadar
The Mater Orchard 2005 (Mater Orchard Building; Sisters of Mercy Community Residence)
POLLEN, Patrick
St Lucy c.1959–60 (in main hospital chapel)

Dublin City, Gardiner Street: CC (St Francis Xavier)
HONE, Evie
Alpha and Omega 1947
Lamb 1947
Fish (Ichthus) 1947
Pelican 1947
Dove 1947
The above five windows were formerly in University Hall Chapel, Hatch Street, Dublin; now installed in the Evie Hone Room
KING, Richard
St Francis Xavier Preaching in the Orient c. early to mid-1930s (Prayer Room. This is the base panel of *St Francis Xavier* which was recently installed in Belvedere College Chapel, Dublin.)
(Created at Harry Clarke Studios.)

Dublin City, Grafton Street: Bewley's Oriental Café
CLARKE, Harry
Two decorative windows (A) 1928
Four decorative windows depicting the Corinthian, Doric, Ionic and Composite Orders of Architecture (A) 1928

Dublin City, Great Denmark Street: Belvedere College
DOWLING, William
Stations of the Cross V, VII, IX, X 1940–1 (opus sectile mosaic in opal glass)
Our Lady with the Young Christ 1946 (opus sectile mosaic in opal glass)
KING, Richard
St Francis Xavier c. early to mid-1930s, companion window to that of Irish or European Saint with Crozier and Tonsure in St Patrick's College (P.J. Brophy Library), Carlow
Our Blessed Lady of the Magnificat 1934–5
Stations of the Cross I, II, III, IV, VI, VIII, XII, XII, XIII, XIV 1935–9 (opus sectile mosaic in opal glass)
Apparition of the Sacred Heart to St Margaret Mary 1938 (2 lights)
SIMMONDS, Charles (Cecil)
St Stanislaus, Virgin and Child, St Aloysius 1930 (3 lights; sketch designs, TCD)
St Francis Xavier 1934 (sketch designs, TCD)
St Ignatius Loyola 1934 (sketch designs, TCD)
(All above created at Harry Clarke Studios.)

Dublin City, Haddington Road: CC (St Mary's)
CHILD, A.E.
St Cecilia 1904
EARLEY, William (Bill) E.
Lamb of God, Our Lady, and the Four Evangelists c. early 1940s (rose)
*Christ the King c.*1940s
O'BRIEN, Catherine
The Baptism of Christ 1910

Dublin City, Holles Street: National Maternity Hospital Chapel
EARLEY, Gerard
Madonna and Child mid–late 1960s (3 lights; design by Gerard Earley with fabrication undertaken by staff at Earley Studios)

Dublin City, James Street: CC (St James's)
KELLY, Kevin
*Nativity with the Shepherds and Three Kings c.*1993 (in light box)
*Nativity c.*1998 (in light box)
(Both made at Abbey Stained Glass Studios and donated by Ken Ryan, the former in memory of the artist and the latter in memory of the artist's wife.)

Dublin City, James Street: former C of I (now a distillery)
HEALY, Michael
Faith, Hope and Charity * 1915–16 (2 lights)
(Removed in 1966 by donor's son to be reinstalled in St Brendan's C of I, Sydenham, Belfast, though this did not occur. Present location untraced.)

Dublin City, Kilmainham: Irish Museum of Modern Art (former Royal Hospital)
CHILD, A.E.
Heraldic Window * (Arms of General Sir William R. Mansfield, Field Marshal Lord Grenfell, Field Marshal Sir Hugh Henry Rose, and General Sir Neville G. Lyttelton, with a caryatid, gargoyles and putti) 1912 (in the Great Hall, 2 lights)

Dublin City, Leeson Park: C of I (Christ Church) (currently Romanian Orthodox Church)
CHILD, A.E.
The Nativity 1936 (2 lights)
The Supper at Emmaus 1936 (2 lights)
WALSH, George Stephen
Moses and the Burning Bush, Abraham Sacrificing Isaac, Christ with Chalice, Christ Healing a Woman, Christ Healing the Daughter of the Syrophoenician Woman 1956 (3 lights)

Dublin City, Lower Abbey Street: The (original) Abbey Theatre vestibule
PURSER, Sarah
*Two rectangular lights and three lunettes featuring symmetrical trees in leaf, based on designs by Christopher Whall c.*1904 (They survived the fire of 1951 where they remained until the building was demolished in 1961 though it is understood they were removed at that time. Present location untraced.)

Dublin City, Lower Abbey Street: The Flowing Tide Pub
INGLIS, Tony or TOMLIN, Stanley
Dublin Characters: Theatre Goers, Street Traders, Students, Drinkers, Artists, with the Custom House and Nelson's Pillar * *c.*1940s/1950s (3 panels)
Tragedy and Comedy Masks * *c.*1940s/1950s (panel)
There are also three depictions of Neptune and other sea-themed images which were apparently installed after the Talbot Street Bombings of 1974 when the original pub windows shattered. Artist/studio unidentified.

Dublin City, Lower Gloucester Place: Rutland National School (visits strictly by appointment)
YOUNG, Peter
Big Cheese 2009 (10 panels)

Dublin City, Lower Kevin Street: Former Moravian Church (now offices)
RHIND, Ethel
Various windows installed between *c.*1916 and 1922 (including three leaded lights on front facade featuring neo-classical swags; six monochrome portraits were removed in 1959 when ceased to be a church, reinstalled in Gracehill Moravian Church, County Antrim)

Dublin City, Merchant's Quay: CC (Immaculate Conception, known as Adam and Eve's)
EARLEY, Willie
Seven suspended panels depicting full-length portraits of 'modern' popes: Pius IX, Leo XIII, Pius X, Benedict XV, John XIII, Pius XI, Pius XII 1959–61

Dublin City, Merrion Square, North: American College Dublin
LAMB, Peadar
Oscar Wilde Window 1995

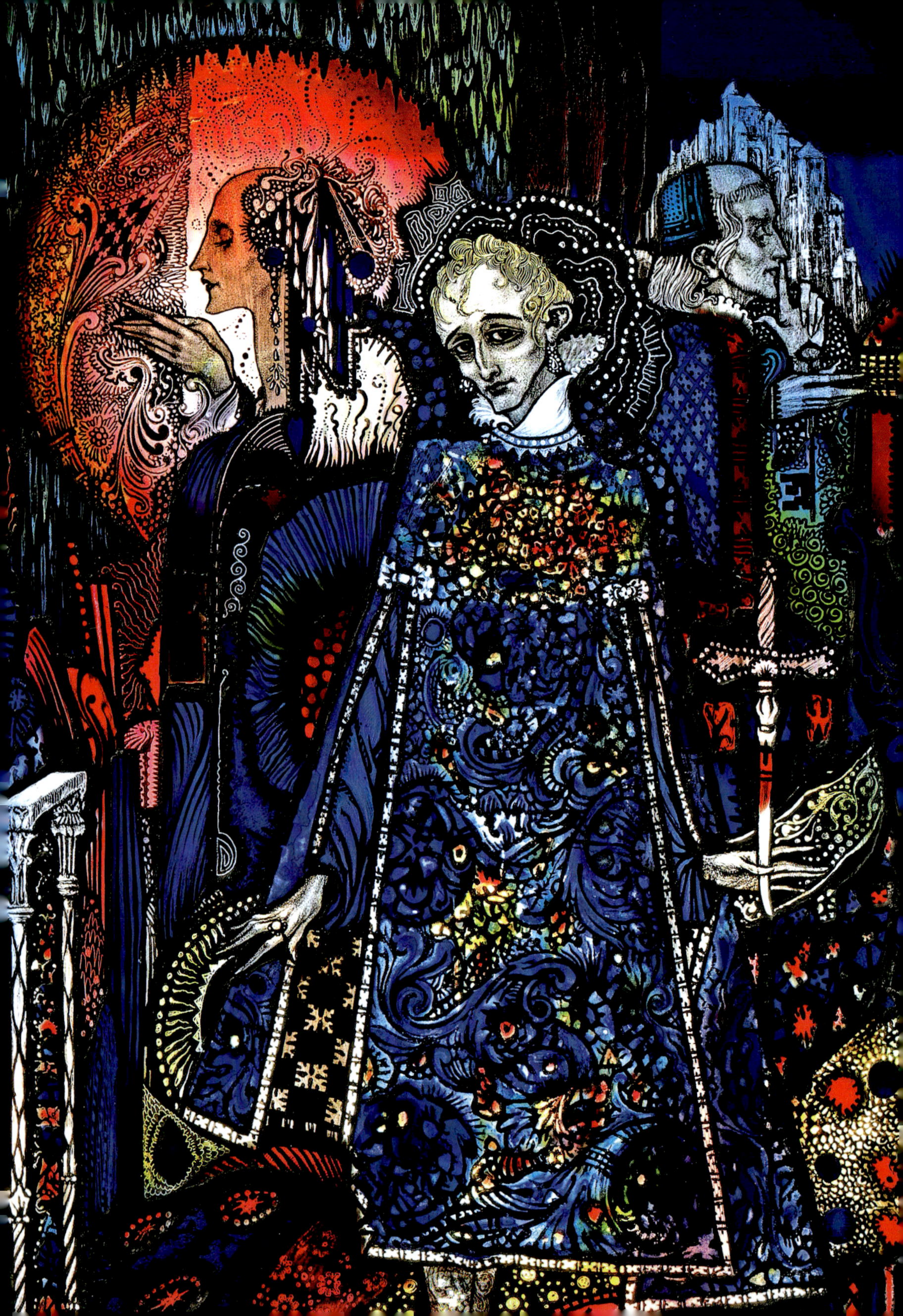

Dublin City, Merrion Square, South: Arts Council Collection
SCANLON, James
Growth Cycle 1985 (panel)

Dublin City, Merrion Square, South: Notre Dame Dublin Global Gateway
KELLY, Kevin
Blessed Virgin Mary with St Patrick and St Columba 2004
(Made at Abbey Stained Glass Studios and adapted from an original Harry Clarke Studios cartoon made for a window for New York World's Fair, 1939. See Camarillo, California, USA.)

Dublin City, Merrion Square, West: National Gallery of Ireland
CLARKE, Harry
The Song of the Mad Prince 1917 (panel)
The Mother of Sorrows 1926 (3 lights; originally made for the Convent of Notre Dame, Dowanhill, Glasgow)
HEALY, Michael
St Ita 1924–5
St Brigid 1924–5
The Good Shepherd 1924–5
St Patrick 1924–5
St Columcille 1924–5
(all five windows formerly in the Convent of Mercy Chapel, Ballyhaunis, County Mayo)
HONE, Evie
The Cock and Pot, Vulgo The Betrayal 1945 (panel)
Head of St John c.1949 (panel)
The Three Children in the Fiery Furnace c.1947 (panel)
Two Apostles 1952 (panel)
Resurrection 1947 (panel)
St Christopher 1944 (panel)

Dublin City, Mount Street: C of I (St Stephen's, also known as the Pepper Canister Church)
ELVERY, Beatrice
Christ Among the Doctors 1907

Dublin City, North Brunswick Street: Morning Star Hostel Oratory
BREEN, Lua
St Louis Marie de Montfort 1970

Dublin City, North Circular Road: Chapel of former Female Convict Prison at Mountjoy
KING, Richard
Our Lady of Perpetual Succour with Angels Carrying Symbols of the Passion 1939 (3 lights)
(Created at Harry Clarke Studios.)

Dublin City, North William Street: CC (St Agatha's)
INGLIS, Tony
St Agatha c.1940s (in former mortuary chapel)
Immaculate Conception c.1940s (in former mortuary chapel)
Christ the King c.1943 (in former nuptial chapel)
St Cecilia c.1943 (in former nuptial chapel)
St Patrick c.1943 (in former nuptial chapel)
St Lawrence O'Toole c.1943 (in former nuptial chapel)

Dublin City, Parkgate Street: Ashling Hotel
MURPHY, Johnny
Four Winds of Erin (4 panels in light boxes, moved to lower ground floor) c.1968 (cartoons, NIVAL)

Left:
Harry Clarke,
The Song of the Mad Prince (1917), National Gallery of Ireland, Merrion Square, Dublin. Collection NGI. Photograph © National Gallery of Ireland

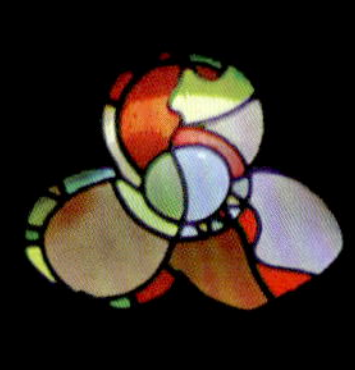
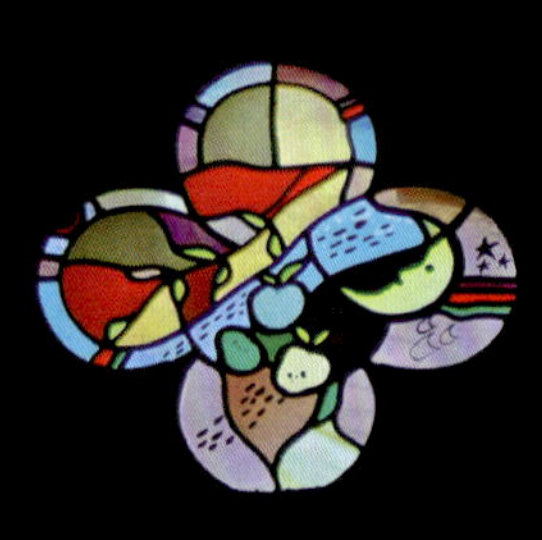
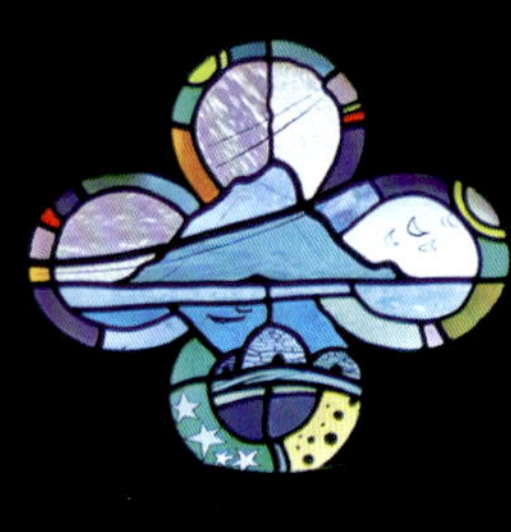
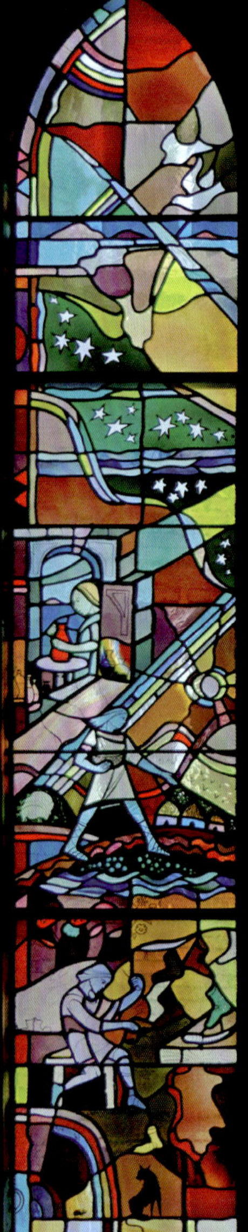
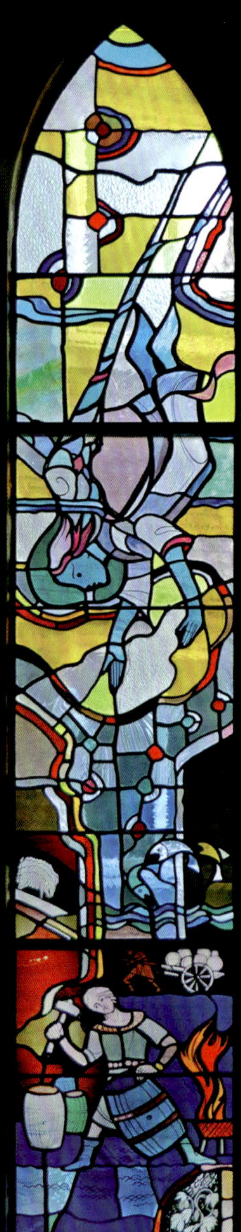
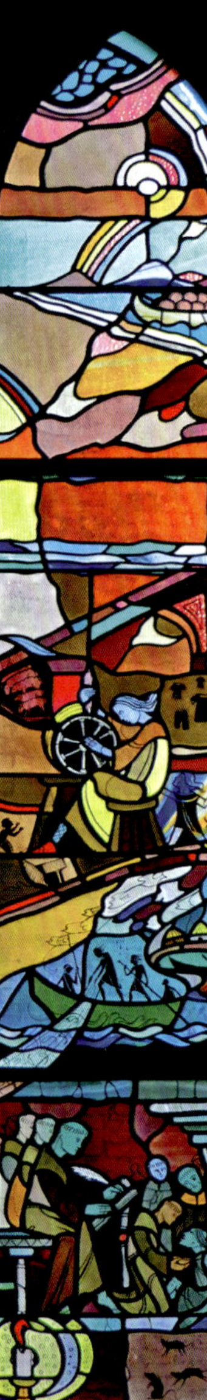

Dublin City, Parnell Square, North: Dublin City Gallery The Hugh Lane
CLARKE, Harry
The Eve of St Agnes 1924 (22 panels in one window) (preliminary designs, Crawford Art Gallery, Cork)
CLARKE, Margaret
A Doe and Young Stag (after Franz Marc) no date (panel; in storage)
GEDDES, Wilhelmina
Episodes from the Life of St Colman Mac Duagh 1911(3 panels)
HEALY, Michael
Outside the Courts 1932 (panel; in storage)
HONE, Evie
The Jugs 1947 (panel)
The Cock c.1948 (panel)
The Deposition c.1953 (panel)
SCANLON, James
Study No. 2 for Miró 1985 (panel)

Dublin City, Phoenix Park: The Zoo (Haughton House)
LAMB, Peadar
Tiger, Elephants, Peacock, Monkeys 2008 (4 lights)

Dublin City, St Michael's Hill: Dublinia (museum)
WALSH, George W.
Civic Window 1993 (3 lights, fabricated by Irish Stained Glass, in coffee shop)
St Michael, Surrounded by Craftsmen and Traders of the City 1993 (3 lights, fabricated by Irish Stained Glass, on staircase landing)

Left:
George W. Walsh, *St Michael Surrounded by Craftsmen and Traders of the City* (1993), Dublinia, St Michael's Hill, Dublin

Dublin City, St Patrick's Close: C of I Cathedral (St Patrick's)
ELVERY, Beatrice
Angel Musicians 1908–9
MACBRIDE, William
Chivalry (war memorial) 1917
PURSER, Sarah
Cormac of Cashel 1906 (painted by A.E. Child) (sketch design, NGI)

Dublin City, St Patrick's Close: St Patrick's Cathedral Grammar School
EARLEY, James
Time Signatures (theme interprets the interconnected nature of St Patrick's education system and the school's role within the wider community of Dublin 8) 2020

Dublin City, St Stephen's Green, South: CC (University Church)
CAMPBELL, George
The Scourging at the Pillar c.1960s (panel) (painted by George W. Walsh)

Dublin City: St Stephen's Green, South: Staunton's on the Green Hotel
CLARKE, Harry
Blessed Julie with Two Children, and the Visitation of Our Lady to St Elizabeth (1927) (originally made for thc Chapel of the Convent of Notre Dame, Dowanhill, Glasgow, Scotland)

Dublin City, St Stephen's Green, West: Unitarian Church
CHILD, A.E.
Discovery, Truth, Inspiration, Love, Work, with Christopher Columbus, Martin Luther, Christ in the Temple, Florence Nightingale, and William Caxton 1917–18 (5 lights)
O'BRIEN, Catherine
Courage, Efficiency, Kindness 1943 (trefoil)
RHIND, Ethel
The Good Samaritan 1937 (2 lights)

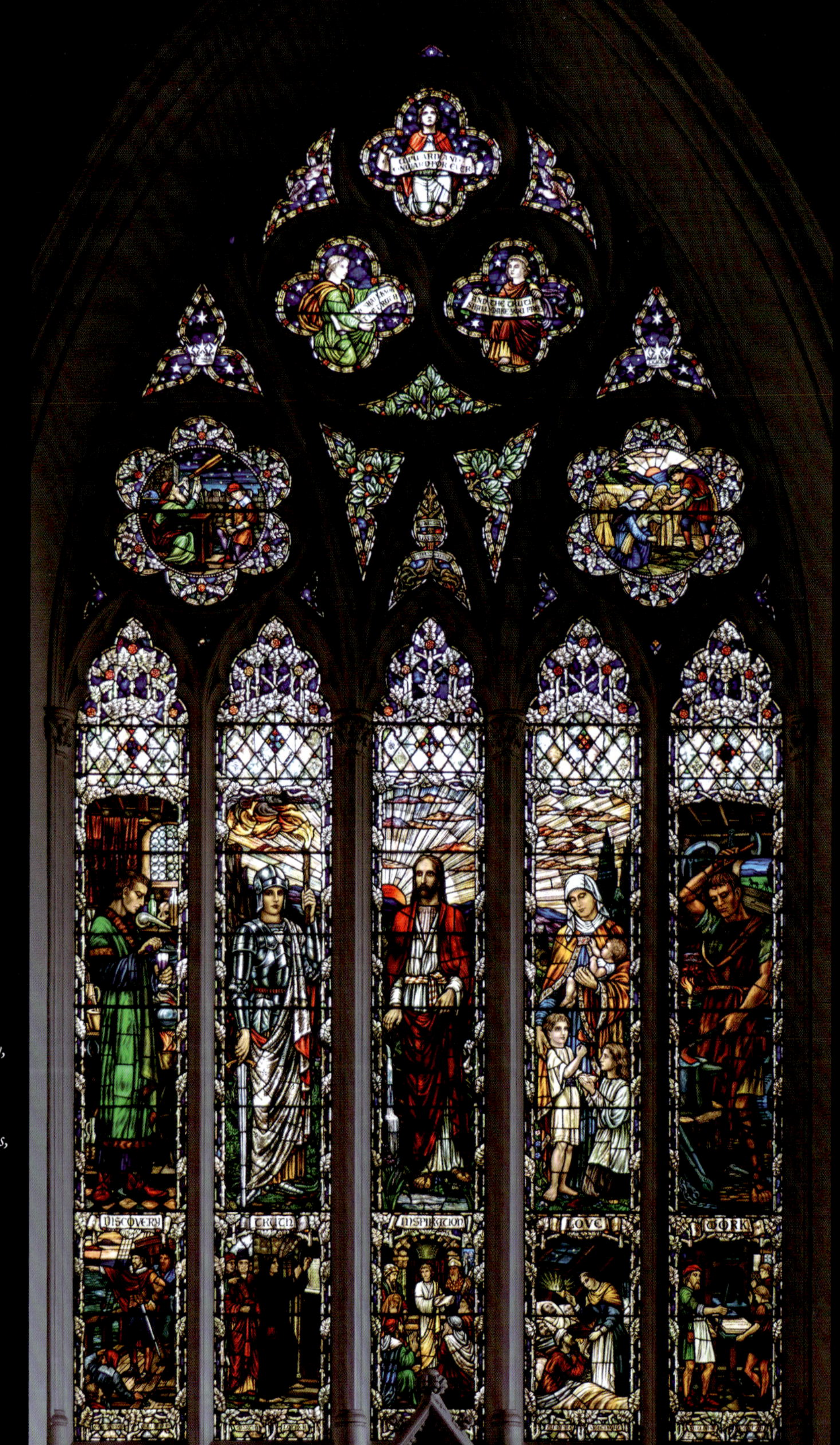

A.E. Child, *Discovery, Truth, Inspiration, Love, Work, with Christopher Columbus, Martin Luther, Christ in the Temple, Florence Nightingale, and William Caxton* (1917–18), Unitarian Church, St Stephen's Green, Dublin

Dublin City, St Stephen's Green, West: Royal College of Surgeons of Ireland
CLARKE, Terry
Crucified Christ 1953 (panel; in Chapel of Meditation)
Blessed Virgin with the Christ Child and St John the Baptist 1954 (panel; in Chapel of Meditation)
O'BRIEN, Catherine
Heraldic Window with RCSI Coat of Arms 1959–60 (in President's Office)
Heraldic Window with Colles Coat of Arms 1961 (in President's Office) (sketch design, NGI)
WALSH, George W.
Medical Oath 2002 (centre light, Albert Lecture Theatre)
Key figures in development of surgery and medicine through the ages (I): René Laennec, Joseph Lister, Abraham Coles, William Harvey, Imhotep; and *Vesalius Anatomy* 2002 (left light, Albert Lecture Theatre)
Key figures in development of surgery and medicine through the ages (II:) Joseph Murray, Florence Nightingale, Alexander Fleming, William T.G. Morton, Wilhelm Roentgen; and *RCSI Dentistry* 2002 (right light, Albert Lecture Theatre)

Dublin City, South William Street: Grogan's Pub
LAMB, Katharine
The Day People (featuring customers of the pub) 1993
The Night People (featuring customers of the pub) 1995

Dublin City, Temple Bar: The Green Building, Temple Lane
COTTER, Maud
Absolute Jellies Make Singing Sounds 1994

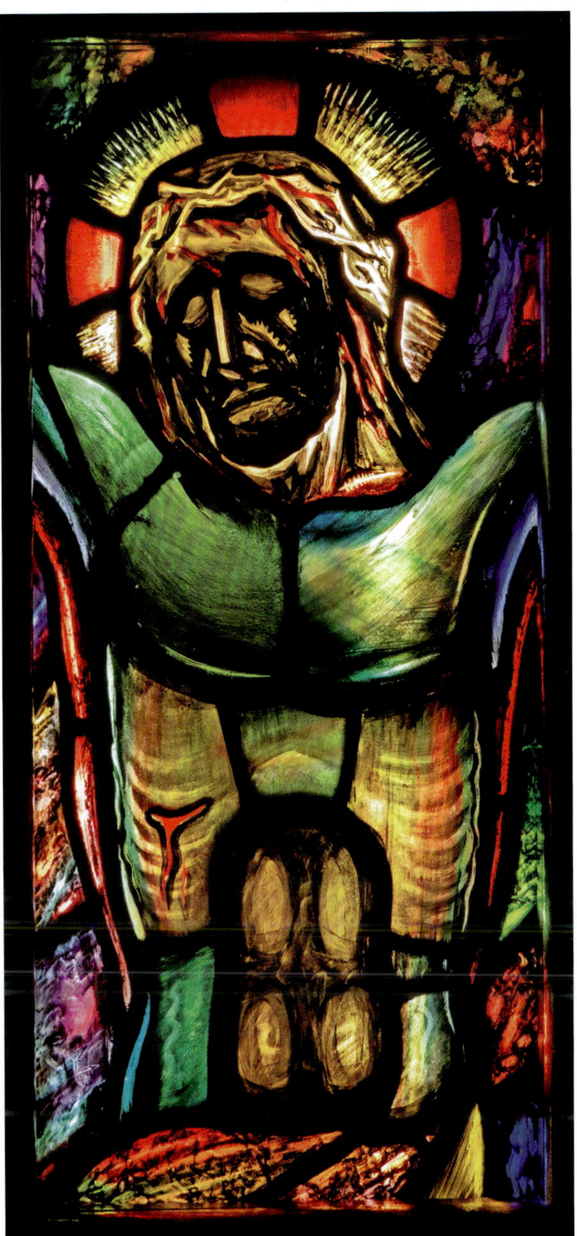

Above:
Terry Clarke, *Crucified Christ* (1953),
Royal College of Surgeons (Meditation Chapel),
St Stephen's Green, Dublin

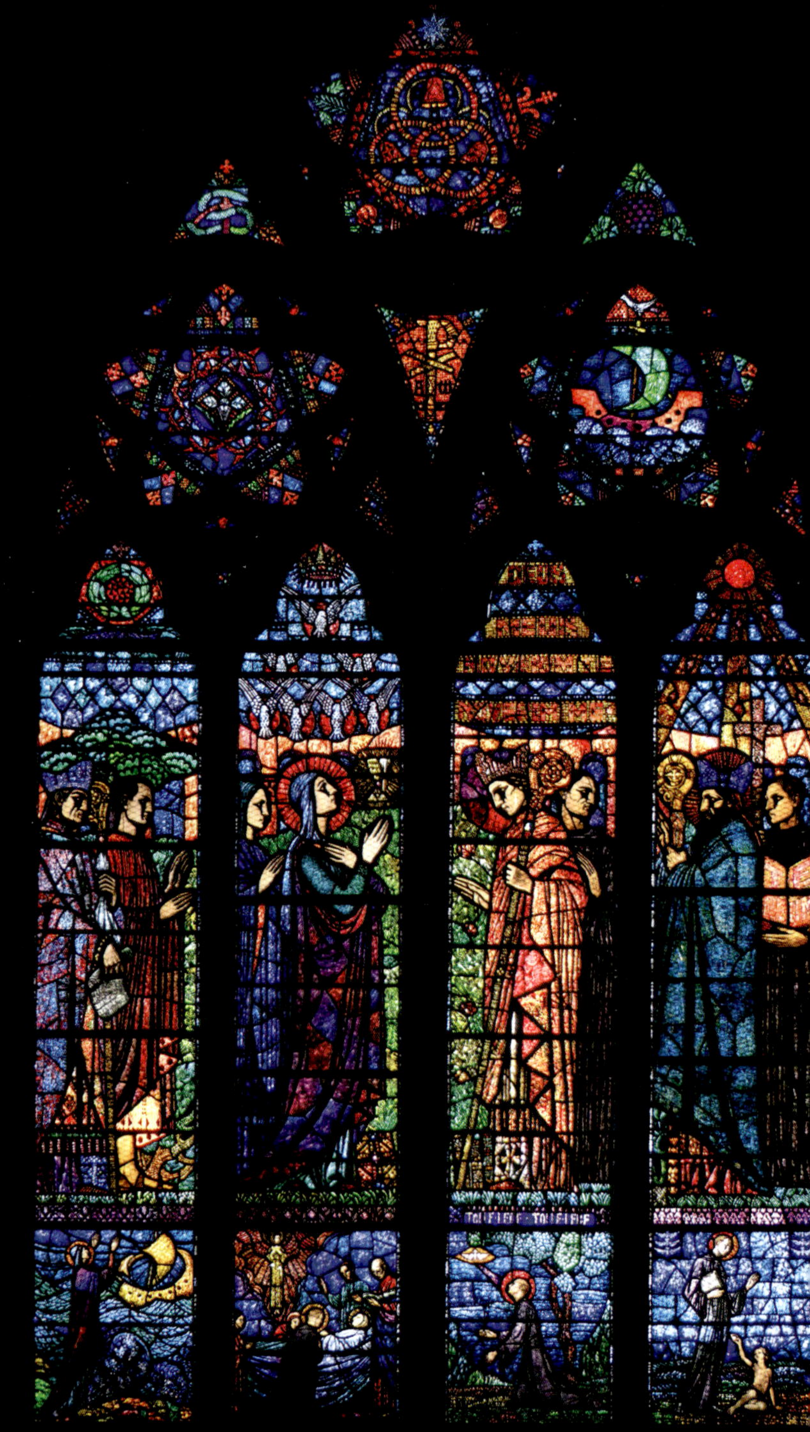

Dublin City, Temple Street: former C of I (St George's), now offices
MacBRIDE, William
Slain Soldier Greeted by Christ and Attendant Angels * (war memorial) *c.*1920
McGOLDRICK, Hubert
Three decorative opus sectile mosaic panels with Alpha and Omega 1933 (panels apparently removed and currently untraced)

Dublin City, Temple Street: Convent of the Sisters of Charity
CLARKE, Harry
Decorative window with Crown of Thorns and Nails (B) 1927 (formerly in the Jesuit Fathers' Retreat House Chapel, Rathfarnham Castle, Dublin, along with two similar windows which went to the Catholic Church, Tullamore. Temple Street Convent also has three decorative windows by Harry Clarke Studios which came from the Jesuit Fathers' Domestic Chapel, Rathfarnham Castle, as follows:
Decorative window with Symbols of Christ's Passion: Gall and Vinegar, Cock, Host and Chalice, Seamless Robe *c.*1929–31
Decorative window with Symbols of Christ's Passion: Crossed Palms, Lantern and Bludgeon, Shroud on Cross *c.*1929–31
Decorative window with Symbols of Christ's Passion: Agnes Dei, Grapes and Wheat, Pelican *c.*1930–1

Dublin City, Thomas Street: CC (St Augustine and St John's)
HEALY, Michael
St Augustine and St Monica 1933–4 (4 lights) (sketch design, NGI)

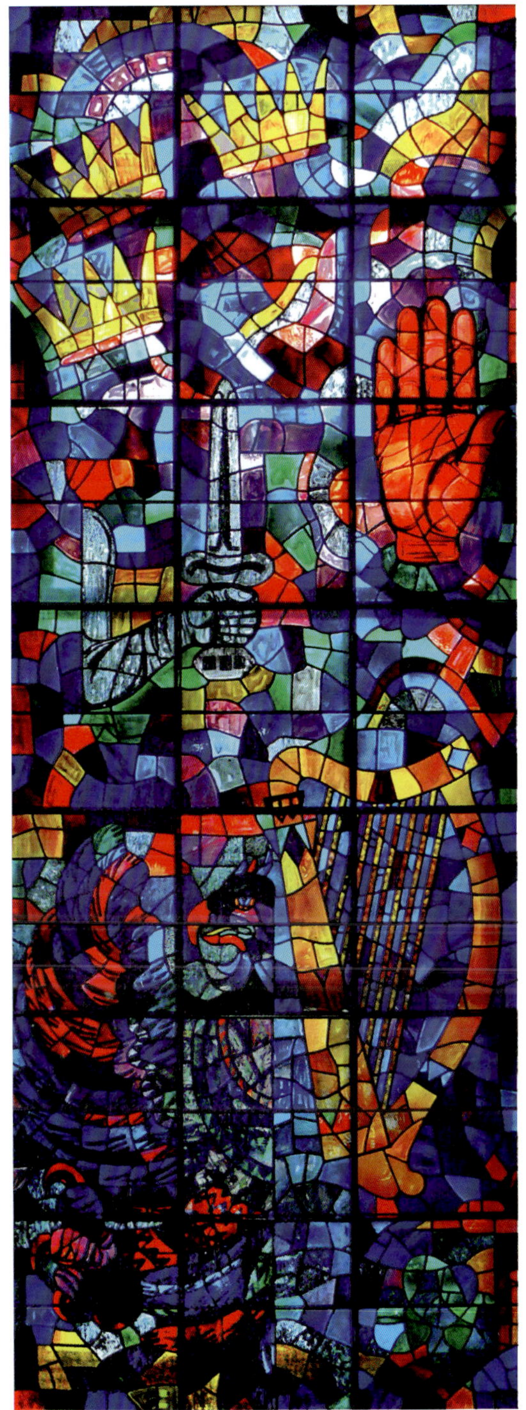

Left: Michael Healy, *St Augustine and St Monica* (1933–4), Catholic Church (St Augustine and St John's), Thomas Street, Dublin
Right: Evie Hone, *My Four Green Fields* (1938–9), Government Buildings, Upper Merrion Street, Dublin

Dublin City, Thomas Street: National College of Art and Design
CLARKE, Harry
The Baptism of St Patrick 1912 (panel)
MOLLOY, Austin
The Book of Job 1915 (panel)

Dublin City, Upper O'Connell Street: Dublin Bus building (formerly Córas Iompair Éireann)
BURKE, Phyllis
Crests of the Four Provinces c.1959 (four panels in coloured acrylic made in the manner of stained glass) (designs, NIVAL)

Dublin City, Upper Merrion Street: Government Buildings
HONE, Evie
My Four Green Fields 1938–9 (Window originally created for the Irish Pavilion, New York World's Fair, 1939) (sketch design, NGI; sketch design, Manresa House, Dollymount, Dublin)

Dublin City, Upper Merrion Street: Merrion Hotel (The Cellar Bar)
YOUNG, Peter
Triptych 2017 (3 panels)

DUBLIN NORTH

Dublin North, Airport: CC (Our Lady Queen of Heaven)
CORCORAN, Sheila
Stations of the Cross 1964 (fused layers of painted glass, not leaded. Initially removed at the behest of Archbishop McQuaid who disliked them. Subsequently reinstated.)
DUNNE, Michael
Abstract glazing c.1964

Dublin North, Artane: CC (Our Lady of Mercy), Brookwood Grove
CAMPBELL, Christopher
Baptism of Christ c.1968
Our Lady of Ransom/Our Lady of Vallarpadam c.1968
The Risen Christ c.1968

Right:
Sheila Corcoran, *Stations of the Cross* (1964), Catholic Church (Our Lady Queen of Heaven), Dublin Airport

Dublin North, Artane: CC (St John Vianney), Ardlea Road
MULDOWNEY, Patrick
Dove, Miracle of Loaves and Fishes, Crucifixion, Last Supper, Agnes Dei 1993 (in entrance porch)
There are four pairs of 'Jubilee Windows', as follows:
Jubilee Windows I:
The Angel Gabriel, the Star Leads the Wise Men to Jesus (left) 2000–1
Blessed Virgin, Pentecost, View of Dublin from the Millennium Bridge (right) 2000–1
Jubilee Windows II:
St Brigid (left) c.2000
Noah's Ark (right) c.2000
Jubilee Windows III:
The Creation (left) c.1999
Christ Yesterday, Today, Forever (right) c.1999
Jubilee Windows IV:
Infant Moses is Rescued from the Nile (left) c.2000
Burning Bush, Moses with the Twelve Commandments, the Golden Calf (right) c.2000
Additional decorative glazing 2003

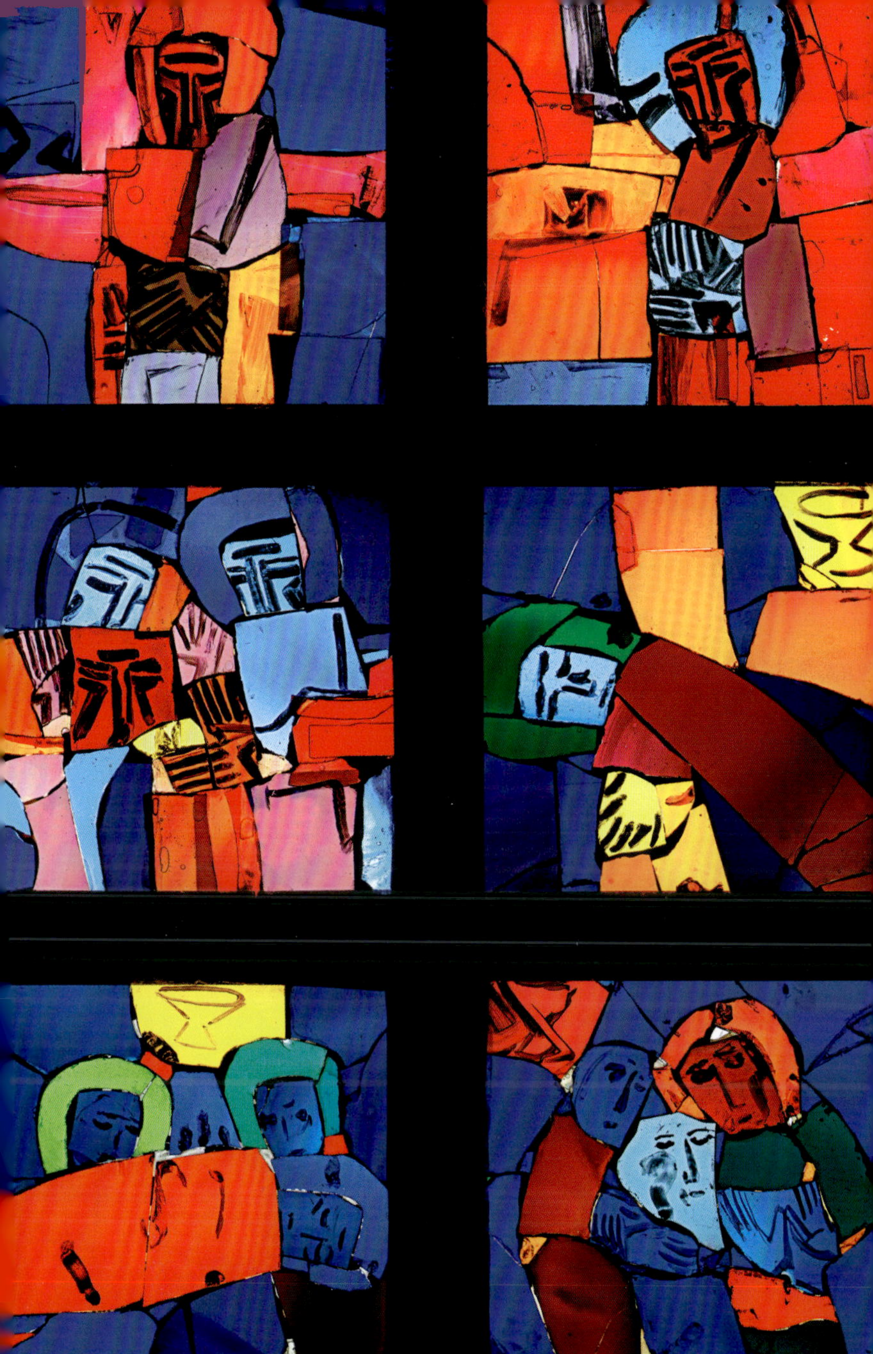

This page, from left: Christopher Campbell, detail of *Baptism of Christ* (*c.*1968), and detail of *The Risen Christ* (*c.*1968), Catholic Church (Our Lady of Mercy), Brookwood Grove, Artane, Dublin

Facing page: Patrick Muldowney, details of *The Angel Gabriel* (2000–1); of *Noah's Ark* (2000); of *View of Dublin from the Millennium Bridge* (2000–1), Catholic Church (St John Vianney), Ardlea Road, Artane, Dublin

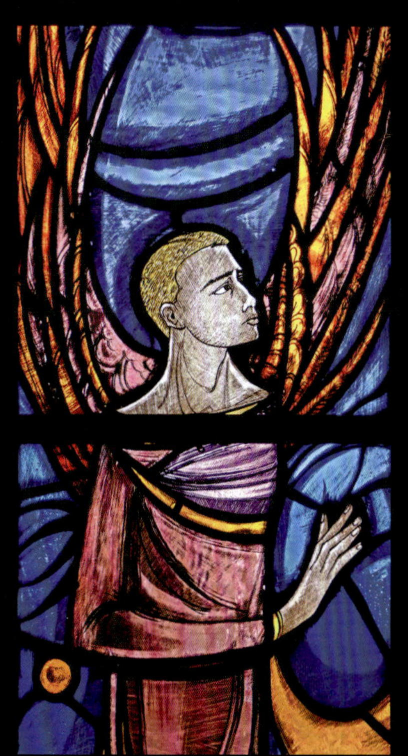

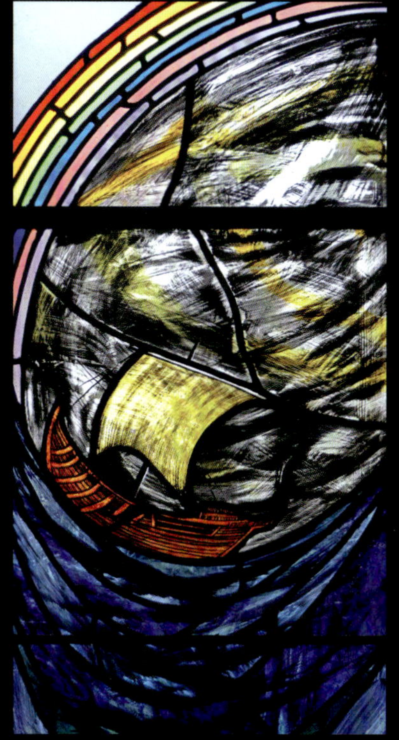

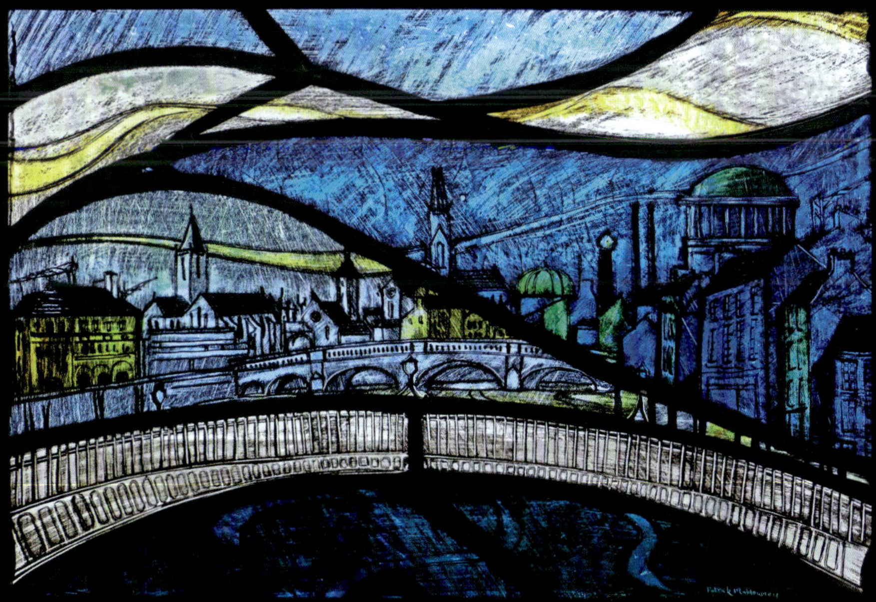

Dublin North, Artane: Oratory of the Resurrection of the Lord, Kilmore Road (currently Parish of St George, Serbian Orthodox Church)
BRANDT, Ruth
The Resurrection 1983
The Good Shepherd 1983
Blessed Edmund Ignatius Rice with Pupils 1983
The Nativity 1983
Abstract 1983 (circular band of stained glass at ceiling level)

Dublin North, Balbriggan: CC (St Peter and St Paul's)
CLARKE, Harry
The Widow's Son 1924 (2 lights)
The Visitation 1924 (2 lights)
DOWLING, William
Presentation in the Temple * 1944 (2 lights)
Christ Healing Lepers * 1944 (2 lights)
Miracle of the Loaves and Fishes * 1944 (2 lights)
Finding in the Temple * 1944 (2 lights)
Healing of the Woman who Touched the Hem of Our Lord's Garments * 1944 (2 lights)
St Patrick and the Princesses * 1944 (2 lights)
Resurrection * 1944 (single light)
Raising of Lazarus * 1944 (single light)
KING, Richard
Joachim and Anna 1936–7 (2 lights)
Blessed Virgin Mary and St Joseph 1936–7 (2 lights)
St Philomena and Blessed Oliver Plunkett 1936–7 (2 lights)
St Patrick and St Brigid 1936–7 (2 lights)
Also, *Annunciation* 1944 (2 lights) which may be by either William Dowling or Terry Clarke.
(All windows in the church were created at Harry Clarke Studios.)

Dublin North, Balbriggan: C of I (St George's)
O'BRIEN, Catherine
The Presentation in the Temple 1938 (2 lights)

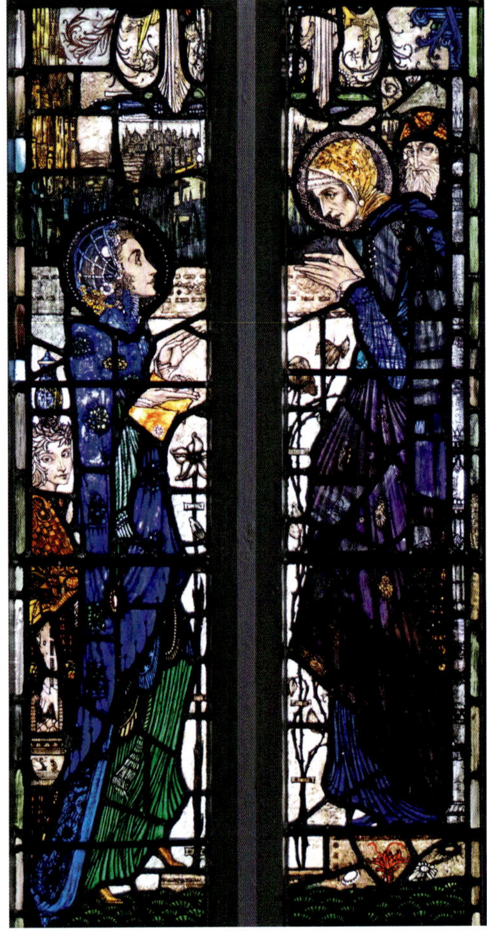

Above: Harry Clarke, detail of *The Visitation* (1924), Catholic Church (St Peter and St Paul's), Balbriggan, County Dublin

Dublin North, Baldoyle: St Patrick's Nursing Home, Dublin Street
WALSH, George W.
*St Patrick c.*1964 (painted by Willie Earley; originally one of three windows in Emmaus Retreat and Conference Centre, Swords. See separate entry.)

Dublin North, Ballyboughal: CC (Assumption of Our Lady)
KELLY, Kevin
*Assumption c.*2002
*Resurrection c.*2002
(Both created at Abbey Stained Glass Studios.)

Dublin North, Ballymun: CC (Our Lady of Victories), Ballymun Road
CORCORAN, Sheila
Man, Symbol of St Matthew 1968
Eagle, Symbol of St Mark 1968
Ox, Symbol of St Luke 1968
Eagle, Symbol of St John 1968
Dove 1968 (in the former baptistry, now the shop)
Christ the King 1968 (in Sacred Heart Chapel)
Madonna and Child 1968 (in Our Lady Chapel)
Decorative Glazing at Lower Level 1968
(Willie Earley assisted Sheila Corcoran in the making of these windows)
MOLONEY, Helen
Symbols including Lamb of God, Tree, Serpent and Apples, Dove, Flames of Pentecost, Cross and Five Wounds of the Crucifixion, Water of Baptism, Tree of Jesse, Crown of Victory, Anchor of Hope and Steadfastness, Keys of the Kingdom 1968 (8 windows creating octagonal lantern over altar)
WALSH, George W.
Stations of the Cross 1968
St Joseph 1968
St Patrick 1968
Madonna and Child 1968 (enclosed balcony above entrance)
(All above windows created at Abbey Stained Glass Studios.)

Dublin North, Bayside: CC (Church of the Resurrection), Bayside Boulevard
WALSH, George W.
Large Abstract Window 1968 (subsequently altered by others to incorporate figurative element from elsewhere)

Dublin North, Beaumont: Beaumont Hospital Chapel, Beaumont Road
BURKE, Phyllis
Creation 1987

Dublin North, Blanchardstown: CC (St Brigid's), Church Avenue
BURKE, Phyllis
St Brigid 1978 (in extension)

Dublin North, Blanchardstown: Blanchardstown Shopping Centre (oratory), Navan Road
KELLY, Kevin
Nativity 2002
(Created at Abbey Stained Glass Studios.)

Dublin North, Carpenterstown: CC (St Thomas the Apostle)
DOWLING, William
Immaculate Conception 1947 (3 lights; originally in the Dominican Convent, Dún Laoghaire)
(Created at Harry Clarke Studios.)

Dublin North, Castleknock: C of I (St Brigid's)
CLARKE, Harry
St Hubert, St Luke and St George (A) 1928 (3 lights)

Dublin North, Clonsilla: C of I (St Mary's)
CHILD, A.E.
The Angel of the Resurrection 1927
HONE, Evie
St Fiacre 1938

Dublin North, Clontarf: CC (St John the Baptist's)
MacBRIDE, William
Virgin Mary and St Elizabeth * *c.*1923 (2 lights)
St John the Baptist and Christ * *c.*1923 (2 lights)

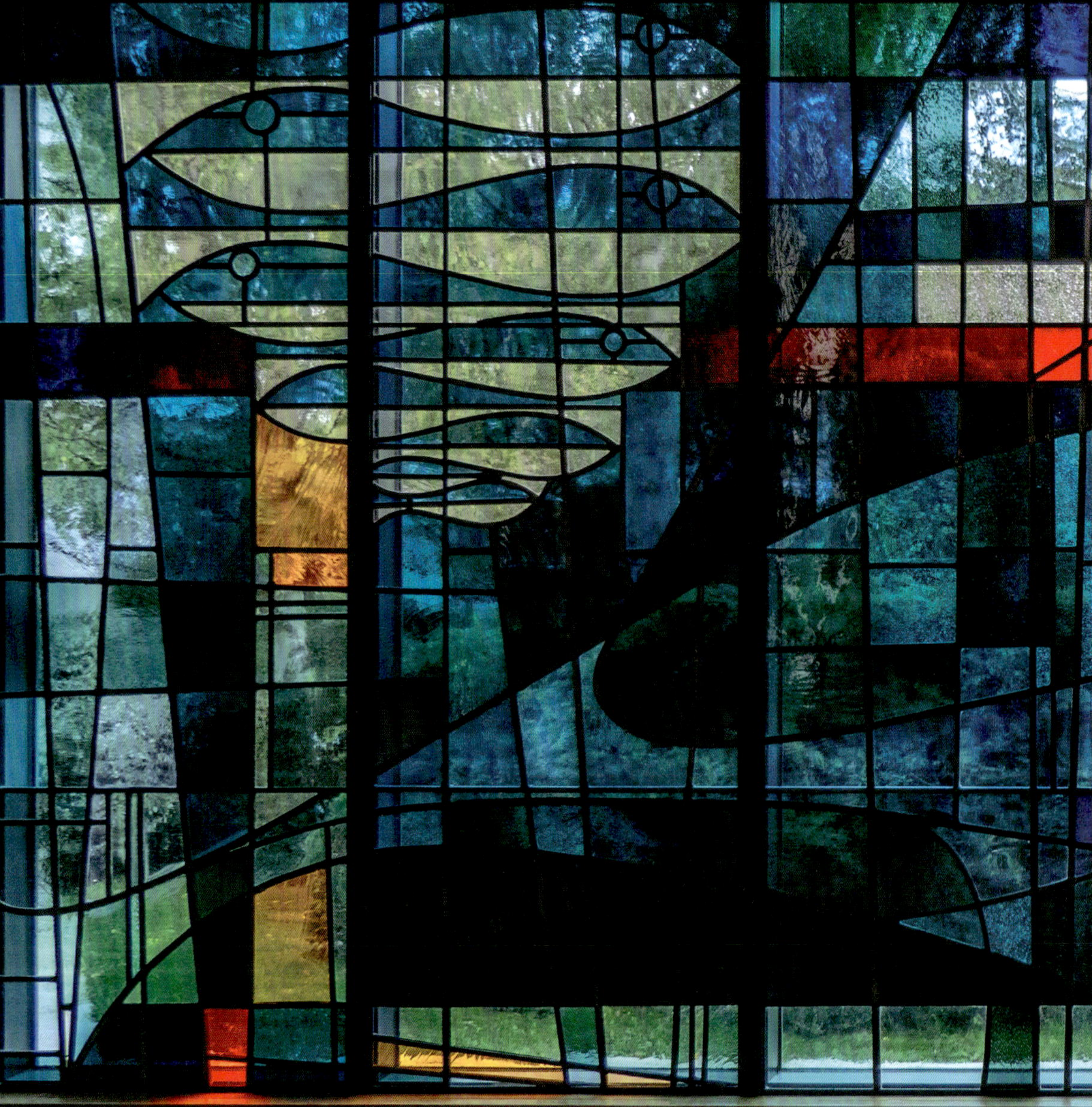

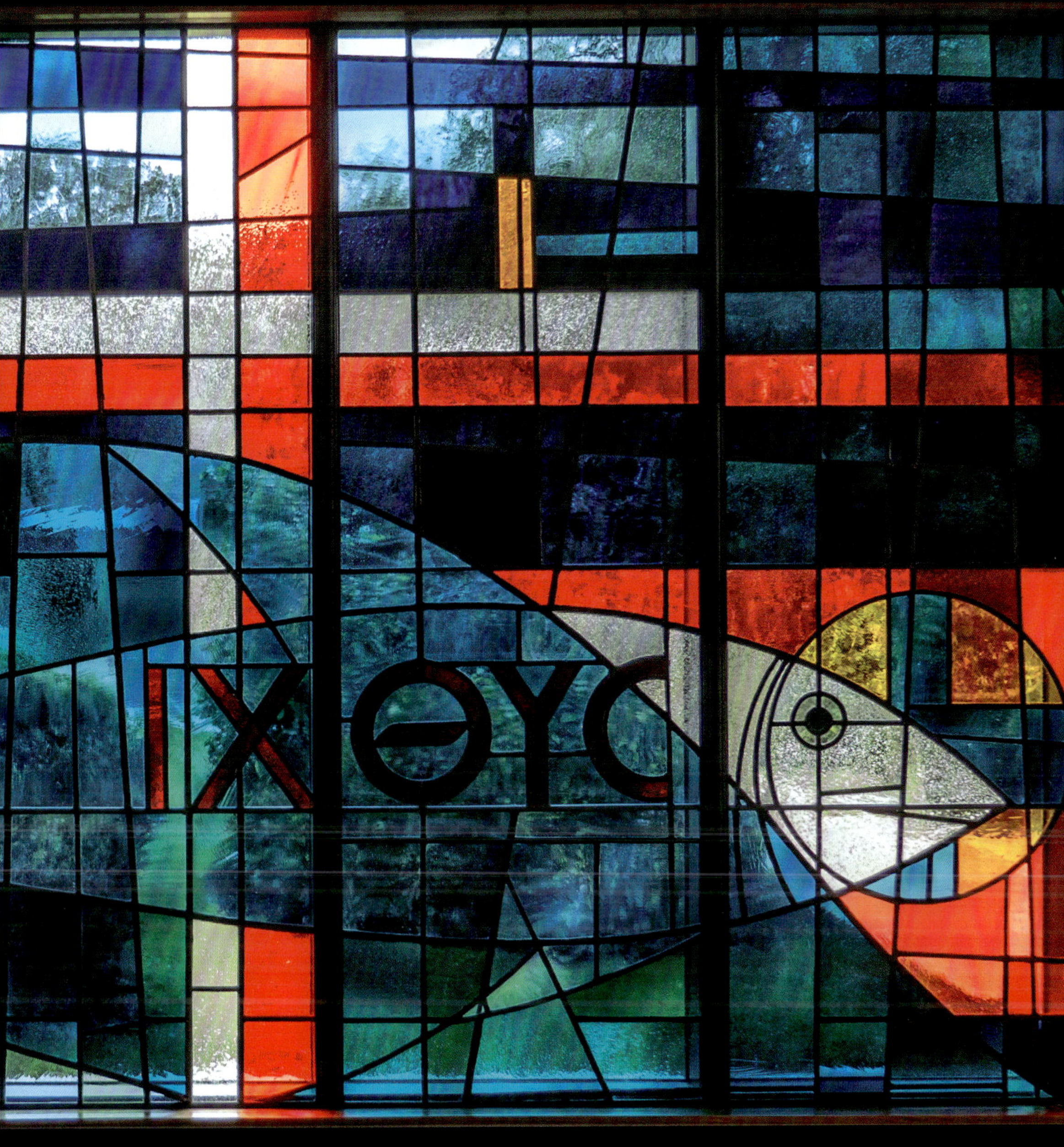

Richard King, *The Fish (Christ)* (1969–70),
Nazareth House Chapel, Clontarf, Dublin

Dublin North, Clontarf: C of I (St John the Baptist), Clontarf Road
O'BRIEN, Catherine
Christ Blessing Little Children 1950 (lower portion damaged)

Dublin North, Clontarf: Nazareth House Chapel, Malahide Road
KING, Richard
The Fish (Christ), Mary, the Passion, the Resurrection, the Pascal and Apocalyptic Lambs, and the Holy Spirit 1969–70 (seven windows in abstract stained glass)

Dublin North, Clontarf: Chapel of Daughters of Charity of St Vincent de Paul, Mount Prospect Avenue
KING, Richard
Stations of the Cross 1962–3 (fourteen single lights)

Dublin North, Clontarf: Clontarf and Scots Presbyterian Church, Clontarf Road
CLARKE, Harry
Pietà and Resurrection (war memorial) (A) 1919 (4 lights)

Dublin North, Clontarf: Former Verville Retreat Centre, Vernon Avenue
POLLEN, Patrick
St Dympna 1962–3 (sketch design, NIVAL)
St Brigid 1962–3
(Both these windows were removed and are now in a private collection, Dublin)

Dublin North, Coolock: C of I (St John the Evangelist's), Tonlegee Road
CHILD, A.E.
Faith * 1920
Valour 1920
Angels of Sorrow and Joy * (2 lights)

Dublin North, Dollymount: CC (St Gabriel's), St Gabriel's Road
DOWLING, William
Virgin Mary Flanked by Saints Daniel and Zachary with Archangel Gabriel above and Lion at Base 1956 (3 lights; drawing and photograph of cartoon, TCD)
(Created at Harry Clarke Studios.)

Dublin North, Dollymount: Jesuit Fathers' Manresa House, Clontarf Road
HONE, Evie
The Nativity 1945 (sketch design, NGI; sketch design, Manresa House, Dollymount, Dublin North; cartoon, NGI)
The Sacred Heart and Jesuit Saints 1945
Pentecost 1946
The Last Supper 1946
The Beatitudes 1946 (cartoon, NGI)
The above five were originally in St Stanislaus's College Chapel, Tullabeg, County Offaly.
Christ and the Soldier c.1940s (panel)
Madonna and Child with St Stanislaus c.1940s (panel)
Head of Christ c.1950 (panel)
PYE, Patrick
St Ignatius 1957 (panel, now in Community Dining Hall; formerly in the Jesuits' House, Emo, County Laois)

Dublin North, Donabate: CC (St Patrick's), Main Street
CLARKE, Harry
'Suffer Little Children' (B) 1926 (2 lights)
Also of note in this church is the rose window depicting *Angel Musicians* c.1937, though the artist as yet remains unidentified.

Right:
William Dowling, *Virgin Mary Flanked by Saints Daniel and Zachary with Archangel Gabriel above and Lion at Base* (1956), Catholic Church (St Gabriel's), Dollymount, Dublin

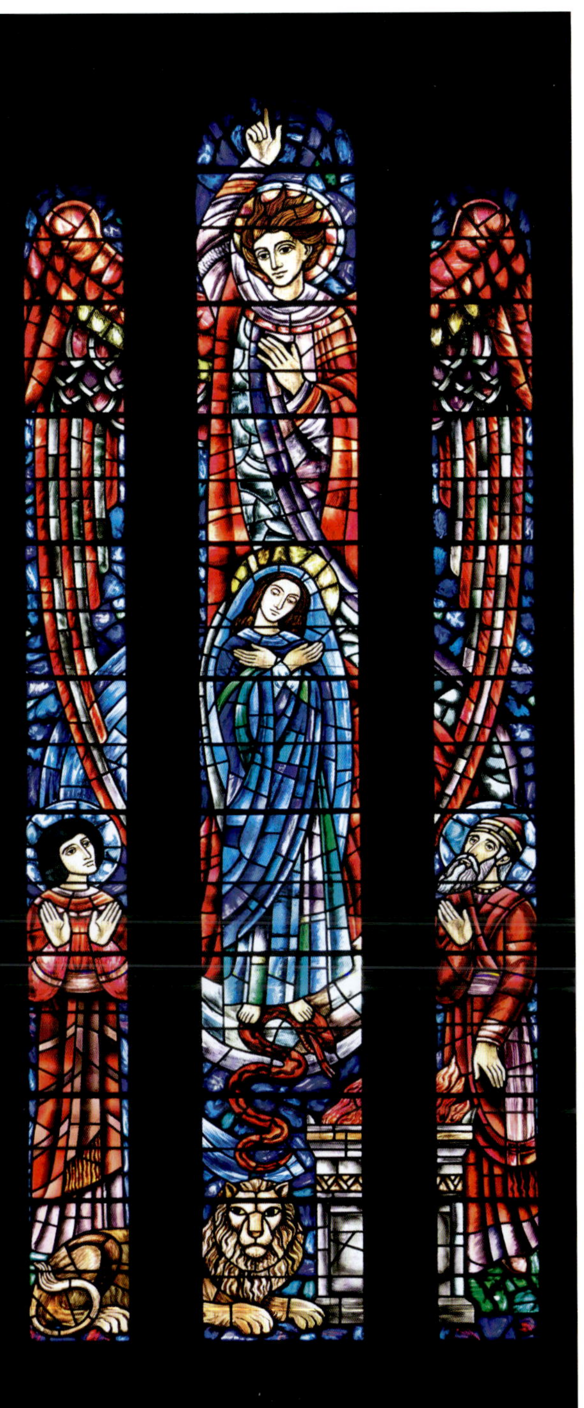

Dublin North, Donnycarney: CC (Our Lady of Consolation), Malahide Road
MURPHY, Johnny
Abstract lights in stained glass and slab glass 1968
Holy Spirit 1968 (in former baptistry, now repository)

Dublin North, Drumcondra: All Hallows College Chapel (Dublin City University), Grace Park Road
HONE, Evie
The Assumption 1954 (rose)

Dublin North, Drumcondra: CC (Corpus Christi), Home Farm Road
DOWD MURPHY, Róisín
Annunciation 1991 (2 lights)
Baptism of Christ 1991 (2 lights)
Agony in Garden 1991 (2 lights)
Ascension 1991 (2 lights)
(sketch designs and cartoons, NIVAL)

Dublin North, Drumcondra: Dominican Convent, Griffith Avenue
ELVERY, Beatrice
St Patrick 1909 (formerly in Dominican Convent, Eccles Street, Dublin)

Dublin North, Drumcondra: St Patrick's College, Dublin City University ('Quiet Space', former Vincentian oratory, first floor), Drumcondra Road Upper
PYE, Patrick
Holy Spirit in the Form of an Angel Guiding Vatican II, with Arrival of Pope John XXIII 1966
Holy Spirit in the Form of a Dove Coming Down on the Apostles, and They Head Out into the World 1967
(cartoons for both windows in the collection of St Patrick's College)

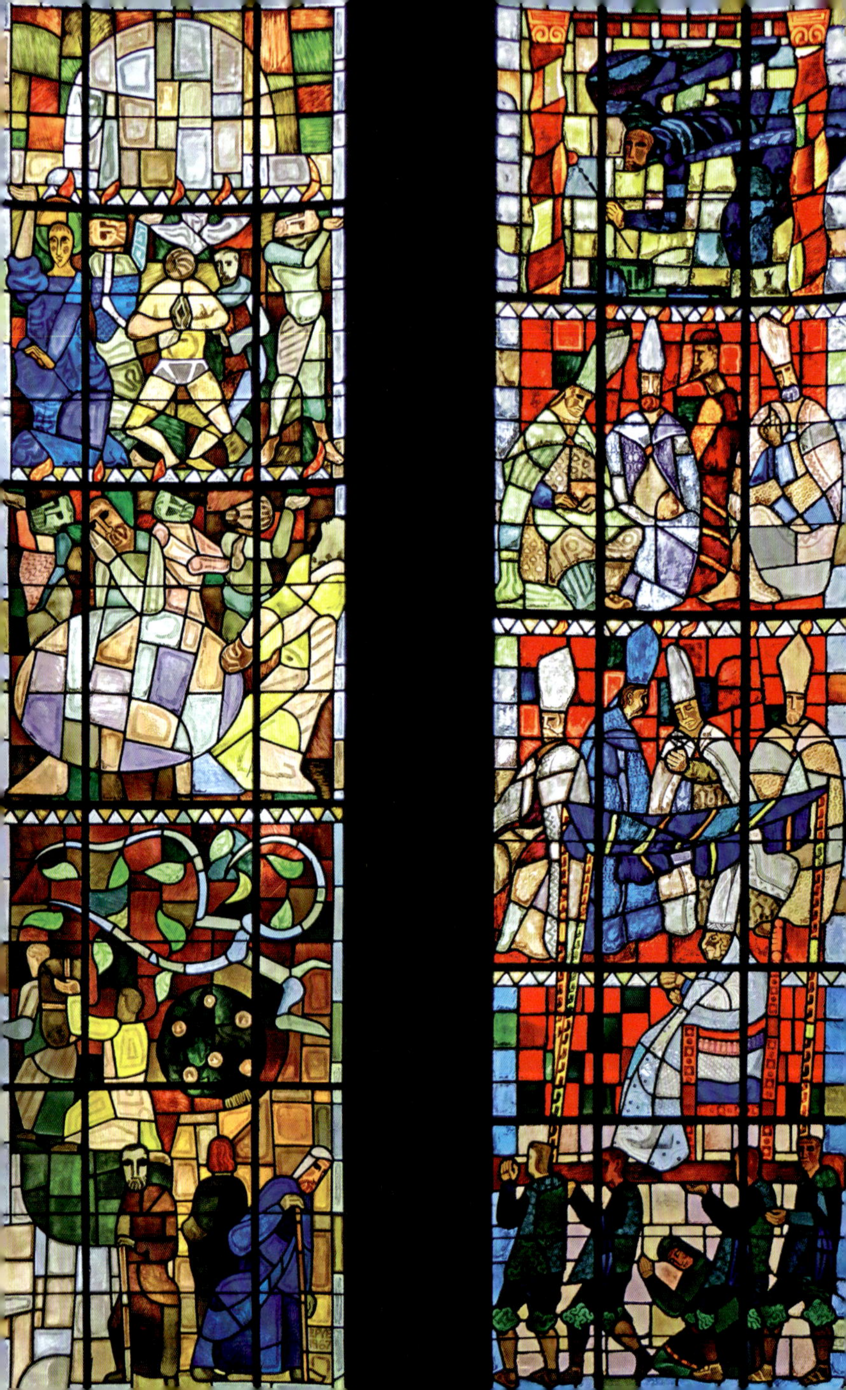

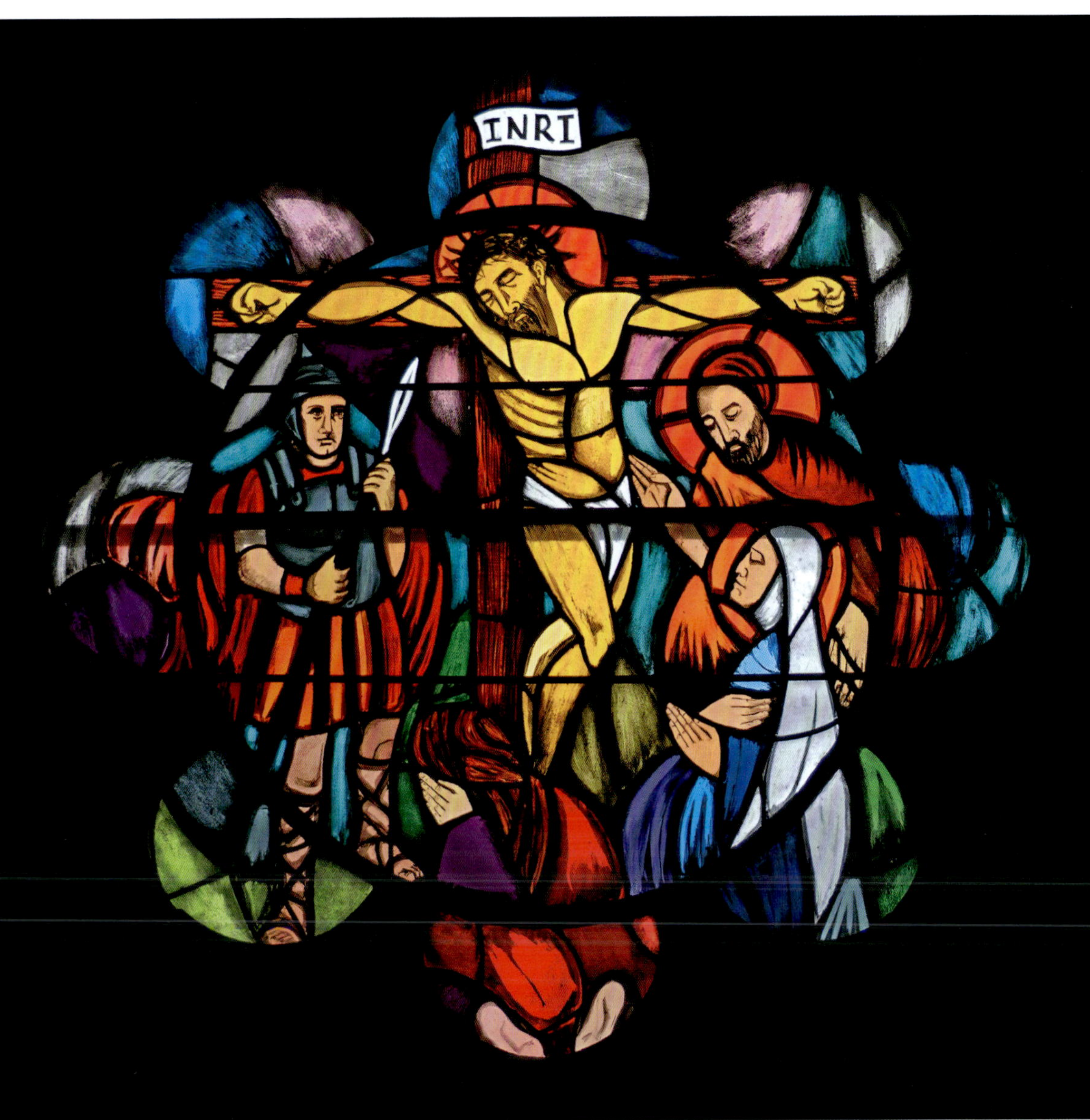

Above: Margaret Becker, detail of *Crucifixion, Surrounded by Eight Scenes from Christ's Passion* (1980), Catholic Church (Church of the Assumption), Howth, County Dublin

Left: Patrick Pye, *Holy Spirit in the Form of a Dove Coming Down on the Apostles, and They Head Out into the World* (1967), *Holy Spirit in the Form of an Angel Guiding Vatican II, with Arrival of Pope John XXIII* (1966), 'Quiet Space', St Patrick's College, Drumcondra, Dublin

Dublin North, Finglas: National Orthopaedic Hospital Cappagh (chapel), Cappagh Road
MURPHY, Johnny
*Scheme with religious symbols c.*1965 (sketch design for the tall window in NIVAL)
*Small abstract window c.*1965

Dublin North, Finglas West: CC (Church of the Annunciation), Cappagh Road. (Currently closed and due for demolition, to be replaced by smaller church on same site, incorporating some of George Stephen Walsh's stained glass and opus sectile mosaics.)
WALSH, George Stephen
Annunciation and abstract glazing 1967
Stations of the Cross 1967 (opus sectile mosaic)
Baptism of Christ 1967 (opus sectile mosaic)

Dublin North, Grangegorman: C of I (All Saints), Phibsborough Road
O'BRIEN, Catherine
Ruth and Naomi 1914
Memorial to Rev. Joseph Bewley who is Depicted Instructing Children on the Road through Life 1923
RHIND, Ethel
Archangel Michael 1921 (opus sectile mosaic on exterior wall) (sketch design, NGI)

Dublin North, Howth: CC (Church of the Assumption), Main Street
BECKER, Margaret
Crucifixion, Surrounded by Eight Scenes from Christ's Passion 1980 (rose)

Dublin North, Howth: C of I (St Mary's), Howth Road
PURSER, Sarah
Faith, Charity, and Hope (painted by Catherine O'Brien and Hugh Barden) 1905 (3 lights)
HONE, Evie
Scenes from the Lives of Christ and St Andrew 1943 (2 lights) (left-hand side cartoon, Our Lady's Hospice, Harold's Cross, Dublin south)
O'BRIEN, Catherine
The Baptism of Christ 1961 (2 lights) (sketch designs, NGI)
RHIND, Ethel
Fortitude 1910
Saints Killian, Michael and George 1920 (3 lights)
TOMLIN, Alan
Risen Christ with Angels 2004 (3 lights)
TOMLIN, Alan and Stanley
Blessed Virgin Mary 1973

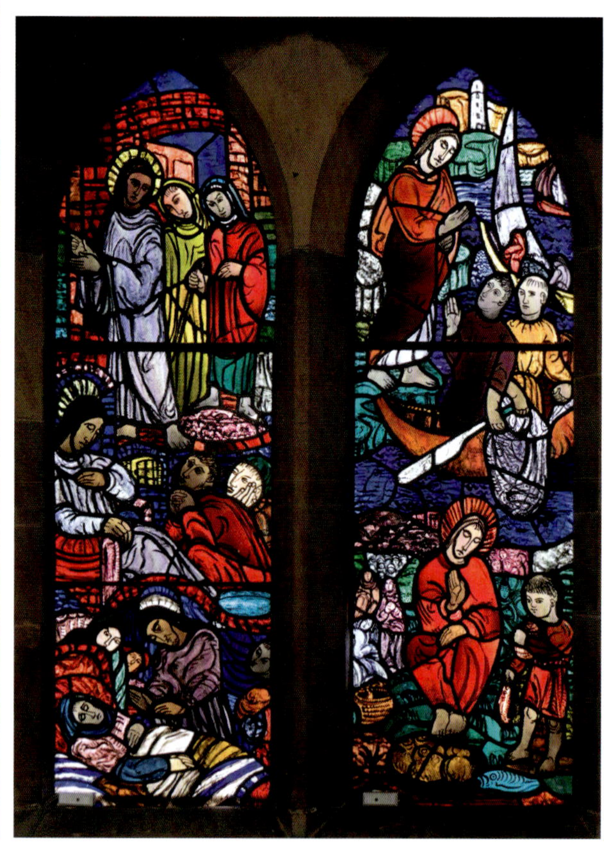

Dublin North, Kilmore West, near Beaumont: CC (Church of St Luke the Evangelist), Kilbarron Road
COX, James
St Patrick and St Bríd 1979 (2 lights)
St Fursa and St Íde 1979 (2 lights)
St Luke Painting the Virgin's Portrait * date unknown
KING, Richard
Untitled stained glass window of The Crucified Christ with Mary His Mother c.1963
Pietà c.1963

Dublin North, Kilsallaghan: C of I (St David's)
HEALY, Michael
Christ as Salvator Mundi 1917 (sketch design, NGI)

Dublin North, Lambay Island: Lambay Castle (private chapel)
POLLEN, Patrick
Trinity and Symbols of the Evangelists (three panels in cruciform shape) *c.*1966

Dublin North, Lusk: CC (St Maculind's), Chapel Road
CLARKE, Harry
St Maculind (A) 1924
Nine decorative chancel windows with floral ornament (A) 1924
CLARKE, Terry
Risen Christ 1941
Saints Brigid, Patrick and Colmcille 1944 (3 lights)
DOWLING, William
Virgin Mary, Christ Child with Holy Spirit above, and St Joseph * 1943 (3 lights) (colour schemes, preliminary design, TCD)
(Windows by Terry Clarke and William Dowling were created at Harry Clarke Studios.)
POLLEN, Patrick
Baptism of Christ 1957–8 (sketch design, NIVAL)

Left: Evie Hone, *Scenes from the Lives of Christ and St Andrew* (1943), Church of Ireland (St Mary's), Howth, County Dublin

Dublin North, Malahide: CASA (Caring and Sharing Association) Break House, Árd na Mara
WALSH, George W.
Washing of the Feet 2014

Dublin North, Malahide: CC (St Sylvester's), Prayer Chapel (right of church), Main Street
YOUNG, Peter
Seasons 2014 (4 panels)
Creation 2014 (8 panels)
Eden 2014 (4 panels)

Dublin North, Malahide: CC (Sacred Heart), Estuary Road
MURPHY, Johnny
Abstract clerestory windows 1991 (sketch designs, NIVAL)

Dublin North, Malahide: C of I (St Andrew's), Church Road
O'BRIEN, Catherine
Our Lord Blessing Children 1950 (2 lights) (sketch design, NGI)
RHIND, Ethel
St Andrew 1927
WALSH, George W.
The Sea as Symbol of Healing and Renewal, the Creator's Hands, Eucharist, Holy Spirit, Lighthouse as Symbol of Guidance 2006 (wheel window, above gallery)
Fishers of Men 2006
The Creation, History, Events and Individuals Relating to Malahide including St Oliver Plunkett, St Marnock, Church Festivals 2006 (five clerestory windows in the adjoining Chapel of St Marnock)

Dublin North, Malahide: Presbyterian Church, Dublin Road
MURPHY, Johnny
Sowing and Reaping 1956 (3 lights, with lettering by Michael Biggs) (sketch designs and cartoons, NIVAL)

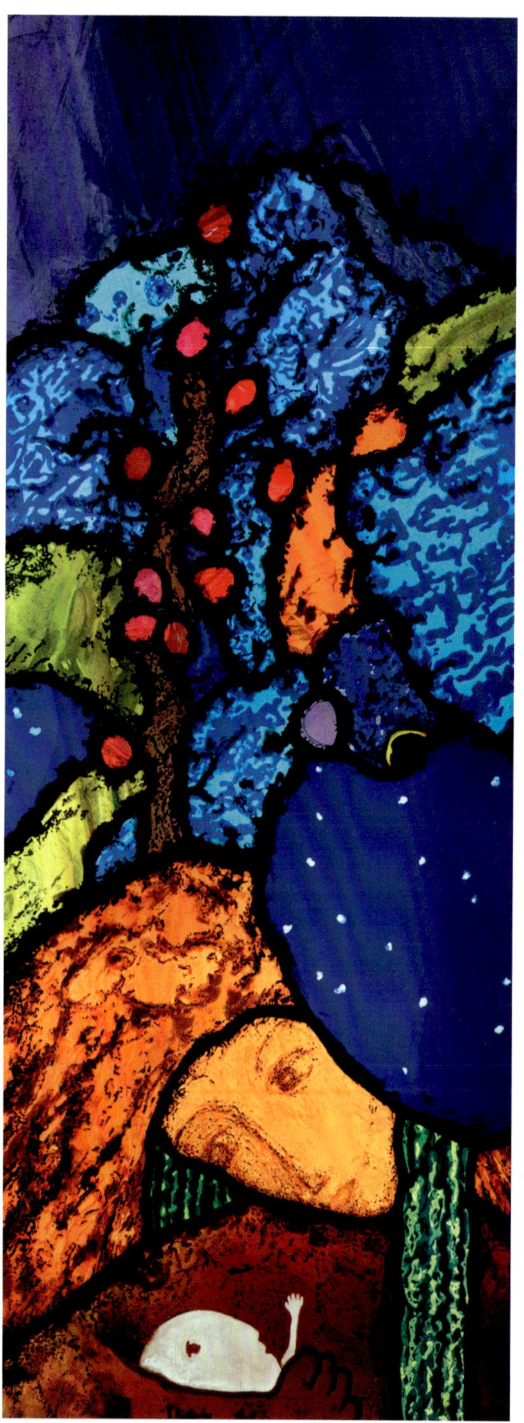

Dublin North, Mulhuddart: CC (St Luke the Evangelist)

EARLEY, Willie

Return of the Prodigal Son 1993 (when the sanctuary was extended *c.*2005 the window was, to its detriment, relocated to a high position under a skylight)

Dublin North, Phibsborough: CC (Vincentian Fathers' Church of St Peter), Cabra Road

CLARKE, Harry

The Sacred Heart, St Margaret Mary and St John Eudes 1919 (3 lights; the window was altered and the tracery lights were destroyed when re-sited in 1972).

Four ornamental windows, with amber quarry slabs and Symbols of the Passion 1924 (each 2 lights, former mortuary chapel)

Fanlight comprised of rose and two spandrels 1924 (former mortuary chapel)

Dublin North, Porterstown: CC (St Mochta's), Luttrellstown Road

BURKE, Phyllis

The Resurrection 1993

Dublin North, Raheny: CC (Our Mother of Divine Grace), Howth Road

WALSH, George W.

Abstract 1962 (15 triangles in *dalle de verre* above entrance)

Abstract 1962 (wall of glass in *dalle de verre* leading to former baptistry)

Dublin North, Raheny: C of I (All Saints), Howth Road

RHIND, Ethel

Censing Angel, Trumpeting Angel 1917 (2 lights)

Left: Peter Young, *Eden II* (2014), Prayer Chapel adjoining Catholic Church (St Sylvester's), Malahide, County Dublin

Right: Johnny Murphy, *Sowing and Reaping* (1956), Presbyterian Church, Malahide, County Dublin

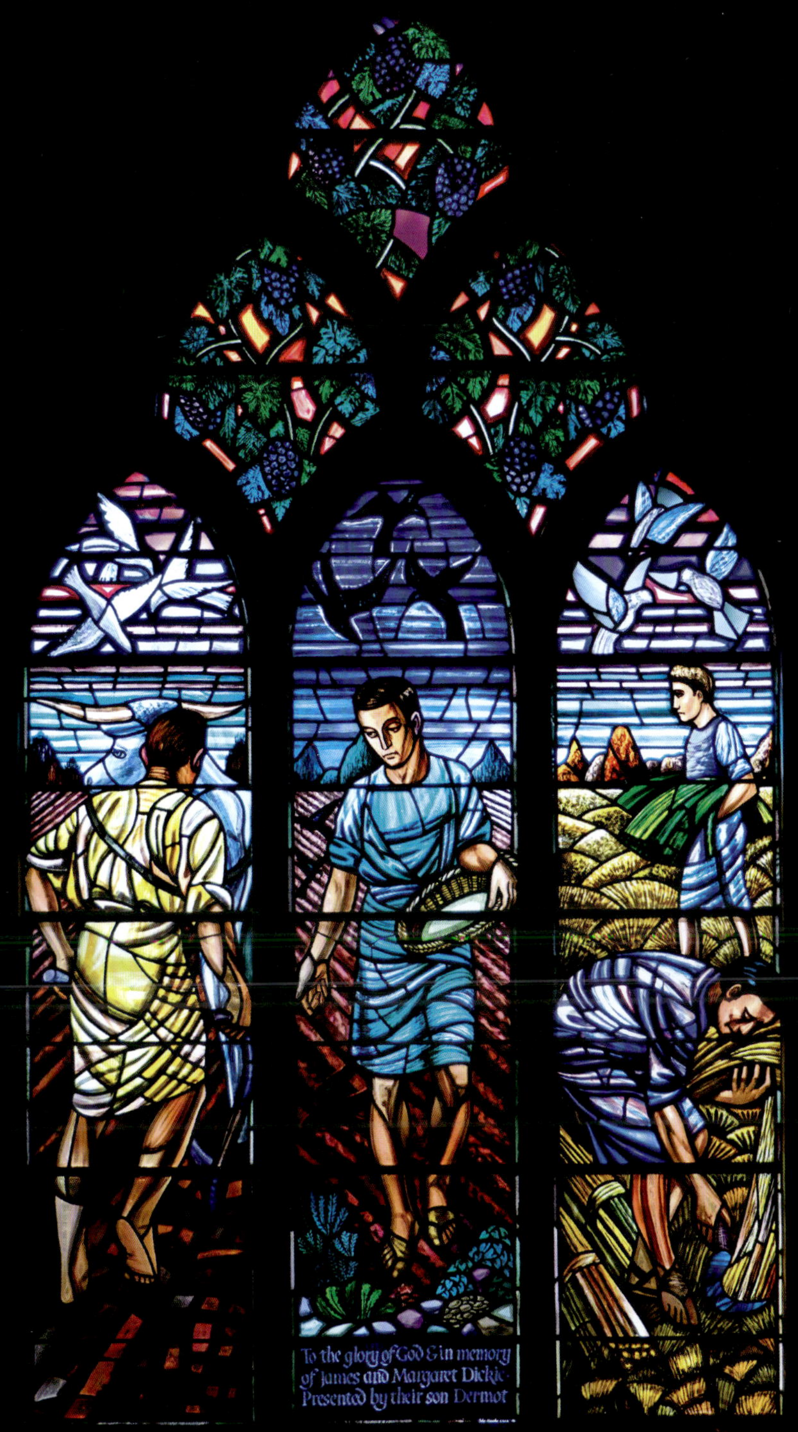
To the glory of God & in memory
of James and Margaret Dickie
Presented by their son Dermot

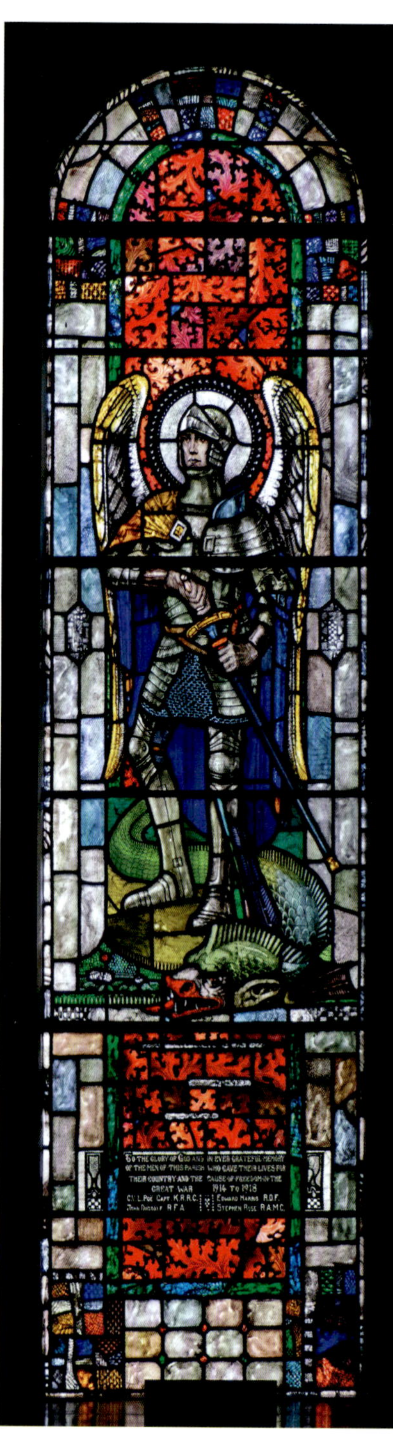

Dublin North, Raheny: St Francis Hospice, Station Road
HONE, Evie
*St Anne with the Child Mary c.*1943 (panel; formerly in St Anne's Hospital, Northbrook Road, Dublin)

Dublin North, Raheny: Former Chapel of the Novitiate of the Oblate Fathers of St Mary Immaculate, Belcamp Hall (windows currently off site in OPW storage)
CLARKE, Harry
St Kevin and St Laurence O'Toole (A) 1925 (2 lights)
The Two Princesses, Eithne and Fidelma, and St Gobnait (A) 1925 (2 lights)
St Patrick and Blessed Oliver Plunkett (A) 1925 (2 lights)
St Malachy and St Brendan (A) 1925 (2 lights)
St Brigid and St Dymphna (A) 1925 (2 lights)
St Doulough and St Columcille (A) 1925 (2 lights) (borders altered in late 1950s)

Dublin North, Rush: CC (St Maur's)
WALSH, George W.
Nativity 1990–3
Crucifixion 1990–3
Resurrection 1990–3
Assumption 1990–3
Crucifix 1990–3 (behind altar) 1990–3
St Thérèse of Lisieux 1990–3
St Catherine 1990–3
St Joseph 1990–3
Miraculous Draft of Fishes 1990–3

Dublin North, Santry: C of I (St Pappan's), Santry Villas
McGOLDRICK, Hubert
Michael 1921–2
Phoebe * 1929
O'BRIEN, Catherine
Fortitude and Justice, with Job and St John the Baptist 1935 (2 lights)

Left:
Hubert McGoldrick, *Michael* (1921–2), Church of Ireland (St Pappan's), Santry, Dublin

Dublin North, Stoneybatter: Sisters of Charity Convent Chapel, Stanhope Street
MURPHY, Johnny
Abstract with Cross motif 1988 (*dalle de verre*)

Dublin North, Swords: Emmaus Retreat and Conference Centre, Balheary Demesne
WALSH, George W.
Our Lady of Perpetual Help c.1964 (painted by Willie Earley)
St Joseph c.1964 (painted by Willie Earley)
(Both windows relocated from their original location in the building.)

DUBLIN SOUTH

Dublin South, Balally: CC (Ascension of the Lord), Cedar Road
HENSEY, Maree
Twenty Lunettes on the Theme of the Creation 2006

Dublin South, Baldonnel: Garrison Church (Our Lady of Loreto and St Brigid's), Casement Aerodrome
TOMLIN, Alan
Commemorative medallions set in leaded lights featuring various models of vintage aircraft, crests and logos, religious symbols 1997– (approximately 50; series ongoing)
Our Lady of Loreto with Emblems 1999 (5 lights)
Memorial to Air Corps Crew of Rescue 111 2000 (3 lights, in porch)

Dublin South, Ballinteer: CC (St John the Evangelist), Ballinteer Avenue
POLLEN, Patrick
The Nativity 1973
The Last Supper 1973
The Crucifixion 1973
The Resurrection 1973
Hand of God, Symbols of the Evangelists, Alpha and Omega, Crossed Keys 1973
The Creation, with symbols and vignettes including Animals, Agricultural Activities, Map, and Galleon 1973

Dublin South, Ballinteer: Wesley College, Ballinteer Road
CHILD, A.E.
Fortitude * 1927 (3 lights; currently in storage)

Dublin South, Ballsbridge: CC (Our Lady Queen of Peace), Merrion Road
EARLEY, Leo
Our Lady Queen of Peace with the Christ Child c.1953 (circular)
Apparition of the Sacred Heart to St Margaret Mary c.1956 (circular)
Annunciation c.1956 (circular) (faces and hands of these windows painted by Jacky Earley)

Dublin South, Ballsbridge: C of I (St Bartholomew's), Clyde Road
McGOLDRICK, Hubert
Christus Salvator Noster 1940 (opus sectile mosaic)
O'BRIEN, Catherine
St Patrick 1925 (south porch) (sketch design, NGI)
St George 1926 (south porch)
St Margaret of Scotland 1938 (north porch)
St Brigid 1941 (north porch)
The Supper at Emmaus 1941
The Adoration of the Magi 1960 (opus sectile mosaic) (sketch designs, NGI)

Dublin South, Ballsbridge: Marian College (Marist Brothers' Oratory), Lansdowne Road
HENEY, Patrick
The Assumption 1959
Saint Marcellin Champagnat 1959 (bottom section with lettering replaced recently)
Jesus with St Joseph in the Workshop 1959

Dublin South, Ballsbridge: St Conleth's College, Clyde Road
KING, Richard
St Conleth 1958

Dublin South, Ballsbridge, St Declan's School, Northumberland Road
MURPHY, Johnny
Five Joyful Mysteries 1959 (sketch design, NIVAL)

Dublin South, Ballsbridge: St John's House (private nursing home), Merrion Road
O'BRIEN, Catherine
*Annunciation c.*1929 (formerly in St Mary's Home, Pembroke Park, Ballsbridge)

Dublin South, Ballsbridge: St Michael's College, Ailesbury Road
EARLEY, Leo
*St Michael c.*1968–9

Dublin South, Ballyboden: CC (Our Lady of Good Counsel), Whitechurch
CARRICK, Desmond
*Resurrection c.*1965 (panel, entrance vestibule)
*Crucifixion c.*1965 (panel, entrance vestibule)
*Crown of Thorns c.*1965 (panel, entrance vestibule)
*Deposition c.*1965 (panel, entrance vestibule)
*Virgin and Child c.*1965 (sanctuary)

Dublin South, Ballybrack: C of I (St Matthias's), Church Road
O'BRIEN, Catherine
*St Brigid c.*1957

Dublin South, Ballyfermot: CC (St Matthew's), Blackditch Drive
MOONEY, Douglas
Scenes from the Gospels 2007–8 (clerestory, behind the altar)
Scenes from Local History 2007–8 (clerestory, facing the altar)
Religious Themes 2007–8 (clerestory, left and right sides)
*Wheat and Vine c.*2010 (side oratory)
*Decorative glazing c.*2010 (Virgin Mary Shrine)

Dublin South, Ballyroan, Rathfarnham: CC (Church of Holy Spirit), Marian Road
MURPHY, Johnny
Scheme of Stations of the Cross 1967 (sketch designs and cartoons, NIVAL)
Abstract and symbolic lights 1967

Dublin South, Belfield: University College Dublin, Charles Institute of Dermatology
KING, Richard
The Kevin Barry Memorial Window 1932–4 (single light window in eight panels)
(Created at Harry Clarke Studios.)

Dublin South, Blackrock: Blackrock College Chapel, Rock Road
HEALY, Michael
The Annunciation 1937–8 (2 lights) (sketch design, NGI)
The Visitation 1937–8 (2 lights) (sketch design, NGI)
HONE, Evie
Decorative window with Armorial Shields 1937
Three decorative windows 1937
Decorative window with Six Episcopal Shields 1938
Fr Jules Leman presenting a model of Castledawson House to the Virgin and Child 1940 (lunette)
*Abstract c.*1937 (panel in staff dining hall; formerly in Kimmage Manor, Dublin)
McGOLDRICK, Hubert
The Sacred Heart 1937

Dublin South, Blackrock: Blackrock College Castle Chapel, Rock Road
HONE, Evie
Pentecost 1940–1 (3 lights) (cartoons, Blackrock College)

Dublin South, Blackrock: CC (St John the Baptist), Temple Road
EARLEY, William (Bill) E.
Scenes from the Life of St Anne c.1933 (5 lights)
HONE, Evie
Virgin and Child, St Brigid and St Patrick 1954–5 (3 lights)

Dublin South, Blackrock: C of I (All Saints'), Carysfort Avenue
GEDDES, Wilhelmina
Archangel Gabriel 1920
Archangel Raphael 1920
Archangel Michael 1920 (destroyed by fire *c.*1937)

Dublin South, Blackrock: CC (Guardian Angels), Newtownpark Avenue
WALSH, George W.
Guardian Angel 1967 (9 lights)
Angel 1967 (sandblasted onto wall)
Abstract windows 1967 (two 15 lights, and additional glazing)
Stations of the Cross 1967 (sandblasted on travertine and filled in with black oil paint)
Eucharist and Baptism, Resurrection and Holy Spirit 2010 (Two pairs of panels of fused glass mounted on free-standing screens, one holding an ambry for holy oils, and one a memorial to deceased of the parish. Executed by Michelle O'Donnell.)
Risen Christ 1967 (3 lights, in former mortuary chapel)

Dublin South, Booterstown: St Andrew's College, Booterstown Avenue
CHILD, A.E.
St Andrew with Angels 1921 (Transferred from St Andrew's College, St Stephen's Green, where it originally was 3 lights composed of six panels. Four panels now remain, two with alterations.)

Dublin South, Cabinteely: CC (St Brigid's)
EARLEY, Leo
Crucifixion 1950s (3 lights)
St Brigid 1950s
St Joseph 1950s
St Therese 1950s
St Patrick 1950s
HENEY, Patrick
Crucifixion 1952 (3 lights, side chapel)

Dublin South, Carrickmines: C of I (known as Tullow Church), Brighton Road
ELVERY, Beatrice
The Prodigal Son and the Good Samaritan 1908 (2 lights)
War Memorial 1919–20 (2 lights)
O'BRIEN, Catherine
The Supper at Emmaus and Christ Welcoming a Soldier 1917
*David and Isaiah c.*1945 (2 lights) (sketch design, NGI)
The Annunciation, the Nativity, the Crucifixion, and Our Lord Appearing to St Mary Magdalene 1959 (4 lights) (sketch design, NGI)

Dublin South, Churchtown: Little Company of Mary Convent, Braemor Park
HONE, Evie
Baptism of Christ date unknown (panel in light box, ground floor)

Dublin South, Churchtown: Notre Dame School, Upper Churchtown Road
EARLEY, Willie
Blessed Virgin Surrounded by Six Angels 1958

Dublin South, Clondalkin: C of I (St John's), Tower Road
CHILD, A.E.
Michael with Two Angels, St Martin, the Centurion, Duty and Sacrifice 1921 (3 lights)

Dublin South, Clonskeagh: CC (Immaculate Virgin Mary of the Miraculous Medal), Bird Avenue
DOWLING, William
Resurrection * 1956–7 (3 lights, in former mortuary chapel)
Baptism of Christ * 1956–7 (in former baptistry)
Christ with Children * 1956–7 (in former baptistry)
Holy Family * 1956–7 (in former baptistry)
(Decorative leaded panels in doors and screens by the Dublin Glass and Paint Company. Decorative windows including gallery window (5 lights) by Earley and Company.)

Dublin South, Dalkey: Our Lady's Manor Nursing Home Chapel, Bulloch Harbour
DOWD MURPHY, Róisín and MURPHY, Johnny
Our Lady of Mount Carmel 1965
Church Symbols 1965 (15 windows)
(cartoons, NIVAL)

Dublin South, Dalkey: Sorrento Park, Coliemore Road
PURSER, Sarah
Memorial to John Dowland 1937 (opus sectile mosaic; executed by Hubert McGoldrick. Face vandalised.)

Dublin South, Donnybrook: Avila Carmelite Centre, Morehampton Road
WALSH, George W.
Holy Spirit and Our Lady of Mount Carmel 2006
Holy Spirit and God the Father 2006
Trinity and Gospel 2006
Ministry 2006 (window above door)

Dublin South, Donnybrook: CC (Church of the Sacred Heart), Stillorgan Road
CLARKE, Harry
St Rita (B) 1924
St Bernard (B) 1924
(these windows flank *Our Lady of Sorrows* by William MacBride)
HEALY, Michael
St Patrick, with St Fidelma and St Eithne 1914 (2 lights) (sketch design, NGI)
MACBRIDE, William
Our Lady of Sorrows 1924

Dublin South, Donnybrook: Muckross Park Dominican Convent Chapel (currently closed), Marlborough Road
MCGOLDRICK, Hubert
*Risen Christ with (at base) Crucifixion c.*1944–5

Dublin South, Donnybrook: Royal Hospital, Morehampton Road
BURKE, Phyllis
Spring 1980s (Chapel)
Autumn 1980s (Chapel)
WALSH, George W.
Pair of abstract windows 1990 (mortuary chapel)

Dublin South, Dún Laoghaire: CC (St Michael's), Marine Road
MURPHY, Johnny and CORCORAN, Terry
Abstract lights and dalle de verre 1973
PYE, Patrick
Baptism of Christ 1972
Annunciation 1972 (sketch design, NIVAL)
Madonna Attending to the Infant Christ 1972 (sketch design, NIVAL)
Our Lady Teaching St John 1972 (sketch design, NIVAL)

Dublin South, Dún Laoghaire: C of I (Christ Church), Park Road
CHILD, A.E.
'I am the Resurrection and the Life' 1909

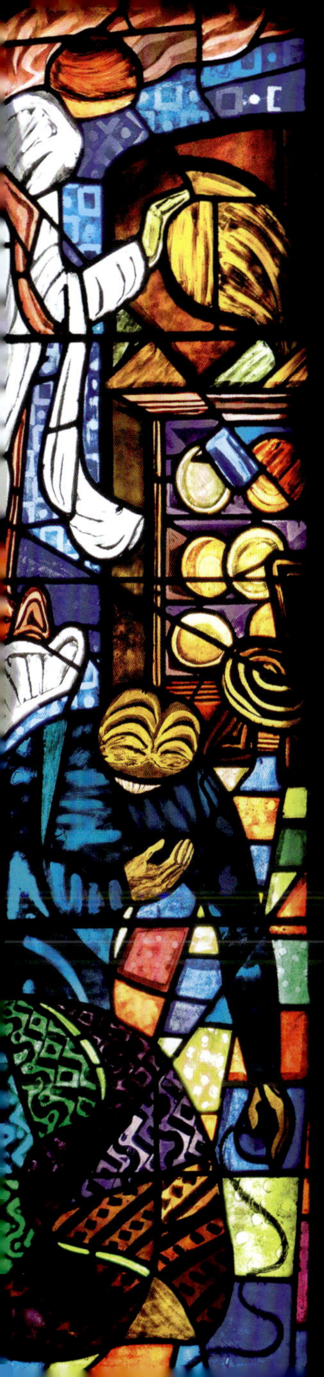

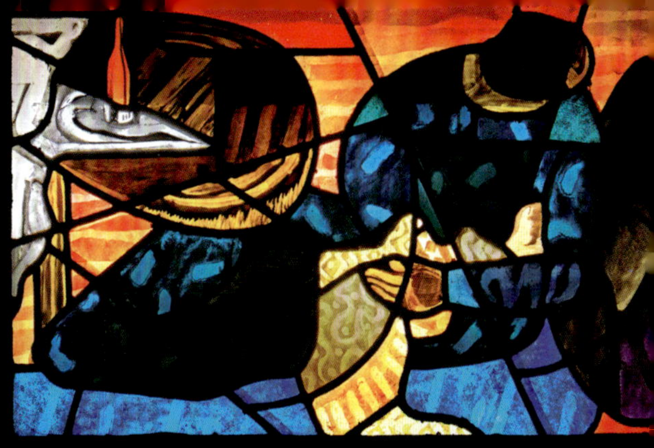

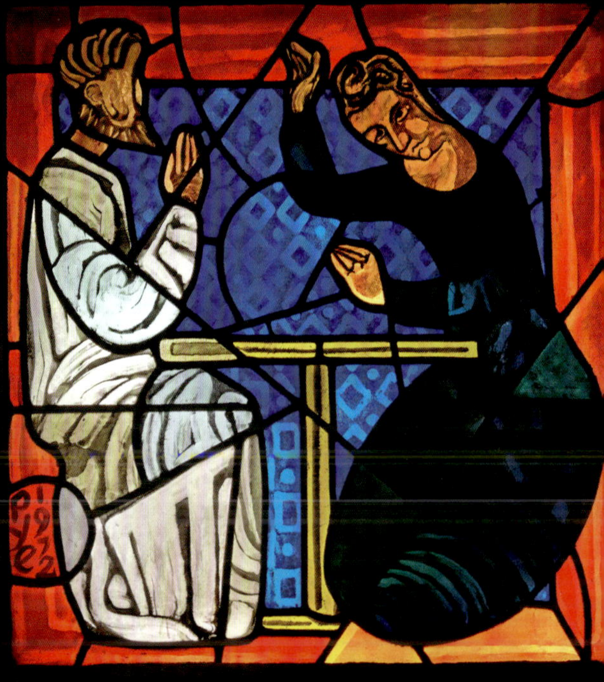

Clockwise from left:
Patrick Pye,
Annunciation,
Madonna Attending to the Infant Christ,
Our Lady Teaching St John (all 1972),
Catholic Church (St Michael's),
Dún Laoghaire, County Dublin

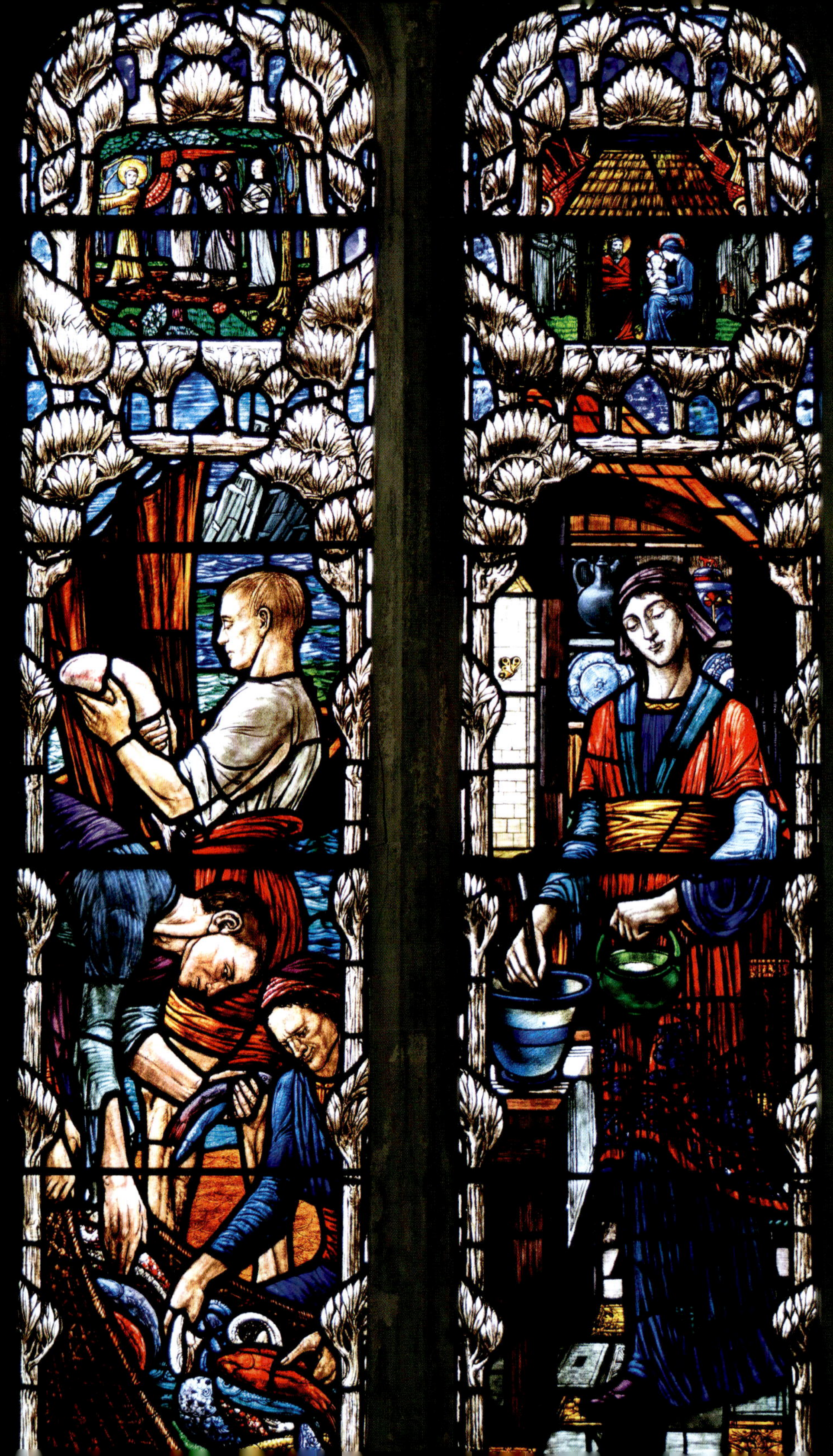

Dublin South, Dún Laoghaire: DLR Lexicon Library and Cultural Centre, Queen's Road
LAMB, Katharine
Untitled (exploring map making, sea charts and floral taxonomy as representations of the geography and nature of the borough) 2014 (light box, Moran Park entrance)

Dublin South, Dún Laoghaire: National Maritime Museum, Haigh Terrace
LAMB, Peadar
Dún Laoghaire Diptych 2010–1 (two separate windows)

Dublin South, Dún Laoghaire: Presbyterian Church, York Road
MACBRIDE, William
Knight and Soldier Receiving Crown from Angel (war memorial) * *c.*1918 (2 lights)
(Created at Joshua Clarke and Sons.)
RHIND, Ethel
The Parables of the Good and Faithful Servant, and of the Prudent Virgins 1909 (2 lights)
The Miraculous Draft of Fishes, and the Parable of the Leaven 1922 (2 lights)
The Good Samaritan, and the Parable of the Lost Groat 1925 (2 lights)
(There is a sketch design for a window, which was not executed, depicting the *Parable of the Talents* by Ethel Rhind for this church, NGI.)

Dublin South, Dundrum: C of I (St Nahi's), Upper Churchtown Road
CHILD, A.E.
The Sermon on the Mount 1929
Our Lord Walking on the Sea 1934
HONE, Evie
The Annunciation 1933–4 (left- and right-hand side cartoons, NGI)
O'BRIEN, Catherine
'I am the Resurrection and the Life' 1914 (sketch design, NGI)
The Disciples at Emmaus 1919
The Miraculous Draft of Fishes 1919
After the Transfiguration 1936 (sketch design, NGI)
Christ Blessing Little Children 1947
RHIND, Ethel
Praise the Lord 1916

Dublin South, Dundrum: CC (Holy Cross), Main Street
HEALY, Michael
Our Lady Queen of the Rosary with St Catherine and St Dominic 1919 (3 lights) (sketch design, NGI)

Dublin South, Dundrum: Sacred Heart Convent Chapel, Mount Anville, Mount Anville Road
KING, Richard
St Elizabeth of Hungary 1934
(Created at Harry Clarke Studios.)

Dublin South, Elm Park: St Vincent's University Hospital Chapel, Merrion Road
WALSH, George W.
All stained glass, non-figurative 1972

Dublin South, Foxrock: CC (Our Lady of Perpetual Succour), Kill Lane
DEEGAN, Philip
Virgin and Child * 1927–8
(Created at Harry Clarke Studios, originally for a private residence, Ardlui, Blackrock, from where it was removed.)
KELLY, Kevin
St Brendan 2001
(Created at Abbey Stained Glass Studios.)

Left:
Ethel Rhind, detail of *The Miraculous Draft of Fishes, and the Parable of the Leaven* (1922),
Presbyterian Church, Dún Laoghaire, County Dublin

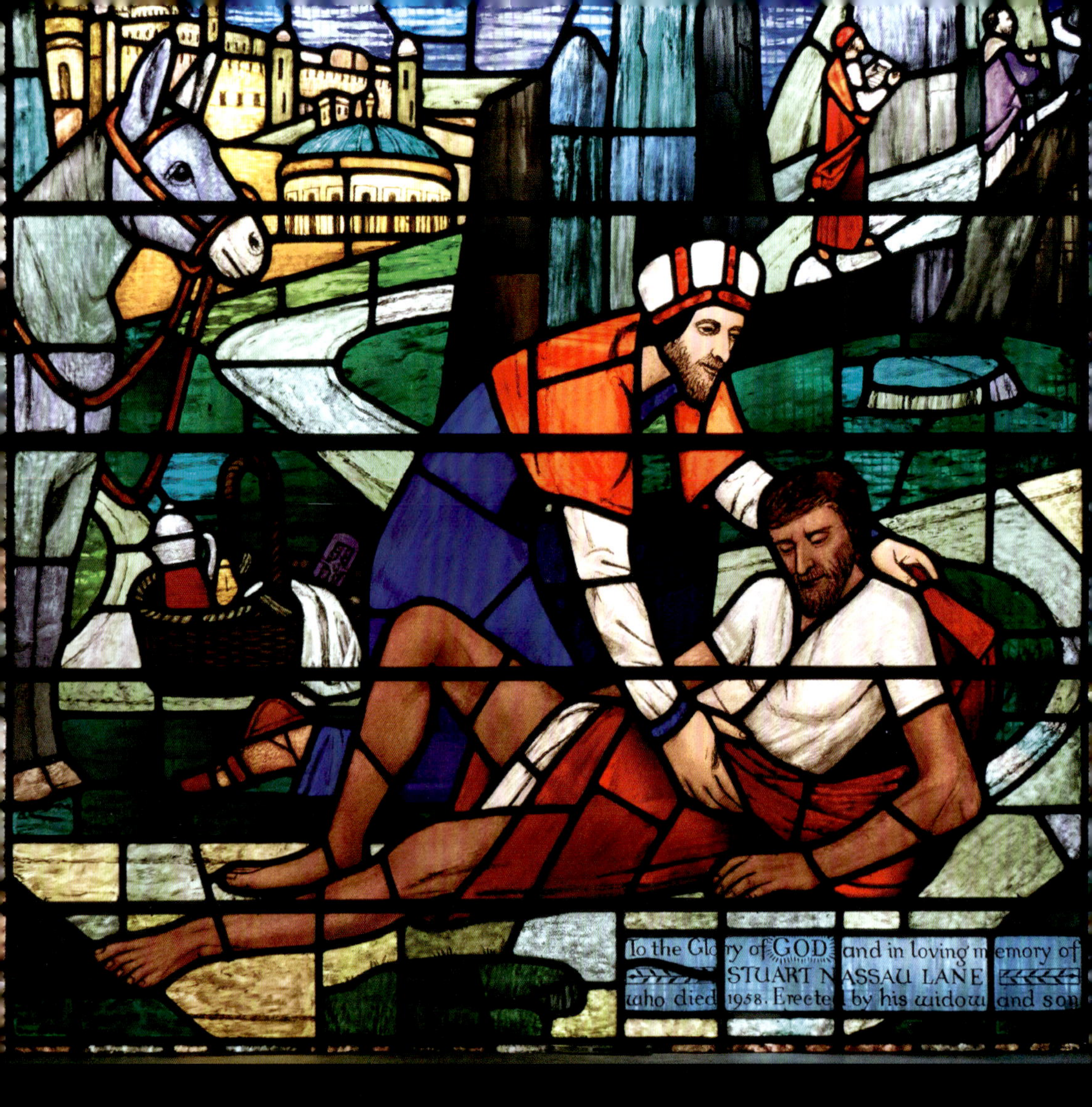

Catherine O'Brien, *The Good Samaritan* (1960), Russian Orthodox Church, Harold's Cross, Dublin

Dublin South, Glasthule: CC (St Joseph's), Summerhill Road
FOX, Kathleen
St Tobias 1909

Dublin South, Glenageary: C of I (St Paul's), Silchester Road
BECKER, Margaret
The Cherry Trees 1995–6 (in rear porch)

Dublin South, Greenhills: CC (Church of the Holy Spirit), Limekiln Lane
KING, Richard
Pentecost 1967–70 (wall of stained glass)
MURPHY, Johnny
Roof glazing abstracts and dalle de verre side windows 1969

Dublin South, Harold's Cross: Mount Jerome Cemetery, Harold's Cross Road
CHILD, A.E.
The Crucifixion 1905 (in the Kincade Family Vault, window now sealed)
HEALY, Michael
Resurrection 1915 (in the O'Shaugnessy Family Vault. It was severely vandalised *c.*1981 and the window is now sealed.)

Dublin South, Harold's Cross: Our Lady's Hospice, Harold's Cross Road
CLARKE, Harry
The Sacred Heart, St Joseph and Our Lady (B) 1928 (3 lights, on back staircase landing, previously in the Jesuit Fathers' Retreat House Chapel, Rathfarnham Castle, Dublin)

Dublin South, Harold's Cross: Russian Orthodox Church (former C of I), Harold's Cross Road
MacBRIDE, William
'Suffer Little Children to Come unto Me' * *c.*1923
O'BRIEN, Catherine
The Good Samaritan 1960 (sketch design, NGI)

Dublin South, Inchicore: CC (St Michael's)
CLARKE, Terry
Five Joyful Mysteries of the Rosary 1945 (5 lights)
DOWLING, William
St Michael, Virgin Mary, Sacred Heart, St Joseph, St Lawrence O'Toole * 1945 (5 lights)
(Both windows created at Harry Clarke Studios.)

Dublin South, Inchicore: Sacred Heart Fathers Oratory, Inchicore Road
MULDOWNEY, Patrick
Parables from the Old Testament: Moses on Mount Sinai, and God Punishes the Israelites 2003
Ecce Homo with Alpha and Omega, The Passion of Christ and Lamb of God 2003
Parables from the New Testament: Jesus and the Woman of Samaria at the Well, and Jesus Heals the Paralytic at Capernaum 2003

Dublin South, Killiney: C of I (Holy Trinity), Killiney Hill Road
CLARKE, Harry
The Angel of Hope and Peace 1919
McGOLDRICK, Hubert
The Annunciation and the Crucifixion 1943 (2 lights)

Dublin South, Killiney: CC (St Stephen's), Killiney Hill Road
BECKER, Margaret
St Joseph with Christ as a Child 1982
MOLONEY, Helen
Christ Crucified with St Stephen and Saul, with Symbols of the Life of Christ and the Redemption 1982 (sketch designs and scaled cartoon, NIVAL)

Dublin South, Killiney: Holy Child School Chapel, Military Road
NEVIN, Stanislaus
Scheme of windows in dalle de verre, featuring abstract geometric patterns (executed by Goddard and Gibbs of Shoreditch, London) 1961–2

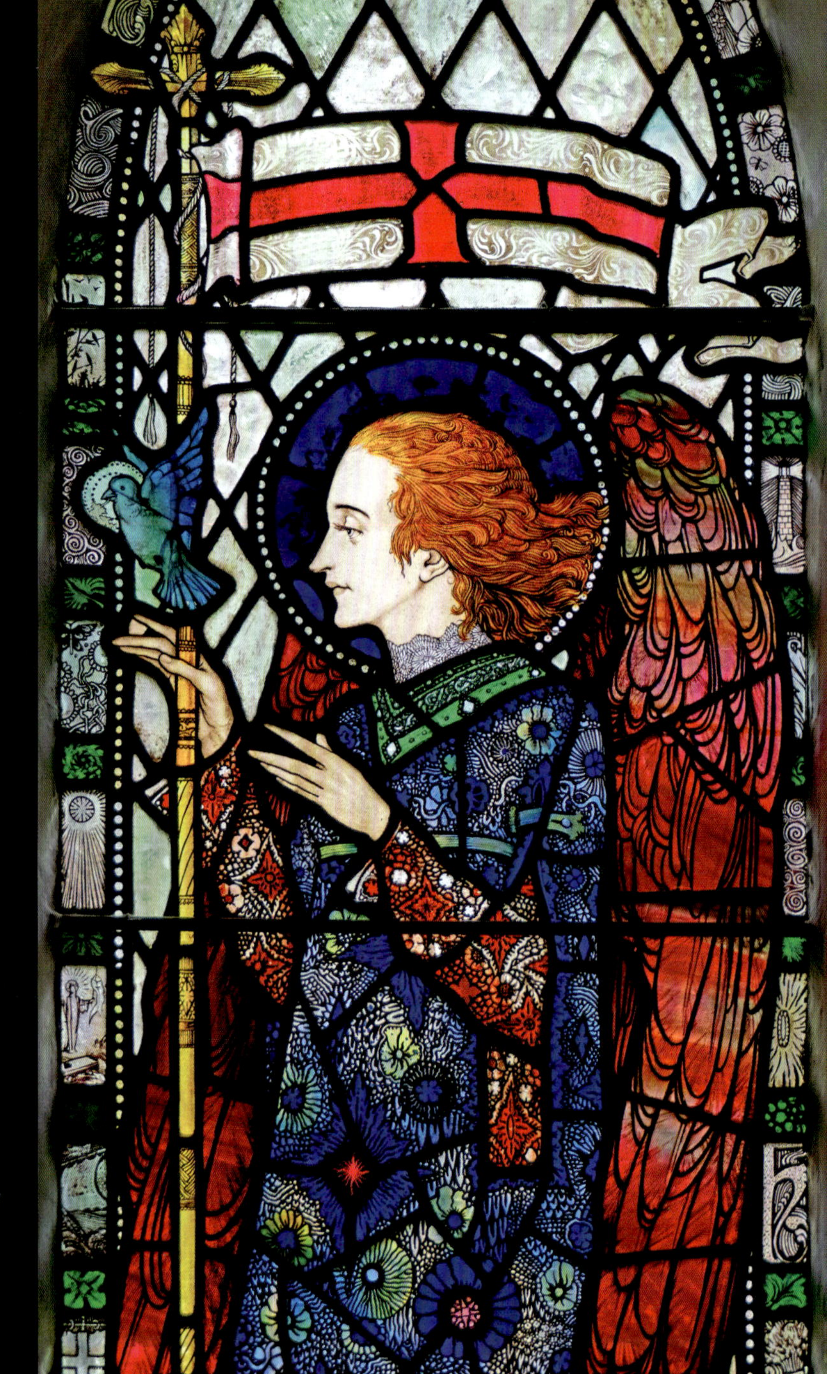

Harry Clarke, detail of *The Angel of Hope and Peace* (1919), Church of Ireland (Holy Trinity), Killiney, County Dublin

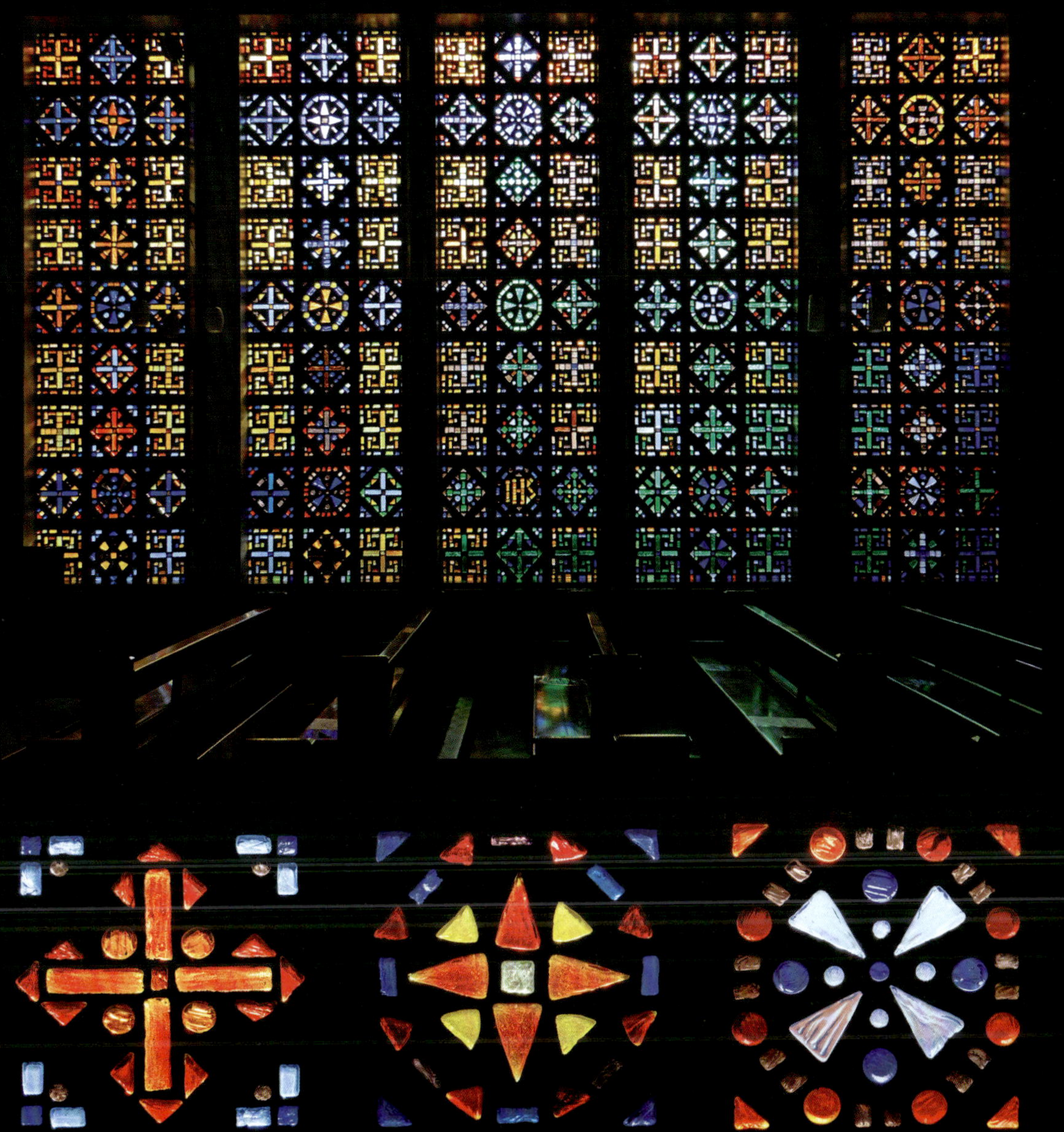

From top:
Stanislaus Nevin, section of right-hand wall, with details below, from *Scheme of windows in dalle de verre featuring abstract geometric patterns* (1961–2), Holy Child School Chapel, Killiney, County Dublin

Dublin South, Kill o' the Grange: CC (Holy Family), Kill Avenue
WALSH, George W.
Scheme of abstract windows, including three windows (8 lights each) with acid-etched Christian symbols 1972–3

Dublin South, Kill o' the Grange: C of I, Rochestown Avenue
McGOLDRICK, Hubert
The Good Shepherd 1931
(NGI has two sketch designs by Michael Healy, *The Good Shepherd* and *St Peter*, which were prepared as alternates for this window.)
O'BRIEN, Catherine
'Let Light Perpetual Shine Upon Them' 1947 (2 lights)

Dublin South, Kilmacud: CC (St Lawrence O'Toole's), Lower Kilmacud Road
BURKE, Phyllis
The Last Supper, with Entombment, Crucifixion, Resurrection 1969
St John the Baptist 1969 (in Prayer Room)
Baptism of Christ 1969 (in Prayer Room)

Dublin South, Kilternan: C of I (Golden Ball), Enniskerry Road
MOLLOY, Austin
'The Searcher after Wisdom' 1913–4 (panel)

Dublin South, Kimmage: Holy Spirit Church, Kimmage Manor, Whitehall Road
CLARKE, Terry
Zacharius * c.1940 (clerestory)
DOWLING, William
St James the Greater 1940
St Edward the Confessor c.1940
Immaculate Conception * c.1940
St Anne with the Young Mary 1940
St Peter c.1940
Sacred Heart c.1940
St Michael c.1940
Annunciation c.1940
St Joseph * 1941 (opus sectile mosaic in opal glass)
Cross (with bronze case for relic) 1941 (opus sectile mosaic in opal glass)
Stations of the Cross c.1941–2 (opus sectile mosaic in opal glass)
KING, Richard
St Brigid 1940
St Paul 1940
St Thomas Aquinas 1940
(Of the 28 windows in the church – plus *St Peter Claver* in ancillary room – all were made at Harry Clarke Studios with the exception of *St John Evangelist* which was made at Earleys. It is likely that either William Dowling and/or Terry Clarke designed the other windows not identified here.)
McGOLDRICK, Hubert
St Columba 1941 (Room of Reconciliation)

Dublin South, Kimmage: Kimmage Manor, Whitehall Road
KELLY, Kevin
St Claude Poullart des Places and St Francis Libermann 1999–2000 (in Main Reception, Marian House)
(Created at Abbey Stained Glass Studios.)

Dublin South, Lucan: C of I (St Andrew's), Main Street
O'BRIEN, Catherine
The Good Shepherd 1923–4 (3 lights)

Dublin South, Lucan: Lucan Public Library, Lucan Shopping Centre, Newcastle Road
LAMB, Katharine
Lucan Portrait 2000–1 (light box in foyer)

Right:
Phyllis Burke, *The Last Supper, with Entombment, Crucifixion, Resurrection* (1969), Catholic Church (St Lawrence O'Toole's), Kilmacud, Dublin

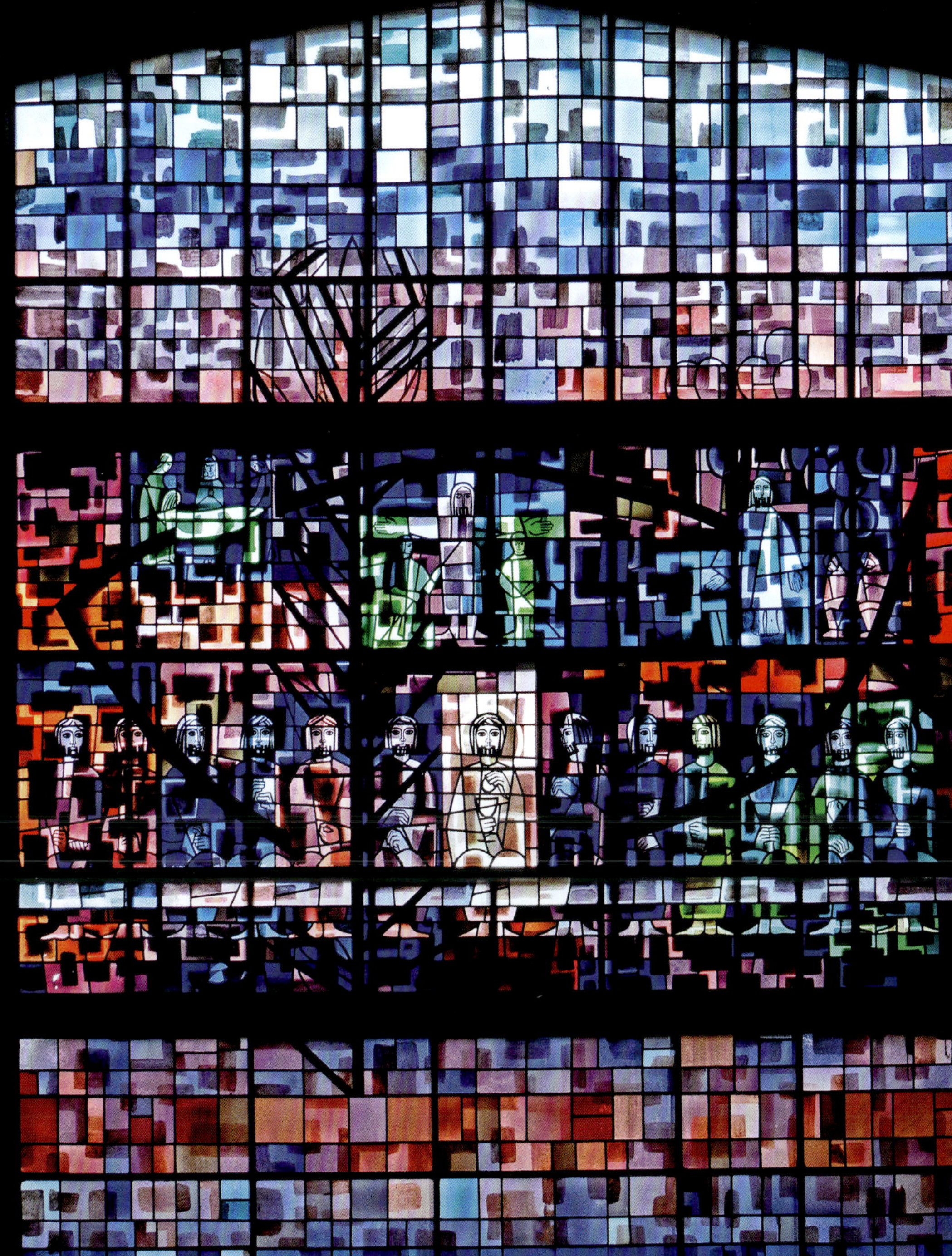

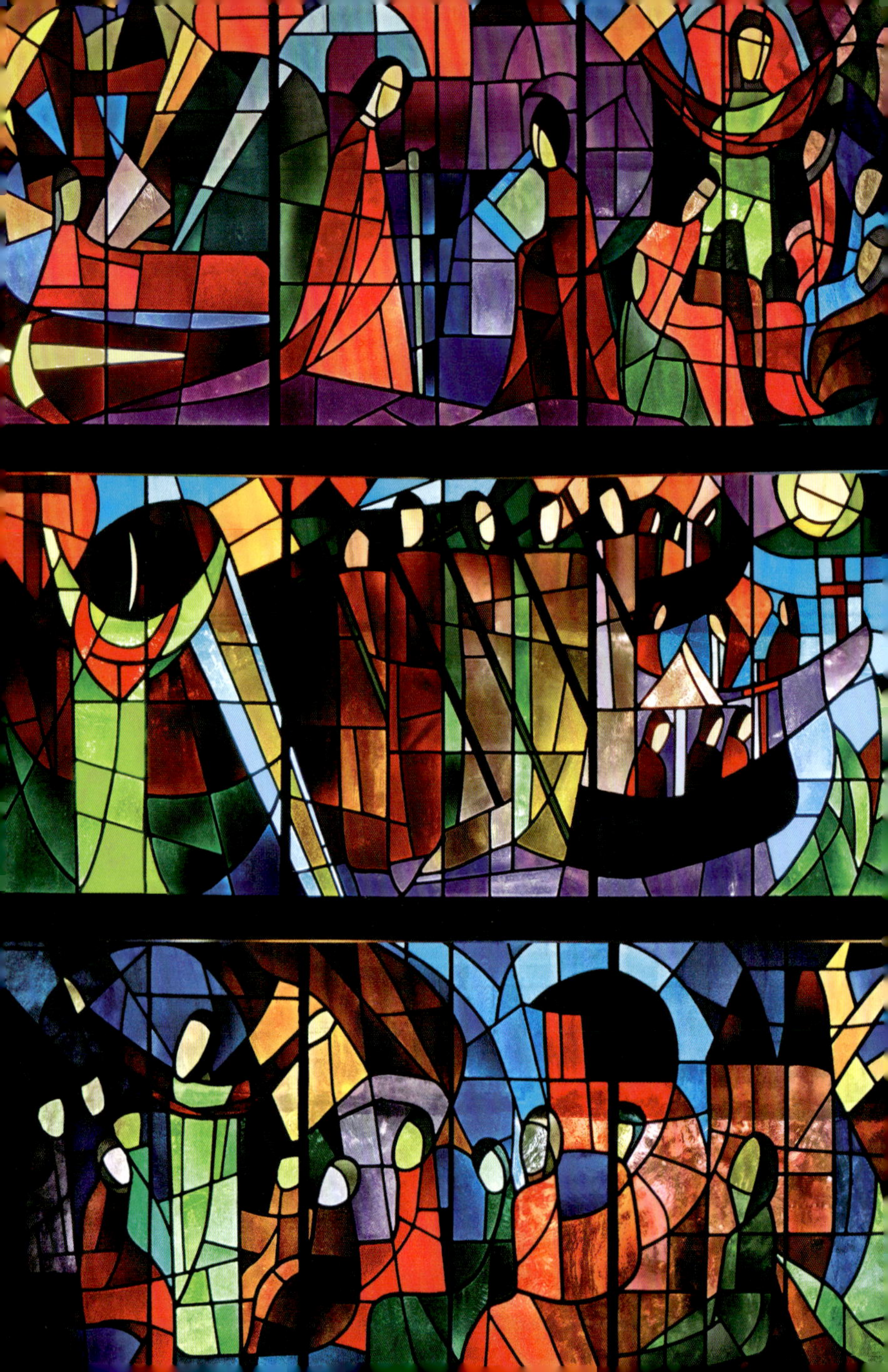

Dublin South, Milltown: C of I (St Philip's), Temple Road
CHILD, A.E.
Sacrifice, Victory, Peace 1920 (3 lights)

Dublin South, Milltown: Jesuit Provincialate, Milltown Park, Milltown Road
HONE, Evie
Head of Christ 1950 (panel) (cartoon, Manresa House, Dollymount, Dublin North)
POLLEN, Patrick
Conversion of St Paul 1962 (panel)

Dublin South, Monkstown: CC (St John's; Society of St Pius X, former C of I), Upper Mounttown Road
O'BRIEN, Catherine
Te Deum 1951

Dublin South, Monkstown: Sacred Heart Convent (closed in 1977 and subsequently demolished, windows presumed destroyed)
BURKE, Phyllis
Twelve windows of abstract designs (cartoons, NIVAL) 1967

Dublin South, Mount Merrion: C of I (St Thomas's), Foster Avenue
CHILD, A.E.
Knight in Armour 1920
Christ with Kneeling Knight 1920
HONE, Evie
St George 1941 (entrance porch)

Dublin South, Parnell Road: Christian Brothers Monastery Chapel (demolished post 1994, unclear if windows salvaged)
MURPHY, Johnny
*Abstract windows c.*1968 (sketch design and photographs, NIVAL)

Left:
Frances Biggs, *Scenes from the Life of St Ignatius Loyola* (*c.*1980), Gonzaga College Chapel, Ranelagh, Dublin

Dublin South, Ranelagh: Cherryfield Lodge Nursing Home (Jesuits), Milltown Park, Sandford Road
HONE, Evie
Symbols of the Four Evangelists 1953 (four panels)

Dublin South, Ranelagh: C of I, Sandford Road
CLARKE, Harry
St Peter and St Paul (A) 1927 (2 lights)
WALSH, George W.
St Francis of Assisi 2007 (2 lights)

Dublin South, Ranelagh: Gonzaga College Chapel, Sandford Road
BIGGS, Frances
*Abstract: Mystery of the Trinity c.*1969 (in the sanctuary)
*Let There be Light! c.*1980
*The Firmament: Planet, Stars and Worlds c.*1980
*All Things that Grow: Flowers and Plants c.*1980
*Fish and All Things that Fly c.*1980
*Man c.*1980
*God Rested and Was Pleased! c.*1980
*Episodes from the Life of Mary: the Annunciation, the Nativity, the Flight into Egypt c.*1980
*Episodes from the Passion of Christ: the Last Supper, the Crucifixion, the Resurrection c.*1980
*Scenes from the Life of St Ignatius Loyola c.*1980 (3 lights, above entrance)
*Abstract c.*1980 (12 narrow lights)

Dublin South, Ranelagh: The Devlin Hotel, Ranelagh Road
EARLEY, James
Gothic I 2018 (light box)
Gothic II 2018 (light box)

Dublin South, Rathfarnham: CC (Church of the Divine Word), Marley Grange
WALSH, George W.
Sanctuary windows and screen 2006
Side windows 2008
Stations of the Cross 2008 (designed by George W. Walsh and made by Laura O'Hagan)

Dublin South, Rathfarnham: C of I, Main Street
McGOLDRICK, Hubert
The Good Shepherd 1928

Dublin South, Rathfarnham: Loreto High School Beaufort, Grange Road
WALSH, George W.
Madonna and Child, Mary Ward, Education 2007

Dublin South, Rathfarnham: Rathfarnham Castle, Rathfarnham Road
All windows by Harry Clarke/Harry Clarke Studios were removed in the 1980s and distributed between Tullamore CC, County Offaly; Our Lady's Hospice Harold's Cross, Dublin; Sisters of Charity Convent, Temple Street, Dublin.
McGOLDRICK, Hubert
The Good Shepherd 1929 (removed in 1980s; current location untraced)

Dublin South, Rathfarnham: St Columba's College, Whitechurch (in chapel unless otherwise indicated)
HONE, Evie
*The Annunciation c.*1950 (in lightbox, library)
O'BRIEN, Catherine
Richard Caulfield Orpen Memorial – featuring medallions of buildings he designed for the school 1940 (4 lights, in hall, Hollypark)
*St Columba c.*1940 (trefoil, in stairwell off dining hall)
'When the Morning Stars Sang Together' 1947 (sketch design, NGI)
PURSER, Sarah
The Good Shepherd: Gwynn Memorial 1904 (painted by Michael Healy)
The Good Shepherd: Irwin Memorial 1912 (painted by Ethel Rhind)
RHIND, Ethel
The Risen Christ 1921 (opus sectile mosaic)

Dublin South, Rathgar: Methodist Church, Brighton Road
O'BRIEN, Catherine
*The Good Shepherd c.*1952

Dublin South, Rathgar: C of I, Zion Road
CHILD, A.E.
St Luke 1914
'Of Such is the Kingdom of Heaven' 1932 (2 lights)

Dublin South, Rathgar: The High School, Zion Road
MacBRIDE, William
Peace, Victory and Justice (war memorial) 1919 (3 lights)

Dublin South, Rathgar: Presbyterian Church (Christ Church), Highfield Avenue
GEDDES, Wilhelmina
St Peter Preaching to the Jews 1914–5 (3 lights) (sketch design, NGI)

Dublin South, Rathmichael: C of I, Ferndale Road
CHILD, A.E.
The Nativity 1939
Rabboni 1939
O'BRIEN, Catherine
The Crucifixion 1938 (sketch design, NGI)
PURSER, Sarah
The Good Samaritan 1903 (painted by Catherine O'Brien and Miss Townsend)

Dublin South, Rathmines: C of I (Holy Trinity), Cambridge Villas
CHILD, A.E.
St Christopher * 1924
HEALY, Michael
St Philip, St Peter, St Paul, St Andrew 1909 (4 lights)

Right:
William (Bill) E. Earley, *God the Father, Crucifixion, with Our Lady, St Patrick and St Brigid* (*c.* early 1940s), Catholic Church (St Patrick's), Ringsend, Dublin

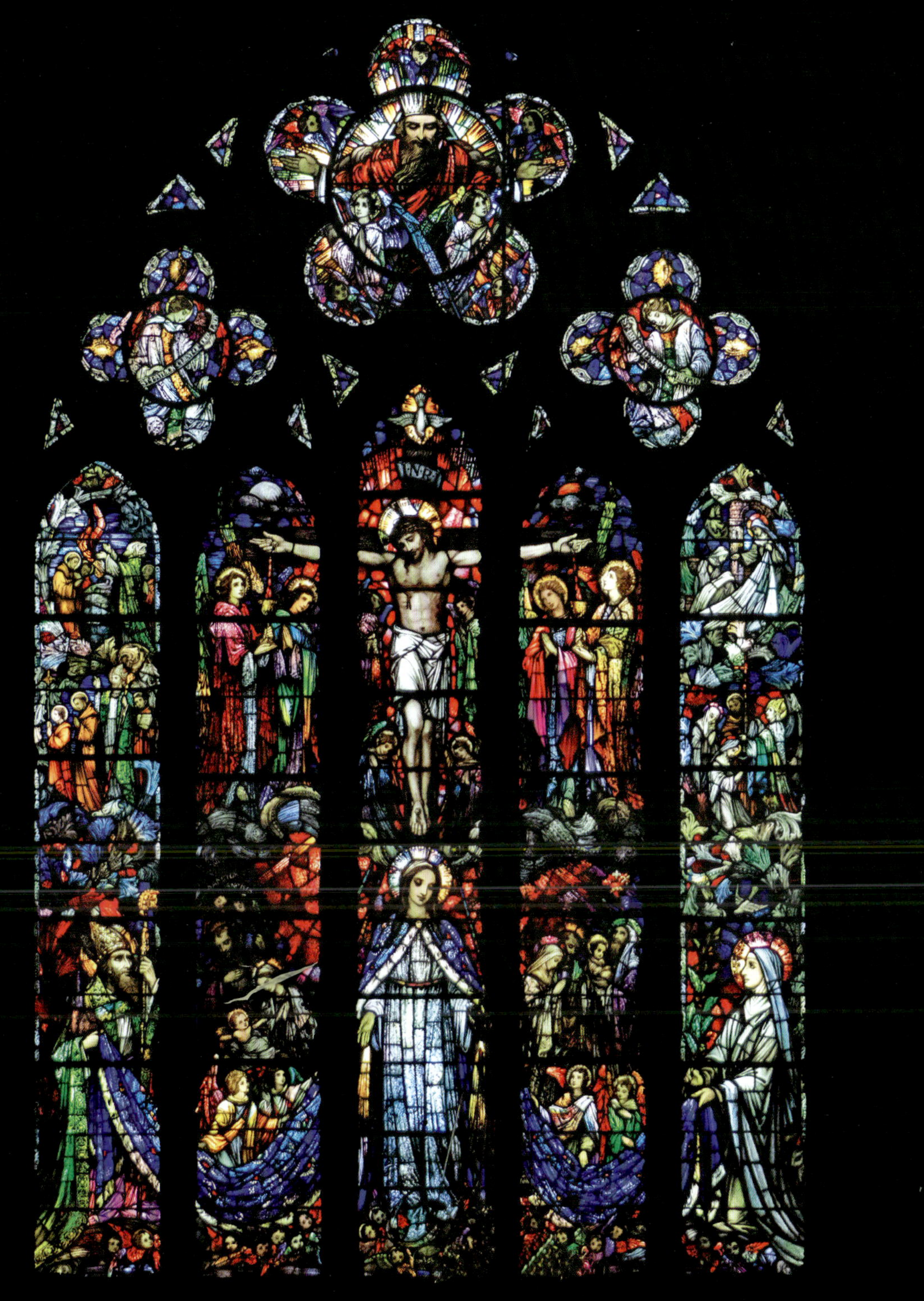

Dublin South, Rathmines: C of I College of Education Chapel, Upper Rathmines Road
McGOLDRICK, Hubert
The Bible, Diocesan Arms of Armagh and Dublin, Christ Teaching in the Temple 1937 (3 lights, with replacement border)

Dublin South, Rathmines: Portobello Barracks Chapel, off Lower Rathmines Road
HONE, Evie
The Good Shepherd, with St Joseph Holding the Christ Child, and St Patrick 1937–8 (3 lights) (See also: **England, Surrey:** Royal Army Ordnance Corps Church (St Barbara's), Deepcut, Camberley.)

Dublin South, Rathmines: St Louis High School Chapel, Charleville Road
MURPHY, Johnny
St Louis (3 lights) *c.*1963
St Patrick (3 lights) *c.*1963
*Church Symbols c.*1963 (12 windows)
*Holy Spirit c.*1963
(Celia Harriss Crampton of Murphy-Devitt Studios worked on these windows) (sketch designs and cartoons, NIVAL)

Dublin South, Ringsend: CC (St Patrick's), Thorncastle Street
EARLEY, William (Bill) E.
God the Father, Crucifixion, with Our Lady, St Patrick and St Brigid c. early 1940s (5 lights plus tracery)

Dublin South, Sandymount: Mount Tabor Nursing Home Chapel (private), Sandymount Green
MULDOWNEY, Patrick
Spring: Sparrows Nesting 1999
Summer: Miracle of the Loaves and Fishes 1999
Autumn: Harvest Scene 1999
Winter: Jesus Calms the Storm 1999

Dublin South, Sandymount: United Presbyterian and Methodist Church, Sandymount Green
CHILD, A.E.
St Paul 1921
HONE, Evie
Abstract composition with the Arms of James Robertson Coade 1943
Rock of Ages 1945–6
RHIND, Ethel
Dorcas Seated 1933

Dublin South, Tallaght: CC (St Dominic's), St Dominic's Road
WALSH, George W.
Life of St Dominic, Resurrection, Creation 1999 (clerestory windows)

Dublin South, Tallaght: CC (St Aengus's), Balrothery
MULDOWNEY, Patrick
Scheme of windows with Holy Spirit theme 2005

Dublin South, Tallaght: C of I (St Maelruain's)
HONE, Evie
Head of the Virgin date unknown (panel, a gift to the church from Patrick Pye)
(Both Evie Hone and Patrick Pye are buried in the adjoining graveyard.)

Dublin South, Tallaght: Dominican Priory, Tallaght Village
CAMPBELL, George
*Twelve abstract lights c.*1969 (painted by George W. Walsh and Willie Earley, and created at Abbey Stained Glass Studios.)

Right:
Evie Hone, *The Annunciation* (*c.*1940) (panel), Terenure College Chapel, Terenure, Dublin

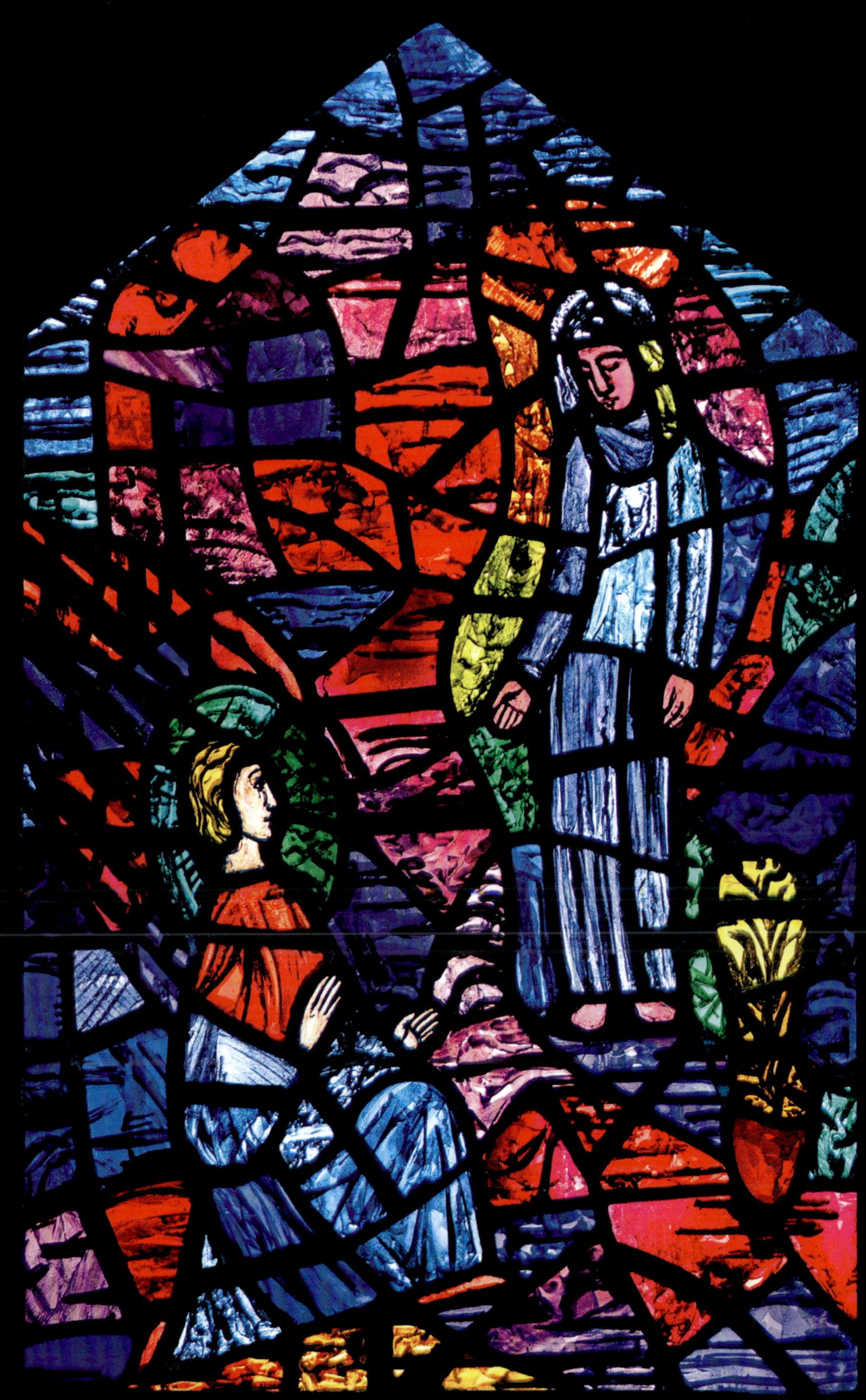

Dublin South, Tallaght: Tallaght University Hospital
HONE, Evie
Penal Days c.1936 (panel in light box, Chapel of Rest; previously in Adelaide Hospital, Dublin)
SCANLON, James
Untitled with Theme of 'Healing' 2001
Untitled with Theme of 'Struggle' 2001
(both windows in Hospital Chapel, ground floor)
YOUNG, Peter
Nádúr (inspired by Lough Tay, County Wicklow) 2018 (panel in light box, Viewing Room, Rosheen Suite, ground floor)

Dublin South, Terenure: CC (St Joseph's), Terenure Road East
CLARKE, Harry
The Crucifixion and the Adoration of the Cross by Irish Saints 1920 (3 lights)
The Annunciation 1922 and
The Coronation of the Virgin in Glory 1923 (companion windows; Lady Chapel)
DOWLING, William
Holy Spirit 1946 (rose, above organ gallery)
KING, Richard
The Resurrection 1935–6
Baptism of Christ 1937 (2 lights)
Apparition of the Sacred Heart to St Margaret Mary 1934–6 (circular)
The Coronation of the Virgin or *Queen of Heaven* 1934–6 (circular)
The Little Flower before Pope Leo 1939–40 (circular)
The Virgin Mary and St Anne 1939–40 (circular)
(Windows by William Dowling and Richard King created at Harry Clarke Studios.)

Right:
Phyllis Burke, from left:
Carmelites as Missionaries (2007–8)
and *Carmelites as Educationalists* (2007–8),
Terenure College Chapel, Terenure, Dublin

Dublin South, Terenure: Terenure College Chapel, Templeogue Road
BIGGS, Frances
Blessed Titus Brandsma 1986
St Thérèse of Lisieux c.1987
St John of the Cross 1988
St Teresa of Avila 1988
The Annunciation to St Joseph c.1989–2000
Elijah, Prophet of Carmel c.1989–2000
Mary, in the Carmelite Tradition c.1989–2000
Albert, Lawgiver of Carmel c.2000–1
BURKE, Phyllis
Carmelites as Missionaries 2007–8 (sketch design and cartoons, NIVAL)
Carmelites as Educationalists 2007–8 (sketch design and cartoons, NIVAL)
HONE, Evie
The Annunciation c.1940 (panel)
Virgin Mary c.1949 (panel)

Dublin South, Terenure: Synagogue (Dublin Hebrew Congregation), Rathfarnham Road
TOMLIN, Stanley, Alan and Fergus
Wall of stained glass featuring *Ten Panels Celebrating Jewish Festivals* 1967
TOMLIN, Alan and Fergus
Wall of stained glass featuring *The Second Temple (centre) with Western Wall (left) and Citadel of David (right)* c.1968
TOMLIN, Alan
Five Star of David-shaped abstract windows in shades of blue * c.1968 (Ladies' Gallery)
Five abstract rectangular windows in shades of blue * c.1968 (Minyan Room)
Abstract window: Holocaust Memorial * c.1968 (staircase)

Dublin South, Whitechurch: C of I, Whitechurch Road
EARLEY, Willie
Tobias and the Angel 1998

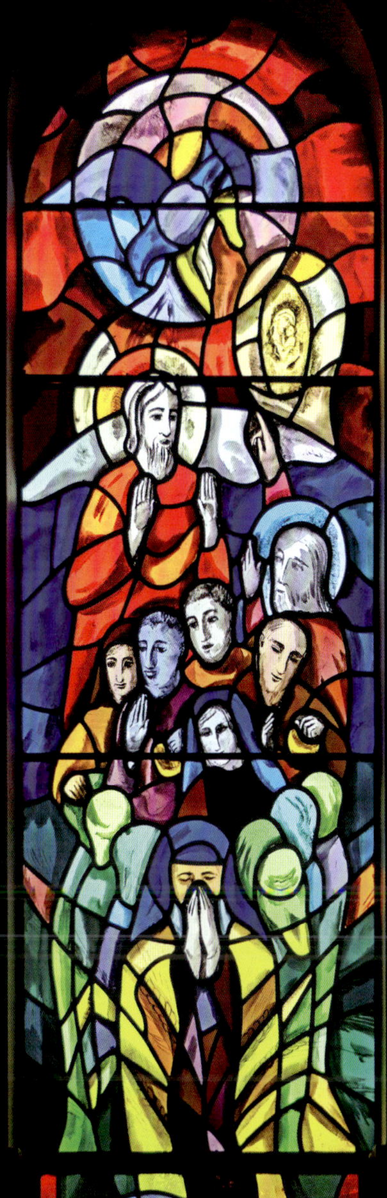
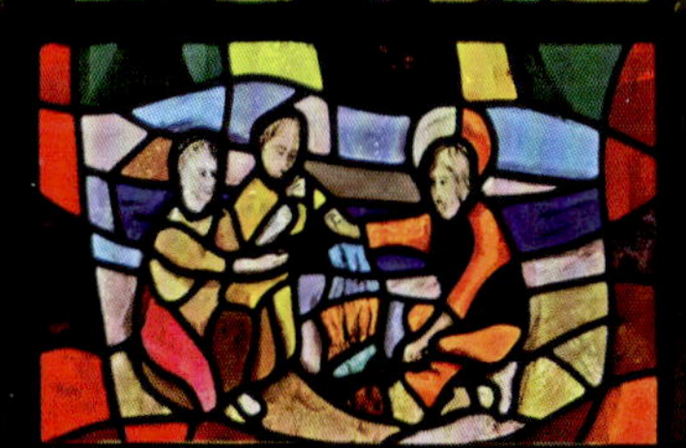
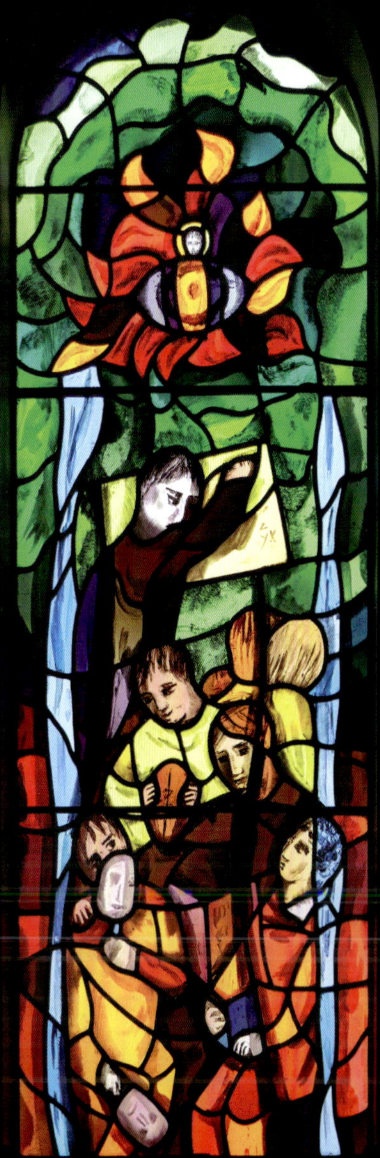
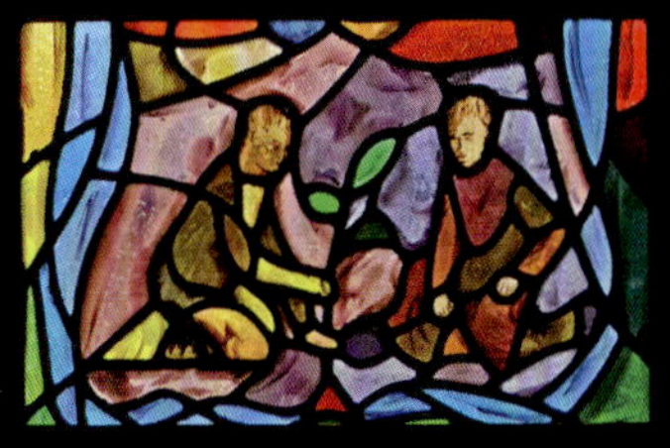

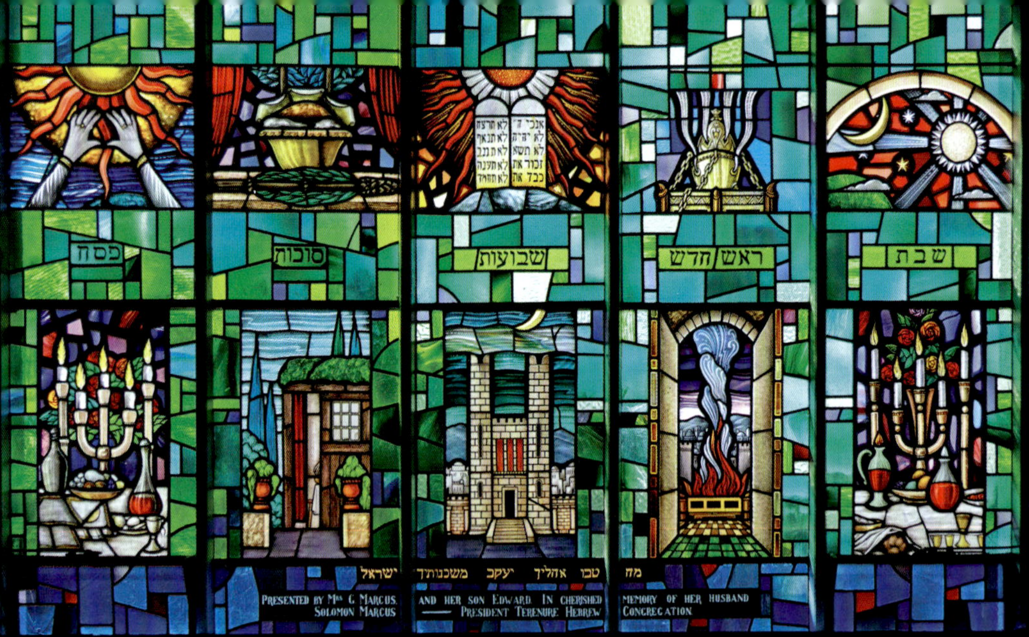

פסח
סוכות
שבועות
ראש חדש
שבת
מה טבו אהליך יעקב משכנותיך ישראל
PRESENTED BY MRS G. MARCUS. AND HER SON EDWARD IN CHERISHED MEMORY OF HER HUSBAND
SOLOMON MARCUS —— PRESIDENT TERENURE HEBREW CONGREGATION

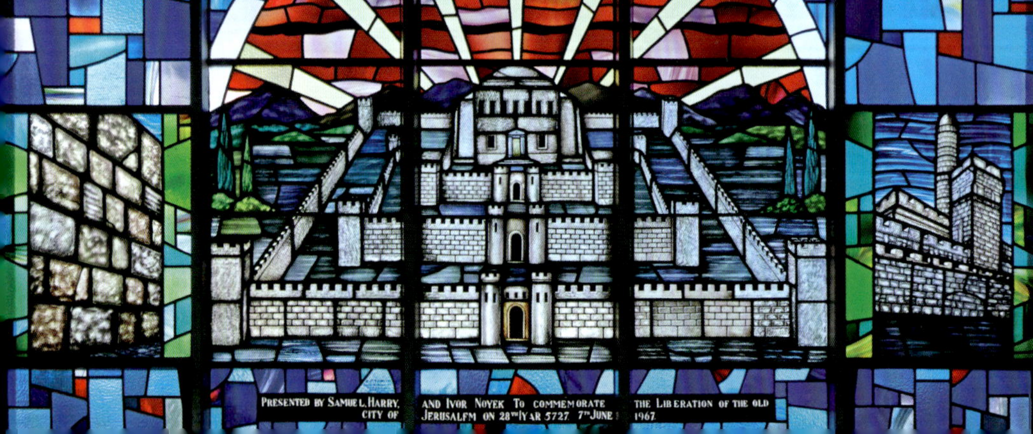
ירושלים
אם אשכחך
תשכח ימיני
PRESENTED BY SAMUEL, HARRY, AND IVOR NOYEK TO COMMEMORATE THE LIBERATION OF THE OLD
CITY OF JERUSALEM ON 28TH IYAR 5727. 7TH JUNE 1967.

COUNTY FERMANAGH

Belleek: C of I
ESLER, David
The Potter's Wheel 2009 (3 lights)

Enniskillen: Convent of Mercy Chapel
CHILD, A.E.
St Mark 1905
St Matthew 1905
The Good Shepherd 1905
St Luke 1905
St John 1905
Angel with Candle 1905 (painted by Catherine O'Brien)
Angel with Censer 1905 (painted by Catherine O'Brien)
ELVERY, Beatrice
Christ 1905
St Margaret Mary 1905
St Joseph 1905
Virgin and Child 1905
St Macartan 1906
The Immaculate Conception 1906
HEALY, Michael
St Patrick 1905
St Brigid 1905
St Columba 1906 (partly painted by Catherine O'Brien)
St Benignus 1906
St Benedict Joseph Labre 1906
St Anthony 1906
O'BRIEN, Catherine
The Angel of the Annunciation 1906
Our Lady of the Annunciation 1906
PURSER, Sarah
St Michael 1905 (painted by Catherine O'Brien)
St Elizabeth 1905 (painted by Catherine O'Brien)
AN TÚR GLOINE STUDIO
Additional decorative slab glass windows 1905

Castle Archdale: C of I (St Patrick's)
CHILD, A.E.
Te Deum 1907–8 (5 lights)
St George and St Patrick 1910 (2 lights)

Derrybrusk: C of I (St Michael's)
ELVERY, Beatrice
Moses, the Good Shepherd and the Prodigal Son * 1907

Inishmacsaint, Derrygonnelly: C of I (St Ninnidh's)
GEDDES, Wilhelmina
The Angel of the Resurrection 1912

Monea: C of I (St Molaise's)
GEDDES, Wilhelmina
Innocence Walking in the Fields of Paradise 1913 (sketch designs, NGI)

Rossorry: C of I
COURTNEY, Dorothy
The Ascension * 1910–1 (3 lights) (painted by A.E. Child, Catherine O'Brien and Hugh Barden)
O'BRIEN, Catherine
Te Deum 1921 (3 lights)

Trory, near Ballycassidy: C of I
O'BRIEN, Catherine
Christ Enthroned 1922

Left, from top: Alan, Fergus and Stanley Tomlin, detail of wall of stained glass featuring *Ten Panels Celebrating Jewish Festivals* (1967); Alan and Stanley Tomlin, detail of wall of stained glass *featuring the Second Temple* (centre) *with Western Wall* (left) *and Citadel of David* (right) (*c.*1968), Synagogue, Terenure, Dublin

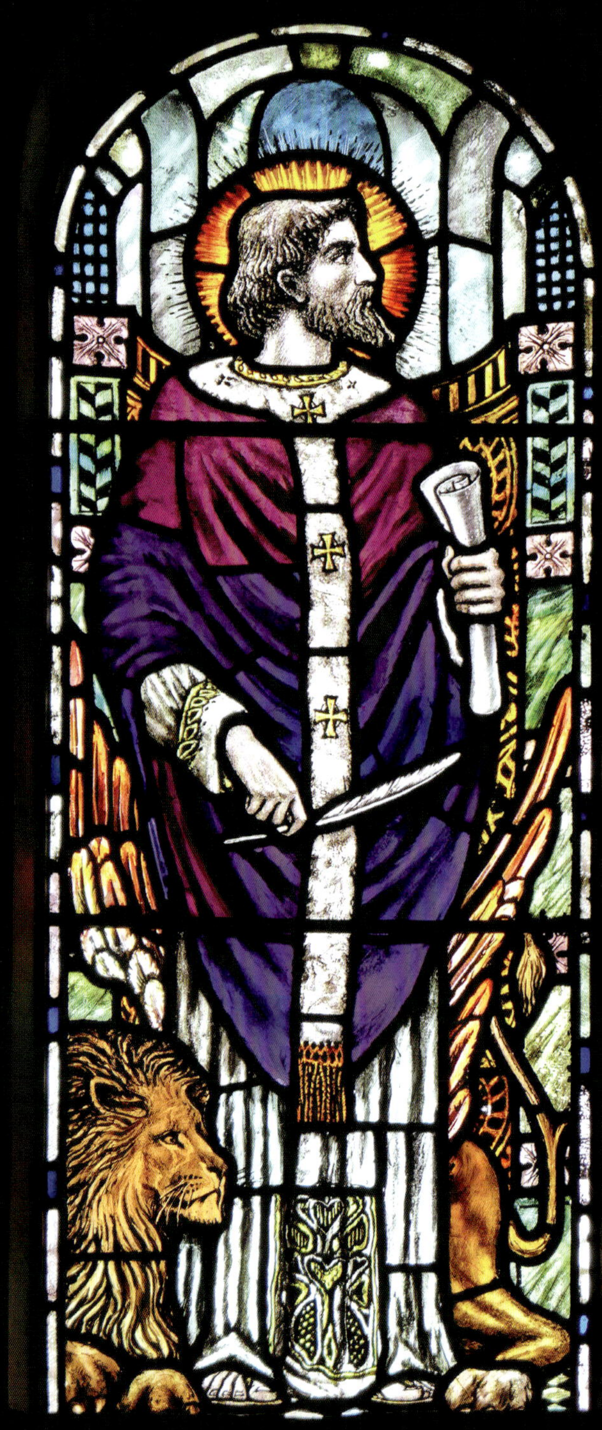

A.E. Child,
St Mark (1905),
Convent of Mercy
Chapel, Enniskillen,
County Fermanagh

COUNTY GALWAY

Abbeyknockmoy CC (St Bernard's)
WALSH, George W.
The Apparition at Lourdes 1970s (2 lights)

Aran Islands (Inis Meáin): CC (Holy Mary of the Immaculate Conception)
KING, Richard
Blessed Virgin Mary with St John the Baptist and St Enda 1939 (3 lights)
St Breacan 1939
St Caomhán 1939
St Máire Maighdilín 1939–40
(Created at Harry Clarke Studios.)

Ardrahan (Labane): CC (St Teresa of Avila)
CHILD, A.E.
*St Elizabeth c.*1902 (largely designed by Christopher Whall and made by A.E. Child at Earley and Powell, Dublin)
PURSER, Sarah
St Andrew 1903 (cartoon probably designed by A.E. Child, painted by him and Michael Healy, assisted by Catherine O'Brien and Miss Townsend)
RHIND, Ethel
*St Peter Enthroned c.*1910
(This church also contains two windows commissioned by Edward Martyn from the British Arts and Crafts artist, Selwyn Image, *St Robert* (1902) and *St Anna* (1906).)

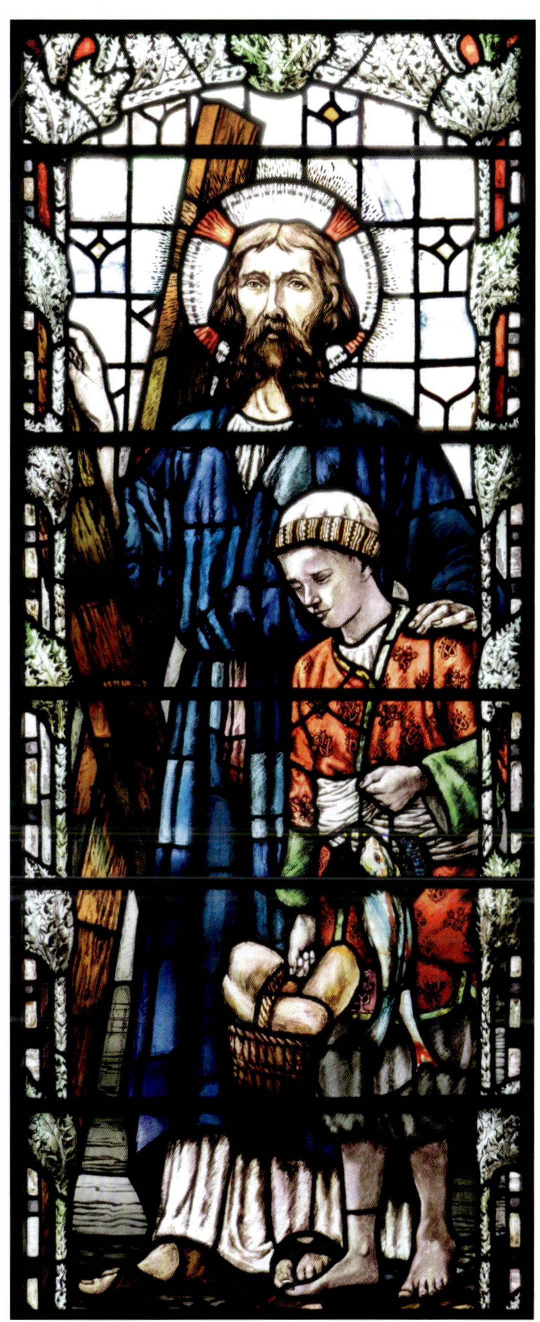

Right:
Sarah Purser, detail of *St Andrew* (1903, cartoon probably designed by A.E. Child, painted by him and Michael Healy, assisted by Catherine O'Brien and Miss Townsend) Catholic Church (St Teresa of Avila), Ardrahan (Labane), County Galway

Aughrim: C of I
TOMLIN, Alan
St Joseph 1969 (3 lights)

Ballinakill: CC (St Joseph's)
BURKE, Phyllis
Twelve windows with symbols 1973

Ballinasloe: CC (St Michael's)
CLARKE, Harry
St Patrick and St Rose of Lima (B) 1925 (2 lights)
POLLEN, Patrick
Our Lady Spinning, with the Nativity, St Joseph and Jesus in the Workshop, with the Flight into Egypt (latter panel significantly repaired in recent years following damage) *c.*1957–8 (2 lights)
*Raising of the Daughter of Jairus c.*1957–8 (2 lights)

Ballinasloe: Former Presbyterian Church (now privately owned), Society Street
RHIND, Ethel
St Michael 1911 (in Whigham Memorial Hall, rear of church)

Ballinderreen: CC (St Colman's)
BURKE, Phyllis
Seven abstract windows 1973
DONAS, Marthe
The Deposition * 1916 (made at An Túr Gloine with, most likely, assistance from one of the other artists; sketch design in the Musée Marthe Donas, Ittre, Belgium)

Barna: CC (Church of Mary Immaculate Queen)
WALSH, George W.
Aspects of Christ's Life: The Carpenter, The Fisherman, The Sower, along with local scenes 1977

Belclare: CC (Sacred Heart)
O'BRIEN, Catherine
The Sacred Heart, St Patrick and St Brigid 1924 (3 lights)

Bullaun: CC (St Patrick's)
WALSH, George W.
St Patrick 1972
Sacred Heart 1972
Virgin Mary 1972
Abstract clerestory windows 1972

Camus: CC (Church of the Assumption/Séipéal Deastógála)
WALSH, George W.
Holy Spirit, Lamb of God, Holy Communion early 1970s (3 lights)
Marian Window early 1970s

Cashel: CC (St James's)
RIVERS, Elizabeth
St Joseph 1964–5 (designed by Elizabeth Rivers and completed by Frances Biggs after her friend's death, made in Patrick Pollen's Studio, Upper Pembroke Street, Dublin)

Claddaghduff: CC (Star of the Sea)
BURKE, Phyllis
*Twelve nave windows c.*1974

Creagh, near Ballinasloe: CC (Our Lady of Lourdes)
POLLEN, Patrick
Madonna and Child date unknown (circular, above gallery)
PYE, Patrick
Scenes from the Lives of Mary and Joseph 1961 (2 lights, in porch)
*Christ Praying in Gethsemane, the Entombment, and Resurrection c.*1986 (2 lights)
(Additional windows, attributed to Richard King, were made in 1932–3 at Harry Clarke Studios, Dublin.)

Creeragh: CC (Our Lady of the Wayside)
BURKE, Phyllis
Our Lady of the Wayside 1968

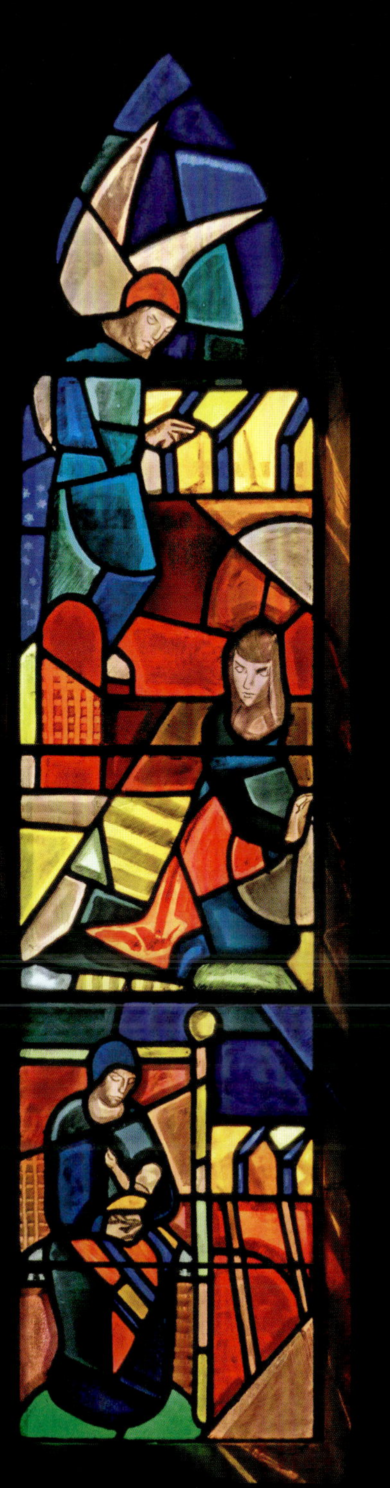

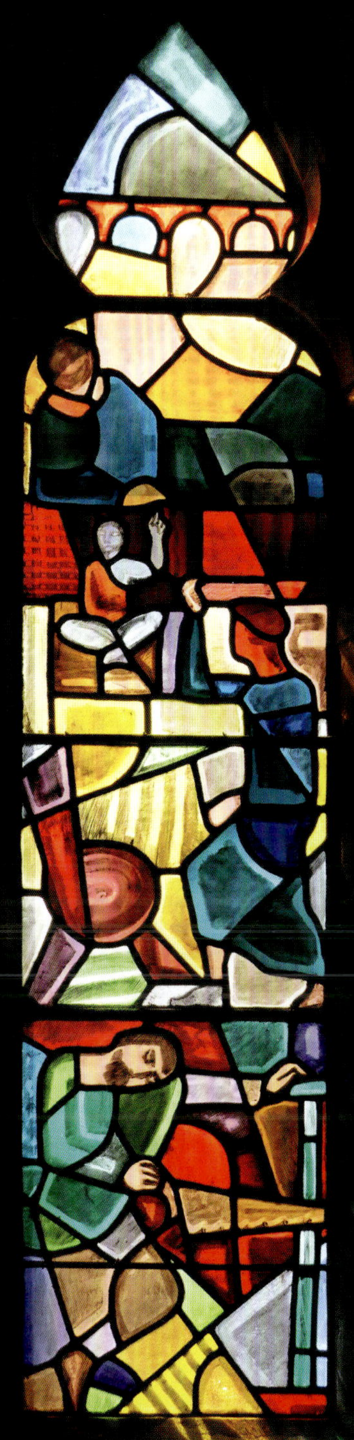

Patrick Pye,
Scenes from the Lives of Mary and Joseph (1961),
Catholic Church (Our Lady of Lourdes), Creagh,
near Ballinasloe, County Galway

Dunmore: CC (Our Lady and St Nicholas)
MURPHY, Johnny
Scheme of abstract lead-lights and dalle de verre 1967 (sketch design, NIVAL)

Galway City, Claddagh: CC (St Mary's Dominican Church)
HEALY, Michael
St Dominic Receiving the Rosary 1934–5
McGOLDRICK, Hubert
St Dominic Carrying the Icon of the Madonna of San Sisto and Leading Nuns Across the Tiber to their New Home, the Dominican Convent of San Sisto 1939

Galway City, Distillery Road: National University of Ireland Galway (Chapel of St Columbanus)
WALSH, George W.
Risen Christ 1989
Christ Debating with Students 1989
Bible 1989
Saints Arriving by Boat 1989
Monastic Learning 1989
615 (Death of St Columbanus) 1989
Madonna and Child 1989
Mary and Elizabeth 1989
Marriage Feast at Cana 1989
Last Supper 1989
Ascension 1989

Galway City, Forster Street: CC (St Patrick's)
WALSH, George W.
Scheme of windows on Life of St Patrick 1972

Galway City, Forster Street: COPE Galway, Modh Eile House (formerly Sisters of Mercy, Chapel of Magdalen Convent)
HONE, Evie
The Blessed Virgin Mary, the Sacred Heart, St Joseph and St Mary Magdalen 1952 (rose)

Galway City, Gaol Road: Catholic Cathedral (Our Lady Assumed into Heaven and St Nicholas)
BURKE, Phyllis
Carrying the Ark, Aaron High Priest 1999 (sketch design and cartoon, NIVAL)
Moses Striking the Rock 1999 (sketch design and cartoon, NIVAL)
The Fall of Jericho 1999 (sketch design and cartoon, NIVAL)
CAMPBELL, George
The Joyful Mysteries c.1965
The Sorrowful Mysteries c.1965
The Glorious Mysteries c.1965
(George Campbell's three rose windows were painted by George W. Walsh and Willie Earley, and created at Abbey Stained Glass Studios.)
DOWD MURPHY, Róisín
Elijah c.1999
Raphael and Tobias c.1999
By the Rivers of Babylon c.1999
Isaiah: His Call c.1999
Jeremiah and the Potter c.1999
Daniel in the Lion's Den c.1999
(sketch designs and cartoons for all, NIVAL)
DOWD MURPHY, Róisín and MURPHY, Johnny
Melchizedek 1964
Isaac 1964
Jacob 1964
Joseph 1964
DEENY, Gillian
The Adoration of the Magi c.1965–70
Jesus Teaching by the Sea of Galilee c.1965–70
St Peter Receives the Keys c.1965–70
The Curing of the Paralytic c.1965–70
(Gillian Deeny's windows were designed and painted by the artist in Abbey Stained Glass Studios.)
EARLEY, Willie
Medallions with Christian Images, Symbols and Emblems set in 69 Leaded Lights c.1965 (located in various offices adjoining the cathedral)
(Created at Abbey Stained Glass Studios.)

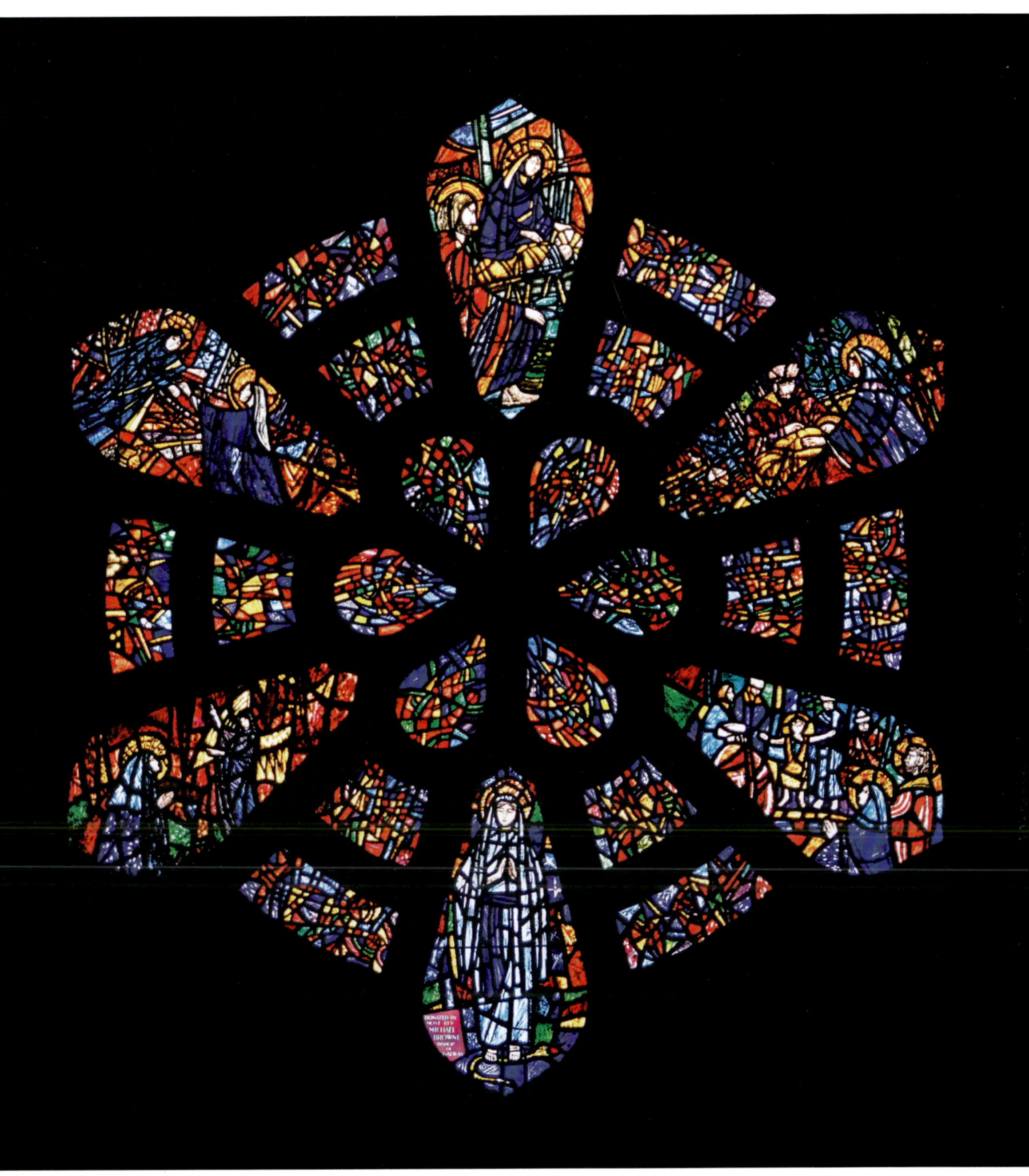

George Campbell, *The Joyful Mysteries* (*c.*1965) (painted by George W. Walsh and Willie Earley), Catholic Cathedral, Galway

POLLEN, Patrick

Temptation of Our Lord in the Desert 1965 (sketch design, NIVAL)

*The Multiplication of the Loaves in the Desert c.*1965 (sketch design, NIVAL)

*The Transfiguration of Our Lord c.*1965 (sketch design, NIVAL)

*The Sending of the Apostles c.*1965 (sketch design, NIVAL)

*Baptism of Christ by St John the Baptist c.*1966 (sketch design, NIVAL)

*St Michael c.*1966–7

*St Gabriel c.*1966–7

*Miracle of Naim, a Widow with a Young Son c.*1966–7

*Daughter of Jairus c.*1966–7

*Lazarus c.*1966–7

*Our Lord Looking to the Three Whom He Had Raised from the Dead c.*1966–7

*Martha and Mary c.*1966–7

*St Brigid c.*1968

*St Patrick c.*1968

*St Fachtna Curing the Blind Man c.*1968

*St Columcille c.*1968

*St Enda c.*1968

St Nicholas 1969 (sketch design, NIVAL)

The Holy Family 1969 (sketch design, NIVAL)

Jesus Blessing Children 1969

Wedding Feast at Cana 1969 (sketch design, NIVAL)

*Good Shepherd c.*1969–70

*Jesus Washing Peter's Feet c.*1969–70

*Jesus Walking on the Water with St Peter c.*1969–70

*Jesus Calming the Storm c.*1969–70

*Mary Magdalen Anointing the Feet of Jesus c.*1969–70

SCANLON, James

*The Creation of the World c.*1999

*The Creation of Adam and Eve c.*1999

*The Fall and Expulsion c.*1999

*Cain and Abel c.*1999

*Noah, the Ark and the Rainbow c.*1999

The Call of Abram 1999

WALSH, George W.

Moses Receiving the Ten Commandments 1999

Passover 1999

The Finding of Moses 1999

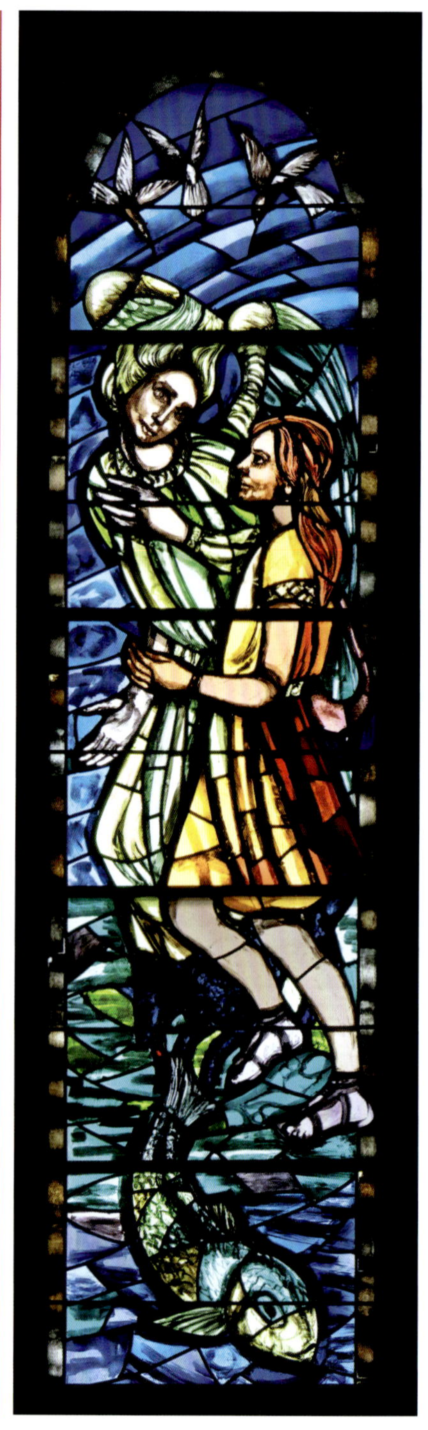

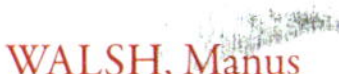

WALSH, Manus
*Samuel Anoints Saul c.*1965
*David After Slaying Goliath c.*1965
*David, King and Psalmist c.*1965
*Solomen's Judgement c.*1965
*The Last Supper c.*1965
(Manus Walsh's windows were created at Abbey Stained Glass Studios.)

Galway City, Middle Street: CC (St Augustine's)
WALSH, George W.
The Resurrection 1968 (3 lights)
St Augustine 1968
Abstract laylight 1968
Windows with symbols 1968

Galway City, Newcastle Road: National University of Ireland Galway (formerly St Anthony's Franciscan College)
POLLEN, Patrick
Crucifixion 1970s (glass inlaid in pierced concrete sections; currently boarded up as a protection from potential vandalism) (sketch design, NIVAL)

Galway City, Newcastle Road: University Hospital Galway
WALSH, George W.
Symbols of Cleansing and Healing 2003 (4 panels, in New Chapel)

Galway City, Presentation Road: CC (St Joseph's)
DEEGAN, Philip
St Joseph * 1924 (Created at Joshua Clarke and Sons.)
MacBRIDE, William
*Madonna and Child c.*1922
MURPHY, Johnny
*Baptism of Christ c.*1960 (sketch design, NIVAL)
MURPHY, Johnny and DOWD MURPHY, Róisín
Resurrection 1967 (cartoon, NIVAL)

Left: Róisín Dowd Murphy, *Raphael and Tobias* (*c.*1999), Catholic Cathedral, Galway City

Galway City, Presentation Road: Presentation Convent Chapel (connecting door from chapel gives access to St Joseph's Church; see separate entry)
WALSH, George W.
Five windows with Religious Symbols 1970s (2 lights)

Galway City, St James Road, Mervue: CC (Holy Family)
BURKE, Phyllis
The Annunciation 1968
The Nativity 1968
The Presentation 1968
The Crucifixion 1968
The Resurrection 1968
The Ascension 1968
(sketch design and cartoons, NIVAL)

Gort: Convent of Mercy Chapel
ELVERY, Beatrice
Our Lord and Blessed Margaret Mary 1904–5 (2 lights) (painted by Catherine O'Brien and Michael Healy)

Inishbofin Island: CC (St Colman's)
DOWLING, William
Christ Calming the Waters, with Madonna and Child, Miraculous Draft of Fishes 1977 (3 lights)

Inverin (Tully): CC (St Colmcille's)
BECKER, Margaret
*Nave windows and sanctuary windows, all abstract c.*1963–4
(Note: window over entrance, *St Colmcille,* was made later by another, unidentified, artist/studio)

Killererin: CC (St Mary's)
WALSH, George W.
Risen Christ 1980s (3 lights)

Kilmilkin: CC (Holy Nativity)
HONE, Evie
St Brendan 1950 (cartoon, NGI)

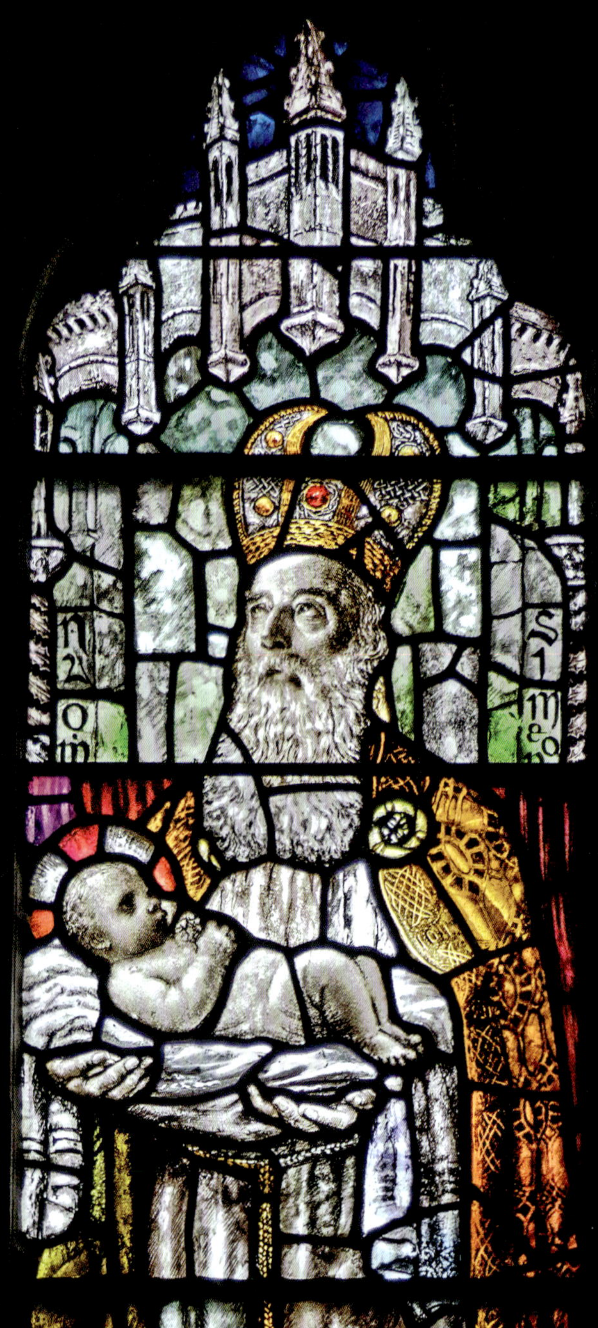

Michael Healy, detail of *Simeon* (1904), Catholic Cathedral, Loughrea, County Galway

Kiltartan: CC (St Attracta's)
WALSH, George W.
St Colman MacDuagh Baptised at Corker 1977
St Colman MacDuagh at Kiltartan 1977
St Colman MacDuagh at Clonmacnoise 1977

Kinvara: CC (St Joseph's)
BURKE, Phyllis
Mother and Child c.1974 (in porch)
St Joseph c.1974 (in porch)

Loughrea: Catholic Cathedral (St Brendan's)
CHILD, A.E.
The Annunciation 1903 (2 lights) (based on original designs by Christopher Whall, painted by A.E. Child, Michael Healy and Catherine O'Brien)
The Agony in the Garden 1903 (2 lights) (based on original designs by Christopher Whall, painted by A.E. Child, Michael Healy and Catherine O'Brien)
The Resurrection 1903 (2 lights) (based on original designs by Christopher Whall, painted by A.E. Child, Michael Healy and Catherine O'Brien)
The Baptism of Christ 1904 (2 lights)
St Clare and St Francesca 1927–9 (2 lights)
Faith: The Roman Centurion 1934
St Patrick 1937
HEALY, Michael
Simeon 1904 (sketch design, NGI)
Virgin and Child with Saints Patrick, Brendan, Colman, Jarlath, Columba, Brigid 1906–7 (rose)
Holy Family and Six Angels 1907 (rose)
St Anthony of Padua 1907
St John 1927
Tu Rex Gloriae, Christe 1929–30
Our Lady Queen of Heaven 1933
St Joseph 1935
The Ascension 1935–6 (3 lights)
The Last Judgement 1936–40 (3 lights)
HONE, Evie
St Brigid 1942
The Creation 1950 (rose)
McGOLDRICK, Hubert
Christ of the Sacred Heart Appearing to St Margaret Mary 1925 (2 lights) (sketch design, NGI)
PURSER, Sarah
St Brendan c.1903–4 (in right porch: this is one of only about five panels of stained glass actually painted by Sarah Purser herself.)
St Ita 1904 (painted by Catherine O'Brien)
The Passion 1908 (3 lights) (painted by Beatrice Elvery)
The Nativity 1912 (3 lights) (painted by A.E. Child)
PYE, Patrick
St Brigid 1957 (in left porch)
RHIND, Ethel
Stations of the Cross 1929–33 (opus sectile mosaic)

Loughrea: Carmelite Priory
BURKE, Phyllis
Edith Stein c.1995–6
The Good Shepherd 2002 (cartoons, NIVAL)

Milltown: CC (St Joseph's)
WALSH, George W.
Joseph 1970 (clerestory) (designed by George W. Walsh and painted by Willie Earley)
Virgin and Child 1970 (clerestory) (designed by George W. Walsh and painted by Willie Earley)
Lower level, non-figurative windows 1970
Stations of the Cross 1970 (black on white background, in oils)

Oranmore: CC (Immaculate Conception)
BURKE, Phyllis
The Immaculate Conception 1974 (4 lights)
Abstract with Fish, Grapes and Cross Motifs 1974 (5 lights)
Lamb of God 1974 (in porch)
WALSH, George W.
Risen Christ 1972 (etched glass panel)
Stations of the Cross 1972 (oil paint on marble)

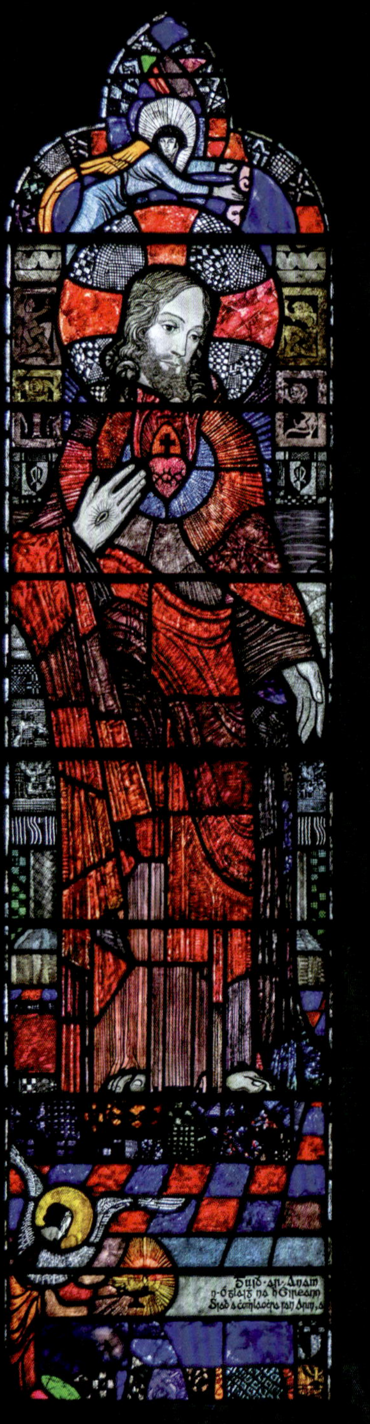

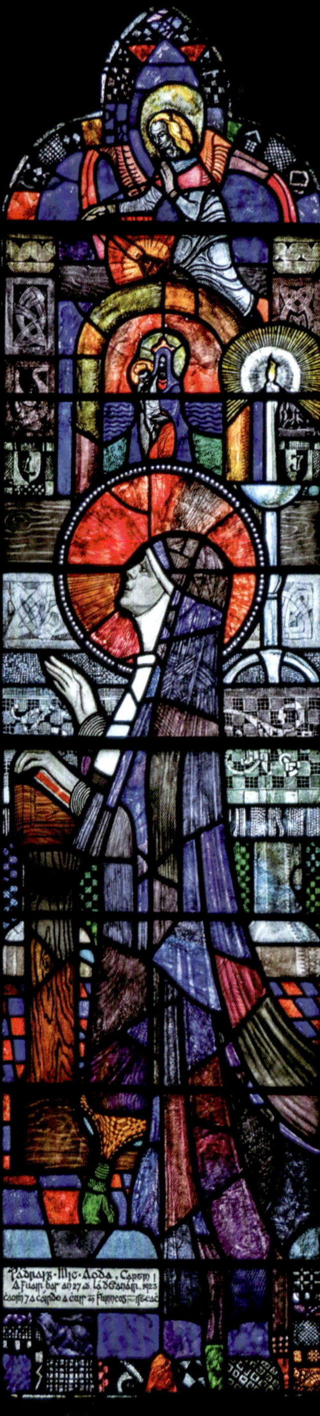

Oughterard: CC (Immaculate Conception)
KING, Richard
Crucifixion 1934 (3 lights)
(Created at Harry Clarke Studios.)

Peterswell: CC (St Thomas's)
HONE, Evie
Our Lady of the Rosary 1950

Renmore: CC (Garrison Church, St Patrick's)
WALSH, George W.
Crucifixion 1973
Blessed Virgin 1974
Last Supper 1974
Joseph and the Young Jesus 1975
Christ Healing the Lame Man, date unknown (circular)
(Additional windows by or attributed to Willie Earley, Kevin Kelly and Alan Tomlin.)

Ryehill: CC (Sacred Heart)
CONNON, Evan
Ascension of Christ into Heaven date unknown

Spiddal: CC (St Enda's)
BURKE, Phyllis
*I Have Fought the Good Fight c.*2000
O'BRIEN, Catherine
St Enda 1906
St Michael 1907
'Let Perpetual Light Shine Upon Them' 1919 (sketch design, NGI)
St Martin 1931
RHIND, Ethel
Stations of the Cross 1918–28 (opus sectile mosaic)
WALSH, George W.
St Fainse 1970 (2 lights)
St Enda 1970 (2 lights)

Left:
Hubert McGoldrick, *Christ of the Sacred Heart Appearing to St Margaret Mary* (1925), Catholic Cathedral, Loughrea, County Galway

Tierneevan, near Gort: CC (St Colman's)
CAMPBELL, George
The Sower Sowing the Seed 1963 (executed by George W. Walsh)
WALSH, George W.
St MacDuagh 1975
Holy Family 1975

Tuam, Bishop Street: Catholic Cathedral (Assumption of Blessed Virgin Mary)
KING, Richard
St Jarlath 1961
St Patrick 1961

Tuam, Bishop's Street: St Jarlath's College
HONE, Evie
St Legend of Jarlath 1940 (panel, inserted into unsympathetic modern stairwell window)

Tuam, Vicar Street: former Bon Secours Hospital chapel (subsequently Courthouse, currently unoccupied)
DOWD MURPHY, Róisín and MURPHY, Johnny
Madonna and Child 1962 (3 lights)
Saints and church symbols 1962 (2 lights)
(cartoons for both, NIVAL)

Tullycross, Renvyle: CC (Christ the King)
CLARKE, Harry
St Bernard and St Barbara with Christ Revealing the Sacred Heart (A) 1927 (3 lights)

COUNTY KERRY

Ardfert: CC (St Brendan's)
MURPHY, Johnny
Abstract lights 1978

Ballinskelligs: CC (St Michael's)
KING, Richard
St Michael of the Skelligs c.1972 (2 lights)

Ballybunion: CC (St John's), Church Road
WALSH, George Stephen
Resurrection date unknown (2 lights)

Brosna: CC (St Moling's)
O'BRIEN, Catherine and PURSER, Sarah
St Moling, Virgin and Child, St Carthage 1908 (3 lights; middle light, except for top angels, was designed by Sarah Purser, rest is by Catherine O'Brien)

Dingle: Díseart Institute of Education and Celtic Culture (former Presentation Convent Chapel), Green Street
CLARKE, Harry
The Nativity (A) 1924 (2 lights)
The Baptism (B) 1924 (2 lights)
The Sermon on the Mount (B) 1924 (2 lights)
'Suffer Little Children' (B) 1924 (2 lights)
The Apparition of Jesus to Mary Magdalen (B) 1924 (2 lights)
The Garden of Gethsemane (B) 1924 (2 lights)

Fieries: CC (St Gertrude's)
WALSH, George W.
Eucharist, Mary 1997 (3 lights)
Risen Christ 1997 (3 lights)
Trinity, Justice 1997 (3 lights)

Fieries: National School, Church Lane (visits strictly by appointment)
YOUNG, Peter
Homeland 2011 (4 panels)

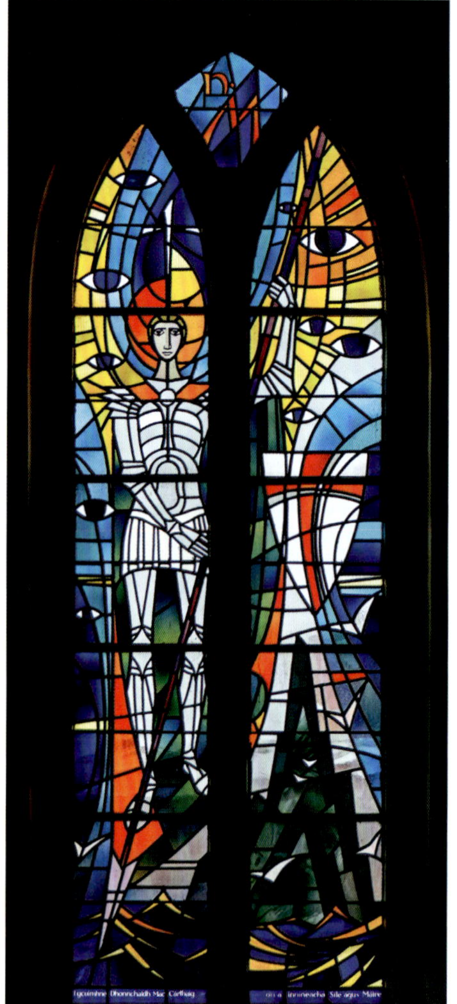

Glenflesk: CC (St Agatha's)
KING, Richard
St Joseph 1932
Christ the King 1932
St Michael 1932
St Gabriel 1932
Blessed Virgin Mary 1932
All formerly in the Presentation Noviciate, Oakpark, Tralee.
(Created at Harry Clarke Studios.)

Left: Richard King, *St Michael of the Skelligs* (*c.*1972), Catholic Church, Ballinskelligs (St Michael's), County Kerry

Kilcummin: CC (Our Lady of Lourdes)
WALSH, George W.
Saints Matthew, Mark, Luke, John, Peter, Paul, James, Jude 1972 (8 panels)
Non-figurative 1972 (8 panels)
Rosary 1972 (above door)

Killarney, Fair Hill: Franciscan Friary
KING, Richard
Seven Joys of Mary, St Francis of Assisi and the Trinity 1929–30 (5 lights with tracery)
(Created at Harry Clarke Studios.)

Killarney, New Road: St Brendan's College Chapel
RHIND, Ethel
The Legend of St Brendan (I) 1914 (2 lights)
The Legend of St Brendan (II) 1914 (2 lights)
Each of these two-light windows has been incorporated into a five-light window in the new chapel, with the first panel by a different artist.

Killarney, New Street: Bank of Ireland
WALSH, George Stephen
Abstract, Featuring Financial and Monetary Symbols date unknown (wall of glass comprised of six vertical panels)

Killarney, New Street: Catholic Cathedral (St Mary's)
MURPHY, Johnny
Abstract lights 1972

Killarney, Park Road: CC (Church of the Resurrection)
BURKE, Phyllis
Symbols of the Eucharist 1993

Killorglin: CC (St James's)
COX, James
St Brendan date unknown
McGOLDRICK, Hubert
Mater Dolorosa and *St Joseph* 1932
WALSH, George Stephen
St Brendan 1966
St Ita 1966
St Luke 1966
St James 1966

Sneem: Slí na Síoga
SCANLON, James
Environmental sculpture with abstract stained glass windows 1989

Tralee, Castle Street: CC (St John's)
KING, Richard
Woman Clothed with the Sun 1957 (rose)
POLLEN, Patrick
*Trinity c.*1956–7 (rose; in former baptistry)
*Saints Matthew, Mark, Luke and John c.*1956–7 (2 lights, in former baptistry)

Tralee, Day Place: CC (Holy Cross, Dominican Church)
HEALY, Michael
Sacristy door panels: decorative with symbols 1913

Tralee, Prince's Street: Kerry Group HQ
SCANLON, James
Three abstract windows 1991 (currently in storage)

Tralee, Strand Street: Bon Secours Hospital Chapel
DOWD MURPHY, Róisín and MURPHY, Johnny
*Figurative and abstract lights c.*1963

Tralee, Upper Rock Street: CC (Our Lady and St Brendan's)
MURPHY, Johnny
Our Lady 1970
St Brendan 1970
Abstract lights 1970

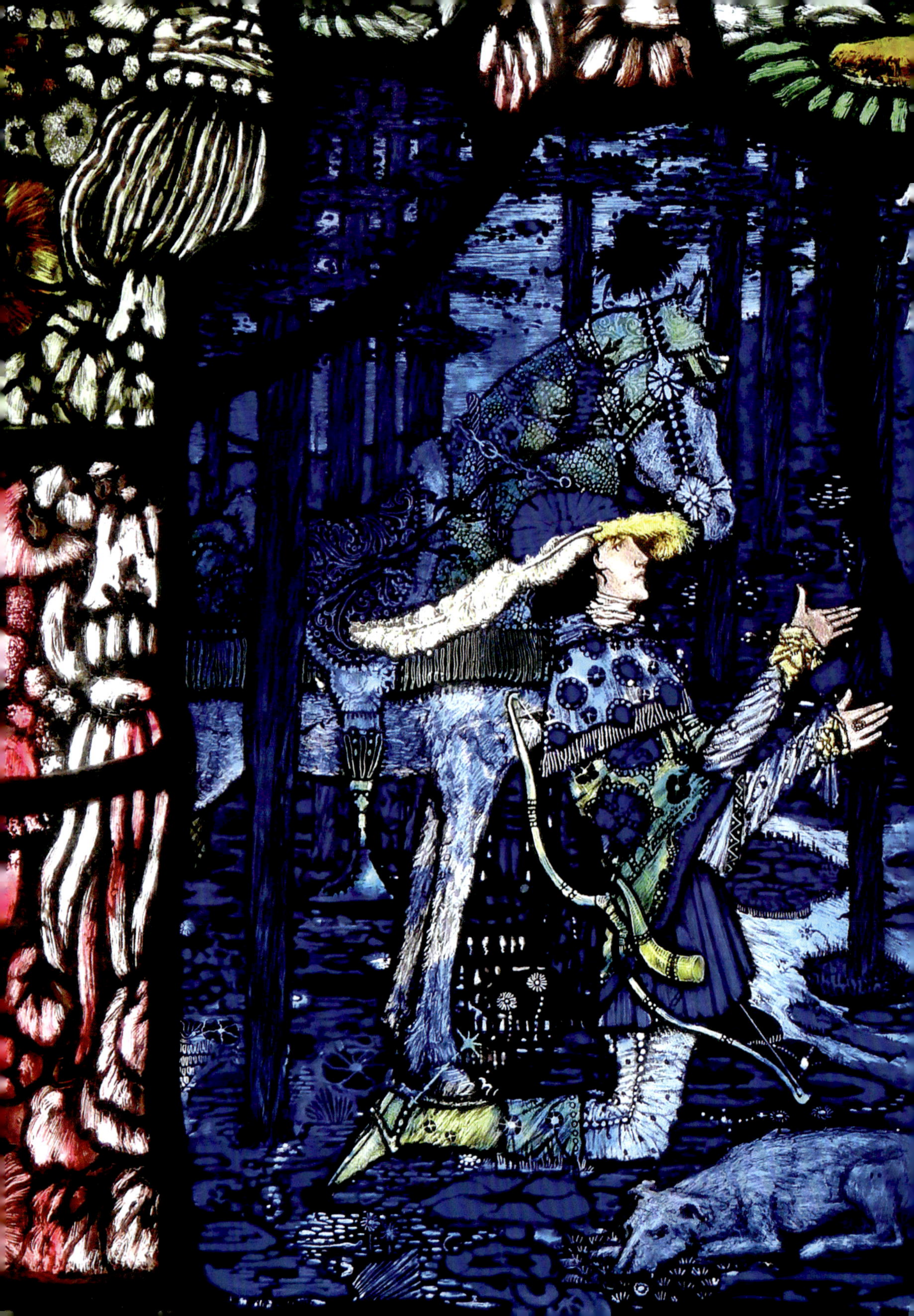

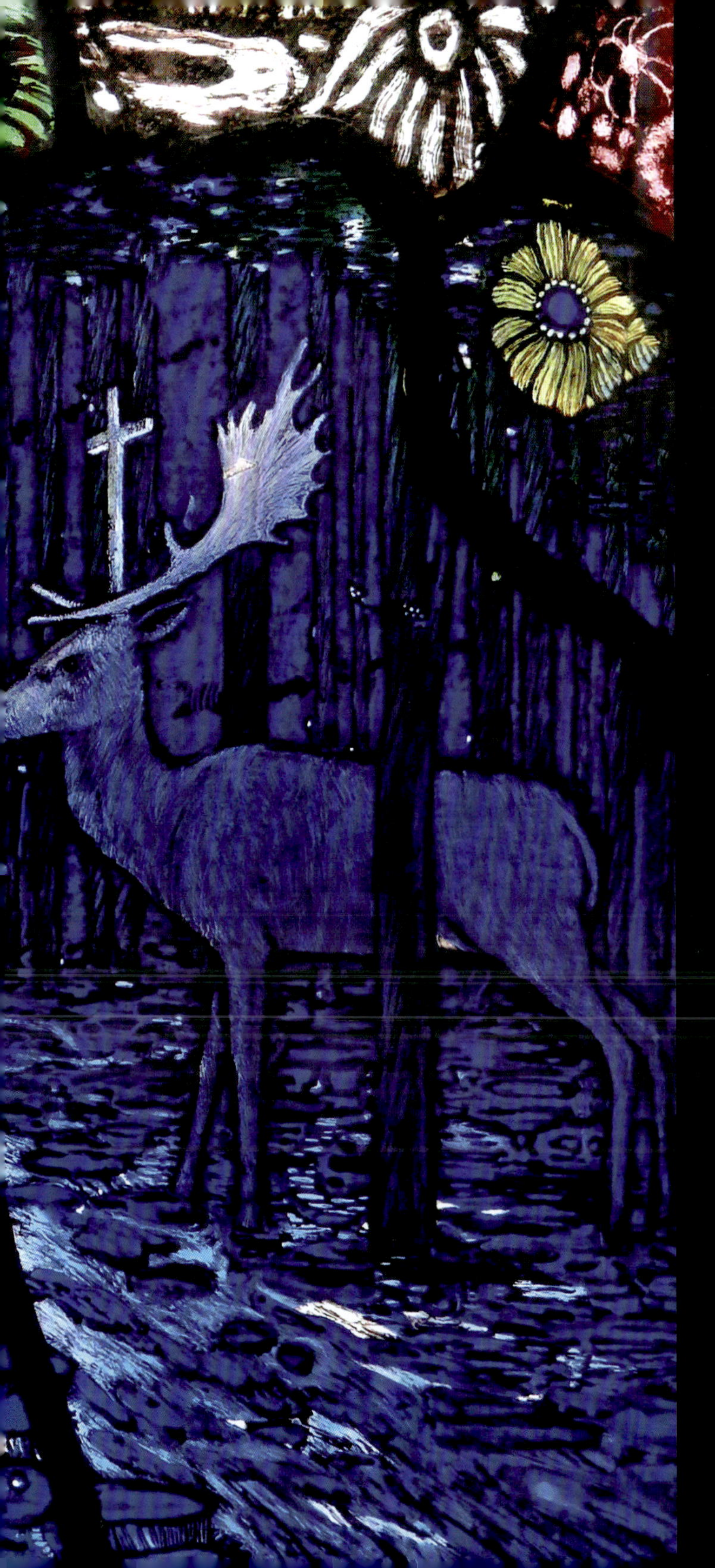

Harry Clarke,
detail of *St Hubert* (1921),
Church of Ireland (St Patrick's),
Carnalway, Harristown,
near Kilcullen, County Kildare

COUNTY KILDARE

Athy: Library (former Dominican Church), Convent Lane
CAMPBELL, George
Abstract stained glass scheme, including very large windows, two dalle de verre windows, and clear windows with etched angels 1964
(Created at Abbey Stained Glass Studios.)

Ballycane, near Naas: CC (Church of the Irish Martyrs), Ballycane Road
WALSH, George W.
Scheme Commemorating the Lives of Seventeen Irish Martyrs Who Died in the 16th and 17th Centuries 1991
Screen incorporating Tabernacle 1991
Baptistry screen 1991

Carbury: C of I
O'BRIEN, Catherine
The Good Shepherd 1913
'Behold I Stand at the Door and Knock' 1913
These windows, now in light boxes, originally formed a two-light window when previously in Rahan C of I, County Offaly.

Carnalway, Harristown, near Kilcullen: C of I (St Patrick's)
CLARKE, Harry
St Hubert 1921

Castledermot: C of I
O'BRIEN, Catherine
The Sower 1925–6 (sketch design, NGI)

Coolcarrigan, near Timahoe: C of I
O'BRIEN, Catherine
Decorative window with Celtic Ornament 1911 (sketch design, NGI)
Decorative window with Celtic Ornament 1912
Decorative window with Symbols of the Four Evangelists, Based on those in the Book of Armagh * 1916 (2 lights)
Decorative window with Celtic Ornament * 1927
POLLEN, Patrick
Decorative window with Celtic Ornament 1980 (sketch design, NIVAL)

Cooleragh: CC (Christ the King)
MURPHY, Johnny
Christ the King 1963
Apostles 1963
St Brigid 1963
St Patrick 1963
St Conleth 1963
Holy Spirit 1963
Church Symbols 1963
(Celia Harriss Crampton of Murphy-Devitt Studios worked on these windows; sketch designs and cartoons for all, NIVAL)

Clane: Clongowes Wood College Chapel
BECKER, Margaret
The Seventh Dolour (The Entombment) (designed by Evie Hone in 1942, made by Margaret Becker in 2014–15) (cartoons, Clongowes Wood College; left-hand side cartoon, Our Lady's Bower Secondary School, Athlone)
HEALY, Michael
St Joseph's Dream, St Joseph Searching in Bethlehem, the Flight into Egypt 1916 (3 lights)
St Patrick and St Brigid 1920 (2 lights)
The First Dolour (Prophecy of Simeon) 1935–8 (2 lights)
The Second Dolour (Flight into Egypt) 1938–9 (2 lights)
The Third Dolour (Search for the Holy Child) 1938–41 (2 lights)
The Fourth Dolour (Christ Meets His Mother) 1941 (2 lights) (begun by Michael Healy and completed by

Evie Hone after his death) (Sketch design by Michael Healy, NGI; sketch design for tracery by Evie Hone, NIVAL)
HONE, Evie
The Fifth Dolour (The Crucifixion) 1942 (2 lights)
The Sixth Dolour (The Deposition) 1942 (2 lights) (sketch design and cartoon, Manresa House, Dollymount, Dublin)
PYE, Patrick
The Trinity 1987 (currently in storage)

Clane: Clongowes Wood College, Ignatian Chapel
HONE, Evie
Head of Christ Crucified 1949 (circular panel)
St Ignatius and St Francis Xavier 1955 (2 lights)
WALSH, George W.
St Peter Claver 1982 (2 lights)

Clane: Clongowes Wood College, 'The People's Church'
BECKER, Margaret
John Sullivan Memorial Window c.2010

Crookstown, Ballitore, near Athy: CC (St Mary and St Lawrence's)
MULDOWNEY, Patrick
St Palladius 1992
St Francis of Assisi 1992

Curragh Camp: CC (St Brigid's)
MURPHY, Johnny
Lamb of God with Alpha and Omega, and names of various apostles and saints 1958 (cartoons, NIVAL)
Abstract lead-lights 1958

Derrinturn, Carbury: CC (Holy Trinity)
O'BRIEN, Catherine
The Annunciation 1904 (2 lights)
St Conleth and St Brigid 1904 (2 lights)
WALSH, George W.
Apparition at Knock 2007 (2 lights)

Kilberry, near Athy: C of I
O'BRIEN, Catherine
Landscape with horse and cattle (W.H.F. Verschoyle Memorial) c.1943 (opus sectile mosaic panel)

Kilcullen: C of I (St John's)
O'BRIEN, Catherine
The Resurrection * 1920 (quatrefoil)
RHIND, Ethel
'He Hath Delivered my Soul in Peace * 1920 (quatrefoil)

Kildare Town: CC (St Brigid's)
PYE, Patrick
Resurrection and Descent from the Cross 1971 (2 lights, mortuary chapel)
St Brigid Punishing Two Offending Nuns 1971 (shrine to the Madonna and Child)
Five abstract panels creating a screen 1971 (entrance portico, formerly in Blessed Sacrament Chapel)
Scenes from Christ's Passion: (six small windows, from left to right) *The Agony in the Garden, Jesus before Pontius Pilate, Christ Meets His Mother, The Crucifixion, Mary Magdalene and the Angel of the Resurrection at the Tomb, The Resurrection* 1975 (in Blessed Sacrament Chapel)

Kildare Town: C of I Cathedral (St Brigid's)
FRÖMEL, Gerda
St Luke c.1964

Kildare Town: Kildare County Council Municipal Collection
HONE, Evie
Three Fish c.1947 (roundel; formerly in the collection of the Arts Council who purchased it from novelist Kate O'Brien)

Kilkea: Kilkea Castle (Baronial Hall)
WALSH, George Stephen
Lady Emelinda date unknown
Silken Thomas date unknown
Wizard Earl date unknown

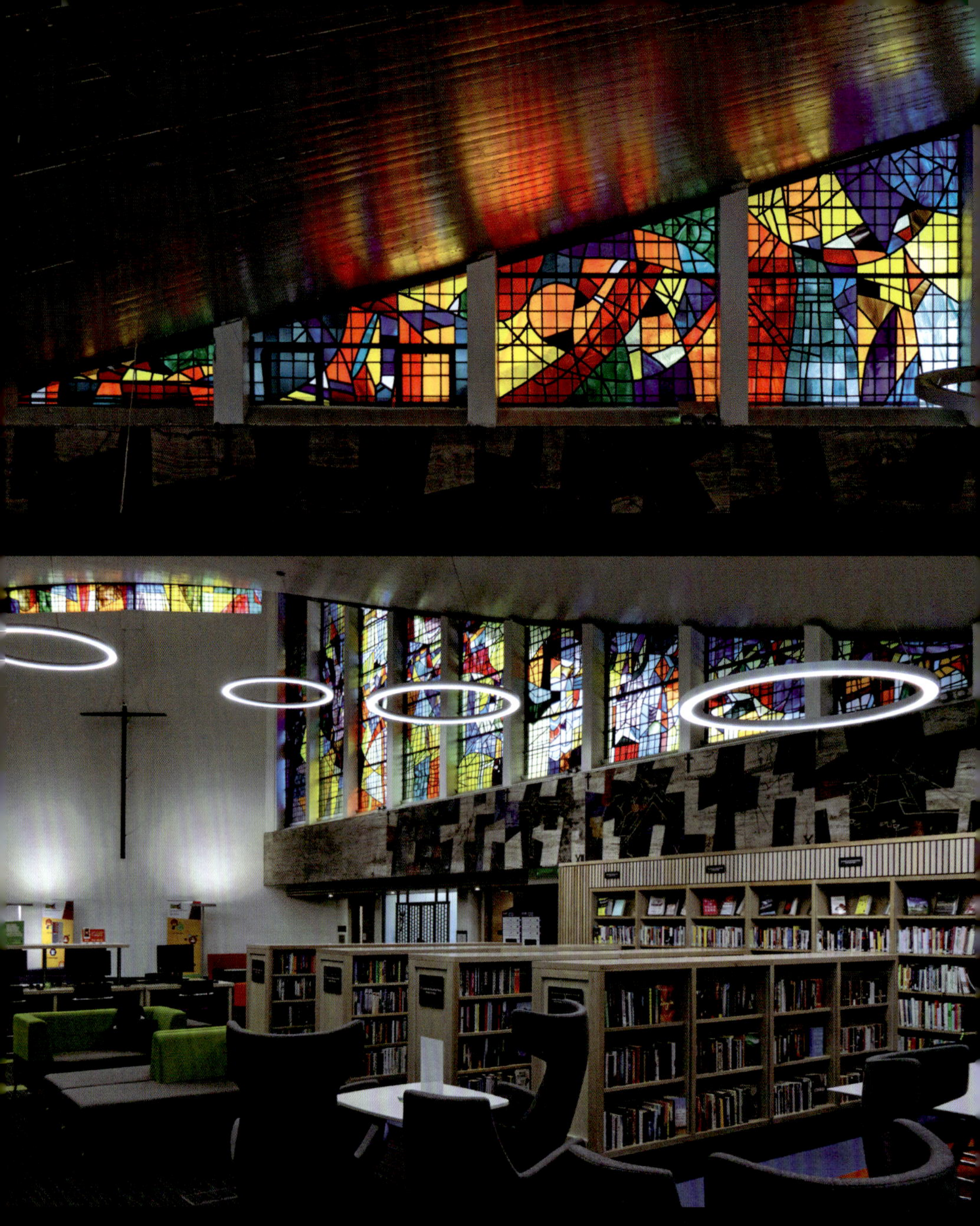

George Campbell, *Abstract stained glass scheme* (1964),
Athy Library (former Dominican Church), Athy, County Kildare

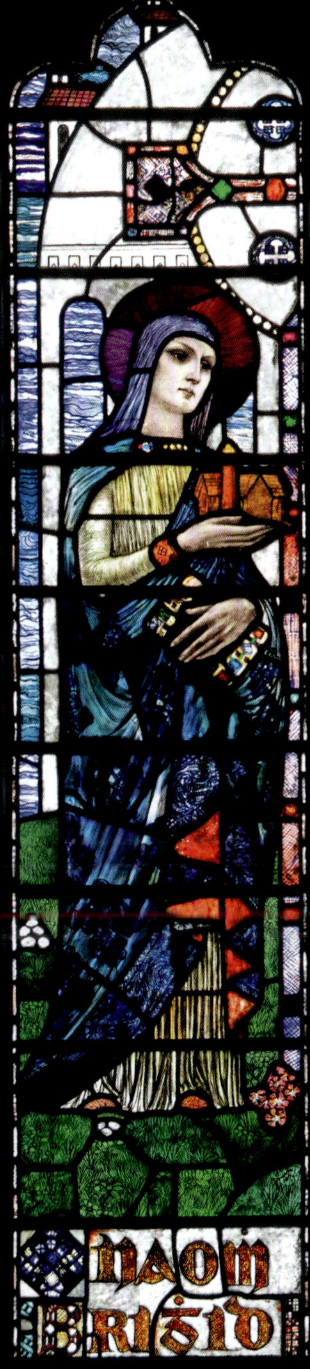

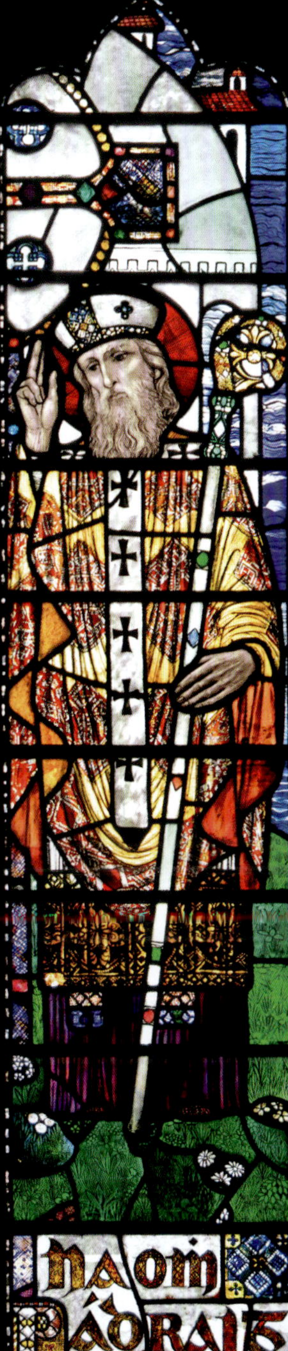

Michael Healy, detail of *St Patrick and St Brigid* (1920), Clongowes Wood College Chapel, Clane, County Kildare

Kilkea: C of I
CHILD, A.E.
St Lawrence O'Toole, St Patrick and St Cathach 1926 (3 lights)

Kilmeague: C of I (St Brigid's)
CHILD, A.E.
St Paul and St Luke 1919 (2 lights)

Maynooth: St Mary's Oratory, St Patrick's College
EARLEY, William (Bill) E.
Nativity, Annunciation 1939 (4 lights, 2 above 2)
Coronation of the Virgin, Visitation 1939 (4 lights, 2 above 2)

Monasterevin: C of I (St John the Evangelist's)
CHILD, A.E.
Crown of Life, Knight with Angel 1918

Naas, Kerdiffstown Road: Kerdiffstown House Oratory
MULDOWNEY, Patrick
Blessed Frederic Ozanam SVP 1999
Blessed Virgin Mary 1999

Naas, Sallins Road: CC (Our Lady and St David's)
WALSH, George W.
Abstract baptistry alcove window 1991

Naas, Sallins Road, Oldtown: Scoil Bhríde (visits strictly by appointment)
YOUNG, Peter
Aesop's Fables 2014 (2 panels)

Newbridge, Ballymany: CC (Cill Mhuire)
BREEN, Lua
Stained glass scheme based on Hallel Psalms 1984

Newbridge: Newbridge College Chapel (St Eustace's)
DOWD MURPHY, Róisín and MURPHY, Johnny
Four Horsemen of the Apocalypse and Other Scenes from the New Testament Book of Revelation, abstract lights 1965–8 (cartoons, NIVAL)

Newbridge: Liffey Lodge (former Patrician Monastery) chapel, Naas Road
DOWD MURPHY, Róisín and MURPHY, Johnny
Crucifixion 1963 (5 lights)
Our Lady 1963
St Joseph and the Christ Child 1963
St Patrick 1963
St Brigid 1963
St Colmcille 1963
St Therese 1963
St Conleth 1963
Rev. Dr Delaney 1963
Loaves and Fish 1963
Wheat and Grapes 1963
Ubi Petrus Ibi Ecclesia 1963 (heraldic)
Fratres Sancti Patricia Pro Deo et Patria 1963 (heraldic)
(sketches and cartoons for most, NIVAL)

Newtown: CC (Nativity of Our Lady)
WALSH, George W.
Multiple Christian symbols, the Creation, local saints, way of life, flora and fauna 2000 (5 windows, including one behind altar)

Straffan: C of I
CHILD, A.E.
Christ Blessing Little Children 1913
The Crucifixion 1913
The Resurrection 1913
O'BRIEN, Catherine
The Ascension 1948 (3 lights)

Two Mile House, near the Curragh: CC (St Peter's)
POLLEN, Patrick
The Assumption 1983 (sketch designs, NIVAL)

COUNTY KILKENNY

Bennettsbridge: CC (St Bennett's)
HONE, Evie
*Christ Meets Veronica (VI Station of the Cross) c.*1940s (panel in light box)

Bigwood, near Mullinavat: CC (St Paul's)
POLLEN, Patrick
Entire scheme of abstract windows 1964–5 (sketch designs, NIVAL)

Callan: CC (Brother Rice Memorial Church)
MOLONEY, Helen
Repeated motifs of the Lamb, Holy Spirit, Crucifix, Sun within a Star, Symbolising Jesus and Mary, all set within abstract framework 1969 (16 lights) (sketch designs, NIVAL)

Castlecomer: C of I (St Mary's)
HEALY, Michael
St Christopher, the Angel of the Resurrection, and St Martin 1920 (3 lights)
O'BRIEN, Catherine
War Memorial 1946 (opus sectile mosaic panel)

Clara: CC (St Scuithin's)
HONE, Evie
*Dove of Peace c.*1940s (panel, in left-hand side sacristy)

Below: Helen Moloney, *Scheme of abstract windows with symbols* (1969), Brother Rice Memorial Chapel, Callan, County Kilkenny

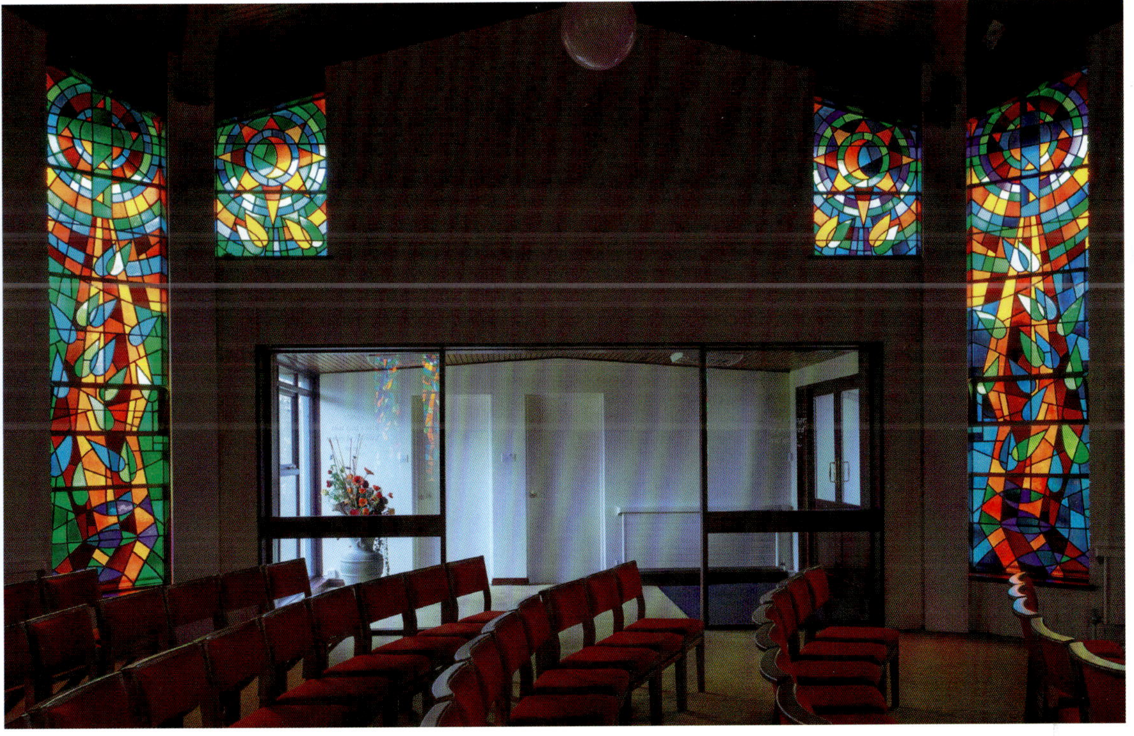

Ennisnag, near Stoneyford: C of I (St Peter's)
O'BRIEN, Catherine
St Ciaran and St Moling 1940 (2 lights) (sketch design, NGI)

Freshford: C of I (St Lachtain's)
TOMLIN, Stanley
St Cecilia * *c.*1956

Gowran: Former C of I (designated a National Monument, in the care of Gowran Development Association and Office of Public Works)
HEALY, Michael
War Memorial 1918 (2 lights) (sketch design, NGI)
McGOLDRICK, Hubert
Sorrow and Joy 1920 (2 lights)

Graiguenamanagh: Duiske Abbey
POLLEN, Patrick
St Fiacre and St Moling (sketch design, NIVAL) *c.*1979 (2 lights)
*Dove c.*1979 (rose window, flanked by 2 abstract lights)
Abstract * *c.*1979 (small quatrefoil)

Inistioge: C of I (St Mary and St Columba's)
O'BRIEN, Catherine
Valour, the Resurrection and Charity 1919 (3 lights)

Kilfane: C of I
McGOLDRICK, Hubert
The Good Samaritan 1932 (2 lights)

Kilkenny City, Abbey Street: CC, Black Abbey (Dominican Priory)
WALSH, George W.
Sun, stars and moons with Cross motif 1973 (4 lights, with tracery)
Abstract with moons 1973 (2 lights)

Kilkenny City, College Road: St Kieran's College
KING, Richard
Saints Patrick, Kieran, Ailbe, Ibar, Canice and Brendan 1932 (6 lights with tracery)
St Lawrence and St Stephen 1933–4 (2 lights)
St Augustine and St John Chrysostom 1933–4
(George Stephen Walsh assisted in the painting of these windows. Created at Harry Clarke Studios.)

Kilkenny City, Loughboy: CC (St Fiacre's)
MULDOWNEY, Patrick
St Fiacre 1992
Baptism of Christ 1992
Tabernacle 1992
Madonna and Child 1992

Kilkenny City, The Close, Coach Road: C of I Cathedral (St Canice's)
CHILD, A.E.
The Nativity 1931 (2 lights)
ELVERY, Beatrice
The Parables of the Sower and the Lost Sheep 1908 (2 lights)
RHIND, Ethel
The Crown of Life (war memorial) 1918 (2 lights)

Knocktopher: CC (formerly the Carmelite Priory)
POLLEN, Patrick
St Patrick, Virgin and Child with St Simon Stock, St Joseph 1958–9 (sketch design, NIVAL)

Talbot's Inch: Convent of Mercy Chapel
MURPHY, Johnny
Abstract lights 1984

Right:
Ethel Rhind, *The Crown of Life* (1918), Church of Ireland Cathedral, Kilkenny City

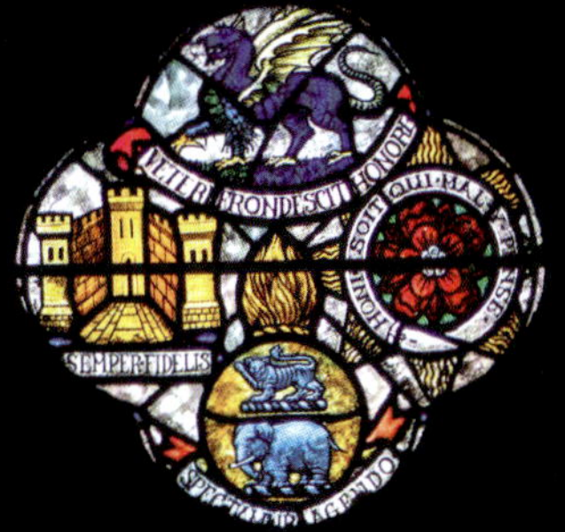
FRONDESCIT HONORE
HONI SOIT QUI MAL Y PENSE
SEMPER FIDELIS

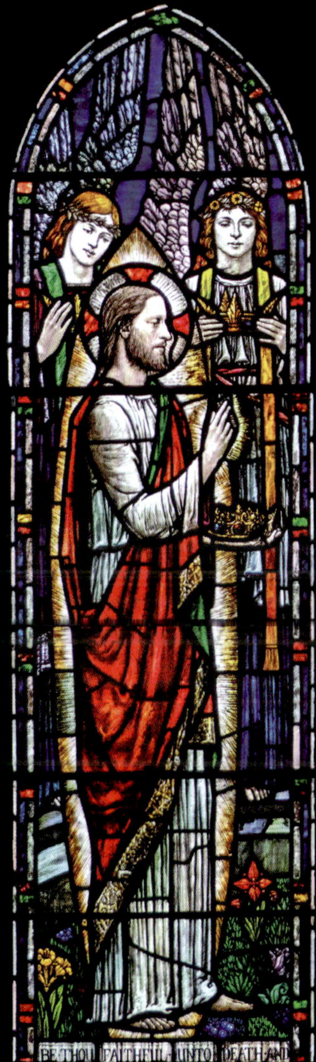
BE THOU FAITHFUL UNTO DEATH AND

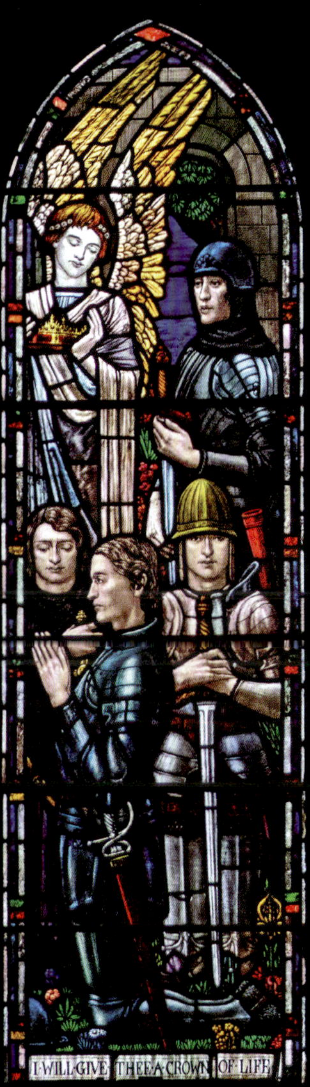
I WILL GIVE THEE A CROWN OF LIFE

COUNTY LAOIS

Abbeyleix: C of I (St Michael and All Angels)
CHILD, A.E.
Christ as Good Shepherd 1929
O'BRIEN, Catherine
St James and St Martha 1942 (2 lights)
Flowers, donkey and squirrel 1944

Ballintubbert: C of I (St Brigid's)
CHILD, A.E.
Centurion, St George, Angel of Light 1906 (3 lights)

Clonaslee: CC (St Manman's)
MULDOWNEY, Patrick
Crucifixion 2017 (in sacristy)

Errill: CC (Our Lady Queen of the Universe)
TOMLIN, Alan
Abstract scheme incorporating Stations of the Cross 1972

Portarlington: Mount St Anne's Retreat and Conference Centre
DOWD MURPHY, Róisín and MURPHY, Johnny
Nativity 1964
Presentation in the Temple, Finding in the Temple 1964
Holy Spirit Descends 1964
Resurrection 1964
Assumption 1964
Ascension 1964
Queen of Heaven 1964
Abstract 1964 (cruciform-shaped)
(cartoons for all, NIVAL)

Portlaoise: C of I (St Peter's)
CHILD, A.E.
Christ Blessing Little Children 1938

Mountmellick: Presentation Convent Chapel
MURPHY, Johnny
Abstract 1958 (3 lights)

Rosenallis: CC (St Brigid's)
MULDOWNEY, Patrick
The Creation 2010–1
Holy Family 2010–1
Risen Christ 2010–1
St Patrick 2010–1
St Brigid 2010–1
Eucharist 2010–1
Lamb of God 2010–1
Crown of Thorns 2010–1
The Holy Spirit 2010–1
Spring 2010–1
Summer 2010–1
Autumn 2010–1
Winter 2010–1

Stradbally: C of I (St Patrick's)
ELVERY, Beatrice
Risen Christ Appears to Mary Magdalene 1905 (2 lights) (Catherine O'Brien assisted in the painting of this window)

Timahoe: CC (St Michael's)
HEALY, Michael
The Sacred Heart 1921–2 (sketch design, NGI)
The Immaculate Conception 1921–2 (sketch design, NGI)

COUNTY LEITRIM

Carrick-on-Shannon: CC (St Mary's)
MULDOWNEY, Patrick
Rejuvenation 2010

Drumcong: CC (St Brigid's)
WALSH, George W.
*Madonna and Child c.*1994
*Risen Christ c.*1994
*Church building c.*1994
*Creation c.*1994
*St Brigid c.*1994 (rose)
*Jesus Hominum Salvator c.*1994 (side room)

Farnaught: C of I
RHIND, Ethel
Angel of Mercy 1919
Fortitude 1923
St Modomnoc 1937

Gorvagh: CC (St Joseph's)
WALSH, George W.
Holy Spirit 1987
Eucharist 1987

Leitrim Village: CC (St Joseph's)
WALSH, George W.
Risen Christ 1988 (3 lights)
Creation 1988
Ancient Ireland 1988
Coming of Christianity 1988
Elements 1988
Shannon 1988
Work of local people 1988

Mohill: C of I (St Mary's)
CHILD, A.E.
The Good Shepherd 1937

COUNTY LIMERICK

Abington: C of I (St John's)
CHILD, A.E.
Virgin and Child with Infant St John the Baptist 1908

Bruff: Former C of I (now community, performance and meeting space)
CHILD, A.E.
The Good Shepherd 1913

Castleconnell: Castle Oaks Hotel (former Presentation Convent)
MURPHY, Johnny
*Church symbols c.*1960

Castletroy: CC (Our Lady Help of Christians), Milford Road
MURPHY, Johnny and MURPHY, Reiltín
Scheme of symbolic abstract single lights and three lights 1981

Castletroy: University of Limerick
CHILD, A.E.
Symbols of the Four Evangelists (based on the designs for these in the Book of Armagh) 1914 (four small trefoil panels, Foundation Building, garden level)
HONE, Evie
*St Brigid Kneading Bread c.*1940 (panel; Irish American Cultural Institute's O'Malley Art Collection, Plassey House)

Croom: C of I
RHIND, Ethel
The Adoration of the Shepherds, Christ in Glory, Supper at Emmaus 1913–14 (3 lights)

Kilmallock: C of I (St Peter and St Paul's)
CHILD, A.E.
The Good Shepherd 1906 (painted by Catherine O'Brien and Ethel Rhind)

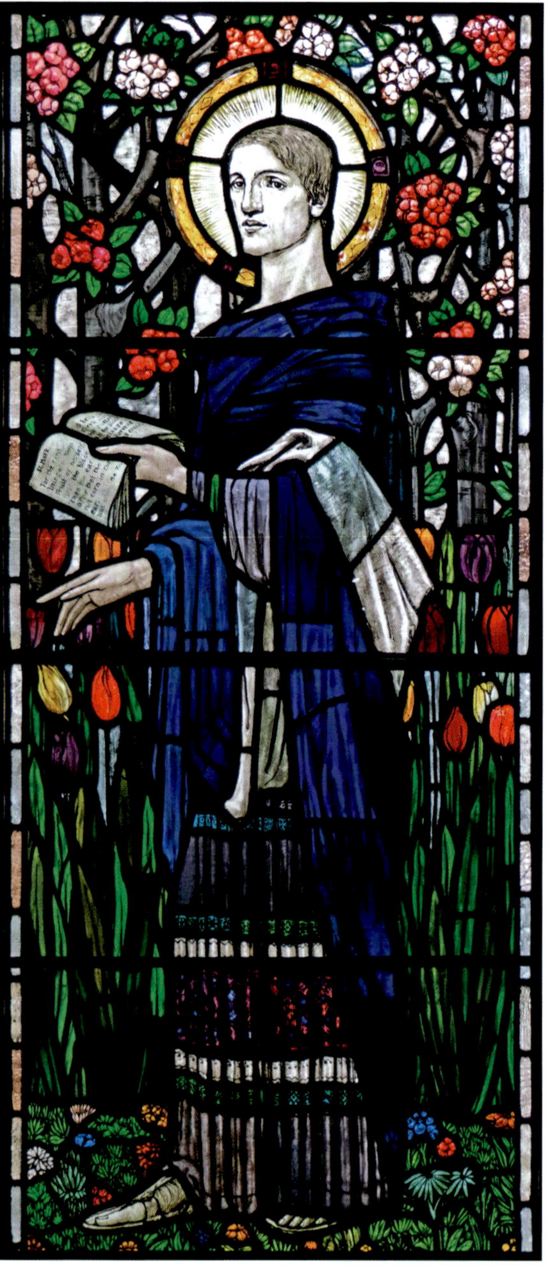

Ethel Rhind, detail of *St Mark* (1919), Knockainey Historical and Conservation Society (former Church of Ireland), Knockainey, County Limerick

Kilmurry: Kilmurry Arts and Heritage Centre (former C of I)
CHILD, A.E.
River, Tree, Doves, and Sword * *c.*1920
'Blessed Are the Pure in Heart' * 1925

Knockainey: CC (Church of Our Lady)
DOWLING, William
St Brigid and St Ita 1930
St Peter and St Paul 1930 (sketch design, TCD)
Christ the King with, at the base, Three Scenes from the Life of Christ * 1931
Blessed Virgin with, at the base, St Brendan, St Patrick and St Ailbe * 1939
Adoration of the Magi * 1940
Coronation of the Virgin * 1940
Christ Blessing Children * 1943
Annunciation * 1943
(All windows created at Harry Clarke Studios and were relocated from the old – since demolished – church at Knockainey in the 1970s.)

Knockainey: Knockainey Historical and Conservation Society (former St John's C of I)
RHIND, Ethel
St John 1911
St Mark 1919

Limerick City, Bridge Street: C of I Cathedral (St Mary's)
DOWLING, William
Ascension, with St Catherine, Prodigal Son, Annunciation, Good Samaritan and St Nicholas 1960–1
O'BRIEN, Catherine
History and Architecture 1912 (2 lights)
St Luke Drawing the Virgin and Child 1914 (2 lights)

Limerick City, Corbally Road: St Munchin's College
HENEY, Patrick
St Colmcille, St Patrick and St Brigid 1962 (3 lights, in chapel)
Past Bishops of Limerick 1962 (nine medallions set into leaded lights, in school)

Limerick City, Dooradoyle Road: Crescent College Comprehensive
BIGGS, Frances
Supper at Emmaus 1987 (panel, prayer room)

Limerick City, Ennis Road: CC (Our Lady of the Rosary)
DOWD MURPHY, Róisín
Nativity and Resurrection 1979 (each side of the central Evie Hone *Baptism* panel; cartoons, NIVAL)
HONE, Evie
The Baptism of Christ 1950 (in the baptistery) (sketch design, Manresa House, Dollymount, Dublin)
WALSH, George W.
Six Scenes from the Life of Christ, separated by sandblasted glass in abstract pattern 1979

Limerick City, Glentworth Street: CC (St Saviour's Dominican Church)
MURPHY, Johnny
Holy Spirit 1959 (3 lights)
Crucifixion 1960 (4 lights)
*Four abstract lights c.*1959–60 (above oratory windows)
*Abstract c.*1959–60 (rose, above gallery)
MURPHY, Johnny and MURPHY, Reiltín
Martyrdom of Bishop Terence Albert O'Brien Observed by Sorrowing Women and Children, his Final Testimony, the Sarsfield Chalice, his Pectoral Cross, Sarsfield's Ride, the Pikes of '98, Burned Homes, Emigrant Ship, Rising Sun of Easter, Abundant Harvests, the Shannon Scheme, Planes over Foynes, Joining the EEC, Culminating in Visit of Pope John Paul II to Limerick 1982 (two adjoining walls of stained glass in Bishop O'Brien Memorial Chapel) (sketch designs, NIVAL)

Limerick City, Henry Street: Former Presbyterian Church (now offices, windows removed, location untraced)
AN TÚR GLOINE STUDIO
Decorative windows with symbols (I) (2 lights) 1938–9
Decorative windows with symbols (II) (2 lights) 1938–9

Limerick City, O'Connell Avenue: CC (St Joseph's)
KING, Richard
St Patrick * 1932–3
(Created at Harry Clarke Studios.)
MURPHY, Johnny
Two abstract lights 1974

Limerick City, O'Connell Street: CC (St Augustine's)
DOWLING, William
St Joseph 1940
St Monica 1940
Our Lady of Consolation 1940
St Nicholas of Tolentine 1940
St Augustine 1940
There is a large four-light window, also created at Harry Clarke Studios, designer as yet unidentified, depicting *Scenes from the Life of St Augustine c.*1941

Limerick City, Pery Square: Limerick City Gallery of Art (former Carnegie Library)
AN TÚR GLOINE STUDIO
Fanlight with Limerick City's crest 1906

Limerick City, South Circular Road: CC (Mount Saint Alphonsus, Redemptorists)
EARLEY, Willie
Rainbow-themed windows * 1961 (a pair of 2 lights, tentatively attributed to Willie Earley)
(Created at Abbey Stained Glass Studios.)
There is also an abstract three-light window with central medallion by Abbey, 1967.

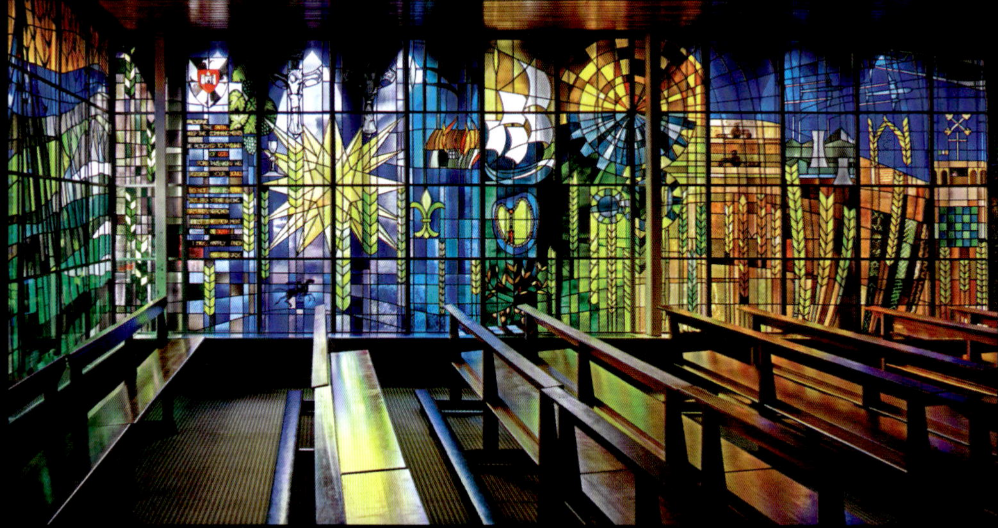

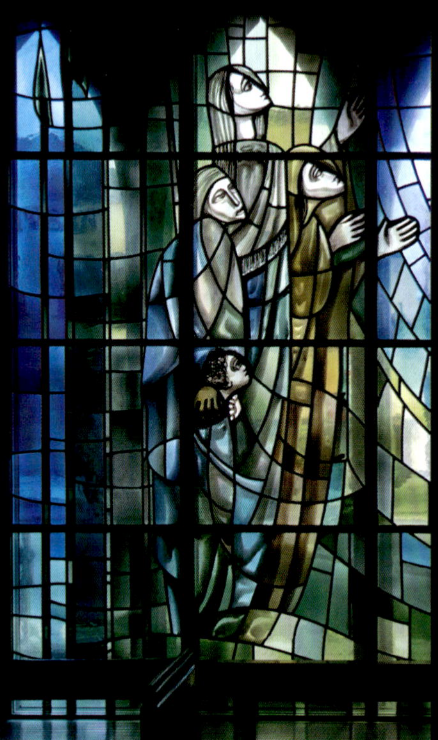

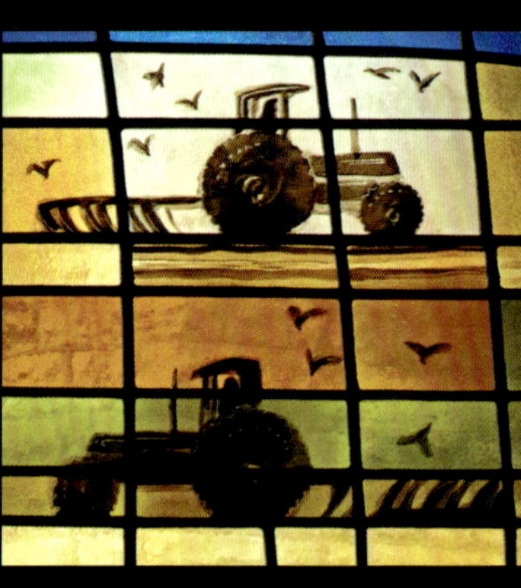

This page: Johnny Murphy and Reiltín Murphy, *Martyrdom of Bishop Terence Albert O'Brien and Scenes from the History of Limerick* (1982), Catholic Church (St Saviour's Dominican Church), Limerick City

Facing page: Margaret Becker, *St Michael Vanquishing Lucifer, St Jarlath, St Martin and the Beggar* (c.1975–80), Patrick Pollen, *St Malachy, St Bernard, St Columbanus* (1960); Patrick Pye, *The Calling of St Peter, St Peter and St Paul at the Gates of Jerusalem, St Paul Meeting the Faithful at the Three Taverns* (1960), Glenstal Abbey Church, Murroe, County Limerick

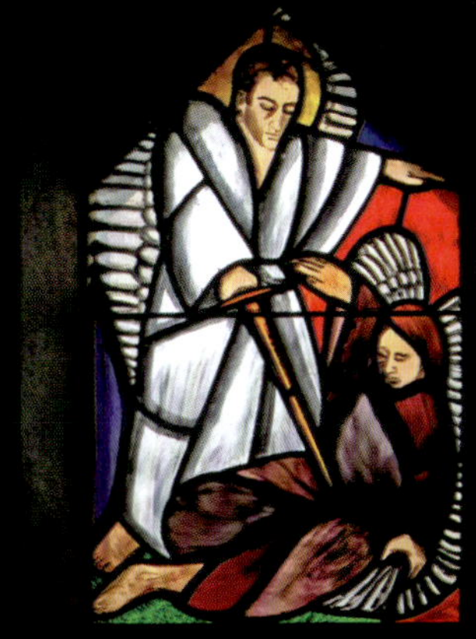
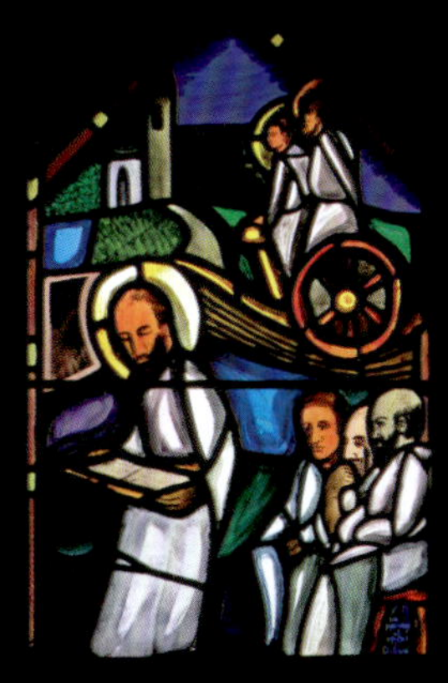
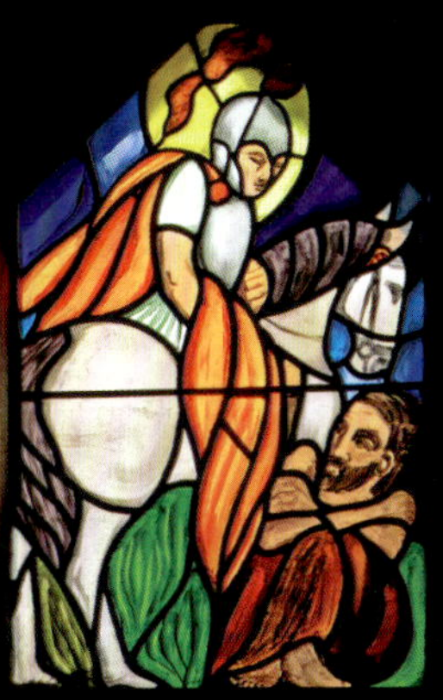
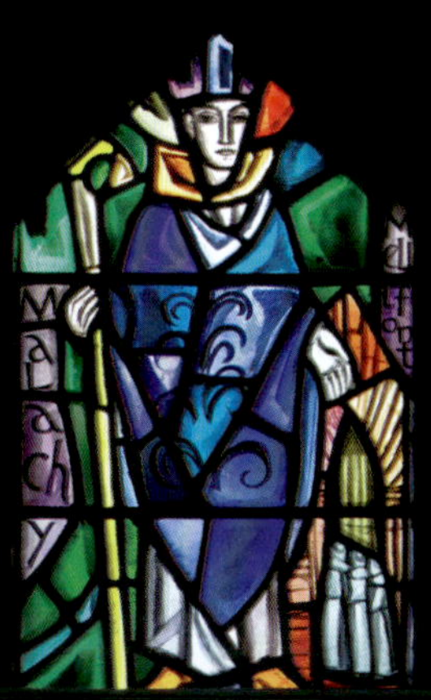
Malachy
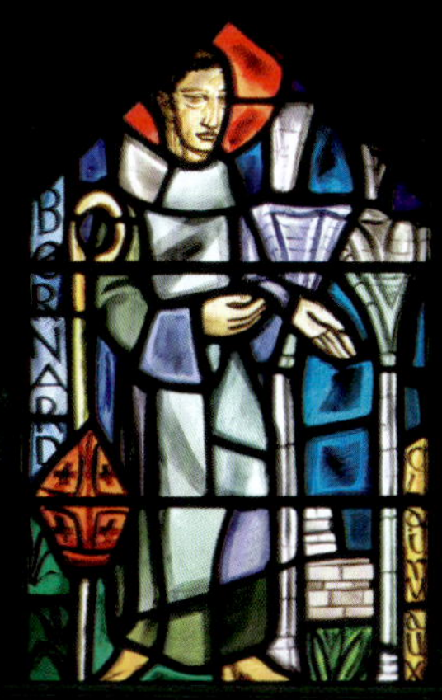
Bernard
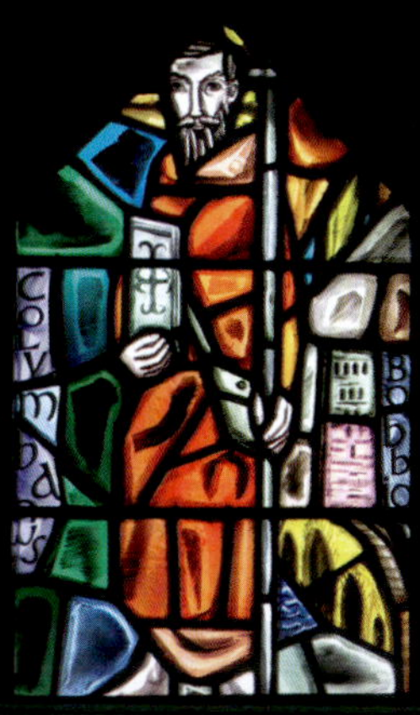
Columba
Bobbio
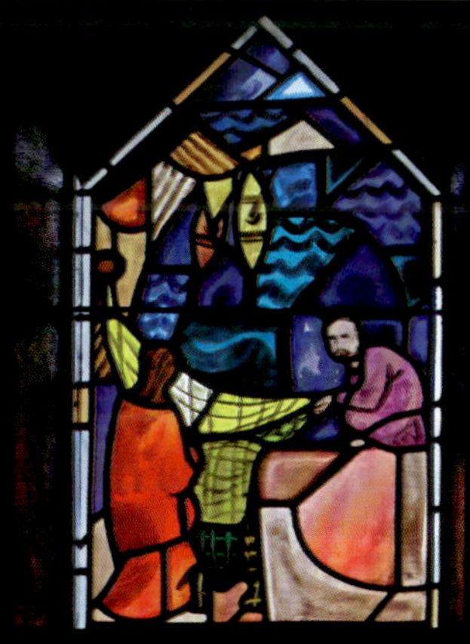
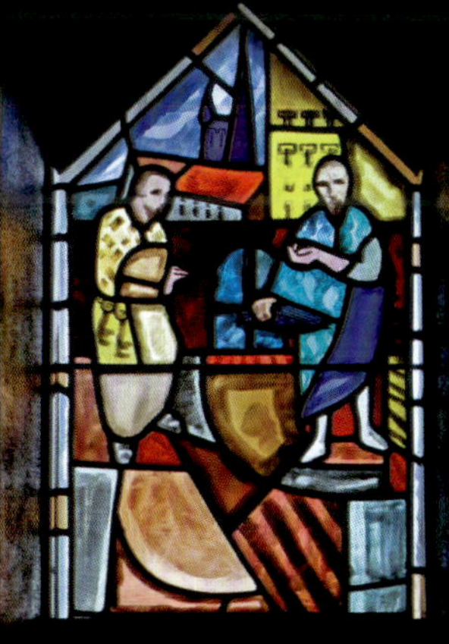
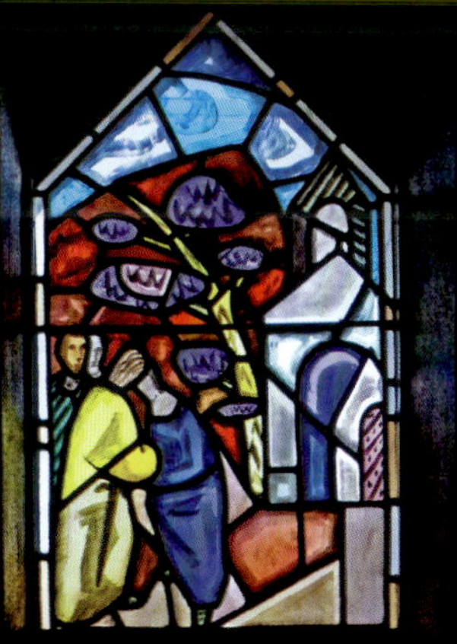

Limerick City, Southill: CC (Holy Family), O'Malley Park
DOWD MURPHY, Róisín and MURPHY, Johnny
Annunciation, Visitation, Nativity, Presentation in the Temple, Christ Among the Doctors, Archangel Michael *c.*1958 (six medallions, formerly in the chapel at CBS Sexton Street, Limerick, now in light boxes. There is a coloured cartoon for the *Annunciation* in NIVAL)
KELLY, Kevin
Holy Family *c.*1995 (light box)

Lisnagry: St Vincent's Centre Chapel
MURPHY, Johnny
Two abstract lights 1969

Murroe: Glenstal Abbey Church
BECKER, Margaret
St Michael Vanquishing Lucifer, St Jarlath, St Martin and the Beggar *c.*1975–80 (3 lights)
BRAUN, Sebastian
St Scholastica and St Gertrude *c.*1957 (design freely interpreted by unknown artist, possibly Christopher Campbell; in school-choir robing chapel)
Leaded lights with decorative borders (clerestory level no longer extant) *c.*1956 (made at Irish Stained Glass)
CAMPBELL, Christopher
St Sebastian *c.*1956
POLLEN, Patrick
St Malachy, St Bernard, St Columbanus 1960 (3 lights)
PYE, Patrick
St Patrick and the Black Birds, St Patrick Driving Out the Snakes, St Patrick and the White Birds 1959 (3 lights)
The Calling of St Peter, St Peter and St Paul at the Gates of Jerusalem, St Paul Meeting the Faithful at the Three Taverns 1960 (3 lights)
Old Testament Themes 1963–4 (3 lights, in Blessed Sacrament Chapel) (executed by Margaret Becker and painted by Patrick Pye)
Wedding Feast at Cana, Virgin of the Apocalypse, Lamb of God and the New Jerusalem 1963–4 (3 lights, in Blessed Sacrament Chapel) (executed by Margaret Becker and painted by Patrick Pye) (cartoons, NIVAL)
TUTTY, Benedict
Saint Teresa of Ávila and Saint Thérèse of Lisieux 1966
There is also a panel in the church depicting *St Michael* by an, as yet, unidentified artist.

Murroe: Glenstal Abbey Icon Chapel (visits by appointment)
SCANLON, James
St Matthew 1988 (circular panel)
St Mark 1988 (circular panel)
St Luke 1988 (circular panel)
St John 1988 (circular panel)
Centre of Cosmos 1988 (circular panel)
Two narrow abstract panels (one red-themed, one blue-themed) 1988

Patrickswell, near Knockainey: CC (St Patrick's)
CLARKE, Terry
Coronation of Our Lady 1942
DOWLING, William
Christ the King * 1940
Christ among the Doctors (medallion set into diamond-patterned lancet) * 1943
Presentation in the Temple (medallion set into diamond-patterned lancet) * 1943
Crucifixion, with (below) Annunciation, Nativity, Holy Family in the Carpenter's Shop 1943 (preliminary designs, TCD)
(All windows created at Harry Clarke Studios.)

Rathkeale: C of I (Holy Trinity)
O'BRIEN, Catherine
The Sower 1931 (3 lights) (sketch design, NGI)
St Paul and St Luke 1937 (2 lights)

Templeglantine: CC (Most Holy Trinity)
WALSH, George W.
St Patrick *c.*1970–1
St Brigid *c.*1970–1

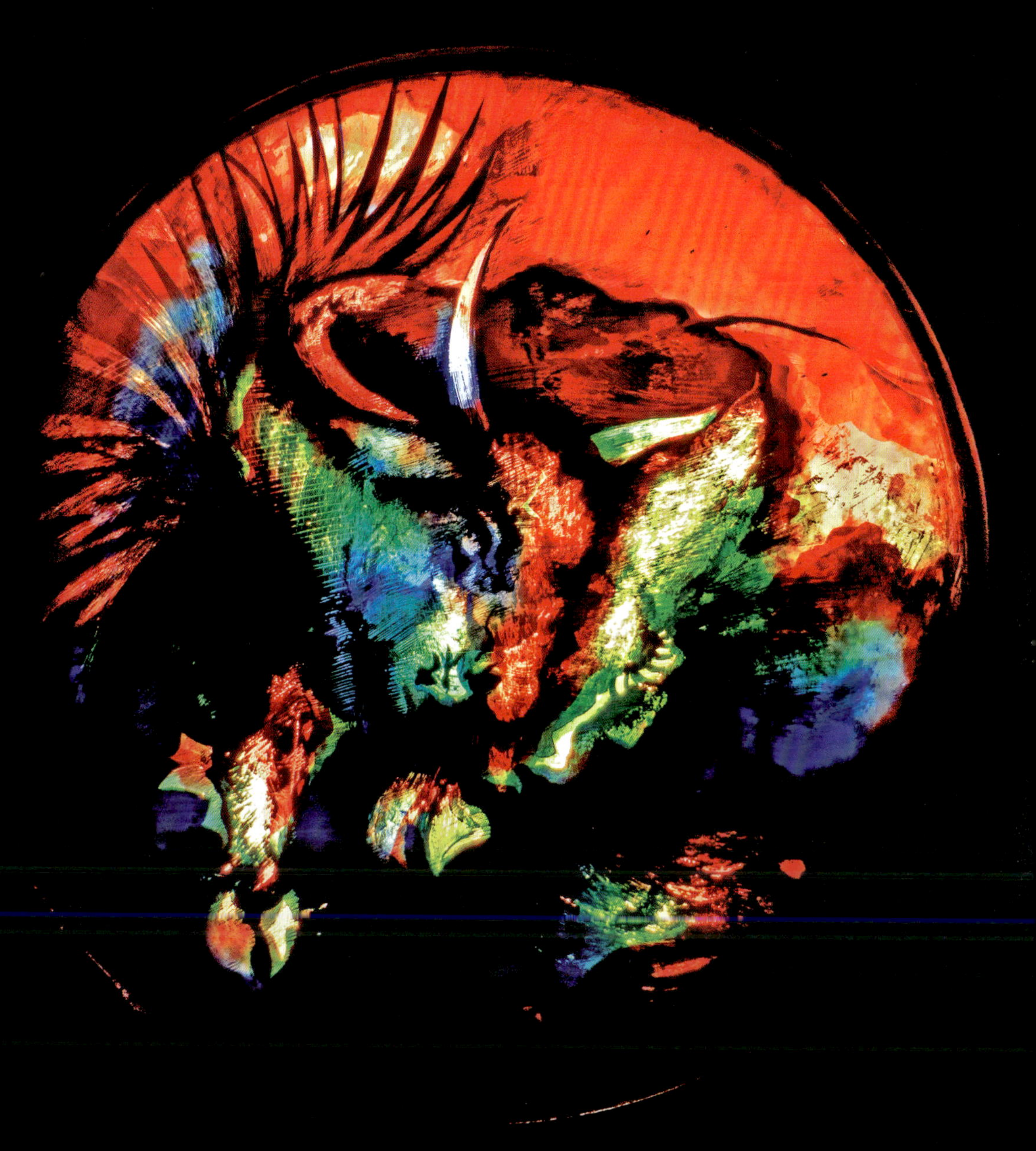

James Scanlon, *St Luke* (1988), Glenstal Abbey Icon Chapel, Murroe, County Limerick

COUNTY LONGFORD

Ardagh: CC (St Brigid's)
MURPHY, Johnny
Abstract lights 1977

Ballinamuck: CC (St Patrick's)
WALSH, George W.
Baptism and Renewal 1960–1 (baptistry)

Ballymacormick: C of I (St Catherine's)
RHIND, Ethel
Decorative window with an Angel in a Medallion (I) 1915
Decorative window with an Angel in a Medallion (II) 1915

Carrickedmond: CC (Sacred Heart)
WALSH, George W.
Sacred Heart, St Sinód and St Sinneach with images of Early Christianity 2011 (3 lights)

Clonbroney: CC (St James's)
SIMMONDS, Charles (Cecil)
Christ the King, Surrounded by Symbols of the Evangelists * 1931 (circular; preliminary designs, TCD)
(Created at Harry Clarke Studios.)

Longford Town: Catholic Cathedral (St Mel's)
KING, Richard
St Anne 1932–3
(Created at Harry Clarke Studios and restored by Abbey Stained Glass Studios after the disastrous fire of 2009.)
The Resurrection 1932–3
(Created at Harry Clarke Studios and restored by Abbey Stained Glass Studios after the disastrous fire of 2009.)
SCANLON, James
Eleven abstract lights 2013–4 (clerestory lunettes, west side of nave. The remaining lunettes are by Kim En Joong, who also created other windows for the cathedral.)

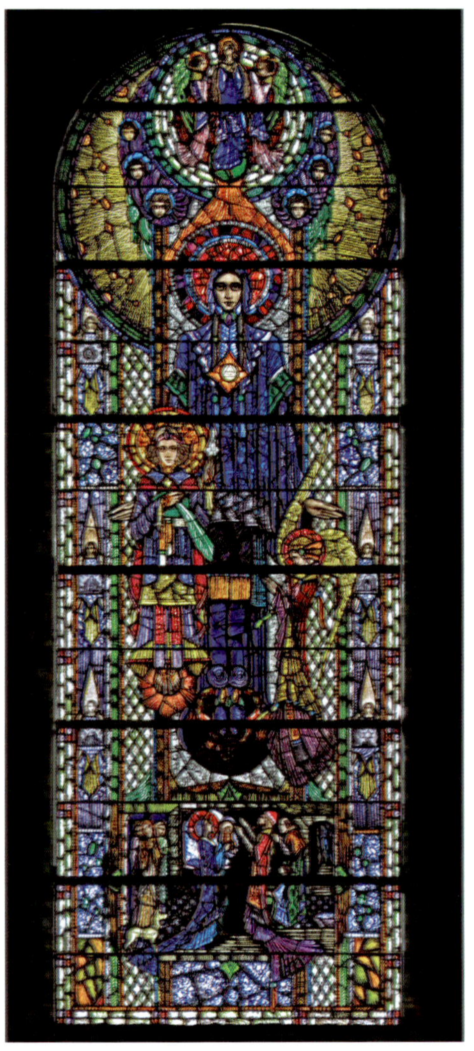

Above: Richard King, *St Anne* (1932–3), Catholic Cathedral, Longford Town

Moydow: CC (St Mary's)
WALSH, George W.
*Risen Christ c.*1970

COUNTY LOUTH

Bridge a Crinn: CC (Most Holy Rosary)
CHILD, A.E.
St John the Baptist before Herod, and the Head of St John the Baptist on a Dish * 1912
HEALY, Michael
Doubting Thomas, and Judith 1923 (sketch design, NGI)

Drogheda, Ballsgrove: CC (Holy Family)
BECKER, Margaret
Baptism of Christ 1995 (in baptistry)

Drogheda, Beechgrove: Medical Missionaries of Mary Community House
BURKE, Phyllis
*Christian symbols, including the Four Evangelists, Holy Spirit, Angel, Dove of Peace, Wheat, Fish c.*1963
Reconfigured from a much larger scheme in the former Chapel of the Medical Missionaries of Mary Nurses' Training Hostel, Drogheda. (cartoons, NIVAL)

Drogheda, St Laurence Street: Highlanes Gallery (former Franciscan Friary church)
MacBRIDE, William
St Francis of Assisi, Immaculate Conception, St Clare of Assisi * 1929 (3 lights)

Drumcar: CC (St Mary's)
KING, Richard
St John of God and Children 1958
The Holy Family 1958

Dundalk, Anne Street: CC (St Malachy's Dominican Priory)
HEALY, Michael
Christ with Symbols of the Eucharist, The Last Supper, St Dominic Receiving the Rosary 1913
Nine plain-glazed lancets, each with a star and roundels containing different emblems or symbols 1932–3 (in nave; sketch designs, NGI)
KING, Richard
Apparition of the Sacred Heart (St Margaret Mary in Glory) 1933–4
St Teresa 1934
St Malachy 1934
(The three windows by Richard King were created at Harry Clarke Studios.)
McGOLDRICK, Hubert
Two plain-glazed lancets, each with a star and roundels containing different emblems * 1942 (in transepts)

Dundalk, Church Street: C of I (St Nicholas's)
POLLEN, Patrick
*Salvaged Netherlandish and modern roundels set in coloured glass c.*1960 (sketch design, NIVAL)

Dundalk, St Mary's Road: CC Cerdon (Marist Fathers)
KING, Richard
Virgin and Child, Auxilium Christianorum (Our Lady Help of Christians) 1939–40 (opus sectile mosaic in opal glass)
(Created at Harry Clarke Studios.)

Jenkinstown: CC (Our Lady of the Wayside)
BREEN, Lua
Jesus and the Tax Collector in the Tree 1993–4 (sketch design, NIVAL)
Feeding the Five Thousand 1993–4 (sketch design, NIVAL)
Streams of Life, John 7:37:39 1993–4 (sketch design, NIVAL)
Baptism of Christ in the Jordan 1993–4 (sketch design, NIVAL)
Symbols of the Sea 1993–4
Alpha and Omega 1993–4 (sketch design, NIVAL) (circular)
MULLINS, Brendan
The Good Shepherd 2013
(Created at Abbey Stained Glass Studios.)

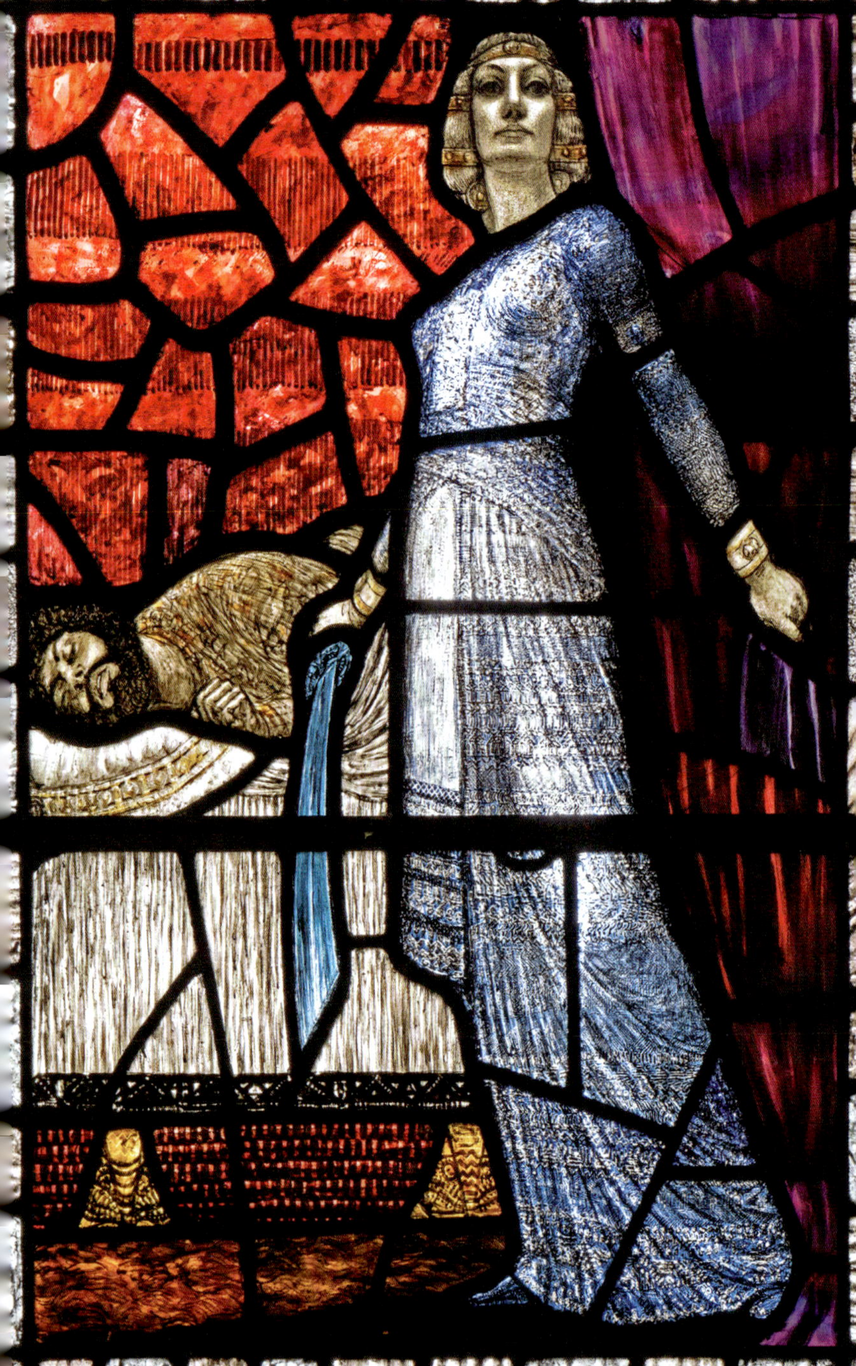

Kilcurry: CC (St Brigid's)
EARLEY, William (Bill) E.
Annunciation 1927
O'BRIEN, Catherine
St Columcille on Iona, St Patrick and St Sechnell at Elda in Faughart, St Patrick at the Ford of Ui-Lilaigh, with St Brigid and St Dara at Kildare 1914
PURSER, Sarah
Scenes from the Lives of St Columcille, St Patrick and St Brigid 1908–9 (painted by Catherine O'Brien)
Scenes from the Lives of St Fainchea and St Enda 1908–9 (painted by Hugh Barden)
KING, Richard
Sacred Heart * 1933–4
(Created at Harry Clarke Studios.)

Knockbridge: CC (St Mary's)
KING, Richard
Virgin and Child with St Patrick and St Brigid 1932–3 (lunette)
St Patrick 1936
(Both created at Harry Clarke Studios.)

Left:
Michael Healy,
Detail of *Doubting Thomas and Judith* (1923),
Catholic Church (Most Holy Rosary),
Bridge a Crinn, County Louth

COUNTY MAYO

Ballina: St Muredach's College chapel
MULDOWNEY, Patrick
Muredach and followers with symbols of education, boat, Ballina Cathedral, and crests 2016 (11 panels set within internal door)

Ballinrobe: Former Ballinafad College Chapel (now a wedding venue)
DOWD MURPHY, Róisín and MURPHY, Johnny
Holy Spirit 1963
Resurrection 1963
St Teresa 1963
Our Lady Crowned 1963
Scenes from the Society of African Missionary Ministry 1963
Ordination 1963
Portraits of Founders 1963
(Celia Harriss Crampton of Murphy-Devitt Studios worked on these windows) (cartoons for all, NIVAL)

Ballinrobe: CC (St Mary's)
CLARKE, Harry
The Baptism of Jesus in Jordan and the Ascension (B) 1925 (2 lights)
The Presentation in the Temple and The Immaculate Conception (B) 1925 (2 lights)
Ecce Homo, and Jesus with Mary Magdalen in the Garden (B) 1925 (2 lights)
The Assumption and the Coronation of Our Lady (B) 1925 (2 lights)
St Fursey and St Fechin (B) 1925 (2 lights)
St Colman and St Brendan the Navigator (B) 1925 (2 lights)
St Gormgail and St Kieran (B) 1925 (2 lights)
St Enda and St Jarlath (B) 1925 (2 lights)
WALSH, George W.
Our Lady of Cong late 1990s (Lady Chapel/side altar)
River of Life, Eucharist late 1990s (Adoration Chapel)

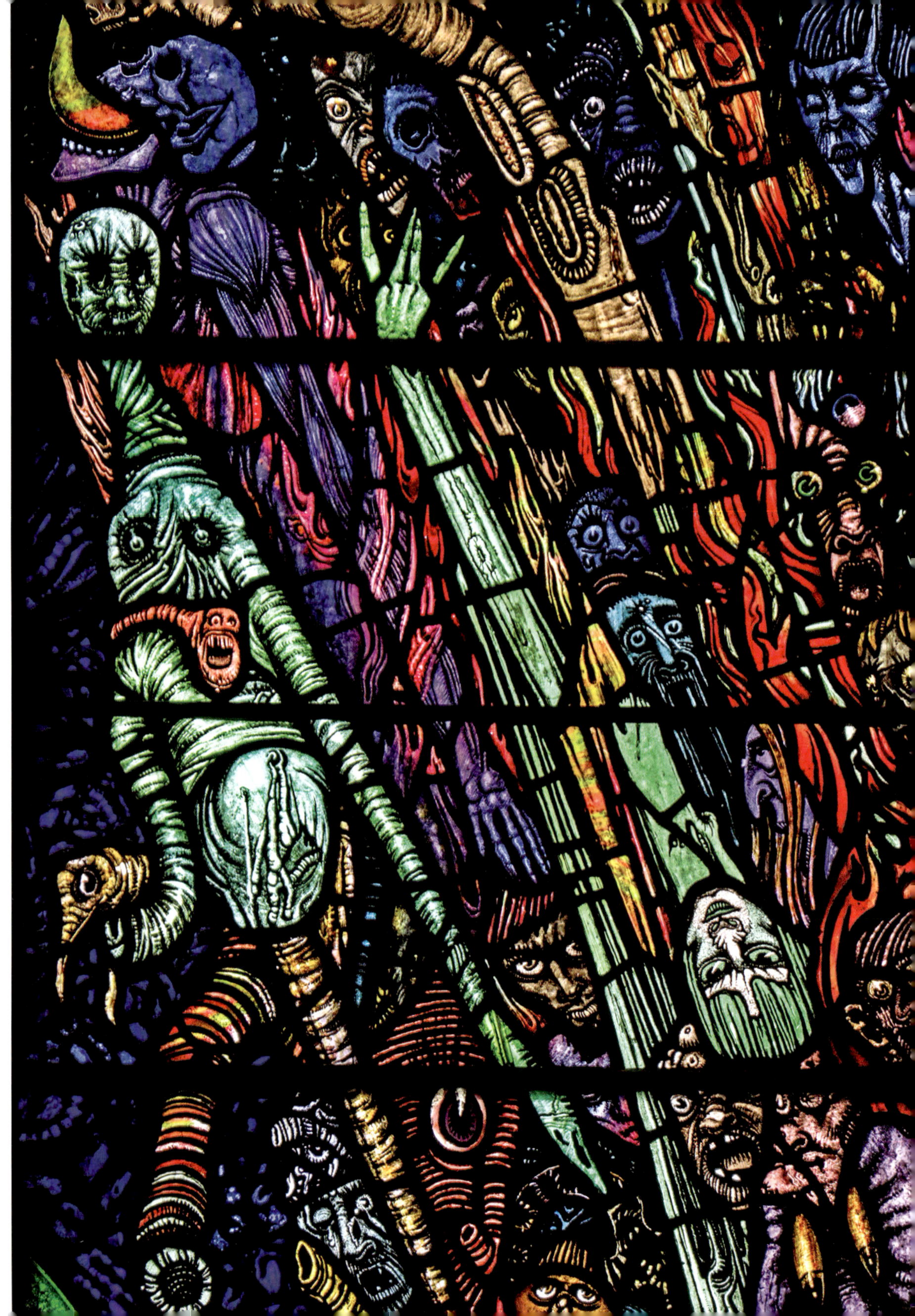

Swinford: CC (Our Lady Help of Christians)
KING, Richard
The Assumption 1952 (3 lights, with rose)
The Old and New Testaments 1964 (2 lights)
McGOLDRICK, Hubert
Our Lady of Lourdes 1940
Christ the King 1940

Tirrane (Mullet Peninsula): CC (St Brendan's)
CAMPBELL, Christopher
Scenes from the Life of St Brendan: St Ita Instructing the Young Brendan, St Brendan and the Sea Beast, St Brendan the Voyager, Inis Glóire Welcomes St Brendan, Consecration of St Brendan 1965 (5 lights)

Westport: CC (St Mary's)
CAMPBELL, George
Crown of Thorns 1960s (rose in *dalle de verre*, made by George W. Walsh)
CLARKE, Terry
St Patrick 1956–7
St Brigid 1960
EARLEY, Willie
*Our Lady of Lourdes c.*1961
*Our Lady of Perpetual Succour c.*1961
*The Holy Family c.*1961
*St Oliver Plunkett c.*1978
*Crucifixion c.*1970
*St Theresa c.*1970
St Francis of Assisi 1978
Our Lady of Knock, the Pope and Archbishop Cunnane 1981
HENEY, Patrick
*St Michael c.*1957–8
*St Elizabeth and St John the Baptist c.*1957–8

Left:
Harry Clarke, detail of *The Last Judgement* (1930), Catholic Church (St Patrick's), Newport, County Mayo

McGOLDRICK, Hubert
Stations of the Cross 1929–31 (opus sectile mosaic)
PYE, Patrick
Madonna and Child, Nativity 1977
*Christ the King c.*1980–2
WALSH, George W.
St Jarlath 1976

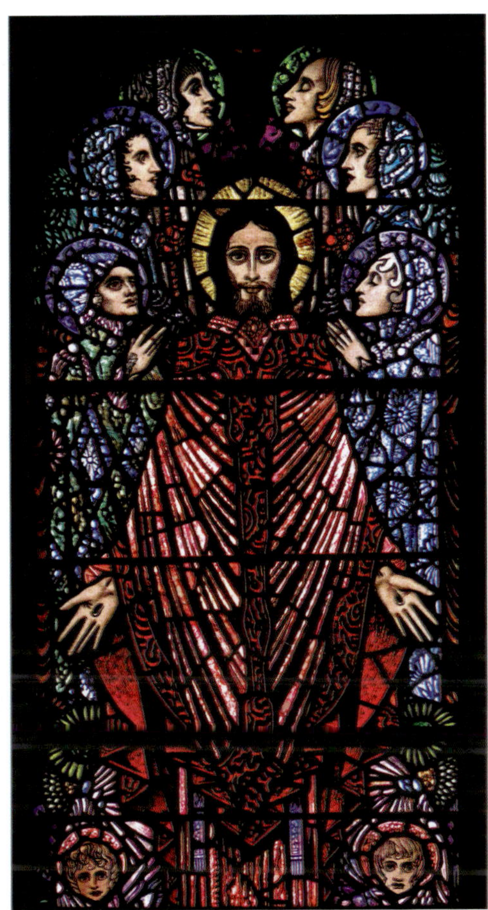

Above: Harry Clarke, detail of *The Last Judgement* (1930), Catholic Church (St Patrick's), Newport, County Mayo

Following page: Richard King, *The Assumption* (1952), Catholic Church (Our Lady Help of Christians), Swinford, County Mayo

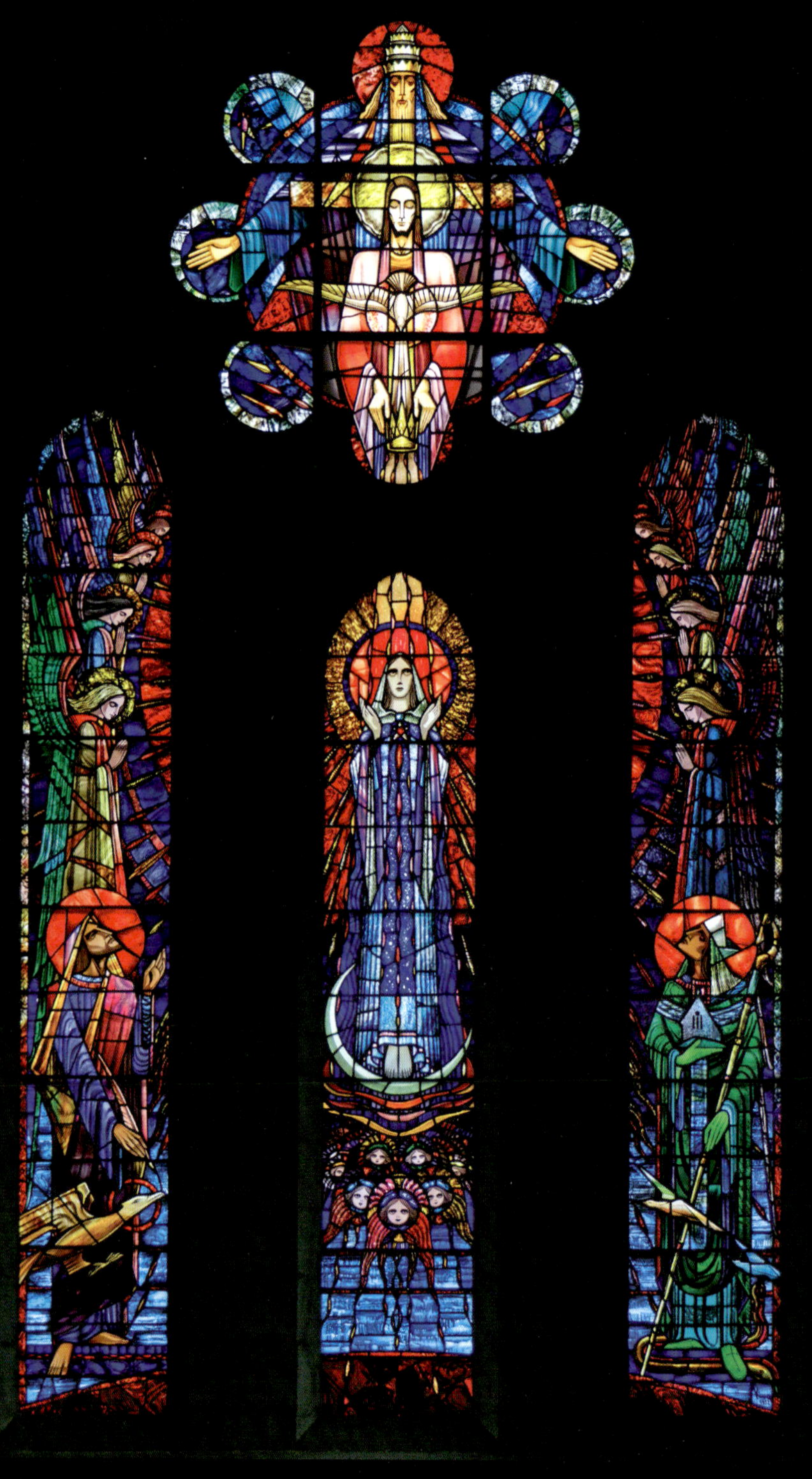

COUNTY MEATH

Ardbraccan: An Tobar, Spiritan Spirituality Retreat Centre
RHIND, Ethel
The Holy Women at the Tomb 1933 (2 lights; relocated from Ardbracken C of I)

Ashbourne: CC (Immaculate Conception)
WALSH, George W.
Broken Chains 1981
Nativity 1981
The Soul's Ascent 1981
Hand of God 1981
Unity 1981
Mater Ecclesia 1981
(Original sketch designs on display in the church.)

Ballinlough: CC (Church of the Assumption)
WALSH, George W.
Memorial window for 9/11 victim Patrick Aranyos 2003

Carnaross: CC (St Ciarán's)
MURPHY, Johnny
Sacred Heart c.1957
Immaculate Conception c.1957
St Patrick c.1957
St Bridget c.1957
Evangelists c.1957
(sketch designs, NIVAL)

Culmullen: CC (St Martin of Tours)
BECKER, Margaret
Christ the King c.1990 (circular)
Assumption of the Virgin Surrounded by Angels c.1990 (3 lights)
Christian symbols and images c.1990 (5 small lights)
Dom Columba Marmion in his Study 1992
Dom Columba Marmion Feeding the Poor c.1992
Dom Columba Marmion on his Deathbed c.1992

Donaghpatrick: C of I (St Patrick's)
PURSER, Sarah
Faith and Hope 1930 (2 lights) (painted by Catherine O'Brien)

Dunboyne: CC (St Peter and St Paul's)
WALSH, George W.
River as Symbol of Cleansing and Renewal 2009 (baptistry)

Dunboyne: CC Parochial House Oratory
MULDOWNEY, Patrick
Abstract 2009
Abstract 2009
Leaf-themed 2009 (2 lights)

Enfield: Enfield Oratory
WALSH, George W.
Blessed Sacrament Window 1991

Johnstown: CC (Nativity of Our Lady)
WALSH, George W.
Diaspora, Missions 2001
Crucifixion, Eucharist 2001
Rebirth, Fellowship 2001
Holy Spirit 2001
Assumption 2001
Baptism 2001
Risen Christ 2001
'And They Were Filled with the Holy Spirit' 2001
'Alleluia the Reign of the Lord our God Almighty has Begun 2001*'*
'I Jesus Have Sent Mine Angel ...' 2001
Doors, abstract and symbolic 2001

Julianstown: C of I (St Mary's)
HEALY, Michael
War Memorial 1920 (2 lights)

Kilberry, Wilkinstown: CC (St John the Baptist)
MURPHY, Johnny
Baptism of Christ 1964 (2 lights)
Resurrection 1964
Assumption 1964
Death of St Joseph 1964
Life of Christ 1964
Lamb of God 1964
Holy Spirit 1964
(sketch design and cartoons, NIVAL)

Kilcloon: CC (St Oliver Plunkett's)
WALSH, George W.
Baptism, Miracle at Cana, Eucharist, Sermon on the Mount, Transfiguration 2009 (5 lights)

Meath Hill: CC (St Patrick and St Brigid's)
WALSH, George W.
Last Supper and Eucharist 1996
Baptism of Christ 1996
St Patrick, St Brigid, and Early Christianity 2012 (cruciform shaped)

Mosney: CC (St Patrick's; currently closed)
MULDOWNEY, Patrick
Christ Blessing Little Children 1996
St Patrick 1996
St Patrick as a Boy 1996 (porch)
St Patrick as Bishop 1996 (porch)
St Brigid 1996(porch)
St Finian 1996 (porch)

Oldcastle: CC (St Brigid's)
KING, Richard
The Martyrdom of Blessed Oliver Plunkett 1936–7

Rathmolyon: CC (St Michael's)
CAMPBELL, Christopher
The Godhead and The Saving of the World through Baptism and the Holy Spirit 1967 (large window in four sections, upper and lower divided by balcony)
Abstract chancel windows and nave windows 1967

Slane: CC (St Patrick's)
WALSH, George W.
Burning Bush 2000 (oratory)

Tara: Hill of Tara Visitor Centre (former C of I)
HONE, Evie
The Descent of the Holy Spirit 1936 (2 lights)

Below:
Evie Hone, detail of *The Descent of the Holy Spirit* (1936), Hill of Tara Visitor Centre (former Church of Ireland), Tara, County Meath

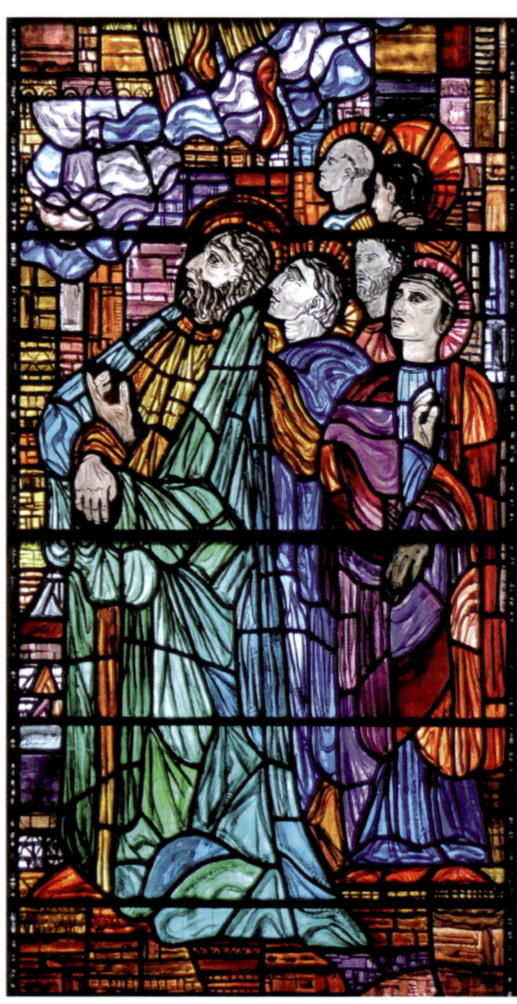

COUNTY MONAGHAN

Ardaghey: CC (St Michael's)
BURKE, Phyllis
Blessed Sacrament 1980s
*Eight abstract nave windows c.*1987–9

Carrickmacross: CC (St Joseph's)
CLARKE, Harry
St Ceara (A) 1926 (2 lights)
St Macartan and St Tigernach (B) 1928 (2 lights)
St Fanchea and St Enda (B) 1928 (2 lights)
St Dymphna (B) 1928 (2 lights)
(The rest in the series of ten two-light windows in the nave and mortuary chapel are by the Clarke Studios.)
KING, Richard
The Crucifixion and Deposition from the Cross 1931–2 (2 lights)
(Created at Harry Clarke Studios.)

Clones: C of I (St Tighernach's)
COURTNEY, Dorothy
The Ascension 1910 (3 lights)

Corduff: CC (St Michael's)
KING, Richard
Annunciation * 1936 (scaled pencil drawing and colour scheme, TCD)
Assumption * 1936 (colour scheme, TCD)
(Above created at Harry Clarke Studios.)
The Baptism of Christ 1954

Inniskeen: CC (Mary Mother of Mercy)
WALSH, George W.
All windows (abstract) 1974

Killeevan: CC (St Livinus's)
CHILD, A.E.
The Agony in the Garden, the Crucifixion with the Blessed Virgin Mary and St John, and the Entombment 1911 (3 lights)

Kilmore: C of I
HEALY, Michael
David, Good Shepherd, St Peter 1911 (3 lights)

Monaghan Town: Catholic Bishop's House Oratory
HEALY, Michael
Saints Macartan, Brigid, Patrick and Dympna 1912 (4 lights)

Monaghan Town: St Macartan's College
KING, Richard
Stations of the Cross 1939–40 (opus sectile mosaic in opal glass)
(Created at Harry Clarke Studios.)

Monaghan Town: Presbyterian Church
O'BRIEN, Catherine
David and Jonathan 1916 (3 lights)

Raferagh: CC (St John's)
KING, Richard
Christ and St John the Evangelist 1954 (2 lights)

Tydavnet: CC (St Dympna's)
BURKE, Phyllis
Eucharist 1980s (rose)

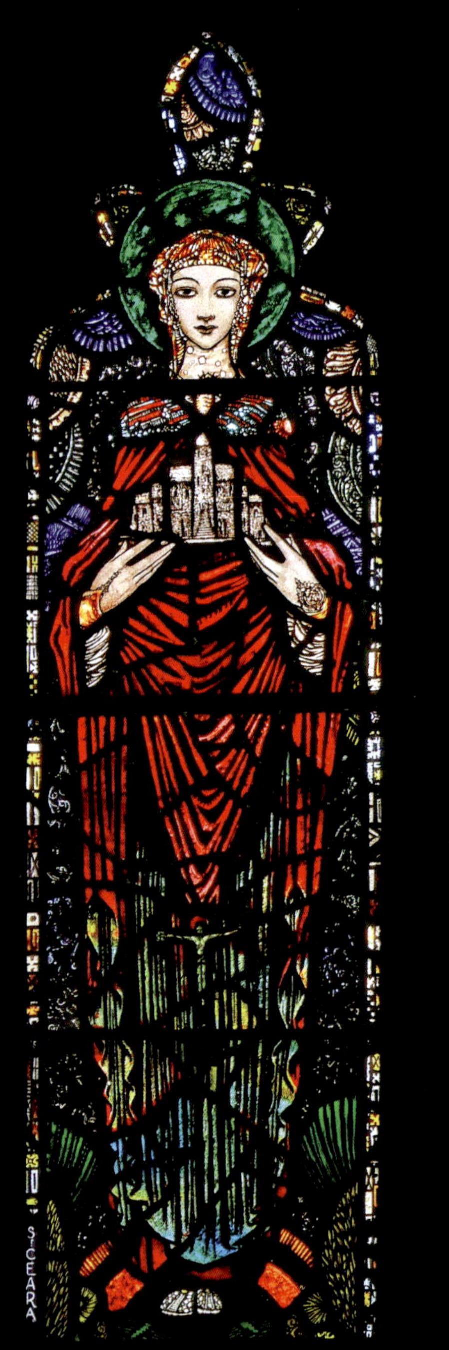
St CEARA

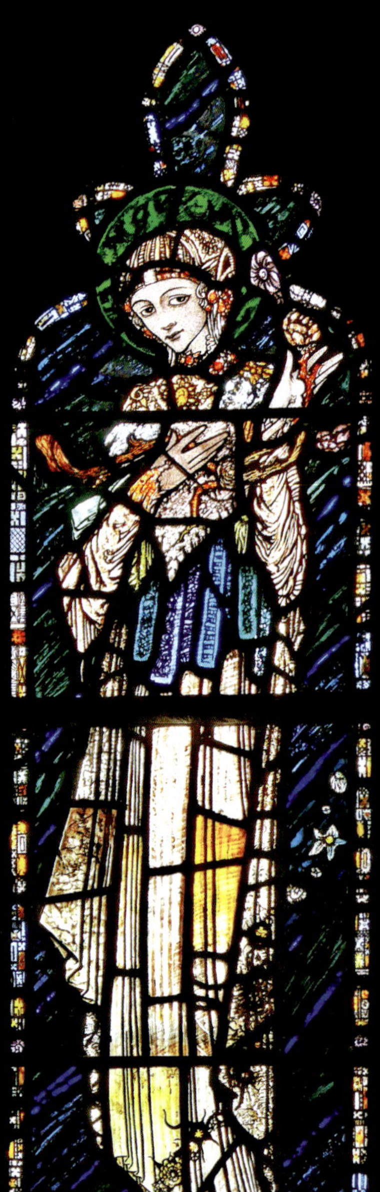
Pray for
Mrs Anne
Carlton &
her living
& deceased
relatives.
St CEARA

COUNTY OFFALY

Ballycumber: Former C of I (now a private residence)
CLARKE, Harry
Music and Literature (B) 1929 (2 lights)

Birr: CC (St Brendan's)
DUNNE, Michael
St Michael, Ascension, Crucifixion, Holy Baptism: Prince of Wales's Leinster Regiment War Memorial 1964 (2 lights)
KING, Richard
Baptism of Christ 1957 (in former baptistry, now Adoration Room)
POLLEN, Patrick
Our Lady of Perpetual Succour with Angels Carrying Symbols of the Passion *c.*1958 (in Crying Room)

Birr: C of I (St Brendan's)
MacBRIDE, William
War, Justice and Victory 1920–1
Archangel Michael Flanked by Kneeling Angels 1920–1
Faith, Hope and Charity 1920–1
Christ Blessing Children * date unknown
St Peter Raising Dorcas * date unknown

Boher: CC (St Manchan's)
SIMMONDS, Charles (Cecil)
St Anne with the Virgin Mary as a Child * 1930 (preliminary designs, TCD)
St Manchan * 1930 (preliminary designs, TCD)
(*Blessed Virgin Mary, Sacred Heart, St Joseph* (3 lights) was also made at Harry Clarke Studios *c.*1930.)
WALSH, George W.
St Manchan 2009 (in porch)

Left:
Harry Clarke, *St Ceara* (A) (1926),
Catholic Church (St Joseph's),
Carrickmacross, County Monaghan

Cloghan, near Banagher: CC (St Mary's)
MULDOWNEY, Patrick
St Lughna of Killourney 2002
St Caimin of Kilcaimin 2002
St Rynagh of Banagher 2002
St Canoc of Gallen 2002

Clonbullogue: C of I (St Kevin's)
CHILD, A.E.
'In Christ Shall All be Made Alive' 1933 (2 lights)

Edenderry: C of I
ELVERY, Beatrice
'Blessed Are the Pure in Heart' 1909 (relocated from Ballyburley C of I, County Offaly)
O'BRIEN, Catherine
The Twenty-third Psalm 1915 (3 lights; relocated from Castlejordan C of I, County Meath)

Eglish: CC (St James's)
BECKER, Margaret
Jesus Walking on Water 1990 (circular)
St James 1990s (circular)
EARLEY, Willie
St Brigid * date unknown
St James of Compostela * date unknown
Madonna and Child * date unknown
WALSH, George W.
Baptism early 1960s
Christ Triumphant early 1960s

Ferbane: CC (Immaculate Conception)
WALSH, George W.
Modern Ferbane 1996
Music and Sport 1996
Monasticism 1996
Communication 1996

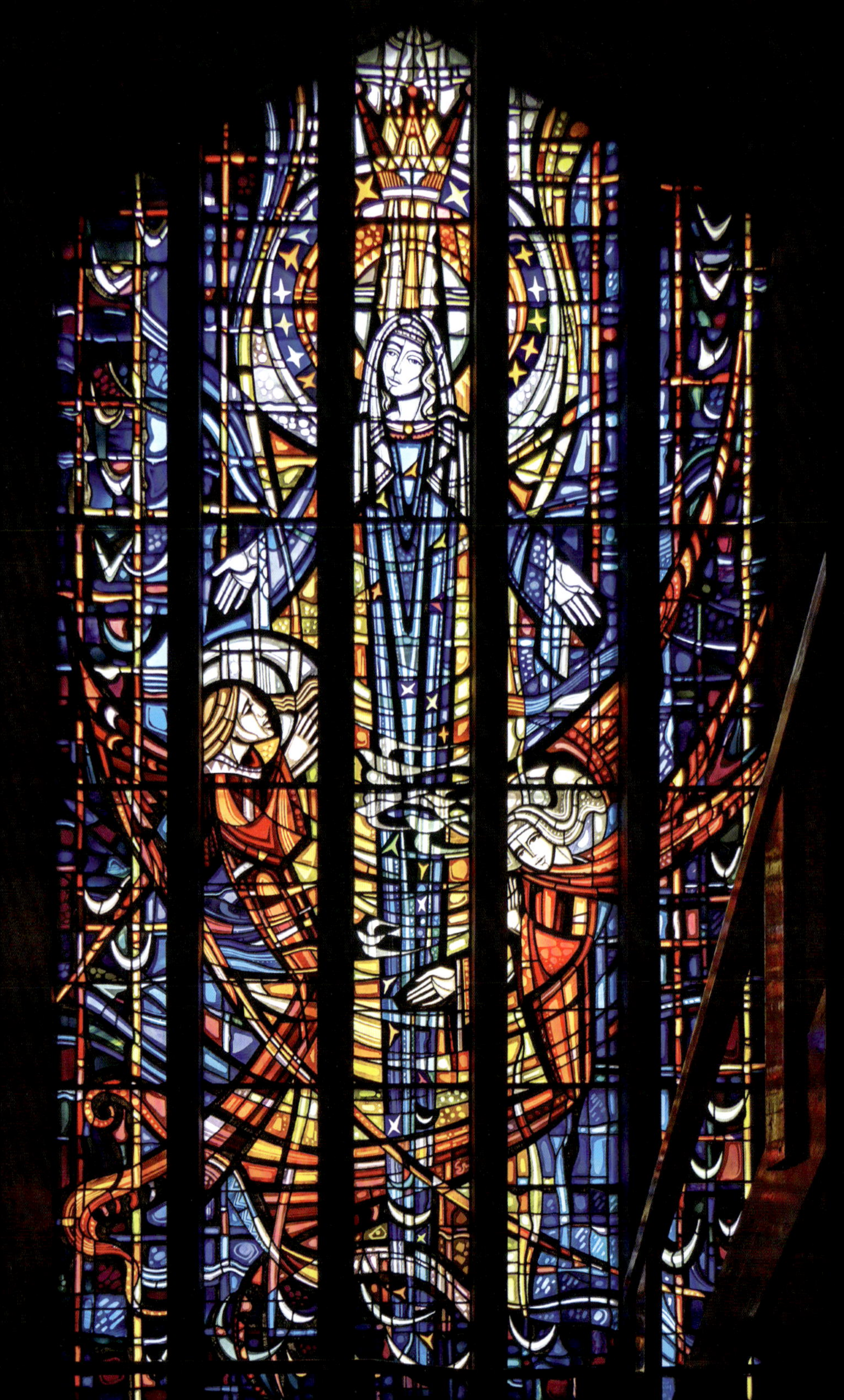

Kinnitty: C of I (St Finnian's)
O'BRIEN, Catherine
The Good Shepherd 1905
RHIND, Ethel
Martha and the Resurrection, Mary Magdalen Washing the Feet of Christ, The Seven Gifts of the Holy Spirit * 1908 (2 lights)

Rath: C of I (St John the Baptist's)
BECKER, Margaret
St John the Baptist panel, and monochrome roundels in six nave windows 1994

Tissaran: C of I, which no longer exists; deroofed in 1979 and fate of the two windows remains unknown.
O'BRIEN, Catherine
Charity 1912
RHIND, Ethel
Faith 1909

Left:
George W. Walsh, *Assumption* (1986) (located behind the organ), Catholic Church (Church of the Assumption), Tullamore, County Offaly

Tullamore: CC (Church of the Assumption)
The following windows by Harry Clarke were formerly in the Jesuit Retreat House Chapel, Rathfarnham Castle, Dublin. When reinstalled in Tullamore Church the five figurative windows were unfortunately radically reconfigured.
CLARKE, Harry
St Peter (now without predella panel) (B) 1928
St Paul (now without predella panel) (B) 1928
Window featuring the reconfigured predella panels with St Peter (top) and St Paul (bottom) (B) 1928
St Ignatius (now without predella panel) (B) 1928
St Patrick (now without predella panel) (B) 1928
Window featuring the reconfigured predella panels with St Ignatius (top) and St Patrick (bottom) (B) 1928
St Brendan (B) 1928
St Brendan's Voyage (predella panel, now isolated from main St Brendan window) (B) 1928
Decorative window with Symbols of Christ's Wounds (stigmata) (B) 1927
Decorative window with Agnes Dei (B) 1927
WALSH, George W.
Nativity 1986
Annunciation 1986
Ascension 1986
Assumption 1986 (now totally obscured by the organ)

COUNTY ROSCOMMON

Ardcarne, near Boyle: C of I (St Beaidh's)
CHILD, A.E.
The Resurrection 1911 (2 lights)
Faith 1921
Patience 1921
HONE, Evie
St Patrick, St Brigid and St Berac 1935 (2 lights)

Ballaghaderreen: Catholic Cathedral (Annunciation of Blessed Virgin Mary and St Nathy)
ELVERY, Beatrice
St John and St Anna 1907 (2 lights)

Clonown: CC (Our Lady of the Wayside)
KING, Richard
Sacred Heart * 1934
Blessed Virgin Mary (Immaculate Conception) * 1934
St Brigid * 1936–7
(All three created at Harry Clarke Studios and were relocated from Kilmurry CC, County Roscommon.)

Cootehall: CC (St Michael's)
O'BRIEN, Catherine
'Come unto Me all ye that Labour and are Heavy Laden' 1917 (painted by Beatrice Elvery)

Fairymount: CC (Sacred Heart)
HEALY, Michael
St John and St Elizabeth, with God the Father 1907–8 (2 lights; quality compromised by well-meaning 'improvements') (sketch design, NGI)
St Peter and St Anne, with the Lamb of God 1907–8 (2 lights; quality compromised by well-meaning 'improvements') (sketch design, NGI)
Ecce Homo and Mater Dolorosa with Dove of the Holy Spirit 1907–8 (2 lights; quality compromised by well-meaning 'improvements')
St Jarlath 1910 (sketch design, NGI)
St Brendan 1910 (sketch design, NGI)
McGOLDRICK, Hubert
St Brigid 1922 (quality compromised by well-meaning 'improvements')

Farragher: Former Franciscan Brothers Monastery, now a private house (window removed when ceased to be a monastery; present location untraced)
CHILD, A.E.
The Crucifixion * 1914

Kilronan: C of I (St Thomas's, currently not in use)
CHILD, A.E.
St Thomas, Christ, St Ronan 1904 (3 lights) (mostly painted by Michael Healy) (sketch design, NGI)

Kilteevan: CC (St Joseph's)
TOMLIN, Stanley
Risen Christ c.1963 (circular)

Kiltrustan, near Strokestown: CC (St Patrick's)
WALSH, George W.
Christ and St Peter 1990

Tibohine: CC (St Baoithín's)
O'BRIEN, Catherine
Four Evangelists 1913 (rose)
RHIND, Ethel
St Asicus * 1913
St Baithen * 1913
Two very small decorative windows * 1913

Tulsk: CC (St Eithne and St Fidelma's)
CHILD, A.E.
The Baptism of Christ, Ecce Homo, The Resurrection, The Ascension 1913–4 (4 lights)

Right: Evie Hone, detail of *St Patrick, St Brigid and St Berac* (1935), Church of Ireland (St Beaidh's), Ardcarne, near Boyle, County Roscommon

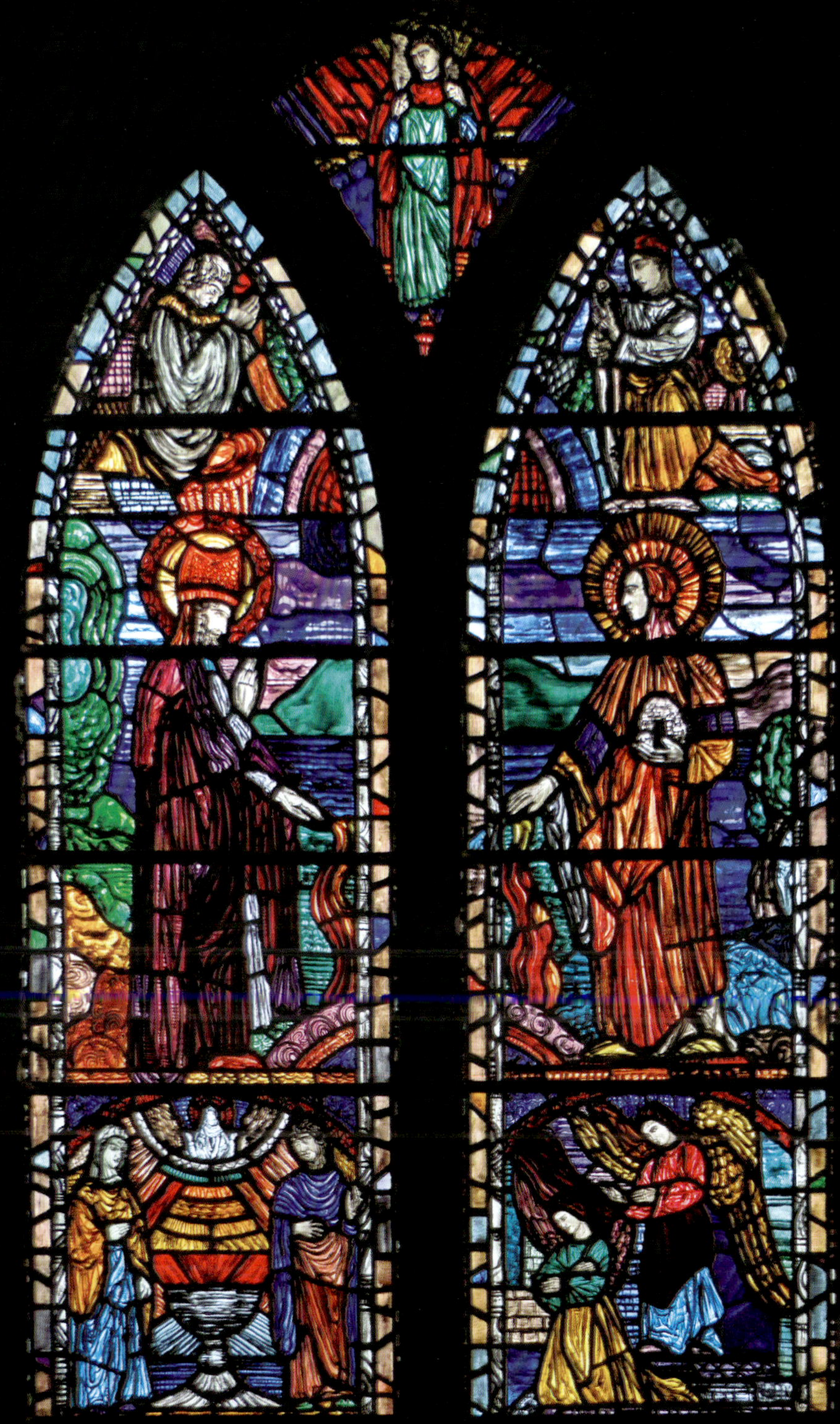

COUNTY SLIGO

Ballytivnan: CC (St Joseph's)
WALSH, George W.
Stations of the Cross 1982
Nativity 1982 (reredos)
Holy Family 1982
Tabernacle and surround 1982
Eucharist 1982 (2 lights, oratory)
WALSH, George Stephen
Life of Christ date unknown (carvings in slate)

Calry: CC (St Patrick's)
WALSH, George W.
St Patrick and Early Christianity 1993 (three windows in side room)

Cloonamahon, near Collooney: Glenbow Intellectual Disability Service (former Passionist Monastery)
POLLEN, Patrick
'God Emptied Himself Taking the Form of a Man' (Philippians 2:7) *c.*1964 (7 lights)
'For Which Cause God Hath Highly Exalted Him' (Philippians 2:9) *c.*1964 (7 lights)
*St Peter's Basilica, Rome, Symbols of the Eucharist and the Good Shepherd c.*1964 (7 lights)
*Host and Chalice c.*1964 (7 lights)
*Abstract glazing with Papal Arms c.*1964 (surrounding double doors)
*Twelve oratory windows c.*1964

Easkey: C of I (St Anne's)
O'BRIEN, Catherine
The Light of the World 1945

Grange: CC (Mary Immaculate)
WALSH, George W.
*Three windows depicting St Molaise c.*1995 (porch)
Holy Family 1982

Lissadell: C of I
O'BRIEN, Catherine
Courage and Love 1950 (2 lights) (sketch design, NGI)
RHIND, Ethel
Harmony and Fortitude 1907 (2 lights)

Maugherow: CC (St Patrick's)
WALSH, George W.
Resurrection and Renewal after Fire 1991
Seven Sacraments 1991
Arrival of Christianity 1991
Annunciation 1991
Teaching of the Gospel 1991 (Sacristy)
Affinity with the Ocean 1991 (Day Chapel)
Stations of the Cross 1991 (wood, carved by James Gannon)
Tabernacle 1991 (bronze)

Riverstown: C of I
CHILD, A.E.
'I am the Resurrection and the Life' 1928 (3 lights; relocated from Toomna C of I, County, Roscommon in 2000)

Sligo Town, High Street: CC (Holy Cross Dominican Priory)
HEALY, Michael
St Raymundus and St Antoninus 1911 (2 lights; transferred from the old Dominican Priory)

Sligo Town, John Street: C of I Cathedral (St John's)
CHILD, A.E.
Christ with Martha and Mary 1927 (2 lights)

Sligo Town, Stephen Street: Sligo County Museum
HEALY, Michael
'E finito' 1929 (panel)

COUNTY TIPPERARY

Ballyporeen: CC (Our Lady of the Assumption), Convent Road
HEALY, Michael
St Patrick 1916 (sketch design, NGI)

Ballylooby: CC (Blessed Virgin and St Kieran's)
McGOLDRICK, Hubert
The Holy Family * 1929 (2 lights)

Cahir: CC (St Mary's)
MURPHY, Johnny
Abstract lights with church symbols 1969

Carrigeen, near Cashel: Rockwell College
DOWLING, William
Madonna of the Woods 1941
Our Lady of Rockwell * 1941
(Both created at Harry Clarke Studios.)
HONE, Evie
Heraldic window with College Crest 1941
Heraldic window with Archbishop McQuaid's Crest 1941
Heraldic window with Congregational Crest 1941

Cashel: Brú Ború (cultural centre), Moor Lane
WALSH, George W.
High Kings 2005 (laminated glass)
Mural 1992 (exterior, carved by David G. Earley)

Cashel: Chez Hans restaurant, Moor Lane
DOWD MURPHY, Róisín and MURPHY, Johnny
Abstract lights, quarried windows with painted details 1968

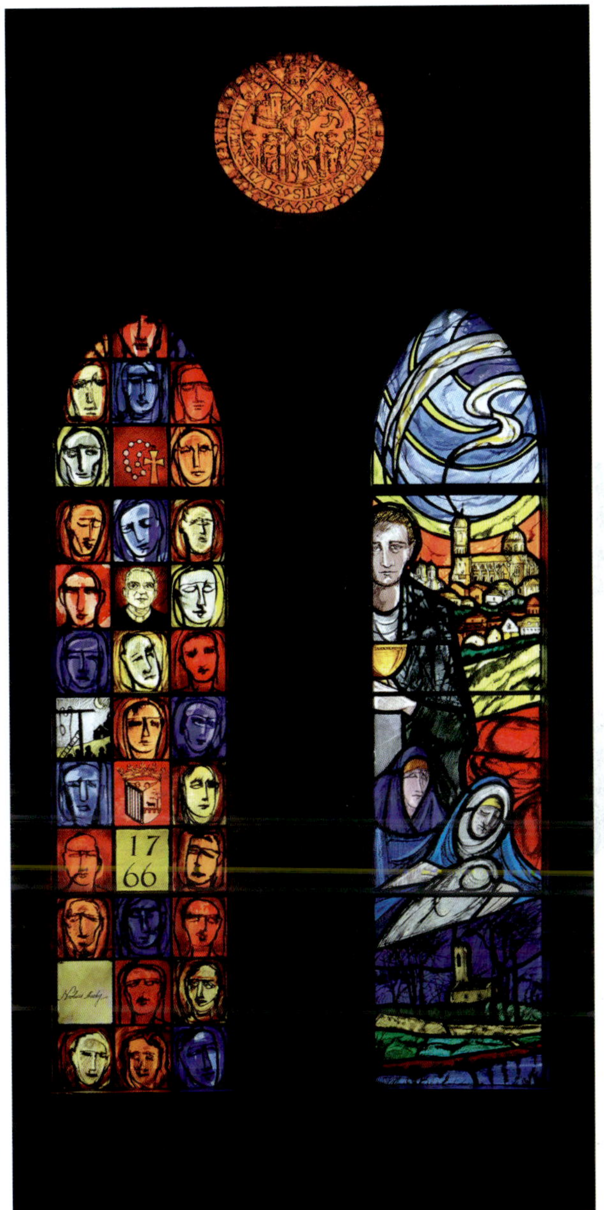

Right: Patrick Muldowney, *Fr Nicholas Sheehy and the 'Unspoken Voices'* (2013–4), Catholic Church (St Mary's), Clogheen, County Tipperary. Photograph © Anthony Hobbs

Clogheen: CC (St Mary's)
MULDOWNEY, Patrick
Fr Nicholas Sheehy and the 'Unspoken Voices' 2013–4 (2 lights)

Clonmel, Abbey Street: CC (Franciscan Abbey Church)
MURPHY, Johnny
*Symbolic abstract east window c.*1960 (5 lights)
*Symbolic abstract lights c.*1960 (including two 3 lights)
Symbols of St Francis 1958 (St Anthony's Chapel)
DOWLING, William
Penal Mass * 1945 (sacristy)
St Francis kneeling alongside another monk celebrating mass at open air altar * 1945 (sacristy)
(Created at Harry Clarke Studios.)

Clonmel, Anne Street: C of I (St Mary's)
O'BRIEN, Catherine
Christ and the Four Evangelists 1931–3 (5 lights, the tracery has ornamental glass dating from *c.*1800)

Clonmel, Davis Road: former Kickham Barracks Garrison Church (currently being developed)
MURPHY, Johnny
Battalion history and church symbols 1956 (3 lights) (cartoons, NIVAL)

Clonmel, Gladstone Street: CC (St Peter and St Paul's)
HENEY, Patrick
St Crispin 1956
MURPHY, Johnny
St Bridget 1956 (sketch designs and cartoons, NIVAL)

Clonmel, Gladstone Street: Place 4U (community space in former Sisters of Charity Convent chapel)
DOWD MURPHY, Róisín
*Assumption c.*1964
MURPHY, Johnny
*Windows with religious symbols c.*1964

Cloughjordan: CC (St Michael and St John's)
CLARKE, Harry
The Ascension with Irish Saints and St Michael and St James (B) 1924 (5 lights)
HONE, Evie
Blessed Virgin Mary and St Joseph 1953 (2 lights)

Duhill, near Ballylooby: CC (St John the Baptist's)
CLARKE, Harry
The Dance of Salome with the Head of St John the Baptist, Watched by Herod and Herodias (B) 1925
The Apparition of Our Lady to Bernadette at Lourdes (B) 1925

Emly: CC (St Ailbe's)
CHILD, A.E.
Archangels Michael, Gabriel and Raphael 1905 (3 lights)
PURSER, Sarah
St John the Evangelist, Madonna and Child, Cormac King and Bishop, with the Coronation of the Virgin 1904 (3 lights) (painted by A.E. Child, Michael Healy, and Catherine O'Brien)

Fairyhouse, near Clonmel: St Joseph's School Chapel (formerly Rosminian Fathers)
BURKE, Phyllis
*'Suffer Little Children to Come unto Me' c.*1988 (cartoons, NIVAL) (triangular window over entrance)
*Symbols of the Rosminians c.*1988 (cartoons, NIVAL)
*Good Shepherd c.*1988

Faugheen, near Carrick-on-Suir: CC (St Patrick's)
BECKER, Margaret
St Martin de Porres 1969

Right: Harry Clarke, *The Ascension with Five Irish Saints and St Michael and St James* (B) (1924), Catholic Church (St Michael and St John's), Cloughjordan, County Tipperary

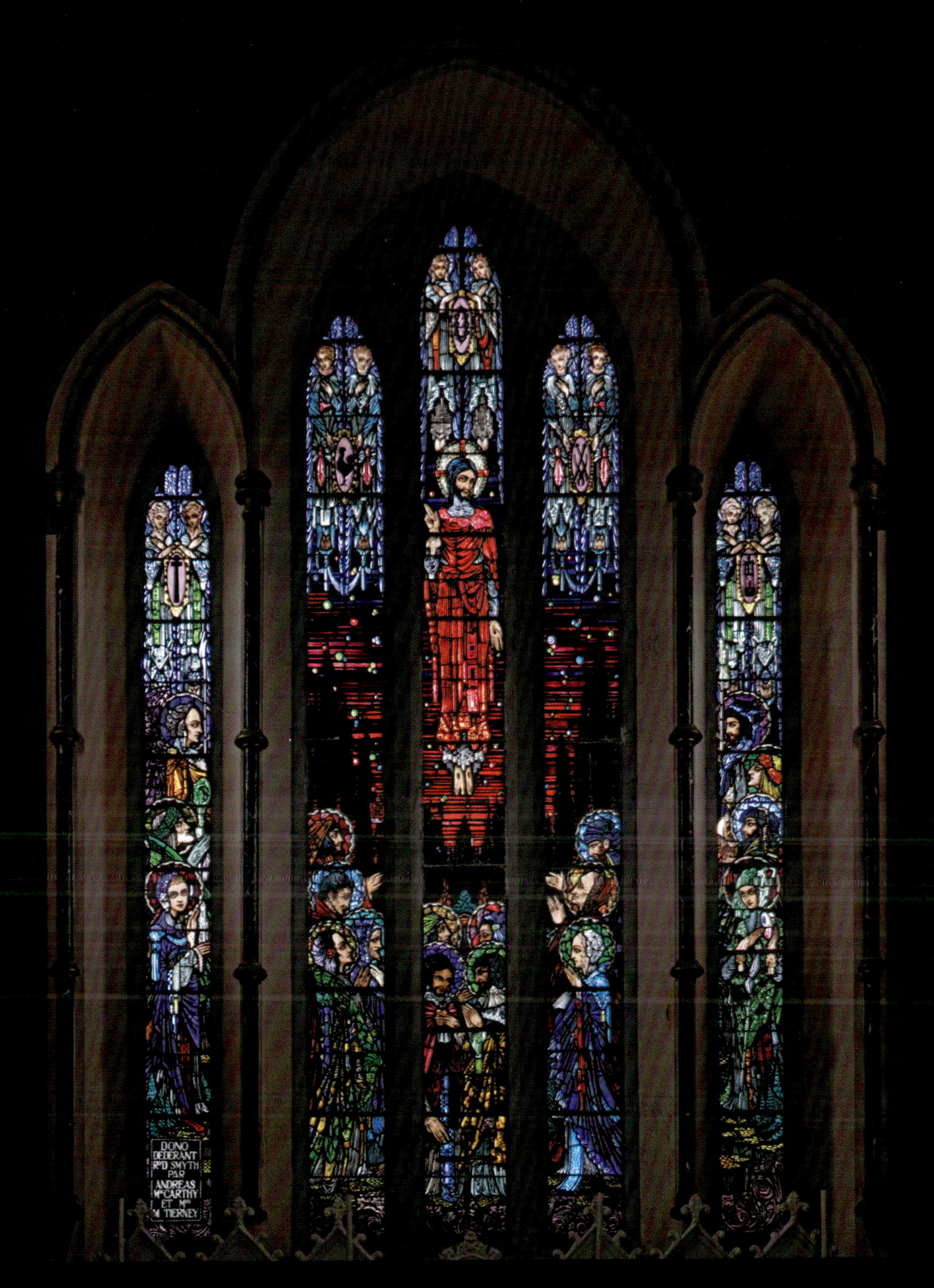
DONO
DEDERANT
RD SMYTH
PAR
ANDREAS
McCARTHY
ET Mrs
M TIERNEY

COUNTY WATERFORD

Ballindud: Former Grace Dieu Retreat and Conference Centre (private), Tramore Road
SCANLON, James
Abstract date unknown (seven panels; in former oratory)

Ballygunner: CC (St Mary's)
WALSH, George W.
Eucharist theme 2014 (wall-mounted tabernacle)

Cappoquin: Mount Melleray Abbey
CLARKE, Terry
Coronation of the Virgin 1942–3 (5 lights with tracery, in Community Chapel)
DOWLING, William
St Philomena 1939–40 (2 lights, in public chapel)
The Apparition of the Sacred Heart to St Margaret Mary 1957–8 (2 lights, in public chapel)
St Joseph the Worker with the Young Christ * 1957–8 (2 lights, in public chapel)
St Peter and St Paul * 1957–8 (2 lights, in public chapel)
Horse Kneeling before the Eucharist held by St Anthony 1963 (2 lights, in public chapel) (sketch design in Dublin City Gallery The Hugh Lane)
KING, Richard
Little Flower before Pope Leo 1940 (2 lights, in public chapel)
(All windows created at Harry Clarke Studios.)

Dungarvan: Sisters of Mercy Primary School
MURPHY, Johnny
Our Lady with Children 1965 (sketch designs, NIVAL)

Dunmore East: C of I (St Andrew's)
QUIGLY, Kathleen
The Good Shepherd 1917
O'BRIEN, Catherine
The Pilgrimage of Life 1948

Glencairn, Lismore: St Mary's Cistercian Abbey
BURKE, Phyllis
Three abstract windows 1990 (sketch designs, NIVAL)
DUNNE, Michael
The Young St Benedict date unknown (in reception)

Tramore: CC (Holy Cross)
BURKE, Phyllis
*The Resurrection c.*1988 (2 lights, in former mortuary chapel, now parish office and shop) (sketch design, NIVAL)

Waterford City, Barrack Street: Edmund Rice Heritage Centre, Mount Sion
KING, Richard
'Suffer Little Children to Come unto Me' or *Jesus the Teacher, depicting Scenes in the Cusps of the Holy Family, Guardian Angel and Child, Entry into Jerusalem, Flight into Egypt, Pentecost, Jesus and the Doctors in the Temple* 1938 (rose) (in the 'Ship Room', formerly the chapel)
WALSH, George W.
Scenes from the Life of Edmund Rice 1979 (*dalle de verre*) (originally designed for the mausoleum chapel which was subsequently demolished and windows relocated to the new Edmund Rice Centre Chapel, 2007)

Waterford City, Cathedral Square: C of I Cathedral (Christ Church)
CHILD, A.E.
Sorrow and Joy 1929–30 (2 lights)

Waterford City, Cork Road Industrial Estate: Bausch and Lomb HQ
WALSH, George W.
Teardrop 1999 (wall-mounted sculpture)

Waterford City, Dunmore Road: Waterford Regional Hospital (Emergency Department)
LAMB, Peadar
Fuinseoig 2012

Waterford City, Ursuline Court: Ursuline Convent (relocated from original convent chapel nearby)
O'BRIEN, Catherine
'Suffer Little Children to Come unto Me' * 1914

COUNTY WESTMEATH

Athlone: CC (St Peter and Paul's)
CHILD, A.E.
Sacrifice 1936 (sacristy)
EARLEY, William (Bill) E.
Last Judgement c.1934–6 (mortuary chapel)
Baptism of Christ c.1934–6
St Peter c.1934–6 (porch)
St Paul c.1934–6 (porch)
KING, Richard
The Blessed Virgin Mary 1934–6
St Joseph 1934–6
St Patrick 1934–6
Sacred Heart 1934–6
Holy Souls (Purgatory) 1935–6
The Shepherds of the Nativity 1935–7 (boys' sacristy)
Angel Panels 1936–7 (sacristy doors)
Seven lead-lights (at clerestory level which includes *Virgin and Child* in organ gallery) 1935–6
(All windows by Richard King created at Harry Clarke Studios.)

Athlone: Former chapel for the convent and boarding school of Our Lady's Bower (now closed), Retreat Road
BURKE, Phyllis
The Curé of Ars and Pope Pius X c.1964 (2 lights)
St John the Baptist and St Ciaran c.1964 (2 lights)
St Patrick and St Brigid c.1964 (2 lights)
The Immaculate Heart of Mary and St Joseph c.1964 (2 lights)
St Augustine and St Ann c.1964 (2 lights)
(cartoons of all, NIVAL)

Athlone: Our Lady's Bower Secondary School, Retreat Road (adjacent to previous entry)
BURKE, Phyllis
Our Lady of Good Counsel c.1964 (panel) (cartoon, NIVAL)

Athlone: Coláiste Chiaráin, Summerhill, Athlone
KING, Richard
St Patrick 1936–7 (Window created at Harry Clarke Studios, and was originally made for Kilmurry CC, County Roscommon.) (drawing, TCD)

Athlone: Franciscan Friary (St Anthony's)
DOWLING, William
St Anthony and the Christ Child 1930
St Francis of Assisi 1930
St Louis IX 1930
St Elizabeth of Hungary 1930
St Clare 1930
KING, Richard
St Bonaventure 1932 (3 lights)
St Pascal Baylon 1932 (3 lights)
(Windows by both William Dowling and Richard King created at Harry Clarke Studios.)
MACBRIDE, William
St Margaret Mary and the Sacred Heart * 1931 (2 lights)
St Anne with St Mary, and St Joachim * 1931 (2 lights)
Scenes from the Life of a Franciscan Saint (possibly St Pascal Baylon) * 1931 (3 lights)
O'BRIEN, Catherine
Abraham and Melchizedek 1936 (opus sectile mosaic) (sketch design, NGI)
The Institution of the Eucharist 1936 (opus sectile mosaic)
Mass in Penal Days 1936 (opus sectile mosaic)
RHIND, Ethel
Stations of the Cross 1934–6 (opus sectile mosaic)
WALSH, George W.
Prodigal Son 1979 (panel in door)
Good Shepherd 1979 (panel in door)

Ballinderry, near Mullingar: La Verna Centre of Spirituality and Hospitality (Franciscan Missionaries of Our Lady)
MULDOWNEY, Patrick
The Eucharist with St Francis and St Elizabeth, with additional leaded colour lights 2011

Dysart: CC (St Patrick's)
HEALY, Michael
Christ the King 1906

Horseleap (Ardnurcher): Former C of I (deconsecrated in 1990, currently closed)
CHILD, A.E.
'Be Thou Faithful Unto Death and I Will Give Thee a Crown of Life' 1917

Killucan: C of I (St Etchen's)
PURSER, Sarah
The Good Shepherd and the Good Samaritan 1926 (2 lights) (painted by Ethel Rhind)

Killucan: St Camillus Nursing Centre Chapel
WALSH, George W.
St Camillus 1996
Last Supper 1996
Washing the Feet 1996
The Good Samaritan 1996
St Camillus's Hospital Work 1996
Local Interest 1996
Our Lady 1996
Reflections on Life 1996
Healing Hands 1996

Moyliskar: Former C of I (deconsecrated)
CHILD, A.E.
Archangel Michael 1906 (removed to All Saints, Mullingar, where now in lightbox)

Right: George W. Walsh, *Last Supper* (1996), St Camillus Nursing Centre Chapel, Killucan, County Westmeath. Photograph © Finola Finlay

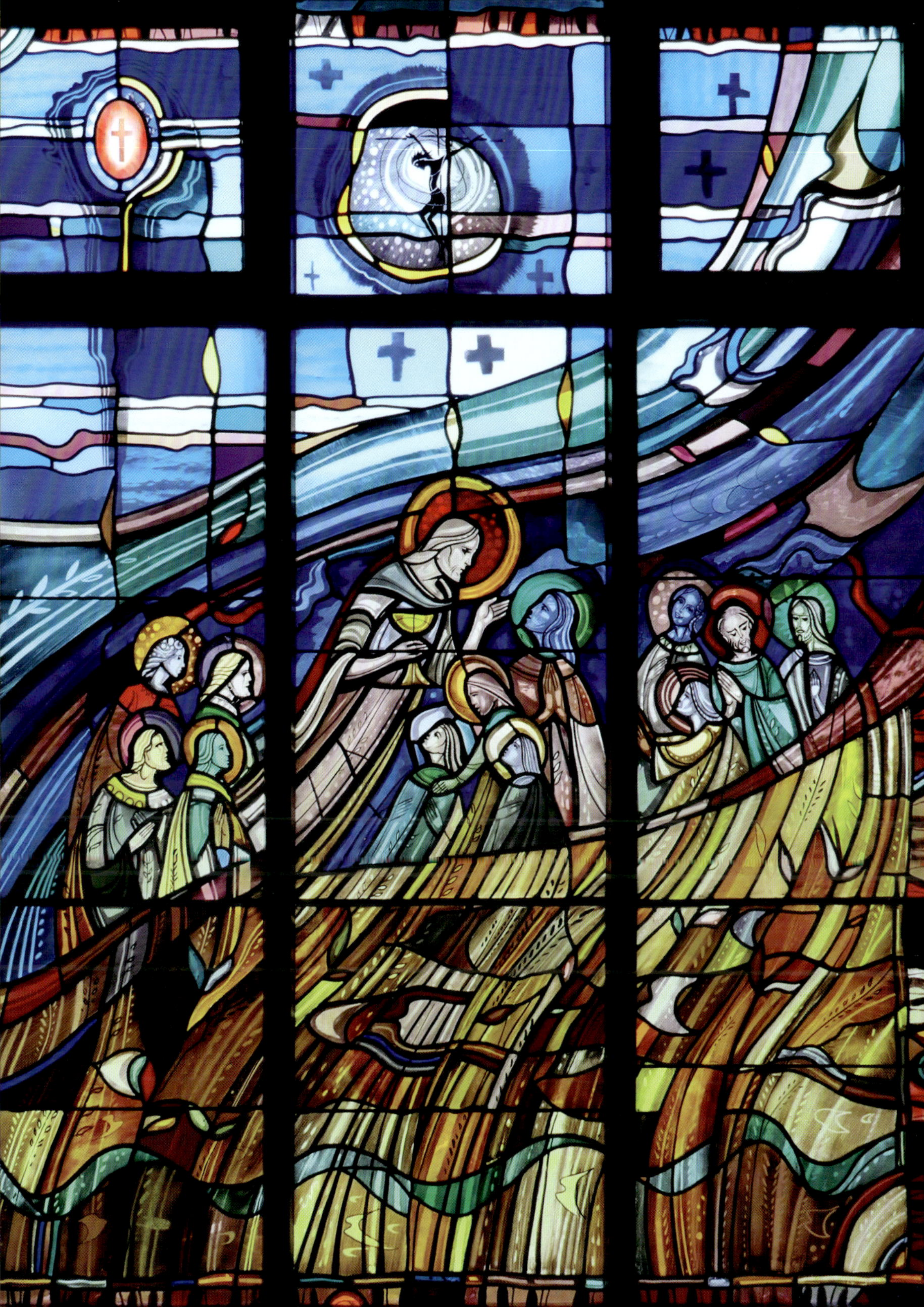

Multyfarnham: CC (Franciscan Abbey)
KING, David
Burning of Multyfarnham Friary in 1601, with (above) a Friar Celebrating the Eucharist on a Mass Rock, Friar Mícheál Ó Cléirigh working on 'The Annals of the Four Masters' in 1628 (left light), a Franciscan Friar Preaching (right light) 1974–7 (3 lights)
Children of Lir I: Their First 300 Years on Lough Derravaragh 1974–7 (2 lights)
Children of Lir II: Their Second 300 Years on the Straits of Moyle 1974–7 (2 lights)
Children of Lir III: Their Final 300 Years on Inis Gluaire 1974–7 (2 lights)
Children of Lir IV: They Are Transformed from Swans Into Humans and Are Baptised by St Machaomhóg 1974–7 (2 lights)
St Patrick Lighting the Paschal Fire on the Hill of Slane 1974–7 (2 lights)
'A Woman Clothed With the Sun, With the Moon Under Her Feet, and on Her Head a Crown of Twelve Stars' (Revelations 12: 1-2) 1974–7 (2 lights)
Window inspired by St Francis's 'Canticle of the Sun' 1974–7 (2 lights)
A Figure Scattering the Seed of Faith 1974–7 (2 lights)
Archangel Michael in Battle with a Dragon 1974–7 (2 lights)
Window inspired by Micheál Ó Síocháin's poem 'Ag Críost an Síol' 1974–7

Rochfortbridge: CC (Immaculate Conception)
CLARKE, Terry
Immaculate Conception 1949 (3 lights)
(Created at Harry Clarke Studios.)

COUNTY WEXFORD

Bunclody: C of I (St Mary's)
O'BRIEN, Catherine
Charity and Faith (with Hope in tracery) 1927 (2 lights)

Coolcotts: Scoil Mhuire (visits strictly by appointment)
YOUNG, Peter
Legends 2008 (7 lights)

Ferns: CC (St Aidan's)
BREEN, Lua
Stained glass scheme based on themes of Evolution of Man from Primeval Slime, through Judaism, through Conflict with the Devil, leading to the New City of Jerusalem 1976
McMurrough, King of Leinster, Donating Lands to St Aidan 1976 (porch)
St Aidan Bidding Farewell to St David 1976 (porch)

Ferns: C of I Cathedral (St Edan's)
O'BRIEN, Catherine
St Patrick 1931

Glynn: CC (St Lawrence's)
KING, Richard
Blessed Virgin Mary and *The Sacred Heart* 1936–7
St Patrick and *St Joseph* 1937
St Lawrence, St Brigid and *The Little Flower* 1939–40 (seven windows; medallions set in decorative glazing; created at Harry Clarke Studios)

Right:
Harry Clarke, detail of *Our Lady and Child Adored by St Aidan of Ferns and St Adrian* (1919), Catholic Church (Church of the Assumption), Wexford Town

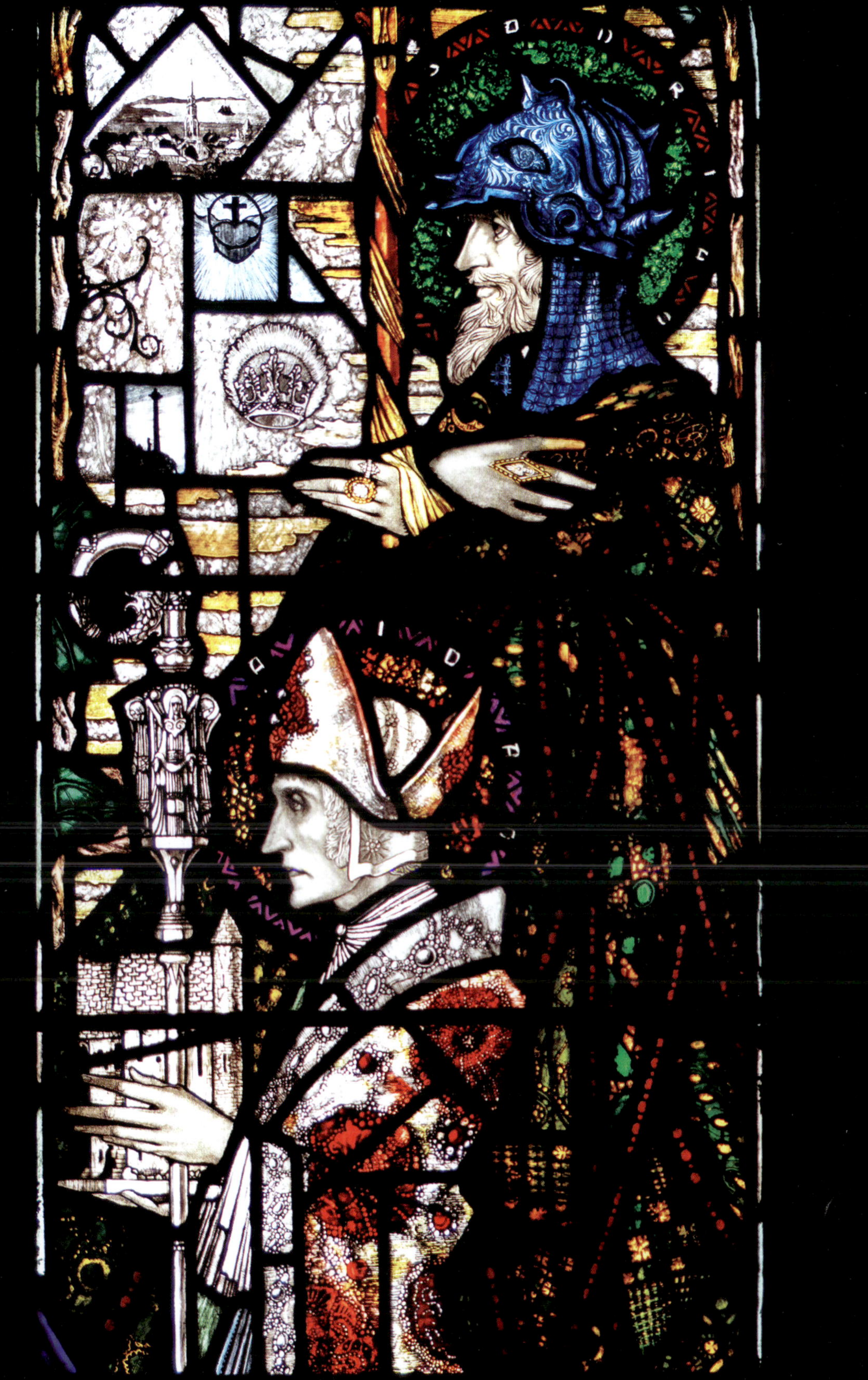

Gorey: C of I (Christ Church)
CLARKE, Harry
St Stephen 1922
Gideon (A) *c.*1922 (companion to *St Stephen*, and also in memory of Percival Lea-Wilson)
St Luke and St Martin of Tours (A) 1923 (2 lights) (cartoon, TCD)
DOWLING, William
St Brigid and the Beggar 1942
(Created at Harry Clarke Studios.)
O'BRIEN, Catherine
The Angel of Peace 1910
Our Lord and St Peter Walking on the Water 1956–7 (sketch design, NIVAL)

Inch: C of I
DOWD MURPHY, Róisín
Christ Blessing Children 1984 (sketch design, NIVAL)

Killanne: C of I (St Anne's)
O'BRIEN, Catherine
The Good Shepherd 1938 (3 lights)

Killurin: C of I
CHILD, A.E.
Sorrow and Joy *1910 (2 lights)

Kilmore Quay: CC (St Peter's)
WALSH, George W.
'I Shall Make you Fishers of Men' 2010 (porch)

Kilmuckridge: CC (St Mary's)
HEALY, Michael
St John 1904 (in former mortuary chapel)

Kiltennel, Courtown: C of I
McGOLDRICK, Hubert
St Brigid 1936

New Ross: Good Counsel College, Bosheen Street
MURPHY, Johnny and MURPHY, Reiltín
Abstract scheme 1984

Rosslare Harbour: CC (St Patrick's)
WALSH, George W.
St Patrick Baptising 1969 (3 lights)
Abstract windows 1969
Stations of the Cross and cross behind altar 1969 (painted antique glass, laminated on marine ply background and mounted on marble)

Tagoat: CC (St Mary's)
WALSH, George W.
Pugin, Church Architect 1992
Prodigal Son 1992
Good Samaritan 1992
Sowing Seed 1992
Suffer the Little Children 1992
Miraculous Draft of Fishes 1992
Abraham and Isaac 1992

Wexford Town, Bride Street: CC (Church of the Assumption)
CLARKE, Harry
Our Lady and Child Adored by St Aidan of Ferns and St Adrian 1919 (2 lights)

Wexford Town, Clonard Road: CC (The Annunciation)
DEENY, Gillian
Stations of the Cross 1998
Doves, Loaves and Wheat 2009
Butterflies and Boats 2009
EARLEY, Willie
The Annunciation 1974 (in the 'Day Chapel', which was the original church)

COUNTY WICKLOW

Bray, Church Road: C of I (Christ Church)
CHILD, A.E.
The Entombment and the Crucifixion * 1928 (2 lights)
'Return to Thine House', and Christ Calms the Storms 1932 (2 lights)
Our Lord and the Woman of Samaria, and 'I Shall Make you Fishers of Men' 1932 (2 lights)

Bray, Church Terrace, Main Street: Cornerstone Church at the Well (former St Paul's C of I)
CHILD, A.E.
'Woman Behold Thy Son', and *'I Was in the Spirit on the Lord's Day'* 1918 (2 lights)

Bray, Killarney Road: CC (St Fergal's)
WALSH, George W.
All stained glass and etched glass windows 1980
Stone sculpture depicting St Fergal 1980

Delgany: C of I (Christ Church)
O'BRIEN, Catherine
The Good Samaritan * 1910

Dunganstown: C of I (St Kevin's)
O'BRIEN, Catherine
Christ Blessing Little Children 1961 (sketch designs, NGI)

Grangecon: C of I (The Ascension)
O'BRIEN, Catherine
Memorial tablet with crests 1944 (opus sectile mosaic)

Greystones, La Touche Road: CC (Holy Rosary)
HONE, Evie
The Good Shepherd 1948
Our Lady of the Rosary 1948 (cartoon, Catholic Church, Aughrim Street, Dublin)

Greystones, La Touche Road: Kilian House Family Centre (adjoining Holy Rosary Church)
CLARKE, Terry
St Teresa, St John of the Cross, and the Blessed Virgin Mary 1940–1
(Created at Harry Clarke Studios. This window was relocated from the former Carmelite Convent, Delgany.)

Johnstown, near Arklow: CC (St David's)
BREEN, Lua
Stained glass scheme based on themes of the Pre-Crucifixion Agony, Humiliation, Death and Resurrection of Christ, incorporating the Stations of the Cross 1971
Cockrel 1971
Palm leaves 1971
The Last Supper 1971 (wrought iron, behind altar)

Kilbride (Eneriley), near Arklow: C of I (St Brigid's)
CLARKE, Harry
Ecce Homo with Scenes from Christ's Ministry (quatrefoils) and *The Crucifixion* (rose) 1924 (3 lights)
Abstract window with slab glass 1924 (small lancet in south transept over a door)

Killamoat, near Rathdangan: CC (St Mary's)
WALSH, George Stephen
Nativity * 1935
There is a second window, *Crucifixion c.* early 1920s, also made at Clarke's Studio.

Nun's Cross, near Ashford: C of I
O'BRIEN, Catherine
Christ's Entry into Jerusalem 1935

Tinahely: C of I
CHILD, A.E.
The Good Shepherd 1931 (3 lights)

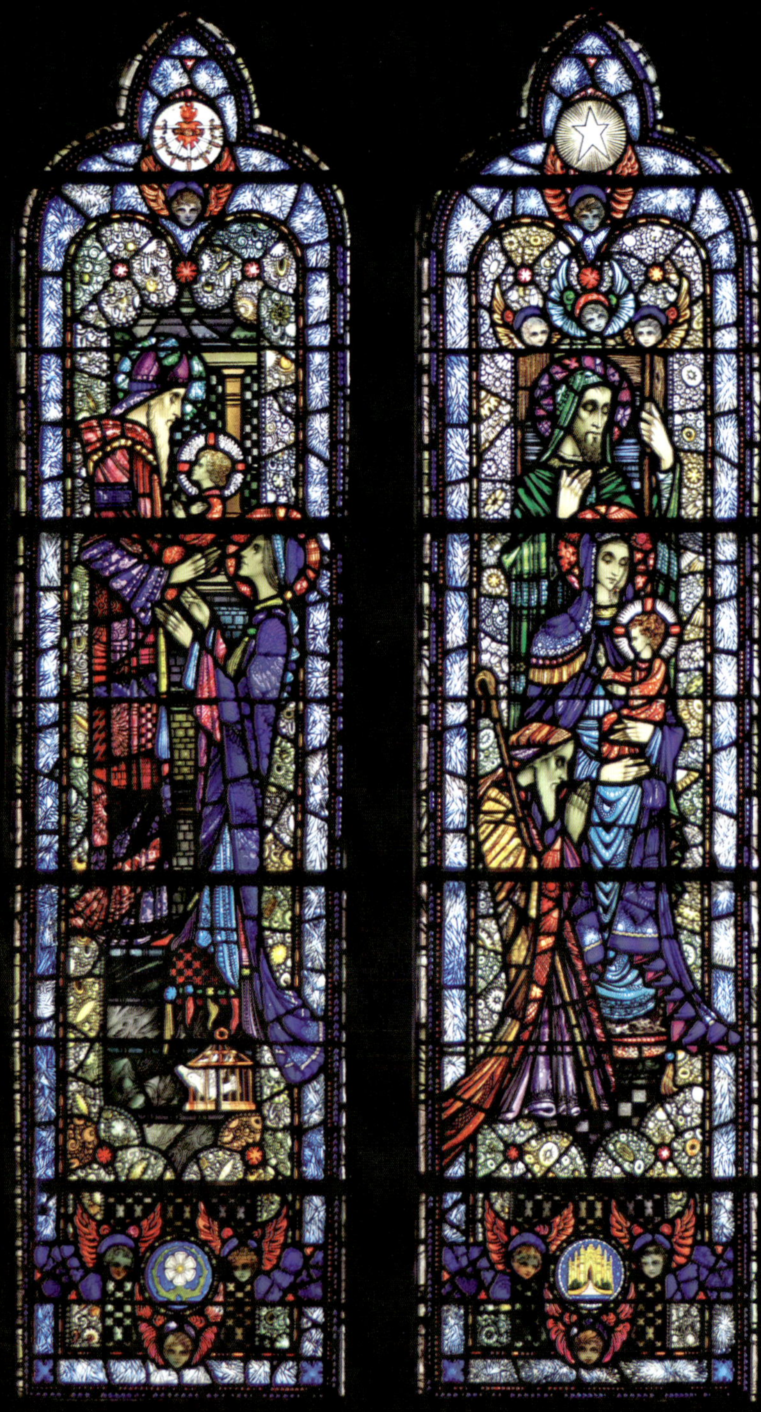

Valleymount: CC (St Joseph's)
McGOLDRICK, Hubert
Rex Regum and Attendant Angels 1933 (originally a three-light window in St Anthony's CC, Clontarf, Dublin, now three separate lights in apse)

Wicklow Town: C of I, Church Hill
O'BRIEN, Catherine
The Ascension 1929
POLLEN, Patrick
Grape Vines and Leaves I c.1967–8 (sketch design, NIVAL)
Grape Vines and Leaves II c.1967–8 (sketch design, NIVAL)
Leaded light with Ship c.1968–9 (sketch design, NIVAL)
Leaded light with Lifeboat c.1968–9

Wicklow Town: Dominican Convent Chapel, Convent Road
DOWLING, William
Fifteen Mysteries of the Rosary 1938–9 (eight two-light windows. Richard King may have collaborated with William Dowling on these windows regarding decisions about iconography, colour, design and symbolism) (sketch designs, TCD)
(Created at Harry Clarke Studios.)
KING, Richard
The Paschal Lamb 1966–7 (rose)
Windows Depicting Angels 1966–7
The Trinity 1967 (rose)

Left: William Dowling, *Fifteen Mysteries of the Rosary: Presentation in the Temple, Nativity* (1938), Dominican Convent Chapel, Wicklow Town

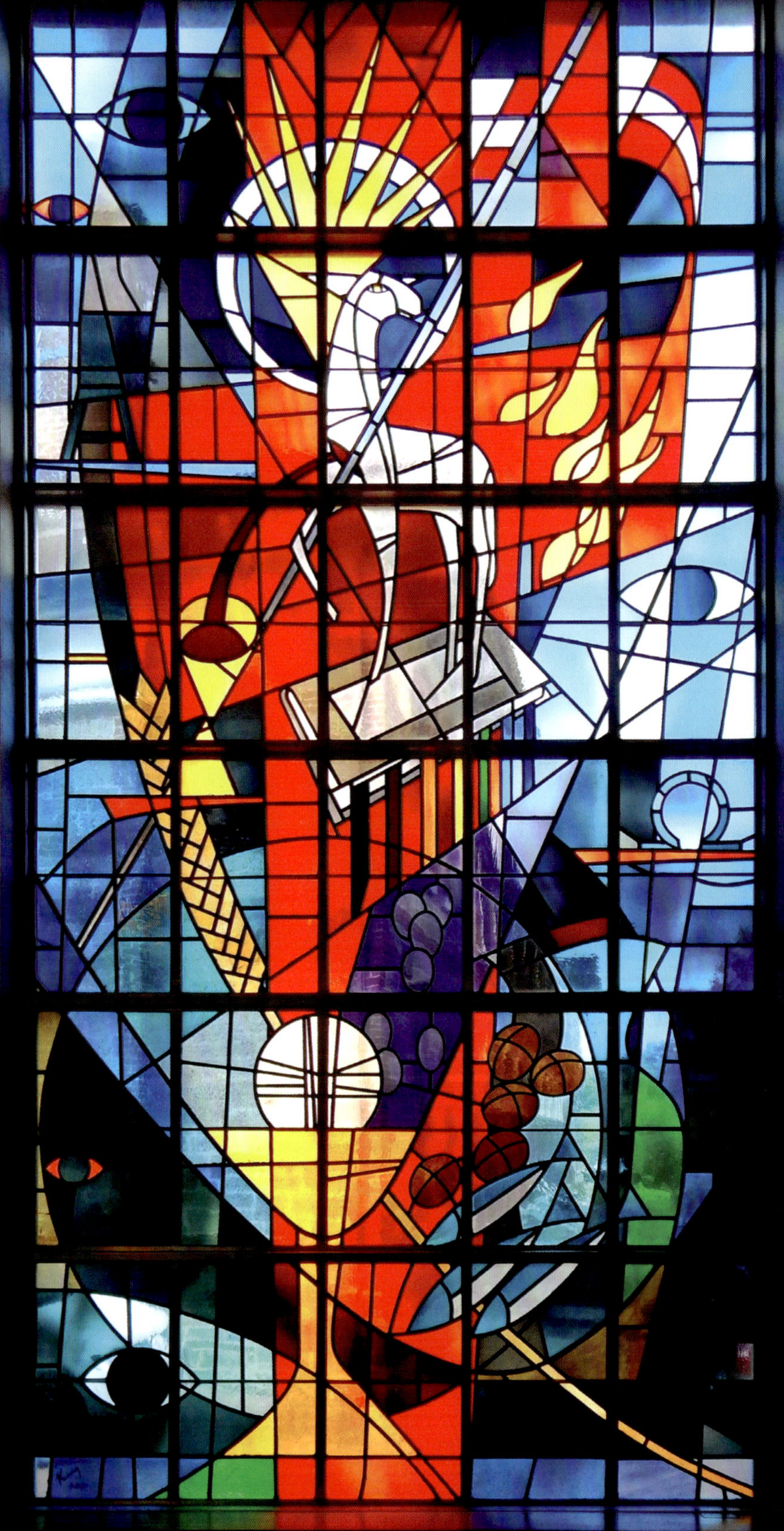

WINDOWS ABROAD, ARRANGED BY COUNTRY

AUSTRALIA

Australia, Queensland: Catholic Cathedral (St Stephen's), Elizabeth Street, Brisbane
CLARKE, Harry
The Ascension (B) 1923 (3 lights)

Australia, Queensland: CC (St Thomas Aquinas), Central Avenue, St Lucia, Brisbane
DOWLING, William
Christ as King and Priest 1975
Melchizedek 1975
Risen Christ 1975
St Joseph 1975
St Pius X 1975
St Thomas Aquinas 1975
St Pascal Baylon 1975
Our Lady and St John 1975

Australia, South Australia: Catholic Cathedral (St Mark's), Norman Street, Port Pirie
KING, Richard
The Immaculate Conception 1957
St Mark 1957

Australia, South Australia: CC (St John the Baptist), Anzac Highway, Plympton, Adelaide
KING, Richard
Our Lady Queen and Mother 1964–5
Baptism of Christ 1964–5

Australia, South Australia: Sisters of Saint Joseph of the Sacred Heart, Convent Chapel, High Street, Kensington, Adelaide
KING, Richard
Our Lady 1965–6
The Eucharist Window 1965–6
St Joseph 1965–6
Stations of the Cross 1965–6

Australia, Victoria: CC (Immaculate Conception), Burwood Road, Hawthorn
KING, Richard
The Nativity and Adoration of the Magi 1961 (3 lights)

Australia, Victoria: CC (St Dominic's), Riversdale Road, Camberwell East, Melbourne
KING, Richard
St Dominic 1938–40 (3 lights)
St Catherine of Siena 1938–40 (3 lights)
St Thomas Aquinas 1938–40 (3 lights)
Our Lady of Fatima 1956 (3 lights)
The Resurrection with Lazarus and Job 1956 (3 lights, mortuary chapel)
Our Lady of Lourdes 1956 (3 lights)
(First three created while he was at Harry Clarke Studios.)

Australia, Victoria: CC (St Joseph's), Kepler Street, Warrnambool
EARLEY, Leo
*Our Lady Surrounded by Angels c.*1954 (5 lights)
*Christ with Martha and Mary c.*1954 (3 lights)
*Christ Among the Doctors c.*1954 (3 lights)
*St Patrick and St Joseph c.*1954 (2 lights)
*St Maria Goretti and St Theresa c.*1954 (2 lights)

Australia, West Australia: CC (Our Lady of the Most Blessed Sacrament), Corfield Street, Gosnells
KING, Richard
The Christus (They Knew Him in the Breaking of the Bread) 1969–71
Our Lady of the Blessed Sacrament 1969–71

Left:
Richard King, *The Eucharist Window* (1965–6), Sisters of Saint Joseph of the Sacred Heart, Convent Chapel, Adelaide. © Sisters of Saint Joseph, CentreWest Region, SA Archives

Australia, West Australia: St Thomas More College Chapel, Mounts Bay Road, Crawley, Perth
KING, Richard
Christ, Priest and Teacher, Our Lady Seat of Wisdom, the Holy Spirit, Cardinal Newman, Cardinal St Robert Bellarmine SJ, St John Fisher and Blessed Contardi Ferrini 1957–8 (wall of stained glass comprising seven windows and Stations of the Cross in stained glass underneath) (sketch designs/scale drawing, NGI)

Australia, West Australia: CC (St Columba's), Forrest Street, South Perth
KING, Richard
Saints Columba, Brigid and Patrick 1935–7 (rose) (Created at Harry Clarke Studios.)
The Holy Family 1950 (sketch design, NGI)
Our Lady Queen of Heaven 1950 (sketch design, NGI)
Holy Child of Prague 1950 (sketch design, NGI)
St Anne and the Blessed Virgin Mary 1950 (sketch design, NGI)

BELGIUM

Belgium, Brussels: Justus Lipsius Building (Headquarters of the Council of the European Union), Rue de la Loi
SCANLON, James
Abstract 1994 (in foyer)

Belgium, Ypres: Catholic Cathedral (St Martin's), Vandenpeereboomplein
GEDDES, Wilhelmina
Te Deum: King Albert Memorial 1934–8 (rose)

CANADA

Canada, Alberta: Anglican Cathedral (Church of the Redeemer), Seventh Avenue, Calgary
CHILD, A.E.
Faith, Hope, Charity * 1907–8 (3 lights)

Canada, Newfoundland: Cathedral Basilica (St John the Baptist), Military Road, St John's
EARLEY, Leo
Nineteen decorative windows, each with Two Medallions Featuring Heads of Saints c.1954–5 (2 lights)
Visitation c.1954–5 (2 lights)
Annunciation c.1954–5 (2 lights)
Nativity, Simeon with the Christ Child c.1954–5 (2 lights)
Jesus in the Temple (2 lights)
Christ Crowned with Thorns, Christ Carrying His Cross c.1954–5 (2 lights)
Agony in the Garden, Christ at the Pillar c.1954–5 (2 lights)
Crucifixion, Resurrection c.1954–5 (2 lights)
Ascension, Descent of the Holy Spirit c.1954–5 (2 lights)
Assumption, Coronation of the Virgin c.1954–5 (2 lights)
Eight North American Jesuit Martyrs c.1954–5 (2 lights)
EARLEY, William (Bill) E.
Risen Christ c. late 1940s
Baptism of Christ c. late 1940s
Immaculate Heart of Mary c. late 1940s
Immaculate Conception c. late 1940s
Our Lady of Fatima c. late 1940s
Assumption c. late 1940s

Canada, Newfoundland: CC (Mary Queen of Peace), Torbay Road, St John's
WALSH, George W.
Our Lady Crowned Queen of Peace 1984
Christ, with Symbols of the Passion 1984
Stations of the Cross 1984 (etched in polished black limestone)

Canada, Newfoundland: CC (St Anne's), Conception Harbour, near St John's
HEALY, Michael
St Anne and the Blessed Virgin 1925 (circular) (sketch design, NGI)

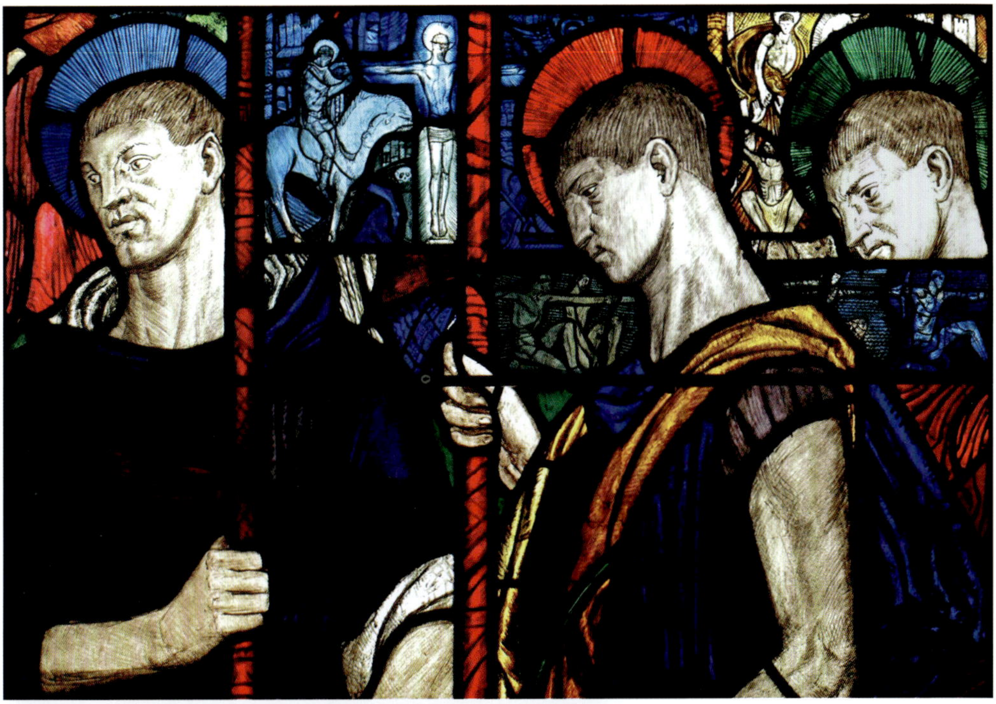

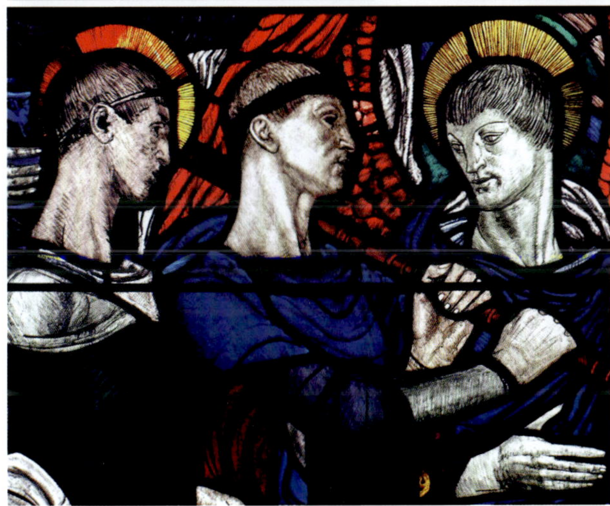

Wilhelmina Geddes, details of *The Duke of Connaught's War Memorial to his Canadian Staff: The Welcoming of a Slain Warrior by Soldier-Saints, Champions and Angels* (1919), St Bartholomew's Church (parish church of Government House), Parliament Buildings, Ottawa. Photographs © Kevin McQuinn

Canada, Ottawa: St Bartholomew's Church (parish church of Government House), Parliament Buildings, MacKay Street

GEDDES, Wilhelmina

The Duke of Connaught's War Memorial to his Canadian Staff: The Welcoming of a Slain Warrior by Soldier-Saints, Champions and Angels 1919 (3 lights) (sketch design, NGI)

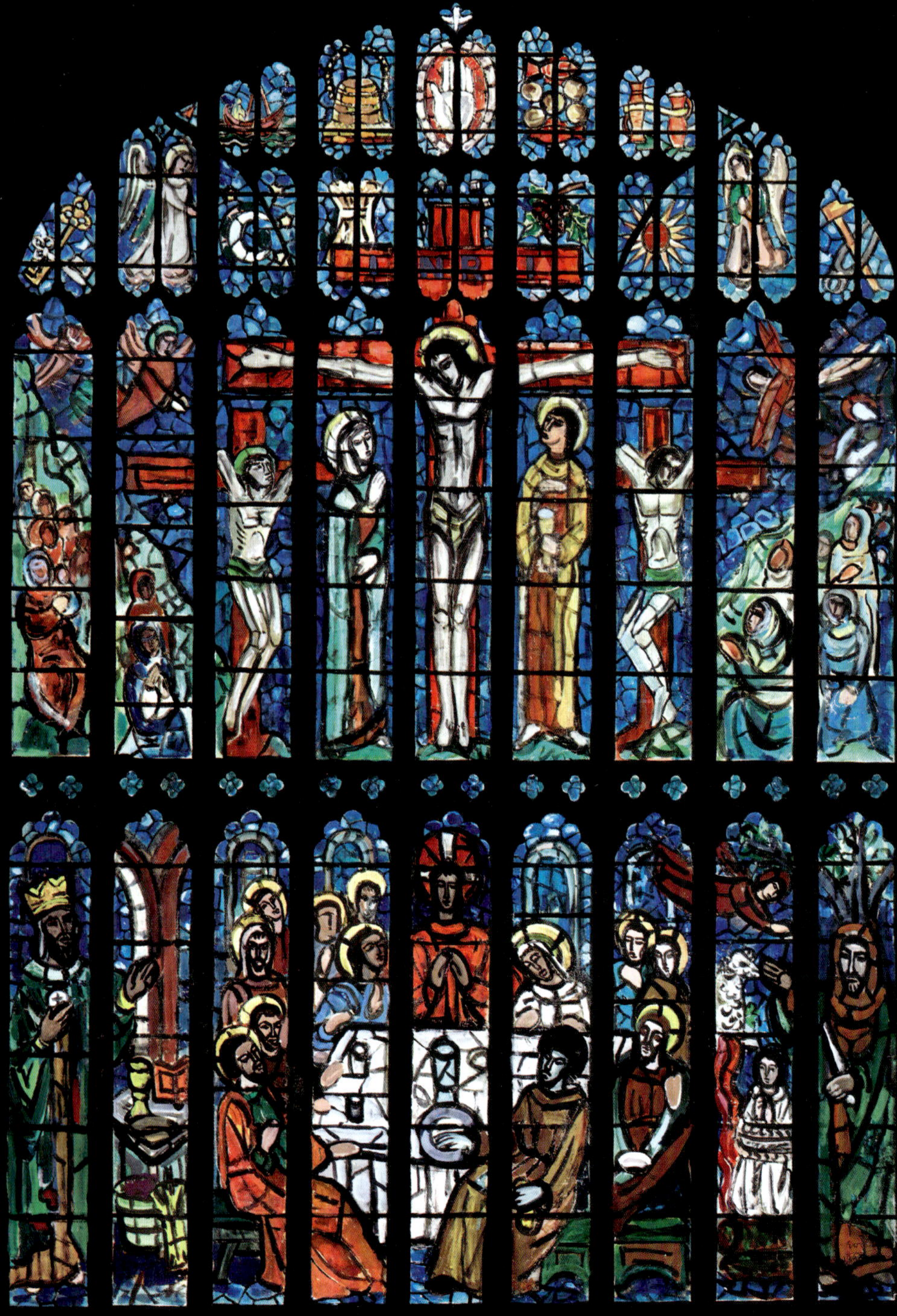

ENGLAND

England, Berkshire: Eton College Chapel, Windsor
HONE, Evie
The Crucifixion and the Last Supper 1949–52 (9 lights) (sketch designs, NGI; sketch design, Manresa House, Dollymount, Dublin; sketch design, Tate Gallery, London; sketch design, Eton College; cartoons, Maynooth College, County Kildare)

England, Bristol: Chapel of the Three Kings of Cologne, Foster's Almshouses, Colston Street
POLLEN, Patrick
Epiphany 1968 (4 lights) (sketch design, NIVAL) (cartoon for *Madonna and Child* light, Jesuit Fathers' Community House, Leeson Street, Dublin)
Armorial window 1968 (3 lights) (sketch design, NIVAL)

England, Cambridgeshire: Ely Cathedral, Stained Glass Museum
CLARKE, Harry
St Wilfred and St John Berchmans, and the Presentation of Our Lady to St Elizabeth in the Temple 1927 (made for the Lady Chapel, Convent of Notre Dame, Dowanhill, Glasgow)
GEDDES, Wilhelmina
Faith, Hope and Charity 1955–6 (3 lights; design and cartoons prepared by Wilhelmina Geddes; window executed by Charles Blakeman)
*St Joseph and the Angel c.*1930 (panel)
HONE, Evie
*Christ Meeting His Mother c.*1950 (panel)
Annunciation 1938 (panel)
YOUNG, Peter
Sure Enough the Duck 1992 (panel)

Left:
Evie Hone, *The Crucifixion and the Last Supper* (1949–52), pen, ink and watercolour preliminary design for Eton College Chapel, Windsor, Berkshire. Collection NGI. © The Artist's Estate. Photograph © National Gallery of Ireland

England, Cheshire: C of E (St Mary's), Church Lane, Nantwich
CLARKE, Harry
The Virgin and Child with St Cecilia and Richard Coeur de Lion 1920 (3 lights)

England, Cumbria: C of E (Holy Trinity), Bardsea, near Ulverston
GEDDES, Wilhelmina and HEALY, Michael
The Baptism of Christ 1923–4
The Crucifixion 1923–4
The Resurrection 1923–4
(sketch design by Geddes, NGI; windows executed by Healy)

England, Cumbria: Lanercost Priory, near Brampton
HONE, Evie
St Cecilia 1947

England, Dorset: CC (Church of the Annunciation), Charminster Road, Richmond Park, Bournemouth
HONE, Evie
The Virgin, The Annunciation, The Visitation 1948 (3 lights) (sketch design, Clongowes Wood College, County Kildare; right-hand side cartoon, Our Lady's Hospice, Harold's Cross, Dublin south)

England, Dorset: C of E (St Mary's), Church Lane, Sturminster Newton
CLARKE, Harry
Madonna and Child with St Elizabeth of Hungary and St Barbara 1921 (3 lights)

England, Durham: CC (St Cuthbert's), Old Elvet
CLARKE, Harry
St Cuthbert, William Bede, Thomas Plumtree and Blessed Thomas Percy (A) 1930–1 (2 lights)

England, East Sussex: CC (St Mary's), Queen's Road, Crowborough
POLLEN, Patrick
St Bernadette of Lourdes 1960

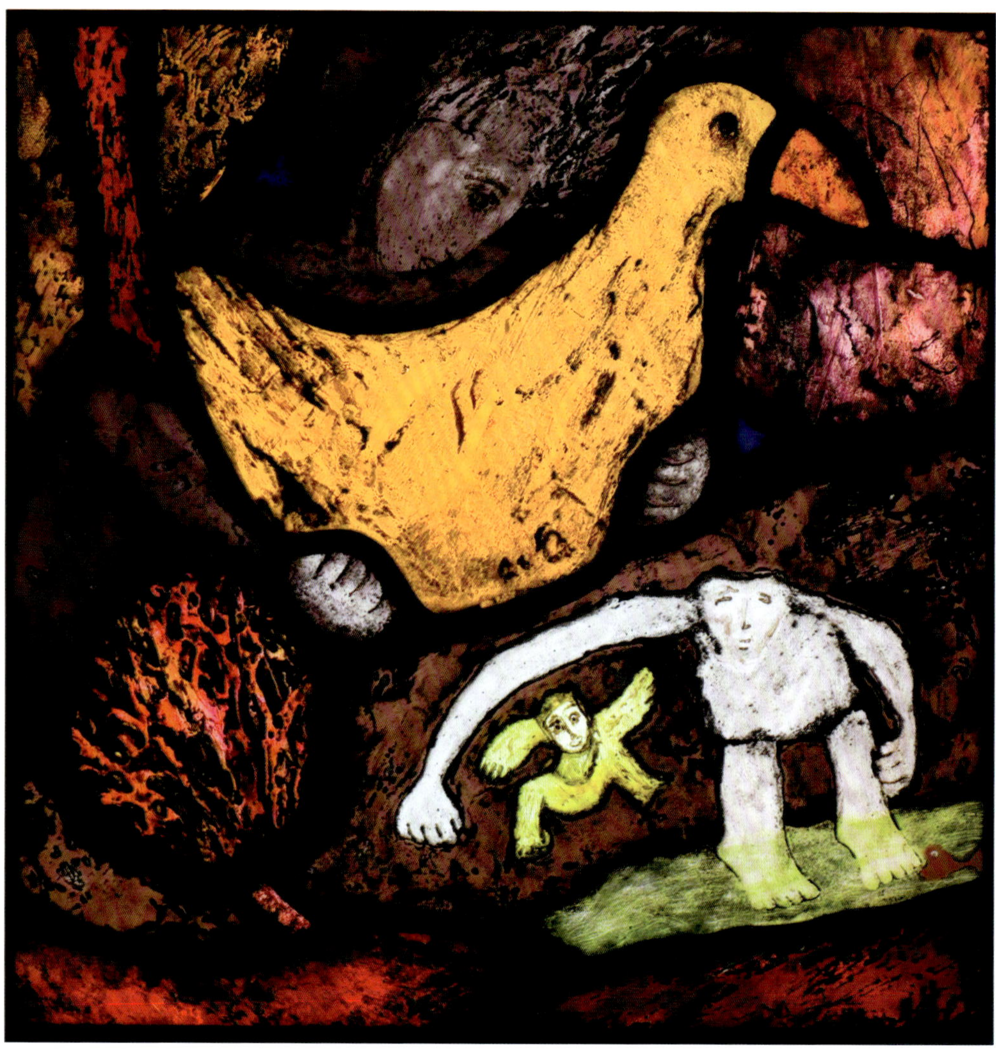

Above: Peter Young, *Sure Enough the Duck* (1992), © Stained Glass Museum, Ely Cathedral, Ely, Cambridgeshire (ELYGM:1992.5)

England, East Sussex: CC (St Thomas More's), Church Close, Patcham, Brighton
DOWD MURPHY, Róisín and MURPHY, Johnny
Holy Family 1969

England, East Sussex: C of E (St Pancras's), Kingston, near Lewes
COTTER, Maud
Rev. Michael Scott Memorial Window 1991

England, Greater London: C of E (All Hallows), Horsenden Lane North, Greenford
GEDDES, Wilhelmina
Madonna and Child with Angels and Figures of Isaiah and St Simeon 1951–2 (circular)

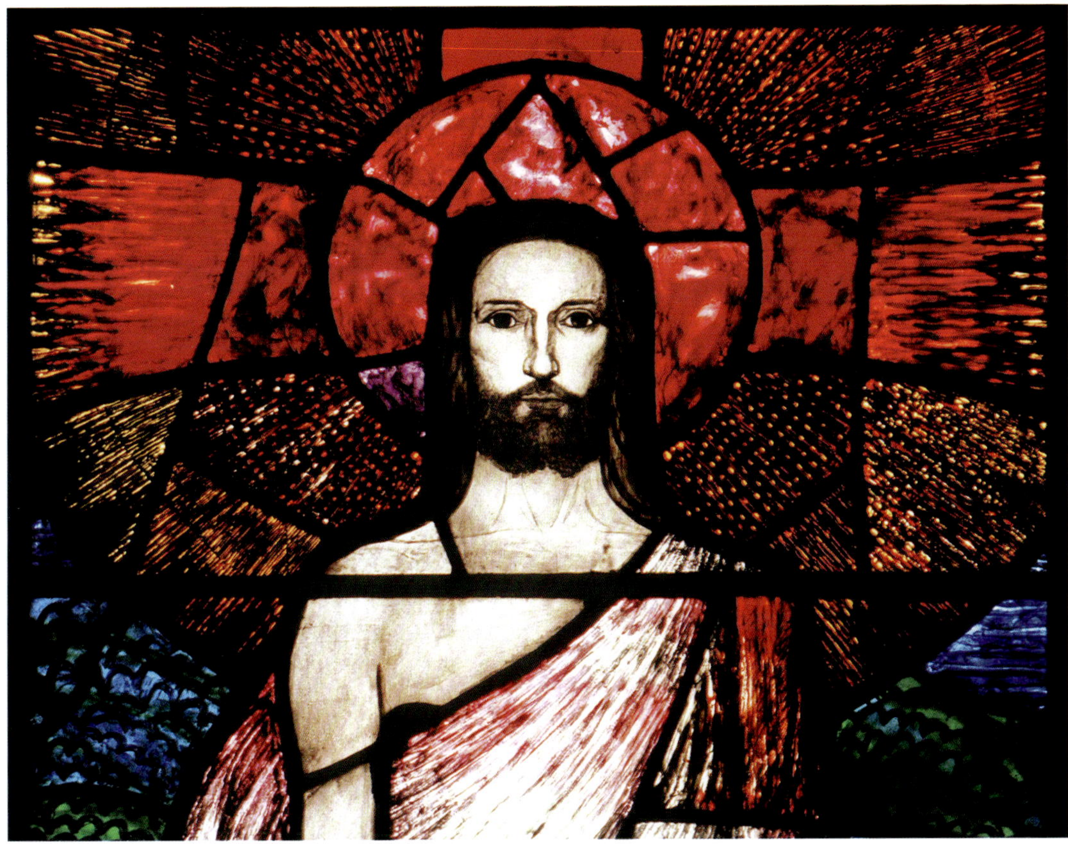

Above:
Wilhelmina Geddes, detail of *The Baptism of Christ, The Crucifixion, The Resurrection* (1923–4, executed by Michael Healy), Church of England (Holy Trinity), Bardsea, near Ulverston, Cumbria.
Photograph © David Caron

England, Greater London: C of E (St Nicholas's), St Nicholas Way, Sutton
RHIND, Ethel
Title unknown (destroyed in war) 1907 (3 lights)

England, Greater Manchester: CC (St Oswald and St Edmund's), Liverpool Road, Ashton-in-Makerfield
CLARKE, Harry
Seven glass windows depicting saints devoted to the Eucharist:
St John the Evangelist (A) 1930
St Clare (A) 1930
St Ita (A) 1930
St Juliana Falconieri (A) 1930
St Paschal Baylon (A) 1930
St Catherine of Siena (A) 1930
St Tarcisius (A) 1930
KING, Richard
St Agnes 1930–1

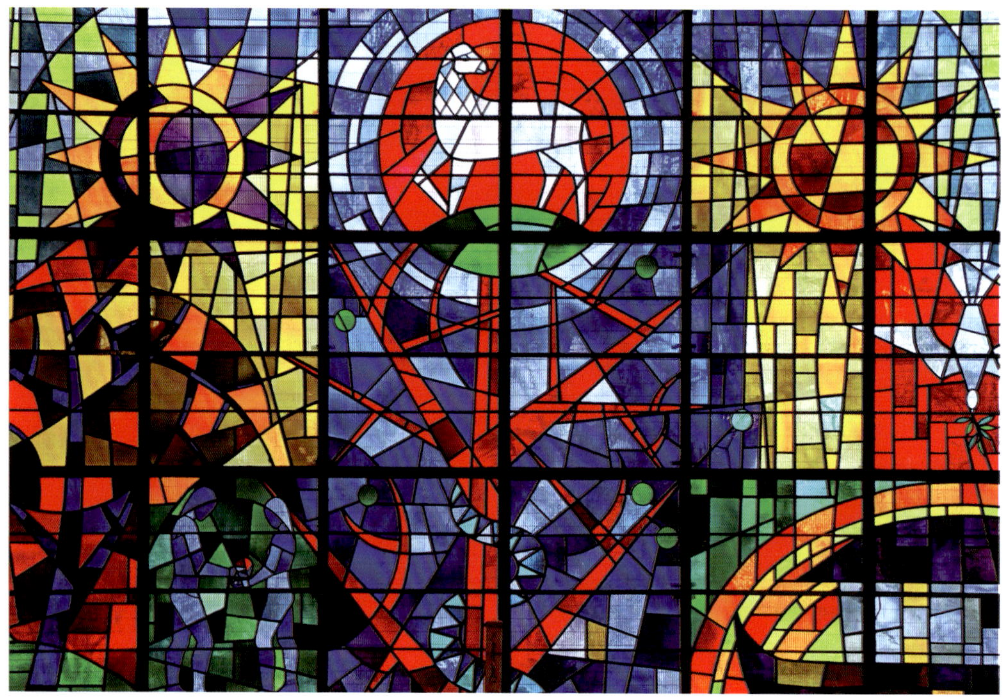

England, Greater Manchester: CC (Our Lady of the Assumption), Wood Street, Middleton, Manchester
KING, Richard
The Assumption 1961 (3 lights, with free-form lunette above)

England, Greater Manchester: C of E (Christ Church), Liverpool Road, Patricroft
CHILD, A.E.
The Crown of Life * 1922 (2 lights)

England, Greater Manchester: Manchester University Settlement Chapel, Ancoats Hall, Every Street, Ancoats
RHIND, Ethel
Memorial to Eva Gore-Booth 1928 (building demolished and window remains untraced)

Above:
Helen Moloney, details of *Creation, Fall and Redemption of Mankind* (1966),
Catholic Church (Holy Family), Southampton, Hampshire. Photograph © Fr James Bradley

England, Hampshire: CC (Holy Family), Redbridge Hill, Southampton
MOLONEY, Helen
Creation, Fall and Redemption of Mankind 1966 (wall of stained glass)
Holy Family 1966 (sanctuary window)
(sketch designs, NIVAL)

England, Hertfordshire: C of E (St Michael and All Angels), Waterford, near Hertford
CLARKE, Harry
St Cecilia and a Listening Angel (designed by Harry Clarke in 1921, executed freely from Clarke's cartoon by Karl Parsons in 1929)

England, Kent: CC (St Michael and All Angels), Crofton Road, Farnborough, Orpington
DOWD MURPHY, Róisín
Annunciation 1964 (3 lights)
Nativity 1964 (3 lights)
Agony in the Garden 1964 (3 lights)
Ascension 1964 (3 lights)
Assumption 1964 (3 lights)
Archangel Michael Defeating Lucifer 1964
Holy Spirit 1964

England, Kent: C of E (St Mary's), High Street, Downe, Orpington
HONE, Evie
The Crucifixion, with the Blessed Virgin Mary and St John 1949 (3 lights) (cartoon, Milltown Park, Dublin)

England, Kent: C of E (Wheler family chapel, private), Otterden Place, Eastling, near Faversham
GEDDES, Wilhelmina
St Joseph of Arimathea 1933

England, Kent: Carmelite Shrine of St Jude, Tanners Street, Faversham
KING, Richard
Untitled window of Mary and the Christ Child with the Holy Spirit or the Immaculate Conception 1954–7
Our Lady of Mount Carmel 1954–7 (3 lights) (window severely damaged in a fire of 2004 and recreated in 2005)
God the Father 1954–7
The Resurrection of Christ 1954–7
Crucifixion with Priest Celebrating the Eucharist and Souls in Purgatory on either side 1954–7 (3 lights)
St Brocard 1954–7
St Simon Stock 1954–7
The Prophet Eliseus (or Elisha) 1954–7
The Prophet Elias (or Elijah) 1954–7

England, Lancashire: See Greater Manchester and Merseyside

England, Leicestershire: C of E (St Edward King and Martyr), Clapgun Street, Castle Donington
POLLEN, Patrick
*Memorial Window Depicting St Luke Painting the Virgin and Child, the Baptism of Christ by John the Baptist, and other scenes c.*1950s (2 lights) (sketch design, NIVAL)

England, London EC4: Dr Johnson's House, 17 Gough Square
GEDDES, Wilhelmina
The Tour of the Hebrides 1928 (panel; stolen *c.*1976)

England, London E11: CC (Our Lady of Lourdes), Cambridge Park, Wanstead
SCANLON, James
*Two abstract windows c.*2004–5

England, London N6: C of E (St Michael's), South Grove, Highgate
HONE, Evie
The Last Supper, and Christ Washing the Feet of the Disciples 1954 (5 lights) (sketch design, Manresa House, Dollymount, Dublin)

England, London NW5: La Sainte Union Secondary School, Highgate Road, Highgate
POLLEN, Patrick
The Annunciation 1959–61 (panel, located at school chapel entrance; formerly in the Covent of the Sacred Heart, Highgate, London)

England, London SE12: C of E (St Mildred's), St Mildred's Road, Lewisham
GEDDES, Wilhelmina
St Elizabeth, the Virgin and Child, St Mildred 1953–4 (3 small windows)

England, London SE22: CC (St Thomas More's), Lordship Lane, East Dulwich
PYE, Patrick
An Apparition of St Columba 1970 (3 lights)

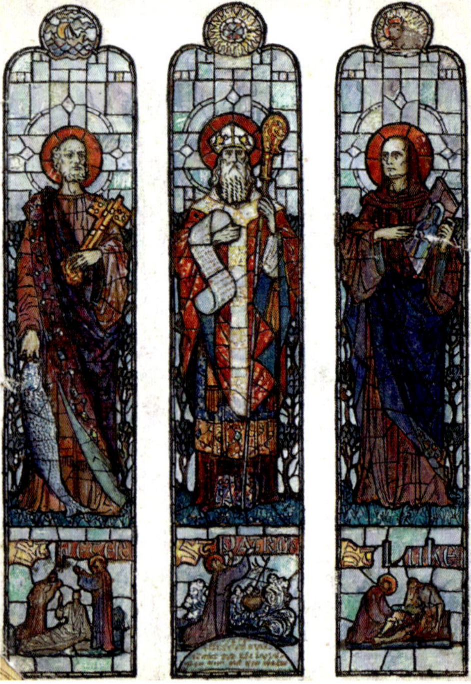

Above:
Michael Healy, *St Patrick, St Peter and St Luke* (1913), watercolour preliminary design for the Church of England (St Peter's), Wallsend. Collection NGI. Photograph © National Gallery of Ireland

England, Tyne and Wear: C of E (St Luke's), Frank Street, Wallsend
GEDDES, Wilhelmina
The Crucifixion with Blessed Virgin Mary and St John, Moses, Joseph of Arimathea, and the Deposition 1922 (5 lights)

England, Tyne and Wear: C of E (St Peter's), Church Bank, Wallsend
HEALY, Michael
St Patrick, St Peter and St Luke 1913 (3 lights, in former Lady Chapel, refitted as a vestry) (sketch design, NGI)
Our Lord Blessing a Woman, with the Nativity and the Shepherds 1919 (3 lights, in former Lady Chapel, refitted as a vestry)
Angel of the Resurrection, with St George and St Christopher 1921 (3 lights)
Our Lord Walking on the Water 1921 (3 lights)
RHIND, Ethel
The Good Shepherd, Mary of Bethany, David 1921 (3 lights)

England, Tyne and Wear: C of E (St Paul's), Askew Road, Gateshead (church demolished; window possibly destroyed, currently untraced)
McGOLDRICK, Hubert
Saints Martin, George, Michael, Paul 1921 (4 lights) (sketch design, NGI)

England, Warwickshire: CC (Our Lady and St Benedict's), Wootton Wawen
HONE, Evie
Christ Washing the Feet of the Apostles * *c.*1950 (panel)

England, Warwickshire: C of E (All Saints), High Street, Bedworth
CLARKE, Harry
Saints Peter, Paul, Luke and John (B) 1929 (4 lights)

England, Warwickshire: Ettington Park Hotel (former home of the Shirley family), Stratford-upon-Avon
HONE, Evie
Christ in Judgement 1950 (3 lights) (cartoons, NGI and NIVAL; centre light cartoon, OPW Glebe House, County Donegal)
St Nicholas of Bari, with Stories from his Legend 1950 (3 lights)

England, West Midlands: CC (St Augustine's), Avenue Road, Handsworth, Birmingham
POLLEN, Patrick
St George 1960s
St Patrick 1960s
Baptism of Christ 1960s

England, West Midlands: CC (Christ the King), Westhill Road, Coventry
WALSH, George W.
Scenes from the Life of Christ 1970 (clerestory)

England, West Midlands: CC (St Thomas More's), Watercall Avenue, Styvechale, Coventry
POLLEN, Patrick
St Thomas More *c.*1968 (3 lights) (sketch design, NIVAL)
Christian symbols *c.*1968 (3 lights)
All other glazing *c.*1968

England, West Sussex: Ashdown Park Hotel (formerly Chapel of Our Lady, Convent of Notre Dame), Ashdown Park, Wych Cross, East Grinstead
CLARKE, Harry
The Immaculate Conception with St Anne (A) 1925 (3 lights, in the Memorial Chapel tower)
Scenes from the Life of Our Lady with base panels, depicting Emblems of Her Litany: (A) 1925
The Immaculate Conception (Emblem: The Queen of Virgins) *and the Visitation of Our Lady and St Anne* (Emblem: Morning Star) (2 lights)
Our Lady's Presentation (Emblem: Mystical Rose) *and the Annunciation* (Emblem: Ivory Tower) (2 lights)
The Visitation (Emblem: Mother of Good Counsel), and *The Espousal* (2 lights)
Our Lady of the Angels (Emblem: Queen of Angels) (2 lights)
The Family of Our Lady and the Presentation of Our Lord (Emblem: Queen of Martyrs) (2 lights)
The Adoration of the Magi and the Descent of the Holy Ghost (Emblem: Seat of Wisdom) (2 lights)
The Assumption (Emblem: Gate of Heaven) *and the Coronation* (Emblem: Queen of all Saints) (2 lights)

England, West Sussex: CC (Holy Family), North Road, Lancing
MURPHY, Johnny
Holy Family 1970 (cartoons, NIVAL)

England, West Sussex: C of E (St John the Baptist), Church Walk, Crawley
CHILD, A.E.
Sorrow and Joy 1907 (2 lights)

England, West Sussex: C of E (St Michael and All Angels), Northchapel, near Petworth
GEDDES, Wilhelmina
St Francis of Assisi and his Canticle of All Created Things 1930 (3 lights)

England, West Sussex: C of E (St Bartholomew's), Habin Hill, Rogate
CHILD, A.E.
St Catherine * *c.*1912

England, West Sussex: Sisters of Mercy Convent Chapel, Salisbury Road, Worthing
DOWD MURPHY, Róisín and MURPHY, Johnny
Risen Christ (sketch designs, NIVAL)
Our Lady Crowned (sketch designs, NIVAL)
Church symbols 1967

England, West Yorkshire: C of E (St James the Great's), Barnsley Road, Flockton
POLLEN, Patrick
St Eustace and St Christopher 1957 (2 lights) (sketch designs, NIVAL)

England, West Yorkshire: Former C of E (St Marie's), Low Moor, Bradford (now a private residence)
O'BRIEN, Catherine
The Good Samaritan 1937 (3 lights)

England, Yorkshire: See North Yorkshire, South Yorkshire, West Yorkshire

GERMANY

Germany, North Rhine-Westphalia: CC (St Clement's), Mülheim, Cologne
FRÖMEL, Gerda
St Wendeler and his Wife 1959

Germany, North Rhine-Westphalia: CC (Christ the King), Uellendahl-Katernberg, Wuppertal
FRÖMEL, Gerda
*Abstract c.*1960 (baptistry)

GREECE

Greece, Andros Island: Goulandris Memorial Chapel
POLLEN, Patrick
Three small panels (subjects not recorded) 1962

INDIA

India, Hazaribagh: St Kiran's Girls School Chapel (former Dublin University Mission), near Muffasil Thana, Ranchi-Patna Road, Hazaribagh 825301
CHILD, A.E.
Angel * 1925 (circular; adapted from a design by Sarah Purser)

India, Hazaribagh: St Columba's Hospital Chapel (former Dublin University Mission), Rabindra Path, Hazaribagh, Jharkhand 825301
RHIND, Ethel
Woman with the Anointment, The Good Shepherd, Parable of the Ten Virgins * 1912–3 (3 lights)

KENYA

Kenya, South Kinangop: CC (St Francis's), South Kinangop (current location untraced)
O'BRIEN, Catherine
*St Francis of Assisi with European and African Animals c.*1953 (sketch designs, NGI)

MALAYSIA

Malaysia, Penang: Colonial Penang Museum, Jalan DS Ramanathan (Scott Road), Pulau Tikus, George Town
McGOLDRICK, Hubert
The Spirit of the Morning 1926–7 (lunette; commissioned for Rose Lands, Grange Road, Singapore, a private residence since demolished)
O'BRIEN, Catherine
The Spirit of the Night 1927 (lunette; commissioned for Rose Lands, Grange Road, Singapore, a private residence since demolished) (sketch design, NGI)
QUIGLY, Kathleen
Pan, Bacchus, Ceres and Proserpina 1926 (lunettes; commissioned for Eu Villa, Grange Road, Singapore, a private residence since demolished)

NEW ZEALAND

New Zealand, Wellington: Crematorium Chapel, Old Karori Road, Karori
GEDDES, Wilhelmina
Faith 1914
Hope 1914
HEALY, Michael
Charity (St Martin of Tours) 1930
Love, Two in a Garden 1931 (sketch design, NGI)
Wisdom 1936–7
McGOLDRICK, Hubert
Gethsemane 1939

NIGERIA

Nigeria, Delta State: Catholic Cathedral (Our Lady of the Waters), Bomadi, Ughelli
MULDOWNEY, Patrick
Entire scheme of abstract lights incorporating Christian symbols 1995

Nigerian, Imo State: CC (Our Lady of Mount Carmel), Emekuku, Mbaise
DOWD MURPHY, Róisín
Assumption 1966 (cartoon, NIVAL)
Ascension 1966 (cartoon, NIVAL)

Right:
Wilhelmina Geddes, *Faith* (1914),
Karori Crematorium Chapel, Wellington.
Photograph © Joseph McBrinn

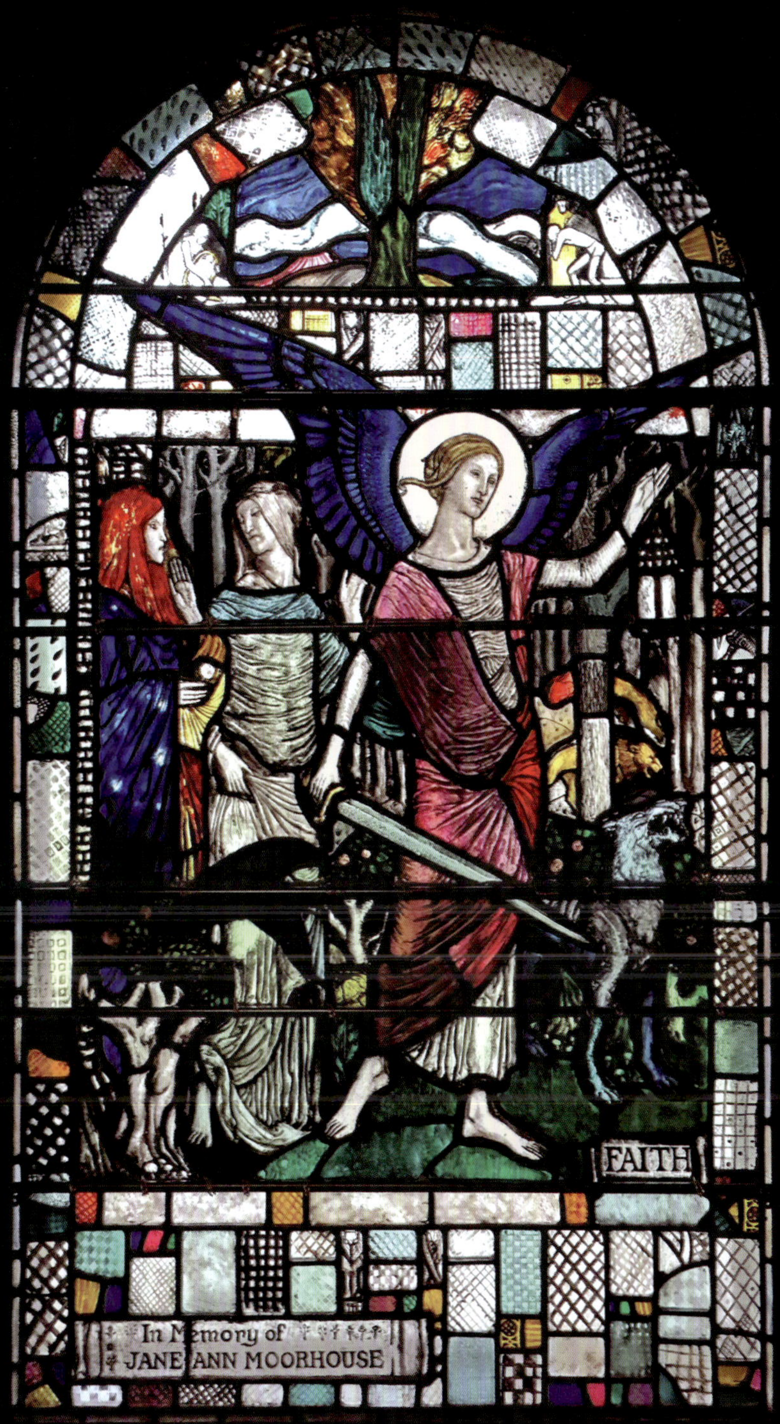
FAITH
In Memory of
JANE ANN MOORHOUSE

Nigeria, Akwa Ibom State: CC (St Peter and St Paul's), Essene, Ikot Abasi LGA
BURKE, Phyllis
*Stations of the Cross c.*1958

Nigeria, Plateau State: CC (St Theresa's), Church Street, Jos
KING, Richard
Crucifixion 1936–9
(Created at Harry Clarke Studios.)

Nigeria, Oyo State: CC (St Gabriel's), Mokola, Ibadan
MURPHY, Johnny
Abstract 1971 (*dalle de verre*)

Nigeria, Cross River State: Catholic Cathedral (St Benedict's), Monaya Road, Ogoja
MURPHY, Johnny
Stations of the Cross 1957 (cartoons, NIVAL)

PAKISTAN

Pakistan, Punjab Province: CC, Presentation Convent, Wah
MURPHY, Johnny
Our Lady 1955
St Joseph 1955 (sketch design, NIVAL)

PHILIPPINES

Philippines, Negros Oriental Province: CC (Our Mother of Perpetual Help, Redemptorist Church), Dumaguete
MURPHY, Johnny
*Holy Spirit c.*1960 (circular laylight)

SCOTLAND

Scotland, Aberdeenshire: C of S (St Kentigern's), Invercauld Road, Ballater
CHILD, A.E.
St George and the Dragon 1907

Scotland, Edinburgh: Royal College of Surgeons of Edinburgh, Nicolson Street
WALSH, George W.
Coat of Arms and Symbols of Surgery 2008 (5 lights; gift from RCSI, Dublin to RCSEd to celebrate the latter's 500th anniversary)

Scotland, Glasgow: Kelvingrove Art Gallery and Museum, Argyle Street
CLARKE, Harry
The Coronation of the Blessed Virgin 1923 (3 lights) (made for the Convent of Notre Dame, Dowanhill, Glasgow)

Scotland, Glasgow: CC (St Vincent de Paul), Main Street, Thornliebank
EARLEY, Willie
Abstract scheme with symbols, images and text 1959
(Created at Abbey Stained Glass Studios.)

Scotland, Inverclyde: CC (St Ninian's), Gourock
KELLY, Kevin
The Holy Family, with the Finding of Jesus in the Temple, the Wedding Feast at Cana, John the Baptist Baptising Christ, Pietà 2002
The Nativity, with the Annunciation, the Visitation, the Adoration of the Magi, the Flight into Egypt 2002
(Both windows created at Abbey Stained Glass Studios.)

Scotland, Midlothian: Rosslyn Chapel Crypt, Chapel Loan, Roslin
POLLEN, Patrick
Transfiguration 1954 (sketch designs, NIVAL)

Scotland, Stirling: C of S, Buchanan, near Drymen
CHILD, A.E.
Knight and Dragon * 1914 (in storage)

SINGAPORE

Singapore: De La Salle Brothers School (St Patrick's) Chapel, East Coast Road

O'BRIEN, Catherine

St Patrick 1931

Below:

Patrick Pollen, *Flight into Egypt* (1957–9), ink and watercolour preliminary design for the Catholic Cathedral, Johannesburg. Collection NIVAL, NCAD, Dublin. Reproduced courtesy of the Pollen family.

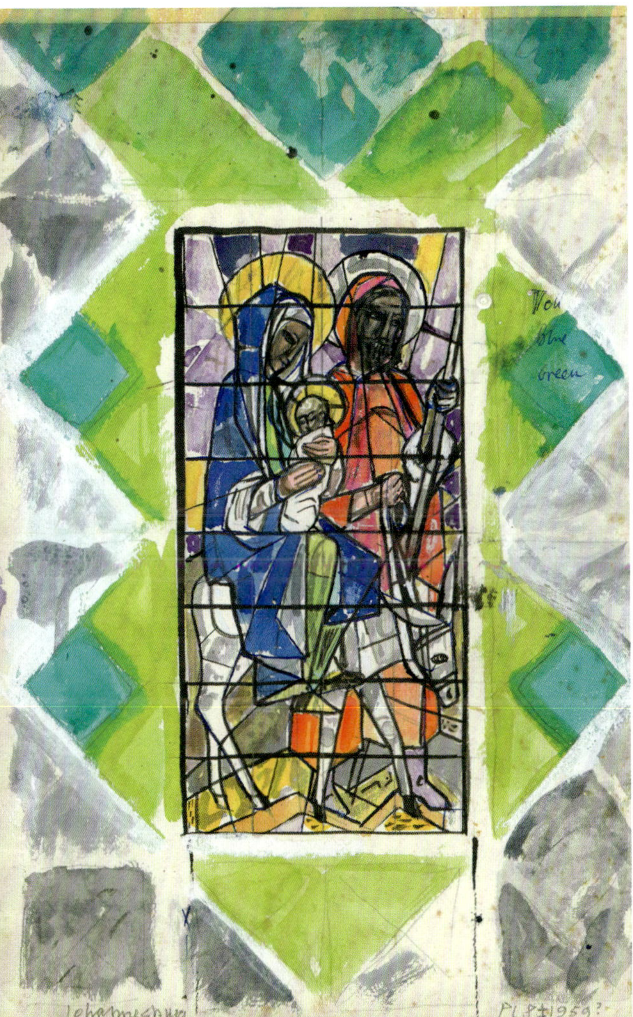

SOUTH AFRICA

South Africa, Johannesburg: Catholic Cathedral (Christ the King), Nugget Street, Berea

POLLEN, Patrick

Christ Meets His Mother 1957–9 (sketch designs, NIVAL)

Flight into Egypt 1957–9 (sketch designs, NIVAL)

Nativity 1957–9

Immaculate Conception 1957–9

Christ the King 1957–9

Feed my Sheep 1957–9

Pentecost 1957–9

Assumption 1957–9

Cross and Nails 1957–9 (sketch designs, NIVAL)

Virgo Potens 1957–9

Lamb of God 1957–9

Rose Mystica 1957–9

Chi-Ro and Crown 1957–9

Sheep 1957–9

Holy Ghost 1957–9

Vas Honoris 1957–9

The Angel (St Matthew) 1957–9

The Lion (St Mark) 1957–9

Chi-Ro in Circle of Eternity 1957–9

Wheat (bread) 1957–9

Anchor (faith) 1957–9

Pelican (Christ's Church) 1957–9

The Trinity 1957–9

Fish and Net (net of souls) 1957–9

Bull (St Luke) 1957–9

Eagle (St John) 1957–9

Fish (IXOVS) 1957–9

Grapes (wine) 1957–9

Ship (ship of the church) 1957–9

Chalice 1957–9

Host 1957–9

Alpha and Omega 1957–9

Keys (of St Peter) 1957–9

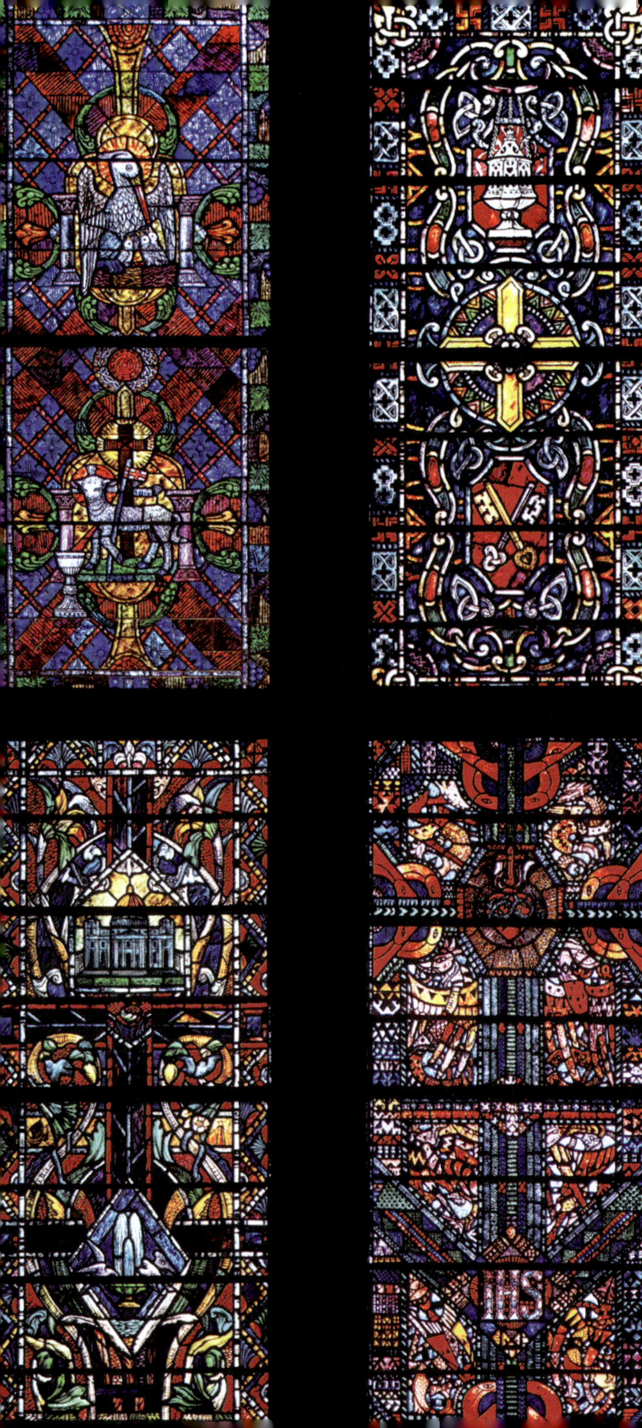
IHS

TURKEY

Turkey, Izmir: C of E (St John's), Talatpasa Boulevard, Alsancak
O'BRIEN, Catherine
'Blessed Are The Pure in Heart' 1905 (north porch)

USA

USA, Arizona: Brophy College Chapel (Jesuit Fathers), North Central Avenue, Phoenix
CHILD, A.E.
Alpha and Omega c.1930–1
Butterfly, Crossed Palms and Crown 1932
Symbol of the Holy Trinity (triangle) with Omniscient Eye of God, Sceptre and Crown 1934
Smoking Thurible, Crossed Keys 1934
HEALY, Michael
IHS, Sacred Heart 1937 (sketch design, NGI)
McGOLDRICK, Hubert
Symbols of the Blessed Virgin, The Burning Bush and Lily Among the Thorns * 1934
Dove, Fire and Torch 1934 (sketch design, NGI)
O'BRIEN, Catherine
Wheat and Grapes, Host and Chalice 1937 (sketch design, NGI)
Pelican and Lamb 1937 (sketch design, NGI)
RHIND, Ethel
St Peter's Basilica, Rome, Fountain of Grace c.1934

USA, California: CC (Mary Star of the Sea), West 7th Street, San Pedro
CLARKE, Terry
Miraculous Draft of Fishes 1958
(One of more than fifty windows made at Harry Clarke Studios for this church in 1958–60 and 1969–70.)

Left, clockwise from top left: Catherine O'Brien, *Pelican and Lamb* (1937); A.E. Child, *Smoking Thurible and Crossed Keys* (1934); Michael Healy, *IHS and Sacred Heart* (1937), Brophy College Chapel, Phoenix, Arizona. Ethel Rhind, *St Peter's Basilica, Rome and Fountain of Grace* (c.1934); Photographs © David Caron and Jake Kelly

USA, California: CC (St Mary of the Immaculate Conception), Bean Avenue, Los Gatos
WALSH, George Stephen
Crucifixion c.1962
Melchizedek c.1962
Preparation of the Passover c.1962
Jesus Lamb of God c.1962
Manna in the Desert c.1962
Multiplication of Loves c.1962
Giving of the Law c.1962
Transfiguration c.1962
Adam and Eve c.1962
Moses Goes up the Mountain c.1962
Sermon on the Mount c.1962
David Brings the Ark to Jerusalem c.1962
Christ Enters Jerusalem c.1962
Elias Raises a Boy from the Dead c.1962
Raising of the Widow's Son c.1962
Good Samaritan c.1962
Prodigal Son c.1962
Martha and Mary c.1962
Adoration of the Magi c.1962
Stations of the Cross 1970s/early 1980s (opus sectile glass mosaic)

USA, California: St John's Seminary, Seminary Road, Camarillo
EARLEY, William (Bill) E.
The Annunciation c.1939 (3 lights, Seminary Chapel)
KING, Richard
Ireland's Homage 1938–9 (3 lights, Seminary Chapel)
(Created at Harry Clarke Studios.)
MacBRIDE, William
Saints Brigid, Patrick and Colmcille * c.1939 (3 lights, Seminary Chapel)
O'BRIEN, Catherine
Saints Patrick and Brigid c.1939 (2 lights, Faculty Chapel)
Above windows were exhibited at the Irish Pavilion, New York World's Fair, 1939.

USA, California: CC (Sacred Heart), 39th Street, Sacramento
DOWLING, William
St Peter * 1949–50
St Paul * 1949–50
DOWLING, William and/or KING, Richard
Symbols of the Evangelists * designed 1938, executed 1948 (rose)
Symbols of the Sacraments * designed 1938, executed 1948 (rose)
KING, Richard
St Margaret Mary and the Sacred Heart of Mary 1931–2 (2 lights)
The Sacred Heart and St Francis de Sales 1931–2 (2 lights)
The Baptism of Christ 1931–2
St Patrick 1931–2
Rose window with abstract pattern 1931–2
St Michael 1935–7
St Anthony of Padua 1935–7
St Thérèse (The Little Flower) 1935–7
St Joseph 1935–7
Mater Dolorosa 1938–40
St John the Apostle and Evangelist 1938–40
St Stephen 1938–40
St John the Baptist de la Salle 1938–40
St Rose of Lima 1938–40
DOWLING, William
St Brigid 1949–50
(All above created at Harry Clarke Studios.)

USA, California: CC, St Mary's Mausoleum, Fruitridge Road, Sacramento
DOWLING, William
Symbols of the Eucharist 1978
Symbols of the Passion 1978
Symbols of the Holy Trinity 1978
Symbols of the Virgin Mary 1978

USA, Florida: Wolfsonian-Florida International University, Washington Avenue, Miami Beach
CLARKE, Harry
The Geneva Window (A) 1930 (single window in eight square sections, comprising 15 panels; commissioned for the International Labour Building, League of Nations, Geneva) (preliminary design, Dublin City Gallery The Hugh Lane)

USA, Florida: CC (St Helen's), 20th Street, Vero Beach
O'BRIEN, Catherine
Stations of the Cross, The Chalice, The Lamb 1957 (16 roundels)

USA, Iowa: Waterloo United Methodist Church, Kimball Avenue, Waterloo
WALSH, George Stephen
*Scheme of stained glass on Old and New Testament themes c.*1960 (painted by George W. Walsh)

USA, Massachusetts: Boston College (James Jeffrey Roche Room, Bapst Library), Commonwealth Avenue, Chestnut Hill, Boston
KING, Richard
Lugh Triumphing over Balor and Christ Triumphing over the Devil 1951 (2 lights) (cartoon, NGI)
Monk/Scribe 1951 (cartoon, NGI)

USA, Massachusetts: Boston College (John J. Burns Library), Commonwealth Avenue, Chestnut Hill, Boston
HONE, Evie
Virgin 1938 (panel, in light box)
RHIND, Ethel
The Mystic Marriage of St Catherine 1938 (panel)

Right: Harry Clarke, the *Geneva Window* (1930), detail of the panels depicting *St Joan* by George Bernard Shaw, *The Demi-gods* by James Stephens, and *Juno and the Paycock* by Sean O'Casey. Published with the permission of The Wolfsonian – Florida International University Miami, Florida

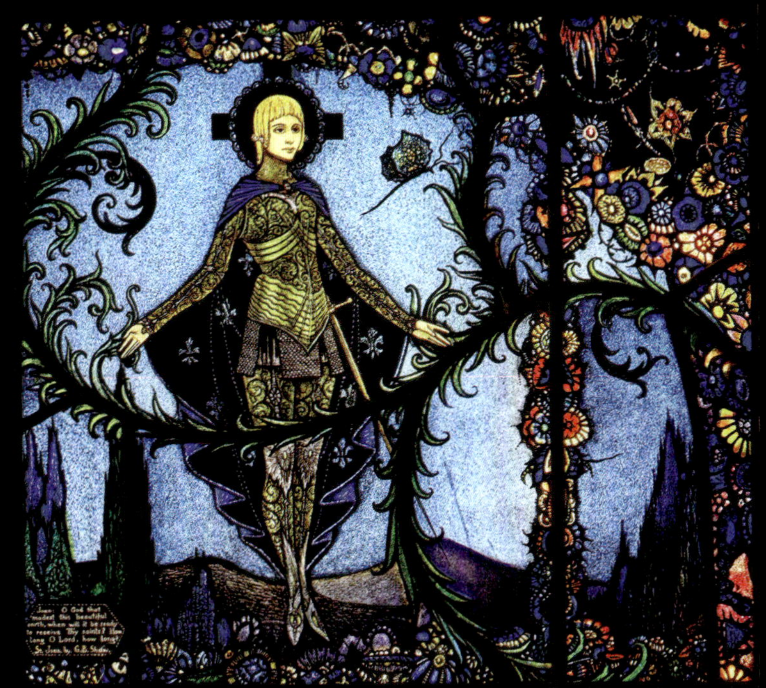
Joan: O God that madest this beautiful earth, when will it be ready to receive Thy saints? How long O Lord, how long?
St. Joan by G.B. Shaw.

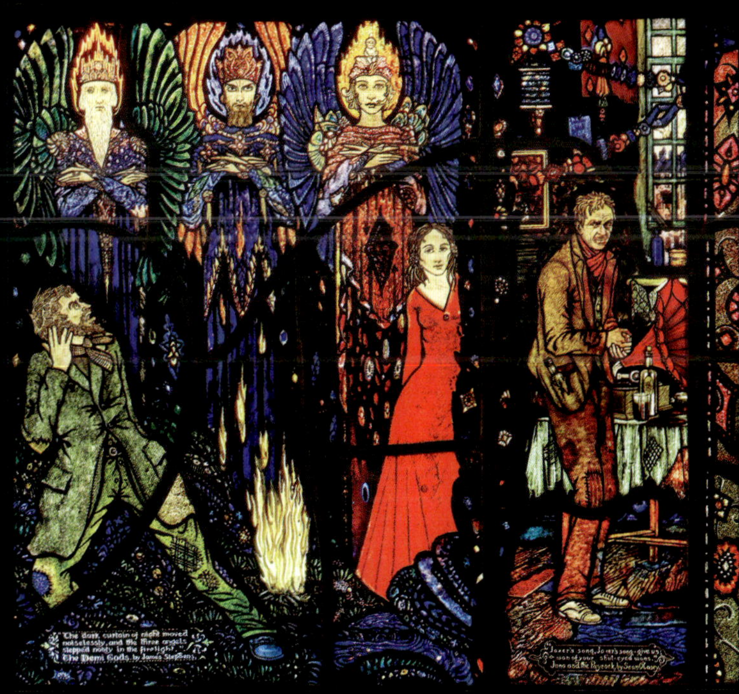
"The dark curtain of night moved noiselessly, and the three angels stepped noddy in the firelight."
The Demi Gods, by James Stephens.
"Joxer's song, Joxer's song - give us wan of your shut-eyed wans."
Juno and the Paycock, by Sean O'Casey.

USA, Massachusetts: Newton Country Day School of the Sacred Heart Chapel, Centre Street, Newton
CHILD, A.E.
St Cecilia 1927 (3 lights)
HEALY, Michael
St Helena 1927 (3 lights) (sketch design, NGI)
St Teresa 1927–8 (3 lights) (sketch design, NGI)
McGOLDRICK, Hubert
Sacred Heart 1927 (rose)
St Margaret Mary 1927 (3 lights)
O'BRIEN, Catherine
St Catherine of Siena 1927 (3 lights)
QUIGLY, Kathleen
St Madeleine Sophie Barat 1927 (3 lights)
RHIND, Ethel
St Catherine of Alexandria 1927 (3 lights)

USA, Michigan: Cranbrook Academy of Art Museum, Woodward Avenue, Bloomfield Hills
HEALY, Michael
St Patrick Lighting the Paschal Fire on the Hill of Slane *c.*1914 (cinquefoil panel) (sketch design, NGI)

USA, Minnesota: University of St Thomas (O'Shaughnessy-Frey Library Center), Summit Avenue, St Paul
WALSH, George Stephen
Medallions depicting vignettes, portraits, crests and symbols 1958
Of the 246 medallions, many were designed and painted by George Stephen Walsh, including ones depicting Science, Alice in Wonderland, Androcles and the Lion; others most likely by Conrad Pickel, at whose studio they were made.

USA, New Jersey: CC (St Vincent de Paul's), Avenue C, Bayonne
CLARKE, Harry
Nine chancel windows depicting angels bearing symbols of the Mass:
The Stole (B) 1929
The Cross (B) 1929
The Thurible (B) 1929
The Wine and Water (B) 1929
The Chasuble (B) 1929
The Maniple (B) 1929
The Candle (B) 1929
The Ciborium (B) 1929
The Book (B) 1929
(preliminary designs, TCD)
KING, Richard
St Joseph and St Vincent de Paul 1934–6 (2 lights)
St Patrick and Blessed Virgin Mary 1934–6 (2 lights)
Mass of Dedication and Solomon's Sacrifice for the Dedication of the Temple 1939–40 (2 lights)
First Communion Mass and the Loaves of Proposition Given to David 1939–40 (2 lights)

USA, New Mexico: Catholic Cathedral of the Sacred Heart, East Green Avenue, Gallup
WALSH, George Stephen
*Bishop Lamy and La Conquistadora c.*1961
Father Anselm Weber and Mother Katharine Drexel *c.*1961
Fray Juan Ramirez and the Mission Church at Acoma *c.*1961
*Fray Marcos de Niza at the Pueblo of Hawikuh c.*1961
(above windows painted by George W. Walsh)

Right:
Peadar Lamb, *Long Day's Journey Into Night, Cré na Cille (The Graveyard Clay)* From a series of five panels (2009) for the Irish Repertory Theatre, New York City. Photographs © Roland Paschhoff

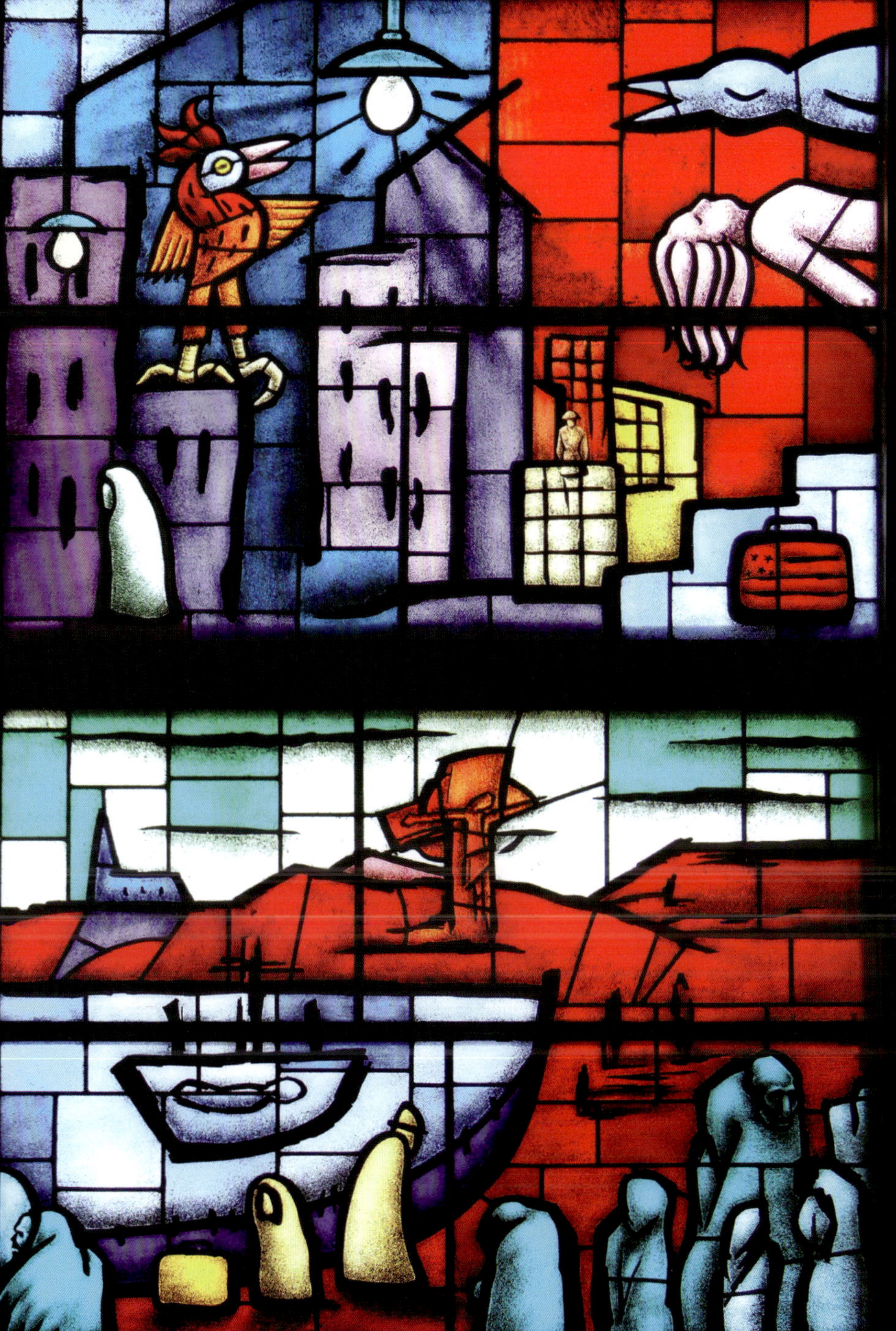

USA, New York: CC (St Vincent Ferrer's), Lexington Avenue, New York City
AN TÚR GLOINE STUDIO
Patron saints of music: Saints Cecilia, Gregory, Dunstan, Caedmon, Odo and Germaine 1932–3 (3 lights)
This large window was executed by An Túr Gloine Dublin, to the design of the American Charles Connick. It was the combined work of A.E. Child, Catherine O'Brien, Michael Healy and Hubert McGoldrick, with Healy as overall supervisor.

USA, New York: Irish Repertory Theatre, West 22nd Street, New York City
LAMB, Peadar
The Stars, Godot, Long Day's Journey Into Night, Cré na Cille (The Graveyard Clay), Imirce (Emigration) 2009 (five panels)

USA, New York: Episcopalian Church (Christ Church), Pelhamdale Avenue, Pelham
ELVERY, Beatrice
Christ Blessing Children 1912 (3 lights)

USA, North Carolina: CC (Our Lady of the Holy Rosary), Main Street, Lexington
POLLEN, Patrick
*Ascension c.*1988 (2 lights on either side of sculpture of Christ) (sketch designs, NIVAL)

USA, North Carolina: CC (Our Lady of Fatima), Link Road, Winston-Salem
POLLEN, Patrick
Nativity 1985–6
Crucifixion 1985–6
Resurrection 1985–6
St Joseph with the Christ Child 1985–6
Blessed Virgin Mary or *Female Saint* 1985–6
Four single lights featuring symbols and text 1985–6

USA, Pennsylvania: Dominican Convent Chapel, Lititz Pike, Lancaster
DOWLING, William
Mysteries of the Rosary Scheme 1954
(Created at Harry Clarke Studios.)

USA, Pennsylvania: Mercersburg Academy Chapel, Mercersburg
HEALY, Michael
Archangel Michael 1926 (sketch design, NGI)

USA, Washington DC: Episcopalian Cathedral (St Peter and St Paul's), Wisconsin Avenue
HONE, Evie
The Raising of the Daughter of Jairus, The Holy Women Leaving the City of Jerusalem to Visit the Tomb of Christ, Noli me Tangere, Christ Appearing to Two of the Disciples on the Road to Emmaus 1953 (2 lights) (sketch design, NGI; cartoons, Hunt Museum, Limerick City)

USA, Wisconsin: Boe Memorial Chapel, St Olaf College, Northfield
WALSH, George Stephen
Creation 1957 (3 lights)
Promise 1957 (3 lights)
Incarnation 1957 (3 lights)
Preparations 1957 (3 lights)
Teachings 1957 (3 lights)
Miracles 1957 (3 lights)
Crucifixion 1957 (3 lights)
Resurrection *1957 (3 lights)
Pentecost 1961 (3 lights)
St Paul 1961 (3 lights)
The Early Church 1961 (3 lights)
Pre-Reformation 1961 (3 lights)
Reformation 1961 (3 lights)
Post-Reformation 1961 (3 lights)
World Mission 1961 (3 lights)
Lutheranism in Latin America 1961 (3 lights)
Transfiguration *c.1957 (5 lights)
(all painted by George W. Walsh)

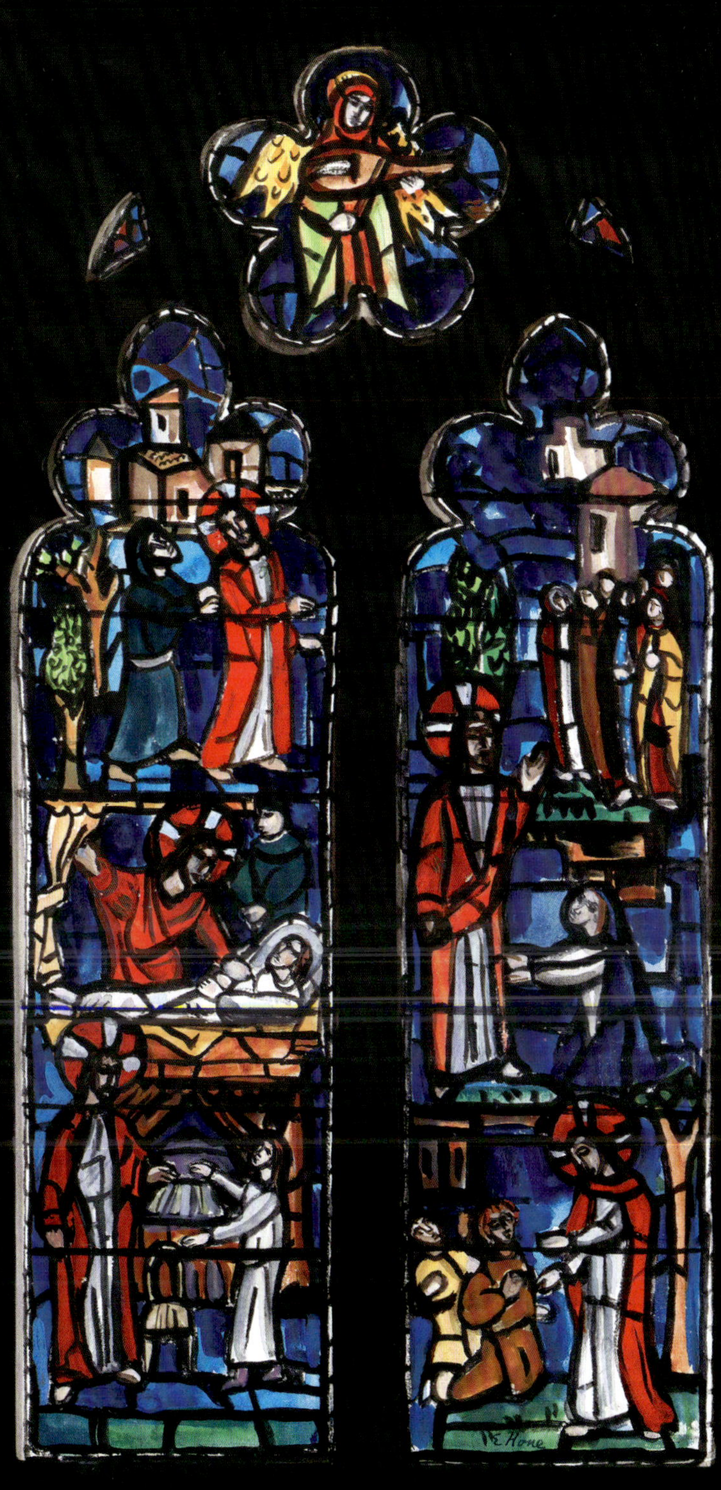

Evie Hone, *The Raising of the Daughter of Jairus, The Holy Women Leaving the City of Jerusalem to Visit the Tomb of Christ, Noli me Tangere, Christ Appearing to Two of the Disciples on the Road to Emmaus* (1953), preliminary pencil and watercolour design for the Episcopalian Cathedral, Washington. Collection NGI. © The Artist's Estate. Photograph © National Gallery of Ireland

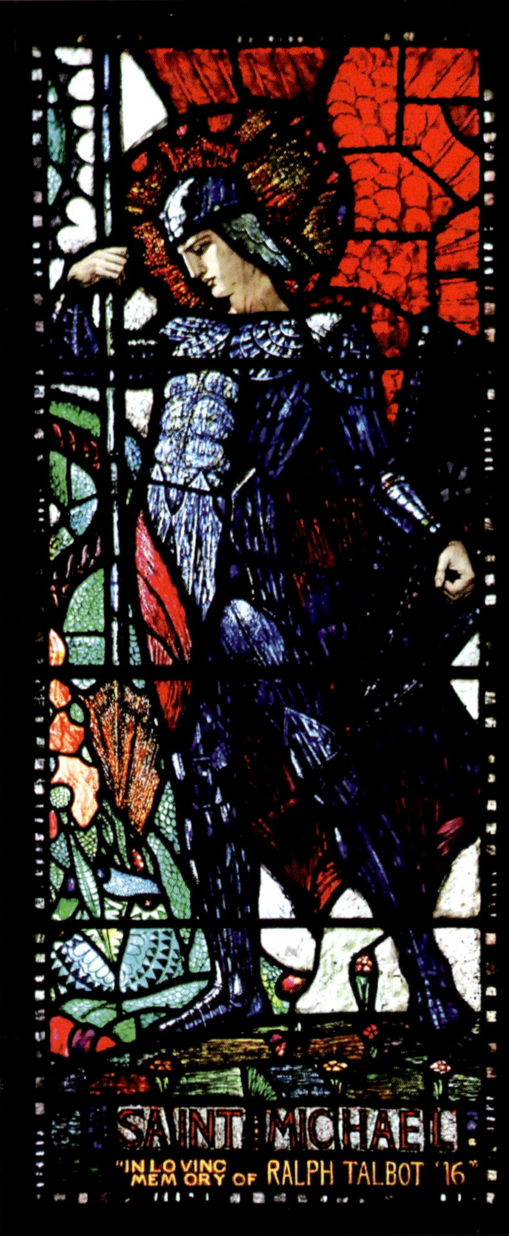

Above: Michael Healy, *Archangel Michael* (1926), Mercersburg Academy Chapel, Mercersburg, Pennsylvania. Photograph courtesy of Mercersburg Academy

USA, Wisconsin: Milwaukee CC (All Saints, formerly St Agnes'), North 25th Street
WALSH, George Stephen
St Agnes c.1961 (painted by George W. Walsh)

USA, Wisconsin: CC (St Mary's), East Washington Avenue, Tomahawk
WALSH, George Stephen
Madonna and Child 1961 (*dalle de verre*, over the entrance, made with George W. Walsh)

USA, Wisconsin: Lutheran Church (Trinity), White Rock Avenue, Waukesha
WALSH, George Stephen
The Institution of the Lord's Supper c.1958–9
Christ Spreading the Gospel Across the World (movable window) c.1958–9
Christian symbols (movable window, composed of seven panels) c.1958–9
Scenes from the Book of Revelation (movable window) c.1958–9
God Created the Heavens and the Earth c.1958–9
God Created Lands, Sea, Vegetation, and the Sun, Moon and Stars c.1958–9
God Created the Fish and Birds, and All Living Creatures of the Land c.1958–9
Satan Led Adam and Eve into Sin c.1958–9
The Flood c.1958–9
Throughout the Ages God Gave Many Promises of a Saviour from Sin c.1958–9
The Birth of Jesus c.1958–9
The Baptism of Christ c.1958–9
Jesus Gathers His Disciples c.1958–9
Jesus's Transfiguration c.1958–9
Jesus Taught the People in Parables c.1958–9
Jesus Performed Many Miracles c.1958–9
Jesus was Crucified for Our Sins c.1958–9
Jesus Conquered Sin and Rose from the Dead c.1958–9
Luther's Seal (back window) c.1958–9
(above windows painted by George W. Walsh)

WALES

Wales, Cardiff: C of E (All Saints), Victoria Square, Penarth
CLARKE, Harry
The Aged Simeon Holding the Infant Christ (B) 1928
St Michael and the Giving of the Laws to Moses, with St Gabriel and the Annunciation (B) 1930 (2 lights) (both windows destroyed in 1941 during Second World War bombing raid)

Wales, Ceredigion: CC (Our Lady of the Angels and St Winefride), Queen's Road, Aberystwyth
KING, Richard
The Assumption 1955

Wales, Ceredigion: C of E (St Peter's), Church Street, Lampeter
GEDDES, Wilhelmina
Christ with St Peter and St Andrew 1943 (3 lights)

Wales, Ceredigion: CC (Church of the Holy Cross), Victoria Street, Aberaeron
KING, Richard
Our Lady of Ireland c.1958

Wales, Conwy: CC (Y Bugail Da), Talybont Road, Llanrwst
MURPHY, Johnny (unidentified NCA student/graduate, supervised by Johnny Murphy)
Abstract window with church symbols 1960 (reconfigured when relocated from Betws-y-Coed CC)
Baptism of Christ 1960 (relocated from Betws-y-Coed CC)
DEENY, Gillian
Madonna and Child c.1960 (relocated from Betws-y-Coed CC)

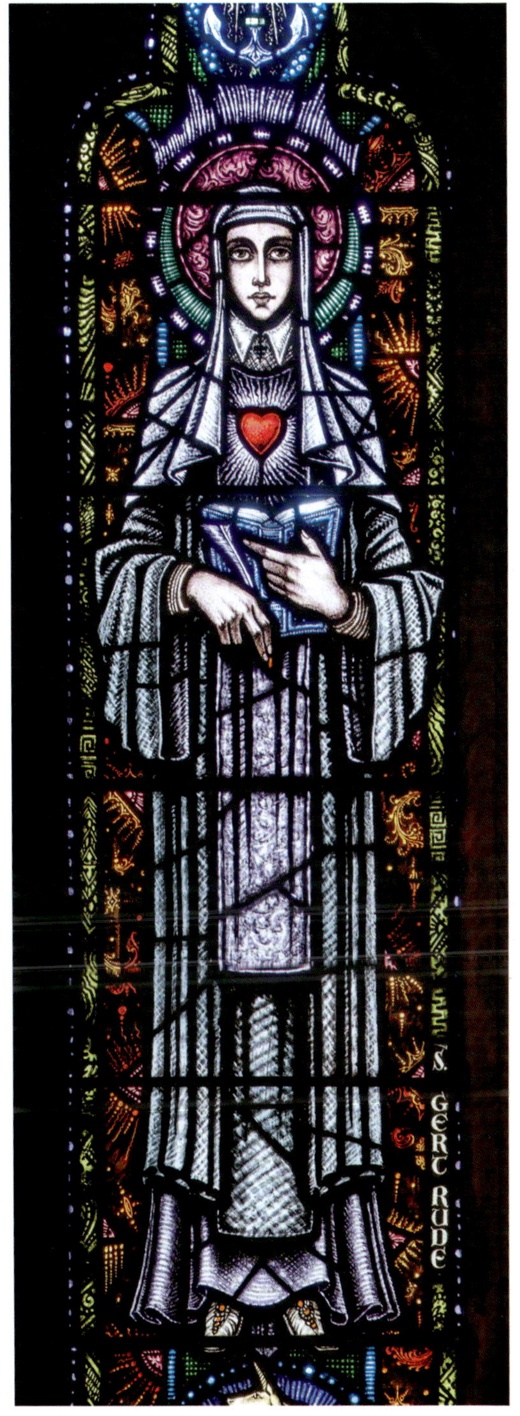

Right: Richard King, detail of *St Gregory and St Gertrude* (1932), Catholic Church (St David's), Monastery Road, Pantasaph, near Holywell, Flintshire, Wales. Photograph © Martin Crampin

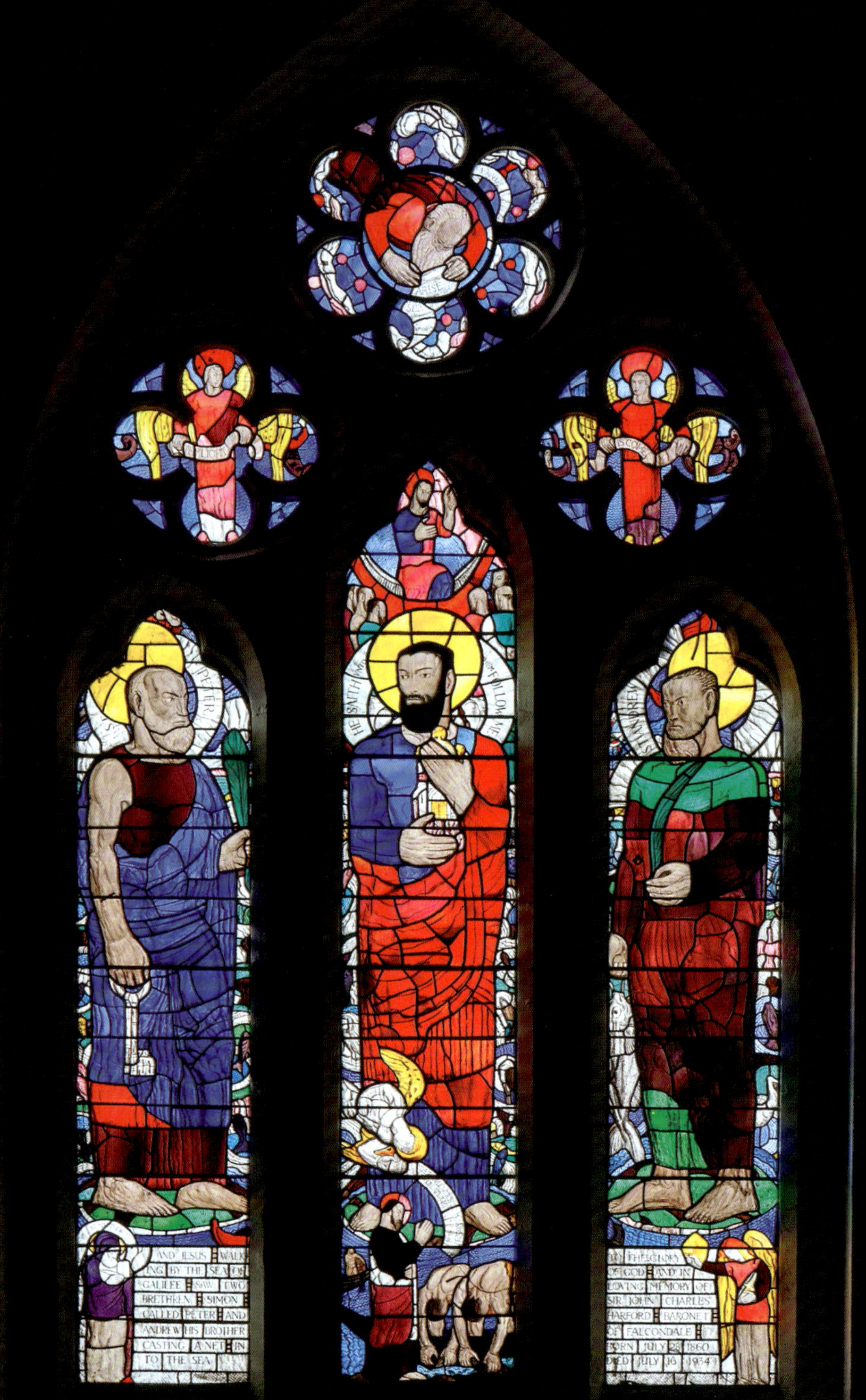
PETER
FOLLOW ME
ANDREW
AND JESUS WALK
ING BY THE SEA OF
GALILEE SAW TWO
BRETHREN SIMON
CALLED PETER AND
ANDREW HIS BROTHER
CASTING A NET IN
TO THE SEA
TO THE GLORY
OF GOD AND IN
LOVING MEMORY OF
SIR JOHN CHARLES
HARFORD BARONET
OF FALCONDALE
BORN JULY 28 1860
DIED JULY 16 1934

Wales, Flintshire: C of E (Emmanuel), Mold Road, Buckley
CHILD, A.E.
Angel of Peace 1929–30

Wales, Flintshire: CC (St David's), Monastery Road, Pantasaph, near Holywell
KING, Richard
St Gregory and St Gertrude 1932 (2 lights)
St Teresa and St Catherine 1933 (2 lights)
(Both created at Harry Clarke Studios.)

ZIMBABWE

Zimbabwe, Harare Province: Ashkenazi Synagogue, Milton Park, Harare
WALSH, George W.
Menorah and *Star of David* *c.*1977
(Two small circular panels created at Abbey Stained Glass Studios.)

Zimbabwe, Harare Province: CC (St Joseph's), Hatfield, Mashonaland East, Harare
CAMPBELL, George
The Crucifixion *c.*1960s
(Created at Abbey Stained Glass Studio; installed in 1990s.)

Zimbabwe, Harare Province: St Anne's Hospital, King George Road, Avondale, Harare
KELLY, Kevin
Immaculate Conception *c.*1995
(Created at Abbey Stained Glass Studios.)

Zimbabwe, Manicaland Province: Catholic Cathedral (Holy Trinity), First Avenue, Mutare
CAMPBELL, George
The Resurrection 1971 (cartoons by George W. Walsh and executed by him in conjunction with George Campbell at Abbey Stained Glass Studios. Bottom section subsequently repaired locally.)
WALSH, George W.
Stations of the Cross 1971 (etched on travertine and executed at Abbey Stained Glass Studios by studio staff)

Left:
Wilhelmina Geddes, *Christ with St Peter and St Andrew* (1943), C of E (St Peter's), Lampeter, Ceredegion. Photograph © Martin Crampin

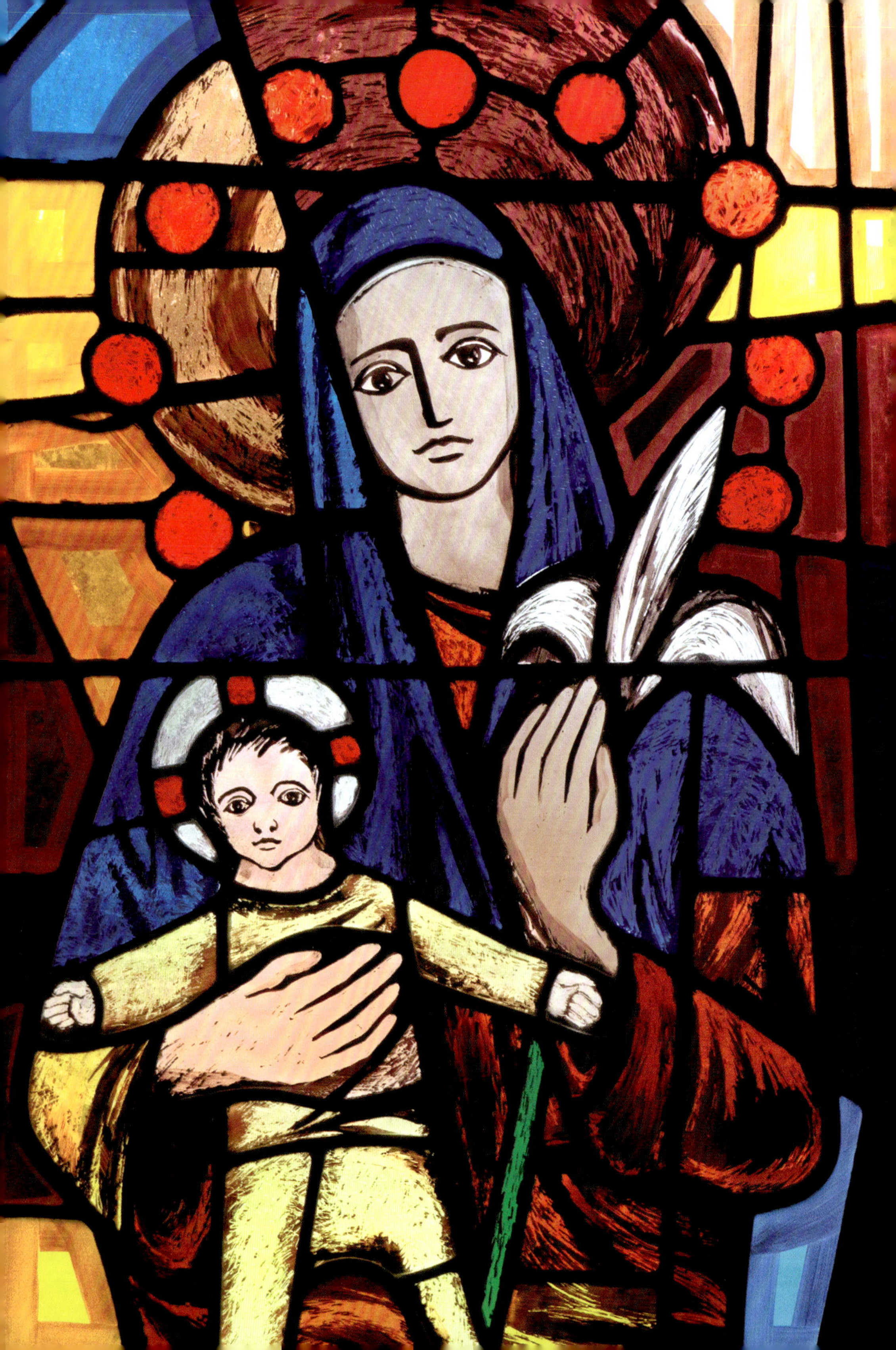

Biographical Notes on Artists

LUA BREEN (b.1942)

David Caron

Lua Breen was born in Dublin and received his secondary education at Newbridge College, County Kildare. A graduate of the National College of Art (NCA, later NCAD), he was awarded a Royal Dublin Society Travelling Scholarship for his stained glass work and his travels brought him to France, Belgium and Germany, studying both historical and contemporary stained glass.

Breen initially developed a career in education, firstly as a secondary school teacher, in both London and Dublin, before being appointed as a lecturer in NCAD, specialising in metal and jewellery. His earliest commissioned work in stained glass dates from 1970 and although he continued to work in the medium, it was only upon taking a sabbatical in 1990 from which he never returned – and moving to rural north Donegal that he had the opportunity to fully develop this aspect of his career, while continuing to produce a smaller output in metal, often cast bronze. Over the next two decades Breen was awarded several major commissions for entire stained glass schemes, often for new-build churches replacing older ones which had been firebombed and destroyed during 'The Troubles'.

Left:
Lua Breen, detail of *Madonna and Child* (1996), Catholic Church (St Brigid's), Derryvolgie, Malone Road, Belfast, County Antrim

Collaborating with highly regarded church architects, such as Richard Hurley, or working for receptive parish priests often allowed Breen considerable scope in choice of theme and imagery. Although at ease creating windows in a more traditional, figurative mode with plenty of painted detail, it is in his non-painted and more abstract ones, such as the large sanctuary window for St Brigid's Church, Belfast, and the accompanying series of two-light windows, all inspired by the *Hallel Psalms*, which bring together a skilfully orchestrated combination of exuberant, often complex lead lines and joyous colour to striking effect. Breen's windows, frequently made up by the Irish Stained Glass Company, Dublin, are distinctive not only for their array of often vivid colours, but also for utilising areas of lighter glass to allow the surrounding landscape – sometimes dramatic as in the case of the Catholic Churches at Holywood and Carnlough – to be glimpsed, thereby connecting the internal and external.

The artist donated small-scale preliminary designs for virtually his entire stained glass output to the National Irish Visual Arts Library (NIVAL), Dublin, in 2019.

❧

PHYLLIS BURKE (b.1930)

David Caron

Phyllis Burke was born in Kildare Town in 1930 and when she was 15 the family moved to Dublin. She began attending the National College of Art as an evening student in 1948 where she studied drawing and painting under Maurice MacGonigal and Seán Keating, and sculpture under Domhnall Ó Murchadha. At weekends she, along with a small group of fellow students, went sketching and painting and it was on one of those occasions in 1950 that she met her future husband, the architect Arthur Gibney.

When Johnny Murphy (later of Murphy-Devitt Studios) began teaching evening classes at the College of Art in 1954, Phyllis was among his early students, and by around 1958 she had embarked on her first stained glass commission, a series of small square Stations of the Cross for a church in rural Nigeria at the behest of an Irish architect. However, before being despatched, two of the stations were exhibited at the *Irish Exhibition of Living Art* in Dublin and those in turn led her to being commissioned by Liam McCormick, the distinguished church architect, to create three windows (1961) depicting Irish saints for the church he was then designing at Milford, County Donegal. Phyllis Burke made her Milford stained glass windows with guidance from Patrick Pollen in the half of An Túr Gloine he was then renting from Catherine O'Brien. That pivotal commission placed her windows in the company of those made by two much more established stained glass artists – Pollen and Patrick Pye. Commissions quickly followed, such as those for chapels at Our Lady's Hospital, Ennis, Our Lady's Bower, Athlone, and an entire scheme for a new chapel attached to the hospital at Drogheda, all of which were made in Pollen's studio.

Church building in Ireland was booming post-Vatican II and Phyllis's experience was that one local commission often led to another, such as her series of windows for several Galway churches. She regularly worked directly with priests, and enduring friendships developed with various diocesan clergy and with members of the Carmelite Order in particular. She also worked for several architects rather than one in particular. Like many stained glass artists of her day, she moved comfortably between abstract leaded windows and highly narrative ones, and everything in between, always responding to the architecture of the location. Many of her windows of the 1960s show evidence of a marked design sensibility and a modernist flavour. From around 1967 she began to share a stained glass studio with the artist Michael Dunne which he had built in the back garden of his family's house in Lennox Street, Dublin.

From 1974 onwards Phyllis worked with one particular glazier, Dermot McLoughlin (who also worked with Frances Biggs), and they teamed up for what was perhaps her best-known commission – a series of twelve single lights (eight of which measure 15.5 ft x 6.5 ft) for the Carmelite Church in Clarendon Street, Dublin. These windows, which appear more painterly and understated than her earlier works, span the years 1990 to 2006. Phyllis also designed two windows for the Carmelite community in Loughrea, County Galway; a window depicting Edith Stein – one of the windows she was most proud of, and a subject she returned to in her Clarendon Street series – and the *Good Shepherd*. After Frances Biggs died in 2006, the Carmelites in Terenure College turned to her to complete the final two windows for their school chapel, figurative single lights depicting the Carmelites as missionaries, and the Carmelites as educationalists.

In addition to working in stained glass, Phyllis Burke also created work in enamel, usually of religious subjects. She donated a substantial collection of preliminary designs and cartoons for windows covering all decades of her career to NIVAL in 2019.

❧

ALFRED ERNEST (A.E.) CHILD (1875–1939)

David Caron

A.E. Child was born in London. As a teenager he began a career as a trainee accountant but spent so much time drawing in the margins of the ledgers that his father was persuaded to allow him to enrol at the Central School of Arts and Crafts instead, winning a scholarship around 1890. Child's next major step was to join Christopher Whall's stained glass studio, most likely as a paid studio assistant. Whall was by then a key figure in the Arts and Crafts Movement, and Child has been described as his 'chief helper' and 'favourite pupil'. While there, Child made something of a name for himself designing decorative plain glazing, and he is also known to have assisted Whall on his magnum opus, a magnificent series of windows for Gloucester Cathedral, begun by the master in 1895.

The year 1901 was a turning point for Child: early in the year he married his childhood sweetheart, Annie Haines, and in October they emigrated to Dublin. The following month their first child was born and the same month he began teaching stained glass classes at the School of Art in Kildare Street. On 1 January 1903 An Túr Gloine, a custom-built stained glass studio at 24 Upper Pembroke Street, formally opened with Child as official manager, and his School of Art students would trail up to the studio with their glass to have it fired in the little gas-fired kiln.

The first entry in the An Túr Gloine work journals was for a two-light apse window, the *Annunciation*, for Loughrea Cathedral, which was designed by Child, though closely adapted from a slightly earlier window by Whall, as was the case with the second and final apse windows. All three were executed by Child with assistance from Michael Healy and Catherine O'Brien. In due course Loughrea Cathedral became a showcase for work by An Túr Gloine artists, including several more by Child himself.

Child's importance in the history of twentieth-century Irish stained glass cannot be underestimated. He was an excellent craftsman, a dedicated and

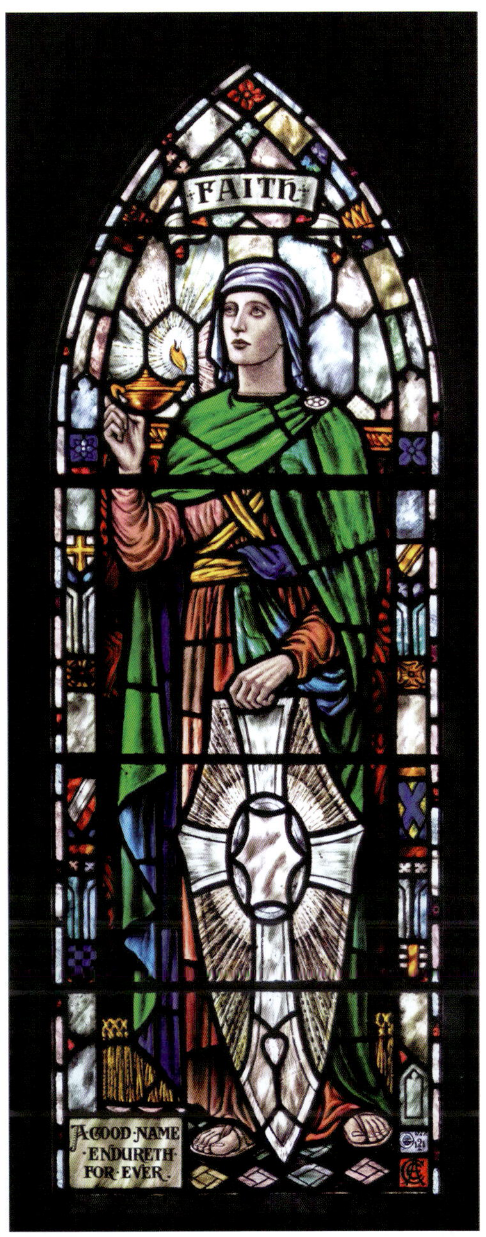

A.E. Child, *Faith* (1921), Church of Ireland (St Beaidh's), near Boyle, County Roscommon

exacting teacher, and was solely responsible for instructing a generation of Irish stained glass artists in the craft, including Harry Clarke, Michael Healy and Wilhelmina Geddes. His teaching principles, his design philosophy and visual aesthetic were all closely derived from his mentor Whall, and he rarely deviated. Like Whall, he had a preference for large areas of pale quarries, loosely matted to diffuse the light, contrasted with rich, deep colours, always using the finest of pot-metal glass. As with Whall, nature was a constant source of inspiration and often, as in Whall's windows, saints were surrounded by frames and canopies of boughs, stalks and leaves, appearing both sinuously organic and highly symmetrical at the same time.

Aside from teaching the craft at the School of Art and managing An Túr Gloine (though Sarah Purser appears to have largely dealt with the clients), Child designed and made around 130 windows during his career in Ireland. Throughout this time his style and technique remained remarkably consistent, though over the decades his formulaic approach to framing saints with organic structures gradually diminished and he correspondingly eschewed deep colours for a brighter palette. Child also introduced elements of Celtic ornamentation, such as strap work designs, in his windows from time to time, as did the other An Túr Gloine artists, and he and his wife received instruction in Irish from Padraig Pearse as he felt it would assist him in writing inscriptions in windows. One of Child's weaknesses was his inability to instil much individual personality or expression into the faces he painted, many having a bland, generic quality to them. Following the Second World War he undertook a significant number of war memorial commissions. These, and allegorical figures generally, suited him as they offered the opportunity to paint idealised, heroic figures, often in suits of armour, which he was adept at rendering, with backgrounds filled with beams of celestial light, something at which he excelled.

The window he thought was his best was also his largest, a five-light (1918) for the Unitarian Church, Dublin which consumed over a year of his life. Featuring five principal figures, including one with children, for whom it's likely his own were the models, five predella panels and extensive tracery, including three rose windows, it represents *Discovery, Truth, Inspiration, Love, and Work*. In many respects it is the detailed predella panels, rather like children's book illustrations, which are the most successful aspects of this monumental work, although one doubts if his mentor Whall, who was against overly pictorial windows ('Keep your pictures for your walls and your windows for the holes in them'), would have fully approved. Another feature of this window are the tiny details throughout, which are barely visible to the human eye but are a delight to discover, including the little colophon of a tower.

Despite failing sight in his latter years, A.E. Child continued designing and painting windows apace, even completing three in his final year, 1939.

❧

HARRY CLARKE (1889–1931)

Nicola Gordon Bowe

Harry Clarke was born on 17 March 1889 in North Frederick Street, Dublin, where his father, Joshua, had set up a stained glass and ecclesiastical decorating business three years earlier. He was educated at Belvedere College but left aged 14 on his mother's death, to help his father in the family business. As a result of this invaluable training, night classes in stained glass at the Metropolitan School of Art in Dublin and a short period in London, he won a scholarship to study full-time at the Dublin School (1911–13) under A.E. Child and in France (1914). The panels which won him the National Competition Gold Medal three years running reveal an accomplished Whall-inspired technique behind a rare gift for imaginative and symbolic expression. The *Judas* (1913) panel, an entirely original and poignantly dramatic interpretation of a medieval theme can be seen as a bridge between the Middle Ages and the

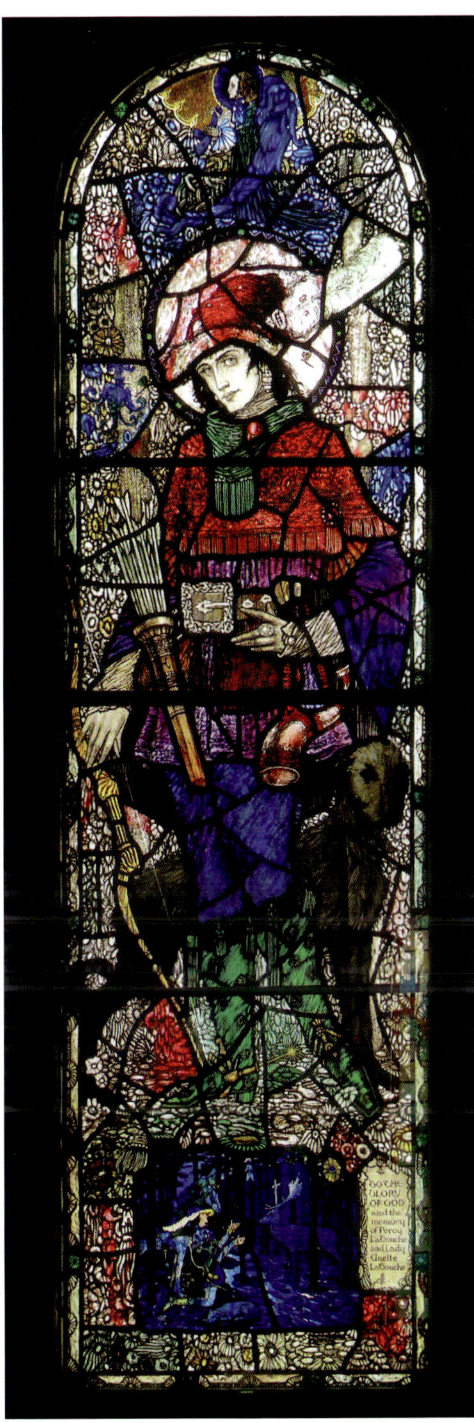

Left:
Harry Clarke, *St Hubert* (1921),
Church of Ireland (St Patrick's),
Carnalway, County Kildare

early twentieth-century Symbolist and Arts and Crafts movements.

His first public commission in stained glass resulted in his eleven windows (1915–17) for the Honan Chapel in Cork, which firmly established his reputation as a young artist of rare technical and imaginative ability; they confirm Ruskin's opinion that 'the true perfection of a painted window is to be serene, intense, brilliant like flaming jewellery, full of easily tangible and quaint subjects and exquisitely subtle yet simple in its harmonies'. At the same time, his black and white and colour illustrations for Hans Christian Andersen's *Fairy Tales* received acclaim. Over the next few years, apart from church windows, he made a unique series of miniature stained glass panels, which combined his fondness for literary illustration, rich colour and microscopic and fantastic detail on a minute scale, such as Synge's 'Queens', Walter de la Mare's 'Song of the Mad Prince', Flaubert's *S. Julien*, Perrault's *Bluebeard*, Shakespeare's *A Midsummer Night's Dream* and Keats's 'Eve of St Agnes'. Although all originally in private collections, the last is now on view in Dublin City Gallery The Hugh Lane. The Geneva Window, depicting scenes from Irish literature, which he made towards the end of his life for the staircase at the League of Nations building in Geneva, has recently been removed from loan exhibition at the same gallery and is at present in storage in London.[1]

By 1921, when his father died and he had to take over the stained glass side of the business, he had already completed a number of windows, completely original and of the highest quality. In Ireland these include *The Nativity* (1918), Castletownshend, West Cork with its inventive treatment of clear quarries; *The Sacred Heart* (1919), Phibsborough, Dublin, partly vandalised when removed to its present position; exquisitely orchestrated war memorials in Killiney (1919) and

Wexford (1919); the monumental and influential *Adoration of the Cross* (1919), Terenure, Dublin; and the dramatically posed *St Hubert* window, Harristown, County Kildare (1921) with its Dürer-inspired predella panel, a superb example of Clarke's intricate aciding technique. Windows in Nantwich, Cheshire (1920) and Sturminster Newton, Dorset (1921), both in England, were well reported in *The Studio*. These windows reveal the principal characteristics of his highly idiosyncratic and already mature style. Elegant, entranced, exquisite saints in richly ornamented and decorated attire, redolent of the Russian ballet and curiously like the most theatrically fashionable clothes today, gaze dreamily through us, as though hypnotised or lost in their own mystical visions. They are surrounded by strong, rich colours and intriguing tiny details which range from the bizarre and macabre to the exquisite and evocative, always impeccably painted and imaginatively realised. Celtic and Japanese art, the Diaghilev ballets, European Symbolism and the tenets of Art Nouveau, the Arts and Crafts movement and proto-Art Deco designers and craftsmen are as much echoed as Brueghel, thirteenth-century stained glass and the Elizabethan icon.

By 1924, under Clarke's inspired direction, the radically improved studios employed twenty-seven men, had moved across the road to two large Georgian houses and were inundated with work, some of it made by him, most of it designed by him and all supervised by him. The superhuman amount of work and responsibility, the constant travelling and deadlines, both for his own and the studios' designs, gradually took its toll on his never very strong constitution. He was always keen to experiment and was particularly excited by amber and blue slab glass, which he incorporated into an abstract window in Kilbride (Eneriley), County Wicklow and a series of four semi-abstract windows in Phibsborough, Dublin (both 1924). Evie Hone showed interest in his treatment of deep blue quarries in his *St Maculind* window (1925) in Lusk, County Dublin. When the pressure of work became too great, he would escape to the Fulham Glass House, where Geddes also worked, and for several years entertained hopes of starting a studio in London. He felt constricted by the demands of most clients (particularly clergy) in Ireland, and longed to do more experimental work on secular windows and panels. Sadly, a number of schemes in England did not materialise.

By 1925 he had done all his best work. In February 1926, on the advice of colleagues at the Glass House, he employed the photographic services of Raines in Ealing to enlarge his small-scale sketches for use as cartoons; this enabled him to turn out more designs, but their execution by the studios lacked his master touch. Later that year, a nearly fatal accident accelerated a general decline in his health, which he valiantly countered by taking on more and more work. Before his 42nd birthday he died of consumption in a Swiss sanatorium. In 1930 the studios had been registered as Harry Clarke Stained Glass Limited. They closed in 1973.

Clarke's own work is easily distinguishable from that of his successors and many imitators. His imagination was magical, fertile, bizarre, his vision frequently microscopic, and the archetypes which flowed from his brush and pen creatures of a fantasy more closely related to European Symbolism than the Celtic Revival. George (Æ) Russell commented in 1925:

> There can be no doubt that Harry Clarke has a genius which manifests itself at its highest in stained glass ... I do not feel the full soul of the artist is manifested until he can let light pour through his design ... I imagine that if one scraped a little the subconscious mind of the artist you would let in a flood of rich colour out of some inner luminous aether, where the fire is more brilliant than the eye can see, and the only way he could recreate that colour for us was by the art he practises. There is not a square inch in these windows which is not invented. Everywhere one looks one sees the creative faculty at work ...

Clarke was a member of the RHA, a vital force and frequent exhibitor in the Irish Arts and Crafts Society, a member of the Guild of Irish Art Workers, a tutor in graphics at the Dublin School of Art and a renowned book illustrator on both sides of the Atlantic. He wrote intelligently about the technique of stained glass and was a versatile graphic artist. He designed posters, advertising booklets, stationery, theatre programmes, bookplates, Christmas cards, handkerchiefs and textiles, was an able caricaturist and painted and designed murals.[2]

1 Subsequent to Nicola writing this biographical note the Geneva Window was sold and is now on display in the Wolfsonian-Florida International University, Miami, Florida, USA.

2 For further reading see G. (Æ) Russell, 'The Work of Harry Clarke', *Irish Statesman*, August 1925; J. White and M. Wynne, *Irish Stained Glass* (Dublin: The Furrow Trust 1963); N. Gordon Bowe, *Harry Clarke*: Monograph and Catalogue of the Exhibition (Dublin: Trinity College, 1979); N. Gordon Bowe, *The Life and Work of Harry Clarke* (Dublin: Irish Academic Press, 1989); N. Gordon Bowe, 'The Miniature Stained Glass Panels of Harry Clarke' *Apollo*, February 1982; N. Gordon Bowe, *Stained Glass*, in the Recent Irish Art series published by the Arts Councils (Belfast and Dublin: 1983); N. Gordon Bowe, 'Harry Clarke: Miniatur-Glasscheiben aus den Jaren 1917–1927', *Weltkunst*, 15 January 1986.

WILLIAM J. DOWLING (1907–1980)

Paul Donnelly

William (Willie) Dowling was born in Dublin and on finishing his secondary education at O'Connell School took up an apprenticeship in the printing trade. His artistic abilities soon became evident and he began classes at the Dublin Metropolitan School of Art in October 1925.

In late 1927, when Harry Clarke sought an assistant artist to help meet the demand for his stained glass work, Austin Molloy recommended Dowling for the position and in January 1928 he started working at the studio.[1] Dowling worked with Clarke, learning the craft of making stained glass according to his standards and design aesthetic. He had the benefit of Harry Clarke's direct instruction for more than a year before ill health forced Clarke to seek medical treatment in Switzerland. One of the first windows Dowling worked on was *St Brendan* (1928), which was designed by Clarke for the Jesuit Retreat House in Rathfarnham.[2] Through the 1930s Dowling worked on a number of important commissions for the Clarke Studios, including *The Sacred Heart Appearing to St Margaret Mary* (1933) for the Sacred Heart Convent on Leeson Street, Dublin,[3] *Crucifixion* (1934) for Puckane Catholic Church, Tipperary, and *Fifteen Mysteries of the Rosary* (1938) for the Dominican Convent, Wicklow.

In 1940 Dowling was appointed manager of the Clarke Studios, a position he held until the company closed in 1973. Throughout this period, in addition to managing the business on a day-to-day basis, he continued to design windows for patrons in Ireland, Britain, Australia, New Zealand, Africa and the United States.[4]

In his role as a principal designer, Dowling was charged with delivering work which was derived from the distinctive artistic legacy left by Harry Clarke. Dowling wrote that the aim of Clarke Studios was to 'avoid the mundane and commonplace. That was the ideal of Harry Clarke and one which we have done our very best to follow.'[5]

Dowling travelled to France a number of times to visit the cathedrals of Chartres, Bourges, Rouen and Paris, and while he strove to retain the original ideals of medieval stained glass, he imbued his later work with a contemporary sensitivity, producing designs which could be described as 'modern traditional' in style. While the majority of his work was in that style, he also produced work which included more modern elements, such as in his three-light *St Gabriel* (1955) in St Gabriel's Church, Clontarf, Dublin, and his *Mysteries of the Rosary* scheme (1954) for the

Dominican Convent Chapel, Lancaster, Pennsylvania.

Dowling was a strong advocate for the Irish stained glass industry, recognising its potential for employment and enhancing the country's cultural image all over the world. He continued to work as a freelance artist after the Clarke Studios closed. Among his finest works in this period was three lights for St Colman's Church on Inishbofin, *Miraculous Draft of Fishes*, *Madonna Queen of Heaven* and *Christ Calming the Storm* (1977). He also completed commissions for St Mary's Mausoleum, Sacramento, California and the Church of St Thomas Aquinas, St Lucia, Brisbane.

1 Molloy, a good friend of Harry Clarke, replaced him as teacher at the Metropolitan School of Art when Clarke could not keep up both his teaching and business commitments.
2 Relocated to the Catholic Church, Tullamore, County Offaly.
3 *Sacred Heart Appearing to St Margaret Mary* (1933) was subsequently transferred to the Catholic Cathedral, Cavan.
4 The design duties for the majority of new commissions were divided between Dowling and Harry Clarke's nephew, Terence (Terry) Clarke.
5 TCD MS6028.

❧

BEATRICE ELVERY (1883–1970)

David Caron

Beatrice Moss Elvery was born in Dublin into a comfortably off artistic family. Following after her mother and aunt (Phoebe Traquair, a leading light in the Scottish Arts and Crafts movement), she started attending classes at the Dublin Metropolitan School of Art and over the next eight years won many prestigious awards, mostly for life drawing and modelling. By 1904 she was tutoring at the School of Art, illustrating children's books, drawing dissections for doctors and archaeological finds, and it was around this time that Sarah Purser – who had provided her with a little corrugated-iron studio in the yard of An Túr Gloine in which to do her sculpture – suggested she enrol in A.E. Child's stained glass classes at the School of Art.

In her autobiography, *Today We Will Only Gossip*, Beatrice Elvery recounted her life at An Túr Gloine: 'I became an employee of the stained glass studio [in late 1904] at a wage of ninepence an hour. I put away my clay and my modelling stands and used my tin studio as a place for drawing cartoons on windows; all the other parts of window-making I did in the large Stained Glass Studio across the yard ... As we were being paid by the hour there was a lot of "going slow" in the cutting and glazing part of the shop ... I worked so fast that Sarah Purser decided to pay me by the job. Otherwise I only got about a quarter of the pay of the other artists. If I was having a window cut I kept the cutter so hard at work that he would cry "You're turning this place into a blooming sweated industry ..."'

Beatrice Elvery's capacity for draughtsmanship, particularly of older male faces, is evident in *Christ Among the Doctors* (1907) for St Stephen's Church of Ireland, Mount Street, Dublin. Again this skill and her ability to capture emotion and humanity can be seen in her window of the following year, the *Good Samaritan and the Prodigal Son* for Tullow Church of Ireland, Carrickmines, County Dublin, which she considered to be among her two best works. Tullow Church was the Elvery family's parish church and it also holds a bronze lectern by her, a carved oak prie-dieu she designed, and her final stained glass window, a war memorial, created in 1919–20.

Elvery's other favourite stained glass work was her three-light of 1910 for the tiny Catholic Church on Tory Island, which features two scenes from the life of St Columba and, in the centre, a Crucifixion; rich colours in the three panels contrasting with plenty of pale milky quarries seem to sit well in this island location. Also in 1910 she designed a huge rose window

Right:
Beatrice Elvery, detail of *The Prodigal Son and the Good Samaritan* (1908), Church of Ireland (Tullow Church), Carrickmines, County Dublin

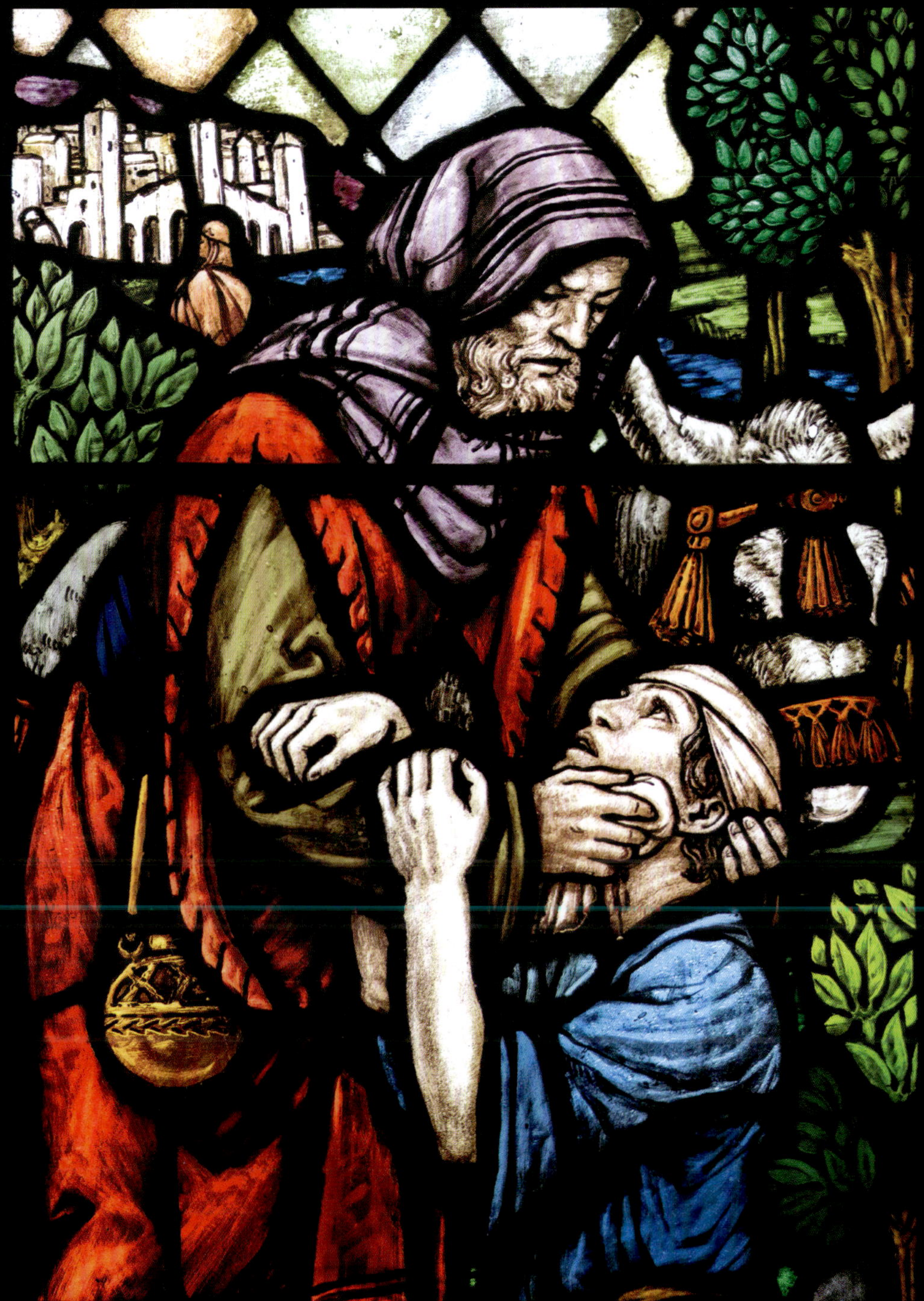

for Letterkenny Cathedral depicting nine scenes from the life of St Colmcille with additional tracery. In it, as in several others over the following years, her natural talent as an illustrator comes to the fore, though as she remarked about her windows generally, perhaps in a somewhat self-deprecating manner, 'They are rather like coloured illustrations to a child's book. I never got the right feeling for glass or the detached, austere quality necessary for ecclesiastical work.'

In 1912 Elvery was commissioned to undertake a three-light window for the Episcopalian Church, Pelham, New York, by a family descended from the patriot Robert Emmet; it was to be the first of many An Túr Gloine commissions for the United States, though her only overseas one. Only located recently, it depicts Christ blessing children and, like her window for Tory, incorporates plenty of pale quarries, offsetting the colourful pictorial elements. The year 1912 was also the year Beatrice Elvery married and moved to London with her barrister husband, Gordon Campbell, later Second Baron Glenavy. At that point, with the exception of the memorial window for her childhood parish church and one other, Beatrice Elvery ceased to work in the medium, though over an intense eight-year career in stained glass she had managed to create about twenty-seven windows and a number of small domestic panels.

Two children later, in 1917 she and Gordon returned to Dublin, though life was not easy; both her father-in-law and her husband were targets in the Civil War and their own newly acquired home, 'Clonard' in Kimmage, was razed. In 1934, by now styled Lady Glenavy, she was elected an Academician of the RHA, which coincided with the beginning of the final phase of a richly creative and diverse career; she then focused on painting and developed a unique surrealist style, often featuring still-life compositions or stylised figures in Arcadian landscapes.

WILHELMINA MARGARET GEDDES

(1887–1955)

Nicola Gordon Bowe

Wilhelmina Margaret Geddes, the eldest of four children, was born at Drumreilly, County Leitrim on 25 May 1887, when her father was working as a site engineer with the Sligo and Leitrim Railway. The family soon moved back to Belfast (where he set up on his own as a building contractor) and where she attended the Methodist College and, from the age of 16, the Belfast Art School, where she was awarded many prizes for her drawing, watercolour and graphic illustration. From 1910 she also attended Orpen's classes at the Metropolitan School of Art in Dublin and that year exhibited an illustration of *Cinderella and an Ugly Sister* at the Arts and Crafts Society's Fourth Exhibition. Sarah Purser was so struck by this work that she suggested Wilhelmina take up stained glass and invited her to join An Túr Gloine. Her first panel, made at the Belfast School in 1911, depicted a conventional *Sir Walter Raleigh,* but the three panels illustrating *The Life of St Colman MacDuagh* made later that year from the Pembroke Street studio for Sarah Purser (now in Dublin City Gallery The Hugh Lane) reveal a deeply coloured, brooding, flickering, expressionist line in an entirely original style, reminiscent of El Greco, if anyone. In 1911 she was awarded a travelling scholarship to London from Belfast, much of which she spent in the British Museum.

Her first window, *The Angel of the Resurrection* (1912) at Inishmacsaint, County Fermanagh, shows her successfully working on a large scale, with a commanding central figure dramatically positioned; details such as the lantern illuminating the ominous scene above and the Whall-inspired semi-abstract symbolic quarries beneath, where clear glass is ingeniously painted and juxtaposed with tiny squares of distinctively bright colour, would recur throughout her work. Nearby at Monea, her next window, *Innocence in Paradise* (1913), is much closer to the Whall school, except for the small, mysterious

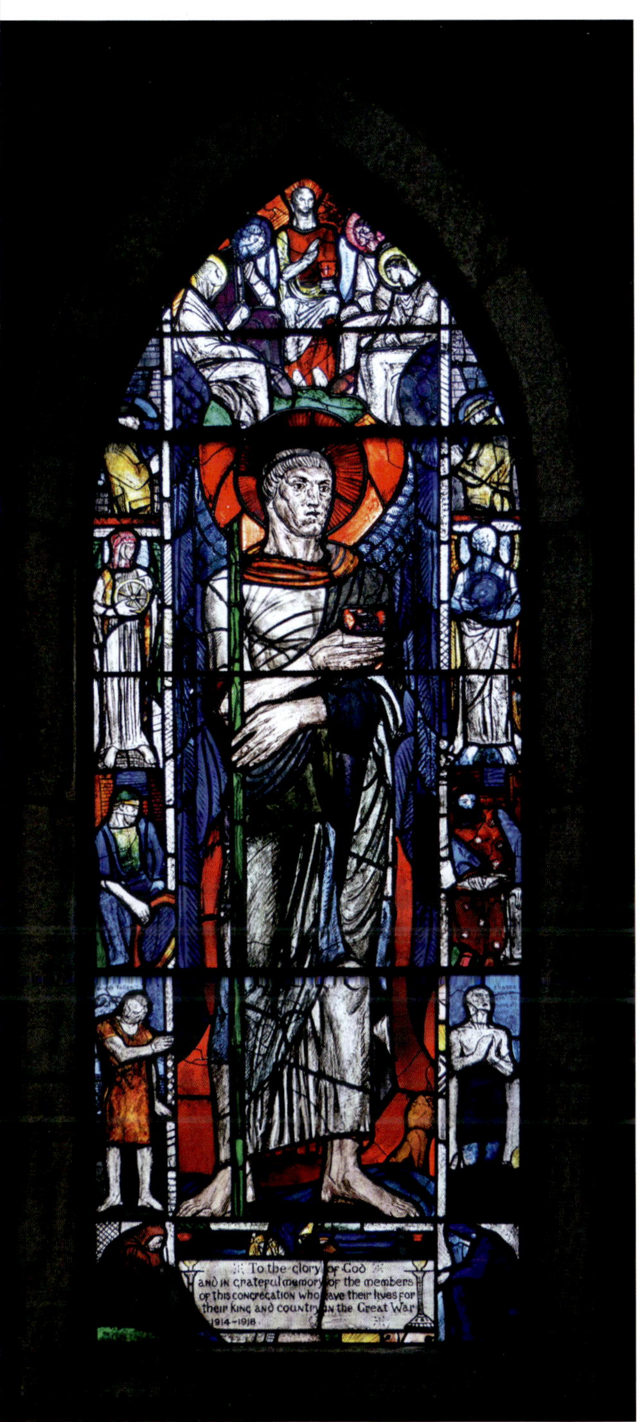

entombment beneath. Next year, her *Charity* window in St Ann's Church of Ireland, Dawson Street, Dublin and *Faith, Hope and Charity* window in Townsend Street, Belfast are more conventional than the lilting, attenuated, draped figures she would develop from archaic and medieval sculpture and set in richly patterned symbolic settings, for example in Karori Crematorium Chapel, Wellington, New Zealand and Southport, Lancashire (both 1914). That year she went on one of Sarah Purser's trips to French cathedrals. Her *St Peter Preaching to the Jews* (1914–15) in Rathgar, Dublin and *Parables* window (1916) for Belfast's Presbyterian Assembly Hall reveal her powerful drawing and a deeply spiritual and solemn intensity, alleviated by intriguing details lurking in the borders around the principal figures.

> She had a gift for the simple rendering of essential action which seems to have come straight from the Middle Ages ... Miss Geddes, like so many women artists, matured quickly and even her early work has in its detail the strong expressive drawing, the power of simplifying without loss of meaning, which remains her chief characteristic (Stephen Gwynn).

Her *Archangel* windows (1918) in Blackrock, County Dublin and *St Michael* (1918) in

Left:
Wilhelmina Geddes, *St Gabriel* (1920), Church of Ireland (All Saints), Carysfort Avenue, Blackrock, County Dublin

St Ann's, Dawson Street, Dublin mark her artistic maturity, characterised by an entirely original choice and treatment of the most beautiful, unusual colour harmonies and her stylised, elemental, almost defiant figures. These, usually draped in wet folds, are ideally suited to stained glass in their timeless but strangely modern depiction. A commission from the Duke of Connaught to commemorate members of his staff killed in the Great War by a three-light window in Ottawa drew considerable attention to both her work and An Túr Gloine. The window was greatly admired on exhibition in London at the Glass House before its dispatch to Canada in 1919. The hauntingly beautiful *Leaves of The Tree were for the Healing of the Nations* (1920) in the Malone Road, Belfast, composed of small figures in a rich tapestry of tiny pieces of deeply glowing colour, contrasts dramatically with the last two windows she made at An Túr Gloine – the monumental Wallsend *Crucifixion* (1922), whose brooding figures seem intent on bursting their architectural confines, and the smouldering *Patrick and Columba* (1923) for Larne, County Antrim. The menacing *St Brendan* she designed for the 1924 British Empire Exhibition at Wembley eventually had to be made by Michael Healy and Ethel Rhind (Sarah Purser later had it installed in Curraun Church near Achill Island, County Mayo). She had officially left An Túr Gloine in 1922, following a protracted period of ill health which was to persist throughout her life. Three years later she moved to London, where she rented a studio in the Fulham Glass House and lived in lodgings. The first window she made from London, a three-light *St Christopher* (1926) for Laleham in Middlesex is arguably her greatest – inventive, affecting and entirely unprecedented from a technical, design and iconographical standpoint. Her Wallasey *Psalm 100* window (1935), on a much larger scale, shows her skill at manipulating light and handling a number of small figures in a powerfully unified composition. Every window she made reveals her skill and profoundly spiritual expressive power. Her angular, tubular figures, with wistful disturbed expressions became increasingly sinewy and monumental; her lead lines and brushwork simpler, looser and more intent on bringing to life larger pieces of glass in smouldering, ardent colours. Her massive, even titanic figures, painted in a cubistic, sometimes deceptively washy manner, bear comparison with the work of such European glass artists as Georges Desvallières.

Although her windows are still to be found in Ireland, England, Wales, New Zealand, Canada and Belgium, too many have been destroyed, neglected or ignored. She is one of the very few artists who instinctively understood the importance of a schematic approach if a window was intended to be seen from a height or distance and on any scale. She was a totally dedicated craftswoman. Gwynn has remarked how, 'not content to indicate to the workmen "ruby", "violet" or the like, she herself picks out every piece and fixes on it the section of the cut line design'. Her skill, craftsmanship, energy, originality, artistry and powerful imagination remain unparalleled even today and she is now beginning to receive long overdue attention from a wider circle than those who worked with her or knew her and hold her work in the greatest admiration. She died after prolonged ill health on 10 August 1955.[1]

1 For further reading see Gwynn, S., 'The Art of Miss W.M. Geddes', *Studio*, October 1922; Bowe, N.G., 'Wilhelmina Geddes' *Stained Glass* (Journal of the Stained Glass Association of America), vol. 76, no. 1, Spring 1981; Cormack, P., *Women Stained Glass Artists of the Arts and Crafts Movement*: Catalogue of the Exhibition (London 1985); Bowe, N.G., *The Dublin Arts and Crafts Movement 1885–1930*: Catalogue of the Exhibition (Edinburgh 1985); Bowe, N.G., *Catalogue of the Centenary Exhibition of Wilhelmina Geddes (1875–1955)* (Belfast 1987); Bowe, N.G., 'Wilhelmina Geddes', *Irish Arts Review*, vol. 4, no. 3, Autumn 1987; Bowe, N.G., *Wilhelmina Geddes: Life and Work* (Dublin: Four Courts Press, 2015).

MICHAEL HEALY (1873–1941)

David Caron

Michael Healy was born in a Dublin tenement house and as a child was noted for sitting apart and drawing incessantly; by 14 he was out earning a livelihood. Following a brief stint as a part-time student at the Dublin Metropolitan School of Art, Healy's deep religious faith led him to present himself as a postulant lay-brother at the Dominican noviciate in Tallaght, Dublin. He only stayed for a limited period and rarely spoke about it afterwards. He then re-enrolled at the School of Art, where he remained a part-time student for three years, and at that stage he was considering a career in book illustration. Healy's first stroke of good fortune was when the benevolent editor of a fledgling Dominican publication, the *Irish Rosary*, offered him illustration work and then sponsored him to live in Florence for eighteen months arranging for him to undertake further illustrations and copying work while there. In Florence, Healy attended the Life School of the Accademia di Belle Arti though more importantly it was the exposure to Italian Renaissance painting while there which was to have a lifelong, recurring influence on his artistic development.

Returning to Ireland in spring 1901 Healy was appointed art master at Newbridge College, County Kildare, a role to which he was ill-suited and he left. His second stroke of good fortune was to be recommended – due to his drawing prowess – by the sculptor John Hughes to Sarah Purser when she was seeking her first recruits for An Túr Gloine. It was not until January 1903, with the official opening of the studio, that Healy's career really got underway; he was then in his 30th year and was about to discover his true vocation as an artist in stained glass.

For his first two years at An Túr Gloine Healy executed or assisted in the execution of thirteen windows; in the majority of these he assisted in the painting of windows which had been designed by Purser or A.E. Child. The first window designed and painted entirely by Healy, *Simeon* (1904), demonstrates his finely honed drawing ability and his natural affinity for the craft that would ensure he would soon eclipse his instructor (Child) and his peers.

In 1909, having undertaken mainly small single-light windows, Healy was assigned a large four-light window for the Church of Ireland, Rathmines, Dublin, which can be seen as the culmination of his first six years as a maturing stained glass artist. However, this was quickly eclipsed by his five-light of the following year, the *Convention of Drum Ceat* for Letterkenny Cathedral, with its heightened palette and panoramic cast of nearly thirty figures, all with richly expressive faces. By now he was regularly employing the 'aciding' technique to create a jewel-like affect, not dissimilar to Harry Clarke, which allowed windows to sparkle and come to life as the external lighting conditions changed.

In 1916, though somewhat interrupted by the Easter Rising, he created his impressive three-light for the chapel of Clongowes Wood College, County Kildare, which depicts three incidents – all nocturnal scenes – from St Joseph's life which occurred around the time of Christ's birth. It was only on the conclusion of the First World War that war memorial windows were commissioned from An Túr Gloine in significant numbers, and it was mainly Healy and Child who specialised in this genre. Between 1918 and 1921 Healy designed twelve windows and half of these were war memorials, probably the finest of which were for the Church of Ireland, Castlecomer, County Kilkenny, and a variant which he created for the Church of England, Wallsend.

The year 1923 saw Healy create two windows (for the Church of Ireland, Donore Avenue, Dublin and the Catholic Church, Bridge a Crinn, County Louth), both of which show how he excelled at creating single-light windows which combined principal figures with multiple vignettes; windows which have impact from a distance but also draw the viewer in for close inspection in order to relish the beguiling details and narrative content. Another window for Donore Avenue Church, *St Victor* (1930), incorporates many small scenes depicting episodes relating to the parish's history spanning several centuries, and ranks among his finest.

By this time an interest in Byzantine art had emerged and can be seen in his *Tu Rex Gloriae, Christe* (1929–30) and *Our Lady Queen of Heaven* (1933), both for Loughrea Cathedral, the latter a sumptuous symphony of pinks and mauves created by two layers of flashed glass plated together with extensive aciding. A few years later his style had evolved further, using stronger black outlines, almost in the manner of woodcuts, faces often depicted in profile as can be seen in his majestic four-light, *St Augustine and St Monica* (1934–5) for John's Lane Church, Thomas Street, Dublin.

Between 1936 and 1941, the year of Healy's death, he executed nine windows and a few small panels. Some of these, particularly the larger works, took as long as four years. There were two overseas commissions, for New Zealand and Arizona, the others comprising three distinct sets: a pair of three lights, the *Ascension* and *Last Judgement* for Loughrea; a pair of two lights for Blackrock College Chapel (a homage to Fra Angelico); and a trio of two lights for Clongowes. All nine of these windows number among the finest he executed in a stained glass career that spanned thirty-nine years. However, the two that stand out are those for Loughrea, which are stunning in terms of technique and dramatic interpretation.

In addition to his stained glass career, Healy was a habitual recorder, in rapid pencil and watercolour impressions, of Dublin street characters going about their daily business, often done on his lunch break from An Túr Gloine. He also painted in oil, both portraits and landscapes of the surrounding Dublin countryside and mountains, though he only very rarely exhibited.

A fairly solitary character, Michael Healy developed a close bond based on mutual regard with the much younger Evie Hone, whom he worked alongside in An Túr Gloine. In his private life he was fortunate to find a sympathetic landlady with whom he was to develop a deep and loving relationship which endured for close to thirty-five years up to his death in hospital from pneumonia in 1941.

❧

EVIE HONE (1894–1955)

Joseph McBrinn

Evie Hone is unique in the history of modern Irish stained glass in that she did not descend from the revival of stained glass that flowered as part of the Gothic Revival and the Arts and Crafts movement. She trained as a painter and became a pioneer of abstract art before embarking on a career in stained glass, aged 38, without any formal training. She was born on 22 April 1894 into an affluent Dublin family that had come to Ireland from Flanders in the seventeenth century. They were well-known merchants, manufacturers and maltsters, and widely accomplished in the arts. In 1906, just before her 12th birthday, Hone contracted a viral infection, later diagnosed as poliomyelitis (infantile polio), which initially left her completely paralysed and subsequently with life-changing disabilities in both legs and her right arm. Hone's mother had died shortly after her birth and when her father died in 1908 she was sent to London for treatment. From early on she had expressed a keen interest in art and in 1912 she enrolled at the Byam Shaw School of Art. Although she excelled at designing 'compositions', her great epiphany did not come until 1914 when she travelled to Italy. Profoundly moved by the emotion and empathy embodied in the volumetric forms and pure, prismatic colours of medieval art, she became determined to forge a career as an artist.

In 1917, she moved to the Central School of Arts and Crafts and came under the influence of Bernard Meninsky. She also studied briefly with Walter Sickert at the Westminster School of Art, where she met fellow Dubliner, Mainie Jellett. In the autumn of 1920, following Meninsky's advice, Hone went to Paris. Initially, along with Jellett, she enrolled in the studio of André Lhote, who encouraged his students to absorb the lessons of Cubism but not abandon representation entirely, often sending them to study Old Masters in the Louvre. All this felt routinely academic, as Hone was more interested in the radical ideas emanating from Cubism such as pictorial flatness, simultaneity of viewpoints, the dynamic exploration of space, time and rhythm and the repudiation of subject matter. She and Jellett left to work under Albert Gleizes, a utopian theoretician as much as a painter, who had been one of the earliest proponents of Cubism. Aside from adhering to Gleizes's austere method of 'translation and rotation', Hone's abstract paintings of the 1920s and 1930s show a marked fascination with strong, sonorous colours and simplified, modulated forms that betray her interest in the Italian Primitives but, also, increasingly in the medieval stained glass she encountered at Chartres, outside Paris, and earlier in the collection of the Victoria and Albert Museum in London.

By 1932 she had started to work out ideas of her own for glass, but when she approached Sarah Purser about the possibility of joining An Túr Gloine she was rejected as untrained. Purser advised her to enrol in A.E. Child's class at the Dublin Metropolitan School of Art. She duly registered, but Child thought little of her sketch of a Cubist-inspired still life and discouraged her from making it into a panel. Encouraged by two of the most brilliant contemporary stained glass artists, Wilhelmina Geddes in London, who taught Hone basic techniques, and Richard Roland Holst in Amsterdam, who voiced admiration for her ability and originality, she completed her first window. This single light, depicting *The Annunciation* flanked by Romanesque-inspired abstract patterns, all in smoulderingly dark ruby reds, inky blues and pink golds, was installed in St Nahi's, Dundrum, Co. Dublin (1933–4). Its success earned Hone her first commission and in need of a studio to work, and a kiln to fire glass, she returned to An Túr Gloine where Purser reluctantly admitted her. Her subsequent windows show the progressive development of a monumentalism and primitivism akin to that of other contemporary 'medieval modernists', especially the French painter Georges Rouault. Like Rouault, Hone's work was often described as possessing the sincerity, humility and religious feeling of 'medieval humanism'. Devout and spiritual, she converted to Roman Catholicism in 1939. In the same year she completed a window to represent Ireland at the New York World's Fair. *My Four Green Fields* measured 21ft by 9ft and was an astonishingly bold matrix of abstract symbols.

However, it was on the success and strength of her equally audacious windows for Irish churches (Clongowes; Tullabeg; Kingscourt) that Hone was awarded the prestigious commission for the new east window of the fifteenth-century chapel at Eton College (1949–52). It comprised nine lights, measured 50ft in height and contained 1,000 square feet of glass. Hone broke its soaring perpendicular mullions into two planes, the upper depicting *The Crucifixion*, and the lower *The Last Supper*, flanked by 'figures of priestly sacrifice' and symbols of the 'miracles and parables'. From early on Hone seemed especially attuned to the graphic possibilities of lead calmes and understood that glass should only 'be employed in accordance with its nature and capacity'. She wrote that the 'radiance and beauty' of the work of the twelfth and thirteenth centuries was the 'standard' to which all modern stained glass artists must aspire. She rejected Ruskin's description of stained glass as 'flaming jewellery', countering that the purpose of a stained glass window 'is primarily not to represent something but to arrange forms and colours in such a way as will produce an effect of beauty, a living organism with rhythm and balance and not a chaotic juxtaposition of brilliant scintillating colour like jewelled stones'. Hone's approach and technique were deceptively simple. She avoided aciding and plating as well as detailed and decorative painting, and used large pieces of glass to construct a design of interlocking panels of pure colour. It is generally believed that she turned to stained glass as she tired of non-representational art, but she exploited and delighted in the abstract potential of glass. She continued to align with the avant-garde and to produce and exhibit non-figurative painting after she started working with glass. Subsequently, she positioned stained glass where it was rarely seen, such as in the venues of the innovative exhibition societies to which she belonged. She had been a founder member of the Irish Exhibition of Living Art in 1943, for instance, and regularly showed her stained glass there.

By the 1940s Hone had also begun to make drawings after medieval Irish stone carvings in churches and other monastic sites, as well as from high crosses and penal crucifixes. Her friend Derek Hill commented: 'In some ways the finding of these Celtic stones, after her researches among the Primitives, Chartres and Rouault, which led up to them in natural sequence, seem to have crystallised the various elements of her work.' In 1944, when An Túr Gloine closed, she opened a studio in her home at Marlay in Rathfarnham, County Dublin. Friends and visitors described her as indefatigable, as 'a dynamo of activity' who possessed an astonishing 'appetite for work'. It is estimated that she 'carried out some forty-eight commissions consisting of 112 lights or separate openings together with upwards of 150 domestic panels'. She trained no pupils, but her influence on the post-war generation of stained glass artists was pronounced. After her death a major retrospective exhibition of her work was mounted in Dublin and London.

❧

RICHARD KING (1907–1974)

Ruth Sheehy

Richard Joseph King was born in Castlebar, County Mayo, on 7 July 1907 and was educated by the Christian Brothers in Westport. Having moved to Dublin in 1927, King enrolled at the Dublin Metropolitan School of Art to study life drawing with Seán Keating and design/illustration with Austin Molloy. The latter artist, who recognised King's talents in draughtsmanship, arranged for him to meet Harry Clarke. King entered the stained glass studios of Joshua Clarke & Sons in March 1928, where he became apprenticed to Harry Clarke from 1928–30 and began his career in stained glass. After Clarke's death in January 1931, King became principal designer and later manager of the Harry Clarke Stained Glass Studios from 1935–40. The influence of Harry Clarke on Richard King's artistic formation was pivotal for his development in the medium of stained glass and in religious art which had integrity. Colour symbolism, iconography, design, decoration and the Celtic Revival were all part of this training from Clarke which stood to King for the remainder of his career. Apart from the religious stained glass windows and Stations of the Cross in opus sectile mosaic made of opal glass which King designed during the period 1930–40, while in the Clarke Studios, another salient secular work is the *Kevin Barry Memorial Window* (1932–34).This stained glass window in the Charles Institute of Dermatology, Belfield, University College Dublin, reveals the stylistic impact of Harry Clarke on King's work during this early period.

Richard King left the Clarke Studios in May 1940 to have an independent career and to develop his own individual artistic style. In 1936 he found an outlet for his gifts in graphic art by submitting illustrations to *The Capuchin Annual* and *The Father Mathew Record*. King was staff artist of the *Annual* from 1940–53, but continued to submit illustrations to it on the basis of commissions until 1972. His distinctive stamp designs during the 1930s and 40s expressed his deep religious sense and his understanding of Irish culture, nationalism and the Celtic Revival. Due to the difficulties of importing stained glass into Ireland during the Second World War and the Emergency, King did not resume his work in this medium until 1949–50.

An awareness of modernism, which became apparent in King's work from the late 1940s onwards, contributed to the eclectic manner of his constant stylistic and technical experimentation. He worked in a variety of media, such as scraperboard, airbrush, oils and watercolour, in the 1940s. Apart from stained glass, King also painted in oils on masonite and canvas in the 1950s and 60s. During the 1960s and early 70s, he produced Stations of the Cross and crucifixes in vitreous and non-vitreous enamels, illustrations and stained glass windows. Artists such as Georges Rouault, Evie Hone, Mainie Jellett and Wilhelmina Geddes influenced his work in painting, illustration and especially in stained glass. King designed stained glass windows for churches in many parts of Australia, England, Ireland, USA and Wales.

The religious dimension of King's stained glass windows benefited from his interests in theology and the Scriptures. Vatican II and his study of the theological works of Pierre Teilhard de Chardin SJ enabled King to grow at the spiritual level and have a more profound understanding of the mystery of Christ. These aspects brought a deeper meaning and richer symbolism to his interpretation of theological themes in his stained glass windows from 1960–73. These late stained glass windows in Ireland and overseas, distinguished by movement, colour and light, reveal the influences of cubism, expressionism and abstraction. King admired modern French and German stained glass such as the work of Alfred Manessier, Fernand Léger, Gabriel Loire, Anton Wendling, Hermann Gottfried, Wilhelm Buschulte and Georg Meistermann. The culmination of King's artistic achievement, seen in his work from 1965–73, is the combination of the original legacy of Harry Clarke with a style which was modern and ultimately unique to him. The last part of his career reveals that King had found his authentic voice as an artist, which also facilitated the expression of his theological vision. After a rich, varied and productive life and artistic career, Richard King died on 17 March 1974.

HUBERT MCGOLDRICK (1897–1967)

David Caron

Hubert Vincent McGoldrick, the youngest of a large family was born in Rathgar, Dublin and is first recorded as having attended classes at the Dublin Metropolitan School of Art at the age of 13. Two years later, in 1913, he joined Earley and Company of Upper Camden Street, Dublin, the city's largest and long-established stained glass company. During his apprenticeship he continued attending A.E. Child's stained glass classes at the DMSA. In 1918 McGoldrick exhibited designs for stained glass at the annual exhibition of the RHA which may indicate that he saw himself as an artist and not as a typical Earley's worker who was but one member of a very large production team.

In 1920 Hubert McGoldrick was invited to join An Túr Gloine at a point when the studio was particularly busy undertaking commissions for war memorial windows. He was the first male and the first Catholic to join the studio since Michael Healy's arrival some fifteen years earlier. Like Healy, he was a devout Catholic, but in personality was very different; while Healy was reclusive and introvert, McGoldrick was theatrical and flamboyant.

His first window, *Sorrow and Joy* (1920), for Gowran, County Kilkenny, indicates a strongly developed personal style and choice of palette which would have been quite at variance to the prevalent house style at Earley and Company. Like Harry Clarke and Michael Healy, he revelled in rich detail, particularly evident in his works of the 1920s. One of his finest windows was produced early in his An Túr Gloine career, *The Sacred Heart Appearing to Saint Margaret Mary* (1925) for St Brendan's Cathedral, Loughrea, a window which revels in sonorous warm colours and detailed vignettes.

Arguably his most noteworthy window, and certainly one of the most unusual commissions to come to the studio, was a massive lunette, *The Spirit of Morning* (1926–7), for a private home in Singapore. It was commissioned – along with a less dynamic companion window by Catherine O'Brien – by an Irish architect who was based there and who was a friend of Sarah Purser. Following several decades in storage, it is now on public display in the Penang Colonial Museum, Malaysia. Of all McGoldrick's works, this one has the most sense of the period that it was created in, possibly since the secular subject matter allowed a more contemporary representation of womanhood. By this time the studio was receiving several substantial international commissions – championed in the USA by the distinguished Boston-based stained glass designer Charles Connick – and McGoldrick was among six of the An Túr Gloine artists whose work featured in the Chapel of the Sacred Heart, Newton

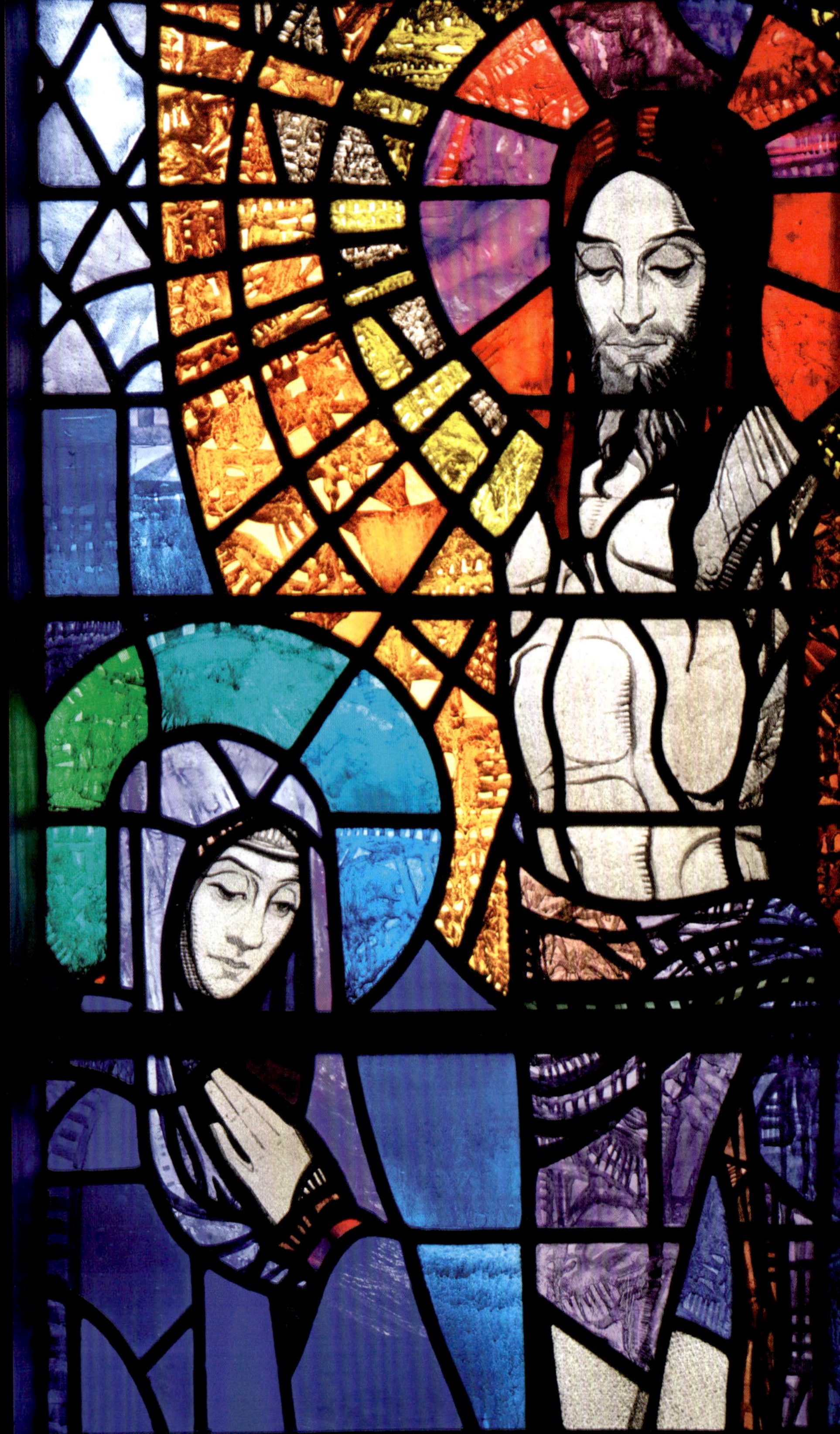

Left:
Hubert McGoldrick, detail of *The Annunciation and the Crucifixion* (1943), Church of Ireland (Holy Trinity), Killiney, County Dublin

Country Day School, Newton, Massachusetts.

In the 1930s another commission to fill an entire USA church with An Túr Gloine stained glass came to the studio, this time for the Chapel of Brophy College Preparatory, Phoenix, Arizona and McGoldrick depicted *Symbols of the Blessed Virgin Mary; The Burning Bush and the Lily Among the Thorns* (1936). McGoldrick's final overseas commission was for a crematorium chapel in Karori, near Wellington, New Zealand; his *Gethsemane* (1939) was one of six An Túr Gloine windows for that small chapel. In many of his later works, such as his *Annunciation and Crucifixion* (1943) for the Church of Ireland, Killiney, County Dublin, he eschewed the detail so prevalent in his earlier work for a simplified approach, often using deep tones of blue and gold and little aciding.

Noteworthy is that, parallel to his stained glass career, McGoldrick – like Ethel Rhind and to a lesser extent Catherine O'Brien – also worked in opus sectile mosaic, a sideline at An Túr Gloine. His greatest achievement in this medium is a series of *Stations of the Cross* for the Catholic Church, Westport, County Mayo (1929–31).

Hubert McGoldrick worked at An Túr Gloine until 1943, when the artist and unofficial manager, Sarah Purser, died and, reluctantly, the two remaining artists, McGoldrick and Catherine O'Brien, decided to dissolve the co-operative studio. Whereas O'Brien continued to work at the premises for another two decades, McGoldrick essentially retired at that point, his final commission being a window for the chapel of Dominican College, Muckross Park, Dublin. Having lived in the same house in Rathgar all his life, he died in 1967.

❧

HELEN MOLONEY (1926–2011)

Bart Felle

Helen Moloney, initially trained as a painter, came to stained glass in her early 30s, spending two decades producing sacred art before effectively retiring. She was the stained glass artist of choice for Liam McCormick (1916–96), the pre-eminent church architect of his day. Moloney worked not only in stained glass, but also in enamel and appliqué design.

On graduating from the National College of Art in 1948, she spent a year in Paris studying and absorbing art, before returning to Dublin in 1951, where she worked as an art teacher. Inspired by the 1958 retrospective exhibition of Evie Hone's stained glass, she decided to study the medium, and returned to the NCA to learn the craft under Johnny Murphy. Graduating in 1961, Moloney worked with her friend Patrick Pollen prior to establishing her independent practice two years later. Moloney's stained glass work was exclusively religious and, with one exception, commissioned for new churches, where usually she was the sole stained glass artist.

When she commenced her practice in 1963, the Catholic Church was on the cusp of major change, which was to have profound architectural implications for church buildings and art in the coming decades. Liam McCormick was to become the outstanding church architect of a generation and a pioneer in commissioning modern Irish art for his buildings. Moloney commenced a two-decade-long working relationship, the most important in her career, with the architect in 1964; Desertegney Church, County Donegal, being the first of twelve stained glass commissions she was to undertake for him. She also worked with other prominent ecclesiastical architects, including Richard Hurley, Wilfrid Cantwell and Philip Shaffrey. Painstaking in her approach, her total output was limited to some eighteen stained glass commissions. Never having a kiln, she worked with various studios to have her designs realised, including Dublin Glass and Paint Company, Abbey Stained Glass, Caldermac of

Belfast, Cathedral Glass, and Murphy-Devitt Studios.

In her earlier years in the National College of Art, Moloney had been exposed to modern Irish and European art through the *Irish Exhibition of Living Art* held there annually. Her niece noted that 'She talked about art all the time. She adored Patrick Scott, Van Gogh, Picasso, of course, and Gauguin, Nolde, Rouault, Braque, Chagall, Matisse, Monet, Henry Moore, El Greco, the Flemish primitive Memling.'[1] Moloney's interpretation of religious iconographic symbolism reflected the vibrancy of colour of the stained glass she saw in Notre Dame and the Sainte-Chapelle during her time in Paris,[2] which was to become her trademark. Her appeal was not to the sentimental, but to the harmony of her designs and their architectural settings, to her understanding of colour balance, her use of strong colours and carefully thought out lead lines. Largely eschewing figurative design, her approach was that of abstract or semi-abstract elementalism. Ultimately Moloney's designs, while relatively simple, are yet highly complex and she had a number of favourite graphic symbols which she reused, that of the Lamb instantly recognisable yet subtly different in some eight of her schemes. Her approach was wholly in sympathy with McCormick's vision of buildings rooted in their landscape.

By the early 1980s new church commissions were getting scarcer and for Moloney, an artist lacking commercial sensibilities in a decade of successive economic shocks, the requirement to sell her art must have been a strong contributory factor in her stopping work at the age of 56. She died in 2011, mourned by her family and a loyal circle of friends. Patrick Pye anticipated her legacy when he stated that 'Helen Moloney is an artist whose achievement in stained glass and designs for enamel work in churches will bring deserved repute when the grapevine of younger art experts reaches out to the sometimes remote churches where they bear silent witness away from the gallery and beaten track of the art world.'[3]

1 Dr Helen Callan email, 9 August 2018.

2 Nicola Gordon Bowe, *Irish Stained Glass* (Dublin: The Arts Council, 1983), p. 18.

3 The Arts Council / An Chomhairle Ealaíon Archive, 6783/19181/1.

JOHNNY MURPHY (1921–2006) and RÓISÍN DOWD MURPHY (1923–2006)

of **Murphy-Devitt Studios**, Dublin

David Caron

Johnny Murphy was born in Cork and initially won a scholarship to attend the Crawford College of Art, transferring to the National College of Art, Dublin, in 1940 where, as a student of painting, he remained for four years. In 1947 he again won a scholarship, this one allowing him to spend an exhilarating year studying and travelling in Paris and Rome. Murphy joined the Harry Clarke Studios around 1952 and a year later he married the painter Róisín Dowd whom he had known from their Dublin college days. She was from the opposite end of the country, having grown up in Belfast and Bangor before the family had moved to Dublin.

In 1954 Johnny Murphy was appointed part-time lecturer in stained glass at NCA (now NCAD), re-establishing classes in the craft which had been in abeyance since 1938, the year before the previous instructor, A.E. Child, had died. The year 1955 marked the time Murphy joined forces with a former Clarke master craftsman and NCA student, John A. (Des) Devitt and they began undertaking commissions together, and three years later they formally established Murphy-Devitt Studios. Initially based in a mews in Monkstown, they subsequently moved to a purpose-built studio in Blackrock at Anglesea House. Johnny

Right:
Róisín Dowd Murphy and Johnny Murphy, *Second, Third and Fourth Horsemen of the Apocalypse* from a scheme of windows (1965–8) for Newbridge College Chapel (St Eustace's), Newbridge, County Kildare

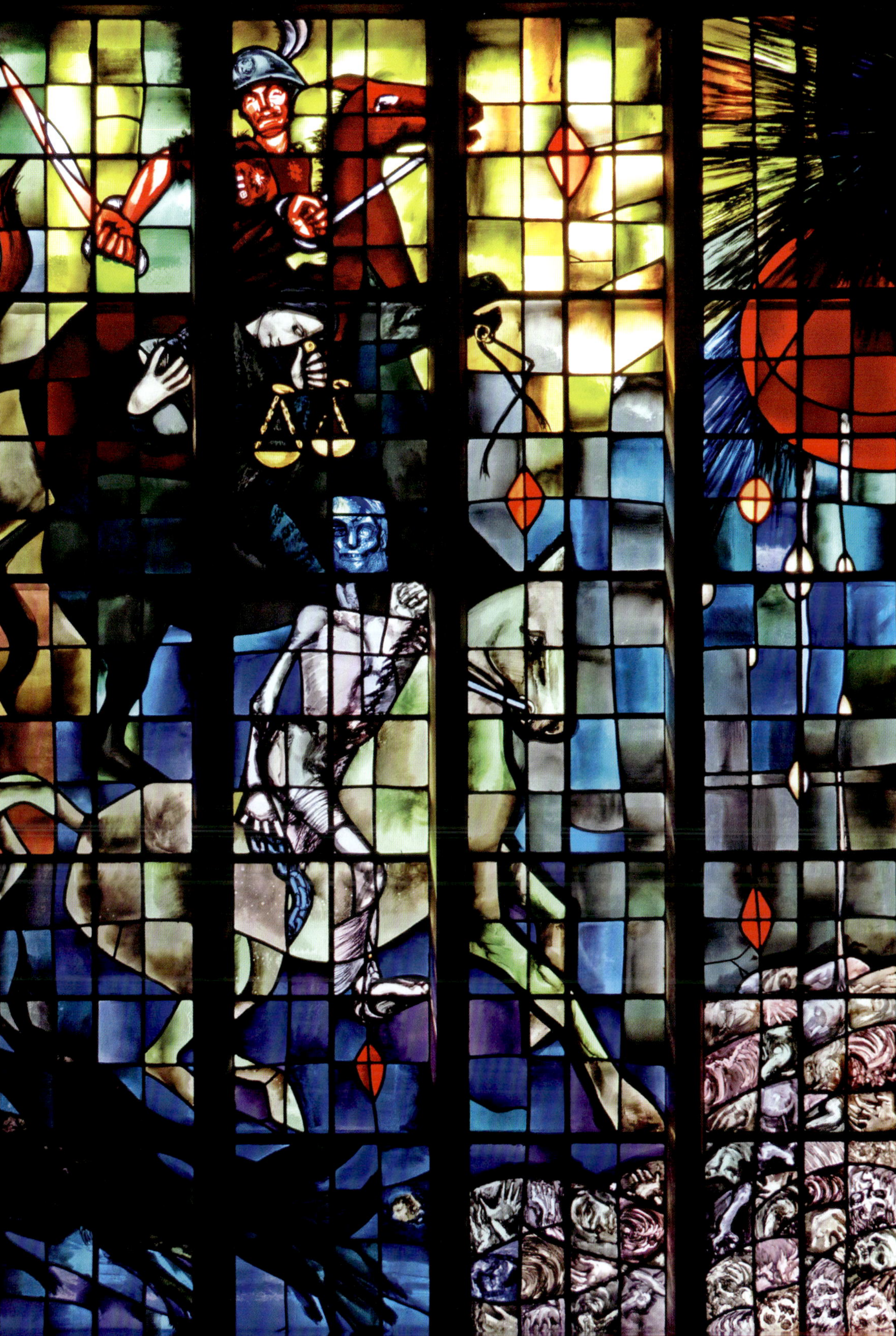

Murphy was the principal artist in the studio, while Róisín Dowd Murphy played a key role in many of the commissions and undertook solo windows, with their eldest daughter, Reiltín, assisting on commissions from time to time.

In addition to a small number of expert craftsmen, specifically brothers Paddy, Dermot and Mikey McLoughlin, Murphy-Devitt encouraged students or young artists to work with them for short periods, including Ann FitzGibbon and – after the studio proper closed – Michael Timlin, both of whom, in addition to developing careers as artists, also went on to become lecturers at NCAD. Another artist, Terry Corcoran, subsequently emigrated to the USA where he continued to work in stained glass and other media. The studio's longest serving recruit, Celia Harriss (later Harriss Crampton), remained with Murphy-Devitt for four years before moving to England where she continued her stained glass career, culminating in a conservation role in Canterbury Cathedral, and much later developed a distinguished reputation as a botanical illustrator.

During the 1960 and early 1970s, which would have been the peak period of activity for Murphy-Devitt, the studio was often called upon to create a 'scheme', a complete set of designs of windows, for new churches. This gave Johnny Murphy the opportunity to excel at what he did best; to devise an overall vision for a large number of lights, sometimes including clerestory windows and walls of glass, all contained within a contemporary space. He appears to have relished scale and drama (perhaps harking back to an earlier period when he had been employed painting huge cinema posters and theatrical backdrops). His own preference was for the bold 'graphic' treatment of saints and other figures, regularly interspersed with passages of understated abstract glass. Like a composer, all elements would come together in effortless harmony, though often with great visual contrast. His daughter Reiltín remembers his interest in music and him drawing an analogy with a fugue 'whereby the same melody or image is played in different ways. His abstracts are often flipped, turned, twisted to be similar but not identical.' She also noted his keen appreciation of the actual glass, always using the best of quality from Saint Gobain in France, with additional glass coming from Pilkington's in the United Kingdom. 'He loved its kinetic effect in its flaws, its trees moving outside, its changing light and colours from passing clouds, its seeming to be alive.'

Róisín Dowd Murphy often contributed windows, or painted significant aspects of windows in schemes which Johnny Murphy had devised, and her style, while distinct, would always integrate effectively, sometimes almost seamlessly. If Johnny was in essence a designer, then Róisín was at heart a painter. Reiltín summed up her mother's windows as being 'full of colour and movement, vigour and life. Róisín loved the Renaissance artists, such as Michelangelo and Botticelli, and her images echo theirs with her love of flowers, of dressmaking, textiles, braided hair, of children and musical instruments. Róisín's windows give a moment in time: her saints are real people with busy lives, her images are "snapshots" rather than "icons". Róisín was never happier than when she was covered in charcoal while drawing a full-size cartoon or, covered in pigment, painting those figures and details onto the glass.'

Murphy-Devitt Studios closed in 1980 but Murphy and Dowd Murphy – and Des Devitt too – continued to work together until 2005, after the Murphy family had moved to live in a former mill near New Ross in County Wexford. Johnny Murphy, Róisín Dowd Murphy and Des Devitt all died in 2006.

❧

CATHERINE (KITTY) O'BRIEN (1881–1963)

David Caron

Catherine O'Brien was born in Durra House, near Ennis, County Clare, and her background and family circumstances were in many ways similar to Sarah Purser's: born into a middle-class country Anglo-Irish Protestant family, she enjoyed a comfortable, privileged upbringing until dwindling family funds forced her to move to Dublin to acquire training for a career. Catherine O'Brien is first recorded as being enrolled as a student at the Metropolitan School of Art in 1901 and she, along with Michael Healy, were the first two artists to be recruited by Purser when An Túr Gloine formally opened in January 1903.

Although the philosophy of An Túr Gloine was that each artist would be responsible for the entire creative process, in the early years O'Brien and the other new recruits were still very much learning their craft and often assisted in the painting of windows designed by Child and Purser. The earliest windows which she designed and executed in their entirety show the legacy of Christopher Whall as transmitted by his student A.E. Child to his own students. In these windows O'Brien regularly utilised plenty of pale quarries in the background, often with delicately painted designs and characteristic 'architectural' canopy constructions of branch and leaf encasing saints. Not as talented a draughtsperson as Healy, Elvery or Rhind, she was most comfortable with fairly straightforward representations of the human form and her attempts to capture gestures and movement sometimes resulted in an awkward rigidity.

By the mid-1920s An Túr Gloine had achieved significant international recognition and O'Brien was among the artists who designed and executed windows for prestigious overseas clients, among them a massive lunette, *The Spirit of the Night*, for a private home in Singapore, and two windows each for school chapels in Newton, Massachusetts and Phoenix, Arizona.

In time O'Brien eschewed her preference for lighter, mellow tones in favour of a brighter palette and by the early 1930s had adopted regular use of pulsating intense oranges, reds, blues and greens, sometimes evoking a folk art quality in her windows.

Throughout her career smaller-scale, intimate windows rather than large multi-light windows seemed to suit her style better (though among the exceptions are a fine five-light, *Crossing the Bar* for Kinsale Church of Ireland). These works often had a simplicity and modesty in execution and ambition which seemed most at home in country churches. The majority of her windows can be found in Church of Ireland churches of which she was a committed member. Unlike most of the other An Túr Gloine artists, she regularly signed her windows, either as 'K. O'B' or 'K. O'Brien', sometimes accompanied by a tiny tower. Like Ethel Rhind, though to a lesser extent, O'Brien also worked in opus sectile mosaic, a sideline of the studio.

In 1940, on Purser's retirement, Catherine O'Brien took over as manager of An Túr Gloine until its closure in January 1944. She then bought out the studio and its contents, and from 1954 she rented out space to fellow artist Patrick Pollen. In the 1950s her work is characterised by simpler designs with less painting, recalling children's book illustration. A fire in 1958 destroyed the premises, and while the cartoons were lost, many of the small-scale preliminary designs, including over 140 by O'Brien herself, survived and in time were donated by Pollen to the National Gallery of Ireland. The studio was rebuilt a year later, but by then O'Brien was in her late 70s, though still actively undertaking new commissions.

Among her final commissions were a pair of colourful heraldic windows for the Royal College of Surgeons in Ireland. She herself is commemorated by an understated window depicting St Luke in his guise as patron saint of artists by Patrick Pollen which is in Christ Church Cathedral, Dublin.

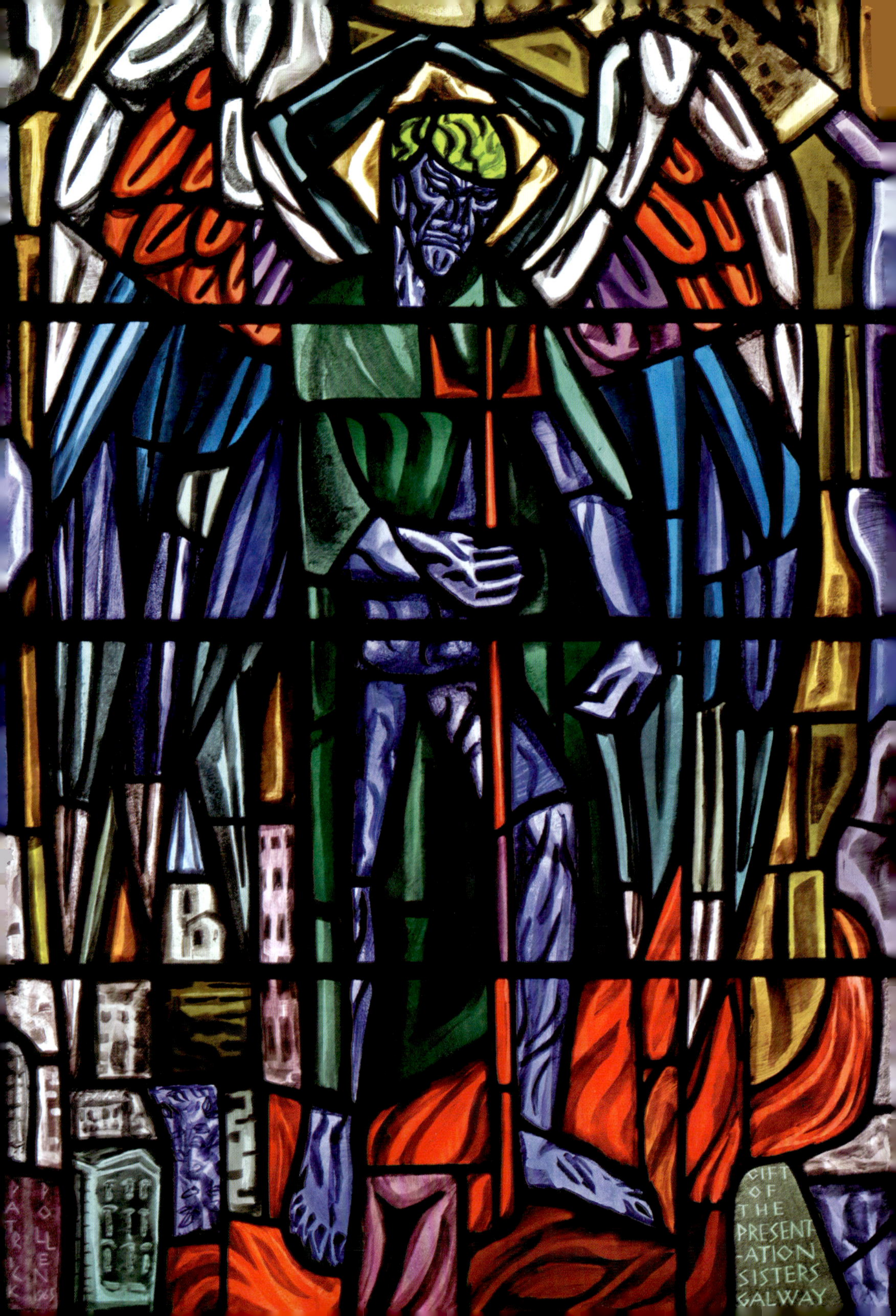
PATRICK POLLEN 1965
GIFT OF THE PRESENT-ATION SISTERS GALWAY

PATRICK POLLEN (1928–2010)

William Earley

Patrick Pollen was an English stained glass artist with strong Irish connections who made his career in Ireland. He was the great-grandson of John Hungerford Pollen, who was engaged by John Henry Cardinal Newman to be Professor of Fine Arts at the new Catholic University of Ireland and who was the architect of Newman's University Church on St Stephen's Green, Dublin. His father, Arthur, was a well-known sculptor of largely religious work. His mother, also a distinguished artist, forming the main Irish connection, was the Hon. Daphne Baring, daughter of Cecil Baring, third Lord Revelstoke, whose family owned and had a home on, Lambay Island off the coast of Howth, north County Dublin.

After travelling for a period in Europe and having completed his military service, Pollen first went to train in art at the Slade School in London in 1949. He stayed there only eighteen months and then spent a brief time studying at l'Académie Julian in Paris.

Pollen was fascinated by Evie Hone's stained glass window at Eton College, *Crucifixion and Last Supper*, encountered during a visit to Eton College in 1952. He came to Dublin to work under her tutelage at her Rathfarnham studio at Marlay Park, remaining until 1954. He then moved to premises rented from the stained glass artist Catherine O'Brien at the old An Túr Gloine co-operative studio in 24 Upper Pembroke Street, central Dublin.

Pollen's windows can be seen all over Ireland and the United Kingdom and as far afield as the United States and South Africa. He exhibited his stained glass regularly in the 1950s at the annual Irish Exhibition of Living Artists. He worked with many architects, notably Liam McCormick on his churches at Milford and Murlog, both in County Donegal. His largest Irish commission was twenty-six windows in 1965 for the Cathedral of Our Lady Assumed into Heaven and St Nicholas, Galway.

Pollen's work was a product of many influences: the artistic tradition of his family, with both its modern influences and the tradition of design and craft which came through J.H. Pollen and his association with the Arts and Crafts Movement; the strong Catholic faith which heavily influenced his artistic formation and which had been with him since his youth; and the dominating presence of Evie Hone and, through her, Georges Rouault. His early work of 1955, a three-light window in St Georges' Church, Whitchurch, Cheshire, owes much to Hone and may even have been an original commission of hers which she was too ill to take on.

In 1963 Pollen married the sculptor Nell Murphy (1927–2011) and they shared a studio in Dundrum, Dublin. Their work is best seen together in Liam McCormick's St Patrick's Church, Murlog, County Donegal where Pollen made two large windows on the theme of *St Patrick's Breastplate* and Murphy made the Stations of the Cross.

Pollen's style has been described as one of rugged directness, well exemplified by his windows in Galway Cathedral. He went to immense lengths to choose his glass and was steeped in the hands-on production of stained glass arising from the Arts and Crafts tradition. He was also a subtle colourist, as may be seen in particular in his window on the theme of the canticle Benedicite in St Paul's Church of Ireland church, Ramelton, County Donegal.

After an active period in the 1960s and early 1970s Pollen, as with many stained glass artists, found commissions increasingly hard to find. He moved with his wife and family in the early 1980s to Winston-Salem in North Carolina in search of better opportunities but found finding commissions no easier there. He and his wife returned to Ireland in the early 1990s. They lived for a time on Lambay Island before settling in Wexford. Pollen died in 2010 and his wife, Nell, died in 2011.[1]

Left:
Patrick Pollen, detail of *Temptation of Our Lord in the Desert* (1965), Catholic Cathedral, Galway City

1 For further reading see Nicola Gordon Bowe, 'Patrick Pollen: Metaphysician in Glass', *Irish Arts Review*, vol. 28, no. 2, Summer Summer 2011, pp. 102–7.

PATRICK PYE (1929–2018)

Brian McAvera

Patrick Pye, born in Winchester, is one of the major figures in the revival of stained glass in Ireland, having produced a wide range of panels for churches throughout the country, as well as for private collections. Two aspects are central to his work: the first is that unlike many artists who only produced design cartoons, leaving the fabrication to professional craftsmen, Pye actually made the stained glass himself, installing a kiln and a mill for stretching lead in his studio in the late 1960s; the second is that he was a committed Catholic, a convert who took his theology seriously yet who, paradoxically, did not wish to recreate the medieval 'layman's Bible' in stained glass, but was 'more anxious to set a mood by virtue of colour and harmony', ensuring that no extraneous symbolism would 'conflict with the shapes and the colours'.[1]

As well as attending night classes with John Murphy, who taught the practicalities of making stained glass at NCAD in the 1950s (the art historian John Turpin regards Murphy as being responsible for the revival of stained glass in the college from 1954 onwards),[2] the artist also studied under Professor Albert Troost, studying the techniques of stained glass at the Jan Van Eyck Academie in Maastricht in 1957–8. His interest in the Romanesque and the Gothic, fuelled by assiduous travelling, overlapped with the influences of John Piper (in particular his almost abstract baptistery window at Coventry Cathedral)[3] and Evie Hone, the latter reinforced by his close friend and mentor Elizabeth Rivers, who had a long working relationship with Hone's stained glass studio.

Pye's work can be seen both north and south of the border: some of the highlights would include Glenstal Abbey in Limerick, Milford Church in Donegal, Creagh Church in Ballinasloe and St Brendan's Cathedral in Loughrea, both in Galway. In 1983 Nicola Gordon Bowe singled out his 'ingenious' Convent of Mercy Chapel at Cookstown, County Tyrone,[4] to which might be added the church at Cladymore, County Armagh and the *Agony in the Garden* window for the former Methodist Church in Donegall Square, Belfast, amongst others.

As with both Piper and Hone, what attracted Pye most to stained glass was colour. 'If you can visualise the differences of tone that can be attained in painting, the range (between one and a hundred) might be from thirty-one to fifty-two. But the tonal range of God's own sunlight and the absolute obscurity of a bit of dark glass would be more like from one to a hundred. It's a very dramatic art form in that sense.'[5] No matter what the ostensible subject was, Pye's concerns were colour, form and an equipoise between abstraction and figuration. While he respected the theology, what interested him more was empathy. Technically, he talked of the 'need to modulate the highlights of bright colours with relatively neutral colours ... Pattern is very important. The shape of the leads is a vital matter. The curious thing about glass is that in a single piece of glass, if there is a certain texture or variety of tone, this will give the form a sort of sculptural quality. It's amazing that a patterned surface can have a depth of colour and space.'

There are two other elements worth noting about Pye's work. The first is that it is a visual counterblast to Harry Clarke and his imitators: there are no pretty, decorative details, no bejewelled romantic versions of medieval figures. Instead there is an uncompromising, steely-eyed intensity of vision, a sparseness, an economy, a simplification of forms, a linear emphasis with abstracted stylised shapes. The second is that he liberated Irish religious art from sentimental pietism and the highly damaging effects of nationalism.

In the artist's work, as Frances Spalding remarked of John Piper, 'colour is both representational and abstract at the same time; and made sonorous by the use of echoes and repetitions'.[6] Unlike Piper, however, but very much like a medieval Catholic craftsman, Pye possessed what Herbert Read called the necessary 'instinct to make the best use of the arbitrary effects which chance [in the process of physically making the stained glass] might throw into his hands'.[7] The result was a personal vision expressed in that personal calligraphy which one can also see in his paintings and prints.

1 All unattributed quotations come from conversations with the artist in the period 2011–13.
2 John Turpin, *A School of Art in Dublin since the Eighteenth Century* (Dublin, 1995), pp. 388–9.
3 See especially Frances Spalding, *John Piper, Myfanwy Piper: Lives in Art* (OUP, 2009), pp. 371–9.
4 Nicola Gordon Bowe, *Stained Glass*, in the Recent Irish Art series (Dublin and Belfast: The Arts Councils in Ireland, 1983), Sheets 16 and 17.
5 From an article in the artist's studio, Donovan, 'A Touch of Glass', in *The Irish Times* (1998).
6 Spalding, *John Piper, Myfanwy Piper*, p. 33.
7 See Herbert Read, John Baker and Alfred Lammer, *English Stained Glass* (Thames & Hudson, London, 1960), p. 7.

SARAH PURSER (1848–1943)

David Caron

Sarah Purser, noted painter and first female full member of the RHA, played an important role in Irish cultural life, in particular helping to develop Dublin's Municipal and National Galleries. In her early 50s she, along with Edward Martyn, founded An Túr Gloine and her ongoing commitment over the decades to ensuring it was a success cannot be underestimated. Although A.E. Child was official manager of the studio, it would appear that it was Sarah Purser who mainly dealt with clients, a significant number of whom were known to her personally from her days as a society portrait painter; aside from this she was a supreme networker, whether at the popular monthly salons in her Dublin mansion, Mespil House, or while travelling by rail, working her way through railway carriages to strike up conversations with ministers of religion. She also had a key role as 'art director' of the studio and took particular pains to match up the individual artists with commissions which best suited their artistic strengths.

Regarding which stained glass windows Purser herself designed, and particularly to what extent she was engaged in their execution, can be difficult to define. Although Purser had no formal instruction in the craft, unlike the other artists in the studio, she obviously would have acquired considerable knowledge by virtue of the amount of time she spent in the 'shop' each week and since she was not paid by the hour – as was the case of the other workers – the time she spent on windows is not recorded in the studio's work journals.

In the early years of An Túr Gloine press reports regularly referred to it as 'Miss Purser's Stained Glass Works' and likewise articles often erroneously gave her credit for windows designed and made entirely by other artists. In a slim ATG pamphlet, *List of Principal Stained Glass Windows Executed in Ireland from 1903 to 1928*, it states that Purser was the artist responsible for fourteen windows, which again adds somewhat to the confusion. In reality these were mainly executed by other artists in the studio.

At a high-profile reception to celebrate twenty-five years of An Túr Gloine in 1928, Sarah Purser somewhat self-deprecatingly told the audience: 'I myself, though I hope I am some judge of glass, am not a stained glass worker in the sense we give the word ... My only output is a tiny window in the porch at Loughrea, something in the nature of a curiosity. I designed ... some of our early windows, but though the real artists obligingly painted them, we never found it satisfactory.' Aside from her window depicting *St Brendan the Navigator* referred to by her above – and a small number of panels created as personal gifts – Sarah Purser produced approximately twenty designs for windows which were realised, though she did not necessarily draw the cartoons and

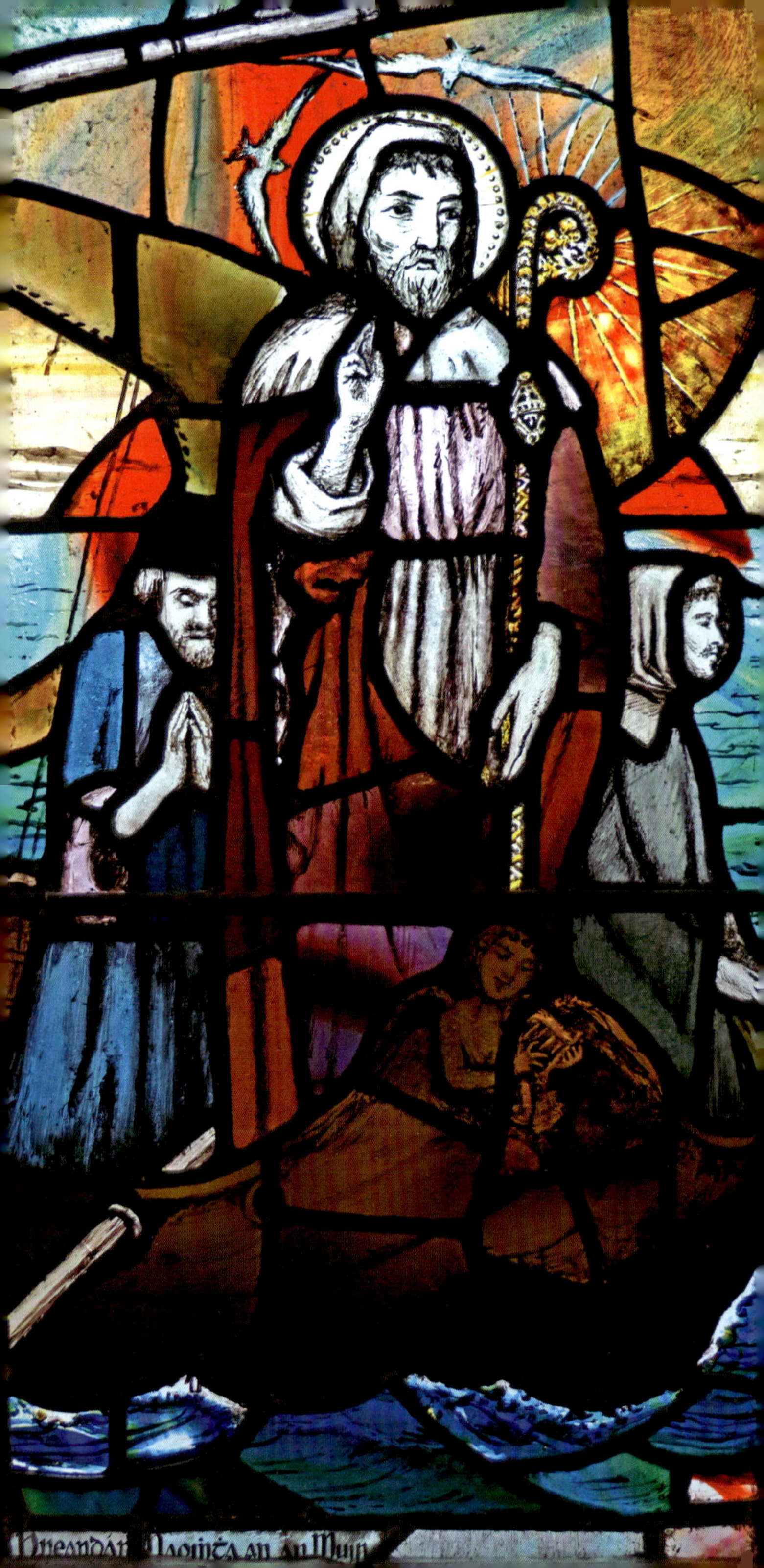
Breandán Naoṁṫa ar an Muir

Left:
Sarah Purser, *St Brendan* (*c.*1903–4), Catholic Cathedral, Loughrea, County Galway

would most likely have done some painting of 'her' windows.

A rare photograph of Purser, A.E. Child, Michael Healy and glazier Tommy Kinsella in An Túr Gloine features a cartoon of *St Andrew* (1903) for Labane Catholic Church, near Ardrahan, one of An Túr Gloine's earliest windows, and although the *List of Principal Windows* states that Purser was the artist in this instance, it is much more likely that it was A.E. Child who drew up the cartoon, which he subsequently recycled for an almost identical window of the same subject in 1921. Often a close examination of the ATG order books and work journals – where information was entered as the work was being undertaken – reveals which artist(s) was involved in painting Purser's windows: Child, Healy, O'Brien, Rhind, Elvery and Hugh Barden (the last being a freelance artist) all executed her designs. By 1912 Purser had ceased to design any windows with the exception of two, for Killucan Church of Ireland (1926) and Donaghpatrick Church of Ireland (1930).

A rare secular and also culturally significant commission was a set of five windows (two rectangles and three lunettes) which Purser designed – derived from designs by the great Christopher Whall, teacher of A.E. Child – for the vestibule of the original Abbey Theatre in 1904. These decorative designs featured symmetrical trees in leaf and remained in situ for a decade after the disastrous fire which had destroyed the auditorium. Around the time the cut-stone vestibule was being carefully dismantled in 1961 they sadly disappeared without trace.

❧

ETHEL RHIND (1877–1952)

David Caron

Ethel Rhind was born in India to a Scottish father, who was then working as an engineer for the Indian Civil Service, and a mother from County Antrim. She acquired an art teacher's certificate at the Belfast School of Art, moved to Dublin and in 1902 took up a scholarship to study mosaic under Miss Holloway at the Metropolitan School of Art. By 1904 she was also attending A.E. Child's stained glass class owing to her particular aptitude for mosaic, which never left her. Like Catherine O'Brien, she scooped up many of the awards at the School of Art and Sarah Purser's invitation to her to join An Túr Gloine in 1906 must have been influenced by these achievements.

Ethel Rhind's earliest window is a small *St Eunan* (1906) for Raphoe Cathedral which she executed based on a design by Sarah Purser. A year later she designed and painted two-light memorial window, *Harmony and Fortitude* (1907), for her distant relatives the Gore-Booths of Lissadell. Like Catherine O'Brien, when designing and painting her own windows, the strong Arts and Crafts-influenced aesthetic of A.E. Child (passed on from his own teacher, Christopher Whall) remained evident for a decade or so, although she did demonstrate a preference for richer colours. One of the qualities which distinguished Rhind from both O'Brien and Child was an ability to instil greater individual character and personality into the figures she depicted.

In 1909 Rhind designed and executed the first of three fine two-light windows for York Road Presbyterian Church, Dún Laoghaire, County Dublin, though her later two (1922 and 1925) are considerably more imaginative, both featuring richly textured detail and a delight in decoration, as do a pair of two-lights for Townsend Presbyterian Church in Belfast, *Pilgrims Progress* (1913) and *Parables* (1921–2). Animals feature in her windows from time to time, such as a wide variety of fish in *Praise the Lord* (1916), a prominent tabby cat in her *Parables of the Good Samaritan and the*

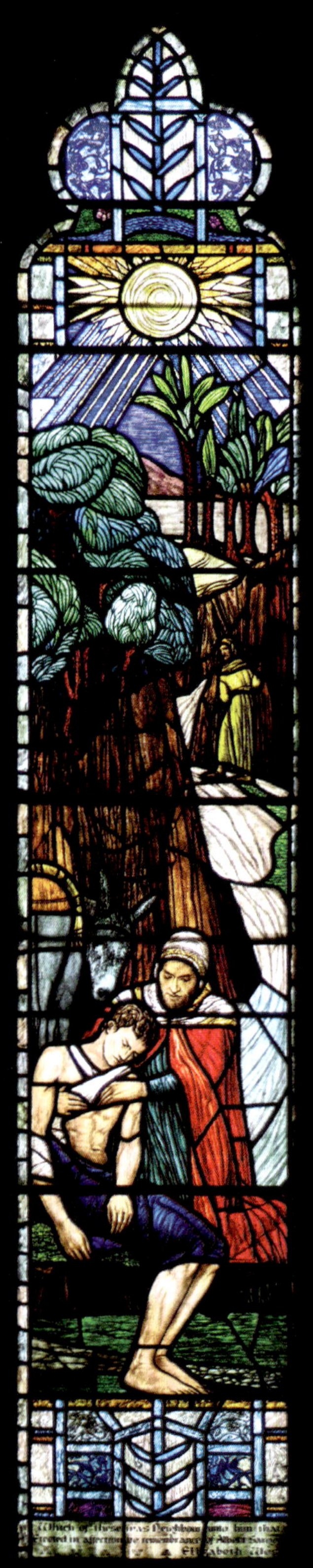
Which of these was Neighbour unto him that
Erected in affectionate remembrance of Albert
Elizabeth

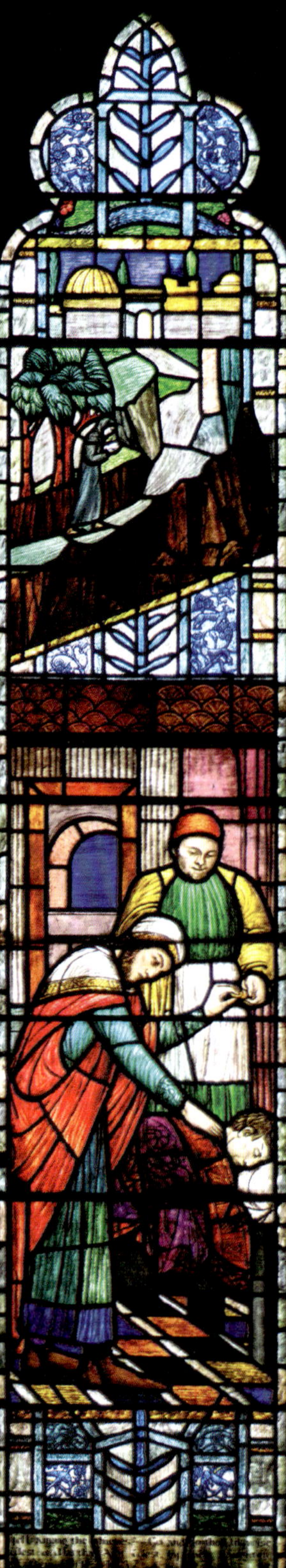

Lost Groat (1925), and an eagle and fish in *St John the Evangelist* (1929).

Parallel to her career in stained glass, Ethel Rhind also excelled in opus sectile mosaic, a type of mosaic which used larger, custom-cut pieces of glazed ceramic tile (similar in approach to stained glass) rather than the conventional tiny square tesserae. It seems that Joshua Clarke and Company were the first to offer work in this medium in 1903. The *Irish Builder and Engineer* of that year explained its special attributes: 'It is a modification of mosaic, and can be used for all classes of church and mural decoration at less cost than glass mosaic. Another feature is that the material is absolutely damp proof, thus overcoming one of the long-standing difficulties in artistic wall decorations. Any scheme of colouring can be worked out, and the material so prepared that surface glitter is altogether avoided.'

Her greatest achievement in this medium are three sets of Stations of the Cross for West of Ireland churches. The process was both time-consuming and noisy, irritating the other An Túr Gloine staff. Her first Station was for the charming Hiberno-Romanesque Church in Spiddal, commissioned from her by Lord Killanin in 1918. It was a decade before all fourteen were completed and they were followed by sets for Loughrea Cathedral (1929–32) and the Franciscan Friary, Athlone (1934–6). In contrast to her stained glass windows, her work in mosaic is more muted and restrained, with less detail and a reduced colour palette. With reference to her mosaic work, Nicola Gordon Bowe discerned 'the effective influence of Wilhelmina Geddes's earlier stiffly stylized archaicised style'. Aside from her Stations, the majority of her fifty-plus windows can be found in Protestant churches.

Ethel Rhind retired from An Túr Gloine in 1939 and died in a Dún Laoghaire nursing home in 1952.

Left: Ethel Rhind, detail of *The Good Samaritan* (1937), Unitarian Church, St Stephen's Green, Dublin City

GEORGE STEPHEN WALSH (1911–88)

David Caron

George Stephen Walsh was born into an artistic family at Garden View, Ranelagh, Dublin, his father being a coach painter. At the age of 14 Walsh became an apprentice in Joshua Clarke and Sons by which point Clarke's son, Harry, had established himself as an exceptional talent. While serving his apprenticeship, Walsh also attended the Metropolitan School of Art, and panels made during that period demonstrate not only considerable technical skill but imagination, love of drawing the human form and a keen sense of composition. On completion of his apprenticeship Walsh stayed on at Clarke's – which formerly became Harry Clarke Stained Glass Limited in 1930 – working as a stained glass painter and remained with the studio until about 1941, when, due to diminishing commissions in Dublin, he moved to James Powell and Sons in London where, among other jobs, he worked on cartoons for Liverpool Cathedral.

In 1948 Walsh and his young family relocated to Belfast where he was appointed head designer at Clokey's. A singularly large window made by Walsh while he was at Clokey's is a six-light with tracery celebrating the virtues of work and featuring different occupations and trades, which dates from 1956 and was made for the Fisherwick Presbyterian Church, Malone Road, Belfast. It is a synthesis of traditional design motifs featuring plenty of decorative interlacing and modernity, with several contemporary figures painted in a crisp graphic style recalling a faux wood-cut technique.

In 1957 George Stephen Walsh and his family moved to Wisconsin where he and his son, George W. Walsh (b.1939, see next entry), began working for the Conrad Pickel Stained Glass Studio in Waukesha, a small though well-regarded company which had been established ten years previously. George Stephen was the chief designer, and George W., who was still completing his seven-year apprenticeship, painted many of his father's windows. Commissions often comprised entire schemes of stained glass for a church, something unheard of in Ireland at this date. One particularly notable scheme of nineteen windows (*c.*1958–9), designed by George Stephen and painted by his son, was for the Trinity Lutheran Church in Waukesha. These mainly narrative windows, with the *Creation* as one of the principal themes, are rich with exuberant detail, full of energy and visual excitement, and have a distinctly modern appearance, a major departure from the work he undertook at Clokey's.

In addition to traditional stained glass, Pickel's also employed the *dalle de verre* technique which often complemented modern architecture, a technique where thick pieces of coloured glass, sometimes chipped or faceted to increase the refraction and reflection effects, are set into a matrix of concrete and epoxy resin. Both father and son quickly became skilled in the technique and examples of George Stephen's work in the medium can be seen in his large *Madonna and Child* (1961) for St Mary's Church, Tomahawk, Wisconsin.

During the six-year period at Pickel's, the Walsh family returned to Ireland for short periods a few times and ultimately, due to the harsh climate of Wisconsin, a decision was made that the family would return permanently in 1963. George Stephen established his own small independent studio in Drumcondra under the title *George S. Walsh Stained Glass Studio*, advertising that he undertook 'stained glass windows, mosaics, murals, bronze work'. Before departing Wisconsin, Walsh had begun designing, though not executing, windows for the long-established Hiemer and Company Stained Glass Studio of Clifton, New Jersey, whereby he would be briefed on commissions, devise schemes and do preliminary drawings (sometimes cartoons too) and these would then be sent to New Jersey for the company's staff to execute. This arrangement intensified after he returned to Ireland and continued until about 1984.

Throughout his career, though increasingly as he grew older, Walsh was happy working in a wide variety of media, exhibiting regularly. An accomplished painter, skilled in scraperboard, and a talented sculptor working in bronze and other materials, he had a remarkably productive career, though he will be chiefly remembered as a stained glass artist of distinction.

❧

GEORGE W. WALSH (b.1939)

Finola Finlay

Thoroughly grounded in his own modernist practice, George Walsh nevertheless represents a link with the great tradition of stained glass of the first half of the twentieth century.

George Stephen Walsh, George's father (see previous entry), apprenticed under Harry Clarke and worked in Clarke's studio, later moving to Clokey of Belfast. There George served his apprenticeship under his father, attending the Belfast College of Art concurrently.

In 1957 George Stephen moved the family to Wisconsin, the first of several trips across the Atlantic for the Walsh family. Father and son worked in the Conrad Pickel Studio in Waukesha, Wisconsin. When George's father and family returned to Ireland, George moved to the Conrad Schmitt Studio in Milwaukee, mastering *dalle de verre* and, for George, expanding the range of his artistic vision.

Frank Ryan of Abbey Stained Glass Studios asked George to return to Ireland in the early 60s to join the studio along with their lead artist William Earley. For Abbey he developed expansive *dalle de verre* windows (e.g. Raheny) and traditional leaded-glass pieces, such as the huge windows for Guardian Angels in Blackrock or St Augustine's in Galway, which hint at the influence of Gabriel Loire, the *dalle de verre* master, in their size and swathes of swirling colour.

Right:
George W. Walsh, *Christ Debating with Students* (1989), National University of Ireland Galway (Chapel of St Columbanus), Galway City. Photograph © Finola Finlay

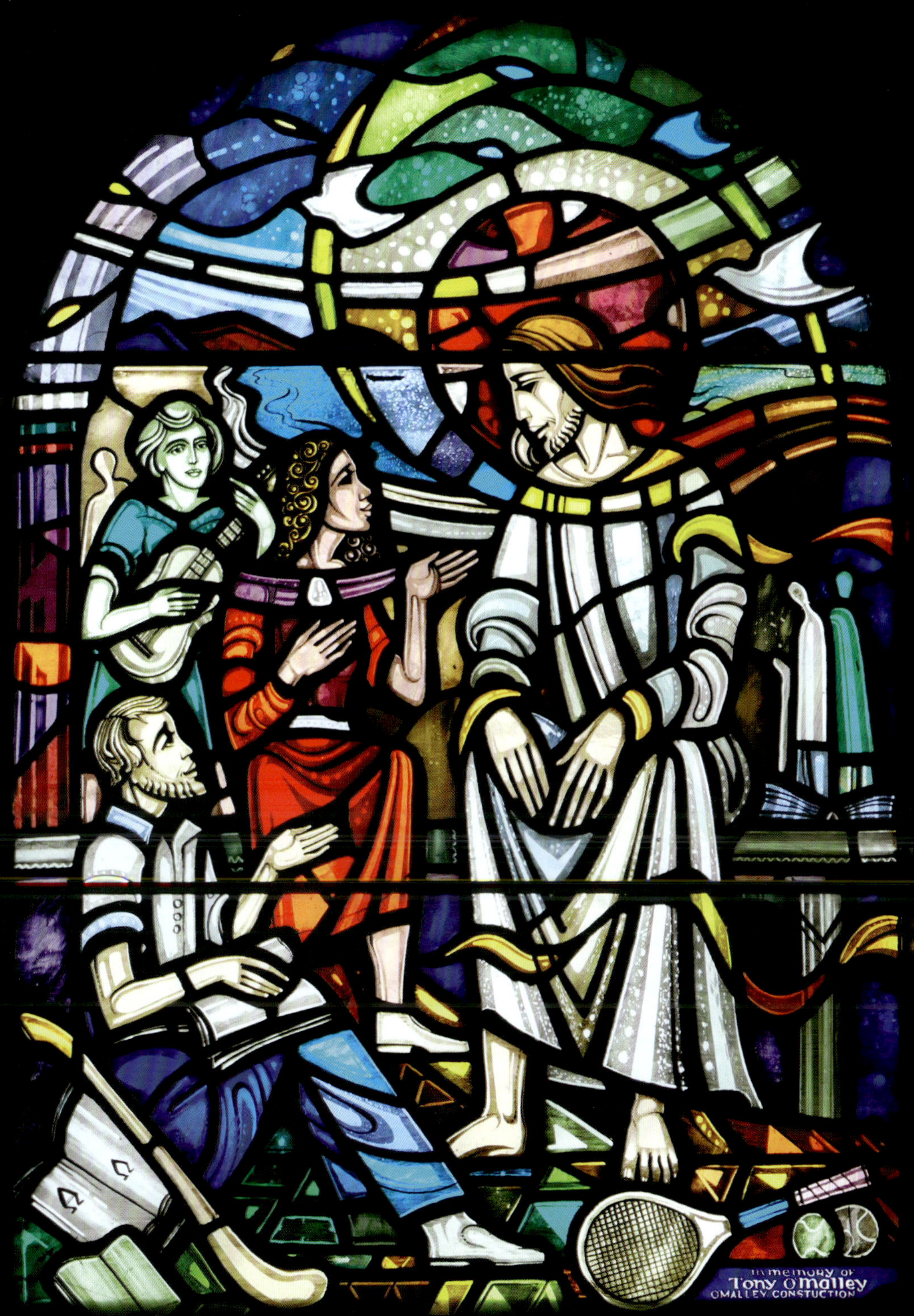
In memory of
Tony O'Malley
OMALLEY CONSTUCTION

George went out on his own in the 1970s, his distinctive style evolving into his signature blend of the sacred and the secular, executed in brilliant colour and complex lead lines. He formed creative partnerships with several architects, most notably Eamon Hedderman of Holly Park Studio, Dr Richard Hurley, Dublin and Paddy Rooney in Sligo, who were re-interpreting liturgical spaces after Vatican II. At its most interesting, this movement led to a whole new approach in church design, but George took the principles into his windows as well. He wanted the images in glass to tell the story of the place and the everyday lives of its people, as well as the sacred iconography chosen by the parish.

Outstanding examples of George's work using this principle abound. In the remote Beara Peninsula, the plain facade of St Kentigern's Catholic Church in Eyeries belies the blaze of colour within. The eleven windows tell the story of Eyeries interwoven with religious themes, beginning with seismic upheavals, dinosaurs and cosmic storms, leading on to ancient Ireland and passage grave-inspired images. Themes of emigration, communication, farming and fishing mingle with depictions of the *Resurrection* and *Nativity*.

The lives of those residing on the fault-line between Protestant and Catholic areas are reflected in the award-winning Church of the Holy Family in Belfast. This church is a re-imagining by Eamon Hedderman, Holly Park Studio, of how the building shell, the furniture and the decoration can seamlessly create a fully integrated experience. Here, George designed and executed the windows, bronze tabernacle and stations, the latter executed by Laura O'Hagan. The site context is the framework for a set of extraordinary statements: the crucifixion station uses an automatic weapon to shoot nails into Jesus's hands and feet; a nearby window shows two faces separated by barbed wire, while through the glass the reality of razor wire on an outside wall is visible.

Only an artist that has been classically trained in stained glass techniques could produce the complex images in which George specialised. Larger pieces of coloured or flashed glass (always painted, acided or textured) were balanced by areas in which each colour was a separate fragment of glass, all cut and shaped in different ways and leaded together to produce a final arresting effect.

Motifs repeat in George's work: water undulates around the space; hands clasp in friendship and reconciliation; sun and wind reference great elemental forces; beehive huts and monks conjure up the past; animals, fish, birds (often extinct types) and insects leap, swim and fly by. Knights ride horses into battle and a postman delivers mail on his bicycle. These details enrich the spaces between larger-scale depictions of the *Risen Christ*, the *Nativity* or local saints. This mixture of the sacred and the secular, the devotional and the quotidian, embedded in richly coloured, abstract and sophisticatedly leaded glass has become his hallmark.

In between commissions George has focused on his personal art practice, ranging from large windows, small-scale display pieces in both leaded and fused glass, paintings in oils and water colours, and collages. He has exhibited widely and is currently represented by the Trinity Gallery, Dublin.

Select Bibliography

An Túr Gloine commemorative booklet, *List of the Principal Stained Glass Windows Executed in Ireland from 1903 to 1928 at An Túr Gloine* (Dublin: Helys, 1928).

An Túr Gloine commemorative booklet, *Twenty-fifth Anniversary Celebration of An Túr Gloine Stained Glass and Mosaic Works* (Dublin: Sign of the Three Candles, 1928).

Black, E., 'Olive Henry' in W. Ryan-Smolin, E. Mayes and J. Rogers (eds), *Irish Woman Artists From the Eighteenth Century to the Present Day*, (Dublin: National Gallery of Ireland and Douglas Hyde Gallery, 1987), p. 167.

Brett, D., and McKeown, J., 'Windows on a World', *Circa Art Magazine,* 68, Summer 1994, pp. 128–31.

Brown, S.A., 'Wilhelmina Geddes' Ottawa Window', *Irish Arts Review*, Yearbook 1994, pp. 181–8.

Butler, R.J., 'All Saints, Drimoleague and Catholic visual culture under Bishop Cornelius Lucey in Cork, 1952–59', *Journal of the Cork Historical and Archaeological Society*, 120 (2015), pp. 79–97.

Butler, R.J., 'All Saints, Drimoleague: clarifications and new discoveries', *Journal of the Cork Historical and Archaeological Society,* 121 (2016), pp. 141–3.

Butler, R.M., 'Modern Stained Glass', *Architectural Review*, vol. 59, 1926.

Callen, A., *Angel in the Studio: Women in the Arts and Crafts Movement 1870–1914* (London: Astragal Books, 1979).

Caron, D., 'An Túr Gloine Stained Glass in Arizona', *Irish Arts Review*, Yearbook 1994, pp. 174–80.

Caron, D., 'City Under Siege', *Irish Arts Review*, vol. 33, no. 1, Spring 2016, pp. 116–19.

Caron, D., 'Four Horsemen', *Irish Arts Review*, vol. 36, no. 2, Summer 2019, pp. 116–21.

Caron, D., 'From Dublin to the Far East: An Túr Gloine Stained Glass in Singapore', *Irish Arts Review*, vol. 17, Yearbook 2001, pp. 114–21.

Caron, D. 'Illuminating Faith', *Irish Arts Review*, vol. 20, no. 3, Autumn 2003, pp. 121–5.

Caron, D., 'Divine Delights', *Irish Arts Review*, vol. 37, no. 3, Winter 2020, pp. 114–17.

Caron, D., 'Michael Healy's Stained Glass Window of "St Victor"', *Irish Arts Review*, vol. 9, Yearbook 1993, pp. 187–91.

Connick, C.J., *Adventures in Light and Colour* (London and New York: Random House, 1937).

Cormack, P., *Arts & Crafts Stained Glass* (London and New Haven: Yale University Press, 1985).

Cormack, P., *Christopher Whall 1849–1924: Arts and Crafts Stained Glass Worker*: Catalogue of the Exhibition (London: William Morris Gallery, 1979).

Cormack, P., *Women Stained Glass Artists of the Arts and Crafts Movement:* Catalogue of the Exhibition (London: William Morris Gallery, 1985).

Costigan, L., and Cullen, M., *Dark Beauty: Hidden Detail in Harry Clarke's Stained Glass* (Dublin: Merrion Press, 2019).

Costigan, L., and Cullen, M., *Strangest Genius: The Stained Glass of Harry Clarke* (Dublin: The History Press, 2010).

Coxhead, E., *Daughters of Erin* (London: Secker and Warburg, 1962).

Curran, C.P., 'Evie Hone: Stained Glass Worker 1894–1955,' *Studies*, vol. 44, Summer 1955.

Curran, C.P., 'Michael Healy: Stained Glass Worker 1873–1941', *Studies*, vol. 31, March 1942.

Curtin-Kelly, P., *Harry Clarke and His Legacy; the Stained Glass in St Joseph's Church, Terenure* (Dublin: Liberties Press, 2017).

Felle, B., 'Radiant Legacy', *Irish Arts Review*, vol. 37, no. 1, Spring 2020, pp. 120–5.

Finlay, F., 'Sacred Lights and Secular Ground', *Irish Arts Review*, vol. 36, no. 1, Spring 2019, pp. 112–17.

Frost, S. (ed.), *A Tribute to Evie Hone and Mainie Jellett* (Dublin: Browne & Nolan Ltd, 1957).

Gordon Bowe, N., 'A Forgotten Masterpiece: The Fate of the Children of Lir', *Irish Arts Review*, vol. 24, no. 1, Spring 2007, pp. 78–85.

Gordon Bowe, N., 'A Host of Shining Saints: Harry Clarke's Stained Glass in Cork', *Country Life*, 12 July 1979.

Gordon Bowe, N., *Catalogue of the Centenary Exhibition of Wilhelmina Geddes (1887–1955)* (Belfast: Arts Council of Northern Ireland, 1987).

Gordon Bowe, N., 'Fallen Sons and Warrior Angels', *Irish Arts Review*, vol. 32, no. 1, Spring 2015, pp. 118–21.

Gordon Bowe, N., 'Four Green Fields, *Irish Arts Review*, vol. 30, no. 3, Autumn 2013, pp. 108–11.

Gordon Bowe, N., 'Glazing Images', in A. Whitty (ed.), *The Light Fantastic: Irish Stained Glass Art* (Kilkenny: Crafts Council of Ireland, 2007).

Gordon Bowe, N., 'Harry Clarke, An Túr Gloine and the Early Twentieth-Century Irish Stained Glass Revival', in J.M. Hearne (ed.), *Glassmaking in Ireland: From the Medieval to the Contemporary* (Dublin: Irish Academic Press/NMI, 2010), pp. 196–214.

Gordon Bowe, N., 'Harry Clarke's Geneva Window', *Irish Arts Review*, vol. 30, no. 1, Spring 2013, pp. 118–27.

Gordon Bowe, N. *Harry Clarke: The Life & Work* (Dublin: The History Press Ireland, 2012 [Revise–d Edition]).

Gordon Bowe, N., 'Harry Clarke: Miniatur-Glasscheiben aus den Jahren 1917–1927', *Weltkunst*, 15 January 1986.

Gordon Bowe, N., *Harry Clarke:* Monograph and Catalogue of the Exhibition (Dublin: Trinity College, 1979).

Gordon Bowe, N., 'Harry Clarke', *Stained Glass* (Journal of The Stained Glass Association of America), vol. 73, no. 4, winter 1978–9.

Gordon Bowe, N., 'Michael Wynne, 1937–2003', *The Journal of Stained Glass*, vol. 38, 2004, pp. 208–10.

Gordon Bowe, N., 'Patrick Pollen, Metaphysician in Glass,' *Irish Arts Review*, vol. 28, no. 2, Summer 2011, pp. 102–7.

Gordon Bowe, N., *Stained Glass*, Recent Irish Art series, no. 3 (Dublin and Belfast: The Arts Councils in Ireland, 1983).

Gordon Bowe, N. 'The Art of Beatrice Elvery, Lady Glenavy (1883–1970)', *Irish Arts Review Yearbook*, vol. 11 (1995), pp. 168–75.

Gordon Bowe, N., with Cumming, E., *The Arts and Crafts Movements in Dublin and Edinburgh 1885–1925* (Dublin: Irish Academic Press, 1998).

Gordon Bowe, N., *The Dublin Arts and Crafts Movement 1885–1930:* Catalogue of the Exhibition (Edinburgh: Edinburgh College of Art, 1985).

Gordon Bowe, N., 'The Irish Arts and Crafts Revival (1894–1925) with particular reference to Harry Clarke', *Journal of the Decorative Arts Society*, no. 9, 1985).

Gordon Bowe, N., *The Life and Work of Harry Clarke* (Dublin: Irish Academic Press, 1989).

Gordon Bowe, N., 'The Miniature Stained Glass Panels of Harry Clarke', *Apollo*, February 1982.

Gordon Bowe, N., 'Wilhelmina Geddes', *Irish Arts Review*, vol. 4, no. 3, Autumn 1987, pp. 53–9.

Gordon Bowe, N., *Wilhelmina Geddes: Life and Work* (Dublin: Four Courts Press, 2015).

Gordon Bowe, N., 'Wilhelmina Geddes', *Stained Glass* (Journal of the Stained Glass Association of America), vol. 76, no. 1, Spring 1981.

Graves, J., 'Ancient Irish Stained Glass', *Transactions of the Kilkenny Archaeological Society*, vol. 1, part 2, 1850.

Griffith, A., Helmers, M., and Kennedy, R. (eds), *Harry Clarke and Artistic Visions of the New Irish State* (Dublin: Irish Academic Press, 2018).

Gwynn, S., 'A Dublin School of Stained Glass', *Spectator*, 28 January 1928.

Gwynn, S., 'The Art of Miss W.M. Geddes', *Studio*, October 1922.

Haggerty, A.J., 'Stained Glass and Censorship: The Suppression of Harry Clarke's Geneva Window, 1931', *New Hibernia Review/Iris Éireannach Nua*, vol. 3, no. 4, Winter 1999, pp. 98–117.

Hanley, J. 'Drama Through the Window', *Irish Arts Review*, vol. 27, no. 1, Spring 2010, pp. 112–13.

Hatrick, C., 'Irish Stained Glass', *Ulster Architect*, February 1992, pp. 61–2.

Hatrick, C., 'Subduing the Light', in T. Reeves-Smyth and R. Oram (eds), *Avenues to the Past* (Belfast: Ulster Architectural Heritage Society, 2003), pp. 27–32.

Hayes, M. and Rogers, J., 'Lost in Translation', *Irish Arts Review*, vol. 29, no. 4, Winter 2012, pp. 128–31.

Hurley, R., *Irish Church Architecture in the Era of Vatican II* (Dublin: Dominican Publications, 2001).

Kennedy, S.B., 'Hone, Evie, Irish painter and stained glass artist, 1894–1955', in Delia Gaze (ed.), *Dictionary of Women Artists*, vol. 1 (London and Chicago: Fitzroy Dearborn, 1997), pp. 706–8.

Kreilkamp, V. (ed.), *The Arts and Crafts Movement in Ireland: Making it Irish* (Boston: McMullan Museum of Art, Boston College, 2016).

Larmour, P., *The Arts & Crafts Movement in Ireland* (Belfast: Friar's Bush Press, 1992).

Larmour, P., 'A Patron of Church Art', in Paul Larmour and Shane O'Toole (eds), *North by Northwest: The Life and Work of Liam McCormick* (Kinsale: Gandon Editions, 2008), pp. 150–71.

MacGreevy, T., 'St Brendan's Cathedral, Loughrea 1897–1947', *Capuchin Annual*, 1946–47.

McAvera, B., *Patrick Pye, Life and Work, a Counter-Cultural Story* (Dublin: Four Courts Press, 2013).

McBrinn, J., '"A Mouthful of Zephyrs": The Studio Glass Movement in Ireland, 1973–2003', in J.M. Hearne (ed.), *Glassmaking in Ireland: From the Medieval to the Contemporary* (Dublin: Irish Academic Press/NMI, 2010), pp. 229–46.

McBrinn, J., 'Edward Marr, 1905–1973', *Perspective: Journal of the Royal Society of Ulster Architects,* vol. 17, 2008.

O'Connell, J.R., *The Honan Hostel Chapel, Cork – Some Notes on the Building and the Ideals which Inspired It* (Cork: Guy & Co. Ltd, 1916).

O'Donnell, J., *Harry Clarke: The Eve of Saint Agnes* (Dublin: The Hugh Lane, 2012).

O'Grady, J., *The Life and Work of Sarah Purser* (Dublin: Four Courts Press, 1996).

O'Regan, J., *James Scanlon (Profile 12)* (Kinsale: Gandon Editions, 1997).

O'Toole, S., 'The Mastery of Darkness', interview with James Scanlon, *Tracings*, vol. 1, Spring 2000.

Pollard, C., *Liam McCormack: Seven Donegal Churches* (Kinsale: Gandon Editions, 2011).

Pyle, H., 'Cork Glass Now: a Review of the Work of James Scanlon and Maud Cotter', *Irish Arts Review*, Yearbook 1990–1991, pp. 44–52.

Pyle, H., 'Iron in the Soul: Evic Hone', *Irish Arts Review*, vol. 22, no. 4, Winter 2005, pp. 126–31.

Raguin, V., '*An Túr Gloine* (Tower of Glass) at the Newton County Day School of the Sacred Heart', *Interfaces*, 38, 2016–17; available at https://www.holycross.edu/sites/default/files/files/interfaces/virginia_raquin.pdf.

Reihill, K., *George Campbell and the Belfast Boys* (Dublin: Adams Auctioneers, 2015).

Reyntiens, P., *The Technique of Stained Glass* (London: Batsford, 1967).

Rivers, E., 'Evie Sydney Hone', *Journal of the British Society of Master Glass Painters,* vol. 12, no. 1 (1956).

Rogers, F., *Convent Chapel, Enniskillen* (Ballycastle: Impact Printing, 2017).

Rogers, F., *Glass in the Glens: A Study of Stained Glass Windows in Churches in the Glens of Antrim* (Ballycastle: Impact Printing, 2004).

Rogers, F., *Innocence in the Fields of Paradise: A Study of An Túr Gloine Windows in Co. Fermanagh* (Ballycastle: Impact Printing, 2001).

Rowley, E., Andrew Devane's Dublin Churches: Catholic Architecture in Ireland in an Age of Tentative Radicalization, 1960–75', in L. Godson and K. James-Chakraborty (eds), *Modern Religious Architecture in Germany, Ireland and Beyond – Influence, Process and Afterlife since 1945* (London: Bloomsbury, 2019), pp. 62–86..

Ryan, V., 'Divine Light: a century of stained glass' *Irish Arts Review*, vol. 32, no. 2, Summer 2015, pp. 272–5.

Sheehy, J., *The Rediscovery of Ireland's Past: The Celtic Revival 1830–1930* (London: Thames and Hudson, 1980).

Sheehy, R., 'Hope and Resurrection: The Late Work of Richard J. King', *Studies: An Irish Quarterly Review*, vol. 88, no. 352, Winter 1999, pp. 430–47.

Sheehy, R., 'Kevin Barry Memorial Window', *Irish Arts Review*, vol. 11, Yearbook 1995, pp. 208–9.

Sheehy, R. 'The art of Richard King (1907–1974) in Swinford and Newport, Co. Mayo' in *Cathair Na Mart The Journal of the Westport Historical Society*, no. 27, 2009, pp. 30–47.

Sheehy, R., 'The Art of Richard King: Nazareth House', *Studies: An Irish Quarterly Review*, vol. 84, no. 335, Autumn 1995, pp. 267–77.

Sheehy, R., *The Life and Work of Richard King: Religion, Nationalism and Modernism* (*Reimagining Ireland* series) (Oxford: Peter Lang International Academic Publishers, 2020).

Sheehy, R., 'The Liturgical Art of Richard Enda King (1943–95) in Ireland', *Artefact – Journal of the Irish Association of Art Historians*, Issue Seven, 2013 (Dublin: I.A.A.H., 2013), pp. 68–83.

Snoddy, T., *Dictionary of Irish Artists – 20th Century* (Dublin: Wolfhound Press, 1996).

Sweeney, P., *Franciscan Friary Church Multyfarnham: Its History, Restoration and Works of Art* (Offaly: privately published, 2018).

Teehan, V., and Wincott Heckett, E. (eds), *The Honan Chapel: A Golden Vision* (Cork: Cork University Press, 2004).

Walsh, L., *Lumen Christi: The Stained Glass Windows of Mount Joseph Abbey* (Mount Saint Joseph Abbey: Cistercian Press, 2009).

Whall, C., *Stained Glass Work* in The Artistic Crafts Series of Technical Handbooks, ed. W.R. Lethaby (London: John Hogg, 1905).

White, J., *Evie Hone 1894–1955*: Catalogue of the Exhibition (Dublin: 1958).

White, J. and Wynne, M., *Irish Stained Glass:* A Catalogue of Stained Glass Windows by Irish Artists of the 20th Century (Dublin: The Furrow Trust, Gill & Son, 1963).

Wynne, M., 'A Life Concerned with Glass: Evie Hone (1894–1955)', *Country Life*, 14 June 1984.

Wynne, M., *Irish Stained Glass*, in the Irish Heritage Series (Dublin: Eason & Son, 1977).

Wynne, M., 'The Irish Archaeological Inspiration of Evie Hone: A Preliminary Study', *Journal of the County Kildare Archaeological Society,* vol. 14,(1966–7.

UNPUBLISHED

Caron, D., 'An Túr Gloine Stained Glass Windows and Mosaic Stations of the Cross in St Brendan's Cathedral, Loughrea, County Galway', degree thesis, National College of Art and Design, 1982.

Caron, T.D., 'Michael Healy (1873–1941) and the artists of An Túr Gloine', PhD, University of Dublin, 1991.

Donnelly, P., 'The Rise and Fall of Harry Clarke Stained Glass Limited: an analysis of the main influences in the story of the company's success and decline', MPhil thesis, University of Dublin, 2014.

Earley, W., 'The Stained Glass Work of Patrick Pollen', MPhil thesis, University of Dublin, 2014.

Felle, B., 'Helen Moloney, Stained Glass Artist, Her Life and Works', MPhil thesis, University of Dublin, 2018.

Gordon Bowe, N., 'Harry Clarke 1889–1931, His Life and Work', PhD thesis, University of Dublin, 1982.

Wynne, M., 'Stained Glass in Ireland, principally Irish Stained Glass 1760–1963', PhD, University of Dublin, 1975.

ARCHIVES

An Túr Gloine Archive, Centre for the Study of Irish Art, NGI, Dublin

Special collections of original work by the following artists and studios: Patrick Pollen; Helen Moloney; Phyllis Burke; Lua Breen; Murphy-Devitt Studios; Patrick Pye; Earley & Company. Also Evie Hone's papers, NIVAL, Dublin

Clarke's Stained Glass Studios Collection, TCD, Dublin

The Harry Clarke Papers, NLI, Dublin

Watson Archive, Crawford Art Gallery, Cork

The Clokey Stained Glass Collection, Historic Environment Record of Northern Ireland (HERoNI), Belfast